'The second volume of Elizabeth Longford's life of Wellington is as impressive as the first. It covers a long period – from just after Waterloo to just after the Great Exhibition – but the pace is right throughout, each paragraph catching the shifting immediacies of particular and rapidly changing situations. The keynote of the whole period was social change, change which was often associated with dramatic political conflict. Yet it says much both for the personality of Wellington and the skills of his biographer that the man himself, for all his dislike of change, proves as interesting and challenging a subject of study as the turbulent period through which he was living . . . her comments are brilliantly incisive.' *Asa Briggs* – THE GUARDIAN

'Lady Longford paints in the background of the early nineteenth century with the brush of a master . . . her sureness of touch never deserts her' – ILLUSTRATED LONDON NEWS

'The many who have been eagerly awaiting the second volume of Lady Longford's life of Wellington will not be disappointed. It is, if anything, better than the first. To scholarship and research she can add a tart sense of humour, an originality of metaphor and the capacity to invest the intricacies of political manoeuvre with suspense and drama' – IRISH PRESS

Elizabeth Longford

Wellington:
Pillar of State

Panther

Granada Publishing Limited
Published in 1975 by Panther Books Ltd
Frogmore, St Albans, Herts AL2 2NF

First published in Great Britain by Weidenfeld &
Nicolson 1972
Copyright © Elizabeth Longford 1972
Made and printed in Great Britain by
Richard Clay (The Chaucer Press) Ltd
Bungay, Suffolk
Set in Monotype Times

Once more to Frank and in memory of Gerry,
Seventh Duke of Wellington and my daughter
Catherine Pakenham

Contents

Illustrations

Allegory of Wellington at the Crowning of Peace. Watercolour by Thomas Stothard.

Wellington as Master-General of the Ordnance, 1819. Print published by J. Sidebethem.

Wellington in 1818. Engraving by J. H. Robinson from a portrait by Sir George Hayter.

Lord Wellesley as Lord-Lieutenant of Ireland. Print published by McLeary.

Lord Castlereagh by Sir Thomas Lawrence.

George Canning by Sir Thomas Lawrence and R. Evans.

Robert Peel by H. W. Pickersgill.

Wellington in 1824 by Sir Thomas Lawrence.

'Killing Time.' An unsigned print probably by 'HB' (John Doyle).

Wellington in 1829. 'Leaving the House of Lords – Through the Assembled Commons.' Print published by Thomas McLean, March 1829.

The Duel 1829. Print published by Thomas McLean, March 1829.

'Framed but not yet glazed.' Print published by Thomas McLean, 10 June 1833.

'A Sketch in the Park.' Wellington and Mrs Arbuthnot. Artist unknown.

'A Celebrated Commander on the Retir'd List.'

Wellington musing on the Field of Waterloo by B. R. Haydon.

Wellington with his grandchildren in the library at Stratfield Saye by Thorburn.

ACKNOWLEDGEMENTS

The author and publishers wish to thank His Grace the Duke of Wellington for permission to reproduce pictures 13 and 16; the Hon. Mrs Bonham for number 9; Mr Brinsley Ford for number 1; the British Museum for numbers 2 and 12; the Mansell Collection for number 5; the Mary Evans Picture Library for number 4; the National Portrait Gallery for numbers 6 and 7; the Victoria and Albert Museum for number 11; the Walker Art Gallery, Liverpool for number 15; Wellington College for number 8; numbers 3, 10 and 14 are in the possession of the author.

The author would also like to thank Miss Sophie Baker for her photography; Miss Jane Flower, Miss V. Lloyd and Mr W. Clarke for their kind help.

Author's Note

History has a double role: to destroy the illusions of the past and to 'create out of the debris a more extended, a more rational, a more detached sense of human destiny'. On this positive note Professor J. H. Plumb ends his *Death of the Past*, (1969). 'May history step into its shoes,' he reiterates, 'and help to sustain man's confidence in his destiny.'

Wellington's life history seems eminently suited to do just this. And it is no less effective when the hero dives headlong into blunder and odium than when he achieves a spectacular triumph. Nor does it sustain us only as 'rational' beings, but also as creatures of faith, feeling and inspiration.

By gracious permission of Her Majesty the Queen I have again used material from the Royal Archives, Windsor, and by gracious permission of Her Majesty the Queen of the Netherlands, I have used a further letter from the Royal House, The Hague. In thanking Mr Robert Mackworth-Young and the staff at Windsor for their unfailing help, I am struck by a piquant contrast between the approach of Sir Herbert Maxwell (the first Wellingtonian biographer to work in the Royal Archives) and myself. 'I must say it is rather a relief,' wrote Sir Herbert on 4 November 1898 to Sir Fleetwood Edwards, Keeper of the Privy Purse, 'to be told that there is not a mine of unpublished correspondence of the Duke of Wellington.' Each generation of historians has its own idea of a gold-mine, and if I feel relief it is only at not missing a number of letters which seem to me of more than minor interest.

In the most sad loss of the 7th Duke of Wellington early in 1972, it is some consolation to me that he was able to read all the chapters of this volume (as he so kindly did of the first) in manuscript, and to give me the incalculable benefit of his advice and criticism up to the last. Nevertheless his loss to scholarship and culture, and to me personally, is very heavy indeed. The depth and detail of his knowledge of the 1st Duke was unique. I can never thank him and his family enough for the complete freedom they have allowed me in pursuing the path of biography wherever it might lead. Fortunately for the cause of continuity, his son the 8th Duke is the generous guardian of family history and anecdote; and I must express my gratitude to him for many kindnesses, not least for reading the proofs of this book. Recurring to a sad theme, the 7th Duke's distinguished librarian, Mr Francis Needham, pre-deceased him by a few months. In him I have lost a delightful guide to the past who, though properly fastidious, found no by-way too narrow or overgrown to explore. But while lamenting his death, I must again rejoice that his work is continued by one so young and talented as Mr Antony Grant. His constructive criticism of my manuscript, proof-reading and patient help of all kinds have left me greatly in his debt.

I would like to thank again all those whose liberality in lending me material for my first volume has extended to this volume also: Lord Raglan, Mrs Freda Loch, Lady Albemarle, Mr Edmund de Rothschild, Mr Michael Farrar-Bell. To those who have lent me new material or called my attention to it I am deeply grateful: to the 5th Marquess of Salisbury whose kindness will always be remembered, and his librarian Miss Clare Talbot; Sir Arthur Bryant, Lt. Col. J. G. O. Whitehead, Miss Carola Oman, Miss Margery Weiner, Mr J. Bennett, Mr Francis Bamford, Mr John Sparrow, Mrs Georgina Battiscombe, Lord Kenyon, Admiral Sir F. Dalrymple-Hamilton, Mrs Hardy-Roberts, Major John Maxse, Mrs Lettice Miller, the Hon. Mrs Anne Fremantle, Mme Christianne Besse, Mr Kenneth Rose, Lord Dunsany, Mrs N. Tweddell, Mr Tom Cullen, Mrs Margaret Dodger, Mr George Huxley, Mr W. T. Oliver, Brig. K. Thompson, Mrs Ruth Adam, Lady Moran, Mr J. Ford, Mr R. Speaight, Mr Gervase Huxley, Captain P. B. Backhouse, Mr Esmond Warner, Mrs F. B. Maggs, Mr P. Skottowe, Miss Mary Lutyens, Mr J. Bryan III, Brig. P. H. C. Hayward, Mr Brian Inglis, Professor G. Best, Mr H. Bolitho, Dr S. Pasmore, Lady Limerick, the Hon. Mrs Arthur Pollen, Mr R. de Stacpoole, Col. R. J. Longfield, Miss J. Harrild, Mrs Tonge, Mr J. Mannering, Mr R. H. Irrmann, Mr B. G. Buxton, Dr Alec Vidler, Mr Derek Hudson, Mr J. F. Vernon, Group-Captain G. Knocker, Mrs M. R. Cowie, Mr R.

Boulind, Mr E. Franklin, Mr L. Drucker, Mr G. Lewin, Mr J. Showers.

I am most grateful to Mr Victor Percival, Director of the Wellington Museum; Dr Roy Strong, Director of the National Portrait Gallery and his staff; Mr William Reid, Director of the National Army Museum; Commander C. H. Tyers, Naval and Military Club; Mr D. S. Porter, Bodleian Library; Mr P. Hardy, National Library of Ireland; Mr J. T. Eubank, Jr. and Rice University; Brig. D. A. Pringle, Duke of York's Royal Military School; Mr J. R. Dineen, Royal United Services Institute Library; Mr C. Dobson, House of Lords Library; Mr A. E. Barker, S.P.C.K.; Mr A. P. W. Malcolmson, Public Record Office of Northern Ireland; Lord Cromer, Mr T. L. Ingram and Barings Bank; the Public Record Office; the West Sussex and Surrey Records Offices and County Archives; Mr D. W. King and the Ministry of Defence Library; Mr P. Montague-Smith, Editor of Debrett; the Town Clerks of Rye and Winchelsea; the staffs of the London Library and the British Museum.

I would like to acknowledge the help of those who have answered queries relative to this volume or suggested corrections in its predecessor; Mr M. G. Brock, Mr Michael Glover, Mr Jac Weller, Lord Anglesey, the Hon. Gerard Noel, Mr P. J. V. Rolo, Miss Susan Ertz, Mrs J. H. Fisher, Col. A. C. T. White, V.C., Brig. R. G. S. Bidwell, Miss Grizel Grey, Alderman C. Seed, Dr Dorothy George, Mr Richard Ormonde, Professor M. R. D. Foot, Mr A. Brett-James, Mr C. Clive-Ponsonby-Fane, Mr John Terraine, Mrs R. Craddock, Lt. Col. I. H. Stockwood, Brig. S. C. Dumbreck, Mr D. Young, Mr G. Spencer, Lt. Col. A. A. Dean, Mr P. Kivy, Mr B. Sweet-Escott, Mrs S. J. Morton, Mr D. Parsons, Mrs A. Moffat, Brig. H. Bozner, Mr Hugh Farmar and Mr John Ehrman.

As before, I end by thanking most sincerely Mr Harold Kurtz for continuous assistance, Mrs Angela Lambert for invaluable cutting, and my secretary Mrs Agnes Fenner for typing the manuscript yet again. Professor Asa Briggs, Dr G. Kitson Clark and Professor Kevin Nowlan have done me the honour of reading the page-proofs of the chapters on British and Irish political history, of which they are such masters. Miss Anna Collins most generously volunteered research on newspapers and pictures. My warm thanks go to Sir George Weidenfeld for having the original idea of this book and to Mr Antony Godwin and Miss Gila Curtis for helping me to carry it through. My family will be glad to know that their labours are at last ended, especially my daughter Antonia and my sons Michael and Kevin who read the manuscript, and Frank who found much to improve but never found fault.

A Calendar of Events
in Wellington's Career 1815–1852

1815	21 June	Wellington crosses frontier into France.
	21–22 June	Official news of Waterloo reaches England.
	3 July	Surrender of Paris. Treaty of Saint-Cloud.
	8 July	Second Restoration of Louis XVIII. The White Terror.
	7 August	Napoleon exiled to St Helena.
	22 October	Wellington Commander-in-Chief, Army of Occupation.
	20 November	Second Peace of Paris.
1816	February	Wedderburn–Webster libel action.
	25 June	Incendiary attempt on Wellington's house.
	July	Visit to England.
	Autumn	Discussions with Madame de Staël.
	26 December	Flying visit to London.
1817	9 January	Troop reduction announced.
	July	Visit to England.
	October	Appointed Allied referee on French reparations.
1818	10 February	Assassination attempt by Cantillon.
	October–November	Congress of Aix-la-Chapelle.
	21 November	End of Occupation.
	26 December	Appointed Master-General of Ordnance in Liverpool's Cabinet.

1819	16 August	Peterloo.
	Autumn	Six 'Gag' Acts.
1820	29 January	Death of George III. Accession of George IV.
	23 February	Cato Street Conspiracy.
	Summer –Autumn	Trial of Queen Caroline.
	19 December	Appointed Lord-Lieutenant of Hampshire.
1821	5 May	Death of Napoleon.
	5 August	Accident to ear; deafness.
	12 August	Suicide of Castlereagh.
	October– November	British representative at Congress of Verona.
1823–1827		Political duel with Canning.
	10 May	Daniel O'Connell founds Catholic Association.
1824	16 September	Death of Louis XVIII. Accession of Charles X.
	December	Wellington defeated by Canning on recognition of South-American Republics.
1825	March	'Cottage Plot' against Canning.
	April	Wellington propounds plan for Catholic Emancipation.
	1 December	Death of Tsar Alexander I. Accession of Tsar Nicholas I.
	December	Monetary crisis.
1826	February– April	Mission to Russia.
	29 December	Constable of Tower of London.
1827	5 January	Death of Duke of York. Wellington Commander-in-Chief.
	17 February	Lord Liverpool suffers stroke.

	9 April	Canning Prime Minister. Resignation of Tories. Wellington also resigns command of Army.
	8 August	Death of Canning. Goderich Prime Minister. Wellington resumes command of Army.
1828	8 January	Goderich resigns.
	9 January	Wellington Prime Minister. Forced to resign command of Army.
	March–May	Repeal of old Test and Corporation Acts. Cabinet friction over Corn Laws and parliamentary reform.
	20 May	Huskisson and Canningites resign.
	July	Clare election. Irish crisis.
	1 August	Wellington broaches Catholic question with King.
	August–December	Wellington works behind scenes for Emancipation.
1829	20 January	Lord Warden of Cinque Ports.
	10 February	Suppression of Catholic Association, but Tory split on Emancipation issue. Wellington orders 'rightabout face'.
	21 March	Wellington v. Winchilsea duel at Battersea.
	13 April	Catholic Emancipation.
	9 May	Elder Brother of Trinity House.
1829	Winter–	
1830	Spring	Severe economic distress.
	26 June	Death of George IV. Accession of William IV.
	26–29 July	French Revolution of 'July Days'. Flight of Charles X to England; usurpation of Louis Philippe.

	August	Wave of Continental revolutions. Irish agitation for repeal of Union.
	August–November	Rising of agricultural workers under 'Captain Swing'.
	2 November	Wellington refuses parliamentary reform.
	15–16 November	Defeat and resignation. Grey Prime Minister.
1831	22 April	1st Reform Bill thwarted; King prorogues Parliament.
	24 April	Death of Kitty Wellington.
	27 April	Apsley House stoned.
	8 October	Lords defeat 2nd Reform Bill.
	12 October	Apsley House stoned again.
1832	7 May	Lords defeat 3rd Reform Bill; 'May Days' or near-revolution.
	15 May	Wellington fails to form Government; Grey recalled; Wellington abstains.
	7 June	Great Reform Bill becomes law.
1833		Critical period as Leader of Lords.
1834		Chancellor of Oxford.
	8 July	Grey resigns; Melbourne Prime Minister.
	14–15 November	William IV dismisses Whigs, summons Wellington.
	15 November–9 December	Refuses premiership; caretaker for Peel.
	9 December	Foreign Secretary. Peel Prime Minister.
1835	7 April	Fall of Conservatives. Leader of Opposition in Lords for next six years. Bi-partisan policy.
1837	20 June	Death of William IV. Accession of Queen Victoria.

	Summer	Agitation for Six-point Charter and repeal of Corn Laws.
1838	Spring–Summer	Wellington clashes with ultra-Tories. Anti-Corn Law League founded.
1839	May	Bedchamber Plot.
	19 November	Acute seizure.
1840	February	Two more attacks.
	Summer–Autumn	The Hungry Forties. Riots in industrial areas.
1841	Summer	General Election. Peel Prime Minister. Wellington enters Cabinet without office.
1842	February	Peel announces tariff reforms and income tax.
	August	Wellington resumes command of Army, holding it for rest of life. Irrational anxieties over defence. Chartist and Irish agitation.
1843	14 October	Arrest of O'Connell.
1845	October	New of Irish potato famine.
	November	Peel proposes repeal of Corn Laws.
	6 December	Cabinet split. Wellington supports Peel (though against his policy); Stanley opposes. Peel resigns.
	20 December	Russell fails to form Whig Government. Peel recalled by Queen.
1846	Spring	Wellington urges peers to 'right about face' on Corn Laws.
	26 June	Corn Bill passes in Lords; Peel defeated on Coercion in Commons same day; resigns.

1846–1852		Wellington retires entirely from party politics.
1847		The Statue affair.
1848	January	Affair of the Burgoyne letter on defence.
	February	French Revolution, flight of Louis Philippe to England. Wave of European revolutions.
	10 April	Wellington as Commander-in-Chief defuses great Chartist demonstration.
1850		Ranger of Parks.
1851	1 May	Great Exhibition.
1852	February	Fall of Russell; Derby Prime Minister.
	14 September	Death at Walmer Castle, aged 83 years 4 months.
	18 November	Burial in St Paul's.

Part I

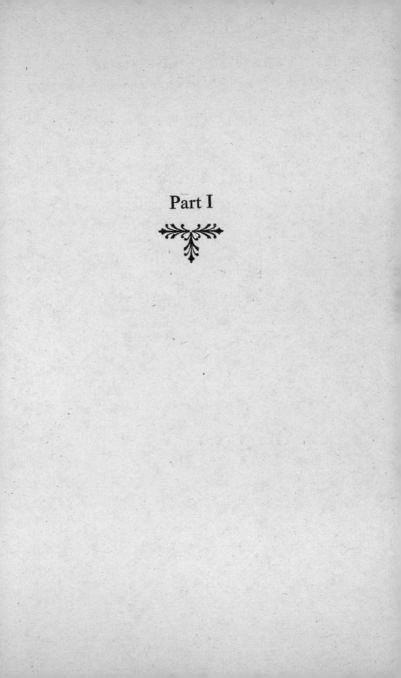

1

Prince of Waterloo

Boney's beat! Boney's beat!
Hurrah! hurrah! Boney's beat.

Highlanders shouted and stamped out the compulsive rhythm as they brought their wounded into Antwerp from Waterloo early on Monday morning, 19 June 1815. No one behind the lines suspected the titanic scale of Wellington's victory. The Highlanders did their best to convey it.

Hearing the noise, an elderly Englishwoman burst out of her hotel bedroom still wearing a white flannel dressing-gown and night-cap stuck on top of her curlers. She stood at the street door laughing, crying and haranguing the universe while the wounded limped by.[1]

A young Scotswoman, Jane Dalrymple-Hamilton, who had chatted to Wellington at the 'Waterloo Ball' and then been evacuated from Brussels to Antwerp, lay in her bed, sleepless and wretched. Suddenly, at 7 A.M., she was startled by a knock on her door. It was the Prussian minister, bringing a note from General von Bülow written on the field of battle. Victory! Immediately her husband, Sir Hew, dressed and rushed downstairs to give the news to Wellington's sister-in-law, Mrs Wellesley-Pole, and his niece, Lady Fitzroy Somerset, who were staying in the same hotel. Both these ladies had been in poor shape the night before, the former begging Sir Hew to take her to England 'as she said she feared all hope of the British being successful was at an end'.

Half an hour after the Prussian message Wellington's Spanish liaison officer, General Alava, came to damp the ladies' soaring spirits with tales of the appalling carnage. He informed Lady Fitzroy that her husband, Wellington's military secretary, had lost his right arm.

'To prove to you that I came from the field of battle,' he added, 'look here.' And he drew from his pocket a handkerchief steeped in blood.[2]

*

Wellington's personal care for the wounded had been shown since the very beginning of the Peninsular War. At one point his army doctors considered themselves so overworked that they resigned in a body. The slave-driver went for them. 'Gentlemen,' he announced, 'I accept your resignations and shall immediately write home for a fresh medical staff.' Then, warming to his task, 'But mark me, until they come out, you shall remain here & you shall perform your duty.'[3]

Now, at Waterloo, every doctor was working frantically round the clock. Hundreds of the wounded had to wait their turn for hospital. They were deposited on lines of straw along the Brussels streets and washed by public-spirited ladies. As the carts rumbled by, fastidious shopkeepers sniffed eau-de-Cologne or camphor. Many French were still lying on the battlefield. When they arrived in Brussels several wore carters' smocks to cover their nakedness, for contrary to Wellington's orders they had been robbed of their rich uniforms. Yet in all their misery and squalor, unquenchable enthusiasm for Napoleon was never more evident, especially on the operating table. '*Vive l'Empereur!*' they would shout hoarsely as an arm or leg was whisked away.

*

It was some days after the battle that the distinguished dead began to return home. The body of General Sir Thomas Picton, who had fallen commanding the 5th Division, was laid on the table at which he had dined in the Vine Inn, Canterbury, a fortnight before, his boots still yellow with Waterloo mud. The poet Thomas Moore was to write a lament for him in a pleasantly optimistic metre:

Oh! give to the hero the death of the brave . . .

Old Tom Picton was given not only the death of the brave but also a monument in Wales and another in St Paul's Cathedral.

The nameless dead of Waterloo lay out under the burning June sun, a growing horror to man and beast. Carriage-horses approaching from Brussels would scream at the smell of corruption. On the Monday and Tuesday piles of dead horses began to be collected for burning. Some were swollen to monstrous size so that the soldiers could hardly lug them to the bonfires. The human dead went into great pits or were burned by peasants protected with handkerchiefs and using the longest possible pitchforks.

Meanwhile on the day after Waterloo the Duke and his friends spent many hours visiting the wounded. Colonel Frederick Ponsonby had been appallingly mauled and left on the field for dead. When he recovered as if by a miracle, the Duke felt bound to keep a friendly eye on him for the rest of his life, which included lending him a large sum of money.[4] William Verner of the 7th Hussars was another young officer who needed a personal visit to recall him almost from the grave. 'You are not nearly so bad as you think,' said the Duke of Richmond briskly. At the end of a month Verner had neither hair on his head nor flesh on his bones, but he was on his feet.[5]

Even Wellington could not work his magic for Sir William de Lancey. The newly married Quartermaster-General lay for nine doleful days in a hovel at Mont-Saint-Jean above the plain of Waterloo, gradually succumbing to the cannon-ball blast which had broken eight ribs though not the skin, while his tragic young wife sat holding his hand. On the Tuesday Wellington drove up in his curricle accompanied by his aide-de-camp, Colonel Felton Hervey. In an hour he was due to join his troops at Nivelles but de Lancey was a special case. He had been struck down while actually speaking to the Duke and had been reported dead. Now the Duke did his best to cheer him with a mild joke, but de Lancey could not raise a smile and the Duke at once changed his tone. He told the dying man that he himself never wanted to fight another battle. 'It has been too much to see such brave men, so equally matched, cutting each other to pieces.'[6] De Lancey died within the week and long afterwards Wellington recalled that mournful sequel to the battle.

'Poor fellow!' he mused, 'we knew each other ever since we were boys. But I had no time to be sorry. I went on with the army and never saw him again.'

*

The time had come for Wellington to complete the overthrow of Bonaparte. He left Mont-Saint-Jean to join his army at Nivelles.

It was Tuesday 20 June. Though his staff had never known him so warm-hearted as on these last two days, the excited Belgian populace found themselves applauding a strangely impassive figure. This was partly due to his necessarily upright seat in the 'Hussar' saddle which he used throughout the Waterloo campaign. Its high pommel in front and spoon behind prevented the rider from bending – a limitation unlikely to worry Wellington. There was also his personal attitude towards popularity. Was he not pleased to be so enthusiastically mobbed? someone asked. 'Not in the least: if I had failed, they would have shot me.'[7]

All around him the grass was white with scraps of paper – letters home, laundry bills, muster rolls, memoranda and love-letters shed by the dead and wounded of both sides. A German *New Testament* and Voltaire's *Candide* caught the eye of a British tourist, and a cavalry officer picked up a small leather notebook with an engraved gold plate on the cover: *'Alexandrine à son Auguste'*. Alexandrine had presented this souvenir to her Auguste on the day he left her to join Napoleon's army. It was a Sunday and she wrote in it her *'pensée'* for that day: 'This Day shall be one of Eternal pain to me. I lose *Everything* – Great God grant it may not be *for ever*.' Another *pensée* was briefer: *'Je t'aime, je t'aime toujours'*.[8]

On Wellington's left as he rode off stood the elm tree which had been his command-post above the field of battle. Ripped and battered by gunfire, it was to be felled in 1818, and twenty years later, in the year of Queen Victoria's coronation, made into two chairs, one for Her Majesty and the other for the Duke.*

> To Field Marshal Arthur Duke of Wellington K.G.
> This Chair
> Made of the Elm which, on the glorious
> field of Waterloo witnessed his triumph . . .
> presented by His Grace's faithful servant
> J. C. Children, 18 June 1838

Long before his chair was carved, honours had been lavished upon him by the crowned heads of Europe. From the Prince Regent came the Royal Hanoverian Guelphic Order and a burst of pious affection: 'I have now, my dearest Lord, only to add my

---

* Wellington's chair still stands in the library of his London home, Apsley House. The Queen's chair is at Windsor.

thanks to the Almighty for having, in His mercy, preserved your life in this most dreadful and sanguinary conflict. . . . George, P.R.'

If there was still any doubt as to who had won the battle, Tsar Alexander I of Russia set it at rest. He presented a diamond-hilted sword to the man whom he named 'Conqueror of Waterloo'.*[9] Kings would henceforth call him '*Mon Cousin*', for William I of the Netherlands had created the Duke a prince – Prince of Waterloo.

The crown meanwhile had slipped from another head, that of Napoleon Bonaparte, Emperor of the French.

*

By the Tuesday evening, 20 June, Napoleon was well on his way to Paris, far in advance of his retreating army. Though his right wing under Marshal Grouchy had mastered the Prussian left on the 19th, he could not afford to remain with them. Trouble was brewing in Paris among the politicians. His only chance was to reach his capital and sweep away all doubts and disappointments with the magic of his presence. The crowds had run gaily to the Palais Royal on 18 June to hear that the Prussian commander, Blücher, was mortally wounded and Wellington dead. How would they take the truth? Napoleon could interpret it for them. He raced ahead and at 8 A.M. on Wednesday, 21 June the small, exhausted figure with bloodless cheeks and dead eyes entered the Elysée Palace. He had been absent nine days A nine days' wonder.

'Prodigies of valour . . . panic. . . . Ney behaved like a fool,' he panted as he began to restore himself in a hot bath. 'I should have crushed the enemy at Ligny if the right had done their duty; I should have crushed him at Mont-Saint-Jean if the left had done theirs.'

This was only the start of a giant operation by Napoleon to shift the blame. Still, it did him good, like the heat and steam.

'All is not lost,' he said more cheerfully, splashing Marshal Davout with bathwater.[10] *Après moi le déluge.*

*

Wellington crossed the border into France on the same date, 21

* Stolen from the Victoria and Albert Museum in 1948.

June, three days after Waterloo. It was a moment of triumph. Nevertheless, the follow-up after a victory had never been his favourite operation. Indeed he was later to inform an agreeable young friend in the diplomatic corps, Philip von Neumann, that 'in view of the exhaustion of the troops, the difficulty of maintaining their energy, & of preventing those excesses to which they are eager to abandon themselves' – there was nothing worse than a battle won except a battle lost.* To which the Austrian replied with that pleasing mixture of tartness and flattery learnt in his profession, that the Duke could not make the comparison because he had never lost a battle.

His troops had little chance to abandon themselves to excesses. Even tough Peninsular veterans were startled by the severities on the march from Waterloo. Special guards were appointed to flog every man found loitering behind his regiment without a pass. For the rest, crossing into France was a merry affair. Regimental bands played 'The girl I left behind me' and raw recruits capered about in cuirasses taken from dead Frenchmen. One Netherlands colonel ordered a *feu de joie*. The shots astonished even Wellington who foresaw trouble rather than joy on the march and thought his army had fallen into an ambush.

It was Napoleon who had been ambushed, by the Minister of Police, Fouché, and the Chamber of Deputies. While the Emperor was preparing to prorogue both Chambers and assume dictatorial powers, the deputies declared themselves in permanent session and forced the Emperor to abdicate in favour of his son, the little King of Rome. Fouché sighed with relief.

'That devil! He terrified me this morning. I thought he was going to begin again. Luckily, there is no beginning again.'[11]

*

Up till the Tuesday only one man in London had received the news of Napoleon's defeat. An agent of Nathan Rothschild, the banker, arrived from Ostend on that evening bringing his employer a garbled account in a Dutch newspaper of a resounding Allied victory. Next morning, Wednesday, 21 June, Roths-

---

* These last dozen words are among the many variants of Wellington's famous aphorism on Waterloo. It was one of his habits to use again and again any phrase which put his point well. In the example above he gave different reasons to support his aphorism from the usual one, namely the appalling carnage (Neumann, vol. 1, p. 48, 11 January 1821).

child's newspaper was in the hands of the British Cabinet. The Prime Minister, Lord Liverpool, did not believe it. The Cabinet sat on it. Throughout Wednesday contradictory reports agitated London. William Wellesley-Pole heard that there had been a terrible defeat. Other rumours were of victory. Bets were laid in the London clubs, many of Brooks's Whigs backing Napoleon for a win. According to one legend, Rothschild had withheld the good news from the Cabinet until early afternoon, standing by his accustomed pillar in the Stock Exchange on the Wednesday morning with a glum face and buying up cheap the funds which he had deceitfully depressed. This of course was a fabrication, though one apparently believed by Wellington. Not until evening did Lord Liverpool discover that Rothschild's news was true.[12]

*

Henry Percy, one of the Duke's very few aides-de-camp to come through Waterloo without a serious wound, brought the news to the Cabinet twenty-four hours after it was known to Rothschild.

He had left Brussels for Ostend on the 20th, Wellington's despatch folded inside a purple velvet sachet given to him by a dancing-partner at the Duchess of Richmond's 'Waterloo Ball'. Still in his blood-stained uniform, he had had to row to the Kent coast after becoming becalmed. From Broadstairs, which he reached about 3 P.M. on the 21st, he dashed to London with two captured French eagles, their banners fluttering from the windows of his chaise-and-four. His first stop was in Downing Street, where Wellington's friend Charles Arbuthnot, husband of the lovely Harriet, came out to see if the shouting was from a Corn Law mob. More than pleasantly surprised, Arbuthnot entered Percy's carriage and directed it to Lord Harrowby's house in Grosvenor Square (now No. 44) where he was host at a Cabinet Wednesday dinner. A noisy crowd followed the eagles, some demanding information, others shouting back, 'Wellington's safe!' The battle had not been a Trafalgar.[13]

Arrived at Harrowby's house, Arbuthnot was sent in first to break the news, which he did with the concluding words: 'In short, the French army is entirely destroyed', to which the incredulous Harrowby replied, 'I beg your pardon, Mr Arbuthnot – but not exactly – I think you are going a little too far.'[14]

It was now Percy's turn to present the despatch. Lord

Harrowby's fourteen-year-old daughter Mary, roused by the uproar from sleep (the time was 11 P.M.), tiptoed to the head of the stairs and was transfixed by the sight of a dusty young soldier plunging into her father's panelled ante-room with a cry of 'Victory! victory!'. Here Wellington's despatch was opened. Then Lord Harrowby read it aloud to the milling crowd under his windows, while Percy galloped off to lay the eagles at the Prince Regent's feet.

His Royal Highness was about to open a ball in St James's Square. Suddenly a mighty wave of huzzas came pouring along King Street and drowned the violins. Percy rushed indoors with his cry of 'Victory' grown fainter from exhaustion. At once the ball broke up, the Prince sobbed at the casualty lists and guests bundled out into the square. For London was catching fire. 'All the world was out of doors,' wrote the diarist Miss Berry, 'during the best part of the night, asking news of their neighbours.'

Next day the mail coaches set forth dressed with oak leaves to bring the news to the uttermost corners of Britain, while relatives of the fallen and sightseers embarked for Antwerp, Ostend and Rotterdam.

*

A fop was among the first civilians to poke around the Château of Hougoumont at Waterloo with cambric pressed to his nostrils. Women noticed small ironies, such as the corn spilt from the forage waggons along the *chaussée* sprouting after a few weeks where all else lay black and blasted. Lighter characters wrote their names on the walls of *La Belle-Alliance* inn or more poetically took home a rosebud from Hougoumont. The poets themselves-hummed round Waterloo like bees. Walter Scott found wheel prints still intact

> *And close beside, the harden'd mud*
> *Still shows where, fetlock deep in blood,*
> *The fierce dragoon, through battle's flood,*
> *Dash'd the hot war-horse on*

while Dorothy and William Wordsworth felt that 'something like horror breathed out of the ground'. The most typical sightseers were a party who called themselves 'the Brentford lads' and

arrived in Brussels in August. The shopkeeping or lower professional classes to which these young bloods belonged formed the
backbone of the England to which Wellington would eventually
return. At Mont-Saint-Jean they hired a guide and bought three
pints of brandy plus plenty of snuff to counteract the 'stench'.
They kissed some girl-harvesters near *La Belle-Alliance*, where a
man's leg lay in the stubble looking 'very fresh'. The peasants
looked even fresher, having made great sums from plunder. But
dinner at the inn was dreadful: fat yellow bacon and almost raw
meat. They could not help suspecting it had been cut off the dead
bodies. Two of the Brentford lads acquired a finger each from a
Frenchman's half-buried hand, to be taken home bottled in
spirits.[15]

Among others who had bought souvenirs were the Duke of
Richmond, Robert Peel, the rising young Tory politician, and
Wellington's Irish political friend, John Wilson Croker.*
Richmond bought twelve cuirasses, Peel one and Croker a cross
of the *Légion d'honneur*.

With whatever indulgence Wellington may have regarded such
curio-collectors, he never allowed himself to buy or even to accept
souvenirs unless they were of intrinsic value. A peculiarly firm
rebuff met those who tried to interest him in the relics of Waterloo. Would he care for the altarpiece of Hougoumont chapel,
guaranteed genuine? Not at all. Or for albums from *La Belle-
Alliance* containing the signatures of visitors to Waterloo in many
languages? The Duke begged to decline to deprive the owner of
them. After the battle he gave away his famous blue Waterloo
cape to his friend Croker, who was later asked by Sir Thomas
Lawrence to lend it for a portrait. 'I was goose enough to consent,' recalled Croker bitterly. A predatory lady made off with it
before he could get it back. What was worse, the Duke left the
lady in possession, merely ordering an exact copy to be made for
Croker. How could he so misunderstand the true value of the
cloak? Croker actually heard him say, 'One cloak is as good as
another.'[16]

*

* John Wilson Croker, 1780–1857. Tory politician and man of letters.
Wellington described him to Lady Salisbury on 21 November 1831:
'Croker is one of the cleverest fellows with the worst judgement in the
world.' (*Salisbury MSS*).

If one cloak was as good as another, only a single account of Waterloo would do – his own official despatch. He discouraged research into the campaign, including the hypothetical question of an Allied retreat, an issue which nagged the Duke.

'Pray, what would your Grace have done,' asked a Waterloo commander, Frederick Adam, one day at dinner, 'if the French Guards had not been dispersed?'

'Oh, I should have retired to the Bois de Soignes and given battle again next morning.'

'But if you could not have done that?'

'It could never have been so bad as that you know,' retorted the Duke, ruffled. He got up and ordered the coffee.[17] In the days of 1814, he had ordered the coffee to cut short an embarrassing flow of compliments. Now the coffee was used to short-circuit a painful recall of that 'close run thing'.

Adam's needling concerned the physical difficulties of retreating through a forest. An answer was given by the Duke ten years later at a dinner given by his niece's husband, Edward Littleton:* he could have retreated if he had wanted to but did not want to. 'I never contemplated a retreat on Brussels. My plan was to keep my ground till the Prussians appeared, and then to attack the French position, and I executed my plan.' As the party left the dining-room Croker exclaimed, 'I never heard the Duke say so much on this subject before.'[18]

There had been a time in August 1815 when Croker hoped to write 'a full history of Waterloo' under the Duke's guidance. The Duke, however, did not want a history. 'The history of a battle is not unlike the history of a ball. . . .' Individuals might remember particular incidents, but 'no individual can recollect the exact order in which, or the exact moment at which, they occurred, which makes all the difference as to their value or importance'.[19]

Compared with other engagements he called Waterloo his 'preferred battle' because he had taken most trouble over it at the time. Certainly it was to cause him most trouble in the future. As time went on his reactions changed from the genial to the sharp. He could still laugh in 1815 when fashionable English visitors to Paris sat in front of him in an opera box and loudly assigned all the glories of the day to the cavalry.

* Edward Littleton, later 1st Lord Hatherton, married the beautiful Hyacinthe Wellesley, natural daughter of the Marquess of Wellesley.

'I have told them that the British infantry won the battle and all our battles,' he whispered to his friend William Napier, the future military historian, who had just sat down beside him, 'but it has been intimated to me that I know nothing of the matter, and I expect soon to be told I was not there.'[20] Again he laughed. But many years later when a baronet, Sir Watkyn Williams Wynn, began asking him in a pronounced Welsh accent whether he had had a good view of the battle, Wellington cut him short – 'I generally like to see what I am about.'[21]

There was also the unknown lady who made a disastrous conversational gambit.

'Is it true, Duke, that you were surprised at Waterloo?'

'No, Madam, but I am now!'*[22] Yet Wellington himself had declared at the Duchess of Richmond's ball, 'Napoleon has *humbugg'd* me, by God.'

Wellington solved his problem with a typical slash at the knot. If he could not stop the historians he would not read their histories. 'Before I knew this,' recalled Lord Ellesmere, 'I once asked him for his opinion on a passage in Napier, with whose work I took [it] for granted he was familiar.'[23] The Duke rapidly disabused him. 'He positively refused to read even an extract.' And this despite the generosity with which he had replied to all Napier's queries.

Added to the 'retreat' and 'surprise' issues was the question of praise. His tributes to his men were mainly verbal. 'There are no men in Europe that can fight like my Spanish [Peninsular] infantry,' he said; 'none have been so tried. Besides, my army and I know one another exactly. We have a mutual confidence, and are never disappointed.'[24]

But he rarely expressed these feelings except casually, and even the magnanimous Sir John Fortescue, historian of the British Army, unbuckled Wellington's sword in 1815 with a qualified blessing:

He deliberately alienated any affectionate feeling of all ranks from him; and, when the war was over he parted from his soldiers without regret, and never troubled himself about them again. He was in fact glad to be quit of them, and made no pretence to the contrary.

* According to another account, a portrait-painter, Pickersgill, asked the question deliberately in order to liven up the Duke's expression.

That this was far from the whole truth will appear in due course. Indeed Fortescue himself seems to have sensed the inadequacy of his valediction, for he added a postscript:

This being so, his ascendancy over the army appears only the more extraordinary; showing forth, in spite of all defects, the extreme greatness of the man.[25]

The great man, meanwhile, prepared to occupy Paris. At times there had seemed a disagreeable prospect of his having to storm some of the French fortresses on the route. One governor had hoped to surrender to Napoleon I, rather than to old Louis XVIII. But Napoleon II, aged four, was in Vienna with his mother, the Empress Marie-Louise. Napoleon I had left for Rochefort on the south-west coast of France, disregarding the excellent advice of his Minister of the Interior, Lazare Carnot, that he should flee to America – 'From there you will again make your enemies tremble' – and the Bourbon royal family were about to enter their capital in the wake of Wellington's army, 'with the baggage', as it was scornfully noted. Wellington proposed to ride in on his bright chestnut, Copenhagen, decked with gold and silver trappings. Madame D'Arblay, the novelist Fanny Burney, who was married to a member of Louis XVIII's bodyguard, wrote to her husband in ecstasy, 'Immortal Wellington! *Vive! vive! vive!*'

Other ladies more dazzling than Fanny were soon to gather round him: Lady Shelley, Mrs Arbuthnot, Lady Frances Wedderburn-Webster, Lady Caroline Lamb, Lady Charlotte Greville and Madame de Staël, not to mention the singers Grassini, Catalani and their sisterhood – all the beauty and seductiveness of Paris to which he was now coming not, as in 1814, a mere ambassador, but to be the country's only effective prince – Prince of Waterloo. It took him four months before he was ready to receive into this galaxy his own sad star, Kitty, Duchess of Wellington, still waiting in England.

At the same time, Paris meant problems as well as parties; problems more urgent than Kitty. One was Fouché, another King Louis XVIII, a third Marshal Blücher, a fourth Marshal Ney and a fifth Napoleon. In Napoleon he faced the odious prospect of the ex-Emperor being either executed by his continental foes, or refurbished across the seas by his American or English friends for a third round.

There was also the private soldier to be christened. The Prince of Waterloo may have found time during the first weeks after victory to invent the Tommy.

A military paper had been submitted to him suggesting a typical name for a private. The Duke crossed out the entry and substituted the name of a veteran in his old regiment, the 33rd Foot. Private Thomas Atkins had been with him during the engagement at Boxtel in 1794. At one tense moment he ordered his 33rd, held in reserve, to form open lanes and let the crumbling first line through to the rear, then fill the gap themselves – a grim manoeuvre. Though they succeeded, Thomas Atkins was one who fell, to become immortal after Waterloo.*

* The above version of the well-known story seems on balance to be the most probable. The RAMC Historical Museum, Aldershot, possesses an original pay-book with the name Thomas Atkins at the top of its specimen page and the date 24 June 1815 at the bottom. The Duke cannot have chosen the name as late as 1843 while Warden of the Cinque Ports according to the usual version, since there is an actual entry in this pay-book (following the specimen pages) as early as 1825. The fact that 24 June 1815 was given as the specimen date on the title page raises the strong likelihood that the Duke changed the name to Tommy Atkins on the proof copy soon after this date. (See A. L. Kipling, *Bulletin of the Military Historical Society*, February 1957; Fortescue, *History of the British Army*, vol. xii., fn. p. 568; *Cornhill Magazine*, June 1915, pp. 755–6; *Winter's Pie*, Christmas 1912, pp. 38–40. I am greatly indebted to Maj.-Gen. A. MacLennan, OBE, Curator of the RAMC Museum, for his kindness, and to Mr Dineen, R.U.S.I., for his tracing of documents.

2

Cases of 'Crim.Con.'?

Grant, O merciful God, that the result of this mighty battle, terrible in conflict but glorious beyond example in success, may put an end to the miseries of Europe, and staunch the blood of Nations.

Such was the form of Thanksgiving Prayer for victory ordered to be said in all churches throughout Britain. Wellington took its concluding words seriously. France restored to tranquillity; the Bourbons restored to the throne. In those two strictly inter-dependent events he saw the end of Europe's misery.

It would be Louis XVIII's second restoration. This was against him, making him look less like a sun king than a paper lantern carried by foreigners. Many British soldiers reflected the contempt in which the French army held this obese, gout-ridden Bourbon. 'His pottle belly Majesty,' wrote Sergeant Wheeler, 'an old bloated poltroon, the Sir John Falstaff of France.' In French, Louis *Dix-Huit* had become 'Louis *Dix Huîtres*', a pun on his passion for oysters. As for his brother the Count of Artois and nephews the Dukes of Angoulême and Berry, they were detested. A British gunner passed the nephews on the road to Paris and reported that their fulsome salutations made even the horses blush.

Nevertheless Louis XVIII possessed one unique asset. He was the legitimate king of France. Ever since the Congress of Vienna had settled for legitimacy it was obvious that no other principle would be accepted by the victorious powers. Wellington, who had returned from the Peninsular War with an open mind, was finally converted to legitimacy by his Cabinet colleagues. The question now was not who should govern France but how to hump old Louis back on to his throne.

By the second day after Waterloo the Duke announced to Louis that he would be re-enthroned but must accept a pair of guardian angels – M. de Talleyrand and M. Fouché, the former a professional turncoat, the latter a regicide. Talleyrand made his

way confidently to King Louis at Ghent, the only obstacle in his
path being the dreadful battlefield, which he managed to skirt.
Fouché's installation was likely to prove a more ticklish operation.

Only because of Fouché's influence with the middle classes and
some of the nobility, and his position as head of the provisional
government, was Wellington prepared to back the man who in
1793 had joined in demanding Louis XVI's death. When Talleyrand first suggested Fouché to Louis, the horrified old man
flushed crimson and shouted 'Never!'. But the British Cabinet
were behind Fouché and the deed was done. Castlereagh called
it 'a great point gained' and the Duke, reminded on occasion
about Fouché's grim record, would shrug his shoulders and
say, 'Why, that is of no account.'[1]

*

With everything now prepared for the Restoration, Wellington's
humane hope was to arrange the capitulation of Paris without
further fighting. He succeeded, though at the cost of misunderstanding and future trouble.

At first there was nothing but profound relief. 'It is true, thank
God!' wrote Wellington's artillery commander at 2 P.M. on 3 July
'Paris has surrendered. . . .' The provisional government under
Fouché agreed to withdraw the French army of some hundred
thousand men to the left bank of the Loire while all disputed
articles in their proposed terms of surrender were dropped except
for Articles XI and XII. Through these articles Fouché intended to
protect the public monuments and those inhabitants of Paris
who by reason of their functions during the Hundred Days
might find themselves in danger. The key sentence in Article XII
ran:

The inhabitants, and in general terms all persons who are in the
French capital at this moment, will continue to enjoy their rights and
liberties. . . .

This was ambiguous. Who was an 'inhabitant'? Would it pro-
hibit King Louis from punishing traitors? When the Convention
of Saint-Cloud was ratified on 4 July Wellington had no thought
whatever of interfering in a future French civil government. His

mind was occupied, as always after a battle, with protecting civilians from military excesses.

*

The Thanksgiving Prayer already quoted had ended by beseeching the Almighty to control the Allied armies:

Let not the story of their progress be stained by ambition, nor sullied by revenge.

As far as the Prussians were concerned, Marshal Blücher saw nothing wrong in reprisals – though when some of his troops entered his own quarters in search of loot the old man expostulated, '*Mes enfants, c'est trop*'. 'He is a famous old fellow,' the Duke told Lady Shelley, 'though he don't quite stop his troops in plundering.'[2]

The difference between British and Prussian ideas had become evident as soon as the two armies left Waterloo. Wellington not only forbade pillaging but ordered his men to respect every inch of the French countryside, crossing the cornfields in single file. 'The impression towards him and his army is indescribable,' wrote Castlereagh from Paris.[3] But the Prussians remained unabashed after indulging in rape and murder on a savage scale. 'England has never been overrun by French armies,' one of them explained, 'or you would act as we do. The French acted a cruel part in Prussia . . . they taught us a lesson we are now come to France to put into practice.'[4]

Though Wellington could not prevent all excesses, he did frustrate Blücher's intention to blow up the bridges of Austerlitz and Jena and Bonaparte's pillar in the Place Vendôme, contrary to Article XI of the Convention which protected public buildings. The story of how Wellington 'kept the bridge' of Jena was rather more Horatian (in the sense that he had several assistants) than his admirers admitted.* Talleyrand was in fact the first to get wind of its imminent destruction by Blücher. But when his government protested under Article XI, Blücher replied that the bridge had already been mined and he very much hoped that M. de Talleyrand would be standing on the parapet. King Louis then declared himself willing (though perhaps not quite able) to

* Both Lady Shelley and Stanhope mention only the part of Wellington in this famous affair.

jump off it, if the Prussians so wished. Wellington promptly posted a British sentry on the bridge. He was amused to hear afterwards that the Prussian engineers, fuses in hand, had requested his sentry to remove himself, to which this stolid Britisher replied, 'Not until I am relieved by the corporal.'[5]

The Prussians went ahead but succeeded only in cracking the arch and tumbling one of their own sentries into the Seine. At this point the three Allied sovereigns arrived in Paris and both bridges were saved, though not the Vendôme statue. When a Peninsular veteran, William Grattan, arrived in Paris hoping to see Boney up aloft, he found that the ultra-Royalists had demolished the hero, leaving in occupation of his pillar nothing but a white Bourbon flag.

A second Prussian project was to exact a stupendous indemnity from Paris, a fifth to be paid within twenty-four hours or Blücher would carry off a number of French bankers as hostages. Wellington knocked this idea on the head, as he was soon to thwart a more orthodox scheme for bleeding France white.

A third clash with Blücher had arisen over Napoleon's fate. The Prussians were for shooting him out of hand. Aghast, Wellington told Blücher bluntly what he thought:

He and I had acted too distinguished parts in these transactions to become executioners . . . if the Sovereigns wished to put him to death they should appoint an executioner, which should not be me.[6]

The object of Wellington's concern, meanwhile, had successfully run the Prussian gauntlet and reached Rochefort.

On 8 July Louis XVIII entered Paris in a state of triumph modified by the black looks among the white cockades. Some British spectators noticed only the dazzle of whiteness and happy tears; Captain Rees Howell Gronow, late of Picton's staff, thought the Parisians looked sulky and stupefied right up to the King's grand entry; then they went mad with joy. To Madame d'Arblay they seemed frighteningly sullen throughout, as if consumed with a mixture of disloyalty and guilt.

Napoleon, having failed to get a guaranteed safe passage to America from Rochefort, decided on 13 July to throw himself on the mercy of Britain's Prince Regent.

Your Royal Highness . . . . I have ended my political career and come, like Themistocles, to seat myself at the hearth of the British people. I put myself under the protection of her laws and address this entreaty to Your Highness as the most powerful, the most steadfast and the most generous of my foes.

Bastille Day, 14 July, was his last day on French soil. On the 15th Themistocles donned his green uniform of the Chasseurs of the Guard, inspected the weeping French sailors who were to row him to Captain Maitland's ship, *Bellerophon*, and sailed for Plymouth to see what his assault on British hearts would achieve.

No British Bastille was ready to fall. True, the Prince Regent's first reaction had been favourable. 'Upon my word, a very proper letter: much more so, I must say, than any I ever received from Louis xviii.' [7]

But on most Tory ears the 'Themistocles' passage grated, and for every radical, like John Cam Hobhouse, who found the whole letter 'very good', there were a hundred citizens longing to have the suppliant hanged, handed back for the purpose to Louis (the Prime Minister's personal wish), immured in some Scottish castle or otherwise disposed of further afield. But it was for the British Cabinet as a whole to decide, which they duly did. Their choice was St Helena.

Napoleon Bonaparte was carried away on 7 August 1815 to a rock in the South Atlantic where, unexpectedly, he founded a new empire, and in the timeless worlds of literature and thought reigned over far more hearts than ever he had conquered as Emperor of the French.

*

See Paris and live! Spending his first night in the Bois de Boulogne which had suddenly been transformed into a white-tented town filled with the British army, George Keppel could not sleep: 'For my part I lay awake all night, thinking of the pleasure in prospect of the following day.' Next morning he went straight to the Tuileries and won a smiling response to his salute from royalty itself, wearing a blue coat with gilt buttons, pantaloons and hessian boots. How odd to find a king dressed quietly 'like an English country gentleman'. Other Majesties were also the objects of cool appraisal. No Britisher thought much of the Austrian, a 'thread-paper of a man'; many preferred the Tsar's 'free open countenance beaming with kindness and condescension on all around him'. White chargers were ridden by the two emperors. Wellington, as usual on his small chestnut, with a plain red coat, one star and no feathers, 'looked nothing as compared with the rest'. Yet every neck was 'on the stretch' to see the hero, and all throats ready to bawl, 'Vive Wellington!'[8]

Dapper young Captain Gronow noticed a female riding-habit at the Duke's side on 25 July 1815. This was the day of the grand review on the plains of Saint-Denis, the rider being Frances Shelley, wife of Sir John Shelley, Bt. At the end of the complicated manoeuvres the Austrian general, Prince Schwarzenberg, paid Wellington a heartfelt compliment. 'You are the only man who can so well play at that game.'

Beautiful Lady Shelley seemed to Gronow to be playing another game. How 'strange' that the Duke should allow her to cavort around him, mounted on one of his horses. Certain French ladies insinuated that she was indecorous.[9] But the Duke continued to lend her a horse whenever she wished. On occasion it would be Copenhagen. It amused him to see her coping with another Waterloo hero. 'I believe you think the glory greater than the pleasure in riding him!'

Lady Shelley was what Dr Johnson used to call a 'rapturist'. Her enthusiasm for Wellington – 'How I adore that great man!' – sometimes bored him. When he had first called on her in Paris that July (they had already met during the London celebrations of 1814), she could hardly restrain her tears, so touchingly simple and unobtrusive did he look. He was exactly the same as last year despite all the new glory, except for even more fire in his eyes and a little added weight. Luckily she managed not to cry, for the hero did not understand 'high-wrought sentiment'.

Nor did Lady Shelley understand all the Duke's tastes. Why did he prefer to listen rather than talk, save about war and politics, so that in general conversation 'he seldom said anything worth noting'? His expression, however, was often revealing. She watched his face at manoeuvres. Why did it stiffen when his soldiers took off their hats to him and shouted? 'I hate that cheering. If once you allow soldiers to express an opinion, they may, on some other occasion, hiss instead of cheer[ing].' Then he relaxed. 'However, I cannot always help my fellows giving me a hurrah!'

She watched his face in his own house. Of course she knew he was tied down abroad at present by his military duties as well as the peace negotiations which opened in July. But did he not look forward to getting back to England? 'Do you know, I never anticipate.' For a moment he allowed himself to dwell on the triumphant return: an extra £200,000 already voted by Parliament, a splendid home of his own to be built at last. 'I think it will certainly be very gratifying, but I am quite happy here.'

Lady Shelley had another question. Would he not dislike peace and quiet after the military life? Surely he would never settle down?

'Oh! yes I shall, but I must always have my house full. For sixteen years I have always been at the head of our army, and I must have these gay fellows round me' – with a glance at his aides-de-camp.

On a different point he showed a lack of taste, she thought, in going so much to the house of Mme. Craufurd, a fat sixty-seven-year-old Frenchwoman, grandmother of the celebrated dandy Count D'Orsay. And in picking up some tiny, dusty French child from the boulevards and eating something horrible it offered him. How could he bear to touch the uninteresting little creature? Frances Shelley much preferred the delightful picnics when his friends would sit on a grassy bank while Colonel James Stanhope (uncle of the Duke's future 'Boswell') recited Byron's *Childe Harold*, Catalani, Grassini and Tom Moore sang, or Kemble talked about Shakespeare and Walter Scott about Mme. de Pompadour. Scott told Frances that Wellington was the only man who had ever made him feel awed and abashed.[10]

*

On 5 August the *St James's Chronicle* copied from the Continental press a sensational story about the Duke.

5 Aug. Brussels 1815 – Fashionable Alliteration.
> '*In the letter W. there's a charm half divine*
> *War – Wellington-Wedderburn-Webster – and Wine,*' F.

The cessation of warfare has, in Paris, enabled scandal to resume her usual influence on the public mind. A report is very prevalent in the first Parisian circles that a distinguished commander has surrendered himself captive to the beautiful wife of a military officer of high rank, in a manner to make a very serious investigation of this offence indispensable.. . . .

The *amour*, said the *Chronicle*, would lead to a 'crim.con.' case.*

Wellington, of course, was the 'distinguished commander', while the military officer and his beautiful wife were Captain James Wedderburn-Webster and the twenty-two-year-old Lady Frances. During the Duchess of Richmond's ball (15 June) it was said that Wellington had flirted with Lady Frances and afterwards walked alone with her in the Park. Not that a couple could be 'alone' in the Park at Brussels during the hot days before Waterloo, since it was a most popular resort.

That Wellington was attracted to this unusual girl (pretty, pious, married at seventeen to a self-confessed libertine and Byron's inamorata though apparently not his mistress) is proved by the fact that he wrote brief notes to her both on the morning of Waterloo and on the day after. That he was her lover is highly unlikely, though the contrary cannot be proved. He had been introduced to her for the first time shortly before the battle and at this date she was seven months gone in pregnancy. It might be argued that in the hectic atmosphere preceding Waterloo anything could happen, that the tensions unwound in Frances Webster's company.† 'I am but a man,' he had said of himself; a man whose wife had gone home to her children with the first batch of refugees from Paris. The argument, such as it is, does not stand up to the contrary statement that Wellington was soon making to his closest friends.

The *St James's Chronicle* continued:

> The husband has laid his damages at £50,000 which it is said the fortunate lover offered to pay; but this affair was too notorious for composition or the party injured had too much sensibility to be content with wearing 'gilded' horns.

Two days later the newspaper followed up with a spread-as-you-deny paragraph.

* 'Criminal conversation', the legal ground for divorce before the 1857 Marriage Act. The *Chronicle*, however, appeared to translate it as 'criminal connection'. See below, p. 42.

† For all his outward calm, there is some evidence that Wellington was feeling the strain. A letter he wrote on the morning of the battle to Sir Charles Stuart contained several small mistakes, such as a word and punctuation left out, and the wrong address, 'Bruxelles', written at the top and then corrected to 'Waterloo'. This was most unusual for Wellington.

Several of the public prints have in some particulars gone too far in their insinuations . . . and have blamed a 'crim.con.' and magnified damages in their usual sweeping way. . . . We may moreover ask, if the rumour of a criminal connection at an antecedent period, while subsequent to it the wedded parties lived & appeared together . . . be sufficient grounds for an action at law?

Predictably, an unctuous denial followed.

We are rejoiced to learn from good authority that there is not the least foundation for a story of criminal intercourse on the Continent. . . .

But a later paragraph reinstated the scandal.

A very beautiful woman of Irish extraction is said to be a party in the amour at Brussels which has made so great a noise on the Continent.

*

All this soon showed in Wellington's face. He began to look ill and worried.

Young William Lennox, his aide-de-camp, never forgot the first impact of the libel. He himself was writing out invitations to a ball when the Duke came in with his Spanish friend, General Alava.

'Have you the newspaper?' he asked William. 'I suppose it's the usual style of attack?'

William handed the paper to Alava, who began searching for the libellous column. Wellington meanwhile played with his watch-chain. As the search went on his face slowly cleared. He looked up. 'Oh! that mine enemy would write a book! better take no notice.' It was not even a book; only a column; and Wellington always knew how to deal with columns.

At last Alava handed him the copy. Suddenly his expression changed to blazing anger.

'That's too bad – the writer's a walking lie – never saw her alone in my life – this must be checked.'[11]

What did the Duke's circle think of the affair? Seeing him with Frances Webster at a ball, Lady Shelley decided it was platonic – at least on his side. 'His manner is the most paternal of any one I ever saw'; he was 'simple and kind' to her in public, but nothing more.[12]

In Ireland, not far from the Duchess of Wellington's old home

at Pakenham Hall, the scandal was being discussed. Maria
Edgeworth cared only about the effect on her beloved friend
Kitty: 'She is not a woman who delights in titles or rank, but she
does enjoy her husband's glory & therefore I hope it will not like
Nelson's be tarnished.'[13]

Arthur's glory was indeed everything to Kitty; but Frances
Webster was no Emma, nor was Arthur the man to look for a
passionate and all-absorbing union outside marriage, however
unsatisfactory the conditions inside might be.

At the end of November 1815 the Edgeworths were puzzled by
a pause in the scandal-mongering. What had become of the
threatened divorce? How was that affair kept out of Doctor's
Commons? Maria's father contributed his masculine reflections
on politics and sex. There had been changes in the French government at the top – Fouché in exile (at least that 'criminal connection' between the Duke and the regicide, as it seemed to many,
was at an end); Talleyrand out of office and the irreproachable
Duke of Richelieu Prime Minister. Now Mr Edgeworth asked
himself whether this prince of dalliance, Wellington, was the type
to retain his popularity under these new circumstances?

*

The public soon heard that Captain Wedderburn-Webster,
instead of instituting proceedings against his wife for adultery,
intended to combine with Lady Frances in bringing a joint action
for libel against the *St James's Chronicle*. Whether or not
Webster at first contemplated a divorce action is not known. But
by the early autumn of 1815 Wellington had convinced him there
was no ground for divorce. The Duchess of Wellington was sent
for in October, which may have been part of the same operation.
Certainly there was a note of relief in Lord Liverpool's letter to
Castlereagh announcing the fact.

The *Lady's Magazine* loyally reported Kitty's arrival in Paris
and her début at the Opera shimmering with humming-birds'
feathers. Homespun Kitty, however, hastily disclaimed the
compliment in a letter to Maria: 'I do not possess any ornaments
of feathers – Do you recollect on a former occasion your telling
me of my having appeared (in the newspapers) blazing with
diamonds – my diamonds are yet in the mine & my humming
birds yet wear their own feathers.'[14]

That was part of Kitty's trouble. The Duke would have preferred the diamonds to be in her hair. But while he was still at the wars Kitty had set her face against fashion. 'My dear Lady Wellington,' said a woman friend in 1813, 'how many times a day do you think of your dress?' 'Why, three times,' replied Kitty. 'Morning, evening and night besides *casualties*.'[15]

To return to the Websters. If the Captain's wife was innocent, his mother-in-law Lady Mountnorris, was guilty – of spreading rumours. Early in the new year, 1816, Webster evidently warned Wellington both verbally and in writing against her. A written reply was sent by Wellington to Webster on 6 January 1816, one of the few footmarks in these sands not to have been washed away either deliberately or by chance:

Dear Sir

I was out when your note came here; and am but just now returned.

I consider what passed between you & me the other day as entirely confidential; and I will have no communication upon it with any body; I am very little inclined to hear family disputes; and am very indifferent as to what is said or may be said about myself, excepting as far as these scandalous stories are turned to affect an innocent Person. Even in that case when I hear them they serve only to put me on my Guard for her sake; and I don't feel the slightest inclination to discuss them with any body whatever.

You may depend upon it that I shall decline to have any communication with Lady Mountnorris excepting that which as a Gentleman I am liable to have with any Lady I meet in Society.

Ever Your's most faithfully,
Wellington.[16]

Next month, on 16 February 1816, before Chief Justice Gibbs in the Court of Common Pleas, was heard the case of 'Wedderburn Webster Esq.' and 'Frances Caroline Webster, his wife, *v.* Baldwin', proprietor of the *St James's Chronicle*. Wellington was in France during the trial, but his name was to the fore and he undoubtedly backed up the two plaintiffs in taking public action.

Counsel for the plaintiffs, Serjeant Best, stated the case. As reported in the press, he explained that a nobleman of rank, like the Duke, would naturally visit, when in Brussels, families of corresponding quality, though 'he was never in his life alone with Lady Webster'. Counsel dwelt on the lady's approaching confinement and the Duke's exalted character as 'the saviour of Europe & the greatest commander of any age & country', who might be 'looked up to by Christendom as the tutelar saint of the world'. Best then called the Duke of Richmond, who pronounced Frances Webster 'a lady of singularly amiable & decorous manners'. Even after reading the libels, neither he nor the Duchess of Richmond had seen fit to lessen the intimacy between Lady Frances and their unmarried daughters.

Overwhelmed by this ducal offensive, Mr Serjeant Lens, for the defence, could only admit his client's utter rout. Little excuse, no justification, nothing but reparation could be offered. In his summing up Sir Vicary Gibbs, known as 'Vinegar' Gibbs for his bitter tongue, directed the jury to exclude from their consideration all matters not immediately concerned with the case, such as the injury sustained by the Duke of Wellington. On the other hand, if the damages given were small, it might suggest that the plaintiffs' case had not been fully proved.

The verdict was £2,000, representing at least £20,000 in today's figures.

On hearing the news, Byron told a friend that he would have had Lady Frances himself rather than leave her to Wellington.

*

The Wedderburn-Websters pass dismally from history. By 1828 the family were in financial trouble, owing to Webster's extravagance, and periodic entreaties reached the Duke for patronage. His polite but steady refusals were understandable.

His two famous letters to Lady Frances, written respectively just before and after Waterloo, were not deemed publishable until his son, the 2nd Duke, included them in the *Supplementary Despatches*. There was also a third letter to Lady Frances which remained unpublished among Wellington's papers, though like the other two it was a pattern of propriety.* When Colonel

* For the first two letters see *Wellington: The Years of the Sword*, pp. 537 and 590. The third letter was dated 18 July 1815, Paris, and was written in answer to Lady Frances's enquiry about the fate of Bonaparte. Having given a factual account up to Napoleon's sailing for England on the 15th, the Duke concluded: 'Exactly in one month after his invasion of the Low Countries, & only one battle, he has been obliged to give himself up to the nation with which he had been at war during his whole career. . . . I hope to see you soon' (*Wellington MSS.*).

Gurwood asked about these letters in 1838 while editing Volume XII of the *Despatches*, Lady Frances had been dead a year but her husband was still living. (He died in 1840.) Wellington replied to Gurwood:

I think it best not to insert these letters to Lady F. Webster. The Gentleman [Webster] who is selling them was in the King's Bench or one of the Prisons for debt; & offered them there for sale for thirty pounds. If they are published without the Names some of those who have seen them will certainly recollect to whom they were addressed; & will add the Names. That would create a nine days' wonder; which . . . it is the object to avoid by omitting the Names. It is best therefore upon the whole not to publish the Letters; as they contain nothing of publick or military interest.*[17]

*

News of the Duke's friendship with another lady also got into English newspapers at this time, but without giving him cause for complaint. This was Germaine Necker de Staël-Holstein, the greatest eccentric in Europe but also the most effective opponent, in the world of thought, of Napoleon's tyranny. Her scintillating intellect and irresistible personality were eventually to make even her advanced political views acceptable to the Duke. She had encountered Wellington as ambassador to the French court in 1814. Waterloo in her eyes was Wellington's apotheosis. In a letter of 9 August 1815 she saluted him as a god: 'My Lord! There is a glory in this world which is unalloyed and without reproach . . . As you wake up in the morning does your heart not beat with the joy of being you?' This hymn of praise, however, was followed some time later by a passionate entreaty on behalf of her 'unhappy country'. Wellington was silent until 24 December. Then he made a bold bid for Mme de Staël's political support, while disclosing that he had lost the support of her friends:

As you are one of us and, as I hope, a moderate, you will have approved all the arrangements which have been made to regulate future relations between France & the rest of Europe. . . .

* According to Richard Ford the artist, writer and close friend of the 2nd Duke, Wellington explained, 'What a fool I must have been when I wrote those letters', on receiving them back. (Note written by R. Ford in the margin of his *Apsley House & Walmer Castle*, 1853; 2nd Duke's copy.)

I see little of your friends . . . I have been forsaken; & all I have now is the memory of those happy hours I spent in your house last year & in your company everywhere.[18]

What had gone wrong in those five months since Germaine de Staël's first ecstatic letter of August? And why did the Duke call a Frenchwoman 'one of us'?

3

At the Court of King Arthur

When Paris surrendered not even Byron had a word to say against the Duke: 'He *is* a man.' The rest of Napoleon's conquerors, especially Castlereagh, Byron dismissed as 'the b . . . s'.

The Paris peace conference had opened on 12 July 1815 with Wellington and Castlereagh as British delegates. The Duke could not have wished for a more fitting partner. Lord Castlereagh had been his friend ever since their early manhood in 'Ascendancy' Ireland. After so long an association it was natural for the soldier to feel complete confidence in the politician's solutions.

Castlereagh believed passionately that only the old Quadruple Alliance of Britain, Austria, Russia and Prussia could preserve the European balance. At Vienna Talleyrand, through his famous secret treaty between the France of the First Restoration, Britain and Austria, had subtly shifted the Alliance towards curbing the ambitious Tsar. With Talleyrand again conducting French affairs, the Alliance would bolster the Second Restoration and leave Austria and Britain riding high on the Continent and the seas. Towards supporting this solution the Duke proposed to apply the full weight of his immense prestige.

It was Wellington's hour and he could say as he had said before the battle of Talavera, 'the ball is at my foot, and I hope I shall have strength to give it a good kick'; but the hour also had its trials.

Louis was not as amenable as Austria's Count Metternich hoped. There were occasions when the Duke needed all his strength to refrain from kicking the King himself. Would His Majesty dine with the Duke of Wellington at his residence in the Elysée Palace? There would be a party of six, including the captain of the guard. His Majesty replied that he could not possibly sit down with a subject. 'The captain of the French guard dines at my table daily,' retorted the Duke, 'and I won't alter my rule.'[1] This time the King required only a gentle kick to make him see reason. He duly sat. It was not always so. People said that the restored Bourbons had learnt nothing and forgotten nothing.

Art provided the first great French grievance. It seemed right to the Allies that the art treasures seized from abroad by the victorious French armies should be returned in defeat.

Wellington's initial plan was mild: gradually to satisfy his Allies' minimal demands for restitution, 'without hurting the feelings of the King of France'. He did not even demand the Bayeux tapestry for England, as someone whimsically pointed out. When Colonel Woodford, one of his ADCs at Waterloo, bought the field of Agincourt and began prodding among French bones, the Duke intervened: 'I gave Woodford a hint to dig no more.'[2]

Notwithstanding the Duke's moderation, it took over two weeks of bitter argument for the French Government to agree to restitution. Then King Louis declared he would yield only to force. The Duke let off steam to Caroline Lamb: 'Nothing could exceed the meanness of Louis XVIII, in his dealings with the English in regard to the pictures in the Louvre.' French concern for the art treasures, he told Castlereagh, was simply national vanity. Better they should realize they were no longer the masters of Europe. Better to teach them 'a great Moral Lesson'.*[3]

On 19 September what was known as 'the storming of the Louvre' began. British soldiers escorted Dutch removers into the building. At once there was a sharp fall in the Duke's reputation. Parisian workmen refused to unhook the Italian pictures, and ladders from a nearby exhibition of performing monkeys were used by Allied soldiers to enable the Titians and Tintorettos to make an ignoble descent. When they carried out the Venus de Medici feet first, a Peninsular veteran named Grattan was accosted by an enraged onlooker.

'Sir, is it not a shame of your General to sanction the removal

* Whether covering up for a subordinate or applying the 'Moral Lesson', the Duke sanctioned the inclusion of some antique arms (now at the Tower) in the Artillery's share of stores captured in Paris. (WO 44/616 and Rotunda Scrap-book; Woolwich.)

of these exquisite models collected by the Emperor with paternal care from every country in Europe and now so well calculated to be seen by all those nations, and free of expense too?'

Soon afterwards Grattan was joined by a young French artist in tears.

'Oh, if the Duke of Wellington would only order the removal of the pictures to take place at night, we should be spared the horror of seeing them torn away.'[4]

In fact the Duke did try this method with the Parisians' favourite trophies, the four horses of St Mark's. Napoleon had set them up on a triumphal arch in the Place du Carrousel, after having liquidated the Venetian Republic by bartering it to Austria in 1797. (Then it was the Venetians who had wept and booed as their horses were let down in chains from St Mark's façade.) Still anxious to spare French feelings, Wellington ordered the bronze horses to be removed by night, assigning the job to a trusted Peninsular veteran, Major Todd. It was hoped that old Louis, under whose windows they stood, would sleep through it. With only a few officers, twenty civilians and some hammers and chisels, Todd set to work. Suddenly there was a loud clatter. The National Guard dashed into the Place du Carrousel followed by an infuriated mob and forced Todd and his chisels to take cover in the Tuileries. Next morning Wellington arrived expecting to find the work done. In a towering rage he ordered three thousand Austrians and Hungarians, their white uniforms and brass cannon flashing in broad daylight, to seal off the Place du Carrousel. They cheered uproariously as Todd brought each horse down, while the mob outside howled. Major Todd was afterwards given a gold snuff-box by the Austrian Emperor.

The 'sack' spread. Spaniards rescued their Murillos and even Sardinians hoped to find something; but having invaded the Louvre when the Austrian guards were absent, they were unceremoniously swept out by cleaners with brooms.

Was there a solution to the 'works of art' problem which Wellington overlooked? It seems unlikely. His troubles derived from the very nature of loot. Loot is not subject to an ethical code. Wellington later defined it as 'what you could lay your bloody hands upon and keep'.[5] In 1815 he had to be satisfied with such morsels of comfort as a letter from Pope Pius VII. His Holiness was delighted to hear that the Vatican treasures were being restored and 'with unexampled generosity' England was paying for the transport.[6]

Napoleon had made the Pope pay the cost of abduction.

*

If the 'art' controversy kept Paris on the boil for three months, the affair of the 'traitors' blazed for twice as long and went on smouldering for years.

For the opening of the drama it is necessary to return to the capitulation of Paris. Article XII guaranteed the liberties of the inhabitants, it will be remembered, irrespective of previous political records. Hardly was the capitulation complete before the British Cabinet received disquieting reports that Article XII might be interpreted as a general pardon. Lord Liverpool had always insisted on 'exemplary punishment' of traitors. The Cabinet therefore urged Wellington to prevent any 'misconstruction' of Article XII.[7]

Never had it entered the Duke's head that his military Convention could impose a political amnesty; in his view it touched nothing political. That did not mean, however, that he pinned his faith like Lord Liverpool on a punitive peace.

There was more than one French 'traitor', meanwhile, who did not stop to test out Article XII. On 6 July Marshal Ney quitted Paris intending to seek asylum abroad. Fouché had provided him with passports (one forged) and a disguise. A week later Napoleon's ADC, La Bédoyère, also decided to be off. He found temporary refuge with the French army on the Loire. The refugees' instincts proved correct. King Louis issued on 24 July his notorious 'Royal Ordinances' containing lists of persons to be banished or executed. The names of Colonel de La Bédoyère and General Lavalette were on the death-list; at its head was that of Marshal Ney. The 'White Terror' was in full swing.

The handsome Charles de La Bédoyère, having been drawn back to Paris for a farewell glimpse of his wife Georgine and baby son, was arrested on 2 August, tried for high treason and on the 19th executed. Georgine had pleaded in vain for his life with Wellington, Tsar Alexander and King Louis. Two traits in the Duke's character helped him to resist: sense of public duty – this time his duty to obey Cabinet orders – and dislike of interfering. The old King denied Georgine with sorrow.

'Madame,' he sighed, 'never has a refusal cost me so much.'[8]

It was to cost his dynasty more than he guessed. Fifteen years later the 1830 Revolution paid off many scores, including the 'White Terror'. Louis xviii's brother, Charles x, lost his throne, while this in turn played its part in Wellington losing the premiership.

The 'White Terror' struck again and again. Ney and Lavalette were arrested (Ney on 3 August) and thrown into the Conciergerie. Once more King Louis had misgivings but Talleyrand, playing along with the British Government, commended Ney's arrest: 'It will be a great example.' Ney, having promised Louis to bring back Napoleon in an iron cage, had treacherously changed sides. For this he had no defence. But his own psychological explanation was correct:

'What could I do? Hold up the floods of the ocean with my hands?' Like Mihailovitch one hundred and thirty years later, he was swept away by the gale of the world. On 6 December his judges decided by massive majorities for death. Only the young Duke of Broglie, future son-in-law of Mme de Staël, stoutly voted '*Non*'.

While Ney was standing his trial Wellington deliberately abstained from intervention. Powerful appeals were made to him but he gently told Ney's beautiful wife, Aglaé, that his was not an independent voice. He was the spokesman of the Allies; a spokesman, moreover, who must on no account make Louis xviii, seem the mouthpiece of the Duke of Wellington. To these two reasons for non-intervention a third must be added which he did not mention to Aglaé.

The story of the third reason was told by the Duke himself to his friend Lord Alvanley many years later. His narrative began:[9]

I daresay you have heard me blamed for not asking Louis xviii to spare Ney: I will tell you what happened & leave you to judge whether I could do anything in such a time.

He then described how he had happened to visit the Tuileries shortly *before* Ney's arrest and on approaching the King,

I was surprised by his turning me a cold shoulder; as I am not given to take offence, I thought I was perhaps mistaken, – so I walked up to him again, & again he showed me a cold shoulder; upon which I immediately left the Palace, feeling very angry & saying to myself 'I'll be

hanged if I come here again to be insulted by the King or any one else':
for there were others . . . who were immediately cold & distant to me
that evening.

Contemporary gossip ascribed some of these other insults to the
French marshals, who turned their backs, thus giving Wellington
the chance, when Louis later apologized, for a *bon mot*:

'Don't distress yourself, Sire: it is not the first time that they
have turned their backs on me.'

The end of Wellington's narrative is important. It was during
his 'estrangement' from the King, he pointed out, that Ney was
executed. If the sentence had been unjust he might have demanded
Ney's life;

but as it was I could only have asked it as a special favour to myself; and
when I had been insulted in this manner, & was not on terms with the
King, I could not think of asking favours of him.

So this was the third reason. Honour forbade him to plead for
Ney. It was not till afterwards, however, that the Duke realized
the point of the insults.

My belief is, that they had offended me on purpose to drive me away,
that I might not interfere to prevent Ney's death. For not long after it
was accomplished, the king sent Comte d'Artois to me to express great
regret a t my absence, & hopes that I . . . had not been offended in any
way.

The Duke received Artois with a resounding volley: 'Monseig-
neur, I am an English gentleman, and no one shall insult me with
impunity.' Whereupon the Count of Artois seized both the
Duke's hands and burst into tears, protesting his brother's total
innocence. The Duke listened 'very coldly'. At last the grovelling
Artois, having been suitably punished, was informed that his
Grace would consent to re-enter the Tuileries.[10]

There is no reason to doubt this story, even though it goes
beyond Wellington's remarks made to Miss Angela Burdett-
Coutts in old age: 'I might or I might not have had great influence
on the King! I did not interfere in any way! I did not consider
it my duty to interfere. . . .'[11] He did not tell her about the King's
cold shoulder. But he implied, in telling the story to Lord
Alvanley, that if Louis had behaved differently he might have
asked for Ney's life as a special favour to himself. Instead he

returned one cold shoulder with another as cold as death.

Wellington's admirers can only regret that he sacrificed the major virtue of magnanimity on the minor though respectable altars of personal honour and public duty. Why, in particular, did old-fashioned ideas of honour weigh so heavily with an otherwise simple and unaffected hero? The answer lay in his own confession, 'I am but a man.' If the man is traced back to the boy, to the despised and 'awkward Arthur' of his masterful mother's biting phrase, it is possible to see why later insults should get under the skin even of 'King Arthur', especially when delivered by other sovereigns.

Ney faced the firing squad with the courage to be expected of 'the bravest of the brave'. When his death sentence was read to him in the small hours of 7 December he interrupted the recital of his former titles with, 'What good can this do? Michael Ney, – then a heap of dust, that is all.' He too was but a man. The tragedy of his execution was swiftly followed by what might be called a Restoration comedy, the escape of Lavalette.

On the night before he was due to be guillotined, Lavalette walked out of prison in his wife's clothes. He was then hidden by three young Englishmen, provided with forged passports and disguised as a British general. Escorted by two of them to the frontier, he reached Bavaria unscathed. The Englishmen, Sir Robert Wilson, Michael Bruce and John Hely-Hutchinson, were all arrested and threatened with death for high treason.

At this point the Duke, who had already defended their right to free speech during Ney's trial – 'an Englishman has as much right to talk in Paris as in London' – intervened. Though unable to resist telling Caroline Lamb that Bruce (whom she had chased in Paris) deserved to be hanged, and Mrs Arbuthnot that Caroline ought to join Bruce in the galleys,[12] the Duke worked hard to get their case tried in an ordinary assize court. He succeeded, and in April 1816 a sympathetic French jury gave them the minimum sentence – three months.

*

Even Wellington could not save Fouché and Talleyrand. The new Chamber of Deputies, elected that August and nicknamed the 'Chambre Introuvable' from its right-wing extremism, combined with King Louis to get rid of both from the Government. At a blow Wellington and Castlereagh had lost their hand-picked moderates.

The Tsar's ambassador in Paris, Pozzo di Borgo, was delighted to see the Duke's two 'little lambs' depart. For in Talleyrand's place there appeared out of Russia an aristocratic French *émigré* with grizzled hair and eagle eyes – the Duke of Richelieu, for years Governor of the Crimea. Russia moved into the lead after Talleyrand's fall. Nevertheless Wellington at first worked closely with Richelieu, supporting the Tsar in his crusade for a fair peace and opposing the Prussians in their policy of dismembering France. At the peace conference he threw all his authority on to the side of moderation. This was decisive.

On 20 November 1815 the Second Peace of Paris was concluded with France. Though Richelieu was deathly white as he signed, afterwards writing, 'all is finished . . . I have put my name to this fatal treaty!', the peace treaty was fatal only to vindictive Prussian hopes. Minor border adjustments were made; French fortresses were dismantled but not seized; there was to be an indemnity of 700 million francs; and France was to be occupied for a minimum of three and a maximum of five years by 150,000 Allied soldiers, fed at French expense and commanded as from 22 October by the Duke of Wellington. Even an army of occupation was not necessarily fatal to future international harmony. But behind the peace terms stood the ominous 'Holy Alliance'. Through this innovation the Duke feared being drawn into perpetual intervention.

The Holy Alliance was the precious brain-child of Tsar Alexander I. Announced at a grand review, it was signed for a start by himself, the Austrian emperor and the Prussian king on 26 September – a combination of mystical dilettantism inspired by the Tsar's personal priestess, Madame de Krüdener; a near-Messianic crusade for a Christian brotherhood of rulers and nations; and a political ambition to extend Russia's influence by sweeping under her wings all Christian nations, including Britain's maritime rival, America. Neither Britain nor America signed. Castlereagh described how he and Wellington had reacted to the invitation: 'The Duke of Wellington happened to be with me when the Emperor called, and it was not without difficulty that we went through the interview with becoming gravity.' *In fine*, it was 'sublime nonsense' – something idealistic and imprecise from which the first British instinct was, and still is, to sheer off.

A second innovation was produced by Castlereagh in a firm tightening of the Quadruple Alliance. He had come to the conclusion that a permanent conference of the four ambassadors at Paris was required during the occupation, not to interfere unnecessarily in the four occupied zones but to keep an eye on France for any signs of revolution. Full-scale congresses of the four great powers would deal with specific dangers to Europe after the occupation had ended. Castlereagh's 'new diplomacy' was admirable as an essay in international consultation. But it was to develop in ways that Castlereagh himself did not approve. In the short run, his five-year plan for nannying France – for such it soon seemed to be – could only damage the popularity of Wellington and his four-pronged army of occupation. If anything went wrong he would be blamed. If it succeeded it would only be for the benefit of Castlereagh and the politicians. Would he not show common prudence and stay out? But no – his friend, Sir John Malcolm, recorded:

He is confident that his opinions may do good, and cannot do harm; & he is ready to encounter all the abuse that can be poured upon him, rather than show the prudence which fights more about personal character than public interests.[13]

*

Early in the new year, 1816, Wellington was able to relax a little in a country mansion he had taken at Mont-Saint-Martin, about twelve miles from his headquarters in the garrison-town of Cambrai. His brother-in-law, Culling Charles Smith, was soon employed, as he had been during the Peninsular War, in sending out animals: four couple of hounds, a spaniel, three stags and three hinds. In addition Benjamin Wyatt, now the Duke's architect but once his clerk in India, was asked to design a huge boar-spear based on Indian hog-sticking. In the autumn of 1817 the Duke was relieved and excited to have killed a 300-lb monster which had gashed his foot. 'I suppose we should have [the Duke of] Berry spearing Boars,' he wrote to Fitzroy Somerset, 'if their Tusks could be drawn.' To Mrs Arbuthnot he called it 'a feat which I assure you delighted me more than the Battle of Waterloo ever did'. The offer of a wolf, however, was declined. 'I am afraid it would be too unpopular in the country for me to venture to import him. . . .'[14]

A troop of spirited girls greatly increased the pleasures of the hunt and of house-parties. Foremost among them was a trio of American visitors from Baltimore. Great-grand-daughters of the wealthy Charles Carroll, who was destined to become at ninety-five the longest surviving signatory to the Declaration of Independence, the Caton sisters were known as 'the three Graces' in a society that was both charmed and envious. Like the three Wellesley brothers, William, Arthur and Henry, the three Caton sisters, Louisa, Elizabeth and Marianne, eventually won a coronet each. One of them, Marianne, was to play an interesting role in the Wellesley family history.

Particularly jealous of their success was clever Betsy Patterson, whose brother Robert Patterson was married to Marianne. 'You would be surprised if you knew how great a fool she is,' wrote Betsy to her friend Lady Morgan, the novelist, 'and at the power she exercises over the Duke; but I believe that he has no taste *pour les femmes d'esprit*.'[15] Betsy, also from Baltimore, was a *femme d'esprit* but the victim of a marriage with Napoleon's brother Jerome Bonaparte which the Emperor had annulled. In the Duke's eyes she seemed hard and too fond of her investments. He much preferred the bewitching Catons, even taking them in 1816 to see the field of Waterloo, a unique concession. Marianne noticed his extreme reluctance to go and his silence during the dinner that followed. Afterwards she confessed that had she realized the 'mental anguish' this sight-seeing tour would cause him, she would never have proposed it.[16]

The Duke vowed to find husbands for Marianne's unmarried sisters and very soon Louisa was wedded to his aide-de-camp, Colonel Felton Hervey. High jinks at Mont-Saint-Martin did not obscure the fact of increasing hostility towards the occupation. King Louis implored Wellington to remain in Paris, when he returned there, as a prop to his Government. The British Cabinet, on the contrary, urged him to return to the safety of Cambrai. Wellington replied bluntly to the Cabinet on 13 February 1816: 'There is not much confidence in anybody either here or in England, excepting myself.' Therefore he must stay in Paris. To his brother William Wellesley-Pole he wrote still more brusquely: 'I wish the British Cabinet would lay aside the notion that I am anxious to be assassinated by a French Mob; & I hope they will allow me to do my own duty in the way I think best myself.'[17]

The attacks continued, becoming personal. Reports of his 'pride' had reached Ireland and reminded Maria Edgeworth that the late Lady Longford (his mother-in-law) had feared for his soul:

> I am not surprised at the account of the Duke of Wellington. Poor Lady Longford . . . was so deeply impressed with the idea of this part of the Duke's character that when the news of one of his victories was brought to her . . . she vehemently ejaculated this prayer, 'God keep him humble!'[18]

Much of this criticism came from party political sources but it was further inflamed by the discontents of soldiers after a war. On one side, the Commander-in-Chief's ineffable glory blazed forth. At regimental feasts his name in laurel leaves would appear level with the Duke of York's.

On the other side was an angry suspicion on the part of the common soldiers that like their Peninsular comrades they would not get even one medal. In 1815 Wellington hoped he had scotched that serpent by ordering an identical silver Waterloo medal for all officers and men alike. Sergeant Robertson praised the Duke's decision: 'As we had all shared equally in the dangers of the day, we should all partake alike in its glories.'

Many officers, however, were dissatisfied with the glories in which Wellington invited them to partake. Colonel Lygon, for example, rejected the Cross of the *Second Class* of the Order of St Vladimir as degrading.

'Won't Colonel Lygon accept it?' said the Duke. 'Well then, give it to Colonel Somebody-else, who will.'[19]

Detesting as he did the whole impossible business of distributing fairly the erratic gifts of foreign princes, Wellington tended to dismiss complaints. Nevertheless, his unassuming frankness still got through to impartial men and women. Cyrus Redding, a visitor to Paris, compared the Wellington of 1816 'at the head of 150,000 men in the proudest position a man could be' with the Wellesley he had known in 1808, humiliated by Cintra: 'He was the same as before, no change was visible – success did not intoxicate him.'

Miss Berry sat by him at dinner. Though she noted that in

speaking of Allied sovereigns he said, '*we* found so-and-so – *we* intend such-and-such things – quite as treating *de Couronne à Couronne*', the thing which struck her most about him was 'the simplicity and frankness of his manners'.[20]

*

The politics of occupation, meanwhile, did not improve. In France it was felt that the feeding of the hundred and fifty thousand would require a miracle. Then Pozzo di Borgo, for Russia, came up with the miracle. What could be easier than to reduce the army of occupation? Let the Duke of Wellington send home thirty thousand men forthwith.

The Duke was in a dilemma. Though personally not unfavourable, a 'Red' disturbance provoked by the 'White Terror' of Artois and his Ultras indicated the dangers of premature evacuation. On the other hand the Russians were playing for French favour. Must he stand aside and let them win? It was crucial to decide whether or not the French people were basically loyal to the occupying forces. He decided they were, if only to be saved from the 'White Terror'. In such a climate it might well be both politic and generous to reduce the army of occupation.

This would mean going to England for discussions and incidentally for the change of air his health needed. On 24 June he wrote privately to the War Minister suggesting a visit to Cheltenham. The public did not know that the Duke had already decided by the 24th to go home. So when a startling event occurred next day, they thought he had been driven out by a gunpowder plot.

On 25 June he gave a great ball in his Parisian mansion, rue Champs Elysées, in honour of the royal princes. It was noted that the princes left early. In the small hours a part of the basement was found to be on fire. Gunpowder, cartridges and shavings had been pushed through the bars of the area window, shattering the iron and setting the floorboards alight. Footmen quickly put out the flames and the host made light of the incident. Nevertheless most people interpreted it as a Royalist crime, and Wellington's nonchalance as an attempt to hush up his quarrel with the Ultras.

*

Crowds visited Cheltenham during July to watch the Great Duke strolling in public with his wife and two sons. Kitty wrote happily about various improvements in her hero. He was 'considerably better both in looks & spirits since his arrival in England', and had more time for his boys. 'I say with delight they are as fond of and as familiar with their noble & beloved Father as if they had never been separated from him. They accompany him on his walks, *chat* with him, play with him. In short they are the chosen companions of each other. . . .'[21]

In private, the rivalries between his admirers such as Lady Jersey, Lady Shelley and Mrs Arbuthnot, which for years were to be a bizarre feature of his social life, made a brief beginning. 'You are all Syrens!' he wrote to Mrs Arbuthnot. 'You the Principal: & want to keep me from where I ought to be'[22] – namely, in the City of London, discussing the financial plight of France. The Salisburys and Westmorlands were clamouring for visits and now the Arbuthnots wanted him, not to mention Colonel Frederick Ponsonby's sister, Lady Caroline Lamb, who needed protecting from herself.

Henceforth Caroline was to be known in his letters as 'Calantha', from the heroine of *Glenarvon*, her novel about Byron. 'Calantha' was of constant concern and interest to the Duke, both for her lurid past and unhappy present. Not that he probed the Byron affair. His object was to see Caroline reconciled to her husband, William Lamb.* He had written to Caroline from Cambrai on 19 April 1816, skimming over the 'strange conduct' of her 'enemy', Byron, who had deserted his wife for his half-sister – 'these modern men of genius are sad fellows', reflected the Duke – and quickly passing on to Caroline's own husband, William Lamb. 'I take yours to be worth half a score such,' wrote the Duke, comparing William with Byron. He then reminded Caroline of their last meeting at Lady Kinnaird's in Paris, when he had made her agree to a treaty of peace with William, sealed by a 'great vow' never to enrage her husband again.[23]

Giving good advice to pretty women with problems was becoming one of the Duke's pleasures. Gossip reported that Lady Kinnaird was about to leave her husband, while Lord Holland in his memoirs observed cryptically that she was 'living in intimacy'

*William Lamb, 2nd Viscount Melbourne (1779–1848), Prime Minister 1834 and 1835–41. Married in 1805 Lady Caroline Ponsonby, who died in 1828.

with the Duke of Wellington. Was this in reality another attempted reconciliation between a husband and wife? If so, it would strengthen the conclusion that Wellington's endeavours (like Gladstone's at the end of the century) were all too likely to start up rumours of affairs with the very women he was trying to help.

During his short London visit of July 1816 the Duke tried to get Caroline admitted to Almack's, the highest imprimatur of social purity – but in vain. Lady Jersey kept her out.

'Poor Calantha!' he wrote to Mrs Arbuthnot, 'what has she done?' He begged his friend not to join in the general abuse, 'and you must not give her up without being quite certain that you have cause'.[24]

In this kindly mood he had written to Richelieu from Cheltenham on 18 July that the British Government would be very sympathetic to a cut of thirty thousand in the occupation troops, provided there was no 'repugnance' on the part of the other powers.[25] Considering that Russia was the moving spirit for reduction, Austria eager to follow and Prussia amenable, Wellington's reply meant 'yes'.

*

Hardly was he reinstalled in France than it appeared that his own attitude to concessions had become one of repugnance. This seemed surprising, considering that while he was in England Louis XVIII had, with his approval, sent the diehard *Chambre Introuvable* packing, and the subsequent elections had produced a more moderate Chamber. Yet the Duke's reception of these political improvements was none the less cautious. Troops could not be reduced before the end of the season. After all, the new deputies had not yet been put to the test by a vote on the indemnity. Would they pay up?

So disgusted was Richelieu by this reversal of policy that he felt Wellington must have been given fresh instructions in London, 'for it is impossible for me to raise the least doubt upon the straightforwardness and integrity of his character'.[26] Bad news from the French countryside had indeed shocked everybody, Wellington included. The harvest was a failure; distress and consequently disaffection were widespread. Even the efficiency of the army of occupation was threatened by a desperate shortage of forage which necessitated the autumn manoeuvres being postponed. In these circumstances Wellington did not feel justified in making more than a minimal concession over troops. He brought down the army, which had risen to 157,886 men, to a strict 150,000. By the winter French finances were so dangerously strained that he was planning the first of three loans to be raised by the British bankers, Barings and Hopes.* Without something of that kind, he wrote to Castlereagh on 6 December, 'France will be aground this year. . . .'[27] Altogether, the general report on the French situation which he submitted to the Cabinet on 11 December was grim in the extreme. Since his return from England he had noticed a great change for the worse: 'There is a general cry throughout France against the occupation, and as usual, particularly against England.' Before, everyone had welcomed the army. Now it was deeply resented by the government officials, ministers and particularly the Royalists. In face of such hostility no reduction was possible. 'I must find matters in a very different state at Paris . . . to alter this opinion.'[28]

A fortnight later this opinion had been altered. He made a dash to England for one day's emergency meeting with Castlereagh on 26 December. What or who had intervened?

A gradual revolution had in fact been taking place once more in Wellington's ideas, though, as was his way, it had not yet been openly expressed. Due in part to his own realization that things could not go on as they were, the credit for this change was also due to Mme de Staël.

*

Already suffering from her last illness, Germaine de Staël had reached Paris in October 1816, equally opposed to Bonapartists and ultra-Royalists. For this reason the Duke had called her 'one of us'. By 1816, however, she too condemned the occupation, having become a vehemently patriotic champion of 'France for the French'. The Duke at first refused to accept this development:

I cannot help observing that you still call yourself *French* in spite of being one of us. I reclaim you; we think too highly of you to let you go

* The dates of the loans were 10 February 1817, 30 July 1817 and 9 and 12 October 1818.

in this manner. . . . I recognize the battle-fields on which we shall meet when I have the pleasure of arguing with you once more.[29]

But when they met and argued in Mme de Staël's salon that autumn, or continued the argument in a great duel of letters, it was the woman of brass, as the British thought of her, who slowly but surely converted the man of iron. While their verbal antagonism was as keen and well matched as ever in December 1816 – she urging him to withdraw every Allied soldier forthwith, he standing pat on conference decisions – the French crisis was sharpening the edge of her arguments, not his.

On the day the Duke arrived in England (26 December) William Napier was passing on the Paris gossip to his wife at home. The French, he heard, could not pay the indemnity and Mme de Staël predicted it would be paid in gold the first year, in silver the second and the third in *lead*. 'She certainly belongs to the brazen age herself.'[30]

Brazen or not, she certainly knew how to phrase an appeal. 'You must become the greatest man, not of our time, but of all times,' she had written to Wellington – 'and give us back France.'[31]

4

End of an Occupation

Wellington was back in France before the new year, 1817, had begun. His volte face about a reduction in the occupying forces was complete. On 9 December 1816 he had declared that a substantial troop reduction was impossible. On 9 January 1817 he notified the permanent conference of the four ambassadors, 'I confess, however, that my opinion has altered. . . . I would propose' – a reduction of thirty thousand men to begin on 1 April 1817. He had realized that only the reduction could give Richelieu that 'moment of popularity' his Government so desperately needed.[1]

Moreover, the contract with Baring Brothers and Hopes for the first loan to the French Government was about to be signed – on 10 February. This great step forward made further advances possible. It had needed all Wellington's persuasiveness to get the other Allies to accept the idea of a loan handled by the British bankers, though at this date the pre-eminence of Barings in floating long-term loans was unchallenged. 'There are Six Powers in Europe,' Richelieu said in 1818, 'Great Britain, France, Russia, Austria, Prussia and Baring Brothers.'

With the troop reduction, Mme de Staël's fervent hope of a free France was half realized. She devoted the last four months of her life to working on her powerful friend for a total end to the occupation, and on 7 May she dictated an appeal as flattering as it was inspiring: 'The conviction has spread that you sincerely intend to do good to poor France and, in fact, to conquer is not enough, one must build in order to be the first man of modern times.'[2]

Wellington replied on the 16th regretting that her need to dictate curtailed the flow of her ideas: 'It would be a great pity if your continued weakness were to deprive us of them for long.'

Despite the tease, Wellington cherished her and during a visit to Paris from Cambrai in June he called on her daily. 'Such compassion,' wrote her great friend, the poet Schlegel, 'well becomes a hero.'[3] Her death-bed conversion to Catholicism astonished the Duke. 'The truth is that she was terribly afraid of Death . . . I doubt however the ability of any Priest to convince her that there is a better world than this, or that if there is she will go to the best place in it.'[4] When she died on 14 July 1817 he felt she had at any rate made this world a better place.

As an old man the Duke would often speak of her. 'She was a most agreeable woman,' he told Stanhope, 'if you only *kept her light*, & away from politics.'[5] Yet it was not really the politics that had jarred him. It was the arguing: the gimlet-like boring of Mme de Staël's sharp intellect into the contradictions of Allied policy. Byron had noticed her insatiable desire to fathom people's characters; his own, he added archly, required a long plumb-line. So did Wellington's, and after exploring his mind she had to change it, a formidable but not impossible task. The bright spark of genius in each created a mutual attachment, bringing her unexpected happiness during her last months and him a clearer vision of the future. Each might have called the other 'one of us'.

*

During the rest of 1817 Wellington needed all his steadfastness and vision. Payment of reparations through the Hope–Baring loan produced a mass of chaotic problems concerning claims. But such was his talent in this financial field that the Tsar finally proposed that he should be sole arbitrator, and at the end of the year he settled down single-handed to a task which today would require a whole department. There were also jealousies to assuage. Sir Alexander Baring, admitted the Duke many years later, had been financially embarrassed by the French failure in 1816 to fulfil their engagements, but afterwards had 'made his fortune' from the French loans. (This phrase was inaccurate and must have been based on the Duke's memory of exaggerated reports about Baring's profits from the loans – from £1,500,000 to £3,000,000. A more reasonable estimate was £170,000.) But he and Castlereagh, the Duke added, had shown no favouritism towards Baring: 'The House of Baring was probably relieved from difficulty as well as others. But neither [Castlereagh] or I ever thought that we had done more upon that occasion than our Duty towards our own Country & the World at large. . . .'*[6]

Lord Castlereagh was no financial wizard and it was through Wellington's labours that the world at large benefited.

Politics, however, were as usual not prospering. A despatch from the Cabinet dated 1 December 1817 showed that they now intended to drag their feet over ending the occupation. Popular impatience in France to get rid of foreigners, wrote Bathurst to the Duke, did not inspire him with a corresponding wish to leave. Bathurst in fact felt that the Cabinet had learnt from events at home how to silence popular discontent.

*

George Keppel, one of the returning Waterloo heroes, noticed the change as soon as he landed at Dover in December 1815. People had gone sour on the war.

The booming wartime economy had collapsed in poverty and suffering. A Corn Law had been passed early in 1815 to keep out cheap foreign corn. Home-coming soldiers competed for employment; and out of whose pockets would come their pensions and half-pay?

'It's us as pays they chaps,' muttered a labourer as Keppel and his men disembarked. When five hundred Irish soldiers went to the bottom in a leaky coal-tub, he heard that the Government were pleased to have got rid of this 'drug in the market'.[7]

Macabre though the Government's pleasure might be, it was probably their only one during the first half of 1816. For the misery of a half-starved rural population, with no alternative but industrial slums, was inevitably declaring itself in social unrest. On 13 May 1816 Castlereagh wrote gloomily to Wellington: 'We have had one of the most disagreeable sessions I ever remember: a sour, discontented temper among our friends, considerable distress throughout the country, & endless debates upon economy. . . .'[8]

A bid to retain income tax, the Government's main means of making the rich bear more of the postwar burden, ended in disaster. It was necessary, Castlereagh declared, to pay for the army of occupation. Criticism redoubled. A peacetime army

* The Duke told Lord Colchester on 14 June 1828 that he and Castlereagh had 'saved Baring from absolute ruin'. (Colchester, vol. III, p. 570).

costing £30 million? A sensitive English nerve began to throb. This was the end of liberty. This was the end of prosperity. City merchants moaned against income tax in poignant petitions. 'The House of *Cummins*,' retaliated Castlereagh with his unlovely pronunciation but unfailing courage, had always shown *ignorant impatience of taxation*.

These four words, spoken of Britain's legislators, did for Castlereagh what four other words – *scum of the earth* – spoken of Britain's soldiers, had done for Wellington.* Men on Castlereagh's own side turned against him. The income tax was defeated by thirty-seven votes and, in Harriet Martineau's exultant but erroneous phrase, 'defeated for ever'.[9]

While the propertied classes rejoiced the hungry people rioted. Food shops were gutted and machines wrecked by Luddites, though not a single shopkeeper was killed. Nevertheless five starving agricultural labourers were hanged. This was to be the pattern all over Britain: not an eye for an eye but a life for a loom; not a tooth for a tooth, but deportation for a looted loaf.

Meanwhile many of the Radical leaders were themselves men of property and had no wish to see an orgy of futile destruction. Their Luddite followers must turn to parliamentary reform.

William Cobbett, who had founded his influential *Political Register* in 1808, now ran a campaign against the classical evil of taxation without representation. He decided to reach more working men by selling single sheets at 2d. His 'Twopenny Trash', as it was called, achieved a circulation of fifty thousand. While Cobbett agitated through print, others took political action. Hampden Clubs were founded throughout the country to organize petitions for reform. On 15 November 'Orator' Hunt organized a great meeting in Spa Fields, an open space with a tavern called Merlin's Cave, to present a petition for universal suffrage. Hunt himself, the demagogic wizard, was also a sincere reformer who rejected force in favour of reason, and an impassioned speaker who ran risks but never ran away. When the crowd at Spa Fields became unwieldy, Hunt postponed the

* After the great victory of Vitoria in 1813 so many of Wellington's soldiers fell to plundering that the pursuit failed. He called them the 'scum of the earth', saying they had volunteered for drink and other ignoble reasons, but later admitted that discipline had made them 'the fellows they are'.

meeting until 2 December. Meanwhile both Whigs and Tories quailed. From the Tory Sir Henry Torrens at the War Office Wellington heard on the 29th that they might not get through the storms ahead.

When 2 December arrived the forces of unreason took over. A detachment of militants, led by Arthur Thistlewood, an embittered reformer, and Edward Castle, an *agent provocateur*, soon had the mob rioting and marching towards the Tower of London, which they intended to occupy. The Tower was duly occupied by the militants, but as prisoners. They were all captured by a force of three magistrates and five constables.*

After stones were thrown at the Prince Regent's carriage on his way back from opening Parliament, a secret ministerial committee on the Hampden Clubs reported their object to be 'nothing short of revolution'. On 24 February the Government struck, with the suspension of Habeas Corpus and 'gag' laws against seditious meetings and literature. They got rid of Cobbett, who fled to America, but not of the meetings and mobs.

The 'March of the Blanketeers' took place on 10 March, when four thousand petitioners met on St Peter's Field, Manchester, with their blankets strapped to their backs in the vain hope of reaching London. It was followed in June by the tragic march of Derbyshire weavers and frame-knitters led by Jeremiah Brandreth, who prophesied that 'northern clouds would roll south, sweeping all before them.' The northern clouds got no further than Nottingham, where troops were waiting. Brandreth was hanged for shooting a man on the march. Two of his friends were also hanged having committed no capital offence, unless it was that of terrifying the Government out of their wits.

What did Wellington make of it all? In 1817 his predictions were sombre – until Metternich congratulated him on England's extraordinary good luck in having a really bad riot. 'The effects of such violent crises,' wrote the Continental statesman, 'always turn in favour of the good party.' Wellington promptly passed on Metternich's opinion to that high Tory, Mrs Arbuthnot, but with a characteristic flavouring of irony: 'I did not know of all the advantage that could be derived from the operations in Spa

* On St Helena, Napoleon heard that a new radical party had been formed as an advance guard of the revolutionaries, known as *'Les Riots'*, who intended to capture London.

fields. . . .' Left to himself in December 1816 he had blamed the upper classes as well as the lower orders for the country's distress, particularly the gentry who indulged a 'rage' for spending money on foreign travel which ought to have given employment at home.[10]

In France, where he could draw on his own experience, he was the most realistic of guides in a worsening situation.

*

Wellington had to face the fact that friction between soldiers and people was serious. Of course there had always been incidents. As early as August 1815 the British 5th Division had done £5,000 of damage to their billets. An enraged Commander-in-Chief made them pay up. His wrath descended also upon a French landlord who, bent on extorting something extra, followed him up the Embassy steps.

'What the devil do you want, sir?' demanded Wellington, who was not in the best of tempers. A bill was thrust into his hand.

'Pooh!' shouted the Commander-in-Chief to an aide-de-camp. 'Kick the rascal downstairs.'

Another time a Cabinet decision embroiled him with the French army. Lord Liverpool insisted on his bringing home the British colours captured at the battle of Fontenoy in 1745 by the Maréchal de Saxe. Wellington answered uncomfortably that they could not be found; if they were, it would be for the Allies as a whole to make King Louis give them up. Unfortunately their hiding-place was discovered and Wellington, despite his plea for joint responsibility, bore the opprobrium for their removal to England.[11]

Hostility between French and British officers was an increasing problem. Most of the incidents took place at theatres or balls. During July 1816 there was an affray at Boulogne caused by a Lieutenant Prior of the 18th Hussars ('a very bad subject') twitting a French actor backstage. After due warning the Frenchman knocked Prior down, Prior's comrades rushed the stage and were in turn attacked by the *gendarmerie*, one of the British officers being seriously wounded. Prior was officially blamed but not without the Duke's insistence. He had the court's verdict revised where it enlarged upon French violence. 'I beg the Court to observe,' wrote Wellington, 'they are not trying the actor but Lt Prior. He was the person who gave the first insult. . . .' He stopped all hunting and coursing at the beginning of 1817 in order to remain on 'tolerable terms' with the inhabitants. Well might Talleyrand reply to a cross-eyed lady who asked him how things were going: 'Just as you see them.'

The Duke's chief solace, as always, was in the performance of his professional duties. He told a young 'Waterloo', James Shaw, that the occupation was not allowed to interrupt his studies:

> He had always made it a rule to study by himself for some hours every day; & alluded to his having commenced acting upon this rule before he went to India.[12]

His personal affairs were also absorbing.

*

'ELOPEMENT IN HIGH LIFE'

Headlines in the Duke's old enemy, the *St James's Chronicle* of September 1815, gave away a family sensation. The Marquess of Wellesley's elder daughter Anne had deserted her husband, Sir William Abdy, and eloped with Lord Charles Bentinck. Her younger sister Hyacinthe, however, persuaded Anne to return home with her, preparatory to rejoining her husband. Soon afterwards their uncle the Duke received a letter from Anne dated 8 October begging him to find Sir William Abdy a job abroad, as a public testimonial to the family's renewed esteem. Before his reply could reach Anne she had eloped again with Bentinck. A second letter (9 November) from the Duke, this time to her shattered sister Hyacinthe, was wholly in character. It was an unfortunate business, he agreed, 'but we must make the best of it'. Hyacinthe should not 'abandon her in her misfortunes. She has not dated her letter to me [almost as great a crime in the Duke's eyes as adultery] & I do not know therefore where to write to her. But I beg you will tell her that if I can be of any use to her she may command me.'[13] (Anne had written again.)

Three of his brothers also were requiring attention. The Rev. Gerald Wellesley had married Lord Cadogan's daughter Emily and been deserted by her, just as his brother Henry had been deserted by her sister Charlotte. Little dreaming how the Prime Minister would regard Gerald's misfortune, the Duke wrote to him about the possibility of Gerald's getting a vacant bishopric.

Liverpool's refusal struck him as bigoted and filled him with deep anger. When, therefore, in February 1816 his elder brother William expressed a wish for the Board of Control, Arthur replied that he would do anything for him except make another private application to Liverpool. An unusually bitter note crept into Arthur's letter. He told William that he had never done himself anything but mischief in being involved with 'this Government's policies'.[14]

A month later, in March 1816, he had to tell his youngest brother, the diplomat Henry, that though the coveted Paris embassy might become vacant, he could not use his influence to get the post for him: 'I have been so unworthily treated by Lord Liverpool.'* It was only through a sweet-tempered intermediary, Charles Arbuthnot, that the Duke's 'fury' with Liverpool was eventually assuaged. 'Gosh', as his family called Mr Arbuthnot, obtained a letter of apology from the Prime Minister.[15] And William Wellesley-Pole in due course found a place as Master of the Mint.

The Duke's two sons were still young enough to give him nothing but pleasure. His Duchess caused little trouble to him, though plenty to herself. It was perhaps as well that Kitty was by no means always with her husband. 'The Duke is here,' wrote Lady Granville from Paris, 'his Duchess is at Cambrai and his loves are dispersed over the whole earth.' If some of them were 'flirts' rather than 'loves', Kitty nevertheless felt it deeply and wept while she worshipped. Her friends encouraged her; indeed Maria Edgeworth heard from Lady Bathurst that she had been more hurt by her friends than her enemies, 'and more by herself than by both put together – but still if she does not quite wash out his affections with tears, they will be hers during the long autumn of life'. As if to confirm this, the Duke said to his sister-in-law, Mrs Wellesley-Pole, 'After all *home* you know is what we must look to at last.'[16]

Kitty's autumn was to be brief but her summer was not always sad.

On Waterloo Day, 18 June 1817, took place the state opening of London's new Waterloo Bridge. A 'Waterloo Fair' was held on

---

* Only the month before, Sir Henry Wellesley had made a second marriage, with Lady Georgiana Cecil, daughter of the 1st Marquess and Marchioness of Salisbury, Wellington's great family friends.

the river bank, and the Thames itself was almost hidden by bob-
bing wherries as the Admiralty barge, with its quota of Waterloo
heroes, approached Rennie's magnificent bridge, hung with
Allied flags. At 3 P.M. began the salute of 202 guns in memory of
the number captured by the British at the battle, followed by a
procession on foot over the bridge with Wellington and Anglesey
immediately behind the Prince Regent and the Duke of York.
The sun shone all day.

Another happy event was Wyatt's discovery at long last of a
site for Wellington's 'palace'. There had been many disappointments. Ravishing Uppark in Sussex, where Miss Hart, Nelson's
future Emma, had once dazzled Sir Harry Featherstonehaugh,
had too steep a drive for the Duke's horses and Sir Harry
demanded 'a Jew's price'. Miserden in Gloucestershire seemed
the last hope by May 1817, though the Duke did not like its
proximity to a fashionable spa: '*I am not* desirous of placing
myself so exactly within a morning's ride of Cheltenham.'[17]

He was saved by an offer from the 2nd Lord Rivers in July 1817
of Stratfield Saye House in Hampshire. Wyatt was enthusiastic:
'I feel no hesitation in saying, that the estate possesses great
beauty & dignity; & is capable of being made a princely Place.'[18]
The happy state of the tenantry, fine carriage drives through
splendid plantations, magnificent park and prospects made it by
far the handsomest estate hitherto proposed. Pope's lovely River
Loddon – 'the nymph Loddona' – glided through it. At the end
of 1817 the nation bought Stratfield Saye for £263,000 and
presented it to Wellington.

Stratfield Saye was to be the Duchess's beloved home for the
rest of her life. It was partly due to her affection for it that the
Duke never proceeded with the grandiose plan conceived by
Wyatt for rebuilding it on higher ground at a cost of
£216,850 15s. 3d. Wyatt's dream of something really sublime – not
'a Confectioner's Device' like Blenheim but a dome copied from
the Pantheon and a circular colonnade from St Peter's; state
rooms not an inch smaller than those at Hatfield; vaulted and
groined arches in the basement; Italian marble, Portland and
Bath stone, the best stock brickwork and £4,000 worth of gilding
– all this and more was to remain forever a paper palace, exqui-
sitely drawn, plainly framed and hung up in a passage of the old
Stratfield Saye.

Kitty had little interest in visionary state rooms or indeed in the more spacious of the apartments already existing. She moved into a small bedroom at the top of the house in the north-east corner (her husband preferred the south-west corner of the ground floor) and her sitting-room next door, which faced the lawns sloping down to the river and the deer park rising beyond, was reassuringly like the old day-nursery at Pakenham Hall in Ireland.

*

The Duke's 'loves' provided an even greater respite in 1817 from French affairs than they had earlier. Lady Shelley had spent much of the previous year in Vienna and Italy making friends with sovereigns. As a student of feminine nature, the Duke chiefly enjoyed the thought of the two rival queens, Lady Shelley and Lady Jersey, competing at the Allied courts. 'I hope she and Queen Willis [Lady Jersey, Queen of Almack's or Willis's Rooms] may not meet in a small town . . . I should like to witness the first meeting.'[19] By spring 1817 Frances Shelley was back in Paris, to the Duke's evident delight and amusement. 'The Shelley is arrived in great beauty!' he announced to Mrs Arbuthnot; 'I have a capital story of her which I must tell you when we meet. I dare not write it.' Nevertheless, he wrote it as follows to his niece Priscilla Burghersh. It appeared that Lady Shelley, with becoming 'pride & Indignation', had rejected the advances of some fat Austrian baron. When asked why, she replied, 'Know, Sir, that I have resisted the Duke of Wellington, and do not imagine, etc. etc. etc,!!!'[20] Wellington commented, 'In my own justification I must say that I was never aware of this resistance!!'*

The Duke's romantic attachment to the lovely Marianne Patterson was no fabrication. Kitty's friend, Mrs Calvert, met Marianne's sister, Mrs Felton Hervey, during amateur theatricals at the Duke of Richmond's in May 1817. Mrs Calvert had to admit that Mrs Hervey was 'a genteel looking young woman', but she added, 'It is the fashion to make a fuss about her because

* *Wellington MSS*, 6 March 1817. Princess Lieven told a similar story to Guizot on 5 April 1840, substituting Prince Metternich for the fat baron and making Wellington comment, 'Devil take me if I ever asked her for anything.' *Lettres de François Guizot et de la Princesse Lieven*, 5 April 1840.

the Duke of Wellington is in love with Mrs Paterson [*sic*].'[21]

At the same time, the Duke's family friendship with the Grevilles focused more and more on Lady Charlotte. Living as she did with her husband and children in Brussels, she was a favoured visitor at Mont-Saint-Martin. Her intimacy with the Duke may have provoked some of the Duchess's tears which so much irritated him.

And of course there was always poor Calantha. 'I see she amuses him to the greatest degree,' wrote Lady Granville, 'especially her accidents, which is the charitable term he gives to all her sorties.'[22]

*

By the beginning of 1818 Wellington feared that the army might be drawn into clashes both with Bonapartists and ultra-Royalists. If the occupation ran its full term of five years this would be certain. So pernicious was the Ultras' influence on the King that he could scarcely see the dynasty surviving:

> The descendants of Louis xv will not reign in France, and I must say & I always will say, that it is the fault of Monsieur [Artois] and his adherents . . .[23]

Various incidents of a sinister new type also reached a climax in February 1818.

What the Duke called 'a nest of libellers' had long been operating in Belgium, and he battled with King William i of the Netherlands for stronger libel laws.[24] But the reform was unpopular, since the libellers were Bonapartist exiles from France with whom many Belgians sympathized. Abuse of the army of occupation reached a peak in August 1817 when a 'Jacobin' poster calling for rebellion was stuck up on a wall!

PROCLAMATION AUX FRANÇAIS

Perfidious England rules France with bayonets . . . and keeps the Bourbon family on the throne.

Français! at the first sound of the tocsin, take up arms; die or live in freedom!

Wellington's reaction was to refrain from warning the army of occupation officially, since this would cause groundless alarm. As he told General Beresford, who was coping with similar troubles in Portugal, 'I never go into any blackguard mob or place in which a fellow might insult me with impunity. In other respects, I ride or walk alone . . .'[25]

By a strange irony, the Duke had narrowly escaped assassination a week or two earlier, though he did not yet know it. On a June evening two French journalists had lain in wait for him in the park at Brussels as he walked home after dinner. He chose a different route, however, strolling with Lady Charlotte Greville and Lord Kinnaird. 'I recollect having a breeze with Kinnaird,' he wrote afterwards, 'about the protection and encouragement he gave to the Jacobins.'[26] The two particular 'Jacobin' assassins meanwhile decided to try again. All the exiles would be able to return to France, they agreed, once 'Le Postillon de la Sainte Canaille' had been laid low. Wellington of course was the 'Postillion of the Holy Scum' and 'Canaille' an anagram for Alliance.

At the end of 1817 a man named Ghirardy, formerly a servant of the Duke's aide-de-camp, was accosted in a Paris street by a French ex-officer.

'Ghirardy? do you recognize me? No? but you have often seen me in the armies. Have you a good job?'

'I don't complain.'

'Oh! it's not as good as the one you used to have. I can put you in the way of one quite as good' – and the ex-officer showed Ghirardy a bursting purse.

'But what is the job?'

'To rid France of the Duke of Wellington.'

Ghirardy refused.[27]

The Commander-in-Chief intended to take up his quarters in Paris towards the end of January 1818, where a violent welcome awaited him.

The affair began on 30 January with a leading French exile in Brussels named Marinet informing Lord Kinnaird, the Jacobins' friend, that Wellington was going to be murdered. Kinnaird very properly communicated with General Sir George Murray in Paris, who replied on 8 February giving the Duke's reaction to the news:

He treats the matter very lightly as you know he always has done everything of the kind; & if there were a chance of getting him in any way to intercede with the French government [for the exiles], certainly the least likely means of doing so would be anything in the shape of intimidation to himself.[28]

As Murray predicted, the Duke made a point of business as usual. On the 9th he had a long talk with Baring about the state of France. Baring was nervous. Could he persuade the Allies to safeguard his loan by occupying France for a further period? The Duke replied firmly that they would do no such thing. The troops would probably be withdrawn at the close of 1818, provided the French fulfilled their obligations.

Next day, Tuesday 10 February, the Duke went to an evening party at the jolly Mrs Craufurd's. On the way home, as the coachman turned into the narrow carriage entrance of his mansion in the rue Champs-Elysées at about 12.30 A.M., there was a flash, a report, and a glimpse of a blond man darting away down the street. No one, not even the carriage, was touched. At first the Duke thought a sentry had let off his musket by mistake. He did not bother to lower the carriage window. Nevertheless it was an attempted murder.

At 6.30 A.M. on the 14th the Paris police, accompanied by Ghirardy, began combing the haunts of Bonapartists. They got on the trail of the ex-officer who had accosted Ghirardy and incidentally had talked murder in the salons. By the end of the day Wellington had found out that the ex-officer's name was Brice. 'He said that he would willingly assassinate me himself; but he had in his service a soldier who would do it freely, & who asked for nothing better than to die'.[29]

In an attempt to cover their own tracks Lord Kinnaird and the Brussels informer Marinet fled to Paris, where they were arrested for interrogation on the 20th. Kinnaird was lodged by the Duke in his house, much to the British Government's horror. But otherwise, explained the Duke, 'he would probably have been lodged in the Conciergerie, which I certainly should not have liked'.

Through the arrest of Marinet on 20 February Decazes, the Minister of Police, got important new clues. Up till then there had been every kind of alarming rumour: was the attempt all Wellington's imagination? suggested the French; on the contrary, did it not herald a nation-wide 'convulsion'? demanded the Prussians; it was a plot by Louis XVIII, thought Colonel Napier;

Kinnaird had fired the shot on a sudden impulse, decided the Italian police; as for the British Cabinet, they dubbed it 'insurrection'[30] and roped in both the Prince Regent and the Duke of York to support their frantic orders for the Duke to quit Paris immediately – orders which he made it abundantly clear he would not obey:

I should give the most fatal shake to everything that is going forward. . . . I have no hesitation in stating it as my opinion that, after assassination, the greatest public & private calamity which could happen would be to obey the order of the Prince Regent.[31]

Instead the Commander-in-Chief gave a very conspicuous ball for the royal family. 'I think it was the most magnificent fête I ever was at,' wrote Lady Dalrymple-Hamilton, and Lady Edward Spencer-Stanhope described it as superb, especially after the Duke left and his aide-de-camp doubled the champagne.[32]

The Commander-in-Chief was to remark many years later that the highest military talent lay in knowing when to retreat and having the courage to do it. But in 1818 his triumph lay in knowing when to stay put and having the courage to disobey orders.

Meanwhile Decazes was after the hired assassin, a soldier named Cantillon.* His shot had failed, it was said, because he was in too great a hurry to get his reward. Others, less friendly to the Duke, said it was because he aimed too high, thinking Wellington was *un grand homme*. Decazes adopted a '*cherchez-la-femme*' policy which proved extremely fruitful. He arrested Marinet's mistress, whom Marinet shared with Kinnaird and who was the wife of an exiled French journalist. Through her Decazes discovered the hiding-place of Cantillon, in the house of '*la fille Julie*'. Cantillon's girl in turn broke her lover's alibi and on 16 March he was arrested.

So far as Wellington was concerned, this was the end of the great 'convulsion'. André Nicolas Cantillon turned out to be a veteran with a fanatical devotion to Bonaparte, who indeed was to reward him handsomely. In his will Napoleon left the would-be assassin 10,000 francs, for had not Wellington assassinated the martyrs La Bédoyère and Ney?

While gaoled, Cantillon wrote a couplet on his cell wall:

* Since the reign of Henry II, there had been Cantillons in Ireland, who curiously enough intermarried with the Crosbies, to whom Wellington was related.

*Through that criminal Wellington
I am in this prison.*

But in fact he left the prison a free man. No one would come forward to pin the actual crime on him, though everyone knew he had committed it.

The Duke was not going to make heavy weather about this result, beyond a wry comment on contemporary morals to Lord Clancarty, Ambassador to the Netherlands: 'In these virtuous days the greatest crime a man can be guilty of is to *dénoncer* the crime of another, even though the crime should be a plot to assassinate a third person!'[33]

In other words, the Duke as usual placed public duty above private conscience. He also ridiculed an age which bred assassins so puny that they would no longer give all for their cause: 'I know that no person in these degenerate days will risk his own life to take mine or that of any other such person. . . .'[34] He spoke too soon. For the murder of the Duke of Berry and the Cato Street Conspiracy in 1820 were to show that dare-all fanatics still existed.

The Cantillon affair did not deflect him an inch from his resolve to end the occupation. The British War Minister objected strongly; the Duke was unmoved. If the occupation continued, he informed the Allied governments, he would have to concentrate the army in a defensive position between the rivers Meuse and Scheldt. This shocked the Allies into evacuation. And when a British general complained to him about the French inhabitants brawling with his men, the Duke replied tartly in the accents of Mme de Staël, 'The occupation of the French territory is not a natural measure, & never was so considered by those who adopted it. . . .'[35]

Now it was to continue no longer. By June 1818 the Duke's extraordinary performance over the Hope–Baring loan, especially his almost superhuman attention to financial detail, had begun to take effect, and he was cautiously optimistic. The funds were rising because of people's 'astonishing avidity' to share in the profits of the new loans, and the country was tranquil. It remained only to settle the terms of evacuation. This, and many other things besides, would be done in the autumn at the Congress of Aix-la-Chapelle.

*

The Congress opened on 1 October 1818 in a dazzle of splendour. Two emperors, a king and many minor royalties mingled with plenipotentiaries, financiers, reigning beauties, actresses and starry-eyed observers in the city that had once been the capital of the Holy Roman Empire. Appropriately enough the Tsar of Russia, with his offering of the Holy Alliance to all men of good-will, was the centre of this galaxy. It was to him that Richelieu turned for political advice, Robert Owen for encouragement in his socialistic housing schemes and Clarkson for support against the international slave trade. It was his expression which Welling-ton and Castlereagh watched most narrowly, the latter agreeing with Metternich that 'the only guarantee against the danger of Russian power was the Emperor's personal character'. Metter-nich, after all, could congratulate himself on having 'the good fortune to know His Imperial Majesty's mind',[36] possibly because he had made a conquest of the Tsar's best-informed Russian subject, the power-hungry Mme de Lieven. 'The hour which I passed at your feet,' wrote Metternich to her, 'has proved to me that it was a good place to be . . . you belonged to me!'

With Wellington and the Tsar both in favour of evacuation, no time was lost in reaching agreement on this issue. The army was to be out of France by 30 November, the indemnity having been reduced to 265 million francs. Now, however, began a tug of war between the Congress system of the Tsar and his 'Holy Allies' on one side, and British interests as represented by Wellington and Castlereagh on the other.

For Castlereagh and Wellington, the 'Concert of Europe' was intended to take concrete shape only on specific issues like the occupation. They still regarded the Quadruple Alliance as the lynch-pin of peace, for it was through this instrument that the Powers controlled France, the revolutionary seed-bed of Europe. Their belief did not prevent them from sponsoring King Louis for the Congress; but for a Congress which was to involve no general supervision of everybody by everybody and no limitation of national sovereignty such as the British Opposition dreaded. Banish the thought of an international Cossack force keeping order in Hyde Park! No; Europe must be regulated by precise treaties as before, the Grand or Quadruple Alliance being simply extended into a 'Grand Quintuple Alliance'.

Not so the Tsar. His team of crowned mystics, which now

included King Louis, saw Aix as directly descended from the Holy Alliance. He proposed that the hitherto constricting Quadruple Alliance should be stretched by the inclusion of Bourbon Spain, while still looking forward to a world-wide Christian union which America, north and south, would join. King Ferdinand VII's tyranny at home and designs against the former Spanish colonies in South America, however, ruled out both him and his Russian sponsor as future Holy Allies of Britain and America; in October 1818 the Tsar's proposal for a 'garantie générale' or 'general alliance' was rejected at Aix-la-Chapelle.

In the end Metternich found a compromise that the Congress could accept. The old Quadruple Alliance was to coexist – but only in secret – with a Concert of Five to be established under a public 'Declaration' of unity signed by Britain, Austria, Russia, Prussia and France. Both sides believed they had won.

*

Alexander I might glitter in Europe for the present and seem to hold out the most seductive hopes for the future; Britain had only one hero – the Duke of Wellington. And his conduct as soldier, administrator and financier over the past three years gave him a position in Europe also which no other Englishman had ever held. He returned to England at the end of 1818 with the batons of six foreign countries in his knapsack.

The Duke was to make his London home in an imposing mansion at Hyde Park Corner, formerly the property of his brother Lord Wellesley – Apsley House. In order to assist Richard's finances Arthur had offered the generous sum of £42,000 for Apsley House without at first disclosing that he was the purchaser. He quickly made some savings. A night-watchman was to be shared with the neighbours at 3s 6d a night each. But the treasures inside Apsley House soon required more than this part-time Cerberus to guard them.

In the hall stood Canova's gigantic nude statue of Napoleon, bought by Britain from the Louvre and presented to Wellington by the Prince Regent. When a British visitor told Canova that the globe in Napoleon's hand looked too small, the sculptor replied, 'Ah, but you see Napoleon's world did not include Great Britain.'

The Portuguese nation honoured Wellington with a silver dinner-service: the merchants and bankers of London subscribed to a silver-gilt 'Wellington Shield'; from the King of Prussia came a service of over four hundred pieces of Berlin china, and from the King of France, who had already given him his highest order of the Saint-Esprit, the famous 'Egyptian service' accompanied by a personal note from Louis: 'Do little gifts [sic] keep friendship alive.'* In London's Hyde Park a colossal statue of Achilles was promised by 'the ladies of England' costing £10,000 and using 36 tons of metal from guns captured at Salamanca, Vitoria, Toulouse and Waterloo; in Dublin's Phoenix Park the first stone for Smirke's granite pillar had been laid on 18 June 1818; in Trim, the now seedy town which young Arthur had once represented, stood a Corinthian column on which a stone Duke pointed his baton towards the ever-diminishing ruins of Trim Castle.

Prize money from Waterloo was distributed in June 1819. To Wellington £60,000 (he gave back two-thirds of his share to the Treasury); generals £1,250 each, subalterns £33, sergeants £9, privates £2 10s.

Loaded with material honours, the Duke also brought home a medley of verbal tributes from the most varied well-wishers. For himself and his troops, General Sir Denis Pack sent a moving farewell: .

When I call to mind . . . that in this long & eventful period . . . I have never seen you discomposed or heard a harsh expression from you to any one under your command, I am beyond all bounds impressed with feelings of admiration for your Grace's character and with deep regret for the separation which has just taken place.[37]

For Northern France, the Prefect felt that he must thank the Duke for his troops' discipline and bear solemn witness to the zeal with which they had carried out 'his Grace's wish to lighten the burden of the Occupation as much as possible'.[38]

For himself and the ladies, Metternich said, 'He's one of the

* The Duke's Saint-Esprit is in the Wellington Museum. King Louis had at first wished to create him Duke of Brunois with an estate at Grosbois, but too many Frenchmen, especially marshals, objected. Contrary to stories, there was never any question of the Duke being made a marshal of France. The Egyptian service was an abortive gift from Napoleon to Josephine.

men I love best in the world, and if I were a woman' – he was
speaking to Lady Shelley – 'I'd love him better than all the
world.'[39]

For himself and his family, Thomas Creevey expressed
astonishment and gratitude that such a character as the Duke
should exist. Creevey wrote a farewell tribute before a new life in
England claimed the Duke:

> . . . considering the imposters that most men in power are – the in-
> sufferable pretensions one meets in every Jack-in-Office – the uniform
> frankness & simplicity of Wellington . . . coupled with the unparalleled
> situation he holds in the world for an English subject, makes him to me
> the most interesting object I have ever seen in my life.[40]

Shortly afterwards Creevey had an unexpected glimpse into the
Duke's future. He happened to be in the Hôtel d'Angleterre in
Brussels where Lady Charlotte Greville was staying. Wellington
came in, saw Creevey, and asked if he had any news from
England.

'None but newspaper news.'

Creevey's brief answer was an attempt to draw the Duke, for
the papers were full of reports that he was to join the British
Cabinet as Master-General of the Ordnance. But Wellington was
markedly uncommunicative.

'Ho!' he replied, 'Ha!' Nevertheless he did not contradict the
reports and his radical friend deduced they were true.

He had indeed accepted that post in the Cabinet – on his own
terms.

Part II

5

A Little *Murder*

Not a few of Wellington's friends deplored his change of career. Why politics, party politics, Tory politics? General Alava, his faithful Spanish ally and a liberal, told Creevey he never was more sorry for an event in his life: 'The Duke of Wellington ought never to have had anything to do with politicks.'

The great man himself was prepared to make some concessions to this feeling. The Duke of Wellington must not be let down by the Master-General of the Ordnance. A compelling manifesto was therefore sent to the Prime Minister stating his own conditions of service. He must be a servant of the country first, of party second. Tories might come and go; the Duke could well go on for ever: 'but I hope that, in case any circumstances should occur to remove them from power, they will allow me to consider myself at liberty to take any line I may at the time think proper.'

His dislike of factiousness in politics dated from the Peninsular War.

The experience which I have acquired during my long service abroad has convinced me that a factious opposition to the government is highly injurious to the interests of the country; & thinking as I do now I could not become a party to such an opposition. . . .[1]

Lord Liverpool, with his usual good sense in man-management, recognized the 'special circumstances' of the Duke's position.

The Ordnance was a partly military, partly civil board responsible for the artillery, engineers and all their equipment including survey maps. As Master-General the Duke followed the Government's postwar line of strict economy, showing no favour towards inventions like Lieutenant Sibbald's, to arm each cavalry horse with a wooden contraption carrying Boadicea-type scythes.[2]

*

Wellington's luck has often attracted attention. He was lucky to fight in India with a brother as Governor-General and in the Peninsula with a friend as War Minister. He was lucky to stop fighting during his prime, while he looked taller than his 5 feet 9 inches, while his complexion was still as fresh as a young man's, his forehead romantic and his expression like a Roman hero's, apart from the mouth. 'His mouth has never been exactly given in pictures,' wrote Cyrus Redding in 1816, and the painter Haydon called it 'a singular mouth like a helpless infant learning to whistle!'[3] The truth was that active service had early destroyed Arthur Wellesley's back teeth, a single stroke of ill-luck which was largely responsible for his 'wretched' utterance in Parliament. His brother Richard, who was an eloquent speaker though subject to black-outs, said of him, 'Arthur can't speak the English language intelligibly – there is only one phrase he can speak, "*our old friend*", and that he can't speak plainly.'[4]

Nevertheless Arthur, having fought his last battle at forty-six, was lucky to enter the Cabinet at forty-nine, a perfect age in his case. But there the luck ended. He struck the unhappiest year in nineteenth-century British history for his first as a peacetime politician.

*

'Mischief and embarrassment' were the two names under which the Duke had learnt to recognize the new enemies of postwar Britain.[5] By 'mischief' his Tory colleagues meant political agitation and by 'embarrassment' economic distress. Repressive measures had reduced the mischief in 1817 to a trickle, while improved trade mitigated the embarrassment during the following year. But in 1819 embarrassment and mischief returned, in that order, with a vengeance.

The harvest of 1818 had been bad and yet the stringent 1815 Corn Law was still in force. Peel attacked the great postwar problem of cash and by the 1819 Act for the resumption of cash payments caused prices to fall. Corn and cash – these were two out of the three spectres which were to haunt politicians for a generation. (The third spectre, Catholics, soon completed the intractable trio.) Mob brutality, said Lord Palmerston, was typical of the times. A matching brutality was the savage penal code. No doubt Sir Samuel Romilly had dented its armour by getting the Com-

mons to vote for abolition of the death penalty for five shillings'
worth of shop-lifting; but Chancellor Eldon defeated Romilly's
reform in the House of Lords.

While still in France Wellington had regarded the Lords as less
of a juggernaut than a spent force. 'Nobody cares a damn for the
House of Lords,' he told Creevey; 'the House of Commons is
everything in England & the House of Lords nothing.'[6] He did
not think so now.

*

Once more it was 'Orator' Hunt who became the catalyst for
popular exasperation. Early in 1819 Hunt and his bodyguard of
Lancashire weavers were involved in an incident with Hussars at
the Manchester theatre reminiscent of clashes reported to Wellington during the occupation of France. A message from Hunt
finally ordered a gathering crowd to disperse before 'the butchers
of Waterloo' massacred them.

Was violence increasing? Not as a policy planned by the leaders
of either side. But violence was in the air; and it was the ghost of
Waterloo itself, especially some of its more dashing associations,
which seemed to provide the Radicals with their counter-
inspiration. The thought of Hussars drove Bamford, one of
Hunt's bodyguard, into a poetic rage: these 'whisker'd whelps'
with 'chicken hearts' would soon be faced by realities –

> *A tougher game they'll have to play*
> *Than that of* Waterloo.

Why were the weavers drilling in the hills on summer evenings?
Bamford truly said their leaders' intention was to turn them from
a rabble into disciplined citizens worthy of the cause for which
they marched. Others noticed that the younger men, desperate
with hunger, handled their walking-sticks like muskets. A Radical
speaker, Sir Charles Wolseley, predicted that a particularly
serious riot near Stockport would become more famous than
Waterloo.

The *doppelgänger* of Waterloo was soon to appear. On St
Peter's Field, Manchester, where later stood the Free Trade Hall,
was 'fought' out in ten unforgettable minutes an engagement of
the utmost horror – Peterloo. It is necessary to put the word

'fought' in inverted commas, since only one side carried weapons of war.

*

'Orator' Hunt had called a reform meeting for 16 August 1819 to be attended by industrial unions from the cotton districts of Lancashire. Since reform meetings were not yet illegal the Cabinet warned magistrates not to disperse the crowds unless they proceeded to felony or riot. If that happened, there was a force of constables and specials commanded by Captain Nadin, as well as the Manchester Yeomanry Cavalry and Colonel L'Estrange's 15th Hussars and 31st Foot, while the Northern Command as a whole was under Wellington's friend General Byng, named by him for valour at Waterloo.

By noon on that fine Monday morning up to eighty thousand men, women and children had converged on St Peter's Field after hours of orderly marching with garlands and the usual reform banners – 'Suffrage Universal', 'Vote by Ballot'. Perhaps the Saddleworth Union struck a sinister note with its black flag inscribed 'Equal Representation or Death'; but on the reverse was 'Love' beneath two clasped hands. Four hundred police already on the field met with no hostility from the crowd. The crowd's vast size, however, struck terror into the heart of 'Miss' William Hulton, the young, blue-eyed chairman of the magistrates.

Hunt had scarcely spoken for twenty minutes to a silent multitude before there was a confused murmur at the top of the field and a wave of pressure towards the hustings. From a window 'Miss' Hulton had read the Riot Act to those who could hear it and ordered Nadin and his police to arrest Hunt. Nadin looked at the warrant and then at the vast concourse between him and the hustings. He told Hulton the job couldn't be done without the military.

'Then you shall have military power,' exclaimed Hulton, '& for God's sake don't sacrifice the lives of the Special Constables. . . .'[7]

It was not their lives that were in danger.

At once the blue and white uniforms of the yeomanry were seen moving into the crowd. Hunt promptly called for three cheers, meaning that the reformers would stand firm and continue their meeting. Some of those with sticks raised them to cheer, some hissed the troops, but nothing was thrown. The yeomanry, brandishing their sabres, advanced under Captain Birley (afterwards known as Hurly-Burly) and at once became engulfed.

'Good God! Sir,' shouted the horrified Hulton at his window to Colonel L'Estrange, 'don't you see they are attacking the yeomanry? *Disperse the meeting!*'

Those three fatal words were the flash-point of Peterloo. Having spoken them, Hulton turned his face away from the window.

There is no unbiased evidence that Hulton was right and that the crowd attacked first. All the testimony of impartial observers agrees that the yeomanry, a body of forty unskilful horsemen, were ordered to squeeze one by one into a crowd two thousand times their number – but were not attacked. 'Not a brick-bat was thrown at them – not a pistol was fired during this period,' said *The Times* reporter, a man 'about as much a Jacobin . . . as is Lord *Liverpool* himself' (*The Times*, 19 August 1819). But from the moment a Waterloo bugle sounded the charge and the 15th Hussars went to the rescue of the yeomanry, all was changed: 'Swords were up and swords were down,' wrote another impartial eye-witness, Edward Stanley, a clergyman and father of the future Dean of Westminster. Hunt and all the platform party including journalists jumped down, Hunt's hand grazed by a sabre and Saxton, editor of the *Manchester Observer*, more seriously threatened.

Not only Hunt and the reform leaders but also *The Times* correspondent were arrested by Nadin – 'Oh! oh! you are one of their writers' – while in a whirlwind of wrath the yeomanry turned on the people with a wild shout: 'Have at their flags!' Suddenly there was a roar and a rumble like low thunder. Every narrow exit was blocked by a terrified stampede. Bamford tried to rally his contingent: 'Stand fast, they are riding upon us; stand fast.' His exhortations were drowned in screams – 'For shame! Break! break! They are killing them in front and they cannot get away. Break! break!'[8]

But the people could not break. Wellington once remarked that anyone could get ten thousand men into a constricted space but it needed a real general to get them out again. At Peterloo there were no generals, only the angry cavalry and unhappy Hulton. Mounds of trampled victims began to pile up on the blood-stained grass. In ten minutes it was over. Silence fell and the August sun beat down on a thick, motionless cloud of dust. Then a light breeze lifted the dust-cloud to reveal something ominously like the aftermath of Waterloo, except that among the torn caps, hats, shoes, ripped-up banners and broken shafts was a wreckage of shawls, bonnets and children's clothes.

*

The aftermath of Peterloo was a political struggle between the two sides.

'Lord Sidmouth!' said the Duke affably to the Home Secretary, 'the Radicals will impeach you for this, by God they will!'[9]

The official letter of thanks sent to the magistrates seemed to many an act of gratuitous callousness; but Wellington was one of the thirteen ministers who believed that unless magistrates were supported in their hour of crisis they would never again do their duty. According to Lady Shelley he approved of their conduct, apart from reading the Riot Act: 'This alone can injure their cause.'[10]

The Government hoped to prosecute the leaders for high treason but evidence only of 'misdemeanour' could be marshalled, for which Hunt was given over two years in prison and Bamford one. An unfortunate woman who had been wounded and lifted into Hunt's carriage went down in Tory mythology as 'Hunt's concubine' –

> His mistress sent to the hospital her face for to renew,
> For she got it closely shaven on the plains of Peter-Loo.

The Times had given a lead to the public sense of outrage with its first full report of the tragedy on 19 August. Like the Waterloo despatch it was embedded in advertisements, but many of them appropriately depressing – aperient sodiac powders for bile and nausea, camphor lozenges for lowness of spirits, aromatic spirit of vinegar for relieving faintness manufactured in Manchester.

The Times's casualty figures, however, put at a hundred, proved to be tragically inadequate. Eleven people were killed and nearly five hundred wounded. 'It was a yeoman's holiday,' said Byron, for a lot of 'bloody Neros'. As the indignation mounted, great Whigs or anti-Tories contributed to the victims' fund and organized protests, while great Tories like the Duke of Wellington prepared to save the country from the agitators' next attempt: 'It

is very clear to me that they won't be quiet till a large number of
them "bite the dust", as the French say, or till some of their
leaders are hanged, which would be the most fortunate result.'[11]

His present business was to minimize the dangers of a revolutionary confrontation between army and people. For the Duke,
like Sidmouth, saw revolution round the corner. In October 1819
he concerted with General Byng further plans for controlling the
North. The two great dangers were that small detachments of
troops would be defeated by simultaneous risings – memories of
the army of occupation – and that troops would fraternize with
the mob – memories of the French Revolution. It was better to
let a few mobs rip than disperse the soldiers. He wrote to Byng on
the 21st: 'As long as no misfortune happens to [the troops] the
mischief will be confined to plunder & a little *murder. . . .*'

Byng informed the Duke with pleasure on 28 October that the
Radicals were weakened by divisions, though with Hunt in prison
most of them favoured Thistlewood as a leader. But thanks to the
Duke's letter he awaited the Radicals' next great meeting of
1 November with calm confidence. 'I consider your letter as
valuable as a reinforcement of a 1000 men. . . .'[12]

The first of November passed off without a revolution. Nevertheless the Government clamped down on the whole country their
retaliatory Six Acts. These temporary measures to preserve order
comprised three laws against the press, two against drilling and
arms and one banning so-called 'seditious' public meetings. In
1819, to quote Professor Norman Gash, 'the wide and sometimes
anarchic tradition of British liberty was still engrained in the
public mind'.[13] Its breach filled the Radicals with horror and
Wellington with satisfaction, a satisfaction which he conveyed to
Pozzo di Borgo, in a letter of 25 November. The debates and the
forthcoming Six Acts, he wrote, had restored the confidence of
good men by exposing the bad to the public. In December he was
urging Sidmouth to enforce ruthlessly the Act against 'insurgents'
drilling with arms:

They are like Conquerors, they must go forward; the moment they
are stopped they are lost. Their adherents will lose all confidence; & by
degrees every Individual will relapse into his old habits of Loyalty or
Indifference.[14]

In a distinctly optimistic mood, he heralded the year 1820 with another strengthening letter to a foreign minister, Baron Vincent, the Austrian ambassador in Paris: 'I did not want to write to you until we were come out of our bad position. Thanks to God and our miraculous Institutions we have reached the end of it. . . .'[15]

Yet God and Britain's miraculous institutions were shortly to receive a last desperate buffet from a genuine revolutionary of the atheistic or agnostic type. Only a very few hours after writing cheerfully to Vincent, the Duke received confirmation of a report that Lord Sidmouth had discovered another plot.

*

While the new plot was allowed to simmer a little longer, those Britons whose loyalty to their invalid king, George III, had for many years been a steadying social influence, received a shock. The King died on 29 January 1820, having been unexpectedly predeceased on the 23rd by his son the Duke of Kent.

It could not be said that the Duke of Kent's death was a blow to Wellington. Creevey recounted how in 1818 he had passed the Commander-in-Chief galloping down a French road in a coach and six in order to escape a session with that eccentric prince. More of a trial was 'Prinny's' elevation into King George IV. The accession of a new monarch meant all the opportunities for disturbance of a general election.

Meanwhile it was Arthur Thistlewood who headed the latest plot, to be known as the Cato Street Conspiracy. Never had conspiracy been more abysmal both in organization and object. Originally planned by Thistlewood for the previous autumn, the coup had been delayed, thus affording a spy named George Edwards ample time both to warn the Government and to foment further trouble. The Cabinet first heard of it on 15 December 1819. Information continued to trickle in until February, when the Lord President of the Council, Lord Harrowby, was stopped in the Park by an informer and given the whole story. The conspirators intended to wait until after the opening of Parliament on 15 February, catch the whole Cabinet at their official dinner in Harrowby's Grosvenor Square mansion and kill the lot. Not quite the incidence of 'a little *murder*' for which Wellington was prepared.

Harrowby's news inspired the Duke and his friend Castlereagh with a sporting stratagem. Each minister should arrive as if to dine but bringing a brace of pistols inside his despatch box. They would then combine with servants and police to hold up the conspirators in the hall until soldiers had surrounded the house and captured all the assassins.

'My colleagues, however, were of a different opinion,' said the Duke regretfully to Gleig some years later, 'and perhaps they were right.'[16]

On 23 February the Cabinet dinner was prepared at 39 (now 44) Grosvenor Square to allay the conspirators' suspicions, while a detachment of soldiers and police were ordered to attack their hide-out in Cato Street, an alley off Edgware Road. Here on 23 February, in the stable-loft of a squat brick building which still looks as unprepossessing today as it did in 1820, there was a fierce scuffle and nine conspirators were arrested by constables and soldiers in pitch darkness. Because the soldiers arrived late on the scene, Constable Smithers was run through the body by Thistlewood, who with thirteen others escaped, only to be rounded up soon afterwards. They were convicted of treason in March, the five ringleaders were hanged and their heads exposed in the City they had hoped to seize.

'Oh God – if there be a God – save my soul – if I have a soul!' said Thistlewood on the scaffold. The illegitimate son of a farmer, he had once served in a line regiment but found his way to revolutionary France and later fought for Napoleon. He was said to have expressed particular hatred for the Duke.

'I had rather kill that D — d villain Wellington than any of them.'[17]

Many of Thistlewood's colleagues were of a very different mould from this professional revolutionary, as they showed by the samples of handwriting which they were required to submit. Under the list of melancholy, gruff names – Ings, Brunt, Strange, Tidd – appeared untutored cries of revenge, religious fervour or fraternal love, most of it in rhyme like the following:

> *wanst i was blind and could not see*
> *but now providence directed me.*

Only poor Tidd threw in the sponge: 'Sir I Ham a very Bad Hand at Righting Richard Tidd.'

The two conspirators who interested Wellington most were

Symonds and Ings. The footman Symonds he considered the worst of the lot: 'He is a Canting Vagabond. He talked to us the other day at the Council like the Duke of Kent of his Philanthropy, of his relieving the distress of his fellow Creatures, of his *crying over them* etc. etc. at the same time that he was concerned in such a Plot of Blood!!'[18]

James Ings, a bankrupt butcher from Portsmouth, admitted to having singled out Wellington for earlier and individual despatch. He had often watched the Duke but never found him alone until one afternoon at the beginning of February when, seeing him leave the Ordnance office, Ings crossed the street and walked after him, intending to stab him in the back when he entered Green Park. But before they reached St James's Palace, a one-armed man met the Duke, turned round and walked back with him through the Park to Apsley House. 'And all this I quite believe,' said Wellington, for the one-armed man was Lord Fitzroy Somerset, who thus accidentally saved his chief's life, perhaps not on the field, but certainly in the park.*[19]

Thus foiled again, Ings decided to bag Wellington with the rest of the Cabinet on 23 February. He volunteered to enter the room first and after the swordsmen had done their work to sever all the heads with a cutlass, 'and Lord Castlereagh's head and Lord Sidmouth's I will bring away in a bag. For this purpose I will provide two bags.'

The Duke promptly sent out a long account of the conspiracy to his dear Mrs Patterson in America. Though no scare-monger he showed how seriously he took it and how easily it might have succeeded. He also explained why the Cabinet had let it run on so long.

In the course of the Tuesday & Wednesday [22 and 23 February] we received Information not only from Spies but from Persons implicated more or less in the Plot who were horrified by its turpitude, & gave Information to put us on our guard but which they desired might be kept secret. We were still therefore under the necessity of letting the conspiracy work its way, as we should have made but a poor figure in a Court of Justice with the support of the testimony of Spies only . . . we were saved certainly by Divine Providence.

* At the battle of Waterloo, Somerset was riding so close to the Duke that his left arm brushed the Duke's right, when he was hit in his own right arm. It is conceivable that the bullet he stopped might otherwise have hit the Duke.

God Bless you my dear Mrs Patterson. Remember me kindly to Mr P. & Believe me Ever Your's most affectionately

Wn.[20]

It took a little while for the Cabinet and country to realize that this was no nation-wide conspiracy, but the plot of a few desperadoes whose horrific dreams matched the squalor of their everyday lives. When James Ings was asked for his handwriting he produced a simple *cri de coeur*: 'If my Life is destroyed in this conspiracy I shall consider I Ham a murderd man the reason is I was not the Inventer of the conspiracy . . . I was drawn [in by Edwards the Spy] because I could not keep my Wife & children.'

In the end the Cato Street Conspiracy, coming on top of Peterloo, did persuade the ruling class that 'mischief' was not entirely due to wickedness. Lord Liverpool was not to fluff his next chance (in 1822) to relax a little the stern, unbending regime.

*

Social issues in 1820, however, were suddenly swept from the board by a new affair. It could be likened only to some all-pervasive stellar influence since it obsessed the whole population, and yet was incapable of adding one crumb or halfpenny to the diet or wages of a single workman in Westminster, where the farce was played.

The question seemed simple. Should Queen Caroline of Brunswick be allowed to take her place beside her husband, King George IV, on the throne of England? The pair had been virtually separated ever since their only child, Charlotte, was conceived in April 1795. The Prince was out of love with Caroline at first sight. She left his roof for her own convivial house in Blackheath and, after the peace of 1814, for a rackety life on the Continent. Why could she not stay in Italy, leaving her husband to the pink-and-white Lady Conyngham, known as the Vice-Queen?

Because Caroline was a political pawn and always had been. While her husband was hob-nobbing with the Whigs, who were so devoted to her interests as the Tories? Tory George Canning became her slave at Blackheath, Tory Lord Eldon sat on her right hand at dinner; but when the Prince Regent backed the Tories in 1812, their Whig and Radical opponents automatically discovered that the Princess's cause was their own.

Queen Caroline landed at Dover on 5 June 1820, entered London on the 6th and was given a rapturous welcome, stage-managed by the radical Alderman Matthew Wood. The Tories put up Wellington to negotiate a compromise settlement with Henry Brougham, her Attorney-General, by which in return for £50,000 a year she would live abroad and allow her name to be omitted from the Liturgy. Alderman Wood, however, decided that Caroline need concede nothing. Two nights running the mob stoned Sidmouth's house, almost catching him, Wellington and Eldon as they arrived in Sidmouth's carriage at the very moment the attack began.

'Let me out; I must get out!' cried Sidmouth to the Duke.

'You shall not alight,' the Duke shouted back, never ashamed to beat a tactical retreat; and to the coachman, 'Drive on!' The carriage, with one pane of glass already broken, was saved by the Duke's decision.[21]

While the Queen stood pat on her privileges the Government examined their secret weapon – a green bag containing eye-witness accounts of Caroline's behaviour abroad, collected by the Milan Commission in 1818. By 24 June the Wellington–Brougham talks had broken down, and on 5 July the Prime Minister introduced in the House of Lords the notorious instrument by which George IV hoped to obtain his freedom: a 'Bill of Pains and Penalties' to deprive Her Majesty of all her prerogatives, and to dissolve the Marriage between his Majesty and the said Queen.'

Some of Wellington's admirers felt that he had been handicapped as a negotiator by his long service abroad. It is indeed hard to believe that a more experienced Wellington would not somehow have prevented the Cabinet and King from plunging into such an unedifying struggle. Mrs Arbuthnot wrote in her journal on 20 October 1820, 'It certainly is not fit that a man like him shd. form one of a Cabinet where his opinion is not asked &, when given, is not attended to.' Henry Brougham went further, writing that but for his handicap the 'wise and firm-minded Duke of Wellington' would have recognized the Cabinet's 'crouching' to the King's command for what it was: an immoral concern to keep themselves in office.

It is certain that had the Duke of Wellington been longer in civil life, and attained his due weight in the councils of the Government, he would have taken this and no other view of the question.[22]

Whether or not Brougham was right in thinking that a more influential Wellington would have handed over the King to the Whigs rather than bring in the bill remains to be seen.

*

Mounting hysteria filled the pause of forty-three days between the first and second readings of the bill (5 July–17 August). In London the problem of law and order caused the Duke such vivid anxiety that his mind began to play with the possibility of a major reform. No proper police force as yet existed, the burden of controlling mobs fell on the military and the Guards gave every sign of siding with the Queen. His Majesty, very gouty and 'in a terrible temper'[23] according to Wellington, dared not show his face outdoors but cowered in Carlton House while the mob screamed 'Nero!' under his window until he withdrew to Windsor. One battalion of Guards mutinied.

It was this last awful event which brought forth a seminal memorandum from the Duke. The emergency, he stated, had produced chaos in the Guards' conditions of service: 'nobody knows who is on or off duty, all the troops are harassed, and the duty is ill done after all' – for which they were savagely punished. How could 'these unfortunate troops' be rescued from their predicament? His answer was historic:

In my opinion the Government ought, without loss of a moment's time, to form either a police in London or a military corps, which should be of a different description from the regular military force, or both.[24]

Eight years later, with Peel as Home Secretary but under the Duke's leadership, 'a police of a very different description' from anything before, even with a different name – 'Peeler' or 'Bobby' after Robert Peel – was formed.

On 17 August 1820, however, it was still the Guards on whom peers had to rely for a passage into the House through a milling crowd around Parliament Square. Everyone expected the worst. The actors in the opening scene of the 'trial' nevertheless reached their House safely on 17 August, though one of them only after an unpleasant experience. As the Duke entered Parliament Square a mob broke into hisses causing his horse to shy. An extraordinary double event: 'The Duke of Wellington – will

England credit it? will the world believe it? – was hissed!' (*Morning Post*) and not only hissed but undoubtedly '*taken by surprise*', a back-handed cut at his Waterloo strategy.

Now began the deployment of the craziest bill-cum-prosecution in history. The Queen wore black artificial ringlets and a white veil over her face, which nevertheless showed through as red as brick-dust. The unqueenly manner in which she lolled in her chair provoked Lord Holland, though her supporter, into a ribald joke: 'Instead of sleeping with Bergami [her majordomo], she sleeps with the Lords.' Small wonder if Caroline shut her ears to some of the green bag's sleazy evidence, dredged up as it was from the muddled memories of foreign menials: the masked ball when Bergami helped her into three indecent costumes, their giggling at fig-leaves on the garden statues, her garment found in his bed. When the postilion promoted to be her livery servant, Teodoro Majocchi, suddenly appeared as a witness against her, she gave a piercing shriek variously interpreted as 'O Teodoro!' 'O *traditore*!' or just 'O!' and fled from the Chamber.

Her counsel, Brougham, his eyes blazing and nose wrinkled, made short work of Majocchi, whose evasive refrain of '*Non mi ricordo*' – 'I don't remember' – became the ironic motto of the mob.

'Well, Creevey,' said Wellington to this keen ally of Queen Caroline after a particularly bad display by the foreigners, 'so you gave us a blast last night.'[25] Creevey heartily agreed, pointing out that foreigners would never be believed in England. 'Oh, but we have a great many English witnesses,' interposed the Duke, '– officers.' Though the officers were unable to give evidence of actual adultery, their description of behaviour on board their ships helped to dispel any lingering doubts that adultery had in fact been committed.

The mob turned out to be good-humoured, except towards the bishops, the Prime Minister and Waterloo heroes. Liverpool lost his nerve and could speak in the House only after dosing himself with ether, whiffs of which drifted into the nostrils of George Keppel, sitting on the steps of the throne. Lord Anglesey they hissed and in return, according to Lady Granville, he made them speeches about his duty. She failed to record what may have been his most notable speech, when the mob one day demanded a tribute to their idol. 'God save the Queen,' he obliged, '– and may all your wives be like her.' An equally persistent tradition gives the famous retort to Wellington,* for whom the roughest treatment was reserved. A climax was reached on 28 August when a hostile mob tried to unhorse him, and *The Times* reported 'considerable difficulty' before he got clear.

Attendance at the trial was compulsory for all peers except the over-seventies, minors, Catholics, those serving abroad or exempted on grounds of sickness or compassion. Otherwise an absentee was fined £100 for each of the first three days and £50 for every subsequent one. Two hundred and sixty peers sweated out the hot August weeks on the bank of the stinking Thames, their physical discomfort surpassed only by their mental wretchedness. By September some were ailing, among them the Wellesley brothers. Richard complained of suffocation, while Arthur developed a feverish cough with touches of his old enemy, rheumatism.

It was a relief to the Duke when Brougham adjourned the opening of the defence from 9 September to 3 October, so that he could retire to Stratfield Saye. When the House returned to the treadmill in October it was again Lord Holland who tried to raise a smile:

> *In this terrible matter which brings us to town*
> *We shall all be knocked up if we are not knocked down.*
> *None surely will gain by this 'Call of the House',*
> *Save eldest sons, witnesses, lawyers and grouse.*

One of the lawyers, Thomas Denman, the Queen's Solicitor-General, now proceeded to indulge in a final flight of fancy which nearly ruined his cause. He reminded their lordships that èven 'the woman taken in adultery' had been told to 'go and sin no more'. Since the defence's whole argument was that Caroline had not sinned at all, Denman's gaffe was monumental. A rhyme appeared in the public prints:

> *Most gracious queen, we thee implore*
> *To go away and sin no more;*

* The present Lord Anglesey defends his ancestor's right (Anglesey, p. 366). Sir William Fraser attributes the retort to the 3rd Marquess of Londonderry (*Words on Wellington*, p. 195). I am indebted to Mr John Wardroper for calling my attention to *John Bull*, 17 December 1820, and *The New Christmas Budget*, 1820, in both of which Theodore Hook makes the joke.

> *Or if that effort be too great,*
> *To go away at any rate.*

Yet M.P.s still could not bring themselves to vote in sufficient numbers for the King's divorce. On the second reading there was a majority of only twenty-eight for the bill. 'This is fatal,' wrote Creevey in triumph. Wellington thought the same. He told Mrs Arbuthnot on 9 November that he expected an even smaller majority for the third reading: perhaps four or five – or they might possibly be beaten. That night there was a 'terrible scene' in the Cabinet. Three-quarters of them wanted to drop the bill and Liverpool went out crying, while Canning's early associations with Blackheath made his position acutely embarrassing.[26] Next day, Friday 10 November, the third reading was carried by a mere nine votes. Someone shouted the news from a window and the crowds cheered themselves hoarse. Strangely enough the Cabinet also was cheerful, for Lord Liverpool immediately withdrew the doomed bill. 'We were all as good humoured & as delighted as possible today,' wrote the Duke to Mrs Arbuthnot, 'so that you need not be afraid of anybody being huffy & breaking up the Government.'[27] Nevertheless it was the King and the Government, not the Radicals, who in Wellington's words of the year before had been made to 'bite the dust'.

*

The danger of the Government's fall was fading less fast than Wellington hoped. Its dismissal by the King had been on the cards up to Caroline's arrival in England, for until that moment the Monarch had been denied his divorce by Lord Liverpool. With the dropping of the bill by the Tories came the chance for the Whigs to drop the Queen. A disloyal riddle was now popular in Whig circles: 'Why is the Queen like the Bill of Pains and Penalties? Because they are both abandoned.' Should the King now abandon the Tories who had failed him? In late November George IV listed the pros and cons for such a revenge.

Pro: The public mind would be diverted from his domestic problems (Lady Conyngham).

The Whigs would make a more popular settlement with the Queen. Human nature likes a change.

Con: The Opposition, being liberal, would liberate Bonaparte, change the Alliance System, perhaps emancipate the Catholics.[28]

Before a royal decision was reached, 'huffy' unhappy Canning resigned. Again the melting-pot. This time Wellington personally urged the King not to change his Government until the Queen's business had been concluded. The King angrily called it 'a letter he ought not to have written to an equal, much less to his Sovereign'.[29] But the Sovereign could see that the crisis was receding. At the play where he at last made a timid reappearance a shout of 'Where's your wife, Georgie?' was immediately silenced by cries of 'Shame!'

Wellington's own unpopularity was slowly subsiding also, and the political tide had finally turned in February 1821 when a last Opposition attempt to get the Queen's name into the Liturgy was defeated by the huge majority of 146. As Emily Cowper put it even before the vote, 'The Queen seems to me *dished* . . .'

On 19 July 1821 Queen Caroline was outside Westminster Abbey on the day of her husband's coronation. A young 'Waterloo', Arthur Shakespear, marked with excitement the dead silence that fell on the multitude when her open carriage arrived. Surely something tremendous would happen? But Caroline had always invited bathos.

> She got out at the end of the platform close to the Hall, intending to force her way in if refused admittance. We ran for the door & got in, the Lord Chamberlain crying out *'close the door!'* There were 6 of the principal *boxers* placed there – Jackson, Spring, & *Cribbe the Champion!*[30]

The sight of her on foot, jostled by the rabble, frantically but vainly rushing from door to door, evoked nothing but catcalls from the spectators. Even the Whig Lady Jersey had deserted her, for the two Jersey boys as well as the Duke's sons were holding up the royal train, inside.

Parliament had voted the enormous sum of £243,000 for the coronation. The Duke of Wellington performed as Lord High Constable of England, his dress together with those of his two sons having cost, according to their tutor, £1,000. Kitty as usual had taken the opposite line, deciding to wear cornelians instead of diamonds because of the economic distress. Wellington's duties were to advance on horseback up Westminster Hall in company with the Earl Marshal and High Steward, escorting various courses of the royal banquet. 'It was very well done,' wrote Mrs

Arbuthnot proudly; 'the Duke of Wellington rode a white Arabian who backed most perfectly.'[31] His Majesty's deportment was far from perfect. The Duke denounced his impiety to the Countess Lieven:

> . . . it is impossible to tell you in one letter about all the follies committed during the ceremony, even the most important and solemn religious part!! The eyes they made at each other, the reciprocal kissing of each other's rings! God alone knows what!!![32]

Emily Cowper thought the King looked at death's door and was only kept alive, apart from sniffing Lady Alicia Gordon's vinaigrette,* by the smiles of the Vice-Queen. But it was the Queen who died. Caroline succumbed on 7 August to inflammation of the bowel brought on, it was thought, by a broken heart. To her partisans it was *murder*.

*

The Queen had no doubt taken the lampooners' advice to go away.[33] A bad odour remained. The establishment was injured as well as Caroline, despite her self-inflicted epitaph, 'Caroline of Brunswick, the injured Queen of England.' The House of Lords felt degraded. 'The calm and gentlemanlike demeanour of the Peers' which George Seymour had so much admired when first appointed Sergeant-at-Arms in 1818 had become a sick grimace.

A man of Wellington's temperament was not likely to remain unscathed in spirit by this political miasma. His imagination, so firmly suppressed in youth by the burning of his violin, was apt to burst out in times of political strain and conjure up visions of a desperate future, with Britain at the mercy of a revolutionary opposition and unworthy throne. It was doubtful whether he regarded the Hanoverians whom he now directly served as much better than the Bourbons he had recently guided in France. In each case, the more degenerate the royal family the less could it be trusted in the hands of extremists, whether French Ultras or English Radicals. As the Duke saw it in 1821, his party must suffer the King for the sake of the country:

> The question for us is . . . whether we shall bear all we have to endure or give up the government to the Whigs and Radicals or, in other words, the country in all its relations to irretrievable ruin.[34]

* Now in the Victoria and Albert Museum.

Strange words indeed for a man who only three years before had denounced party factiousness, refusing to join a Tory administration unless free to do his best for their successors.

As for the throne, despite everything it was still in Wellington's eyes sacrosanct, through its indissoluble bond with the constitution. He was its 'retained servant', in so far as the throne itself was the servant of the constitution. It was the constitution that mattered. In an age of revolution nothing must be done to set it at risk.

From this principle the Duke derived two specific warnings. First, not to submit the constitution to the added stresses of reform when it was supported by a pillar so flawed as the present throne. Second, not to resign, if by doing so his party would be handing over the flawed throne to mischievous politicians. Far from agreeing with Brougham that the Cabinet during the Queen's trial had sacrificed morals for power, Wellington believed he and his colleagues were sacrificing comfort for morals.

*

What, then, was the over-all effect on Wellington of entering high politics at such an unpropitious time?

Politicians would be less than human if they were not influenced by first impressions. Winston Churchill first saw his party, the Conservative victors of 1900, in a tottering state and he learnt, as he himself put it, to rat and re-rat as if it were the most natural thing in the political world. Joseph Chamberlain first saw the Prime Minister (Gladstone) in 1880 being mercilessly baited, and respectful obedience never seemed to him an essential part of politics. Wellington first saw democracy in action during the Queen's trial and it gave him a jaundiced view. For the people were less in favour of the Queen than against all authority: the crown, the aristocracy, the church – what Cobbett called the 'Thing'. A foreigner like the Duke's diplomatic friend Baron Neumann was more impressed by the swiftness of the people's return to common sense: 'Now everything has changed again, Parliament has given its verdict and the people submit to it.' The Duke had his own idea of common sense, which did not include panderings to 'the people'. Take the petitions in favour of the Queen. As Lord-Lieutenant of Hampshire since 19 December 1820 he had dutifully presented a petition with nine hundred signatures. Then came proposals for another petition. Where was the common sense in that? He saw no point in 'going through the farce of a county meeting'.

Immediately the Whig peers, who were the pained recipients of this advice on 25 January 1821, set upon the Duke and in Creevey's words, 'pummelled him black and blue' until he apologized. 'Was there ever such a goose,' asked Creevey, 'as to get into such a mess?'[35]

'The farce of a county meeting.' These words, long remembered against him, exposed his first impressions of democracy. The uninhibited soldier had much to learn as a party politician. By a curious paradox the death of his closest party associate and mentor was soon to give him and the country a fresh start.

Meanwhile he had been picking up many threads, social and domestic, some golden, some hardly glistening at all, since his return to England nearly three years ago.

6

Interlude I:
Almost Private Life

Wellington had just witnessed the dissolution by death of a disastrous marriage. His own married life, though it differed utterly from the King's in being a union of well-meaning rather than monstrous incompatibles, was also going through a tempestuous phase. Indeed during the worst year, 1821, he too felt that he could not live under the same roof as his wife.

Maria Edgeworth drew an appealing picture of Kitty on St Patrick's Day 1819, when she called for the first time at Apsley House. A slight figure whose grey curls and wan skin made her look older than her forty-seven years came towards Maria with a smile of singular sweetness, picked up some shamrocks from a bowl and murmuring in French, 'You are worthy of them', pressed the national emblem into Maria's hand. 'Nothing could be more like Kitty Pakenham,' wrote the delighted novelist, 'former youth and beauty excepted.' As Wellington's ex-aide-de-camp Lord William Lennox wrote of the Duchess, she was 'amiable, unaffected and simple-minded. . . .' She was also 'generous and charitable'.[1] It was these last two qualities which were to be so nearly her downfall.

Mistress of a large establishment in Hampshire, Kitty's pious concern was chiefly for her servants and the poor. The kind of managerial genius which a future great hostess like Lady Palmerston (Emily Cowper) displayed found no place in Kitty's make-up. Yet this was what her husband expected. He asked for a commissary-general and was given a domestic chaplain.

The trouble began at the time of the Cato Street Conspiracy, when the accused men tried to justify their attempt on the Duke's life by citing his alleged harshness to the masses, as reflected in his treatment of his wife. This legend, the Duke held, Kitty had started up herself by her '*foolish* conduct'. He wrote to her angrily on 19 April 1820,

> . . . that you & your family have complained of my conduct towards you without Reason; that your whole conduct is one of watching & spying [on] me, and that you have employed my own Servants in doing so . . . I really don't believe you have any bad Intention. But every day's experience convinces me that you do more foolish things . . . which you must regret . . . upon the first moment of Reflection than any woman in the world.[2]

The truth was that the Duke's habitual reserve and distrust of Kitty's emotionalism had always prevented him from telling her about his day-to-day doings; while she, in fear of a rebuff, dared not ask him necessary questions but would set about finding out in devious ways. This general situation caused a serious incident in the following year.

It was probably on 4 May 1821 that he received from Kitty a letter containing the names of persons to whom he had not given charity. Next day, 5 May, he returned her a rocket:

> I have given all that I chuse to give. Upon this point I cannot help observing upon your mode of enquiry into my Transactions from Servants and other Underlings. It really makes my life a Burthen to me. If it goes on I must live somewhere else. It is the meanest dirtiest trick of which any body can be guilty.[3]

The Duke suspected that his wife was criticizing him for not giving enough to charity. If his suspicions had been correct (which they were not) his anger might have been justified, for his private papers show great generosity in gifts, loans and time. At this period, however, he felt it his duty to concentrate on helping those who had served his armies. When a stray *Chevalier*, who would doubtless have wrung Kitty's heart, asked him '*avec une entière confiance*' for £3,000 sterling, the Frenchman found his confidence was misplaced.

The second part of Wellington's letter to Kitty went further. He hinted that Kitty's system of espionage was motivated by suspicion not only about his charities but also about his private life:

> Yet do or say what I will you cannot avoid adopting some dirty way of trying to find out something which if it could [be found out] & you did find it out would give you the greatest uneasiness.

The Duchess replied on 10 May with four large indignant pages. A list of his charities was required in order that she might not be imposed upon by beggars applying twice over. She would have preferred to get his list from him personally, but since he was at Apsley House and she at Stratfield Saye, she conceived it right to obtain the information from a third person.

> I . . . thought you would have been gratified to be assured that I . . . am neither indifferent nor inattentive to the wants, the comfort or the characters of those about us. You may judge then of the bitterness of my disappointment on receiving the letter which I am not answering . . . I am as incapable of any mean or dirty actions as you are yourself –

– and if he had time to study her character he would find this out for himself.

> With respect to the suspicion so clearly expressed in your [letter] that I cannot misunderstand it, I never had, I have not such a thought [;] dismiss then from your mind so hateful a suspicion. I do not deserve that you should harbour it . . .

Kitty concluded with a request and a hope, both forcefully stated,

> . . . that I may not again be subjected to offensive accusations for which there is positively no grounds whatever.
> I hope this subject so painful to you and so injurious to me now be dismissed forever.[4]

Kitty's hope was not to be gratified. Her letter reached Arthur at the worst possible moment, during a harrowing family crisis. His niece, the beautiful Lady Worcester, daughter of his only sister Anne, had suddenly been taken ill. She died at Apsley House on 11 May, surrounded by a horde of screaming women, two of whom, Lady Jersey and a friend, he had to drag by main force away from the bed. 'I never thought it was so painful to die' were his niece's last words.

That same day both Kitty and Arthur wrote notes which crossed. Kitty offered to come up instantly from Stratfield Saye but also warned Arthur not to overtax Martha Baxter, the housekeeper, whose health was delicate; Arthur returned to the charge:

> It is not extraordinary that I should complain of that which is constantly repeated notwithstanding my remonstrances . . . what I complain of is that I am watched by my own Servants, Aide de camps & dependants and that for your Information! You can't avoid it, you have made it into a habit!

I never received any one list from anybody but five lists and these contained the names of Persons to whom however deserving I gave nothing. You therefore did not get the list for Information of deserving objects; but from motives of Curiosity or others.

But I don't care what your object was. If you are to continue to ask & obtain information of what I do from any Servant or dependant of mine or anybody else excepting myself I'll not live in the same House with you.[5]

This peal of thunder was not calculated to improve Kitty's health. On Monday 9 July she decided it was unlikely she would survive the night. Accordingly she sorted all her unpaid bills, placed them in Martha Baxter's reliable hands and returned to Arthur his two lethal letters of 5 and 11 May, together with a farewell note:

. . . I hope that I forgive you. I would and I am sure I could have made you happy had you suffered me to try, but thrust from you I was not allowed, for God's sake for your own dear sake for Christ sake do not use another woman as you have treated me never write to a human being such letters as those from you which I now enclose they have destroyed me.

God in heaven bless you my husband and bless and guard and guide you and my Children.[6]

Since there is no evidence that Kitty intended to destroy herself, nature must have pulled her through the night of 9 July, despite her melancholy forebodings. Fourteen years ago in 1807 she had longed to die because of Arthur's unkindness, and later repented of such an impious wish. Perhaps both of them felt remorse this time, for six months passed before Kitty was ready for a new trial of strength, and Arthur never again threatened to separate.

Meanwhile it was in this July that the news reached Europe of Napoleon's end.

*

A Parisian party was in full swing at Mme Craufurd's when the death which had taken place at St Helena on 5 May 1821 became known. Wellington and Talleyrand were there to hear the chorus of startled cries.

'What an event!'

'No, it's not an event any more,' corrected the cynical old

diplomat, 'now it's only *an item of news*.'[7]

George IV, expecting to hear from a courtier that Queen Caroline had died, found it was only Napoleon.

'I have, Sir, to congratulate you: your greatest enemy is dead.'

'Is she, by God.'[8]

Talleyrand's attitude was to prove typical; nevertheless, Talleyrand was wrong. For the piteous circumstances of the mighty Emperor's early dissolution under the twin blows of disease and confinement combined with his literary labours to clamp down on posterity a Napoleonic legend which only today is being dislodged.

Naturally the mourning for Napoleon could easily be turned into renewed abuse of his conqueror, as indeed it was by various romantic spirits from Byron downwards. In his 'Detached Thoughts' of 1821 Byron reflected acidly on the vanity of victories:

The Miscreant Wellington is the Cub of Fortune, but she will never lick him into shape: if he lives, he will be beaten – that's certain. Victory was never before wasted upon such an unprofitable soil, as this dunghill of Tyranny, whence nothing springs but Viper's eggs.[9]

Wellington's own immediate reaction to the news, as reported by Mrs Arbuthnot on 4 July 1821, was characteristic of the light but half deferential tone in which up till now he had habitually spoke of his great rival. 'The Duke of Wellington called on me,' wrote Mrs Arbuthnot, '& said, "Now I think I may say I am the most successful Gen[era]l. alive." '[10] Ever since 1814 the Duke had expressed unstinted admiration for Napoleon's generalship. 'I used to say of him,' he often repeated, 'that his presence on the field made the difference of forty thousand men.'[11] This was somewhat warmer than Napoleon's own slighting remarks about the 'Sepoy general'.

There was in fact nothing insensitive or ill-natured in the Duke's comments on Napoleon – until the publication of the codicil to the Emperor's will, with its spectacular legacy and declaration that Cantillon had as much right to assassinate 'that oligarch' as Wellington had to send the Emperor to perish on a rock. Then indeed the Duke's tone changed. In 1831 he said of Napoleon's written works, 'scarcely once has he tripped into truth'; and eight years later he was denouncing him along with all revolutionaries: 'In these revolutionary movements, men take no thought of principle, good faith or religion; they deserve to fail – and in the long run they do fail.'[12]

How these two great antagonists finally compared with one another must wait until the story of Wellington's life has run its course. But Napoleon's savage attack on 'that oligarch' for the harsh conditions of his captivity can be rebutted at once. Wellington deplored Governor Sir Hudson Lowe's blunders, due to his not being 'a man of the world'. Going further, was it wrong to imprison him at all? Lady Bessborough, a Whig, may be taken as speaking in 1815 for England on this perplexing subject:

What an astounding history it has been; but will he not be a puzzling prisoner to take care of? . . . a constant bone of contention he would be, & with his cleverness & friends how sure of escaping before long & setting the world on fire.

The puzzled lady finally decided that Britain ought to have passed the responsibility. 'We had better . . . let the French have taken him.'[13] In which case he would certainly have been shot.

*

The death of Napoleon may have reminded George IV that he had never seen Waterloo, for he ordered Wellington to parade towards the end of September 1821 as historian and guide.

The Duke had recently returned from Paris where he had heard a rumour that Ney's son intended to insult and provoke him to a duel. Nothing happened, beyond Louis XVIII providing the Duke with a perfect answer to young Ney, if required. It should be the reply given by Marshal Saxe when challenged to fight at a masked ball. 'Certainly not, sir,' thundered the Marshal, 'I would have you know that I never fight except at the head of a hundred thousand men. . . .'*[14]

George IV's visit to Waterloo went off without a hitch, apart from the penalties of gluttony. Whether from emotion or a hangover he was strangely silent while riding with Wellington over the battlefield. 'His Majesty took it very coolly; he never asked me a

* Wellington had also seen the baby Duke of Bordeaux, son of the murdered Duke of Berry, whose governess boasted of having been 'un peu' the mistress of Artois, 'un peu beaucoup' the mistress of Berry and 'aussi un peu' the mistress of the Duke of Wellington. The Duke, in telling Mrs Arbuthnot the story, 'disclaimed that distinction for himself . . .'.

single question, nor said one word, until I showed him where Lord Anglesey's leg was buried, and then he burst into tears.'[15] It may have been this martial experience which was responsible for one of George IV's numerous fantasies, namely that he himself had led the Germans' great charge at Salamanca disguised as General Bock.

'Was not that so?' he would shout to the Duke down the dinner-table.

'I have often heard Your Majesty say so,' his Grace would reply.*

After so many conducted tours of Waterloo the Duke had long since learnt to control his own tears. Only once was he said recently to have registered intense feeling, and that was on technical grounds concerned with the correct understanding of the battle. When he saw the monumental Lion Mound erected by the Dutch he burst out:

'They have spoiled my Battlefield.'[16]

*

Kitty's next clash with a distinctly 'Iron Duke' came in January 1822. She wrote to him that, economize as she might, her personal allowance of £500 a year was insufficient. Would he increase it to £670? Arthur refused. For a lady of her rank £500 was generous; only princesses had more.

Kitty was no fairy-tale princess but she was still queen of charity. Indiscriminate charity was what she finally had to admit had run away with her allowance:

I believe I may have given away money very injudiciously, perhaps sometimes [Kitty conscientiously corrected 'sometimes' to 'often' in her fair copy] to spare myself the pain of refusing, and I confess it would be hard to make you pay for my weakness. I will from this time only retain as permanent Pensioners those who are so very old & friendless that they must perish without my assistance –[17]

– a retired miniature painter with an idiot daughter and only £20 a year who had once taught Kitty drawing, a disabled dancing master, the Wellesley boys' wet-nurse, now abandoned by her husband, an old maidservant with a paralytic husband and an old manservant with a crippled child. The sums allowed by Kitty to

* Another version is that the King's hallucination applied to Waterloo itself, but General Bock's great exploit was not at Waterloo but Salamanca (*See* Holland, p. 192).

this poor flotsam and jetsam of great houses were then added up (wrongly, of course; she made the total £216, £9 too little), and after promising in future to stick to her £500 allowance, she bravely asked Arthur to clear her of debt – 'I am ashamed to say of £200. . . .'*

The air was cleared also. She resumed her old practice of addressing her husband in letters as 'My dearest Arthur', having for a time adopted his own brusque style of doing without a beginning. By May 1822 she was willing to abandon even a little of her personal puritanism for his sake, as the following incident shows.

After a rapturous morning on the river at Eton with her two sons, rowing and eating mutton chops, she returned to Apsley House wind-blown and happy – and promptly ran into her husband. He gazed at her dishevelled locks, as she noted, with wonder. Then he lifted them in his fingers and said very gently:

'Had you not better do something with them, had not you better? They are so very grey! had you not better?'

'I feared you hated everything approaching a wig.'

'Oh, no. I am sure you would look better.'

Kitty rushed off to the hairdresser and came home looking 'within a trifle' as young as her niece Kate, to whom she recounted the whole adventure. Kate Hamilton, now married to the Rev. William Foster, had tried in vain, though supported by Kitty's sons, to make her aunt take this step earlier: 'One word or two from one man,' Kitty now wrote in high feather, 'has done what boys and girls and men and women failed in accomplishing. . . . He has not yet seen the change but we shall meet to-night at Devonshire House when I hope he will observe that I have lost no time in complying and O that I had done so about rouge 16 years ago.'[18]

The reference to '16 years ago' means that Kitty was thinking of the year of her marriage, 1806, when Arthur, appalled by his thirty-four-year-old bride's lifeless complexion ('She's grown ugly, by Jove'), entreated her to use rouge. As Kate Foster wrote after her aunt and uncle were both dead:

The gaiety and brilliancy which had won his admiration, were charms

---

* In October 1822 she was ordering baby linen from the matron of Newgate Prison, in response to an appeal from Elizabeth Fry.

after which the Duke naturally yearned and . . . he besought her to supply an appearance of more healthful color . . .

Kitty refused, thus 'inflicting constant pain'. As recently as 1 January 1821, she had written to her evangelical sister, Mrs Stewart:

Do not apprehend a wig for me, my Bess. My boys detest it. Papa sneers at it on others. I never had a fancy for it, and all the world of fashion is reconciled to my white, white hair . . . I never conceal it, for the present.[19]

The wig, when it arrived, was too late.

Less than two months later, towards the end of a garden party on 27 June, Wellington suddenly and for the first time poured out to Mrs Arbuthnot the whole story of his unhappy marriage.[20] First, bitter complaints of their incompatibility — 'he had repeatedly tried to live in a friendly manner with her' — 'she did not understand him' — 'might as well talk to a child'. Next, her obstinacy — 'thinks herself so excessively clever that she never stirs even to accommodate herself to him' — (what about the wig?) — '& never for an instant supposes that when their opinions differ, she may be the one in the wrong' — (what about the debts?). Then his own thwarted domesticity — 'nothing would make him so happy as to have a home where he could find comfort' — and Kitty's failure as a hostess — 'she made his house so dull that nobody would go to it while, whenever he was in town alone and when he had been *en garçon* in France, everybody was so fond of his house that he could not keep them out of it; that he could not but feel & see the difference & that it drove him to seek abroad that comfort & happiness that was denied to him at home.'

The last charge was fully justified. Not only was Kitty shy, short-sighted and badly dressed, but she was also tart and quick to take offence. Two years after Wellington's outburst his comrade and friend, William Napier, was writing indignantly to the Duchess that he heard she would never ask him inside her house again simply because he had expressed what he called 'commonplace opinions in politics'.[21] Kitty was a Tory, William a Whig; but it was sad for the Duke of Wellington when his wife tried to ban his friends in the misguided belief that she was protecting her hero.

It might be thought, however, that Arthur was neither fair to Kitty in his earlier charges, nor accurate in his self-analysis. Eulogies of a quiet home life were all very well; but the women with whom he could have been happy – Lady Charlotte Greville, Mrs Patterson, Mrs Arbuthnot herself – attracted him by their beauty, wit, grasp of politics and social graces rather than by their domesticity. Wellington's ideal life was an army mess and his ideal family the military 'family' of his aides-de-camp. 'My boys', as he called his young staff officers, could never be entirely supplanted in his imagination even by his own sons. Though he thought the opposite, he would not have been the easiest of men to live with as a husband.

Nevertheless an impression emerges from Wellington's tirade of 27 June 1822 that the worst between him and Kitty was over. It was vexation recollected in tranquillity. Would he have confided in Mrs Arbuthnot otherwise?

Mrs Arbuthnot finally arrested the flow of grievances by saying he was a fool to have married her.

He agreed cordially in my abuse of him & I could not think him a greater fool than he did himself. He seemed quite *soulagé* after having made me this confidence, & seemed quite glad to have someone to whom he could say anything.[22]

If Mrs Arbuthnot brought him comfort, the Duchess had her own consolations.

*

The young loved her – from secretaries to the large brood of her adopted children. Six of these besides her own two adored sons brought happiness as well as problems into her house: Arthur Freese, Gerald Wellesley, Kate Hamilton, two Long-Wellesley boys (of whom more hereafter) and Lord Arthur Lennox. Young Freese, like Lennox one of the Duke's numerous godsons, made a successful career in India, thanks to the Duke's money and influence with Charterhouse School and the East India Company, and kept up a glowing correspondence with Kitty, his 'dearest lady' or 'dearest friend'.[23] The younger adopted children treated her with the same uninhibited affection as her own boys. When the Duke of Richmond died of hydrophobia in Canada from the bite of a tame fox, his youngest son, Arthur Lennox, spent holi-

days at Stratfield Saye and wrote Kitty cheeky letters from school:
'My *Dearest* Duchess, *you are a Very* naughty *Boy* for not writing
to *Me*, and I think I must get *Charles* and *Douro* to wip *You*' –
and later, 'I am very much obliged to you for the money you
would have sent me if you had had any cash.'

Douro and Charles were her 'first *earthly* consolation', as she
freely admitted to her sister. She spoilt them, let them bully her
and now and then forgot their needs.

'My dear Mama,' wrote Charles at nine, 'You must have
everything ready as possible or dread the most severe
punishment from me.'[24] Had she remembered, asked Douro, to
prepare for the medieval tournament in the spring holidays of
1820? 'You shall get up every morning at eight o'clock precisely
if you are good and obey my orders,' wrote this thirteen-year-old
from Eton, 'but if you are bad . . . you shall get up at 6 o'clock
without any fire or warm water and then stand in the corner with
a fool's cap upon your head till breakfast time.' He complained
that she sent them back to Eton for the summer of 1822 with 'a
great deficiency' of pocket handkerchiefs – sixteen missing between him, Charles and Gerald.

At fourteen Douro fell madly in love with Dr Hume's pretty
eldest daughter Elizabeth, another 'dear little protégée' of Kitty's,
as Douro called her.* For several years Kitty dithered between
encouraging and checking their secret romance. Douro indeed
seems to have told his mother most of his secrets, with frequent
injunctions to 'keep in silence your Irish tongue and keep shut
your Pakenham mouth'. It was through the Elizabeth affair that
the Duke made his most successful impact on his eldest son's
character. Up till then (1823), the Duke had seemed somewhat of
a pedagogue, ordering Douro at twelve to read a portion of
English every day to stop him speaking so fast, and at fifteen to
send him a weekly letter on his current Latin theme, the letter
being returned with never a word of praise but only the Duke's

* It was with her young protégée that Kitty chiefly indulged her taste for
whimsicality. 'Many happy returns of this day to you, my dear Liz,' she
wrote to Elizabeth Hume on Christmas Day 1823, 'and to all you love and
to all who love you! and to all those that love them that love those that love
those that love them that love you!!' – adding crisply that Douro was working so hard he had turned down all invitations; 'One invitation was from
Lord & Lady Salisbury (who by the way have invited *all* the family except
me . . .)'.

curt corrections: '1. Want of stop. 2. This word repeated, see the preceding line.'[25]

Douro's passion for Elizabeth was confided to a schoolfriend. 'A friend of mine here,' he wrote to Mama in May 1823, 'sends his love to Miss Hume, he has quite fallen in love with the description I have given of her; if she should express any concern to the interesting young man you may tell her his name is Radcliffe.'[26] However, the Wellesley boys' unofficial guardian at Eton, sent with them by Kitty and called the Rev. Henry Wagner, told Douro that the interesting young man must be avoided as a thoroughly bad influence. Douro promptly passed on this opinion to Radcliffe, an 'indiscretion' which produced such an explosion that Papa himself had to be called in to rebuke, explain and calm. He drafted a brilliant letter which, after being rendered legible by Mama in a neat copy, was sent to their sixteen-year-old son.

> ... Of all the evils that surround a person in your situation, bad company is the most fatal. ... God forbid that I should be understood to advise you to keep company with none but persons of your own Rank and Station in life. In all stations there are persons of good and bad Education manners and habits; I earnestly entreat you to associate with the former alone and to avoid the latter, be they of what Rank or Station they may.[27]

There was however one advantage, continued the Duke, in Douro sticking to friends of his own rank. He would avoid flatterers.

> In urging you then to associate with the Good of all Ranks and Stations, I entreat you to recollect that I class among the Bad, those who would endeavour to convince you ... that you enjoy any personal advantage over other Persons. ...

The effect on the impressionable Douro was magical. He replied to his mother on 8 June 1823:

> I intend to keep my copy of it as a memorial of the wisest and best of fathers that ever mortal had; I once thought him the most intense disciplinarian that ever lived, and consequently avoided and feared him accordingly. Lately I have found out what he really is, [so] that now he appears in my eyes the greatest man that ever lived. It seems as if he knows exactly the way to turn me any way he likes, for there is not one word of severity in the whole of these two sheets. ...

When the Duke was severe it was because, as he once told Mrs Arbuthnot, he was afraid that his sons might develop the traits he disliked in their mother. His feelings for his younger son were clouded by 'Charley's' breezy indolence, a quality which the Duke prophesied would ruin even the *jeunesse dorée* in a gritty postwar world, and which drew from him periodic mutterings:

You are now of an age [15½] to be able to feel all the consequences of your idleness, and I therefore take the opportunity of warning you that you will live in times when your Ignorance will be a perpetual drawback upon you, and that no power on earth will be able to place you in any excepting the lowest situations unless you should be qualified to fill higher by your diligence. . . .[28]

Apart from this, his relations with Charles were warm and natural, and he would have agreed with William Napier's enthusiastic picture of him at sixteen as a 'fine, laughing, playful, spirited boy with no pride'.[29] Douro was an entirely different character, thought Napier, 'very much resembling the Duke without his *devil*'.

For '*devil*' read genius in all its manifestations, including demonic energy and fire, and you have the Wellington–Douro problem in a nutshell, a problem that has beset many a famous father of a promising eldest son. How bring him up without either false pride or a destructive sense of inferiority? The Duke of Wellington's extraordinary glamour in the world was altogether too great to give Douro a chance.

There was the small boy hoping in vain to model himself on Papa. 'My Nose is *such a time a-growing*,' Kitty heard him say as he gazed at Nollekens's bust of his father. Then the freshman at Oxford successfully imitating his father, as when a young peer at Christ Church whom he had last seen as a schoolboy made him a condescending bow – 'I only gave him one of Papa's short "how do ye do's?".' Lastly the young man just come of age and ready to blame any shortcomings on his stars rather than himself – 'I wish I had my father's life to begin, for even if perchance I may obtain his power, I never shall have such an age to live in. . . .' Douro particularly liked the reply he heard Napoleon had made when asked whether he was training his son to replace him:

'Replace me? I would not replace myself! I am the child of circumstance.'[30]

Considering the situation between his parents and Douro's inevitable partisanship, it is creditable that the Duke did not make an enemy of his elder son. The young Etonian certainly preferred his mother's mild philosophy to his father's sterner creed.

But is there any truth in a well-known account of Douro's attitude to his father after the great Duke's death? The Duchess of Cleveland was supposed to have asked Douro (by then the 2nd Duke) whether his father had ever shown him any kindness? 'No,' replied the son, 'he never even patted me on the shoulder when I was a boy, but it was because he hated my mother.'[31] On the contrary, the letters of June 1823 show paternal kindness and filial appreciation; indeed judging by a compliment from Douro to his mother it is probable that Wellington succeeded in concealing from his sons the unhappiness of his marriage until they were grown up. When in 1823 Douro first met Wagner's newly married wife, he wrote off to his mother, 'She is an excellent woman, but not the Woman that I like; you know my taste, if you do not I will tell you in three words, "it is Papa's".'[32]

*

Mrs Arbuthnot was once described by the Duke to her husband as 'a pattern of *sensible* women; for she makes the whole world do whatever she pleases!'[33] Did she want Wellington for her lover, and succeed in her desire?

Peel thought so. The man responsible, however, for disseminating the belief that the Duke and Mrs Arbuthnot were lovers was that archgossip, compulsive gambler, father of at least one illegitimate child and bachelor diarist of genius, Charles Greville. In 1824 both Mrs Arbuthnot and a Mrs Lane-Fox received anonymous letters accusing them of love affairs with the Duke. Wellington at once recognized the writing as Greville's. Harriet Arbuthnot then remembered that she and Mrs Lane-Fox had recently taunted Greville with 'unfeeling profligacy'.

The contents of Mrs Arbuthnot's anonymous letter were discussed frankly in her journal for 11 April 1824:

Mr. Arbuthnot & I have been greatly annoyed by another anonymous letter* accusing me of being in love with the Duke of Wellington, of being always in *holes* and *corners* with him, & of being so jealous of

* See p. 126 for a previous anonymous letter.

him that I never can bear him to speak to any other woman! Luckily my dear husband & I live upon terms of such affection and confidence that these base insinuations have only the effect of making us abhor the wicked feeling which could prompt anyone to write such a letter.[34]

Wellington, Harriet and Charles Arbuthnot fumed together over this outrage, particularly the '*holes* and *corners*' phrase. She hardly ever sat by the Duke at assemblies, she wrote, and was always in a large party at the opera; if he called on his way from the Ordnance office it was only after 5 o'clock when 'my door is open to the whole town unless Mr A. is at home & chooses we should be a trio'; and yet the letter said they were together the whole morning.

However, we have agreed that in public we will not talk much together, but go on just the same in private. The anonymous writer would be surprised if he knew how amicably we three had discussed his amiable letter.

If Greville had a personal reason for maligning Mrs Arbuthnot – and not only the above passage but the whole tone and temper of her journal leave no room to doubt that he was maligning her – he had a stronger reason for accusing Wellington. Somewhere about the year 1820 the Duke was certainly involved in a passionate love affair with a woman who was not his wife. That woman was the mother of Charles Greville.

In her journal for December 1824 Mrs Arbuthnot herself was to recall the liaison. Lady Charlotte Greville, she wrote, daughter of the Duke of Portland who had been Prime Minister,

. . . full of grace & talent & the charm of every society she went into was afterwards [i.e. after Waterloo] supposed to have conquered the Conqueror of France. For a long time he appeared to be devoted to her &, though the passion has subsided, they are still great friends.[35]

Two hitherto unpublished letters, or rather parts of letters, unsigned and virtually undated, prove that Charles Greville had indeed had some cause for alarm. First comes a note from Colonel Charles Greville senior (father of young Charles) to his wife Lady Charlotte, whom he had evidently warned of trouble during a previous conversation:

I am extremely sorry to find that the information I gave you, has caused you so much agitation! . . . with respect to Charles, living in the world as he does, & quick & clear sighted as he is, if you had reflected but a moment it would have occurred to you that he could not be blind to your conduct with the Duke of Wellington. But it did not follow that he must know, or even suspect, the degree of intimacy which had subsisted! . . .[36]

Her eldest son, Colonel Greville continued, loved her deeply and desired nothing but her ultimate happiness –

– for God's sake awake from the dream which seems to have taken possession of your mind & look to, as other women do, for your happiness & interest in this world, the affection, the respect & the Welfare of your children. . . .

As for Colonel Greville himself, he must have time to recover from the shock and feel thoroughly convinced that she would no longer allow anybody to lead her into acts derogatory to his honour and her good name.

On 'Friday 17th' an affectionate and clever letter was sent off by Lady Charlotte to her son Charles in which, while not admitting that anything immoral had actually happened, she agreed that a change in behaviour might be necessary:

It is true that I *prize highly* the friendship & confidence of the Duke of Wellington & shd extremely regret to be obliged to renounce altogether his Society . . . but I have no desire to cultivate it in a *clandestine manner* . . . the *fascination* which you do not comprehend is the having for years experienced from him a thousand acts of kindness, friendship & attention with professions of regard & affection for me and all belonging to me which I believe to be very sincere. . . .

At the same time she valued her family and would make the greatest sacrifices for them all.

I need not therefore repeat that I put myself entirely under your guidance & shall if you desire it make the *immediate & unqualified relinquishment* of all intimacy & correspondence with the Duke of Wellington.

But was such a complete break, she asked, really the best policy?

After this unconditional surrender the two Charleses, father and son, must have accepted Lady Charlotte's less drastic suggestion of substituting impeccable conversations with the Duke for what had before been 'crim. con.'. All ended happily except that Charles Greville junior took his revenge. Three days after the great Duke died he dedicated a long passage in his famous diary to the Duke's *'liaisons'*, whether 'innocent', 'very senile' or the genuine article.[37] He became 'the successful lover', wrote Greville, of Grassini and 'some women of fashion, whose weaknesses had never been known, though perhaps suspected'. Mrs Arbuthnot was clearly the leading candidate for this distinction (assuming that Greville had the good taste to exclude his own mother), followed by much less serious contenders like the Ladies Shelley, Jersey and Georgiana Fane, the two last being half-sisters and Harriet Arbuthnot's cousins. The relevant Greville diaries were first published in 1887 and Mrs Arbuthnot's not until 1950, so that Greville's revenge had a free run for over half a century.

*

Despite Greville's attempt to pin down Wellington to the world of gallantry, his influence was on the side of that moral renaissance which began long before the Victorian Age. In matters of sex his greatest friend, Mrs Arbuthnot, was, like Kitty, almost a 'Victorian' prude. Attending the opera with Charlotte Greville, Harriet was deeply shocked by the 'gross indecency' of the French dancers' dress, and Wellington had virtually to apologize for telling her the 'very *odd* story' of how Bonaparte had distracted the French from their military losses in Russia by ordering the female *corps de ballet* to dance 'without their under garments!' At Belvoir Castle Harriet and Kitty had listened with aversion to Lady Shelley and Lady Caroline Poulett boasting of their Cossack trousers with nothing underneath, in contrast to Harriet's three petticoats and riding habit, and had finally left the drawing-room *'toutes scandalisées'* when Lady Caroline accepted an invitation from the Duke of Rutland and an attendant colonel to come and *'be smothered'* behind locked doors.[38]

Unlike 'Old Bags' Eldon, who was no churchgoer and boasted that he upheld the church from outside like a buttress, the Duke always went to church. His only religious trouble was with those tiresome busybodies, the evangelical 'saints', though he found one 'saint', the Duchess of Beaufort, quite agreeable. She did not bore him with her sanctity and was very good-humoured, her only fault being a wish to show him off in church – 'possibly as a conquest of a sinner to the Good Cause'.[39]

In 1819 he became a member of the Society for the Promotion

of Christian Knowledge and, having been reminded by a greatly daring secretary two years later that he had so far paid no sub-scriptions, he gave £50 that year and 5 guineas annually until practically the end of his life.[40] Clergymen, he believed, should be kept clear of 'the *broils* of the county', and he regularly refused to appoint them as magistrates, to the indignation of many Hamp-shire gentlemen.

Heavy gambling disgusted him and the recurrent press stories that he himself was ruined by play made him see red. When the editor of the *Morning Chronicle* used Wellington's name in September 1823 to illustrate an anomaly in the Vagrancy Act – His Grace might be committed as a rogue and vagabond for playing Hazard – the Duke declared that he never played games of chance and had not entered a public place or club for years; nor did he want to hear the old tale again, that his gambling had obliged him 'to sell the offices in the Ordnance himself, instead of allowing them to be sold by others!!'

As a recent member of the landlord class Wellington attracted little personal criticism compared with the growing abuse of the class as a whole. Even Cobbett paid a grudging tribute: 'Accord-ing to all accounts he is no *miser* at any rate; and the estates that pass through his hands may, perhaps, be full as well disposed of as they are at present.'[41]

The Duke would not enclose the common land adjacent to Stratfield Saye when encouraged to do so by Wyatt; nor would he enclose a common near Wellington in Somerset in order that the local gentry might erect him a monument: 'It is much better that it should continue a Common than that I should give or sell a piece of ground which should have become mine in consequence of the Enclosure.'[42]

In that other landlord's perquisite, a pocket borough, he had no private interest, though Reading was available at £6,000.

Wellington was naively dazzled by his new country home. Did Mrs Arbuthnot know that there were white violets growing wild in the park? His friends did not share his enthusiasm. Mrs Arbuthnot wrote in her journal for 11 January 1821, 'It is not a nice place, seems damp & low, and the house but an indifferent one for him.'[43] Lord Francis Leveson-Gower had written it off as 'a miserable imitation of a French Chateau' (though he was glad to spend his honeymoon there later). Despite Wellington's importation of 7-foot-long French beds and Boulle furniture: despite the conversion of an old riding-school into a real tennis court; despite the maroon liveries of his servants, the gay vista of pink-washed stables with rococo curves opposite the front door and the cedar he planted himself in 1817 (still alive today) – Peel in January 1826 was not enthusiastic: 'The house is a wretched one, wretchedly furnished, but warm and not uncomfortable. The drawing-room very small and very low, but a handsome library built, I suppose, by the Duke, with a billiard room only separated by columns from the library.'[44]

Though Peel was a connoisseur of pictures he did not mention those at Stratfield Saye. Contemporary opinion was more impressed by the £1,260 Wellington paid to Sir David Wilkie in 1822 for his *Chelsea Pensioners reading the Waterloo Despatch*, still in Apsley House. The same generous sum was given to Sir William Allan for his *Waterloo* and occasioned one of the most engaging of 'Wellingtoniana'.

'Your Grace,' the artist interrupted as Wellington began counting out interminable banknotes, 'Your Grace might prefer to draw a cheque on your bank to save time and trouble?'

'Do you suppose,' growled the Duke as he went on counting, 'I would let the clerks in Coutts's know what a fool I've been?' *

If society did not approve of the Duke's choice of houses, they were tumbling over themselves to get him into their own. It was in these house-parties that he shone as a man rather than as a hero. As Whigs or Tories got to know him better their liking for the man increased. Even at his own table, with Kitty's lorgnette lifted fiercely against all Whigs, William Napier shed any prejudices against him:

Beyond all question the Duke is a noble highminded man, and I will never believe a story to his prejudice again.[45]

Wellington first stayed with the Shelleys at Maresfield, Sussex, in October 1819. His visit was a memorable one. He was to inform Mrs Arbuthnot three months later while a guest of the Granvilles at Wherstead: 'The shooting has been excellent; but I have shot

* (*Wellington Anecdotes*, p. 70) The painter Landseer told a fellow-artist, W. P. Frith, that when he asked 600 guineas for his commissioned picture of Van Amburgh the lion-tamer, the Duke gave him also 1,200 guineas. 'I could tell you many more instances of his liberality,' added Landseer (Frith, vol. i, p. 323).

worse than usual.' This was a formidable boast if his usual style was that displayed at Lady Shelley's, where he began by peppering a dog, went on to a keeper's gaiters and reached a climax with the bare arms of a cottager hanging out her washing at an open window.

'I'm wounded, Milady.'

'My good woman, this ought to be the proudest moment of your life. You have the distinction of being shot by the great Duke of Wellington!' The Duke had always thought Lady Shelley rather a goose. He quickly produced a sovereign.[46]

The truth was that, as in France, the Duke still loved hunting and shooting more for fresh air and exercise than for the sport itself. At Wherstead again in 1823 he scored another calamitous series of near bull's-eyes:

> I want consolation . . . having had the misfortune of shooting Lord Granville this day. I have put nine shots in his face [on a recount it turned out to be only seven]; luckily his eyes escaped unhurt, and he feels no inconvenience but the smarting pain, I killed the pheasant with the same shot. . . . Lady Granville was very good humoured about it.[47]

Lady Granville could forgive a few pellets in her husband's face. 'I quite love the Duke of Wellington.' It was not that he attracted her as an *héros de roman,* 'but he is the most unpretending, perfectly natural and amiable person I ever met with'.[48] (It was said that in private the 'amiable person' himself took these shooting accidents lightly. 'Bird shot never hurt anyone.')[49]

A touch of the old iron, however, was sometimes necessary. When staying with his niece and nephew, Hyacinthe and Edward Littleton, in Staffordshire, a stranger accosted him:

'Ah, your grace, I have served with you.'

'Where?'

'Why, in Spain.'

'What regiment were you in?'

'In the — Regiment Artillery.'

'Well, and when did you go to Spain?'

'In 1801.'

'Oh, that will never do,' said the Duke, turning on his heel. One could generally catch out impostors with dates. Four hundred less audacious Staffordshire people were content to make up a huge hunt in order to see him. 'I thought this the best mode of showing him,' wrote Edward Littleton in his diary, 'and the Duke himself remarked it was not a bad way of being seen.'*[50]

Fresh air might even compensate for the scanty joys of a house to which he was now in 1822 being summoned uncomfortably often – the King's. 'I have not been quite well for some days,' he wrote to Mrs Arbuthnot on 3 June, 'and I am *frightened* at the disgust I shall feel where I am going!' He was going to stay with the King at his rustic retreat, The Cottage, Windsor. 'But I dare say that being out in the Air all day at the Races will do me good. . . .'[51]

Two years earlier he had noticed the effect of fresh air on another tired statesman, Castlereagh. He was looking better at the end of 1820 than for months, 'owing to exercize and excellent sport'. In this summer of 1822 Castlereagh needed it as never before. True, certain political strains were eased, notably the King's animosity towards his Government. But there were plenty of other anxieties. What Castlereagh called 'embarrassment' and Wellington 'distress' was so acute that 10 per cent cuts were made in ministerial salaries, while HM gave up £30,000 a year from his civil list and was advised not to go abroad for amusement.[52]

Wellington's friend Castlereagh, however, did plan to visit the Continent. The peoples of Europe were again restless. A popular rising in Naples, though summarily suppressed, was a sign of the times. The signs in Spain and Greece were worse. They threatened the 'system'. Two congresses, Troppau and Laibach, in neither of which Britain played an active part, had tried to settle things in a way satisfactory to the monarchies. Now there was to be another congress. This time Wellington's friend must go. But not for amusement.

* Another extract from Littleton's journal dated some years later shows that the Duke's wild shooting was not unique. Littleton took a friend up to a covert on his estate known as the 'Wellington Belt' and the friend proceeded to miss a pheasant, break fifteen panes of glass in a cottage and injure a child. In those carefree times bad shots were blazing away all over Britain.

7

One Gentleman of Verona

It was Saturday evening, 3 August 1822, just under a week before the Duke was due to leave England for the Netherlands on his annual inspection of the frontier fortresses. He and Charles Arbuthnot among others were dining at Cray Farm, Lord Castlereagh's home in Kent, before the Foreign Secretary also went abroad.* The subject of a private conversation between the three of them was blackmail.

A man had been threatening Mr Arbuthnot with exposure of certain public figures unless he were given a government job. The threats had culminated in an anonymous placard accusing Mrs Arbuthnot of a love affair with the Duke. What did Lord Castlereagh advise?

The Duke noticed with astonishment that Castlereagh showed no interest in the attack on Mrs Arbuthnot. He regarded the blackmail as aimed principally at himself. There was a Cabinet meeting on 7 August, the Foreign Secretary appearing 'very low, unwell and dispirited'. He took no part and simply listened in silence to the instructions issued by himself for the forthcoming conference at Vienna and the Congress that was to follow at Verona. On the way home he held Wellington's arm but said nothing. The Arbuthnots meanwhile had heard to their intense astonishment that the Foreign Secretary believed he was being blackmailed not only for having entered a brothel with a woman three years earlier, but also for a homosexual crime: what Harriet called 'a crime not to be named'.[1]

The next – and last – time that Wellington saw his friend was on

* Lord Castlereagh had become 2nd Marquess of Londonderry on the death of his father the year before. For the sake of clarity however he will continue to be called Lord Castlereagh in this story, as indeed up to his death and afterwards he was often so called by his contemporaries.

Friday afternoon, 9 August. As he rode into St James's Square Lady Castlereagh called out to him from her window and at the same moment her husband rushed past him into the house saying he must have a talk. Wellington followed him in.

The Foreign Secretary flung himself down on a sofa and was soon pouring out a tale of unnatural vice and blackmail. Tears streamed down his face as he brought up the recent scandal of Percy Jocelyn, Bishop of Clogher – what Wellington called when writing to Arbuthnot in code, the 'Story of 19'.*[2] Bishop Jocelyn had been discovered with a guardsman in the White Hart, Westminster. Accusing himself of an analogous offence, Castlereagh added that Wellington's coldness at the Cabinet and walking home must have meant he too knew about his crime.

By now the Duke had realized that his friend was 'in a state of mental Delusion', particularly as Castlereagh went on to describe how a stranger had accosted him that morning and told him his horses had been brought from Cray so that he might fly the country.

'Depend upon it,' interposed the Duke, 'this is all an illusion. Your stomach is out of order.' No, insisted Castlereagh, his own servants would bear him out; and suddenly leaping for the bell-pull he rang violently and shouted to the servant,

'Tell me, sir, instantly, who ordered my horses here; who sent them up to town?'

'The horses are at Cray, my Lord, and have never been in town.'

'There, you see it's as I said,' exclaimed the Duke. 'From what you have said, I am bound to warn you that you cannot be in your right mind.' Castlereagh, clutching his handkerchief, covered his face with both hands and lay sobbing on the sofa:

'Well, since *you* say so, it must be so.'[3]

The Duke made his friend promise to see his physician, Dr Charles Bankhead, and took the precaution of immediately going round to the doctor's house himself. Finding him out, he left a note saying that Castlereagh was 'very unwell'. He also found

* See *Wellington and His Friends*, pp. 23–5 and Arbuthnot, vol. II, p. 183. While in India Arthur Wellesley used a simple code in which a letter of the alphabet other than A was given the number 1, and so on. It is possible that in the present code he was using the same principle, where B = 1, J = 9 and BJ = 19, being the initials of Bishop Jocelyn.

time to inform the Arbuthnots of the situation and ask them to visit Castlereagh as soon as they returned to London from their country home, Woodford.

Night had fallen before the Duke was at last able to set out, reaching Dover at 4 A.M. on the morning of Saturday 10 August. His first experience of a Channel crossing in the new, much vaunted steampacket was in keeping with his sombre mood – 'there is a tremulous motion occasioned by the wheels which is very unpleasant'.[4] Still tremulous himself, he unburdened his fears for Castlereagh in a letter to Harriet Arbuthnot that evening:

> I cannot describe to you the Impression it has made upon me. To see a Man with such a sober mind . . . in a state bordering upon Insanity, is not calculated to raise one's opinion of the strength of the Human mind. Poor Human Nature! How little we are after all!

As for the poor Foreign Secretary, Wellington was sure he would not be able to go to Vienna that week, if at all.

A few days later a special courier was on his way from England to summon the Duke of Wellington home. Lord Castlereagh had committed suicide on the 12th.

*

Dr Bankhead had called on his patient as soon as he found the Duke's note, bled him and sent him down to Cray, proposing to visit him next day. Claiming thirty years' knowledge of Castlereagh's peculiarities, Bankhead predicted just a few days' illness followed by restored health.

On the Saturday the patient was no better and on the Sunday delirious. Though remaining at Cray, Bankhead put no restraints on him beyond allowing Lady Castlereagh to remove his razors and pistols. Throughout that day the doctor listened to the ravings of acute persecution mania, among his imagined enemies being the Duke.[5]

Early on Monday morning, 12 August, the climax came. In a paroxysm of rage, Castlereagh seized his wife and accused her also of being in the conspiracy against him. He then demanded to see Bankhead. Lady Castlereagh got out of bed and ordered her maid to warn the doctor. What happened next was told to Wellington in Bankhead's own words sent to him by courier.

Wakened at 7 A.M. by the maid, Bankhead was soon summoned

to the bedroom but found Lord Castlereagh had darted into his little dressing-room next door. (It measured 14 feet by 7 feet.) There the doctor saw him, standing with his back to the room and his chin tilted towards the ceiling.

'My dear lord, why do you stand so?' Still facing the window Castlereagh said: 'Bankhead, let me fall upon your arm; it is all over.'

The doctor caught him, noticing for the first time a small white-handled knife clenched in his right hand. The blood spurted from his throat, he slipped out of Bankhead's arms face downwards on the floor and died without even a sigh.[6]

*

Wellington was back in London on 16 August, haunted by his last interview with the dead man, though ready, as befitted the King's 'retained servant', to concentrate on the problems of Castlereagh's successor.

But first the funeral, which stirred up many contrary emotions in 'Left' and 'Right'. Henry Brougham almost regretted the loss of such an antagonist from the Commons' front bench: 'He was a *gentleman*.' Cobbett had no regrets. He inspired a hostile demonstration outside Westminster Abbey on 20 August as the cortège arrived. Fortunately Castlereagh's family took it to be a round of cheers for the Duke of Wellington, who was a pall-bearer.

Mrs Arbuthnot was devastated. She could not remember a single flaw in her incomparable friend. Unable to face the funeral she came three days afterwards to shed tears on his grave. Then she turned for support to the man who had hitherto been her second-best friend. There is no doubt that the death of Castlereagh resulted in a new relationship between the Duke and Harriet Arbuthnot. Her passion both for friendship and for political discussion, which before had been mainly ministered to by Castlereagh, now found its outlet in Wellington. 'He has promised to fill the place of the friend I have lost.'[7]

There was a corresponding change in the Duke's own feelings. He found himself needing 'the *sensible* woman' as much as she needed him. Up till August 1822 Mrs Arbuthnot had been only the first among equals in that brittle circle of female adorers whose pleasure was to invent rivalries, victories and defeats in the game of winning the great Duke's favour. Wellington had entered into the fun. Mrs Arbuthnot he had nicknamed '*La Tyranna*', the jealous guardian of his engagement-book.

Though it would be quite wrong to suggest that after August 1822 *La Tyranna* finally triumphed over her rivals and made him fall in love with her, she did receive one uniquely self-revealing letter in which the old *badinage* had a different sound and the reticence had vanished. On 13 September he wrote just before leaving England again:

> I hope you will think of me sometimes, and whenever you think of me wherever I may be, you may feel certain that my thoughts and wishes are centred on you, and my desire that every action of my life may please you. God bless you
> > Your most devoted and affectionate Slave.[8]

What did he really feel for her? 'The Duke's feelings,' write the editors of *The Journal of Mrs Arbuthnot*, 'may be described in Landor's words, "There is a middle state between love and friendship more delightful than either, but more difficult to remain in."' For the Duke, his performance on this tightrope was rendered less difficult by Harriet Arbuthnot's own qualities. He recognized that she was neither imaginative nor romantic. When the famous dancer Maria Mercandotti suddenly gave up her career to marry a wealthy *arriviste*, Harriet applauded and the Duke wrote: 'You are right *au fond* in preferring gold to Love! But then . . . you have no *Romance* in your composition! You look to realities; and imagine nothing!'[9]

A deeply conventional and faithful wife, Harriet had no taste for dalliance but a consuming interest in political drama. She was probably the only woman who refused to meet Lord Byron when the prince of romance himself asked for an introduction.

*

One side-effect of Castlereagh's death is interesting for the light it throws on Wellington's magnanimity. As a result of his negligence Dr Bankhead was almost universally pilloried. Creevey said he ought to be tried for manslaughter and Mrs Arbuthnot called him 'that beast'.[10] In a desperate attempt to save his family from ruin, the doctor put it about that Castlereagh had not suffered from overwork – a strain which his physician might be expected to treat – but from guilt over a criminal offence which he had committed in fact, not fancy. The Duke was at first horrified by this story, but having satisfied himself that it was not true, he was even more horrified by Bankhead's behaviour.* After a year, however, when the Duke was certain that few believed the false tale, he turned his attention to the doctor's own plight: he was in a terrible state, 'concealing himself in the fields about Putney'. While it would be impossible to salvage Bankhead directly, provision should be made for his son. But try as he would, Wellington for long could not persuade the Castlereagh circle to let him approach Lord Liverpool in the son's favour. His last attempt, addressed to Lord George Seymour, a relative of Castlereagh's on his mother's side, ended with a characteristic summing-up:

I certainly think that you are all wrong upon this subject – the reputation of our lamented friend does not depend upon what any hearsay [sic] but upon his own actions & conduct! . . . The time is come then when we should no longer be *thin skinned* about him; & we should do [for Bankhead's son] that which in my opinion he would in similar circumstances have done himself.[11]

Bankhead's son got employment as a diplomat and the doctor lived abroad until the age of ninety-one.

Wellington's final arguments as set out above emphasize not only his familiar contempt for gossip and for hypersensitive as opposed to sensible attitudes, but also his strong belief in the dead man's warm, generous nature. Not for the Duke, Croker's famous words about the 'splendid summit of bright and polished frost', which wickedly transformed Castlereagh forever from a man into an ice-cap. Cold and hard he might seem to the world, but beneath the crust were emotional fires. In some ways the Duke was like him.

Each was virile and exceptionally attractive to women. Neither had the classical graces to lift the good sense they often preached in Parliament to the pitch of eloquence. Both looked beyond their own country to Britain's responsibilities abroad, atoning, as it were, for coldness at home by genuine concern for international feelings. If Castlereagh wore a 'mask', as Shelley said, so did the Duke, though one was ice and the other iron. Neither of them

* The truth seems to have been that a man named Jennings and a gang of blackmailers had laid a trap for him when he entered the brothel. The prostitute he had thought was a female turned out to be a male. Before the shocked Foreign Secretary had time to recover his nerve, the gang burst in and began a persecution which ended only with his death.

professed to care a pin for popularity, Castlereagh preferring *unpopularity* – 'it was so much more convenient and gentlemanlike'. The idea of British expansion overseas at the expense of other countries was never favoured by Wellington, while in the final settlement of 1815 Castlereagh kept his colonial demands to a modest minimum for the sake of the European system – an imperial sacrifice which Napoleon considered mad.

It is tempting to trace some of the resemblances between the two political allies, especially their cool detachment, to a common source – their membership not only of the aristocracy but of the Irish Ascendancy. Taught from childhood to feel all the aloofness of an Ascendancy class, utterly apart from the native Irish who were their neighbours, it was only when their eyes were raised to distant horizons that the glance was friendlier.

*

Who would step into the dead man's shoes? Castlereagh had been leader of the House of Commons as well as Foreign Secretary. Speculation was rife, for indeed there was no easy choice. Would the Duke take the latter post himself?

'Are you going to be Minister for Foreign Affairs?' asked Mme de Lieven.

'No, I don't want to be; that would mean deviating from my position and my career. I should be compelled to adopt the opinions of my party and my individual opinion would no longer be free. . . .' On reflection there were two other points against.

'Besides, I have lived too long out of England not to have lost the habit of speaking in the House; I can't do it.' Of course he could learn to do it if the Government wanted him and he wanted to – 'but, just now, I don't.'

Secondly, the 'system' Castlereagh and he had established was so secure that it did not need his personal direction.

'Listen – I have such confidence in the system that, if Lord Grey were to become [Prime] Minister today, he would maintain it just as we do.'[12]

His appeal to Mme de Lieven to 'listen' must have been overheard by some sardonic fate, so soon was his system to be assailed, and through his own chosen agent. That agent was Canning.

George Canning, Irish by birth and now fifty-three years old, was considered a parvenu, or at any rate not a 'gentleman', though he had been educated at Eton and Oxford. His mother, widowed early, had become an actress in order to support her family before she found a second husband in a silk mercer with the ill-sounding name of Hunn. Young Canning, it seemed, had picked up a touch of the Hun himself, what with his destructive, satirical verses and violent personalities in debate. In 1822 he wished to destroy restrictions both on trade and on Catholics. Altogether Canning would be an uncomfortable force to find in a Tory Cabinet – brilliant, iconoclastic, consumed by 'a *love of undoing*' – or so it soon appeared to Wellington and the Arbuthnots in the course of many a ruffled confabulation. Flashy, sarcastic, crooked, cocksure, quarrelsome, high-handed, '*ungentlemanlike*', Canning was all this to them and more. As Charles Arbuthnot was finally to declare: 'They might as well try to amalgamate oil and vinegar as the Duke & Mr Canning.'

Incidentally, the subsequent introduction of Canning's anti-protectionist friend Huskisson into the Cabinet was to cause the disappearance of Wellington's brother William, Lord Maryborough, of which the Duke wrote trenchantly: 'It is certainly true that the removal of Lord Maryborough is considered a blow at me by the wise Publick. But for that I don't care one pin.' Now the Duke cared not one pin that the textures of his mind and Canning's were entirely incompatible. For the sake of the country they must all learn to work with Canning.[13]

Consultations with Wellington and other ministers soon convinced Lord Liverpool that the Government desperately needed revitalizing. Though Canning lacked Castlereagh's urbanity in the House, his scintillating oratory and his alone could stand up to that of Brougham on the other side. He was not what would now be called left wing. He loathed reform at home and all revolutionary movements. But he could stir popular enthusiasm. That in 1822 was necessary.

The new Duke of Buckingham now increased the pressure on Canning's behalf by letting Wellington know on 20 August that unless Canning was made Foreign Secretary he and all his tribe would withdraw their support. Wellington at once told Liverpool, thus giving him the final push towards Canning. There remained only the King. Who should convert HM to Canning but Wellington?

It was indeed Wellington who finally won over George IV.

Writing on 6 September to his Prime Minister, the King stated firmly that Wellington should be the umpire:

As I have reason to hope that the Duke of Wellington may be well enough to come to me tomorrow, I cannot well see you until I have seen him. Under these circumstances I will write to you [with my decision] in the course of the day?[14]

Wellington came, spoke for two and a half hours, and just conquered. As a last resort, the King protested that he had pledged his honour (because of Queen Caroline) not to take Canning.

'You hear, Arthur, on my honour as a gentleman.' By his duty as a king, retorted Arthur, he was bound to take the best man available.

'Very well, gentlemen,' said the King, when he finally met his ministers, 'since you are determined to have him, take him in God's name, but remember I tell you he will throw you all overboard.'[15] Canning found the King's written offer so uncivil that he thought of refusing. It was like being given an entry card to Almacks, he said, and finding written on the back, *Admit the rogue.*[16]

For the third time in these critical days after Castlereagh's death the Duke stepped in. 'We have had the greatest difficulty in keeping Canning straight,' he wrote on 13 September. 'He has been with me all the morning; and is now gone down [to Windsor], and I hope the business will be settled.'[17]

Thanks to the Duke, it was. Mme de Lieven herself heaved a sigh of relief. 'So that is over . . . ,' she wrote to Metternich. 'For the moment, the Duke will be the heart of the administration, the real Prime Minister, I hope he will maintain this position.'[18]

As far as the Duke was personally concerned, he liked Canning no more than the King did. But the Duke was a man on his own; making up his own mind, occasion by occasion, about what was for the public good at any given time. And at this time the public interest demanded a Tory Government tinctured with Canning's brand of liberalism rather than the alternative, a Whig Government tainted by the Radicals. Liverpool, not the King, must stand firm, and it well became the country's 'retained servant' to tell the King so.

*

The Duke had made a crucial intervention in British politics at their most sensitive point. It was to set a pattern for the future. Here and now, however, another duty of the greatest intricacy confronted him. He was to take Castlereagh's place at Vienna and Verona, where in contrast to the Congress of Aix-la-Chapelle he would find the autocrats grown more autocratic, the oppositional movements more active and Metternich the man in control.

Moreover, instead of pulling steadily in double harness with Castlereagh as in 1815 and 1818, he would be continuing the policy of a ghost, and a ghost who had quitted a world grown hostile and vehement. At least Castlereagh had been Foreign Secretary, with all the punch of that great office behind him. Behind Wellington was Canning, a new Foreign Secretary, seen as the exponent of a new word which Peel memorably designated 'odious but intelligible' – the word 'liberal'.*

The conference instructions drawn up by Castlereagh for himself were taken over unchanged by the Duke. They sounded forthright enough: preservation of the European 'system' by maintaining strict British neutrality in all internal disputes abroad. But against the background of upheavals in Spain, Portugal and Greece it seemed exceedingly doubtful whether the late maestro himself, for all his expertise in conducting the Concert of Europe, could have succeeded in preserving harmony and peace.

The explosion in Spain was the most dramatic. It had been sparked off by mutinies in regiments earmarked to fight against Spain's rebellious colonies in South America, but it swiftly became a successful onslaught against the despotism of Ferdinand VII. When the King was forced to accept the liberal constitution of 1812, Spanish ultra-Royalists appealed to the Holy Alliance for help.

The French assembled an army along the Pyrenees to prevent the constitutional infection (as well as yellow fever) from spreading into France. Should that army invade Spain? Since the French Ultras were pressing for invasion and wanted to stage their intervention as a mandate from their Holy Allies, the question to be thrashed out at Vienna and Verona, with Wellington's participation, was whether or not to grant that mandate. The scales, however, were already tipped against peace. The Congress of Verona

* The word 'liberal' had come into usage from the Spanish *liberales*, the opponents of Ferdinand VII.

had been convened for the purpose of letting the French Ultras
deal with the Spanish people as Metternich had already dealt with
the Neapolitans – by forcible suppression. Clearly the Duke
would need to be all eyes and ears when he arrived on the Continent, particularly if he was to fulfil the high hopes of his
admirers. Creevey relied on him 'as the only man who, on this
occasion, could keep those Royal Imbeciles and Villains of
Europe in any order'.[19]

Unfortunately his hearing had been damaged on 5 August
when, as Master-General of the Ordnance, he was present at a
review of howitzers and accidentally got too near an explosion.
Nearly a month later, resolved to be absolutely fit for the international fray, he called in a distinguished aurist, John Stevenson,
to cure his sharp ear-ache and dispel the singing in his left ear.

*

On the morning of 4 September 1822 Dr Hume was sent for
urgently to Apsley House. There he found a spectral figure with
bloodshot eyes and a raging fever huddled in a chair. Stevenson
had treated the Duke's left ear with a strong caustic solution. For
a few hours the patient suddenly heard every sound with torturing
intensity. Then a violent inflammation set in which but for Hume
might have reached the brain. For two days he was unable to eat,
sleep or even write to Mrs Arbuthnot. By the 6th he could scribble
her a pathetic note, totally unlike his normally robust assertions
that health was a function of will-power.

Indeed I never was so unwell, as I do not remember before in my life
having passed a day in bed. All my efforts to bully & bluster failed for
the first time; & strange to say! I was near fainting in the effort to dress
myself, & was obliged to give it up. We are sad Creatures after all![20]

In fact he was to be stone deaf in the left ear for life and subject
during the next few years to severe attacks of illness. His head, on
arrival in Vienna, felt either too heavy or too light, '& sometimes
I feel as if I was drunk & can't walk. I am very tired of being sick,
never having been so before. Even the strength of my Iron constitution tells now against me.'[21]

He proved a bad patient, liable to skirmishes with Dr Hume,
who combined a noisy manner with unremitting anxiety about
the Duke's health and habits. An attempt to keep him at home in
the evenings provoked several outbursts in Spring 1823:

... as if I can sit at home with my hands before me, doing nothing or asleep in my chair!!! ... All doctors are more or less *Quacks*! ... and what they talk is neither more nor less than *nonsense & stuff* ...[22]

A little later Hume was confessing to Kitty that his frankness had offended the Duke and he had not seen him for a month – 'but I cannot help it'.

Wellington's deafness was a family weakness, and the accident of 1822 probably only hastened it. In following Wellington through the problems of the Congress and of Canning, it must not be forgotten that he often felt himself, in his own phrase, 'but a poor Creature'.[23]

*

He stood the journey to Paris well. But once there, his troubles began.

Old Louis XVIII looked wretched: 'His face is like a *scab*; all broke out and blotched.' He had to break it to the Duke that the French 'army of observation' might well be turned into an aggressive expeditionary force. This French situation effectually destroyed the delicate web of Castlereagh's Congress policy. The Duke had hoped to deflect the Congress from the hot Spanish issue on to Greece and Spanish America. All this was now torn to shreds. As he was soon to inform Canning from Verona: 'There is no feeling here about anything except Spain.'[24]

From Paris Wellington had to ask Canning for fresh instructions. When they arrived he found himself stripped of all freedom of manoeuvre. His duty was to declare unequivocally for non-intervention in Spain. This was sending him naked into the conference chamber. He felt his hands were tied. But he was a soldier and would obey orders.

Vienna was a frost. The Tsar left for Verona the day after Wellington arrived. Through some bungle the courier sent to divert the British delegation straight to Verona had missed them on the road. It was 'past bearing' to spend several days with the 3rd Marquess of Londonderry, the former Charles Stewart and up till now ambassador in Vienna. His wife lolled in a chaise longue, not deigning to speak to the Duke because she believed herself to be loved by the Tsar; while his lordship was 'very much out of temper' at Canning's appointment and in fact resigned his post. Wellington bore his cross dutifully and at least managed to keep this petulant but powerful landowner inside the Tory fold.

He was off again as soon as possible, provided with letters of credit by Salomon de Rothschild, and a Quaker escort by sheer chance.[25] This was William Allen, the philanthropist and friend of the Tsar, determined to lecture the Congress on the horrors of the slave-trade. As the Duke was about to start, Allen suddenly walked in.

'Well, Mr Allen, what can I do for you?'

'I must go to Verona.'

'But you can't. Haven't you read that only persons attached to embassies will be admitted?'

'Friend, I must go to Verona, and thou must take me.' A pause.

'Very well, if I must I must; but the only way is to make you one of my couriers.'[26]

So Quaker Allen rode a stage in front of the Duke all the way from Vienna to Verona; through the Styrian mountains which Wellington thought the loveliest country in Europe, and Venice where he would have liked more time to see 'the curiosities of this wonderful city'. But he had caught cold in the Alps and could not sleep. A paragraph from the *Courier*, 19 October, would not have soothed him:

Letters from Vienna announce that persons who had not seen the Duke of Wellington for some years, have perceived a great alteration in his features, and a great change in his person.

His arrival at the Congress created a stir. Every lady longed to be seen promenading on the hero's arm. Byron wrote in his *Age of Bronze*:

> *Proud Wellington, with eagle beak so curled,*
> *That nose, the hook where he suspends the world.*[27]

It was rumoured that if he had been willing to expel the Turks at the head of a Greek army he would have been offered the Greek crown. An official of the French foreign ministry paid tribute to his impact:

The ministers who were to treat with him saw him arrive with pleasure. The grandeur of his position gave his character a loftiness which lent itself unwillingly to the sustained dissimulation of long political intrigues.

He had also drawn from his previous experience a broad way of looking at things which raised him to some extent above national rivalries.[28]

Into the midst of all this fraternal feeling Nosey, with soldierly precision, dropped his bomb, for it is agreed that his bleak refusal to approve the proposed invasion of Spain created as much consternation in the Congress as if he had hurled a bombshell at the Holy Allied feet. In vain he was scolded by diplomats and cajoled by their mistresses. A set-to between him and Metternich ended with his standing in front of the mantelpiece and ostentatiously jamming on his hat. It was his ineluctable duty to oppose the war which everyone but Britain wanted.

In this unenviable task the frustrations ranged from the trivial to the fundamental. Mrs Arbuthnot was given a glimpse of them on 5 November. Endless writing of despatches in a cold house, 'which never receives a ray of the beautiful sun; and yet I have so much to do that I am obliged to pass the entire day in it' – and of dealing with the Tsar-besotted Londonderrys. 'It is quite an affair between her and the Emperor.'

But he must not despair –

I do not lose all hope; and I think there is still a chance of getting to a satisfactory result; and of preserving the Peace of the World – . . . Don't you think that I am strongly tempted to *laisser aller les choses* instead of endeavouring to maintain the Peace?

A week later negotiations seemed no nearer an end, 'and I am more tired of them than I ever was . . . It has been a sad Autumn. Since August nothing has gone right.'[29] His offers to mediate between France and Spain were rejected.

There was perhaps some consolation in the British press reports from Verona.

It is certainly the manly firmness of the Duke of Wellington in opposing propositions which he considers to be at variance with the interests of his country, which is thought one of the greatest obstacles to an early conclusion. The Noble Duke is resolved to maintain his ground to the last. . . .

This was the *Courier*, writing on the same day, 5 November, as his first depressed letter to Mrs Arbuthnot. *The Times* followed up on the 12th with the remark that war was 'only stopped or suspended by the influence of the Duke of Wellington'.

In the evenings at any rate he could *laisser aller les choses* – let things rip – with a clear conscience. True, he was hardly fit to 'parade his glory like a woman-trap across the quadrilles', as

Chateaubriand had said of him in London. But he could play cards with the ex-Empress of the French, Marie-Louise, telling her genially that he would pay his debts in *napoléons*. On the 18th he gave a musical party with his niece Priscilla Burghersh as hostess and Marie-Louise as guest of honour. As he led in the ex-Empress many people asked themselves how she felt, leaning on the very arm which had laid her late husband low.

He was not back in London until December. There was still 'something very extraordinary' about his head despite cuppings and blisters; but the Emperor of Austria had given him riding-horses at Verona if not the imperial confidence, and his general health seemed improved. Even in politics he detected 'a breeze everywhere for Peace' among moderates, though Ultras and Jacobins in all countries wanted war.

In the last effort to avert the invasion of Spain he sent out Fitzroy Somerset to urge upon the Spanish moderates a less extreme constitution than that of 1812. Alas, Fitzroy wrote back that the grandees were not the patriots they had been in 1808 and would rather welcome a French invasion; General Alava, that pillar of the moderates, had grown very grey and melancholy.

Then should Wellington adopt Canning's plan and himself lead a forlorn hope, a mission to Madrid? All his friends expostulated.

The date being now the end of February 1823, it was too late to play any card great or small. On 6 April a French army under Louis xvIII's nephew, the Duke of Angoulême, crossed the Pyrenees and by the autumn had restored Ferdinand vII to absolute power.

The Quintuple Alliance was as dead as Castlereagh – given the *coup de grâce* by the very Bourbons in whose aid it had been invented.

As a result the Duke found himself isolated in a grim no-man's-land between two fires. On the right, the Continental Ultras derided '*la politique Britannique*' at Verona, calling non-interventionist Britain 'an abettor of anarchy', sneering at the Duke's 'narrow patriotism'. On the left, a British mob howled outside the French embassy in London where Wellington was attending a ball, and demanded to know why the Peninsular hero had not saved Spain again.

Wellington could only resort in Parliament to his party's perennial defence in such circumstances: how could the Opposition claim to stand both for keeping the peace and putting down aggression? On this occasion, 24 April 1823, a few sentences from his speech give the dry, pungent flavour of his style at its best:

And here I must call upon the noble Lords opposite, and ask them to state to me whether, at the commencement of these negotiations [at Verona], they would have adopted measures of war or of neutrality for the basis of their future proceedings? As yet (your Lordships will have remarked) they have not declared whether they mean peace or war. Their argument would lead to the alternative of war, but they still seem to lean to pacific measures. I call upon them, therefore, to adopt the one line or the other.

But the Opposition had its perennially convenient way out of this dilemma: by using firm language they would have stopped aggression without provoking war.

In the first few months of 1823 it seemed that Verona had damaged Wellington in many eyes, including, sometimes, his own. The King blamed his intransigence:

He had the great, great disadvantage of being incapable of flexibility or of making a diplomatic approach. He sets about a question like a battery of cannon.

Why had the Alliance suffered such damage at Verona? the Duke asked himself. Was it Castlereagh's death or his own behaviour? Yet he thought he had done his duty.

Wellington was right. He had done his duty, and what seemed a lack of finesse to the King and the Ultras was in fact loyalty to Canning. That loyalty, however, was by no means reciprocated. In the Commons' debates on the invasion of Spain Canning used Wellington as his scapegoat and the Opposition, dazzled by the new Foreign Secretary, were only too delighted to accept this solution.

The truth was that the agonizing paradox of the Duke's position only gradually dawned on his circle. 'He was put with his back to the wall,' said the King in March, now complaining of Wellington's treatment at Verona.[30] Back to the wall, yes; but not a solid wall or a wall he could lean against; rather, a crumbling wall, undermined by Canning's subterranean works.

Wellington did not know that Canning's private instinct had been against sending any British delegate whatever to Verona, and that even Liverpool called him too 'Continental'. He did not yet know of Canning's jubilant comment on the European break-down: 'So things are getting back to a wholesome state again. Every nation for itself, and God for us all.' Nor of Canning's new policy, defined in terms of strictest patriotism: 'For *Europe* I shall be desirous *now and then* to read *England*'; 'for "Alliance" read "England", and you have the clue of my policy.'[31]

Patriotism was no alien concept to the Duke either. But in Canning he was confronting a kind of virulent, insular, ambitious and highly popular patriotism which has its practitioners in every age. He himself remained both by training and conviction a cool, sophisticated European.

Would the Duke, leading spokesman for the old European system based on co-operation between legitimate monarchs, find it possible to march into such a brash new world? Could he 'amalgamate' with vinegar?

*

At least it made no difference to old friendships. The liberal patriot, General Alava, finally driven out of Spain by the triumphant reactionaries, found a refuge at Stratfield Saye. He was given a house on the estate and introduced personally to Coutts's bank.

'This is my friend,' said the Duke; 'and as long as I have any money at your house, let him have it to any amount that he thinks proper to draw for.'[32]

Alava was regarded as quite unique, having fought (on opposite sides) both at Trafalgar and at Waterloo. Highly emotional, he worshipped the Duke and in spite of his black teeth and squat form offered his heart to Mrs Panther, a much bejewelled orna-ment on the fringe of the Duke's intimate set. Even for Alava's sake, however, the Duke would not let Lady Shelley invite Mrs Panther to Maresfield: 'Although a very pleasant and pretty person to have in society, she is not exactly of our old association, that is, of yours, the Tyrant's, and mine; and we must not have an interloper. . . .'[33]

Interlopers were to be a feature of the new era.

8

Redressing the Balance

'Amalgamation' of Wellington and Canning was not yet in question. Up to the early summer of 1823 the oil appeared to float effortlessly on top once more, in both court and cabinet. Canning knew as little about the King as the man in the moon, or so Mme de Lieven deduced from his intensive questioning, whereas court circles were aware that His Majesty's true feeling for the Duke was 'more like Love than anything else!!'.[1] Some members of the Cabinet confidently relied on the Duke's authority and good temper to keep Canning in order and give the Alliance the kiss of life.

By mid-summer, however, Canning had begun to exert noticeable influence over Lord Liverpool. The Court was alarmed. 'The King is very jealous of Mr Canning,' reported Wellington to Mrs Arbuthnot on 19 August.[2] In fact George IV was secretly corresponding with the Continental courts, besides intriguing with his Keeper of the Privy Purse, Sir William Knighton (known as 'the Accoucheur' from his previous profession), to get Lord Liverpool supplanted by the Duke. Canning suppressed the King's Continental correspondence by threatening to expose it in Parliament, while Wellington himself dealt firmly with the plot to put him in Liverpool's place and banish Canning.

By mid-October he had at last convinced the Accoucheur that he would 'not be the means of tripping up Lord Liverpool, as in fact I should never afterwards be of any use to myself or to anybody else'. Canning, moreover, was beginning to find his own way to the King's heart – through patronage. As early as January 1823 he had given a government job to the favourite's son, Lord Francis Conyngham (now known as 'Canningham'), as a result of which the King had been observed walking about with his arm round the Foreign Secretary's neck.[3]

At the same time Wellington believed by the end of the year that his own policy duel with the Foreign Secretary was going fairly well. Though the feeling in Downing Street was hostile to the Allies, he had wrung 'a sort of engagement' from No. 10 not to do any mischief while ministers were away over Christmas – a holiday which the Duke intended to devote to 'bullying' his physical affliction by intensive exercise.[4]

*

Dr Hume agreed he ought to ride and shoot for his health, but not ride and shoot in the glamorous company he chose – with Lord Westmorland, for instance, at Apethorpe. The Duke complained, 'He believes that because a Man is in Society he must be what be calls *"excited"*, that is to say not in his care! This is the whole case.'[5]

Mrs Arbuthnot knew full well it was not the whole case. A few days before this outburst on 27 December 1823 Peel had described how the Duke was overcome by dizziness while out shooting at Lord Hertford's. The Duke himself admitted that only patience and abstinence – but not doctors – would subdue the evil effects of his accident.

Possibly his particular annoyance with Hume was caused by a suspicion that his doctor was in league with his wife to get him out of society and into Stratfield Saye. It would not have been beyond him to take Hume's advice, cancel Apethorpe and go home – as in fact he did – yet remain irritated by the man whose advice he had taken. What with foreign affairs and physicians, the Duke's 'excessively good temper', on which Canning's opponents had counted to overpower him, was being sorely tried.

*

Though the long-awaited Cabinet meeting to decide the Kings' Speech for 1824 was 'very stormy', the Duke felt that his own interventions had succeeded. There would be no insulting attack on France for her aggression; no proposal for recognition of the revolted Spanish colonies. 'Nobody wished it to advance one step,' wrote the Duke to his usual confidante, 'excepting Lord Liverpool, Mr Canning & I believe Robinson.*[6] It certainly will

* Hon. Frederick Robinson (1782–1859), created Viscount Goderich, 1827; Prime Minister, 1827–8; created Earl of Ripon, 1833. One of the Canningites in Lord Liverpool's Cabinet.

not be in the Speech; for that I will answer.' He was not dis-appointed. The Colonial question featured in regard to trade alone.

Two minor setbacks in health were endured that spring, 1824. He took the waters at Cheltenham to break a succession of sleep-less nights, and though the cure failed he recovered from a sub-sequent attack of mild cholera which at least had the merit of making him sleep for thirty-six hours. He was also pleased when a new doctor admitted that his ill-health was due purely to the ear accident and not to '*mouldering* of the constitution' after hard service abroad, as had been suggested. One well-wisher recom-mended a lancet touched with caustic in the back of his neck; another offered 'Galvanism'; yet others suggested that he had cancer of the ear (cure: 'a thorough change in the blood' as practised by a Philadelphian family) or the *tic douloureux* (cure: phosphoric acid in cups of tea, as prescribed at Darmstadt). It must have been a relief when Mrs Patterson's grandfather simply sent him four barrels of American apples.[7]

The Court's excessive devotion to him might have proved more dangerous than the cholera. Even his supporters in the Cabinet were beginning to edge away from the '*King's Favorite*' – but the Duke himself declared once more that he refused to be nominated as Liverpool's successor. Let the King so much as mention it and 'he would immediately quit the Cabinet & go away, for that he never had tried to step into another man's shoes . . . '.[8]

Suddenly Canning's improved position with the King col-lapsed. Was not this the moment to destroy Lord Liverpool's evil genius?

On 29 April 1824 Canning had attended a City Corporation dinner at the invitation of the late Queen's partisans. The out-raged King drafted a letter to Canning which Wellington realized must drive the Foreign Secretary from office. Once more the Duke intervened to save him.

'Ah, I know what you have come to say,' exclaimed the King when his mentor presented himself at Windsor. 'You think that, if I want to get rid of Mr Canning, this is not a proper oppor-tunity, that at all events I ought not to write such a letter as will force him ro resign.'

'Your Majesty knows exactly what I am come about.' So delighted was the King at having read his friend Arthur's mind that he allowed him to redraft the rude letter.[9]

Meanwhile there was again talk of Liverpool's retirement. Wellington reported to Mme de Lieven that he had been approached by the Duke of York's faction with a view to becoming Prime Minister but had refused yet again to lay himself open to the charge of 'coveting' Liverpool's 'cast-off office'. What if the King appointed Canning? asked the Russian ambassadress. Time enough then, retorted the Duke, for 'our party' to refuse to serve. But it could not happen, pursued the Duke hotly. 'Our party is too strong.' It could not be defeated by Canning.

'No, no, no! Impossible! Out of the question! He would be thrown out twenty times before one of us budged.'[10]

It may well be asked why Wellington, the lifelong opponent of factious opposition to authority, was found talking in June 1824 about 'our party' within the Government. The answer is that he believed, with some justification, that Canning was in touch with the Whigs. One cabal deserved another.

On 23 July Canning bounced back, to score a resounding victory on South American trade against Wellington's tenacious arguments in a divided Cabinet. The Duke's disgust at his defeat was unbounded. Again and again he cursed himself for ever having recommended Canning as Foreign Secretary; 'he would cut his hand off,' he assured Mrs Arbuthnot, rather than do it, if he had another chance.[11]

Though so signally defeated in July, Wellington was fighting a holding action in September and October to prevent Canning from descending on Paris and further alienating the Powers. Louis XVIII had at last died (16 September 1824) and been succeeded by his brother Artois, now King Charles X. Canning's pretext for the visit was to pay his respects to the new monarch, a duty which would properly fall to the British ambassador. His true motive was to show that he would not tolerate 'traps & mines' being laid for him at home by foreigners,[12] a reference to the so-called 'Cottage Clique' of foreign ambassadors – the Russian Lievens, Austrian Esterhazys and French ambassador Prince Jules de Polignac, who were voluble spokesmen for the Alliance at the King's *cottage orné* in Windsor Park.

In an atmosphere of distrust and intrigue both Wellington and Canning had cause for annoyance at the other's behaviour. They gave vent to it in a corrosive correspondence which Wellington finally called off, admitting to his friends that if he and Canning fell into a 'war of Words & Phrases' Canning would have the best of it. Verbally Canning had already won – but he did not go to Paris.

Less than two months later the Duke had to concede Canning's greatest triumph so far: Cabinet agreement to full and formal recognition of the South American republics. At the meeting on 15 December all other contestants had fallen away, leaving the Duke and Canning to fight it out in single combat. Canning stumbled away exhausted but victorious. 'I am really quite knocked up with it,' he wrote to Granville. 'The fight has been hard, but it is won. The deed is done. The nail is driven. Spanish America is free; and if we do not mismanage our affairs she is English. . . .'13

Wellington, who had offered to resign on 6 December, took his defeat of the 15th as an incentive to new efforts. Did Canning want to get rid of him? Very well, he would stay on, 'as long as it was possible for him to do so with regard to his honour'. On the day before the next crucial Cabinet of 28 January 1825 when the Spanish colonies' independence would be included in the King's Speech, the Duke found himself giving Carlton House desperate advice. Might not His Majesty find it easier to control a government formed by the Opposition, rather than this Tory party, 'tricked' and duped as it was by Canning?14

His Majesty thought he had a better method of re-establishing control. Banking on the Cabinet's divisions, he demanded to know from each of its members individually whether the principles of the Quadruple and Quintuple Alliances, 1814–18, 'are, or are not, to be abandoned?'15

The royal tactic failed. (Queen Victoria was similarly to fail when she tried to find out the individual opinions of Gladstone's Cabinet.) Canning told a meeting: 'It was all an intrigue of the foreigners to get him out.'16 A chastened Duke proposed that the Cabinet should request His Majesty to accept a collective reply to his gracious letter, viz. that the decision on Spanish America was in no way inconsistent with the principles of 1814–18, and in any case was 'now irrevocable'.17

A fortnight later came an unmerited humiliation for Wellington at the hands of a monarch who had suddenly taken fright. George

IV conveyed a hint through the Accoucheur that 'intrigue' should cease and the Duke and Canning 'amalgamate'.

Amalgamate? This to the man who rightly regarded himself as having time and time again saved Canning from the King's wrath? For once the Duke, to Mrs Arbuthnot's astonishment, swore like a trooper.[18]

*

For a month the Cottage Clique was paralysed. King, favourite, man-midwife, 'the whole gang were beginning to tremble before Canning,' wrote Mme de Lieven despondently. With no spirit left at Court to overthrow him, 'we must put up with this plague until he takes it into his head to break his own neck. . . .'[19]

Towards the end of March, however, the energetic Dorothea de Lieven revived a little and decided to make one more attempt at breaking Canning's neck for him. This was later known as the 'Cottage Plot'.

Mme de Lieven knew that Metternich was in Paris. Why should he not, with the connivance of herself and the Duke, make a secret trip across the Channel, land at Brighton, work out a fresh programme for the Alliance with the King and return to his embarkation point without so much as a nod towards the Foreign Secretary? (That the Duke actually *proposed* this bold breach of protocol to Mme de Lieven cannot be believed, though this was her story to Metternich. The plot would have sounded less implausible put that way round.) But Canning, who had not bought the favourite's son, Lord Francis Conyngham, for nothing, got wind of the intrigue, made it clear he would expose it and thus broke its back.

The New World had won – partly through Canning's threatening to mobilize public opinion both in and out of Parliament, partly through Wellington's preference for retreat rather than a fight in the last ditch.

'And so behold!' wrote Canning in November 1825, when the King agreed to receive the Colombian minister; 'the New World established, and, if we do not throw it away, ours.'

This was the refrain of Canning's nationalistic anthem: Spanish America *English*. The New World *ours*. It grated on Wellington's ears, and indeed he often had cause to remind Canning that other powers besides Britain had a right to legitimate influence in Europe and elsewhere.

A year later, on 12 December 1826, Canning was announcing the Government's decision to send an expeditionary force to the Peninsula because of the deplorable probability that reactionary Spain would invade constitutional Portugal. Then why had he not prevented the earlier take-over of Spain by the French Ultras? demanded a Radical heckler.

At any rate, thundered the Foreign Secretary in reply, it was not a take-over of Spain with the South American colonies attached, the fabled 'Indies' of our island history.

I resolved that if France had Spain it should not be Spain with the Indies. I called the New World into existence to redress the balance of the old.

The House was electrified. Golden phrases, golden as the Indies themselves if not altogether meaningful or modest, seemed to pour from the orator. To others he was too clever by half. A pedestrian style sounded more trustworthy.

Speaking in the Upper House on the same day and on the same subject the Duke was brief. He offered no explanation for the apparent contradiction between the Government's intervention in Portugal and their refusal to intervene in Spain; it was 'altogether unnecessary'. Bathurst had already described the Portuguese situation – how Dom Pedro had abdicated on the death of his father John James VI and bestowed the succession on his little daughter Maria, her hand upon his brother Dom Miguel and a constitution upon the country. The Duke saw no reason to add to or comment on this account. It was enough to picture invasion troops drawn up along the rivers Guadiana and Douro and to remember Britain's treaty obligations to protect Portugal, 'our ancient and near ally'. He only hoped His Majesty the King of Spain would draw back. (His Majesty eventually did so.) Wellington's speech may have taken ten minutes. 'The Duke spoke very well,' wrote Mrs Arbuthnot, '& quite well enough to be Prime Minister.'[20]

*

After his tremendous bouts with Canning a punch-up with the Dean of an Oxford college, Christ Church, should have been child's play. But the Duke was worsted. This was in fact one of those rare occasions when strong feelings, instead of being mastered, led him into indiscretion and unfairness.

On 21 March 1825 the Duke heard that his younger son, after a convivial supper-party in Douro's rooms, had responded to a light-hearted challenge and joined in breaking out of the college gates. (Some weeks before he had helped to paint all the dons' doors red, the Dean's among them.) The Dean had punished him with the stiff sentence of a year's rustication.

According to Alava the Duke 'cried like a child'.[21] Then he counter-attacked. A missile rather than a missive was fired back at the Dean, arguing that the punishment was 'enormous' compared with the crime, and the crime due to the state of indiscipline permitted in the college. There followed exceedingly acrimonious exchanges, which finally put an end both to the correspondence and to the two Wellesley boys' education at Oxford. Within a fortnight Wellington and his family had shaken off the dust of Oxford. Douro was accepted by Trinity College, Cambridge, for the autumn, Charles to follow in spring 1826, after a penitential sojourn with Wagner at Brighton.

The college was to show its displeasure again in 1834 when the Duke's name was put forward as Chancellor of Oxford University. A letter reached Lord Kenyon's son, a graduate of Christ Church, informing him 'of the determination of the Chapter & Common Room to take no part as a body in the Election of Chancellor'.[22] By then, however, the silence of this one voice was hardly noticeable in the University's wild tumult of applause.

*

The sorrow caused to the Duke through the disgrace of his younger son was followed six months later by a traumatic episode involving his elder brother. Again it seemed that his passions might get the better of him, as in the case of Oxford, but this time his good judgement quickly reasserted control. It was probably on 11 October 1825 or a day or two later that the blow fell. A letter from Mrs Patterson announced that she was going over to Ireland to marry, of all people, Richard.

In order to understand the violence of the Duke's reaction to this news it is necessary to remember his peculiar relations both with Richard Wellesley and Marianne Patterson. Lord Wellesley had first forfeited his brother's esteem during the Peninsular War by allowing his womanizing and indolence to injure a potentially brilliant political career. The rift widened during the Hundred Days when Wellesley supported Whig criticisms of the campaign against Napoleon. After Waterloo, Wellesley was jealous of and opposed to his brother in politics, but his debts and temperament continued to reduce his own effectiveness. His first wife, a French actress, after long being separated from him, had died in 1816. Marianne Patterson, on the other hand, had been the Duke's romantic ideal during the years after Waterloo and until she returned to America where her husband Robert Patterson died (the 'Mr P' to whom the Duke sent his love in 1820). So when Arthur heard that Mrs Patterson was to marry the Marquess Wellesley he lost his head and dashed off a furious letter in the hope that he might save her at the eleventh hour from a fate worse than widowhood.

What were the facts about this Marquess, this Lord-Lieutenant, this Knight of the Garter whom Marianne was to marry? The ever-present Mrs Arbuthnot listened aghast to the Duke's summary of his 'very indiscreet' letter:

. . . Ld Wellesley was a man totally ruined; when he quitted Ireland, which he must soon do, he wd not have a house to take her to, or money to keep a carriage; that he had not a shilling in the world, &, moreover, was of a most jealous disposition, a violent temper & that he had entirely worn out his constitution by the profligate habits of his life.[23]

Mrs Arbuthnot tried in vain to console her distracted friend ('I have never seen the Duke more annoyed') with the suggestion that the rich and beautiful Marianne was no better in her own way than Lord Wellesley: 'I told him . . . that it was pretty well for the widow of an American shopkeeper to marry a Marquis. . . .'

No less stunned by the news was the sister of the late 'American shopkeeper', Betsy Patterson-Bonaparte.

'I married the brother of Napoleon the conqueror of Europe,' she said bitterly; 'Mary has married the brother of Napoleon's conqueror.' One of the most curious links in history had indeed been forged.

Wellington was soon writing to Mrs Patterson, 'that a wise man would hold his tongue', and had recovered enough to send the Lord-Lieutenant good wishes on his marriage.[24] Lord Wellesley's ménage, past and future, was one aspect of an Irish scene which daily engaged more and more of the Duke's attention.

Though the Duke rarely declared emotional feelings for any subject or person explicitly, apart from the constitution and monarch, he was deeply and emotionally committed to Ireland. The strength of this feeling was shown by the amount of time he gave throughout his life to research and writing on possible solutions for her problems.

*

The postwar agricultural distress which afflicted England was a thousand times worse in the island next door. Wellington, with his economic flair, saw material poverty at the heart of Ireland's misery; the country lacked a money economy. 'The truth is,' he told Lord Clancarty, an ex-diplomat, 'there is no want of provisions but great want of money to buy them.' He also emphasized the paradox of absentee landlords, especially Opposition supporters, who preferred raising money for the Irish poor at charity balls in England to living on their estates.

> If a few more of the landed proprietors had done what you have done this spring [1822], and gone over to look at their properties instead of *brawling* and *bawling* in London, the distress would have been relieved. . . .
> We want in Ireland the influence of manners as well as laws.[25]

In speaking of 'the influence of manners' the Duke was touching on a more fundamental cause of friction: the Irish had never been assimilated by their conquerors in religion, language or 'manners'. (Throughout the nineteenth century supercilious visitors noted that whereas people at home expressed their joy by a decent hurrah, the wild Irish did it by a howl.) Not that the Duke held the extreme view that the Irish were innately savage and therefore ineducable. He had been born and had spent many years in Ireland, had seen the fighting spirit of disciplined Irish troops in the Peninsula and had acquired in 1819 an Irish Catholic 'liaison officer' to keep him in touch. This was Dr Patrick Curtis, a trusted ally in the Peninsula and now titular Primate of Ireland.

In February 1821 the Duke had dealt a shrewd blow at the heart of Protestant extremism. He refused to join the Orange Order.

... I confess that I do object to belong to a Society professing attachment to the Throne and Constitution of these realms, [from] which ... a large proportion of His Majesty's subjects must be excluded, many of them as loyal men as exist, and as much attachment to the Constitution.

This objection is natural from one who was born in the country in which a large proportion of the people are Roman Catholic, and ... who has never found that, abstracted from other circumstances, the religious persuasion of individuals ... affected their feelings of loyalty. ... .[26]

Nevertheless Wellington had not yet made up his mind to become, in Curtis's words, one of the Catholics' 'patrons'; and when, a few months after his rejection of Orangism, the parliamentary tide turned in favour of the Catholics, the Duke was still found sitting on the breakwater. He joined with Lord Liverpool and the diehards in defeating Catholic emancipation by thirty-nine votes. 'To the thirty-nine who saved the Thirty-nine Articles!' became a fashionable toast.

*

Lord Wellesley's hope, as the new Lord-Lieutenant in 1821, had been to allay violence in Ireland by redressing the balance between Catholics and Protestants.* When the 'Fourth of November' (William of Orange's birthday) came round in 1822, Wellesley forbade the traditional Protestant celebrations; in revenge a Protestant mob hurled a bottle into his box at the theatre and rioted. Some leading Orangemen were dismissed from government posts; in revenge the 'Protestant' Beefsteak Club in 1823 gave the toast, 'Success to the Export Trade of Ireland and may Lord Wellesley be the first article exported'.[27]

As a result of these two incidents a member of Wellesley's staff, Colonel Merrick Shawe, appealed urgently to Wellington. (Shawe had been with Wellesley in India and was well known to the Duke.) It was shocking, wrote Shawe, to see how brazenly the Irish Ultras were conspiring to thwart the Lord-Lieutenant's excellent endeavours. Shawe hoped all would come right. 'But without the protection of your Grace's sevenfold Shield I should

* The Cabinet's original idea had been to send Wellington. They abandoned it after he said that his arrival would give the impression that Ireland was to be put to the sword. Castlereagh added, 'You should not fire your great gun at a sparrow' (Stanhope, 24 October 1833 and 29 October 1842).

apprehend danger.'[28] The sevenfold shield was displayed. Wellington wrote to his brother the very next day, 21 February 1823, offering all possible help from the Ordnance office and making the significant suggestion that he and Wellesley should now embark on 'a correspondence about your govt. in Ireland'; though of course he would await Wellesley's permission before beginning.[29]

Alas, the Duke's offer dropped into a pool of silence. A fortnight later he was explaining to Canning how he thought this rebuff had come about. 'I declined to correspond with Lord Wellesley on the subject of his government when he first went [to Ireland],' thinking that such a correspondence would either do no good or cause 'an awkward relation' with the Home Secretary, Peel; 'but lately having heard from him I expressed a wish to write to him with his permission on the affairs of his government; but he has given me no answer; and I understand that he does not wish to hear from me.'[30]

From Wellington's angle it was a pity that the exchanges with his 'Catholic' brother were each time abortive; first through his own scrupulousness and second through some fear or weakness of Wellesley's combined with an 'almost psychopathic aversion to letter-writing'.[31] A correspondence on Ireland with someone like the Lord-Lieutenant would have helped Wellington and let the world know earlier about the direction in which his own mind was moving.

*

The Catholics meanwhile had been stirred by the winds of change blowing in both Ireland and England. Wellington saw their point only too well. How could the British Cabinet recognize Simon Bolivar's bid for emancipation from Spain while rejecting Daniel O'Connell's claim for Ireland?

Daniel O'Connell had founded the Catholic Association on 10 May 1823, thus screwing up the agitation to an unheard-of pitch. This burly Kerryman, himself a Roman Catholic and proprietor of a small estate, was gifted with a huge voice capable of carrying to ten thousand people and a lawyer's brain astute enough to devise a form of Catholic association which did not actually contravene the law. A Catholic 'rent' of 1d per month was levied by O'Connell on the Irish masses, raising as much as £22,700 that year for the emancipation campaign. It was paid with patriotic pride. Soon an immensely powerful new force was thrown behind the rent – the Irish clergy. Catholic priests became treasurers of their local branches and the pennies were collected at the church doors on 'Rent Sundays' after Mass.

Throughout his life Wellington regarded the formation of political societies, whether Catholic or Protestant, radical or constitutional, with instinctive disfavour. Why should the incomparable British constitution be submitted to these excrescences? They were either dangerous or superfluous. He was therefore fiercely hostile to the Catholic Association. But with its inception in 1823 he was also eager to withdraw from the ultra right-wing Constitutional Association which he had reluctantly joined in 1821, for the purpose of hauling seditious scribblers into court. This egregious society, after coming under heavy fire in Parliament, dissolved itself, to the Duke's relief, in 1823.

All this time the Duke was pursuing his researches into the Irish question, impeded as usual by a flow of uninvited suggestions. A Mr Richard Keene, for instance, was anxious to offer a tract of empty country in Mexico for 'drawing off' the surplus Irish population. The increasing violence in Ireland was reported to him from many Irish sources, among them his old colleague Lord Clancarty, who had retired from the foreign service after offending the King of the Netherlands:

We are in even a worse state [wrote Clancarty], than immediately prior to the Rebellion of 1798. As to the local government [Lord Wellesley's], deprived as it is of all patronage, and without the means of exerting force, what can it do?[32]

Force was a solution which the Duke did not dismiss. Impressed by a book by a Captain Noel which argued that the conquest of Ireland had never been 'perfected', he felt that 'unless measures can be discovered to quiet that country we shall have to compleat the Conquest'.[33] This was in April 1823. Two months later 'conquest' or conciliation seemed even more essential because of fissures in the British Cabinet.

The prematurely aged Prime Minister (he was a year younger than Wellington) was irritable, ill and speaking of resignation. He could not face remedial measures for Ireland, particularly if the Home Secretary resigned on the issue, as he threatened to do.

Wellington saw Peel, urging him to act *'manfully'* at the head of
Irish affairs (Peel had said he was 'sick of the job') and forestall a
Catholic rebellion. 'I fairly scolded him,' he reported to Mrs
Arbuthnot. But he felt he had made no impression except to
prevent Peel from resigning without warning him first.[34]

Wellington's own mind continued to move forward along the
two parallel paths of force and reform. First, suppression of the
Catholic Association.' If we can't get rid of the Catholic Association,' he wrote to Peel on 3 November 1824, 'we must look to
a civil war in Ireland sooner or later.' As Master-General of the
Ordnance it was his duty to warn Bathurst, Secretary for War
and the Colonies, to increase the army in Ireland, though hoping
that Peel's new 'Constable Acts' might enable the Government to
keep the peace through a police force rather than soldiers. On the
other hand, further correspondence with Dr Curtis, the Roman
Catholic Primate, showed him that force was not enough. The
fact of Catholic clergy contributing and collecting funds for the
Association radically altered the position. Could not the
Association be outlawed and the clergy re-attached to the side of
law and order?

Dr Curtis explained, however, that an open society like the
Catholic Association could not be suppressed while secret
Orange societies were permitted to collect large sums of money, to
carry arms, to march with flags and bands playing, 'and all the
rest of their grandeur' for the sole purpose of insulting the
Catholics. While such things occurred the Catholic clergy would
not allow their Association alone to be proscribed.[35] But when
Dr Curtis wrote again on 30 December he announced that despite
everything he was still doing his best to prevent his flock from
breaking the laws, and except when they were under the influence
of spirituous liquors – 'a fatal propensity in this country' – he
was succeeding. Curtis even admitted that the arrest of O'Connell
would be 'a salutary measure', deprecating his 'vain and petulant
display' of Irish eloquence.[36]

In this atmosphere of controversy Wellington began the new
year, 1825, by drafting his own peace policy for Ireland. He spent
all February reading the Irish reports, writing his paper and
intermittently relaxing on his real tennis court. He was also
heartened by the passage of an Unlawful Assembly Act on 9
March, ostensibly aimed at both Orange and nationalist factions,

but which caused the dreaded Catholic Association, now known to Protestants as the 'Popish Parliament', to wind itself up. He did not know that it was to be a case of 'The Association is dead! Long live the Association!' For a new Catholic association arose in July from the ashes of the old.

On 10 April Wellington announced triumphantly to Mrs Arbuthnot that he had at last finished his paper on the Catholic question. He was now making the fair copy, a terrible task, since Fitzroy Somerset was out of town and he was obliged to do it all himself. Not that he was entirely satisfied with the paper. 'But who can be so with the subject who writes to maintain things as they are?'[37]

The precise meaning which the Duke attached to this somewhat cryptic phrase is important. His wish to 'maintain things as they are' certainly did not necessitate opposition to every form of Catholic emancipation. What it did mean was maintenance of the Protestant supremacy. As he saw the Catholic question, peace in Ireland depended on maintaining the Ascendancy but at the same time granting Catholic relief.

*

His answer, reached after tireless consultations and delving into his own Continental experience, involved what was known as an 'Erastian' solution, after the Swiss sixteenth-century theologian who had worked out a scheme for the co-ordination of Church and State, with the secular State on top.

Wellington's analysis was finally reduced to sixteen closely argued points which, with his conclusions, were later to occupy fifteen large pages of small print.[38] He began with the present 'publick apathy' towards the Protestant Church on the part of its own flock; passed on to the fashionable climate of liberal opinion which prevented the anti-Catholic laws from operating effectively; and ended with the rejection of reforms so far suggested, such as Catholic emancipation accompanied merely by appointment of bishops and payment of clergy by the State. This watered-down form of Erastianism did not in the Duke's opinion 'provide security against foreign interference or Papal encroachment'. His own version of Catholic emancipation was more fully Erastian and required a Concordat negotiated in Rome.

'Having settled these measures at Rome,' concluded the Duke, 'they should be recognised by Parliament, and the same Act should repeal every law imposing any disability upon a Roman Catholick.'

Half-way through his analysis the Duke had made a significant plea for reaching a settlement now – now, at a time of 'external peace and of internal tranquillity'. Britain was prosperous. Agriculture had recovered in 1824, commerce was booming. Let a settlement be negotiated from strength and not left to be 'extorted from our fears'.

Nine days after the Duke's paper was ready for Liverpool to see, the House of Commons on 19 April passed the second reading of a Catholic Relief Bill introduced by the radical Sir Francis Burdett, with some Tory support. There followed a Cabinet meeting on the 24th when the Prime Minister suggested a talk with Wellington about his 'Catholic' paper.

'I told him I would call upon him one of these mornings, 'wrote the Duke next day to Charles Arbuthnot. 'I will then state to him the continuance of my opinion that we should turn our minds to a Settlement.'[39]

That very day, 25 April, a speech was made in the Lords which temporarily blew the idea of a settlement out of the sky.

The Duke of York, heir to the throne, was gouty and dropsical but still, in Thackeray's words, 'a man, big, burly, loud, jolly, cursing, courageous'. This man pledged himself in ringing tones to defend the Coronation Oath and Established Church 'whatever might be his station in life, so help him God!'. George IV was older and sicker than York. It seemed like a renewal of George III's hysterical pledge against Catholic emancipation from a man soon to occupy the throne.

The Orange party was ecstatic, Wellington aghast. He dashed off a note to Arbuthnot on the 26th:

There never was such folly. It must render all parties more eager to decide the question at an early period and on the wrong grounds!! It appears to me as if the finger of God was on this family . . . and they were being driven mad.[40]

There had been a time when the Duke thought the finger of God was laid benignly upon himself. Now it was a vengeful finger, incidentally destroying his own careful and complicated plans for emancipation. When he called at 10 Downing Street for a verdict, the Prime Minister could see nothing in his document but difficulties. The cerebrations of Erastus had gone down before the bellowings of York.

On 10 May Burdett's Relief Bill passed its third reading in the Commons, but by only 248 to 227 votes. Enormously relieved, the Tory peers refused to give it a second reading by a resounding majority of 48 (178 to 130). It was said that certain peeresses had locked up their 'Catholic' husbands before the vote was taken, and Tory toasts were drunk to 'The Glorious 48!'.

The Duke of York's oration forced even Wellington off course. He shelved his ideas for emancipation and a Concordat with the Vatican in favour of a snap election, since the country seemed to have swung so far against the 'Catholics' as to offer the chance of a solidly 'Protestant' Parliament being elected for the first time in years – a prospect he could not but welcome. Even if Lord Liverpool decided against an election – as he did – Wellington's conditions for emancipation scarcely obtained after the spring of 1825 and in 1826. Where was the Protestant 'apathy' and economic 'tranquillity'? A backlash against the mood for more liberal domestic legislation of 1824 – repeal of the Combination Laws against trade unions – soon showed itself in many strikes and some violence, while the better off suffered from speculative mania. 'Englishmen, who were wont to be sober, are gone mad,'[41] wrote Lord Eldon of the railway speculators. The workless who had no money with which to speculate were maddened by clear acts of God, a bad harvest and a hard winter.

*

The rage of speculation was partly due to the lure of Canning's sirens, the newly independent South American states. The British responded gladly, pouring money into the new Eldorado, though not all manufacturers had consulted the South American climate when they exported skates and warming-pans.

At the same time the home market became overheated and Harriet Martineau, the radical historian, jeered at rapacious old ladies and retired civil servants who shovelled their savings into such new-fangled enterprises as *steam*-ovens and *steam*-laundries – which naturally ran out of steam. The hair of parents, she heard, turned white in a day at the spectacle of their girls plunging straight from the gambling den into the governess's pit. Boys were as bad, Benjamin Disraeli at twenty incurring a debt which was to dog him until 1849. Even that 'sensible woman', Harriet Arbuthnot, fell for speculation and the Duke had to warn her as early as April 1824 against holding 'bubble securities'. They were still arguing about the subject in the following spring when he prophesied that the bubbles, now of a gigantic size and still expanding, would shortly cause a 'general crash'.

It came at the end of 1825. 'The banks are breaking in every direction,' wrote Harriet with the zest of a born gambler who enjoyed the bust almost as much as the boom.[42] Wellington, to whom heavy gambling and South American politics were equally abhorrent, was glad to concentrate his financial expertise and Rothschild's money on rescuing the Bank of England. The bursting of the speculative bubble and the consequent run on the banks had broken many weaker establishments and threatened even the Bank of England with ruin. It was not the Bank's fault, Wellington told Liverpool, but the fault of the eight hundred uncontrolled banks and of the Government 'in encouraging foreign speculation'. (For Government read Canning.) By the narrowest of margins the Bank was saved, though at the cost of deflation and much suffering during the following months.

The Duke's year ended with one cause for pleasurable anticipation and one for regret. He was booed for a diplomatic visit to Russia; but Marianne Patterson's second venture into matrimony was reported to be disastrous, as he had feared. It affected him politically as well as personally. For the situation in Lord Wellesley's household and the gossip it caused was to make the British Cabinet fear for the stability of the Castle rule.

*

The Wellesley–Patterson marriage had taken place at Viceregal Lodge, Dublin, on 29 October 1825.

'Was the Duke, the Great Bolingbroke, at the wedding?' asked Betsy Patterson-Bonaparte of her friend the authoress Lady Morgan. The Duke was not. The wedding was described by the British Prime Minister as 'this very strange and awkward event'. There had been a celebration of Mass at the Lodge on the following Sunday for Wellesley's Roman Catholic wife.

'That house is as much my palace as the one in which I am,'

burst out George IV when he heard the news, 'and in my palace Mass shall not be heard.'[43]

Nevertheless the Prime Minister felt that apart from the awkwardness of having a Catholic vicereine at a time of Catholic agitation, the wife might well govern her husband 'better than he governs himself'. Unfortunately it turned out to be Lord Wellesley's bastard who governed them both.

Wellesley had appointed a young man named Edward Johnston, one of his illegitimate sons by an early affair, to be his private secretary when he became Lord-Lieutenant in 1821. Four years later Edward, his younger brother and their friends battened on the Lord-Lieutenant and ran his private life. Wellington called them 'the Parasites'. He heard that though Edward Johnston had got a lucrative job at the Board of Stamps in London, he could not be dislodged from Dublin after his father's marriage and continued to rule the roost, against the bride's will, even on the honeymoon. Despite many subsequent battles for her rightful influence in her own house, she appeared to have failed. The Duke believed she would not endure her humiliating position for more than a year, but would leave Richard. Meanwhile he gave what help he could by indirectly sending her the sensible advice to make a tactical retreat. He wrote to her sister, Louisa Hervey, on New Year's Day 1826:

. . . The first of all worldly Duties for a Wife and her connections is to endeavour to raise her husband in the eyes of the World. . . .

I certainly hoped for the sake of your sister but more for that of Lord W that she would have been able to banish from His Presence for ever all the Parasites. . . . But they only deprive her of social comfort. They totally destroy him in Fortune Reputation and every thing which renders life desirable to a Man like him. But bad & noxious as they are, the time is past at which it was possible for her to get rid of them.[44]

It was an earlier generation of parasites, he continued, who had wrecked Wellesley's previous marriage. The contest between the first parasites and the first wife had ended in *her* being turned out of the house. 'Let this example never be forgotten. Your Sister must make up her Mind to do the best she can.'

A week later the Duke was writing similarly to Peel, in answer to a hair-raising account of the feuds in Lord Wellesley's family, according to which the worsting of 'Lady W' was the talk of Dublin. This the Duke believed to be true. Bad as it was, however, he did not think the evil could be cured by the removal of Edward Johnston from Ireland, though he would in fact urge Lord Liverpool to give this solution a trial by recalling Johnston to his London desk at the Board of Stamps.[45] The Duke accordingly did so, but the Prime Minister would not touch this hot potato. A year later the Lord-Lieutenant's political staff were still bemoaning the 'torments' which Edward Johnston inflicted upon them. Nevertheless, Marianne's cause eventually triumphed and the Duke's advice that she should manage the Parasites as best she could and not attempt to turn them out of the house bore fruit. When Richard returned to Ireland in 1833 for a second term as Lord-Lieutenant he left both the Johnstons behind, having quarrelled with the elder and relying on Lord Grey to find a consulate for the younger.

The Duke of Wellington has often been blamed for harshness towards his brother. After the first explosion his impeccable behaviour throughout the little known Marianne episode – to him so poignant – should help to redress the balance.

9

Canning? 'No, No, No!'

A mission to Russia and in mid-winter? Tsar Alexander had died suddenly on 1 December 1825, and Canning told George IV that Wellington was the great personage *par excellence* to bring condolescences and congratulations to the new Tsar Nicholas I.

The Duke caused surprise by the alacrity with which he, still a convalescent, accepted. During the year before, Kitty had been sufficiently worried about him to forget a sharp personal tiff with Charles Arbuthnot and beg him and Harriet to visit Stratfield Saye and help entertain. Mr Arbuthnot, 'exceedingly gratified' by this lifting of a six months' ban, promptly offered his services as a liaison officer between the Duchess and her secretive husband, who still could not get on.[1] If only he were *'civil'* to his wife, expostulated Mrs Arbuthnot. 'He protested he always was very civil to her & never said a harsh word to her in his life.' Mrs Arbuthnot decided that he sincerely believed this, not realizing that his manner, which was extremely abrupt with everybody, became particularly short with her; 'and, as she is frightened to death at him (a thing he detests) she always seems *consterné* [*sic*] when he comes near her.' As a result they abused one another to their friends.

> Poor woman! I am sorry for her . . . I am sorry for him too; it drives him from his home & he is getting tired of running about the world.[2]

Tired or not, when Canning formally proposed the Russian mission on Christmas Eve 1825 Wellington jumped at it. 'Never better in his life', 'ready to start in a week' – such expressions of alertness convinced Canning that the selection of anybody else would have injured the Duke's health far more than all the frosts of Russia.[3] For this was intended to be far more than a courtesy visit.

Events in Eastern Europe had reached a critical point where the Sultan of Turkey might exterminate the Greeks or alternatively the Emperor of Russia decimate the Turks. At the same time Canning saw in these dangers the ideal opportunity for finishing off the old European system and reassembling the pieces under Britain's lead. His policy was to recognize the Tsar's interest in rescuing his Greek co-religionists from further Turkish atrocities and to offer British mediation between Russia and Turkey, and Turkey and Greece. From the watershed that was Britain would flow rivers of concord, for as a great commercial nation Britain always found her supreme good in peace.

It will be noticed that the success of this policy depended on certain nicely adjusted tensions. Too much bellicosity at St Petersburg would precipitate war; too little would give the British mediator no chance to mediate.

It was curious that Canning should have chosen the Duke for such an exercise in brinkmanship. He had been criticized on all sides after Verona for inflexibility and Canning can hardly have expected him to change overnight from a lion into a fox. Some people thought Canning simply wished to get the Duke out of the way. On the other hand, if his mission was primarily to impress Tsar Nicholas there was none so likely to succeed as 'King Arthur'.

*

He was ready to start on 8 February 1826. Although he had shed unexpected tears as he said good-bye to his niece Lady Burghersh and his old mother, his spirits were soaring and his pen scratching energetically as he rolled in his carriage towards Berlin. Having spent his leisure before departure in studying the Moscow campaign of 1812, he was now copying out notes for Napoleon's biographer, Walter Scott. 'It is furiously scrawled, and the Russian names hard to distinguish,' wrote Scott when he received it, adding resolutely, 'It *shall* do me Yeoman's service.' [4]

He reached Berlin on 17 February, to be entertained for two days by the Prussian court and '*better bourgeoisie*'. The British

* The Duke's unmistakable if distant kinship with the White Knight in *Alice* was apparent on the journey and was first noticed by Mr Guedalla. A light-coloured silk anti-vermin cover for his sleeping matress – light in colour to afford no camouflage for the invaders, silk to make penetration more difficult – was all his own invention.

ambassador had not invited him to stay at the embassy, remembering since Verona his 'preference for the inn'.[5] The Duke himself had asked Canning for a minimum staff: 'The fewer we have the better we are likely to get on.'

To get on, and get home again. For the first time abroad he was missing his friends and the open houses they kept for him. 'I cannot tell you what pleasure your letter gave me,' he wrote to Harriet Arbuthnot. 'It appeared an Age since I had heard from you and I am not accustomed now, as I was formerly, to fly off to the end of the World and to hear no more of those I love & regard and with whom I had been living.'[6]

As he sped onward again on the 20th the prospect in Russia ceased to attract. Except for conciliation, he wrote to Bathurst, there seemed little his mission could accomplish. 'I have nearly no means of negotiating in my hands.'[7] On the great issue of Russia versus Turkey he might be able to keep hold of the negotiations if both sides wanted peace.

The Duke's pessimism was justified by events, though not quite in the way he expected. Having arrived on 2 March he attended Tsar Alexander's funeral – 'a terrible Ceremony', with a thawing, months-old corpse – charmed Tsar Nicholas and negotiated the secret Protocol of St Petersburg, by which Britain should mediate between Turkey and Russia to obtain qualified Greek independence. So far so good. Nevertheless, the incompatibility of his own and Canning's approach to diplomacy did in the end produce mystifications and misunderstandings between them. Straightforwardness was made to look crude when the Duke had to carry out subtle schemes – a blunt instrument. Why did he tell the Turks that Alexander had no intention of attacking them over Greece? Even if true – which Canning did not believe – the Turks should have been kept on tenterhooks. Despite his success over the Protocol, he returned to find his relations with Canning had worsened.

On his resumption of British politics at the beginning of May 1826 the Opposition, with Canning's tacit support, dubbed his mission a failure. Before he had left St Petersburg (on 6 April) Mme de Lieven was reporting that he was to be ousted from the Cabinet while abroad and Canning was to make himself Prime Minister: 'He is master. . . .' A month later she wrote that despite Canning's execrable French, 'we are getting to know one another'.

To do justice to the ambitious Dorothea, a change in her feelings for the Duke had begun the moment she saw signs of his losing the long political duel. Three years earlier, on 2 June 1823, she had written: 'I see the Duke of Wellington every day, and every day I am more and more convinced that he counts for nothing in affairs'; and again even more fantastically on the 20th, 'The Duke of Wellington grows stupider every day. It is incredible what rapid progress his malady makes to his brain.'[8] By 1826, though she could still send for him and cry on his shoulder when feeling low, her heart was all in what Mrs Arbuthnot called 'her Canning connection'.

Personally, the Duke was divided between pleasure at being back among scintillating friends and distaste for home affairs in their continuing disturbed state. 'Duke of Wn is in amazing health and spirits,' wrote Lady Cowper on 9 May, 'delighted with all he has seen and looking quite fat and fresh. I never saw such an improvement in any body.'[9] For the gloomy side of the picture he had been prepared while still in Russia by a letter from Lord Westmorland: commercial affairs were worse, the stocks falling and the City critical – 'the grumbling Classes are as you may imagine very numerous' – distress among the silk weavers, bankruptcies in plenty and the Chancellor, Frederick Robinson, promising that 'Banktuptcies past were nothing to what was to come'; at Windsor the King racked with severe gout. 'You are never more wanted at home.'[10]

Wanted or not, the Duke immediately made his presence felt by criticizing government patronage. Let Lord Liverpool, he wrote to Croker, choose whichever of the three peers he preferred to be the new Lord of the Treasury; the Duke would certainly not oppose the Prime Minister's choice:

But I assure you [he told Croker], it would be loss of time and labour to compare the merits of Candidates for Office when in fact there is no merit on the part of any of the three you have mentioned.[11]

There was another nagging case of promotion, however, where the Duke believed personal merit was most certainly involved and the Prime Minister's choice even worse. Lord Liverpool still refused to raise the Rev. Gerald Wellesley to the bench of bishops because of his wife's adultery. In August 1826 Arthur supported Richard's plan to get Gerald a vacant Irish bishopric by sending a personal plea to the stubborn Prime Minister. The result was a flat refusal from Lord Liverpool: 'No clergyman living separate from his wife ought to be raised to the Bench.' In perforce accepting this dictum, Wellington found himself in one of those personal dilemmas which were to damage him unfairly in the eyes of posterity. To quit the public service because of a private quarrel was unthinkable; to be the great Duke yet not serve his family was selfish.

On his return to England, Gerald's was not the only career with which the Duke busied himself. His son Douro needed his attention.

*

From Mrs Arbuthnot's journal it appears that the holidays, as so often happens, had sharpened the father's critical eye and caused the son to avoid him:

> The Duke imagines that the Duchess has set his son against him [wrote Harriet], which only makes him the more irritated against her & mortifies him to the greatest degree. He is unjust, for the Duchess would do anything she possibly can to put him & his children well together if she knew how, but she is such a fool she does not.

Harriet hoped he would soon accept his sons' neglect – 'He is not apt to fret about things which cannot be cured. . . .'[12] She had evidently written off both boys as unworthy of their great father.

It may be, however, that Douro and Charles were reacting against a cultural drive launched by the Duke. Douro was to look into his own mind and ask himself whether he knew about geography, British possessions, ancient history, modern history, national and international law, political economy. Assuming the answer was no, the Duke continued astringently,

> Yet all these are branches of knowledge without possessing which a man can scarcely converse, excepting about his horses & Dogs. . . .[13]

The Duke of Wellington was not a dog lover. In his portraits there are no favourite dogs gambolling around. Nor do domestic animals feature in his letters. The Duke was too cerebral for animals. Even the romance of Copenhagen, his charger, was in time overlaid by other preoccupations. He was not even sure where Copenhagen was buried when the secretary of the United Services Museum asked for his skeleton to join that of Napoleon's charger, which they already possessed. The Duke said he would try to find out.[14] Assuming that he did so, he must have changed his mind about the propriety of Copenhagen leaving Stratfield Saye to run as 'a *Shew*' in double harness with Marengo. For after the rider had followed his horse to the grave, the 2nd Duke erected a tablet in the paddock at Stratfield Saye:

Here lies
COPENHAGEN
The charger ridden by
The Duke of Wellington
The entire Day at the
Battle of Waterloo
Born 1808, died 1836.

God's humble instrument, though meaner clay,
Should share the glories of that glorious day.

But Douro's duty in his early twenties was to forget horses, dogs and even his own rank (the last a very 'untenable' claim to fame) and concentrate on forming his mind – 'and rely upon it that you can make it whatever you please'. With this robust assertion the Duke then produced a formidable reading-list* which Douro was to share with Charles who, as a younger son, would find it even more necessary: 'He may rely upon it that Idleness never did any man any good.' The sad thing was that the reading-list seems to have done little good either; for when Wellington sent the same list fifteen years later to Lady Wilton for her son, he had to issue a *caveat*. 'Mind, I don't tell you that this system has been at all successful.'

* The Duke had borrowed the original list from his Whig friend Lady Jersey, whose sons' tutor had compiled it, and then made various alterations himself. For instance, he added certain works on India and Persia written by his friend Sir John Malcolm, and substituted Burke for the Whig author Lord John Russell. The list consisted of state papers, parliamentary debates and over ninety works, many in several volumes, covering the subjects mentioned to Douro, with special sections on Ireland, Scotland, France and British possessions. The authors included contemporaries like Fouché and Ségur in a long section on the French Revolution. Judging by the Duke's comments, he had read them all himself, except two: 'They talk of Sismondi's *Histoire des Français* (I have never read it)'; 'They talk of Ramsay's *History of the Revolution in America* which I have not read.' Last but one he recommends, 'There is a little French Work entitled *L'Art de Verifier les Dates* which is very useful to have. . . .' (*Private Correspondence*, pp. 44–52).

Notwithstanding any doubts he may have felt, the Duke did not relish interference. When Alava persuaded Mrs Arbuthnot to remonstrate with the boys over their alleged alienation from their father, it was denounced as 'mischief'. In fact Charles was far from being estranged, as Mrs Arbuthnot on an earlier occasion had herself admitted:

Charles is very well with his father; he is a wild, rattling, high spirited boy, full of tricks & not the least afraid of his father, who is amused by his nonsense.[15]

Even Douro she thought would gradually lose his fear in admiration for his father's talents and character.

*

Wellington's private correspondence was full of reports and discussions about his Stratfield Saye estate. Towards the end of 1826 a new steward named John Payn produced drastic plans for reform. Within a year or so he had reduced rent arrears from £1475 to £975. But what dinners he still found going on in the steward's room at Apsley House! In May 1828 – '6 soles 12s. 2 roast fowls 11s. roast lamb 9s. soup 6s. roast beef a guinea, asparagus 9s. young potatoes 5s. Total £3 13s. –.' Opposite this record of debauchery Payn wrote a list of 'What should be proper': namely, 'Leg mutton boiled 6s. 8d. roast beef one guinea, vegetables 5s. Total £1 12s. 8d.' Nine months later the two cooks' expenses, apart from their wages, still amounted to £5,000 a year (perhaps £50,000 in today's currency).

By the end of the following year (1829) there are notes by Payn on relief for the poor, especially coal to prevent them burning up their fences. A glimpse into late summer 1830, when the Duke and the country were driving towards fierce trouble, shows Mr Payn in despair: a bad harvest, arrears mounting again, everybody blaming him. Two months pass and twelve strong men are guarding Stratfield Saye against the agricultural mobs, and the period described by Harriet Martineau as the Years of Peace, 1818–30, is ending in something like civil war.

*

Stratfield Saye beleaguered was the last stage in a gun-powder trail which had been laid in the distressful year 1826.

Wellington was home in time for the general election. In

addition to Lord Westmorland's list of ills, there had been machine-breaking in the North during April with a thousand power looms smashed in one week, followed by a drought. These things forced the Cabinet to promise some relaxation of the Corn Laws even at the cost of fury on the farms. Except in Ireland, however, quarrels within the Whig party saved the Government from disaster. At Waterford, Ireland, O'Connell's Catholic forces won a stunning victory. Whereas in Wales a sharp Radical challenge to the Tory Marquess of Worcester –

> *Shall the sons of Newport free*
> *E'er to Worcester Bow the knee?*

resulted in the labourers' knees still remaining bowed, in Ireland thousands of peasants known as '40s-freeholders' straightened their backs and voted for the first time against their landlords. And what could landlords do when priests threatened to excommunicate all who did not vote straight? Emancipation was only a matter of time.

The Irish poor, meanwhile, were in the plight customary during a bad season. Here Wellington showed an understanding of the country superior to the *laissez-faire* economists who argued in abstract terms. He believed that the systems of land-tenure and labour were responsible for recurrent famines, rather than the size of the population. He and Peel discussed the impending disaster on 20 August. Next day, obsessed with the potential horror, he wrote to Peel picturing a situation in which a million Irish would have to be fed by the State. He also described to Harriet the difference between his and Peel's reaction:

. . . I was astounded by the magnitude of the calamity. He was quite cool & quiet; and said in answer to my observations that we should lose one third of the Population, 'that is the natural course of this great excess of Population'.

The Duke knew that Peel had got these grim ideas from the contemporary exponent of the population explosion. 'He takes his sentiments from Malthus.'*[16] That the food supply was to

* Thomas Robert Malthus (1760–1834) wrote his famous *Essay on Population* in 1798, forty years before Ireland's inhabitants were cut down by famine. Malthus argued that births must be limited since population increased faster than the food supply, and it was said that his friends were careful never to invite him to a party where he might meet a pregnant woman.

explode as fast as the population during the nineteenth century would have been no surprise to Wellington, who showed his disagreement with Malthus in the rest of his letter to Harriet:

It is not true that the Population of Ireland is too great. If the working classes were paid in Money instead of Land & were in the Habit of coming upon the markets for their food, instead of [raising it in potato patches] to pay the rent of which they mortgage their Labour, this misfortune would not have been felt in the same degree or indeed at all.

His solution was neither emigration nor Peel's 'natural course', i.e. death, but a market economy in Ireland to raise the standard of living. Meanwhile, the 'natural course' of change was at work in Britain.

*

The Commander-in-Chief of the British Army, HRH the Duke of York, died on 5 January 1827.

The royal funeral, on 20 January, made sure that as many other people as possible were soon dying also. It took place at night in St George's Chapel, Windsor, with nothing on the flagstones to relieve the rising damp. On returning to Stratfield Saye during the small hours of the 21st Wellington was taken violently ill.[17] Next day Peel, a guest in the house, tried to reassure the Duchess by telling her that before this attack Wellington had looked stouter and heartier than for years.

'That is the effect of age,' said Kitty tremulously. 'People about his time of life get larger.'

'His face is larger.'

'I am so short sighted I cannot remark his features, I can only judge by the colour, and when I look at *that precious face*, it seems to be very pale.' She burst into tears, filling the deeply uxorious Peel with mingled pity and aversion – aversion from those who found it in their hearts, as he told his wife, to usurp Kitty's place. This hit at Mrs Arbuthnot was followed by an even fiercer denunciation of the Duke: 'What wickedness and what folly to undervalue and to be insensible to the affection of a wife!'[18]

While Wellington was recovering from his illness, however undeservedly in Peel's eyes, others were less lucky. The fatal toll of the funeral night was said to have been two bishops, five footmen and several soldiers; while many took to their beds. Canning and his friend Huskisson, both in poor health, caught chills which they never completely threw off. As for the Prime Minister, he was too unfit to attend the macabre event; on 17 February he was found unconscious from a paralytic stroke.

Thus within a few weeks the holders of two great offices of state left the stage. The Duke of York's death, predicted Princess Lieven to Wellington with her acute sense of the political climate, would prove 'the first brutal shock to the old Tory aristocracy'.[19] In Lord Liverpool was removed the untiring, placatory influence which so long had enabled the old aristocracy to absorb this and other shocks.

*

The succession of Wellington to the command of the army was a foregone conclusion. The King no doubt had entertained an intoxicating vision of himself in that post, but it was quickly dissipated by his ministers. 'I will protest against it in the most formal manner,' wrote Wellington to Peel, 'for the sake of the army, for that of the Government, and above all, the sake of the publick.' For a moment the Ultras felt happy, believing that Wellington as Commander-in-Chief would strengthen their cause in the Cabinet; though Charles Londonderry questioned whether the Duke's new office was compatible with his becoming in due course Prime Minister – 'However, there never was a Wellington before; and never will be again' – and to a Wellington all things were possible.[20]

One thing which always came easily to Wellington was to write briefly. He cut down his first General Order to the Army from the immense screed drafted by his staff and full of over-ripe compliments to the late C-in-C. 'I dislike to come before the Army and the world with this parade,' he protested, substituting a few lines of his own in which he simply asked for, and promised, dutiful service.[21]

His main task was how to effect drastic military economies – the country's emphatic postwar demand – while maintaining the army's efficiency. Cuts had been made already. Why was not the late Commander-in-Chief given a military funeral? The answer in Wellington's opinion was obvious: they had not enough soldiers in England to bury a field-marshal.

Other difficulties were connected with the late Field-Marshal's active life. As one of his executors, Wellington heard from the Accoucheur that all the secrets of HRH's debts were to be 'placed in your Grace's bosom', including claims arising out of a legion of mistresses. '*This morning* another female friend presented herself,' wrote Knighton jocularly on 31 May to the Duke, 'with a Bond for a thousand pounds: so that you will see that the disbanded Troops are rather numerous!'[22]

If there were not enough officers in England of the rank to bury a Field-Marshal, there were certainly not enough to discharge his debts, though Londonderry suggested they should do so by a 'voluntary' whip round among officers of all ranks – a plan which the Duke at once vetoed. It was for Parliament to pay up.

However, with Liverpool politically dead, a bigger question arose. Would there be enough men in England willing to raise a Field-Marshal to the highest office in the State? Four years of struggle between Wellington and Canning had reached their climax.

*

Excitement began to build up the moment Lord Liverpool's condition was known. All the Opposition newspapers backed Canning for Prime Minister. The King was torn by doubts. Could the new Government, like the old, contain both Wellington and Canning? Or was it a case of either ... or ...? William Ponsonby, a Whig in the know, analysed the crisis for his sister Caroline Lamb on 20 February:

Everything continues in an extraordinary state & great anxiety is felt to know what will be the consequence. Lord Liverpool is alive, but that is all, & Canning far from strong. His party & the Duke of Wellington's, having been long held together by Lord Liverpool alone, must sever.[23]

Throughout March political fever continued to mount as the committed supporters of each side went into action. Accusations of intrigue flew between the two camps. It was a testing time for both champions: Canning because of physical pain from rheumatic fever, Wellington because he always hated political manoeuvres, particularly in his own interest. He felt too much the master to need them and too much the servant to use them.

The press, in their fanatical devotion to Canning, hinted that

Wellington was courting the King's favour. But in fact the Duke had just asserted his new authority as Commander-in-Chief by refusing to change a regimental appointment at His Majesty's request. From the beginning of the crisis, indeed, Wellington and Peel agreed to use no influence with the King.

One of the turning-points in the great race was 5 March. In the morning the King returned to London, hoping that personal interviews would enable him to do his constitutional duty of choosing the minister. During the afternoon and evening the Government's two 'buggaboos', as Canning called corn and the Catholics, came before the Commons with results not calculated to strengthen Wellington. Canning pleased the moderates of all parties by introducing a liberalized Corn Bill; and a bill for Catholic emancipation was defeated two days later by four votes. Paradoxically this reverse to 'Catholic' Canning got the King off the hook. For it drove that particular buggaboo from the stage at least until the next session. No insurmountable obstacle now stood between the 'Protestant' monarch and a 'Catholic' Prime Minister.

*

Wellington had received a vague rather than 'regular' invitation to visit the King at Brighton during the first critical period up to 5 March; he refused to go, although Canning had at once been wafted to the Pavilion in a sedan chair. As Wellington saw it, he was in the race neither to destroy Canning's career, nor for himself, but to reconstruct Liverpool's masterpiece – the old, old Government of 1812 that had struggled uphill to Waterloo and gone downhill ever since. He was content to serve under any acceptable Prime Minister – say Peel – who was not a 'Catholic'.

The winning-post was now precisely one month away.

10 March: George IV had been nearly a week interviewing his ministers or getting Knighton to do it for him. In the anti-Canning camp a division of opinion had developed. Was Wellington's position as Commander-in-Chief an 'insurmountable obstacle'[24] to his becoming first minister? The two Arbuthnots took opposite sides, but agreed that the King might well appoint Canning; if so, HM would make vast efforts to keep the Duke also. 'I wd almost rather see the Duke die,' wrote Harriet, whose blood now boiled daily in her journal, 'than in a Cabinet of which Mr Canning was the head.'

11 March: Wellington and Arbuthnot saw Knighton separately. Assuming the King did intend to choose Canning, Knighton asked the Duke if he would dare to resign after foisting Canning on HM in the first place. The Duke did not reply, but in a report to Arbuthnot he lamented the state of collapse into which Government had fallen. 'What is wanted everywhere and in every thing is the hand of Authority!!'[25] This had been his own speciality, and this was one reason why he sometimes saw himself as Prime Minister.

12 March: Wellington called on Canning and Peel, the former disinclined to talk politics. Frankly intimating to Peel that he would not serve under Canning, Wellington suggested the Duke of Rutland, Lord Clancarty or Lord Bathurst as possible leaders. Peel countered with the Duke himself. By the end of their discussion Wellington felt satisfied that at least Peel agreed neither of them could serve Canning with 'honour'. The introduction of this word was ominous.

13 March: Knighton again interviewed the Duke and Arbuthnot separately, but merely promised his Grace a massive gold collar from the King. He was told by Arbuthnot that 'no one wd. do but the Duke. . . .' Canning as Prime Minister, rammed home Arbuthnot, would split the Tories without pleasing the Whigs.

14–21 March: Rage filled the Duke at Arbuthnot's unsolicited propaganda. 'I never saw the Duke so much vexed about any thing in my life,' wrote Harriet, '. . . he says . . . that he wd rather serve under Mr Canning than be supposed to quit from any thing like personal pique.'[26] Meanwhile the King had disappeared to Windsor (14 March), having so far failed to reach a solution.

22–3 March: A restive Cabinet sent Wellington to unravel the King's intentions. Besides the 'foolish' gold collar, the envoy received a medley of inconclusive confidences, but the King's only decision was to postpone deciding until the Easter recess, which Wellington bleakly reported to his colleagues.

21–5 March: While trying to silence the Arbuthnots, Wellington faced a more serious menace to his cause from a group of Tory peers. Led by the Dukes of Newcastle and Rutland, they tried to press a 'Protestant' premier (obviously Wellington) upon the evasive King. The annoyance of this Tory pressure-group was to be ably exploited by Canning.

27–30 March: Wellington was once more invited to Windsor. HM must choose between Peel and Canning, stated the Duke to the King on the 28th, or else a third party agreeable to both. Might not the Cabinet *elect* a leader? interposed the King. No. It was HM's prerogative to choose – 'the only personal act the King of England had to perform'.[27] When the King of England inadvertently implied some intrigue between Canning and the Opposition, Wellington, no less unguardedly, let fly.

'And now, Sir, can Your Majesty be surprised that the Tory Party detest Mr Canning? Can you be surprised that they cabal against . . . a man who is himself engaged in such a cabal as this?'[28] Brushing aside this challenge, His Majesty broke instead into furious denunciation of Tory 'cabals and dictation', to which *he would not submit.* And during a subsequent interview with Canning he unforgivably repeated the Duke's accusations. Nevertheless he was as indecisive as ever about the final choice, despite the urgency. That day Lord Liverpool's resignation had been placed in his hands. At parting Canning was ordered to sound Peel on the 29th, and then send him next day to Windsor.

Before setting out Peel called at Apsley House, to find a thoroughly disgruntled Duke who believed, with some justice, that the King and Canning had joined in casting him for the role of ducal caballer-in-chief.

31 March–4 April: Daily more sure of ultimate success, Canning was making desperate efforts to sign up as many non-'Catholic' Tories as possible. He also put up the idea of Robinson going to the Lords as Prime Minister. The Duke knocked it flat. With Canning leader of the Commons, who would be the true Prime Minister?

5 April: Ministerial deadlock, and the King back in town. He saw his senior ministers, including Wellington and Peel. The Home Secretary had hardened against anything other than a replica of Liverpool's old ministry – without Liverpool. But where was the new Liverpool? Peel thought Wellington; Canning knew it had to be himself. Deadlock still.

9 April: The last twist. The King sent Eldon to see whether Peel would bend, and afterwards sent Peel to Canning to see if Canning could bend him. The Home Secretary was immovable. Nothing but a now familiar phrase emerged from this, his final interview: 'Nobody would do but the Duke.' Canning retorted that Wellington was enormously powerful already. If they piled Premier on Commander-in-Chief 'it would be too much'.[29] In that case, said Peel, he could not serve.

10 April: Stalemate now clearly faced the King and it was time to begin a new game. Neither Wellington nor Peel would serve under Canning; Canning would serve under no one but a puppet. King George could not do without Canning, in the sense that no Tory Government could be formed from which Canning was excluded, but he could well do without the advice of high and mighty Tory peers like Newcastle and Rutland. It was said that Canning had won during an audience when he touched the King's pride:

'Sir, your father broke the domination of the Whigs; I hope your Majesty will not endure that of the Tories.'

'No, I'll be damned if I do.'[30]

So the Duke was beaten at last. On the afternoon of 10 April the King commissioned his Foreign Secretary to prepare a plan for the reconstruction of the Government. For Canning, these curiously chosen words held no ambiguities. He was Prime Minister.

10

On the Threshold

When the bolt fell Wellington was strangely sceptical. 'It was said in the House of Lords yesterday afternoon that Mr Canning had been appointed Minister,' he wrote on the crucial 10 April 1827, 'but I have no reason to believe the Report to be true up to this moment, half past two.'[1] So, with the rumours already discounted, he saw no finality in a terse circular letter received from Canning that evening. It simply informed him of Canning's commission from the King to make 'a plan' for the reconstruction of the ministry and trusted that, as the new Cabinet would adhere to the old principles, the Duke would continue to be a member of it. There was no visit from Canning; no offer to elucidate any obscurities such as other colleagues received; just the bare invitation. Wellington was not flattered.

However, he decided to elucidate the main obscurity forthwith. Who was to be Prime Minister? No one was named. He remembered Canning's last suggestion (3 April) of a puppet premier in the Lords. Could it be Robinson? For it was not necessarily Canning himself. Was the King deliberately putting Canning in an ambiguous position?*

Before the Duke could answer Mr Canning's 'obliging proposition' he wished to know 'who is the person whom you intend to propose to His Majesty as the head of the Government?'.

This shaft – for shaft it was in Canning's pride – reached the Foreign Office on 11 April. Canning saw his chance. At one blow he could silence his rival and establish his position with the King beyond any doubt. He drafted a shrivelling reply, submitted it for HM's approval and sent it to the Duke.

* Wellington remembered that in 1812 the future George IV, then Prince Regent, had put his brother Lord Wellesley in just such an ambiguous position.

My dear Duke of Wellington,

I believe it to be so generally understood that the King usually entrusts the formation of an Administration to the individual whom it is His Majesty's gracious intention to place at the head of it, that it did not occur to me . . . to add, that, in the present instance His Majesty does not intend to depart from the usual course of proceeding on such occasions.

Canning did not fail to add that HM had seen his letter as well as His Grace's.

> Ever my dear Duke of Wellington,
> Your Grace's sincere and faithful servant,
> George Canning.[2]

The sharp points in this reply struck Wellington between the eyes, blinding him to political realities. First, he felt certain that Canning had not in fact been appointed Prime Minister, which was why he had taken umbrage at a reasonable query. Second, he did not believe that Canning, if appointed, would maintain the old balance between 'Catholics' and 'Protestants'. Third, Canning's reply seemed deliberately wounding ('faithful servant' instead of the usual 'most sincerely'). Fourth and worst, the King had seen and approved the insults. Conclusion? Neither of them wanted him. He resigned. And not only did he resign the Ordnance but also his position as Commander-in-Chief. While the former, being a Cabinet post, could be justified on political grounds, the latter could not, since Wellington himself held that command of the army was non-political. His dramatic severance of this connection, therefore, was explicable only on personal grounds. Indeed he later admitted that the tone and temper of both Canning's letters, particularly that sent in the King's name on 11 April in terms of 'Taunt and Rebuke', had convinced him he could no longer serve with honour in any capacity whatever.[3]

Wellington's consistent line over the past month and his present protestation that he was not acting 'in cabal and concert' might have carried conviction in other circumstances. Unfortunately the 'Protestant' half of the Government was busily resigning with him. Within a few hours of one another Peel, Bathurst, Eldon, Westmorland, Melville, Goulburn, Arbuthnot and Court functionaries like Londonderry had all walked out. Wellington, aware of the 'cabal and concert' allegation, repudiated it in a letter to Sir John Malcolm on 25 April:

The truth is that I am considered to be the representative of the great Aristocracy. . . . Be assured that . . . I stand alone in the World; am a party to no combination or confederacy or concert. . . .[4]

Nevertheless appearances were against him, and the press thundered at the aristocratic clique who had tried to usurp the functions of the Crown. Outside the windows of Apsley House a statue of Achilles had arisen to honour him. Now in a popular cartoon also the Duke had become Achilles – but Achilles sulking in his tent. So violent and sustained were the attacks that Wellington's friend the Rev. G. R. Gleig boldly proposed to publish an anonymous series of letters putting the record straight, provided His Grace would furnish him with information. Predictably the Duke declined to sponsor any new *Letters of Junius*.[5]

The Duke's instinct against a press war was correct. Peel's advice, however, to defend himself again in Parliament had untoward results. At the opening of the new session the Duke rose on 2 May to explain his resignation from a government which had shifted towards the 'Catholics'. It was led in the Lords by the 'Catholic' Viscount Goderich (formerly Frederick Robinson) while on the Woolsack appeared another 'Catholic', the Whig Sir John Copley, created Lord Lyndhurst; in the Commons Huskisson and Palmerston, as Canningites, still sat on the front bench, but the many vacancies were perforce filled by Whigs and 'Catholics'.

But if the Duke did not now trust Canning to maintain Catholic emancipation as an 'open question', whose fault was it? Moreover, in his anxiety to disprove allegations of personal ambition he went sadly astray. His case was excellent, but he was lured into a sweeping and memorable passage – far too memorable as it turned out – proving that it was 'totally out of the question' for him to be Prime Minister:

. . . a situation for which I am sensible that I am not qualified; and to which, moreover, neither His Majesty . . . nor any wished to see me called. . . . My Lords, I should have been worse than mad if I had thought of such a thing.*

* Not only the Duke's contemporaries but a historian like J. R. M. Butler remembered the Duke's words in *The Great Reform Bill* (1914) and wrote: 'He was totally unfitted for leadership at a time of democratic aspiration.' (p. 99).

There seems little doubt that the Duke's blunder was due on this occasion to his limited experience as an orator. Like so many speakers who lack self-confidence, he tended at a crisis to lash himself into hyperbole, hoping to make up with emphasis where he failed in persuasion.

Meanwhile his admirers, apart from the Ultras, deplored his resignation from the army command. Even Harriet Arbuthnot confessed that he had acted in a 'huff' about a matter of personal dignity. The King affected to be hurt and astonished, proposing to keep the command of the army in his own hands, 'till my friend Arthur recovers his temper'. He made two clumsy attempts to heal the breach, neither of which succeeded. On 21 May he gave the Duke written permission to withdraw his resignation, to which his friend Arthur retorted that nothing but a full apology from Canning for his rebuke of 11 April would enable him in honour to retract.[6]

Mrs Arbuthnot upbraided him for such a '*stiff*' letter, but he insisted it was remarkably civil: 'After all, he cd. not write love letters to the King.' Two months later (19 July) the King inveigled him into paying a courtesy call at the Cottage. As soon as the door had shut behind him there was 'an *earthquake*' in London, as the Duke called it, the press insinuating that he had forced himself upon His Majesty, unexpected and uninvited.[7] It was clear that while Canning remained Prime Minister the points of honour between King George and King Arthur would not be resolved.

How long would Canning remain? His popularity was enormous, his health wretched. At the opening of Parliament, Hobhouse thought he looked 'very feeble and ill'.[8] Of his two major domestic concerns, Catholics and corn, the threads were securely in his skilful hands but he had not even begun to weave a new pattern for either of them. Coaxing the King into Catholic emancipation was relegated to a future session, while argument about the details of the Corn Bill had ended in a political muddle and complete seizing-up of understanding between the Government and the Duke.

Wellington supported the bill in principle, recognizing that the country demanded some lowering of the Corn duties. But as a champion of the agricultural interest he held that the change should be just enough to give minimal satisfaction to the urban masses, and no more. At this date neither Wellington nor many other Tory landlords believed that Corn Law reform could benefit the country as a whole. By lowering the prices of the farm labourer's product they were convinced that it would make the rural poor, in particular, poorer than ever.

Huskisson's bill proposed to free foreign corn from bond when the price of English corn had risen to 60s. a quarter. In an attempt to win an extra 6s. for the agricultural interest the Duke worked out an amendment by which the English price would be allowed to reach 66s. a quarter rather than 60s. before foreign corn came on the market. He submitted his amendment to Huskisson and through some confusion received the impression that the Government would accept it. When the debate in the Lords came on, it was the business of Goderich (Robinson) to convince the Duke that his amendment was not only unacceptable but, if carried, would result in the whole Corn Bill being wrecked. Goderich failed to make the Government's position clear, the Tories insisted on a vote, the amendment was carried and the bill withdrawn.

Unaware of the misunderstandings which had gone to the making of this mess, a large section of the public was deeply shocked. The episode seemed simply to rub in the now widely held view that the great Duke, of all people, was playing party politics. Had he not defeated the very bill to which he had agreed while a member of Liverpool's Government? 'His conduct is bad, perfidious, injurious to the country,' hissed Princess Lieven.[9] And the inventive Sir Robert Wilson announced that instead of the Duke being admired for Wellington boots he would be execrated for a 'Wellington loaf' – odious symbol of the starvation inflicted upon the people by keeping up the corn duties.

The Tory victory over corn brought the Duke no satisfaction, for he was far from captious in intention and indeed had laid down for his own and Charles Arbuthnot's guidance a policy which could not be faulted: 'reasonable conduct' pursued with 'Patience, a great deal of Patience'.[10] Only reasonable conduct would suit their party, he went on, the party of bishops, clergy, the greater aristocracy, landed interest, magistracy and great merchants and banks. 'Factious opposition' could never suit. The object of the press was to mix him up with 'the folly of

Newcastle and Londonderry'.[11] He was neither an ultra-Tory nor a 'Liberal' like Peel and his case was different from either. All these points were made in letters to Charles Arbuthnot between 19 and 23 April. But by 18 June he no longer hoped that even 'a great deal of Patience' would put off the clash indefinitely. When it came he prophesied that his party would take the field against King, Whigs, ultra-Tories and Canningites, with 'nothing for us excepting the good sense of the country'. He was writing on Waterloo Day.

Nevertheless, apart from the Corn Bill's fiasco in the Lords, from which the Duke could have been extricated by a cleverer leader than Lord Goderich, he maintained something like an independent role during Canning's 'Hundred Days', and certainly did not bring on his Waterloo. If any human agency was responsible it was the leader of the Opposition, Lord Grey, whose personal tirades against the Prime Minister so worked upon Canning's excitable temperament that his physician, Dr Farr, told the Duke after his death, 'It was Canning's temper that killed him.'[12] On 3 August Wellington heard that Canning was desperately ill with a stoppage of the bowel and had a blister covering his whole stomach. 'He had no relief.' At Chiswick House in a room above that where Fox had expired twenty years earlier, Canning died on 8 August, exactly a hundred days after he had first faced Parliament as Prime Minister. It happened to be also one hundred days after Wellington's fifty-eighth birthday.

*

It was now getting on for a decade since the Duke had plunged into undiluted politics, and forty years since he had joined the army and become the 'retained servant' of King and nation. Not once in all those years had he refused to serve. The closest shave was over a quarter of a century away, when he had been superseded in an Indian command and thought for a few anguished weeks of resigning his commission. His iron constitution had then succumbed to the Malabar itch, no doubt a physical outlet for Supercession irritation and Resignation fever. In 1827 he went down with the fever again and this time it ran its full course. Without stretching the analogy too far, it is worth noticing that while Canning lay on his death-bed Wellington also was seriously ill. 'The Duke of Wellington has been near dying,' wrote William Napier.[13] For the first and last time in his life the 'retained servant' had said no and stuck to it.

The clue to his uncharacteristic behaviour is set out most vividly in a dialogue which took place between Wellington and the diplomat George Chad in a room at Stratfield Saye on 10 April 1828.

'Canning treated me like a Dog,' burst out the Duke. 'I told the King, "If he had not used your Majesty's name by God I would have called him to account for the treatment."' After reflecting for a moment on Canning's Hundred Days and what had followed, the Duke added,

'The fact is since Liverpool's illness, there was no Minister – Canning never was Minister. . . .'

Chad saw where this was leading, where to lay the blame. He said,

'It was the King.'

'Aye.'[14]

The King was the clue. It was Louis XVIII and Ney over again. The French King had insulted Wellington in 1815 and Wellington had retired from the Tuileries into his tent for four months. Twelve years later a king insulted him again, having been used by Canning just as Louis had been used by Artois. The Duke again retired for four months into his tent. Not that he respected these sovereigns as men or cared a pin what either of them thought of him. But they were that principle of existing order which he had been born to serve. Normally he was neither touchy nor resentful – 'I never had a quarrel with any man in my life,' he wrote to Canning on 12 April 1827[15] – but three or four times in his life when old bruises to his self-esteem were roughly handled he reacted as if he were once more the raw young ensign presenting himself in his first scarlet jacket to a disparaging parent. 'Arthur has put on his red coat for the first time today,' his mother had written to a friend in 1787. 'Anyone can see he has not the cut of a soldier!'[16]

Unfit to be a soldier? Unfit to be a politician? Rubbish from the past. Was he not fit to be Commander-in-Chief and 'perfectly fit' according to his friends to become Prime Minister? Yet for all his brilliant successes he was still vulnerable. Achilles' statue, Achilles' tent, Achilles' heel. That heel, the indefinable weakness which he called his 'honour', had been wounded, and the country's greatest servant lay for four months in his tent as if dead.

*

In Canning a giant had died. 'His one absorbing idea was to be the political Atlas of England, to raise her on his shoulders,' wrote Lady Morgan in her diary, capturing with a novelist's flair both the power and crudity of Canning's vision. A few days before his death the Duke had held forth to the Grevilles on Canning's astonishing talents, fertility and inexhaustible resources – 'the finest speaker he ever heard' – yet able to take criticism. It was only when thinking of the future that the Duke's forebodings got the better of his magnanimity. 'I send you the bulletin from Chiswick this morning,' he had written to Mrs Arbuthnot on 7 August: 'In short he will be dead in a few Hours; after having done as much mischief in four Months as it was possible for a Man to do God knows how it is to be remedied.'[17]

By whom was the 'mischief' to be remedied? That was the real question. Wellington had no illusions about his own chances. They were no more than fifty-fifty. He might or might not be summoned by the King. For no man could rely on His Majesty's whims. He had arranged to stay with the Arbuthnots from the 9th. 'But as it is now possible that I may be sent for I think it best to be found at Home.'[18] How many aspiring politicians have not thought it best 'to be found at Home' when a new government was being formed? The Duke was accordingly at Stratfield Saye when a report arrived that Lord Goderich and Lord Althorp had gone together to see the King.

The Duke at once concluded that 'that fellow our Lord and Master' had ruled him out. 'He hates Peel and me . . .,' he explained to Mrs Arbuthnot, 'and he will adopt any Resource rather than send for us.'[19] Nevertheless, having decided to go to Woodford on the 10th, he again postponed his departure and was still at home on that day, to receive the news that Goderich was to be Prime Minister and an effort made to keep together the Canningite coalition. The Arbuthnots were once more put off. Kitty this time provided the excuse. Her accounts were in arrears up to £10,000 and the Duke had to deal with the mountain of papers on his desk.[20]

By the 14th hope was almost abandoned but on the very next day came the letter from Windsor.

Royal Lodge.

My dear Friend

I write for the purpose of again offering to you the command of my army, and I sincerely hope that the time is arrived when the country will no longer be deprived of . . . your high talents.

Always, with great truth, your sincere friend,

G.R.

It is to be noted that Wellington was invited to resume his position at the Horse Guards, not his Cabinet office.

He immediately sent on the King's letter to Peel and after a prompt and most favourable verdict replied, 'I accept.'

He was far from successful, however, in getting his closest Tory friends to accept the new situation. A note to Harriet Arbuthnot attempted to mollify her and Charles. 'I confess that I was very much surprised,' he wrote, 'as I did not expect that such an offer would be made to me.' But how could he refuse? It would mean 'putting an extinguisher upon myself as an officer of the Army'. On the contrary, snapped Harriet in an unprecedented explosion of temper, he had now put the extinguisher on himself as a leader of any kind and even as a 'fair & honourable' man.[21] Notes flew between Wellington and his two irate friends. Possibly he could not avoid accepting the army, but why had he not made it clear that in so doing he gave no support whatever to the Government? He was '*no politician* but a soldier', grumbled the Duke in reply. 'Ridiculous nonsense,' retorted Harriet, at any rate in her journal. The exchanges culminated in a convincing statement by the Duke to Charles on 21 August:

I stand where I stood before in Politicks. I deny that I was ever the Leader of a Party against the Government. That is the Character which Mr. Canning . . . wished to give me, but which I invariably disclaimed. . . . I stated repeatedly that I should support the Government whenever their Measures were calculated to promote the Honour or interests of the Country. I stand there now.[22]

Wellington was saying no more than he had said many times already, and as long ago as the Peninsular War.* His letter to

* 'I don't conceive that I ought to embark in politicks to such an extent as to preclude my serving the Country under any administration that may

Charles and a Sunday stroll with Harriet combined to heal this most painful breach, though diehards like Lord Falmouth and Lord Eldon still fulminated, while saner colleagues such as Bathurst continued to consider his position embarrassing and delicate. 'God knows it is not one of Joy to myself,' the Duke had admitted to Arbuthnot. But did it really separate him from his political friends? 'I do not think it does, or that it ought to.'[23]

Yet it was the Ultras who in fact sensed a deeper truth. By accepting Goderich's offer the Duke had begun a process of detachment from the extreme Right which words alone could never have achieved.

*

'Goody' Goderich was honest and liberal, but fate had dealt him a cruel blow in 1826 when his daughter Eleanor died aged eleven.* Two months after her death he was asking to retire to the Lords in order to save his wife from evenings alone. Tears were henceforth never far from his eyes, and he was crying as he kissed hands on 9 August and again as he haggled over his Cabinet ministers; 'blubbering fool,' said the King behind his back.

His middle-of-the-road Cabinet, with Huskisson as Leader of the Commons, was the right one for the times. Nevertheless, some ironic remarks made by the King to Lady Maryborough, Wellington's sister-in-law, on 11 November showed how little the Prime Minister was impinging on national life after three months of office. His Majesty, reported Lady Maryborough to the Duke, was determined to govern for himself, 'as there was no man in his kingdom capable of giving him advice on any subject'. HM then winked at her, adding for the Duke's benefit, 'that in Military Affairs it was well known that he [HM] had not a Superior!'[24]

If the King was not altogether displeased to have a weak Prime Minister for a change, the Ultras were now set on getting King Arthur back into the field. They invited him to some of

employ me. . . . I never felt any inclination to dive deeply in party Politics. . . .' (Wellington to William Wellesley-Pole, 22 October 1809. (See *Wellington: The Years of the Sword*, pp. 258–260; Panther, 1971).

* He had already lost a son, but a second son was born a year after Eleanor's death. Cobbett christened him 'Goody' Goderich because of his weakness, having earlier spoken of 'Prosperity' Robinson because of his refusal to recognize economic distress.

their northern estates, where under cover of private hospitality he might make a royal progress among the people. The experiment was variously rated. The mobs had assembled right enough, wrote Gleig, but they were cold; Walter Scott felt that the great Duke had demeaned himself by this manoeuvre. Henry Hardinge on the other hand wrote lyrically to Kitty of the twenty to thirty thousand people huzzaing at Newcastle, Stockton and Sunderland, all of them 'strongholds of Liberalism & Commercial principles'. The Duke's own accounts paid light-hearted tribute to his endurance: 'passed through a *very heavy* fire at York'. By 8 October he was *'cramming'* so much into every day that he had to rise each morning at six to do his routine work for the Horse Guards.[25]

*

Not long after the Duke's return south an event occurred to give the Cabinet a jolt from which it never recovered. On 20 October 1827 Admiral Codrington took pity on the Greeks and sent the marauding Turkish fleet to the bottom of Navarino Bay. When the news reached Britain some three weeks later it appeared to the Whig and Radical part of the country that Greece had been miraculously delivered at the eleventh hour: nothing so tragic and yet so glorious as this destruction had happened since Byron died at Missalonghi. To Wellington and the Tories it was the shocking first-fruits of Canning's four months' 'mischief'.

The teeth which had been put by Canning into the Duke's protocol of 1826 consisted of pressure to be exerted on Turkey, Britain's ally, by the three signatories to Canning's follow-up treaty (6 July 1827) – Britain, Russia and France. Turkey was to be nudged into signing an armistice with the Greeks by 'a friendly demonstration of force':[26] namely, the arrival of Sir Edward Codrington in the Mediterreanean at the head of the combined fleets. In vain Wellington, according to his own account, went down on his knees to make Canning drop this clause.

After Canning's death his cousin, Sir Stratford Canning, ambassador in Constantinople, forwarded some further instructions: Codrington was to cut off the Turkish fleet from their supplies, *'if possible'* without war but if necessary 'by cannon-shot'.[27] Thus when a Turkish frigate fired an unexplained shot during a violent thunderstorm in Navarino Bay, Codrington's flag-ship knew how to reply. Battle was joined and the fleet of Britain's Turkish ally destroyed.

King George IV and his brother William, the Lord High Admiral, put their heads together and decided to give Codrington the Grand Cross of the Bath before a scandalized Wellington could stop them. Afterwards the King is said to have repented sufficiently to observe: 'I send him the ribbon but he deserves the rope.'[28]

*

'The Ministers are frightened to death at the scrape they are in,' wrote Mrs Arbuthnot gleefully; 'quite at *sixes and sevens*, some for peace, some for war, and all despised and derided by everybody. . . .' A special gale of laughter was reserved for Goderich, who darted from one side to the other thinking, in Mrs Arbuthnot's words, of nothing but 'jobs & patronage'.[29]

Jobs for the politicians – the ones who could speak brilliantly in Parliament and pull his crumbling Government together – such jobs were in fact Lord Goderich's only hope. But the eternal dissensions in the Cabinet had given George IV a taste for making his own appointments, which did not extend to Whigs. On 11 December Goderich delivered a tearful ultimatum: he must strengthen the Cabinet with such colourful Whigs as Lord Holland and Lord Wellesley. The King's refusal to consider even a taste of honey for Lord Holland brought on Goody's first resignation, a piece of sham decisiveness which was duly retracted with more tears when chaos supervened.

None of the ensuing manoeuvres appealed to the Duke, least of all those which connected his name with Lord Wellesley's. Canning had relieved the latter of his Irish post, and there were now rumours that the King and Goderich wanted both brothers in the Cabinet. Richard, however, cherished no political ambitions for Arthur. 'I hope the Duke will not be induced to go into the Cabinet,' Arthur heard he was saying.[30] Arthur himself reported dryly to Mrs Arbuthnot, 'You know that I have always suspected this scheme of bringing Lord W & me together. . . .'

To bring anyone together, let alone the Wellesley brothers, was beyond Goody. A lethal quarrel had broken out between two of his essential Cabinet ministers, Huskisson and Herries (Exchequer), over a third minister, Lord Althorp. Heads must roll. But whose? It turned out to be Goody's.

On 8 January 1828 Lord Goderich, dissolved in tears as usual (the King lent him his handkerchief), at last dissolved the Government also. Before 8 A.M. next morning, 9 January, a note was delivered at Apsley House from the Lord Chancellor. While the Duke was still dressing Lyndhurst arrived in person to sweep him off to Windsor. The call had come. He was to be Prime Minister.

'Arthur,' said the King sitting up in bed with a turban night-cap on, 'the Cabinet is defunct!'

Wellington made one condition only: though he would willingly try to form a Government he could not promise to head it, because of his 'very peculiar' professional positions as Com-mander-in-Chief. On the King's side there were two stipulations: first, the administration must be a mixed one of 'Catholics' and 'Protestants', Catholic emancipation remaining an open question; second, it must not contain His Majesty's personal buga-boo, the Whig leader Lord Grey. In respect to everything and everybody else the Duke, as he blithely informed Mrs Arbuthnot, was given *carte blanche*. In high spirits he summed up his pro-spects: 'The Case cannot stand better. . . .'[31]

*

How did his own case stand, now that he had been hoisted to the top of the greasy pole? (Nosey would have appreciated Dizzy's famous metaphor if he had been alive to hear it.) Had he accu-mulated any new capital since he returned from the Napoleonic Wars as a conquering hero? Had he dissipated any of the old?

The winning qualities were still as robust as ever. In the words of Lord Holland, an opponent though a generous one, 'his apprehension is quick, his sagacity marvellous, his application indefatigable, and his decision and courage unfailing'.[32] He was still the pragmatist, the typically British apostle of common sense and 'accommodation'; he was still loved for what Lord Holland, again, called 'the ineffable charm of unassuming simplicity'. Above all he still believed in the almost mystical union between himself and the State, a union which in nearly fifty-nine years he had only once ruptured, and that was when he and Canning flew apart like two hostile elements in a chemical explosion.

In correcting a wax impression of his profile which was to go on a snuff-box, Kitty showed that his physical style in 1828 was vital and lapidary as ever.

The Hair grows rather *up* from the forehead, being naturally inclined to curl, it never lies flat and covers very little of the forehead, which is rather broad, open & beautiful. The nose is hardly large enough but from the Eye to the nostril . . . it is too thick, it should be very fine indeed. . . . The jaw from the ear to the chin requires to be rather more square.[33]

Though this uppish hair was turning from grey to white, Mrs Arbuthnot snipped off two locks for Lady Shelley as a keep-sake, one of which was still brown.

His mastery of unyielding subjects like finance seemed very English; from England too came his attention to detail and concentration; from Ireland doubtless his 'devil', as noticed by William Napier, part devilry, part genius.

His devil expressed itself sometimes in secretivenesss, sometimes in cutting repartee, both habits established during his military career. Lord Holland found him 'very close and his designs quite impenetrable', while Charles Arbuthnot, in offering his interpretive services to the Duchess, wrote:

We all know how great his mind is & how excellent is his heart. We have all our pecularities, & he therefore must have his. If at any time or in any way my knowledge of him . . . can be made instrumental to your happiness, I shall feel that I have done a good deed.[34]

If his political and day-to-day designs were impenetrable, how much more his private relationships? Those magpie collections of gloves, fans, curls and *billets doux* such as the Hanoverian princes loved to assemble were not for the Duke of Wellington. He destroyed his private correspondence and advised his friends to do likewise. 'It is a bad habit to keep personal letters. For my part I have not a line of wirting of any kind which is not official.' * [35]

Occasions when he exhibited his other peculiarity, the crushing retort, were no doubt multiplied by the wit and inventiveness of his contemporaries; but the celebrated exchange between the

* Fortunately for posterity the 7th Duke of Wellington acquired a large number of letters written by the great Duke to his personal friends.

Duke and some minor official from a government office is authentic.

'Mr Jones, I believe,' said the official blandly, accosting the great man in Pall Mall and mistaking him for the secretary of the Royal Academy. The world-famous profile froze.

'If you believe that, you'll believe anything.'*

A soldier's secretiveness could be explained on a mundane level in many obvious ways, such as security, a dearth of first-class staff officers in whom to confide or lack of time for detailed explanations. On a deeper level the Duke's impenetrability was part of his mysterious *daimon* or genius and was first enunciated with clarity in India when he hankered after an independent command.

'I like to walk alone.' That was still what he liked. But he had always felt the compulsive need for the close companionship of a few chosen women. 'I like to walk alone' must be balanced by *A Sketch in the Park*, neither feeling excluding the other. In the elegant print of this title (plate 13) the unknown artist has conveyed all the cool, self-contained intimacy of that magical hour in Hyde Park, when the Duke and Mrs Arbuthnot, his arm crooked to support her hand, walked through the crowds, alone.

*

Wellington's first ten years at home had not taught him to speak the language of Tory politics with fluency. Moreover, he remained impervious to the political exigencies of the House of Commons all his life; hence his imperfect understanding of Peel and his trials, so courageously faced. Far less had his experiences given him a taste for the incantations of the Whigs. The words 'liberal' and 'liberality' provoked sarcastic puns. 'Here is liberality for you again!' he wrote to Harriet in 1826, after hearing from Goulburn that the priests were ruling Ireland:

I likewise see that as we are recovering a little in one part, the Workmen in the Collieries have turned out in another to force their Employers to give them 4 shillings a day instead of 3s. 6d. Here is Liberality again which has occasioned the Repeal of the Combination Laws![36]

* George Jones, RA (1786–1869), painter of military subjects including Waterloo and Vitoria. He was always delighted when, owing to a striking resemblance, people took him for the Duke. 'Mistaken for me, is he? said the Duke on hearing this. 'That's strange, for no one ever mistakes me for Mr Jones.' The Duke spoke too soon (Frith, vol. I, p. 57).

It is almost superfluous to add that he was out of step with the famous 'March of Intellect', 'March of Mind' or 'Spirit of the Age', whose tireless tramp through the press and public meeting-places had begun the movement for 'liberality' and swept along even Tories in its train. Goderich, for instance, was according to the Duke of Rutland an advocate of 'the march of mind, and a parcel of mischievous and infernal trash'. The movement for adult education through the Mechanics' Institutes struck Words-worth as bound to create discontented and presumptuous work-men. He was writing in 1826. Returning from his mission to Russia in the same year, the Duke spoke of the 'dreary vassalage' endured by Russian workmen, but added that they were happier than the British labourers, 'with their comparatively refined, but discontented, ill-informed minds'.[37]

Wellington based his antipathy to the press on long personal experience. As Irish Chief Secretary he had several disagreeable brushes with Dublin newspapers in 1808. They had taught him to take a long spoon when supping with journalists, whether Government or Opposition supporters. The traditionally 'bought' Irish press cost the Government under his direction £20,000, whereas a 'free' press in Dublin went either bankrupt or berserk.[38] The extraordinarily unfettered British and French press gave him no more confidence that the Irish as time went on. By the 1820s England had sprouted a new crop of often scurrilous journals – the *Age*, the *Beacon*, the *Satirist*, *Nimrod*. Wellington was soon calling all journalists with monotonous irony 'the *Gentlemen*' and endeavouring to forget their exist-ence.

As for the 'mob' who could not read, but whose leaders read aloud inflammatory articles to their henchmen in public taverns – they represented Britannia at her worst, worse even than the arch-fiend of revolution, France. 'Our mob is not trained nor accustomed to regular direction as the French was,' he complained to Stanhope when the horrors of 1831 were upon him; 'once let [the mob] loose, and you will see what it will do!' The British settlers let loose on India, with their plunderings and 'base passions', also demonstrated for Wellington the anarchistic flaw in the national character. 'Rely upon it,' he wrote in 1826, 'that with all our civilisation and advantages, we are the nation in Europe the least disciplined and the least to be trusted in a situation in which we are not controlled by the strong arm of authority and law.'[39]

*

The Duke was a suppressed introvert, whose record as a man of action showed the brilliant externalizing of all his talents and genius – perhaps the perfect human syndrome. Hence the external man's willingness to retreat, while the man within remained inviolate and unbeatable; hence the resolution to make persuasive parliamentary speeches when his inner self could be expressed only in music, for ever barred to him since the burning of his violin. Sir Walter Scott described his method of debate as 'slicing the argument into two or three parts, and helping himself to the best'. It sounded both dry and boorish. Yet his table-talk, as Scott also testified, was remarkable for 'the sweetness & *abandon* with which it flowed'.

It was the existence of these natural springs which made him a sociable man, despite the more uncompromising qualities. In the 1820s he became a founder-member of clubs like the Athenaeum and the Oriental, both started in 1824, and Crockford's gambling club, 1827 – the last for companionable reasons, though enemies said it was in order to blackball his son Douro.

Though the Duke was so convivial, it is not altogether surprising that the club stories about him emphasize the iron rather than the charm.

'Very well, think what you are about', he said to the United Services Club, who wished to offer the Athenaeum temporary hospitality; 'but if you let in the bishops, mind your umbrellas.'

While the Guards Club was closed for seasonal cleaning its members were enjoying the hospitality of the Oxford and Cambridge. A young visitor from the Brigade threw himself into a chair next to an elderly gentleman hidden behind a newspaper. 'I say,' drawled the affable visitor, 'you fellows in the middle classes do yourselves well and no mistake!' The newspaper was lowered to disclose the face of the Duke of Wellington, wearing, one may surmise, the expression immortalized by the painter Haydon.

*

The Dutch school of painting was the one which the Duke liked beyond all others. Yet Benjamin Robert Haydon, who lectured on painting, complained of its 'vulgar' taste and 'horrid' subjects.[40] What was it that attracted the Duke? The fidelity to life? The recollection in a glowing tranquillity of emotions and sights experienced in 1815? We are told that the Dutch masters stood for 'the practical social application of the philosophy that things must be made to work'.* Wellington too was that kind of pragmatist. He might be an aristocrat himself, mixing only with the ruling classes, especially the landed interest, but the Britain he hoped to guide as Prime Minister was populated by growing numbers of workers in factories, shipyards and mines. Here in a hundred future Coketowns were not a few men already leading a truly 'horrid' life, 'slaves of an iron-handed despotism'; nor did a man like Cobbett find that all was beauty on his rural rides.†

Such was the picture, such the chiaroscuro of lights and shadows; and while many admired, others wanted to upset the quivering balance. Was the restless 'Spirit of the Times' a true time-spirit or a mere errant fashion? This insistent question, confronting as it does every statesman in his day, now rang its challenge in the Duke's ears.

* Kenneth Clark, *Civilisation* (London 1970).

† Dickens, *Hard Times* (London 1854); Cobbett, *Rural Rides* (London 1830).

11

Prime Minister

The difficulties of forming a general staff were caused by Whitehall sending out the wrong men, not by officers arguing about their postings. 'I say to one go, and he goes.' Forming a Cabinet was the opposite. The Prime Minister would say to one come – and he would come and argue.

Peel at any rate must come. In an unexpectedly high key the Duke summoned his right-hand man:

My dear Peel, I entreat you to come to town in order that I may consult with you . . . everything is open to all mankind, excepting one person [Grey].[1]

That was to be another trouble. Far too many of mankind were open to invitation, and political aspirants required delicate handling.

He managed to impress Peel at their first meeting (10 January) with his friendliness and tact, though immediately afterwards he was writing to Mrs Arbuthnot that 'between ourselves Peel is not easy to deal with'.[2] The future Leader of the House had in fact ruffled Wellington in three separate ways. Through shyness Peel's manner had been cold; he hinted clumsily that the Prime Minister would have to cease being Commander-in-Chief; and he himself insisted on having Canningites with speaking talent in the Cabinet to strengthen his control over a difficult House of Commons.

The Duke misinterpreted Peel's craving for Canningites as due to lack of stamina in facing the Opposition ('Mr Peel, whose fault is not being courageous in the H of Commons, wishes to surround himself with all the speakers,' echoed Mrs Arbuthnot in her journal)[3]; and Peel's insistence on parliamentary orators meant further restriction on the Prime Minister's choice of former associates.

The Ultras had gone out with him in April 1827; they expected to come back with him in January 1828. But like every Prime Minister the Duke had to harden his heart against the claims of auld lang syne, writing again and again the letters which began, 'Nothing has given me more pain . . .'. The search for eloquent speakers was a serious matter and brought the Duke up against one of the more disagreeable episodes of his political career.

Charles Arbuthnot fully expected to be a Cabinet minister, since he regarded himself as a member of the Duke's *private* Cabinet when we were all out together'. But he was a non-speaker. As such Wellington merely reallocated him to his old 'Woods and Forests' without a seat in the Cabinet. The Arbuthnot balloon went up. Poor Gosh thought for a time of refusing to serve, because of 'the sneers & remarks of everyone', while Harriet wailed from Woodford, 'I can't bear it all.' The Duke, as he continued to stand firm, groaned that he was risking 'the break-up of the only private & confidential Relation I have in Life'. When the Arbuthnots eventually caved in, he declared that he had got a better night's sleep than for weeks.*[4]

On the principles agreed with Peel, room could not be found in the Government for either Richard or William, his brothers, a situation which the press gleefully exploited. Richard hoped at least to be reinstated as Lord-Lieutenant of Ireland and bitingly reproached Arthur. This publicized disappointment added another brush-stroke to the false picture of Wellington's family harshness.[5]

Plagued alike by importunities and remonstrances, Wellington stood knee-deep in red boxes and green bags, gesticulating fiercely to Croker: 'There, there is the business of the country, which I have not time to look at – all my time being employed in assuaging what gentlemen call their *feelings*.'[6]

He was a dog with a canister tied to its tail; he was 'very unhappy and uncomfortable'; he would nevertheless push on, alone:

* Many politicians noticed the backwash of this affair without perhaps knowing its cause. One heard the Duke say, 'There is an end of health and happiness for me'; another was told that the Duke was not sleeping and looked very ill, and then that he was 'remarkably well' and looking 'quite young'. (Lady Granville, vol. II, p. 10; Colchester, vol. III, p. 540.)

I must work for myself and by myself; and please God however I may suffer I shall succeed in establishing in the Country a strong Govt.; and then I may retire with Honour.[7]

Was it a coincidence that he had again chosen images so often used during his early days in India: the tormented dog, and walking or working alone? Perhaps the same vision thirty years later of a great country hitherto misruled and relying upon him to evoke order out of confusion produced the same response.

*

By 20 January he had assembled his 'strong' Government, or at least the strongest he was allowed by the conflicting pressures of his own party, the Canningites and the King. Cabinet ministers sitting in the Commons consisted of three Tory 'Protestants' – Peel as Leader and Home Secretary, Goulburn at the Exchequer and Herries at the Mint – and three Canningite 'Catholics' – Lord Palmerston as Secretary at War, Charles Grant at the Board of Trade and Huskisson in charge of the Colonies. When an ultra-Tory reproached the Duke for taking Huskisson, the Whigs' favourite, he is said to have replied, 'Oh! he is a very good bridge for rats to run over.' Palmerston avoided self-reproach for joining Wellington by the thought that here was no 'pig-tail Tory Government', no touch of 'the stupid old Tory Party'; and in any case, he had not joined Wellington's Government, *but they came and joined ours*.[8]

In the Lords were four more 'Catholic' Cabinet ministers – the brilliant but opportunist Lyndhurst as Lord Chancellor, the 'fanciful' and near-mad Dudley as Secretary of State for Foreign Affairs (Lord Redesdale made a neat pun on this strange man's job: *Ses affaires lui ont été toujours étrangères*)* and two able Tory newcomers, Aberdeen and Ellenborough as Chancellor of the Duchy and Lord Privy Seal respectively. Only two 'Protestant' peers returned to office, Bathurst to be Lord President and Melville to the Board of Control (India). It was a Cabinet of thirteen counting the Duke, and the score was seven to six in favour of the 'Catholics'.

Hardly had they settled in before all the Duke's colleagues, banding themselves together as twelve good men and true, gave their unanimous verdict for the Prime Minister resigning his post

* He became totally deranged in 1830.

of Commander-in-Chief. As they expected, he was 'strongly excited' against this move though hardly in a position to resist, having himself suggested less than a year before that command of the army was incompatible with the premiership.[9]

*

The day after the Government was settled (21 January) he sat down to explain his selection to the Tory aristocrats who had been left out. Choosing a government, he told them, was not like forming a dinner or country-house party. He needed the best man for the job. His long string of hand-written explanations sent out on top of all his other work was a measure of the special relationship between himself and the race of Tory grandees. At the same time it was a limited relationship. He owed them a letter each but nothing more.

Wellington could afford to be brief with the myriad other cries for patronage. No, Sir John Shelley could not be made a peer; Captain Elers could not be given a government job, nor could the Rev. G. Gleig get any Church preferment; as for the Rev. W. Groves, champion of a notorious female impostor, 'Princess Olive of Cumberland', his complaints of being treated with disrespect got short shrift. 'I know nothing of you,' wrote the Prime Minister, 'nor ever heard your name. Therefore I could feel no disrespect towards you.'[10]

Much of the press, on the contrary, felt they knew enough about the Duke to administer disrespect with perfect freedom. *The Times*, generally under radical influence, greeted the official announcement of his high appointment by rehashing his speech of 2 May 1827 – 'He knew that he was DISQUALIFIED FOR ANY SUCH OFFICE . . . he should have been MAD AND WORSE THAN MAD, had he ever entertained the INSANE project.' Still harder knocks came from the *Manchester Guardian*. The Duke's military talents, it conceded, could not be questioned, but he was deficient in almost every political quality:

> With a strong bias to arbitrary power, and an utter ignorance of the principles of philosophical legislation [a reference to *laissez-faire* economics], and in a great measure of the state of the country also, he combines inveterate prejudices, very mediocre abilities, and an unteachable disposition.

In concert with the *Globe*, the *Guardian* had believed that this inadequate relic would either fail to form a government or having formed one would retire gracefully to the army.

His erstwhile inveterate enemy, the *Morning Chronicle*, however, was surprisingly able to justify the Duke's appointment: 'In possessing what the French call *caractère* rather than *esprit*, great presence of mind and knowledge of men, he might at last prove a leader capable of keeping his colleagues in order.'

*

On 22 January Wellington's first Cabinet dinner took place at Apsley House. Everyone was scrupulously polite but with the courtesy, noted Ellenborough, 'of men who had just fought a duel'.[11] Only a little over a year later one of the diners was to do just that. Already there was some sort of mental duel going on between Wellington and Peel.

The sad fact was that though they admired and depended on each other's outstanding gifts, their temperaments clashed. Wellington had long known that Peel was really a liberal, and a liberal whose hidden instincts put a brake on his party political attack, making him cautious and sometimes dejected. Though as remote from party factiousness as Peel himself, Wellington received no disturbing signals from alien systems of thought, as Peel did, and so could go into action in a state of either euphoria or exasperation but very seldom of melanchony. Peel shied away from the ebullience conferred by blue blood, the adulation of women and Irish optimism. Wellington had no prejudices whatever against the red blood of the northern merchants to whose class Peel belonged, indeed he prized it; but in Peel's case he felt that water had got into the wine.

All in all, he missed in Peel the 'high tone' which Queen Victoria was later to miss in Gladstone. This alleged weakness of his second-in-command was summed up for Mrs Arbuthnot on 7 April:

The truth is that Peel is afraid of the Opposition, his colleagues and his supporters. He is afraid to place himself on high ground. He never fixes his mind on any good principle to be held in discussion; nor on any principle at all till he gets into the House of Commons; and then he seeks for one which he thinks will be safe.[12]

*

The King's Speech of 29 January was an example of Wellington's determination to play the premiership his own way. He forced a partially recalcitrant Cabinet to acquiesce in describing the Battle of Navarino, when the Turkish fleet was blown out of Greek waters by combined Anglo-French action, as 'an untoward event'. There were anxious moments a little later on, however, when Russia declared war on Turkey (26 April). Some said it was because the British Prime Minister had encouraged the Turks by his sympathy, and so forced the Russians to make a pre-emptive attack. In reality, the 'untoward' remark, Canning's 1827 treaty and the Duke's 1826 mission were all minor events compared with the irresistible dynamism of the times, which destined Russia to increase, condemned Turkey to diminish and put Greece into the van of the fight for national independence.*

> *Yet, Freedom, yet thy banner, torn but flying,*
> *Streams like the thunder-storm against the wind.*

Wellington's policy was to abide by Canning's pro-Greek treaty, while neither joining with nor obstructing Russia in her war. Since the liberals were pro-Greek and the Ultras pro-Turk this pleased neither of the extremes. He told Mrs Arbuthnot on 5 April that there were Cabinet differences over Greece, with Peel and the liberals on one side and himself and the rest on the other. Then he added with just the faintest touch of *hubris* (and the gods were listening), 'However the matter ended by my having everything my own way as usual after a *seance* of $3\frac{1}{2}$ Hours.'[13]

Everything my own way . . . He certainly had his own way over Portugal also, where he insisted on withdrawing the British troops sent out by Canning to cordon off Spain; for the Spanish threat had subsided, whereas Portugal was now in a state of civil war. The Regent, Dom Miguel, had usurped the throne of his young niece, Maria de Gloria, and started a reign of considerable terror against her constitutionalist supporters. The Duke held no brief for Miguel and his 'acts of folly amounting to madness'.[14] Nevertheless the Portuguese crisis seemed to him only a fresh argument for returning to the British policy of non-intervention. Sailing under the flag of Wellingtonian logic rather than liberal

* Though Wellington prevented Greece from getting the Volo-Arta line as her northern frontier, Palmerston as Foreign Secretary successfully reopened the question in 1831.

ideology, the troops were all home by the beginning of April.

Inside the Treasury Wellington also had his way, proving himself as his friend Creevey had predicted, 'the greatest *Economical* Reformer the Country can produce'.[15] It was said that when a Treasury official told him a change in their accounting methods was impossible he replied, 'Never mind; if *you* cannot accomplish it, I will send you half a dozen pay-sergeants who will.'[16]

An important section of the Army itself, however, fell a victim to the country's clamour for economy. In this year 1828, the Royal Waggon Train was reduced to two troops, 124 of all ranks and 110 horses. This, despite Wellington's forcible plea twelve years earlier to retain the corps: 'It is much more easy & there are more facilities to form cavalry & Infantry . . . in a hurry, than it is to form Military Drivers', yet 'the most important operations of War' often depended upon the drivers.[17]

In 1833 a Whig ministry finished the Duke's work by abolishing the Waggon Train completely, with disastrous results some twenty years later in the Crimean War. That it should have been run down during the Duke's own premiership is a grim comment on the priorities which political exigency can establish.

*

Apart from the Army, there was only one matter so far over which the Prime Minister positively failed to have his way – retention on the statute book of the ancient Corporation and Test Acts, by which all members of corporations had to pass the 'sacramental test' of receiving Communion in the Established Church. Lord John Russell had tried without success to make Canning remove this legal disability under which Dissenters had suffered since the reign of Charles II. Wellington decided to oppose Russell's bill, now reintroduced, for two reasons. It would disturb a working compromise, since legal indemnities already enabled Dissenters to join corporations without any test; and in so far as the situation was changed it would weaken the Church of England. But the Commons defied a somewhat half-hearted Peel and on 26 February voted for Russell. The Government then beat a Wellingtonian retreat and repealed the Test Acts themselves. Privately Wellington saw nothing much to criticize in the Repeal Act, but a great deal to fear from the way it had been achieved.

I am very much annoyed [he wrote to Westmorland] about our discussions in the House of Commons upon the Corporation and Test Acts. Not less than 66 friends many of them confirmed government Men voted against us; and 22 stayed away. This does not look well.[18]

Nor did it look any better when Montrose, the Lord Chamberlain, threatened to vote against the Government's own Repeal Bill in the Lords. The Prime Minister wrote severely to this mutinous duke, pointing out that he relied on old friends to be loyal, not to seek out *'curiosities'* to form a party against him. If the servants of the Crown failed to support him either he or they must retire. He would infinitely prefer the former alternative and sincerely hoped His Majesty would have no difficulty in finding a Prime Minister more to their liking.[19]

With a mixture of firmness, sarcasm and minor concessions Wellington managed to quell this kind of insubordination. Throughout April, however, there were other *'curiosities'* to cause division in the Cabinet. The Government's Corn Bill was the immediate cause of trouble between Huskisson and the Duke, reported Princess Lieven to her brother, but quarrels were incessant:

The Lower House does not support the Government, the king does not like Wellington, the nation, which expected mountains and marvels from his firmness, in the absence of talent, is beginning to see that he temporizes on every question, and opinions concerning him are somewhat sobered.[20]

Sobered or not, the country had no one else in mind. 'The Beau is rising most rapidly in the market as a practical man of business,' wrote Creevey at the same date but in a flatly contradictory sense. 'All the deputations come away charmed with him'[21] – even it seems a deputation of Coventry silk weavers who, arriving a shade late, were crisply reminded of the merits of punctuality.

Altogether, despite the many *'curiosities'* proliferating around corn duties and currency regulations, subjects which Wellington averred the people of England could never understand, he felt justified at the end of April in writing buoyantly to his friend the Prince of Orange. Though he had been 'forced' to become Prime Minister and was 'not qualified',

I must say that up to the present the Government have been very successful. There is in fact but little Opposition to it. This state of things cannot last I know.[22]

But since all the country's landed, commercial and monied interests were on his side, he hoped that even when the existing state of tranquillity ended there would still be a strong Government.

As for his treacherous health, it was standing up to the strain famously. Dr Warren had told him there was not a man in London with a better pulse and tongue than his. 'I am damnably worked it's true,' he confessed to his old comrade-in-arms, Colin Campbell, 'but nothing will kill me.'[23]

*

Corn, according to Princess Lieven, was the cause in March of intense friction between the Prime Minister and his Colonial Secretary, William Huskisson. That was so; but the pattern of misunderstanding between these two, first seen over Canning's Corn Bill, had already repeated itself as soon as the Duke's Government was formed. After being duly re-elected for Liverpool, Huskisson had declared that respect for Canningite principles was guaranteed by his presence in the Cabinet. The Tories buzzed angrily at what Mrs Arbuthnot called 'a ridiculous speech' and Wellington denied the existence of any guarantee.[24] It seemed that he and Huskisson could not understand one another.

The next crisis followed quickly. The Cabinet turned on 8 March specifically to corn. Naturally the Duke hoped to see his own amendment, which had been carried during the previous session, embodied in the new bill. Instead he found himself in a minority of one. Huskisson insisted on a greater relaxation of the 1815 Corn Law than the Prime Minister's amendment conceded. Sterile wrangling occupied four days.* At last when Ellenborough and Peel between them had extracted a compromise from the two main antagonists, the second-rate Charles Grant made himself felt by suddenly digging his toes in. Again there was a minority

* The Duke argued as before that no foreign corn should be taken out of the warehouses and put on sale until the price of English corn had risen to 66s. a quarter, when it should be marketed at a duty of 20s. 8d., this duty to be adjusted on a downward sliding scale as the price of home-grown corn rose. Huskisson stuck to his original lower figure of 60s. 'If we break up it will be the Duke's fault,' wrote Ellenborough sharply in his diary.

of one, this time on the liberal side, threatening to break the Government. Even though Huskisson disagreed with Grant, he decided that if Grant resigned he and all the Canningites must go too. This situation enraged the Duke. He saw the Canningites as that blackest of political villainies, a party within a party, ganging up against him. It was only when Huskisson was actually with the King in process of resigning that Grant gave in. The Corn Bill passed.

It was not a bad measure, though it did not move far enough to cope with the four years of scanty harvests which were on their way. British wheat had to reach the high price of 73s. a quarter before foreign wheat could be sold more or less duty free. Nor did the sliding scale of duties promote a healthy trade in foreign corn. Rather it encouraged the cornering of home-grown wheat followed by gambling on price fluctuations in foreign imports. It was against all such acts that the anti-Corn Law associations were to be formed in ten years' time.

The Duke's Government had none the less introduced two long-over-due reforms during their first two months. Repeal of the Test Acts was the heaviest blow to religious bigotry for fifty years; while the Corn Law was the longest step towards free trade since Waterloo. The Duke of Wellington may not have led the vanguard; but he was marching with the spirit of the times, and a Prime Minister must be judged by the direction of his Government as well as by the exact plus or minus (often a matter of guess-work) of his own contributions in Cabinet.

The Test Acts, especially, seemed test cases in a wider context. If the Duke treated the Catholics as fairly as the Dissenters, thought Lord Anglesey, there was hope even for Ireland. And that grimmest of diehards, the Duke of Cumberland, paid repeal the most perfect compliment of which he was capable. He denounced it. 'I look on that repeal of the Corporation and Test Acts to have been our ruin.'[25]

The busy time-spirit, however, was not satisfied with measures of religious and commercial freedom. Before corn had been settled, parliamentary reform was knocking on the door.

*

From the word go Wellington had two monumentally corrupt boroughs on his hands, Penrhyn in Cornwall, that county paradise of rotten boroughs, and East Retford in Nottingham-shire. Parliament had already decided to make an example of them. The only question was, should it be through loss of identity or total annihilation?

As usual the Cabinet was violently divided, at one point the redheaded Peel suddenly losing his temper and turning as pale as death. On the whole Peel supported transference of the franchise to the voteless urban middle class. To the Duke this method seemed both unjust and inexpedient. Why should all the 250 burgesses of Penrhyn lose their votes because twenty-five had taken bribes? Justice demanded that the innocent majority should retain their privileges, but as part of a unit too large to be bribed. Therefore he favoured absorption.

The proposition that a body of voters in early nineteenth-century Britain could be too numerous for bribery was a dubious one; even less convincing was the Duke's further objection to the enfranchisement of big towns. If there were elections in Man-chester, he argued, the mobs would riot and bring pressure to bear on the candidates, whereas under the present system a great Manchester merchant could sit in Parliament for a pocket borough, unmolested by his few constituents and free to represent the true interests of populous Manchester from a safe distance.

Fortunately for the Duke no one but Bathurst and Ellen-borough supported him in ruling out transference absolutely. (Even Croker, regarded as a deep-dyed Tory, told Peel he would have liked both boroughs to be transferred, except that it would seem 'too *reforming*'.)[26] So once again a Cabinet compromise was hammered out. By mid-March it was agreed that one of the corrupt boroughs should be obliterated and the other absorbed: Penrhyn's voting rights handed over to Birmingham and East Retford merged with the adjoining Hundred of Bassetlaw.

But the Cabinet had not reckoned with the House of Lords. When the first (Penrhyn) bill came up to them they took pre-liminary steps towards killing it. This in turn had repercussions on the fate of East Retford, now before the Commons. If the Lords would not give Penrhyn to Birmingham, why should not the Commons give Retford to Birmingham? Huskisson felt him-self pledged to *one* transfer at least. On 19 May neither he nor Palmerston went into their own Government's lobby on the East Retford (absorption) bill but sat tight in their seats and were counted with the Opposition minority. Peel, Leader of the House yet totally unprepared for a front-bench sit-in, was flabbergasted.

It was Wellington's turn to be flabbergasted, though not quite so unpleasantly, when at 10 A.M. on 20 May he received from Huskisson what he and Peel agreed was a letter of resignation.

Huskisson, with his fatal gift for doing the wrong thing in an emergency, had picked up a pen at 2 o'clock that morning and still fevered by the previous night's events conscientiously made bad worse. 'I owe it to you,' he told Wellington, '. . . to lose no time in affording you an opportunity of placing my office in other hands' – in order to prevent any appearance of ministerial disunity on however 'unimportant' a question.

Huskisson did not intend to raise a principle, though he afterwards argued that 'personal honour' forced him to vote as he did.[27] His ill-conceived letter was meant as an *amende honorable* for his demonstration of the night before – in reality an uncalled-for demonstration, since the peers had not yet finally rejected the transference of Penrhyn and might not do so when it came to the crux.

Sensible rather than 'honourable' action, however, happened to be what was required on that hectic Tuesday, 20 May. Huskisson had admittedly not been at all sensible. Was it sensible of the Prime Minister to write him an extremely stiff answer?

Your letter of two this morning, which I received at ten, has surprised me, and has given me great concern. I have considered it my duty to lay it before the King.

That afternoon Lord Dudley and Lord Palmerston, Huskisson's chief Canningite advisers, weighed in with suggestions to their friend for clearing up the misunderstanding. Accordingly at 6 P.M. another letter went off to the Duke from the Colonial Secretary, explaining that his original object had not been to resign but simply to relieve the Prime Minister from any 'delicacy' he might feel at having to ask the Colonial Secretary for his resignation.

Wellington replied roundly on the same evening that he certainly did not understand Huskisson's letter of 2 A.M. as offering him any option at all; nor did he understand the one of 6 P.M. as offering him any other option but to prevent Huskisson's loss by soliciting him to stay in office – an option which in no circumstances would he take up. 'However sensible I may be of this loss,' wrote the Duke, 'I am convinced that in these times any loss is better than that of character. . . .'

Huskisson believed that the Duke wanted to dishonour him by making him withdraw his 2 A.M. letter – the obvious solution to the whole brouhaha – while Wellington felt that he must either accept a resignation which had not been offered or lose caste as Prime Minister by begging a colleague to stay on. Today such dilemmas are inconceivable. The Prime Minister in particular does not hesitate to ask even his most tiresome colleague to reconsider a resignation if he thinks it the lesser of two evils. But 150 years ago when cabinets were smaller, individuals more prominent and premiers had only rudimentary party machines to buffer them against personalities, it was perilous to risk ascendancy as Goody Goderich had, for instance, by pleadings and other admissions of weakness. 'I should soon find myself in the same situation as Lord Goderich,' the Duke noted on the 20th; and then he would have to tell the King (sardonically quoting HM's own words of 8 January) that his Government was *'defunct'*.[28]

Beyond that, the Duke had had enough of Cabinet crises and he was not going to look a gift resignation in the mouth. Mrs Arbuthnot's triumphant opening sentence in her journal of 20 May – 'At last we have *hopes* of getting rid of the Canningites' – was surely a faithful echo of her hero's thoughts. If he had solicited Huskisson to remain, wrote the Duke, Huskisson would have been Prime Minister instead of himself.

Therefore when Lord Dudley came round to No. 10 and explained in person that Huskisson's letter was 'a mistake', the Duke, according to Harriet, said 'very coldly it was no mistake'[29]; according to the more exuberant Gleig, he delivered himself of a declaration which reads like a mixture of Friar Bacon's 'Brazen Head' and the Delphic Oracle: 'There is no mistake, there can be no mistake, and there shall be no mistake.'*

And with this triple affirmation the high priest of firmness slipped out of No. 10 and strolled about in Birdcage Walk, just

---

* When the 'Brazen Head' at last gave tongue it said: 'Time is. Time was. Time is past.' (Robert Greene, *Friar Bacon and Friar Bungay*, Act IV, Scene I).

in case Huskisson should make the mistake of calling.

Every hour of the next few days was crammed with interviews, letter-writing and social events, so much so that he had to apologize to Mrs Arbuthnot for not visiting her. 'God knows that I lead the life of a miserable wretch!!'[30] Nevertheless there were compensations. At a Mansion House dinner on the 21st he was so enthusiastically received that his expression changed from one of strain to elation. Thoroughly roused, he seemed to feel as he did at Waterloo.

The last phase in the 'Battle of Retford' came on 26 May when, with no retraction by Huskisson, the Duke appointed in his place an old Peninsular officer who was now commanding the forces in Ireland, Sir George Murray. Out went all the Canningites in a body; in came more military men, more Tories like young Colonel Maberly and gallant Sir Henry Hardinge minus the arm he had left behind at Ligny. Field-Marshal the Duke of Wellington would soon have his wartime staff complete, sneered the Whigs.

Their sneers further unsettled Lord Anglesey, the Lord-Lieutenant of Ireland, who was in sympathy with the Opposition and had on his conscience some over-friendly encounters between members of his vice-regal court at Dublin Castle and Irish nationalist elements. He now made matters worse by trying to sort out his position in consultation, not with the Cabinet who employed him, but with Lord Holland, by now a prominent Opposition leader. He began feeding to Lord Holland his confidential correspondence with the Government.

The man at No. 10 neither knew about the Lord-Lieutenant's communications with the Opposition, nor cared about the Opposition's criticism of his reconstructed Cabinet: 'all the women are with us', the Duke repeated gaily after sitting between Lady Cowper and Lady Conyngham at dinner. His crony appointments would produce more loyalty than brains or balance for Peel's team in the House of Commons; but loyalty was what he felt the team needed.[31] It never struck him, as he went on taking his airings in Birdcage Walk, that he himself had become the bird in the cage. Through Huskisson's clumsiness and his own willingness to walk alone he was caught in a cageful of nothing but Tories.

12

Emancipation by Stealth

By the end of May 1828 the Duke had some right to feel a 'miserable wretch'. It had been a month of incessant challenge, crucial developments overlapping one another or even occurring on the same day. While the Cabinet had chosen 8 May to begin their protracted arguments about the Corn Law, the Commons had selected it to give a vital vote on Catholic emancipation. For the first time since 1826 the 'Catholics' were successful, Sir Francis Burdett obtaining for his phoenix-like bill a majority of six.

An almost equally important decision on Ireland had been reached by the Cabinet six days before. On 2 May they decided not to renew the 1825 Act against the Catholic Association. This placatory gesture accorded with the advice of Lord Anglesey. If this 'irritating and provoking' act, wrote the Lord-Lieutenant, were quietly allowed to lapse, the extreme Catholic and Orange movements would probably lapse also. 'If, however, we have a mind to have a good *blaze* again' – the Duke should re-enact it.[1]

The last thing Wellington wanted was a good blaze, despite the impression he had given when William Lamb, then Irish Chief Secretary, first suggested dropping the act. 'He looked staggered,' wrote Lamb, '& with that air, which he always has, of a man very little accustomed to be differed from or contradicted, & changed the subject.'[2] Yet he had long been considering how to satisfy the Irish Catholics without imperilling the Union, as reference to his past attitudes makes clear.

'I don't like the Catholick question,' he wrote to his brother William, for instance, in 1812. Ireland had always been inclined to separate from Britain.' It is a Natural Wish in every people to become Independent of their numerous & more powerful neighbours.'[3] While himself serving as Irish Chief Secretary he had been 'astonished' to find how far both Protestants as well as

Catholics had become separatists. It was only the religious divisions which kept Ireland for the Empire, by turning the Protestants into a privileged garrison, afraid of the Catholics. 'Abolish the distinction, & make all Irishmen alike and they will all have Irish feelings; which tend towards Independence & Separation.' Catholic emancipation would inevitably lead to repeal of the Union unless there were political safeguards. But safeguards were available. 'Provided the crown appointed the Catholic Bishoprics as it does in Spain and Portugal,' Wellington thought it might even be best to go the whole length of disestablishing the Irish Protestant Church. In conclusion he denounced politicians for not having 'thought deeply enough upon this great question of Ireland and Britain'. It might be that his brother Richard was the person to settle it, 'upon the largest principles'.

Taking this and his plan of 1825 together, it is clear that the Duke had looked facts in the face. He was prepared for almost any innovation except an Irish breakaway.

Peel was a politician who had 'thought deeply' about Ireland. But his formative years as Chief Secretary (1812–18) left an indelible impression of permanent danger from that quarter. Emancipation to him ultimately spelled separation, with all its historic perils.

*

Huskisson's resignation had an immediate effect in Ireland. In the general liberal exodus Lord Anglesey lost his invaluable Chief Secretary, Lamb, and after some scraping of the barrel by Wellington was sent the latter's amiable, twenty-eight-year-old friend, Lord Francis Leveson-Gower. The Anglesey–Gower combination was nothing like so strong as the Wellesley–Goulburn team of 1821–7, yet it had to face a far more acute situation. For a further result of the exodus was a most crucial Irish by-election.

Wellington chose a progressive 'Catholic' Tory to replace Grant at the Board of Trade. His name was Vesey Fitzgerald, his constituency County Clare. In those days a new minister had to face the electorate at a by-election before receiving his seals of office. Wellington was gambling on Fitzgerald's popularity as a Protestant who favoured Catholic relief and a landlord who favoured his tenants. Why was it then a gamble for Vesey Fitzgerald to face County Clare? Only because the Catholic Association had declared war on the Wellington ministry the moment it was formed; war against a Prime Minister who had never voted for (though often privately planned) Catholic emancipation. Judging by the Waterford election of 1826 alone, where the great Protestant interest of the Beresford family had been defeated by a 'Catholic', every Irish contest could now be a gamble. Wellington's difficulty was O'Connell's opportunity.

*

Unintimidated, the Duke cast yet another vote against Catholic emancipation. This was in line with a frosty remark he had made on 24 April:

. . . there is no person in this House whose feelings are more decided than mine are with regard to the subject of the Roman Catholic claims; and until I see a great change in that quarter, I certainly shall oppose it.

So oppose it he did when Burdett's bill came up from the Commons; and his speech on 10 June made sure of its being defeated by a substantial majority.

Nevertheless it was a speech with a difference. The Duke was genial. He congratulated the House on its good temper and went out of his way to regret the disagreement between himself and his brother Lord Wellesley over 'securities'. The search was not for safeguards against the Catholic religion, he continued pleasantly; he personally did not object to their belief in transubstantiation, purgatory or other 'peculiar doctrines'. The real danger, he implied, was Rome, and here he posed a dilemma; Britain could not have a simple Continental type of Concordat with the Pope, because of the Oath of Supremacy; nor could she control her Catholics through the police like many other countries, since Britain was a free country. Yet control them she must. How was it to be done? The Prime Minister wound up with a fervent plea that these perpetual discussions and agitations should cease – 'then it might be more possible to discover the means of doing something'.

Though some people laughed at the Duke's view that something might be done once everything stopped, it was clear that his whole tone had mellowed already.

Part of the credit was due to Peel, whose advice before the

speech had been as sensible as his own position now became illogical. The Prime Minister, he had argued, was free to leave the door open for Catholic emancipation because of his own relatively moderate record in the past, and Peel urged him to do just this. Peel himself, however, felt that he had been too extreme an anti-Catholic to support the Duke except from the back benches, once the door was opened wide.

Paradox on paradox. Into the chamber goes a Prime Minister to speak and vote against a policy which he rather thinks will prove necessary, while over him hangs the resignation of his second-in-command, timed to take place as soon as he has carried out the manoeuvre which his second-in-command considers unavoidable.

Wellington himself felt as puzzled as anyone. Where were those securities? Where was that 'great change' which on 24 April he had demanded to see before he could act? It will be noted that his hitherto favourite safeguard, the Concordat, had been dropped from the 10 June speech. This was on eccleslastical advice. Yet the Duke apparently did not countenance any of the alternative securities: disfranchisement of the 40s.-freeholders, a police state, military completion of the conquest. What then?

If the securities still eluded him, the 'great change' was not a month away.

*

Daniel O'Connell announced on 24 June that he himself, a Roman Catholic, would stand against Fitzgerald in Clare. The news was stunning. Up till this moment Wellington's candidate had seemed invincible. Indeed O'Connell had finally come to his dramatic decision precisely because the Catholic Association could not find a single candidate of the Protestant religion to oppose Fitzgerald on their behalf. The beauty of it was that while the law forbade a Catholic to *sit* in Parliament it did not forbid him to *stand*. But no one had made use of this legal magic until Daniel O'Connell presented himself at Ennis, the county town of Clare, on Nomination Day, 30 June 1828.

Polling began next day. It was exactly three weeks since Wellington's plea in the Lords for no more agitation. An age seemed to have passed since then, turning the whole Catholic world upside down. Every pulpit was a tribune, boasted the nationalist Shiel, as the peasant voters responded with grave and orderly enthusiasm to the heart-cry of their priests. For five days the disciplined processions set out at 8 A.M. and marched to the polls carrying green leaves, green banners or shamrocks in golden wreaths, while onlookers cheered and further coach-loads of clerics came in from all over Ireland to harangue them at every corner.

It might well become open rebellion, warned Anglesey, and he could see no solution but to invite Messrs O'Connell, Shiel and all the rest of the nationalists into the House of Commons. 'It occurs to me,' he added with a temerity which shook Wellington, 'that if O'Connell can force himself upon the House and thus establish the Catholics, it would probably be a most fortunate event.'[4] Two days later, on 4 July, Wellington and Peel were actually facing this 'most fortunate event' in the form of a threat by O'Connell to thunder at the doors of Westminster. Next day at 11 A.M. the great Dan was carried shoulder high to the Court House of Ennis and there declared elected by 2,057 votes to 982. Such a victory against the odds seemed fit to stand alongside one of the Duke's own coups.

By the end of July O'Connell had done nothing about storming Westminster but a lot to extend popular hatred from Catholic disabilities to tithes and rents. His calm assumption of authority in Ireland contrasted with the hectic relations developing between the Prime Minister and the three persons on whom successful containment of the Irish crisis now depended – the Lord-Lieutenant, the Home Secretary and the King.

There was no confidence between the Duke and Anglesey, though both agreed something must be done in Ireland. There was an antipathetic kind of confidence between the Duke and Peel and agreement about what needed doing; but Peel had made up his mind to resign as soon as it began to be done. There was no agreement or disagreement on the King's part because he had as yet no inkling of what Wellington and Peel were brewing, but he wanted Anglesey to resign.

With all these intractable human problems on the Duke's hands, he had also been landed since the middle of July with a ludicrous 'demarcation' dispute between the Lord High Admiral and his Naval Council. A pitch of frenzy was reached in which the Lord High Admiral ordered the Prime Minister to dismiss the head of the Council; the PM advised the King that the Council were in the right; HM told the LHA, 'You must give way'; and the PM, after 'a grand blow up and explosion' with the LHA, got him back temporarily into more or less of a straitjacket.[5] None of this might have mattered if the Lord High Admiral had not happened to be William, Duke of Clarence, brother and heir to the King.

A king, as so often in the Duke's career, was again to be the factor on which his own success or failure hinged. He dared not let King George IV escape from his political control, nor could he share with any but the fewest of the few his plans for the royal enlightenment over Ireland. He did not guess, however, what a large proportion of his future 'fatigue & labour' was to centre around this man.

The incredible session ended on 28 July 1828 with Princess Lieven laying the blame for the Duke's exhaustion at his own feet. 'He will do everything himself: he is in everything, business, balls, and visits – in a word, he wishes to be the universal man.'[6] Mrs Arbuthnot looked forward to 'comparative repose' for her 'worn out' hero. But once more pacing with him up and down Birdcage Walk, she heard the whole story. He had been racking his brains for a fortnight over the Irish dilemma. Parliament insisted on conciliation first and coercion if necessary afterwards, believing in Catholic emancipation as a cure for agitation; he could not dissolve Parliament in order to get a more 'Protestant' one as long as the 40s.-freeholders could outvote every 'Protestant' candidate in Ireland; yet this Parliament would not vote for the abolition of the 40s.-freeholders until he had pledged himself to Catholic relief. Between them they had him in a vice, or at any rate running round in a vicious circle like a squirrel in a cage. The somewhat awestruck Harriet saw exactly what he meant when he said solemnly, 'This state of things cannot be allowed to continue.'[7]

If there was a point in time when the Duke opted for Catholic emancipation, this was it.

Not for a moment did either of them contemplate his resigning the cage to Lord Grey. That would have been putting His Majesty into the hands of the Opposition. Besides, a statesman does not resign twice.

Three days later, 31 July, the Duke of Clarence and the Duke of

Wellington each began a 'break for freedom'.[8] Clarence hoisted
his flag without telling his Council and sailed away on exercise
with two three-deckers and some smaller craft, no one knew
whither. Wellington put the last touches to a secret plan for
Ireland, about which no one knew except the Chancellor, the
Home Secretary and the Arbuthnots. Next day he was to present
it like a pistol at His Majesty's head.

*

'I shall long to hear the event,' wrote Mrs Arbuthnot. The Duke's
Irish memorandum to the King, dated 1 August, was indeed
startling. It warned of demagogues usurping authority and wise
men advocating emancipation. 'A rebellion is impending. . . .'
At this stage the Duke asked for one thing only: permission to
consider the whole case of Ireland. (Royal leave was then needed
to discuss a measure.) In return he would consult nobody but
Peel and Lyndhurst, so that His Majesty would have the control
of this subject in his hands, 'till the last moment . . .'.[9]

The charm of secrecy worked. The King gave Wellington full
permission on 3 August to make a plan for the pacification of
Ireland, pledging himself to do *'nothing'* until he knew what the
plan was. Three days later he sent for his Prime Minister. Just
one more thing. Remove Anglesey.

That was an operation which the Prime Minister hoped to
avoid. Though Anglesey's presence in Ireland was 'very inconvenient', his removal would be still more so. And thinking of
removals, the Prime Minister already had on his hands the
removal of a character even more inconvenient than Anglesey.
The Lord High Admiral's truancy at sea had brought him up
against his Council's authority once too often. It was them or
him. He had a violent scene with Wellington and though it ended
amicably he handed the Prime Minister a truculent note:

> Therefore, unless it is clearly understood between your Grace and
> myself that I am to be *in future* the judge . . . on what subjects I shall
> consult my Council, *I must resign.*[10]

To the Prime Minister's relief he did so two days later.

Mrs Arbuthnot foresaw trouble; but when trouble came it was
from the King, not his wayward brother. Though the Duke of
Clarence belittled Wellington at a public dinner as 'nothing but
a *lucky sergeant*', in private he told his friend George Seymour 'he

could not help admiring the clearness and straightforwardness with which He had conducted himself to him as Heir presumptive to the Throne'.[11] By contrast George IV, while formally supporting Wellington against Clarence, was far from pleased with the minister who had done his duty. This was to prove in Harriet's words 'very inconvenient & troublesome' at a time when so much revolved uneasily around the King.

Meanwhile the Duke's secret consultations with Lyndhurst and Peel were disappointing. 'I don't make much progress with the Chancellor respecting the Roman Catholick Question,' he wrote to Harriet on 10 August. 'He is afraid of it' – though well aware that something must be done. Peel's contribution was a gigantic memorandum, always, it seemed, pointing out difficulties in the Duke's scheme without having any new ideas.[12]

The Duke had proposed to suspend the anti-Catholic laws annually for seven years instead of repealing them at once: to license and pay the Catholic clergy as a form of control; and to restrict the franchise through a higher property qualification than the present 40s. Only the last point was acceptable to Peel. Suspension would be no good, he said, and payment of the clergy was simply another way of recognizing the Pope and therefore anathema.

Both Wellington and Peel were by now working themselves into a lather through the combination of strict secrecy and interminable drafting. Neither would employ secretarial help for security reasons. So the Duke could not spare a copy to show Charles nor time to visit Harriet. 'In short my Life is a Burthen to me.'[13]

In the middle of Peel's own four-day marathon of composition and copying, his brother-in-law, George Dawson M.P., dropped a clanger at Derry by recommending Catholic emancipation to a public dinner of Orangemen assembled to celebrate their victory over the Catholics on 12 August 1688. Himself a convert from extreme anti-Catholicism, Dawson meant well. His rashness, however, had the opposite effect to the one intended. Instead of pushing the Cabinet towards emancipation he drove the north into a Protestant panic. The suspicious King could not believe that Dawson's speech of 12 August was not officially inspired. His relations with Wellington again deteriorated.

*

The 'Universal Man' had finally been persuaded by anxious friends to take the waters during the second half of August. 'The Duke of Wellington has gone to Cheltenham to recoup,' reported Princess Lieven. 'He is looking very ill. Prime Ministers don't live very long. . . .' At Cheltenham, however, he soon felt well, 'but not very firm upon my legs', as he told Mrs Arbuthnot, 'nor do I know that I shall be so.' His legs none the less carried him for a three-hour walk over the Gloucestershire hills, where he kept a lookout for signs of the over-population and distress about which he read. He saw none. On the contrary, eight women and no men were reaping in a field. 'Yet we are over stocked with people; and are all starving for want of work!!'[14]

From Cheltenham letters still flowed out to his ministers and friends, lucid, well-paragraphed and peppered as always with homely saws – stable doors closed after the steed had been stolen, candles burning at both ends. Lord Aberdeen, now Foreign Secretary, was advised succinctly on the Eastern question – 'It is always best to meet Metternich in front, and to answer him' – and less succinctly on Portuguese affairs, which as usual were causing 'the greatest possible embarrassment'.[15]

The war between Russia and Turkey had meanwhile involved the British Prime Minister in trouble with the partisans of both sides. His ex-colleague Lord Palmerston was intriguing with Princess Lieven to get him out of office. Only then could they feel sure that a British army would not intervene against Russia and, incidentally, Greece.

Whatever his own feelings, the Duke had no intention of pleasing the Ultras by going to Turkey's aid: '. . . if we have the strength of giants, which we have not, we must use it with moderation.'[16] The Turks were defeated and forced by the Russians to sign the Treaty of Adrianople on 24 October 1829. Greece became an independent and constitutional state. Portugal's embarrassments, on the other hand, found a temporary solution when the absolutist Miguel received *de facto* recognition as King of Portugal and the constitutionalists withdrew from Europe to Brazil. Thus one constitutional regime was lost to Europe and another won. The balance had rocked and was still trembling. The struggle continued.

*

At Cheltenham towards the end of August Wellington badly needed any new vigour the waters may have brought him. Disturbing noises were coming from the King, who now hoped to get his brother reinstated at the Admiralty. 'But inventions and Calumnies affect me about as much as the Sea does the Rock against which it washes,' wrote the Duke sternly to Harriet, who wondered whether it would not be politic to appease the King on this issue. 'I'll not take a step to get him back,' declared the Duke. 'He must take his course.' Princess Lieven described his relations with the King as embittered and his 'autocratic ways' as causing so much irritation that His Majesty was said to have exclaimed, 'King Arthur must go to the devil, or King George must go to Hanover.'[17]

Then there was Peel. Wellington felt that Peel did not bear his share of argument with the King about the Admiralty, or indeed about anything except his own Home Office. Peel had just seen the King and sent back a depressing account of their royal master on 25 August. 'He has a deeper *tinge* of Protestantism than when you last saw him,' wrote Peel. And as for the Clarence affair, it would need a personal visit from the Prime Minister to convince him that his brother was really out.

'Between the King and his brothers,' replied Wellington angrily, 'the government of this country has become a most heart-breaking concern.' (The word 'brothers' in the plural referred to Clarence and also Cumberland, whose inflammatory letters from Prussia accounted for the King's more Orange *tinge*.)[18]

Peel's impending resignation over the Catholic question was almost as trying. Harriet wanted the Duke to try appeasement in his case too, but again the Duke was adamant. They could do without Peel, he wrote; at any rate they must look as if they could. Otherwise they would have trouble later.

We may rely upon it that whenever the RC Question is out of the way he will be very troublesome; and out libertize the most Liberal. He is in my opinion a very bad Politician.'

At the end of August the Duke left Cheltenham but was still too busy to squeeze in another visit to the Arbuthnots. 'I must work at the RC Question after I shall have seen Peel & the Chancellor; and prepare it for the Cabinet at an early period.'[19]

At an early period. . . . There was to be no such luck. Wellington could not disclose his secret to the Cabinet until permission had again been obtained from the King. Gout, an excruciating bladder complaint and knock-out doses of laudanum effectively saved the King from any political decisions. Wellington tried to fill in the time by getting forward in his discussions with Peel and Lyndhurst, but after a house-party for the purpose at Stratfield Saye which the Arbuthnots also attended, Harriet wrote, 'I don't know that they made *great progress*.'[20]

He watched the operations of the Catholics, Protestants and Lord-Lieutenant in Ireland with equal disapproval. In September there seemed an off-chance of defeating the Catholic Association at a by-election in Galway. The Duke was against even trying; for if he succeeded and thus showed that the Association was not after all invincible, he might not be able to include its suppression in a package deal for emancipation. Meetings of militant Protestants were no less obnoxious. If he were a Protestant living in Ireland, he wrote to Harriet, he would certainly defend his home against the marauding peasant bands. 'But I would not mix Politics with my actions.'

This was a hit at his friends and relatives who were going in for Brunswick and other anti-Catholic clubs. Lord Longford, Kitty's brother, was one of the offenders. He had founded a Protestant club in July to meet on the first Wednesday of every month while Parliament was sitting, and for many months he showered his brother-in-law with colourful evidence of Catholic sedition: accounts from Limerick of midnight conclaves where there was 'little or no drinking' (a very bad sign) and the members arrived in sinister quietness armed only with books and papers; or a mysterious button worn exactly over the heart by a revolutionary leader; or an RC catechism in cypher with key attached.[21]

'Unpardonable' was how the Duke described the Brunswick clubs in a second letter to Harriet:

Will Lord Aldborough, Lord Longford, Lord Farnham and a long &c. [*sic*] remain in Ireland if there is a cutting of Throats in consequence of the Brunswick Club? . . . No! Their object is Faction and nothing else; and there I leave them. . . .[22]

He could not leave Lord Anglesey so easily.

Anglesey was conducting himself 'in a very extraordinary

manner,' wrote the Duke to Peel. He was openly telling the Catholics that his policy would be to give them all they wanted were not his hands tied by the Government. Policy-making in the eyes of Wellington and Peel was their job, not the Lord-Lieutenant's. His not to reason why but to keep order. Wellington told him so in a trenchant letter of 28 September, pointing out that emancipation could not be considered by the Government until the King consented: 'The first step of all is to reconcile the King's mind to an arrangement'; till then his own duty was to refrain even from discussing it, while Anglesey's duty was to protect life and property.[23]

Anglesey was not diplomat enough to see the sugar on this pill: namely, that the Prime Minister had obviously taken the 'first step', and was in fact working on the King. A prickly letter from Viceregal Lodge crossed Wellington's in which complaints were made against leading Irish Protestants.

Agreement was finally reached that Anglesey should issue a proclamation on 1 October against all illegal meetings, calling on the magistrates to put them down. 'Matters appear critical in Ireland,' the Duke warned Harriet; 'but they will come right.'[24]

Matters in reality were still waiting upon the King's gout. Ten days after the proclamation Wellington at long last got his first audience since early August. It was not a success. The King talked, and talked wildly. Anglesey must be recalled from Ireland, Eldon recalled to the Cabinet and Parliament recalled only to be dissolved and replaced by a new one of a more Protestant hue. Wellington did not try to argue. He went home and wrote the King a long, strong letter amounting to a third memorandum on the state of Ireland, apologizing for the pain he must give but entreating His Majesty to look at the question 'coolly and dispassionately'. The Duke was an optimist.

At the same time some of his own coolness began to desert him as he battled with the rising storm. In response to a proposal by Peel to prosecute Jack Lawless, a nationalist leader who was prancing about Ulster along with 'Kelly boys' and 'Sea-side boys' in defiance of the proclamation, the Duke burst out, 'I am for the prosecution of every body that can be prosecuted.'[25] Anglesey's policy, however, was to avoid prosecutions even under his own proclamation, since there were now signs that the wealthier members of the Catholic Association would control the

militant poor themselves. He therefore refused to dismiss two
magistrates, Tom Steele and the O'Gorman Mahon, who had
failed to make arrests during a communal disturbance. Anglesey's
stock with Wellington seemed to have fallen as far as it could
go.

*

November proved to be a feverish month for the Duke on every
front. The high Tories listened to rumours and did not know
what to think. The Duke of Rutland sent a suspicious letter to
Mrs Arbuthnot which she rashly forwarded to Wellington. 'I
wish that people would leave me and my thoughts and intentions alone,' he replied to her wrathfully. 'God deliver me from
my friends! I'll take care of my enemies myself.'[26] Next time they
met it was scarcely as friends, for he scolded her so loudly as they
walked along the Mall together that she thought passers-by
would think him mad; 'but we ended as we always do,' she
recorded in her journal:

> We made up our quarrel . . . and I must do the Duke justice to say
> that, though he gets into a passion for a moment, he never likes one a
> bit the less for telling him unpleasant truths.

This did not mean that he took her advice.

An active rumour-monger was the Whig Lady Jersey, who tried
to draw the Duke on Lord Anglesey. The Whigs, she said, were
under the greatest apprehension that Lord Anglesey was going
too far and would oblige the Government to recall him.

'Oh no!' said the Duke smiling, 'he is only seeking for a little
Personal popularity!' But in fact the whole Anglesey front was in
flames.

The Prime Minister had rebuked the Lord-Lieutenant on 11
November not only for condoning the magistrates' disobedience
but also for staying with a well-known nationalist and supporter
of the Catholic Association, Lord Cloncurry. The effect of such
behaviour on the Prime Minister's relations with the King and on
his many other difficulties was 'quite incalculable'. Six days later
Anglesey returned the Duke's fire from both barrels: it was
entirely due to the Castle's impartial policy in Ireland, said
Anglesey, that there was a growing state of tranquillity, while in
criticizing this policy the Duke had at least been forced to express

his own views, about which Anglesey had hitherto been left 'entirely in ignorance'. He did not wish to embarrass His Majesty, but if His Majesty desired him to remain as Lord-Lieutenant he would continue as before on his just and stabilizing course.

'You are quite mistaken,' thundered back Wellington, 'if you suppose that you are the first Lord-Lieutenant who has governed Ireland with an impartial hand.'

He did not suppose it, retorted Anglesey; but if the King could see Ireland now he would be pleasantly surprised. He expected Wellington to publish his correspondence and therefore proposed to do the same.

This was the last straw. 'Lord Anglesey is gone mad,' wrote the Duke furiously to Bathurst. 'He is bit by a mad Papist; or instigated by the love of popularity.' He showed Anglesey's last letter to Peel, who saw that the end had come. 'I would not answer this,' he advised. By the beginning of December they were looking for a new Lord-Lieutenant.[27]

The King meanwhile had reacted strongly against Anglesey's correspondence – 'nothing but a proud and pompous farrago of the most *outré* bombast, of eulogium upon himself' – but he saw it as only one more landmark in an altogether hideous prospect.[28]

He had received from Wellington on 16 November yet another memorandum on Catholic emancipation. It did not differ in principle from the plan Wellington had shown Peel and Lyndhurst in August, though the author thought it greatly improved as to detail. 'I am quite satisfied with it myself.'[29] Not so the King; but this time he was not just asked to read it. Wellington now required the royal permission to show it to selected bishops. Inexorably, a new stage had been reached.

'I consider your paper very able,' dictated the King, piteously explaining that he could not hold the pen because of gout; 'but on the point in question I need not tell you what my feelings are.'[30] Nevertheless the Duke, on his own authority, could show his plan to the prelates. The King probably guessed that most of them would prove unfavourable, as indeed they did.

On the same day that Wellington received his Sovereign's reluctant consent, 17 November, the Duke of Cumberland wrote from Berlin to Sir William Knighton: 'My faith is *great* in the D. of W. and I never shall believe that *he* will propose to Parliament any thing like *emancipation*.'[31] It was fortunate for the D. of W. that the King's favourite brother was still abroad.

*

The year 1828 was drawing to an end. How far had the Duke advanced in his task? Hardly at all. Trouble was piling up at Windsor, Phoenix Park, Lambeth Palace and, worst of all, in the Home Office. Peel's pledge to resign still stood and the Duke could no longer buoyantly contemplate walking alone. His feelings about Peel now never fell below smouldering heat and were often impassioned. What disasters would not occur if Peel failed to urge the King to follow his Prime Minister's advice on Ireland? Towards the end of the month, however, his alarm was subsiding, after the most cordial conversation with Peel since the Government was formed. 'I cannot say that he will stay with us. But he has taken my paper away to read it; and I am not without hopes that he will stay.'[32] By 12 December there was another hopeful sign. Peel was showing interest in the date for the opening of Parliament (5 February 1829).

Yet January found Peel back on the resignation tack and Wellington exasperated by his changes of mind. 'It now appears that his real difficulty is that I am the [Prime] Minister,' he wrote bitterly to Harriet on the 7th. Peel had told him the difference between him, Wellington, and Canning was that emancipation had been forced upon Wellington by the circumstances of the times, whereas Canning had taken it up '*con amore*'. But it struck Wellington that if he had been forced, it was by Peel. 'He is *the* person who has forced me forward in the Question.'[33] Wellington himself on the other hand felt it morally impossible to force Peel.

Next day he interviewed Peel again. Still no decision. Would he resign or not? 'God knows what we shall do!' he groaned to Harriet on the 10th. 'Every body says *you must settle it*. If I answer will you support me? I receive a reply which renders all support useless.' Peel was with him again on the morning of the 12th. 'I am nicely worsted,' he confessed afterwards to Harriet, though the interview was to be resumed at 10 o'clock that night.[34]

Suddenly all was transformed. Rather than place Catholic emancipation and the whole Government in jeopardy by resigning, Peel had spontaneously conceded that it was his duty to stay.

He brought round what the Duke called 'a vy. satisfactory paper' and the day's 'communications' were the best ever. The King also had apparently come round. When Peel and other members of the Cabinet visited him at Windsor on the 15th he was in 'remarkably good humour with his Ministers'[35] and showed his *finesse* by asking Peel how he could demand a sacrifice from the King and not make one himself. This clinched the matter for the sensitive Peel. It also meant that stage three had begun. The King had given his consent for the Cabinet to take up the Catholic question.

Next day Mrs Arbuthnot received a jubilant note: 'Peel will stay with us. . . .' The pact was ratified in writing on the 17th as if by high contracting parties. The Prime Minister formally stated to the Home Secretary, 'I do not see the smallest chance of getting out of these difficulties if you should not continue in office',[36] and Peel formally replied that he would continue. It was a double triumph, for Wellington's patience and Peel's public spirit.

On this same happy day Peel thought the bishops also might withdraw their opposition; and to crown all, the protracted search for a new Lord-Lieutenant of Ireland was rewarded. The Duke of Northumberland accepted. Anglesey alone was, in Wellington's words, 'all fire and flame'.[37]

On Christmas Eve Wellington had called a special Cabinet meeting which inaugurated the season of goodwill by warning Lord Anglesey of his imminent recall. Anglesey, however, was to bring on himself a more sudden extinction than Wellington intended.

13

For This Relief . . .

Intense political activity and intrigue marked the run-up to the opening of Parliament on 5 February 1829. The Duke's eighty-seven-year-old friend Dr Curtis, Catholic Primate of Ireland, had inadvertently become the centre of a Catholic campaign in the press. A letter from Wellington, answering one of Curtis's about a possible form of Concordat, was pirated and published in *The Times* on Boxing Day; three days later the audacious Anglesey, though under sentence of recall, weighed in with an open letter to Curtis urging his flock not to be too patient but to keep up their constitutional agitation. Anglesey was dismissed forthwith. His recall, however, only deepened the mystery and confusion, since the Ultras interpreted it as a sortie by the Duke against emancipation.

At the same time Princess Lieven noted that strong hostility to Wellington was being fomented in the House of Lords. According to Wellington's own sources, a house-party at Windsor Castle which included the Lievens, Granvilles and Cowpers was 'regularly employed' in devising a new ministry with William Lamb, now Lord Melbourne, as premier. But the Princess thought battle would be joined over the Duke's 'blunders' in foreign policy, versus his domestic success in showing a huge budget surplus: 'This will sensibly appeal to John Bull's heart.'[1] That the real clash would come over John Bull's other island was a secret hidden even from her.

If success depended on secrecy, secrecy still meant grinding labour, as incessant Cabinet meetings to draft the King's speech began on 18 January. By 1 February a draft was ready for Windsor.

Once again, as over the reforms of last spring, the Prime Minister was overborne on a cherished belief by Peel and his colleagues. All agreed to suppression of the Catholic Association as a preliminary to emancipation, and the majority finally settled on a property qualification of £10 for the country free-holders instead of 40s. But even a modified form of Concordat, such as licensing or registration of Catholic priests in return for clerical stipends paid by the State, was vetoed by the Duke's colleagues. They preferred no control whatever over the Irish clergy to control which acknowledged their existence.

Meanwhile the last weekend of reticence was over and suddenly Wellington's secret was out. The leak had probably begun after a council on Saturday 2 February, when two Tory back-benchers were briefed as seconders to the address. One of them had accepted under the impression that he was to pulverize Catholic emancipation. He seems to have eased the shock of having to support it by unburdening himself at his club. 'I came to town on Monday night,' wrote Greville in his diary of the 4th, 'and found that the concession of Catholic Emancipation was generally known.'

Among members of the Opposition there was at first some natural mortification. The Whigs, looking forward to an exciting session hunting the Ascendancy, were not pleased to find that their fox had been shot by the MFH of a rival pack. But only by occasionally shooting an opponent's fox can democracy be made to work. In the Duke's case his achievement was enhanced by the gravity of the situation in Ireland and the hostility of the King.

The Ultras growled ominously when the news of Catholic relief broke. In an effort to draw their teeth, Wellington saw some of them personally as he had done on the formation of his Government. The results were not beneficial. After his interview Lord Farnborough, for instance, merely told his friend Lord Colchester that the Duke was much impaired in health, 'and in a very disturbed state of mind . . . '.[2]

While the Duke still laboured, the debate on the King's Speech began. The press as a whole, apart from *John Bull*, gave Catholic relief a rousing reception. The Whig *Morning Chronicle* thoroughly approved the encomiums so lavishly bestowed upon the Duke of Wellington, and the Tory *Courier* saw in his whole wise Cabinet a reflection of his own character – 'frank, manly and straightforward'.

In the Commons Peel won most of his cheers from the Opposition. In the Lords, Wellington had to listen to a gloomy display by the Ultras, including a prophecy by Eldon that the moment a Roman Catholic sat in Parliament 'the sun of Great Britain would be set'.[3] This luckily provoked a giggle.* But when Lord Redesdale accused the Duke of bad faith he defended himself vigorously. He had always expressed anxiety for a settlement, he retorted, but with equal consistency had stated that 'a moment of tranquillity' was needed, in order to reconcile the Protestants. Suppression of the Catholic Association would produce that moment of tranquillity, and so justify a settlement. The Duke ended on a sturdier and more democratic note, which greatly angered the Ultras:

My decided opinion is that it is the wish of the majority of the people that this question should be settled one way or other. It is upon that principle and in conformity with that wish that I and my friends have undertaken to bring the adjustment of it under the consideration of Parliament. . . .

The Ultras in Parliament, loathing 'that principle' and denying the existence of 'that wish', redoubled their opposition. They were loudly supported by the Tory parts of the country as soon as the shock allowed them to give tongue. 'Miss' William Hulton, chairman in 1819 of the Peterloo magistrates and describing himself as educated in 'a school of stern unbending politics', swooned away and had to be bled.

The next outraged peer to get the Duke to his feet was his brother-in-law Lord Longford, on 10 February, the day that the Catholic Association Suppression Bill came before the Commons. Hot from the bogs of Westmeath, Longford boldly announced that the Government had exaggerated the bad state of Ireland 'to serve their own purposes' and taken the country by surprise. This attack by his 'noble relative' drew from the Duke a new reason for his having opposed a settlement until now:

It had long been my determination, never to vote for Catholic Emancipation if it were not brought before Parliament for consideration by the Government, acting as a Government, for without such

* Taking Eldon literally, Tory farmers, ladies' maids and no doubt others put down the exceptionally wet September which followed Catholic emancipation to 'the Roman Bill'.

support I considered that the measure would have no probability of success.

How could he ensure this without first obtaining the consent of that 'illustrious personage' who was most involved? And when he did receive that consent, it was too near the beginning of the session to make known what had occurred. Hence the only ground on which he could be accused of taking the country by surprise was unavoidable.

Three more agitated days passed and then on 14 February a new leader descended upon England to weld the mutinous but inchoate Ultras into an organized faction against Catholic relief. The ogre Cumberland, the King's brother, had been threatening to return from Berlin since January: 'only order *good fires* in my rooms,'[4] he had twice reminded Knighton, as if to stoke up the necessary heat for roasting Wellington. Once in England his method was to be skilful and swift. He would work on his brother and get the permission for relief reversed. While Wellington was in the House on the 16th and 17th rebutting charges that the Government had been intimidated, and on the 19th moving the second reading of the Suppression Bill, not to mention his attending the 'corking wedding' on the 20th at The Cedars, Putney, of Colonel John Fremantle, his Waterloo ADC[5] – all this time the Duke of Cumberland was meditating his first great blow. It was struck on the 23rd. He got the Attorney-General, Sir Charles Wetherell, to refuse to draft the Relief Bill (though not unwilling to retain his office). This looked serious.

On the same day, however, there was a promising development for Wellington on the royal front. He heard himself supported by two royal dukes, Clarence and Sussex, in the House of Lords, while Cumberland was reduced to complaining that his brother William had called him 'factious and . . . and . . .'.[6] He had forgotten the other epithet. Clarence jogged his memory.

'Infamous.'

*

Wellington was again in the Lords next day, 24 February, to speak on the third reading of the Suppression Bill. On the 25th the bill passed both Houses without a division. The Government's precondition for Catholic relief had thus been accomplished, though its punitive content by now had little meaning. The astute

O'Connell decided to wind up the Catholic Association, since it had done its job.

On the same day as the third reading, 25 February, the Duke had driven confidently to Windsor to discuss the next step – Catholic relief – with the King. Expecting to find him 'very tranquil' and behaving, as he told Mrs Arbuthnot, 'very fairly & well', he was astounded to be received with a mixture of frivolity and hysteria. The King could not have behaved worse. Mesmerized by the brother he loved and dreaded, the wretched man was 'backing out of the Catholic question'.[7] Wellington drove home in a rage, leaving his Sovereign to the comfort of fantasies about abdication and the polishing of his latest epigram:

'Arthur is king of England, O'Connell is king of Ireland, and I suppose I am Dean of Windsor.' He had left out Cumberland, the lord of misrule.*[8]

*

The decisive battle was now on, and Thursday 26 February was a day of resentment but resolve for both the Duke and Peel. They agreed that the Duke must return to Windsor next morning and bring matters to a head. Either the King must back them or the Cabinet resign.

Peel had the added mortification of seeing the first day of a by-election in his beloved Oxford going against him. Having been elected in 1826 to oppose Catholic emancipation, he now felt in honour bound to give his Oxford constituents a chance to reject him. This they began to do on that Thursday, amid uproar and vilification. It said much for the nerve of both leaders that they could firmly face a crisis so sudden and so violent. All minor personal antipathies were sunk in the overriding need to conquer together.

Within a week Peel was due to introduce the Relief Bill in the Commons. But when the Duke returned to Windsor next day, Friday, the 27th, it appeared that the King was not only apostasizing himself but trying to corrupt as many other Tory voters as possible. The Duke found a plot in existence to make the Royal Household vote against the Relief Bill. This was Cumberland's idea, with whom the Duke began by spending a distasteful and

---

* See above, p. 219, and below p. 243, for variants of this theme.

inconclusive hour. Cumberland's promise to interfere no more did not deceive him. The following five hours which he spent with the King were profoundly painful to both. Wellington could not help pitying the poor old man, whose tears flowed fast for his Protestant conscience. (Cumberland had persuaded him he was betraying it.) But as the committed leader, Wellington explained again that he could not retreat. Either he must introduce Catholic relief or give place to someone else. The King capitulated. Dissolving at last in a flood of assurances and more tears, he gave his trusted Arthur authority to make the Household vote straight, and try to make Cumberland go back home. The traditional royal kiss at parting was bestowed with an arm round Arthur's neck.

That was Friday. On Saturday, however, two unpleasant things happened. Peel was overwhelmingly defeated at Oxford, and though a new seat was quickly found for him, this did not heal the wound. And the Lord Chancellor, who was visiting Windsor, found that Arthur's best friend had slipped back under the influence of Cumberland. Full of anxiety, Lyndhurst hastened to Stratfield Saye and had the Duke roused from sleep at 3 A.M. on Sunday to hear the alarming news.

The rest of Sunday 1 March was to be Wellington's last period of peace for three days. Despite his assiduous visits to Windsor, the King was again absolutely determined that if there was to be any emancipation it was he who would be emancipated from the 'Catholics'. From Monday 2 March to Wednesday 4 March Wellington was to stand and fight a series of actions not unworthy of the ridge of Mont-Saint-Jean; each a close run thing and no certainty that in the end it would not be his rather than Cumberland's Waterloo.

Monday began deceptively well with a vote of thanks from the Common Council of London. The Duke had suddenly become their 'illustrious fellow-citizen', the hero who battled against unfair laws from motives of 'pure patriotism and duty'. That at least was true.

The Duke had arranged with the Lord Chancellor that he would call in at Windsor on his way back to London. There he was met by the King's blank refusal to sanction the letter he had drafted to the Household voters, and abdication talk was again to the fore. The Duke spent altogether three hours at the King's bedside with nothing to show for it.

At the subsequent Cabinet meeting which he joined that afternoon about 4 P.M. it was felt that the time had come for drastic, united action. Peel drafted an ultimatum to the King which the Duke signed on behalf of them all: the Government could not advise His Majesty to give assent to the bill for suppressing associations in Ireland (the Royal Assent to the Suppression Bill was due on 5 March), unless His Majesty gave his gracious assurance that he would continue to approve their general measures. In other words, no suppression without relief. The ultimatum was despatched that day, Monday 2 March.[9]

A flustered line from Windsor dated 11 A.M. on Tuesday informed Wellington that the King would answer properly as soon as he could possibly collect his thoughts enough to put them on paper. This veiled appeal from the victim of duress could no longer wring Wellington's heart. When he, Peel and Lyndhurst were summoned to appear at Windsor at midday on the 4th they all knew that the time for manoeuvres was over and it must be what the Commander-in-Chief used to call bludgeon-work.

*

The three found the King drained of his usual spirits but filling up with brandy and water. Peel, who was destined or not as the case might be to introduce Catholic relief into the Commons next day, explained to the King their accompanying proposals for abolishing the 40s.-free holders, banning Catholic ecclesiastical titles and – adjusting the Oath of Supremacy to fit the new circumstances of Catholic M.P.s.

The moment George IV heard the word 'oath' he objected. He had never understood the Oath was involved. . . . He refused. . . . He withdrew his consent to everything else as well. . . . Then, rounding on Peel, 'Now, Mr Peel, tell me what course you propose to take tomorrow?' Peel answered without hesitation. He resigned on the spot and tomorrow would tell the Commons why. The King then asked Wellington and Lyndhurst, with the same result.[10]

'Why! You promised to stand by me,' he protested to Wellington, 'if I refused to entertain the question.'

'Yes, but that was before the Speech from the Throne, which

equally pledged Your Majesty and your Ministers to bring forward the measure and, as a man of honour, I cannot now retract.'[11]

Ignoring the implication for himself, the King retorted that he would look for other ministers and if he could not find any, return, he supposed, to them. After this gruelling confrontation, which again had lasted five hours, the three ministers, or rather ex-ministers, were dismissed, though not without the kisses which protocol demanded. Wellington left with the added comfort of knowing that two faithful friends of himself and Catholic emancipation, Lady Conyngham and Sir William Knighton, were shortly going in to see the uplifted Monarch. Would they be able to bring him down to earth?*

On arrival in London the Duke could not resist giving the hot news first to the Arbuthnots. Harriet was 'thunderstruck' to hear of a disaster which seemed to her final. That the King's conscience should be made the bugbear was really too bad, 'when everybody knows that he has no more conscience than the chair he sits in'.[12]

She may have been right about the conscience and the chair, but the responsibilities of the throne gave George IV a residual touch of common sense which could do as well.

The Duke and his two colleagues, meanwhile, had gone round just before 10 P.M. to Lord Bathurst's, where the Cabinet were dining. To the diners the news seemed mad rather than bad. How could HM possibly form a 'Protestant' ministry? He would surely have to recall the Duke. They were encouraged by the Duke's own confidence. 'Don't be afraid,' he said; 'before tomorrow morning depend upon it I shall hear from the King again.' As he was speaking, word arrived from Apsley House that a letter from His Majesty was waiting for him there. He returned home at once.[13]

With the help of Lady Conyngham and Knighton the King had quickly realized the enormity of what he had done. Hardly had the Duke reached Lord Bathurst's before a royal letter of retraction was chasing after him along the Windsor road. 'My dear

---

* The contribution to Catholic emancipation of Lady Conyngham and Knighton, those not very favourite characters of historians, is sometimes overlooked. Until Cumberland returned to England, the Duke of Clarence could say to his friend George Seymour, 'It was singular every man about the King was favourable to the Catholics.' 'And every woman too,' added Seymour. Clarence laughed heartily (Confidential Memoranda of Sir George Seymour, 19 August 1828).

friend,' it began:

> As I have found the country would be left without an Administration, I have decided to yield my opinions to *that* which is considered by the Cabinet to be for the immediate interests of the country. Let them proceed as proposed with their measure. God knows what pain it costs me to write these words. G.R.[14]

Peel, after a week of the King's tergiversations, read into this typically ambiguous surrender an unmistakable intention to reserve the right of vetoing emancipation even at the last minute of the last hour, if a suitable alternative Government could be formed. Wellington took Peel's clever advice to counter the King's equivocations by making him approve in writing the actual Cabinet minute of 2 March which he had so violently rejected. 'Do ask him,' wrote Peel, 'to write "Approved" upon your letter of [Monday].' At midnight Wellington did so, though he smoothed Peel's wording into a request for His Majesty's 'gracious approbation' of the Cabinet minute, always assuming that he, Wellington, had interpreted His Majesty's letter correctly as the granting of permission to proceed.[15]

The King's resistance went out with a whimper. Yes, the Duke had put the right construction on his letter, he wrote at 7 A.M. next morning from his bed. But his distress, he insisted, was still great and his sleep had been broken by the Duke's messenger.

At 11 A.M. on that Thursday 5 March the Duke called on the Arbuthnots to tell them 'it was *all set to rights again*'. Harriet was relieved; nevertheless the Duke's situation still seemed to her unenviable. It could not be pleasant to hear that the Sovereign accepted the advice of his Government only because 'he can't get another'.[16]

That the Duke suffered inordinately from this latest unpleasantness may be doubted, He was a realist. Only two years had passed since the King preferred Canning to him. And after all, as Peel truly but tactlessly pointed out, the Duke himself had not taken up Catholic emancipation '*con amore*'. In certain moods he accepted the policy of Catholic emancipation for much the same reason as the King accepted his Government – because he couldn't get another.

*

The great debate on 5 March in the Commons was preceded by a burst of excited speculation about the Government's fate. Had the King bundled them out? 'I rise as *a minister of the King*,' began Peel, deliberately killing the speculation at a blow; and in the four hours of brilliant argument which followed, Peel converted the excitement into the wildest enthusiasm. The anger and despair of Protestant fanatics like Wetherell were correspondingly fanned. As the debates on emancipation proceeded, Wetherell was to work himself into such passions of oratory that he would unbutton his braces and allow his waistcoat to rise up and his breeches to fall down, his 'only lucid interval', according to the Speaker, being between these two garments.

Fortunately the Duke was able to take five days' respite from the Lords, for on the 7th he was prostrated by such an appalling cold that he had to be bled, and temporarily excused himself from argument as 'a sick man'. Something tremendous in the way of tension and reaction was needed to make Wellington plead illness.

Back in his place on 10, 13 and 16 March he answered the accusations of Winchilsea, Eldon and the rest that he was establishing Popery, subverting the Constitution and forcing the King to violate his Oath. As usual Winchilsea roared as if he were addressing a mob in the open on a windy day.[17] It was on the 16th, a Monday, that there was a more remarkable development. A letter appeared in the *Standard* from Lord Winchilsea announcing that he had cancelled his subcription of £50 to King's College, London, because the Duke of Wellington was associated with its foundation.*

*

The audience had been profoundly stirred when the Duke, as Prime Minister, took the chair at the opening of King's College on 21 June 1828. Flanked by three archbishops and seven bishops, he had reaffirmed the place in education of religious teaching. University College in 'Godless Gower Street' had decided, after much controversy, to get on without it. So King's College was the Establishment's ringing answer to the unbelievers.

* Wellington was the proprietor of ten shares of £100 each and donor of £300. King's College was left with heavy debts from the effects of Winchilsea's cancellation and those Ultras who followed his example.

Lord Winchilsea, like the Duke, had seen salvation in a new college based on the King's faith. But what if emancipation brought Roman Catholics not only into the King's hitherto faithful Parliament but into his college also? The possibility of this double infiltration suddenly struck the not very bright Winchilsea and he saw it all as a plot laid by the Duke. King's College was a smokescreen behind which Wellington had advanced upon Westminster:

. . . a blind to the Protestant and High Church party, that the noble Duke, who had for some time previous to that period determined upon 'breaking in upon the Constitution of 1688', might more effectually under the cloak of some outward zeal for the Protestant religion, carry on his insidious designs, for the infringement of our liberties, and the introduction of Popery into every department of the State.

Blind, cloak, outward zeal, insidious designs. . . . Such words in the *Standard* seemed to the Duke to put the struggle on an entirely new footing. They attributed to him 'disgraceful and criminal' motives.

He wrote to Winchilsea on the 16th and again on the 19th giving him a chance to retreat and apologize. But Winchilsea refused to apologize unless the Duke stated publicly that he had not contemplated Catholic emancipation when he inaugurated King's College.

'I cannot admit that any man has a right to call me before him,' replied the incensed Duke on the morning of Friday 20 March, 'to justify myself from the charges which his fancy may suggest.'

In fighting mood the Duke also took the opportunity to send a final blistering answer to the Bishop of Salisbury who, since February, had been writing and publishing scathing letters to him, which had created much excitement. 'Have you seen the Bishop of Salisbury's letter?' a friend asked the Duke after one of these attacks.

'—— the Bishop of Salisbury,' he replied, 'I mean to carry my Bill.'[18] Now on 20 March he brought the correspondence to an end:

As your Lordship is so kind as to give me Your Advice allow me to give you a little; that is to reside in Your Diocese; to attend to the Duties of your High Important and Sacred Office . . . and your Lordship may rely upon it that you will do more to prevent the establishment of Popery and Dissent . . . than you ever will do by your Political writings.[19]

Before evening several more notes had been carried between Wellington and Winchilsea by Sir Henry Hardinge and Lord Falmouth, the one a Cabinet minister and the other a leading Ultra. At 6.30 P.M. the Duke issued a formal challenge:

I now call upon your Lordship to give me that satisfaction for your conduct which a gentleman has a right to require, and which a gentleman never refuses to give.

The seconds, Hardinge and Falmouth, had already arranged for a duel to take place at 8 A.M. next morning.[20]

*

The Duke's doctor, John Hume, was surprised to receive a request from Hardinge on the Friday night to attend a duel between unnamed 'persons of rank and consequence' and to meet Hardinge at his house at 6.45 A.M. on Saturday for instructions, bringing with him a case of pistols. Hume duly appeared; and, instructed in all but the names, was taken alone in a carriage through Pimlico, along the King's Road and over Battersea Bridge, while Hardinge rode off to collect his 'friend'. Hume's carriage stopped at a crossroads half a mile beyond the river. Next moment he was astonished to see Hardinge riding up with the Duke of Wellington.

'Well, I daresay you little expected it was I who wanted you to be here,' said the Duke cheerfully. Hume shuddered.

'Indeed, my Lord, you certainly are the last person I should have expected here.'

'Ah! perhaps so; but it was impossible to avoid it, and you will see by and by that I had no alternative, and could not have acted otherwise than I have done.'

The party proceeded into Battersea Fields. Hume carried the pistols under his greatcoat and hid them beneath a hedge. They waited about.

At last Winchilsea and his second arrived, Falmouth apologizing because his coachman had taken them to Putney by mistake.

'Oh, no; it is no matter,' said Hardinge. This was not the apol-

ogy his principal wanted, and Hardinge proceeded to berate the
agitated Falmouth for letting things reach '*this extremity*'. The
party moved forward into the field, but catching sight of some
farm-workers jumped a ditch into a second field, where they
found suitable ground. Hume then loaded his two pistols for the
one-armed Hardinge and almost had to load Falmouth's also,
since Winchilsea's second was shaking so much with cold and the
effect of Hardinge's continued reproaches.

'Now then, Hardinge,' called the Duke, 'look sharp and step
out the ground. I have no time to waste.' Hardinge hastily
marked out the Duke's position with his heel and then stepped
out twelve paces towards the ditch where Winchilsea was standing. Again the Duke called to him.

'Damn it! don't stick him up so near the ditch. If I hit him he
will tumble in.' The Duke intended to lame his traducer with a
bullet in his leg but not to stop his mouth for ever with ditch-
water.

Before giving the Duke his pistol Hardinge unfolded a piece of
paper and from it read Winchilsea and Falmouth a lecture which
drew tears to Falmouth's eyes. The Duke stood with a good-
natured expression during this performance. Finally the two
pistols were in the principals' hands and cocked.

'Then gentlemen, I shall ask you if you are ready,' said
Hardinge, 'and give the word fire without any further signal or
preparation.' There was an instant's pause. 'Gentlemen, are
you ready? *Fire!*' Hume's eyes were fixed in agony on his friend,
whose blood he might in another moment be staunching, and he
did not notice that Winchilsea kept his right arm glued to his side.
The Duke noticed, and instead of hitting Winchilsea's leg fired
wide. With a seraphic smile Winchilsea then raised his pistol as
if in blessing and fired it off into the air. (Before acting as his
second Falmouth had made Winchilsea promise on his honour,
if he survived the Duke's shot, not to fire back. Falmouth had
always considered him to be 'completely in the wrong'.)

Having stood the Duke's fire, Winchilsea now felt that honour
permitted him to apologize for the *Standard* letter. Falmouth
produced a draft apology which he read aloud to the Duke.

'This won't do,' said the Duke in a low voice to Hardinge; 'it
is no apology.' For though the word 'regret' appeared the word
'apology' did not. Hume promptly pencilled in the words 'in

apology' and initialled them, 'J.R.H.'. This the Duke accepted.
He bowed coldly to the two peers and interrupted another
stream of anguished personal explanation from Falmouth.

'My Lord Falmouth, I have nothing to do with these matters.'
Then he touched the brim of his hat with two fingers. 'Good
morning, my Lord Winchilsea; good morning, my Lord Falmouth' – and cantered off the field. It had been a good morning
for a Prime Minister.*

*

'Well, what do you think of a gentleman who has been fighting a
duel?' asked the Duke of Mrs Arbuthnot an hour or so later,
appearing in the middle of her breakfast. The 'sensible woman'
quickly suppressed her tears when she saw he was presenting it
as an excellent joke. The Duchess, however, was so overcome
that though she tried to write an account to their son Charles,
who was in the army, she was quite unable to do so until five days
afterwards. 'Even now I cannot think without horror that the
precious life of your father should have been endangered by the
violent party spirit of an Enthusiast for such is Lord Winchilsea. . . .' But there was one good result, she added. The duel had
won over the anti-Catholics. 'Last week the Mob were roaming
hooting, abusing your father, now they are cheering him again.'[21]
When the Duke told the King about his duel there was high
delight at Windsor, His Majesty saying he would have done the
same himself.

Public opinion was about equally divided between censure and
approval. The Duke, who possessed no duelling pistols because
he had hitherto had no use for them, did not ignore the ill-effects
of this, his first and last duel. 'I am afraid that the event itself,' he
wrote, 'shocked many good men.'[22] One of them was Jeremy
Bentham, leader of the Utilitarians, who bombarded the Duke
with sheet upon sheet of vivid emotion:

Ill-advised Man! think of the confusion into which the whole fabric of
government would have been thrown had you been killed. . . . Here
am I, leader of the Radicals . . . more solicitous for the life of the leader
of the Absolutists than he himself is! . . . . I cannot afford to lose you.

* Winchilsea's family were said to have consoled themselves with the
false tradition that the Duke and his opponent drove back in the same
carriage to London and had breakfast together at Brooks's.

. . . This moment you present yourself in my mind's eye with a brace of bullet-holes . . . in your body.[23]

The growing body of puritanical opinion was by 1843 to get duelling abolished. Why then did Wellington break the rule of a lifetime on 21 March 1829? He has left behind two personal accounts which explain his very individual point of view.

During a discussion with the Rev. G. R. Gleig he said: 'I assure you I am no advocate of duelling under ordinary circumstances; but my difference with Lord Winchilsea . . . cannot be regarded as a private quarrel.' In other words, his personal honour was not the crux.

Winchilsea had done his best, went on the Duke, to establish the principle 'that a man in my position must be a traitor, unless he adheres through thick and thin to a policy he once advocated'.[24]

In the Duke's opinion the modern traitor did not risk his life. Therefore in freely undergoing the risks of a duel he felt he was proving that, far from betraying his principles by advocating Catholic relief, he was obeying the highest principle of public service.

His attitude comes out more clearly still in a letter to the Duke of Buckingham written exactly a month after the duel.

The truth is that the duel with Lord Winchilsea was as much part of the Roman Catholick question, and it was as necessary to undertake it . . . as it was to do every thing else that I could do to attain the object which I had in view.[25]

He had been living, he continued, for quite some time in such an atmosphere of calumny that he had therefore seized upon Winchilsea's 'furious letter' as a heaven-sent opportunity to dispel the miasma. The magic worked. In consequence of the duel moderate 'Protestants' had come forward to remonstrate with the extremists. Men were ashamed at having believed lies. 'The system of calumny is discontinued.'

Put briefly, the gesture of the duel was delivered to extremists in language they understood. This showed Wellington's instinctive knowledge of his wild men. It also showed once again the dramatic sense which lurked in the Iron Duke. With a sweep of his cocked hat he had cried 'Farewell Portugal!' in 1813; he waved it again in 1815 to start the Waterloo charge. This man in

1829 found it not unnatural to scatter the past and salute the
future by cocking a pistol.

*

After the duel Wellington went on to attack ultra-Protestantism
in the Commons as well as the Lords. He got the King's permission, while reporting his own encounter with Winchilsea, to
liberate Peel from the awful Wetherell. Lord Bathurst had
sagely advised him to sack the Attorney-General without
explanation: 'I never knew a reasoned removal end well.'[26]
Wellington took Bathurst's hint and sent Wetherell the curtest of
dismissals. A last fling by the ultra-Protestant nobility was dealt
with less briskly.

'Old Bags' Eldon appeared at Windsor on 28 March armed
with anti-Catholic petitions. Next day the news of this interview
brought hope to those who longed for Wellington's fall. He
himself, while still fuming over Eldon's foray, heard that the
Duke of Newcastle also proposed to invade Windsor, but at the
head of a huge procession carrying an address from the 'London
and Westminster Protestant Society'. This was the last straw. He
dashed to Windsor on the 30th and warned the King not to
receive petitions except officially through Peel: the Westminster
mob, he added shrewdly, would turn their pilgrimage into an
attack on Lady Conyngham.

At first the King had tried his usual tactic of changing the
subject. Wellington listened patiently, letting him ramble on for
an hour about irrelevancies; then he firmly brought the conversation back to the Westminster petition. He came away with a
royal veto on Newcastle's project. Later on that same day the
Commons passed the Catholic Relief Bill by 320 votes to 142, a
majority of 178. For him and Peel it had been a good day's work.

On the 31st the Duke moved the bill's first reading in the House
of Lords, allowing an interval of only one day before he opened
the debate on the second reading on 2 April. Speaking slowly,
with folded arms and no notes, he was forceful but not vehement,
and entirely free from his usual hesitations. His speech contained
the most moving and effective passage he ever delivered. He had
described Ireland as on the brink of civil war and was appealing
to noble lords who argued that he could put down the Catholic
Association by means other than concession. By force.

But, my Lords, even if I had been certain of such means of putting it down, I should have considered it my duty to avoid those means. I am one of those who have probably passed a longer period of my life engaged in war than most men, and principally in civil war; and I must say this, that if I could avoid by any sacrifice whatever, even one month of civil war in the country to which I was attached, I would sacrifice my life in order to do it.

The 'Great Captain's' simple, sincere and direct plea for peace went straight to the nation's heart. He wound up on 4 April with a good-tempered reminder to noble lords that even as a soldier his services had not always been approved; that nevertheless

I rendered them through good repute and through bad repute, and that I was never prevented from rendering them by any cry which was excited against me at the moment.

Nor would he be prevented now.

Catholic relief obtained a majority of 105, 217 voting for it and 112 against. Wellington had predicted a 'very substantial' majority, meaning about 50; the Ultras told the King it would be only 5. The size of the majority stunned everyone. 'Really it seems like a dream!' wrote the generally unimpressionable Ellenborough. Agitation would end in England and tranquillity dawn in Ireland. But Ellenborough's first thought was, 'This will quiet Windsor.' Princess Lieven foresaw the same triumphant sequence of everybody submitting to the Catholic bill. 'The king, therefore, naturally submits also. Amen.'[27] It was not quite Amen for Cumberland.

The result of the second reading on Windsor was an outburst of royal passion which tried even the Duke's monumental patience. Aberdeen reported on the 6th that the King in his paroxysms talked of a disgraced Parliament and a revolutionary people – Wellington's name he did not deign to mention. Wellington's corresponding anger with the King took Mrs Arbuthnot's breath away.

He abused him most furiously, said he was the worst man he ever fell in with in his whole life, the most false, the most ill-natured, the most entirely without one redeeming quality. . . .[28]

But when the day of the great Protestant procession came, only four carriages rolled down to Windsor, containing four Ultra peers with addresses, and the Westminster organizer. The Duke had ordered Sir Richard Birne, the police chief, to stand by and Peel was waiting to accept the petition on the King's behalf, which he duly did. Lord Skelmersdale, one of the Ultras, heard perhaps not for the first time that his Majesty would retire to a spa in Hanover, his brother William would make a good Roman Catholic king, and they could send for Dr Doyle (the famous Catholic bishop) to educate Princess Victoria.[29]

Next day, 10 April, the Prime Minister moved the third reading of the Relief Bill. He expressed gratitude to the Tories who had stuck to him and warmly thanked the Whigs: 'I had no right to expect the cordial and handsome support they have given me.' Then he congratulated everybody on having brought the measure to its final stage and confidently awaited the vote. The House divided: Contents, 213; Not Contents, 109. Majority, 104. Running into Lord Dungannon, a prominent Whig, outside the Chamber, the Duke said gaily, 'Well, I said I would do it, and I have done it handsomely, have I not?' The gaiety was short-lived.

The Royal Assent was extracted rather than given on 13 April and among the 109 Not Contents were men who had been the Duke's close friends. When he went down to the House on the 13th his cold had returned in force. He left the Chamber with his cloak drawn tightly round him. 'His anxious wish, I may say determination,' Mrs Arbuthnot had written with her usual percipience towards the end of March, 'is to draw the Tories round him again. . . .'[30]

One penalty of being a reformer was having to go out into the cold. The full impact of Wellington's party problem, however, was yet to be felt.

There were also the long-term effects on Ireland. Catholic emancipation was not a cure-all. In 1828 the Duke had written about the need to discover 'a remedy for the existing Evils,'[31] – evils in the plural. High among those evils were absentee landlords, inability of the peasants to 'come on the market' for lack of money, dependence on the potato as a food, insecurity of land tenure and the labour system. The Emancipation Act could do no more than make sure that Catholic voices were heard at Westminster to air these grievances.

Nor did the Duke believe that the actual form of legislation he had had to adopt in 1828 was the best possible. He once called

Catholic emancipation a 'cant term', because it implied that the Catholics in Ireland could have freedom without giving securities. In time to come he would often lament what seemed to him a lost opportunity for stabilizing the country, through salaried clergy and a modified Concordat with the Vatican. It is more than doubtful whether the Irish hierarchy would have accepted his proposals; it is certain that even if they had, the demand for repeal of the Union would not have been inhibited. The shriek of famine would have drowned the whisper of the stipend. Nevertheless there was civilized wisdom in the Duke's ideas not found elsewhere.*

*

For a long, golden moment national thankfulness flooded all party bounds, giving Wellington a lustre which some thought outshone Waterloo. The endearing Duke of Sussex who, with the late Duke of Kent, represented the royal left wing, said his laurels had changed into olive, a change into greater glory. There was a deep conviction that where so many statesmen had tried and failed none but the great Duke could have steered the country into its religious haven. 'He is the only Man living,' wrote Colin Campbell to Kitty, 'who could have carried the measure, & he has saved his Country from a Civil War by his firmness & manliness.'[32] Wellington's vast prestige, combined with his vigour and courtesy in the lengthy debates, undoubtedly won over many waverers. Princess Lieven put his personal vote in the great Lords debate at 150. He also commanded an army of hero-worshippers outside Parliament, among whom was numbered the thirteen-year-old Charlotte Brontë. Never could she forget Papa opening his newspaper and reading aloud the drama of the debate:

> . . . the anxiety was almost dreadful with which we listened to the whole affair; the opening of the doors; the hush; the royal dukes in their

---

* Apparently because of the Oath of Supremacy, the Duke had turned against paying the Catholic clergy by 1828. 'I was at one time bit by this mania', he wrote scornfully to Lord Redesdale on 9 August 1844 (MSS.). But he always believed in some kind of Concordat. (See below, pp. 496-7). As for the hierarchy, Miss Edgeworth heard that Bishop Doyle, at least, was won over to a paid Catholic clergy by the Rev. Sydney Smith's enticing picture of a clerical nest-egg in every bank. 'Oh, Mr Smith, you do have a way of putting things.' (Edgeworth, vol. II, p. 304).

robes and the great Duke in green sash and waistcoat; the rising of all
the peeresses when he rose; the reading of his speech – papa saying his
words were like precious gold; and lastly the majority – in favour of the
Bill.

A few months later, on 28 July, Charlotte began writing a
magical tale called 'The Search After Hapiness [*sic*]', in which it
transpired that happiness depended on living under the benign
rule of a great 'military King' – the Duke of Wellington.

Charles Greville, as Clerk to the Council, was aware above all
of the Duke's unique service in converting the King. Having
noted that 'extra-ordinary circumstances' had already raised him
higher than any subject in modern times, and that he 'dictates'
to his Cabinet, Greville went on:

> He can address the King in a style which no other Minister could
> adopt. He treats with him as with an equal, and the King stands com-
> pletely in awe of him. . . . The greatest Ministers have been obliged to
> bend to the King, or the aristocracy, or the Commons, but he com-
> mands them all.[33]

Or as Lord Clarendon explained cynically to Macaulay, the
Whig M.P. and famous historian, the Duke had only to say, 'My
Lords! Attention! Right about face! Quick march!' and the
troops would obey.

There were humbler English worthies whose trust in their
great Duke was rudely shaken. The most serious charge against
him was launched by Conservative England: he had callously
turned his coat, taken his party by surprise and betrayed those
who trusted him. Even Sir Herbert Maxwell, his Conservative
biographer who wrote seventy years later, thought that for the
sake of party unity and his own reputation he ought to have
resigned and left the job to its natural executors, the Whigs.

From Wellington's angle such a view gets too far away from
the centre of his web, the King. Wellington knew that George IV
would never take Grey as Prime Minister because of his support
for Queen Caroline. To resign would be to force a constitutional
crisis and, instead of splitting the party, split the country. He
could not do it.

Taking his friends by surprise had been largely unavoidable
and was not the real weakness of his policy. Wellington had been
taken by surprise himself. He had gone on voting against

Catholic emancipation up to 1828 in the belief that the volcano would remain dormant until the question of safeguards was settled. The voters of Clare took him by surprise and forced him to adopt their timetable.

From a wider angle, there is always an element of betrayal in a bi-partisan policy. Yet to argue that Conservatives must act only conservatively and Radicals radically is to destroy the balance between opposition and co-operation on which the British party system rests.

The Duke's contemporaries, both Irish and English, realized the difficulties with which he contended, especially his 'infamous army' of half-convinced Tory recruits, and honoured him accordingly. There was a public meeting on 6 May at the London Tavern to celebrate 'the heroes of Catholic Emancipation' – Peel, Anglesey and 'many other illustrious names both living and dead', but pre-eminently the Duke. Nationalists like a Grattan and a Curran, Radicals like Hunt and Burdett were the most vocal sponsors. A Wellington Testimonial Committee was set up in Dublin for the addition of bas-reliefs to the Wellington obelisk in Phoenix Park.* Not even the name most prominent in previous battles against the Government was missing from the list of subscribers – Daniel O'Connell Esq., M.P.

A change was detectable in the Duke's own feelings also. Quoting his great speech, Ireland was the country to which he was 'attached' in more than one sense. Why should he not revert to Anglo-Irish custom and spend part of the year (and of his money) there? His brother Richard was trying to sell the last of the family estates. After his great victory the Duke began negotiating with Richard's agent to buy them. Perhaps he too might share some of 'the peace, the happiness and the prosperity' which, in his speech, he hoped he had brought to the country of his birth.†

---

* These were not completed until 1861.

† Lord Clifden was so 'exhilarated' by the King's Speech that he ordered his agent in Ireland to buy a large landed property to add to his other possessions. 'This is a story worth telling as the act of an old Irishman,' wrote Lord Ashley to the Duke in giving this good news. (*Wellington MSS.*, 9 February 1829.)

14

. . . Little Thanks

The Duke expected to reap the benefits of his triumph in a firmer political position. For a time he did so, though the immense international prestige which Princess Lieven had predicted for whoever carried Catholic emancipation was not always visible. When young Dr Wiseman, the future Cardinal, illuminated the front of the English College at Rome with the mystic words '*Emancipazione Cattolica*', the natives stared up in deep perplexity.

At home, however, the Duke's Government was seen to be a reforming one, and enthusiasts like Jeremy Bentham and Robert Owen (who offered him a socialist plan to recast the whole of his domestic and foreign policy)[1] rightly assumed that he had not exhausted his appetite for change. 'Head it, Duke!' cried Bentham, sending him the prospectus of a new Law Reform Association drawn up by himself in magnificent Gothic lettering and even more Gothic language. Though Jeremy got no more out of his hero than the usual 'Compts.' and thanks, his high hopes were not unreasonable. For Catholic emancipation had been quickly followed by another historic reform.

The creation of the Metropolitan Police force was in every sense the child of Peel's foresight and labour. As Home Secretary he had worked for years at penal reform as well as at the police. Nevertheless Wellington's call for an absolutely new kind of police in 1821 must not be forgotten, nor the active support which as Prime Minister he gave to Peel in 1829. He introduced the Metropolitan Police Bill himself in the Lords in June, after Peel had done the same in the Commons on 15 April, just two days after Catholic emancipation became law.

'In one parish, St Pancras,' said the Duke, 'there are now no fewer than eighteen different establishments . . . not one of which has any communication with another. The consequence is that the watchmen of one district are content with driving thieves from their own particular neighbourhood into the adjoining district.' This ludicrous beating of game which was never brought down represented only one aspect of an utterly inefficient and often corrupt system, if system it could be called. Leaving out the City which managed its own affairs, less than 350 men protected the million and more inhabitants of London. Some of these were parish constables, some special constables, some watchmen. Their duties were defined by a series of statutes, but lack of personnel as well as total deficiency in organization prevented them from being carried out. Crime was annually increasing.*

For the first time in the history of Parliament a Select Committee had reported (July 1828) in favour of a single streamlined police force for the metropolis, under the Home Office. Peel's bill, based on this report, was passed on 19 June 1829. Within eight weeks the two Police Commissioners had recruited their new force, with headquarters at Scotland Yard.

The Duke well understood, though he did not share, the ingrained British fear, not only among the criminal classes, of a centralized police force. It smacked of arbitrary power. In a year's time the London mob were calling them 'raw lobsters' in contrast to their hard-boiled scarlet colleagues, for they hated the blue-uniformed police even more than the red-coats. But the public christened them 'bobbies', a sure sign of incipient warmer feelings. As for the Duke, by November 1829 he was already congratulating Peel on the entire success of the new force. 'It is impossible to see any thing more respectable.'[2]

The same could not be said of the militant Irish. A habit of violence was not easy to break. Moreover the Government were to blame for alienating O'Connell. Instead of admitting him to Parliament forthwith, they compelled him to stand again under the new Catholic laws. He denounced the mean spirit of the Ascendancy and Union, and swept in unopposed. As Creevey said, the Beau was immortalized by his measure apart from this 'one damned thing'. In July and August proclamations were issued against Orangemen and Ribbonmen respectively.

* The figures Peel sent to Wellington were: 2,539 committals in 1822, 2,902 in 1825, 3,516 in 1828.

Nevertheless Wellington's reward from Catholic emancipation was substantial. Ireland as a whole was quieter at the end of 1829 than it had been for two years, and the Duke was studying a hopeful thirty-page memorandum from his friend Maurice Fitzgerald, the Knight of Kerry, on how to cure Irish unemployment through more public works and less absenteeism. Everyone who could afford it left Ireland for part of each year, wrote Fitzgerald; perhaps it was his eloquence which gave Wellington the idea of travelling in the opposite direction, to acquire his brother's estates.

He felt calm and confident enough about Ireland that autumn to answer some unusually crazy advice from wellwishers with perfect good temper – a suggestion for silencing all Irish political meetings by pensioning off five leading Orangemen and five leading Catholic orators at £2,000 per annum each; and a request from Valentine Blake of Galway to be created a peer, descended as he was from a Knight of King Arthur's Round Table and willing as he would be to serve the modern 'King Arthur' in a similar capacity.

*

Notwithstanding Wellington's successes the session had ended on 24 June with lugubrious feelings among his friends. Without his legendary good luck, part of which consisted in the Opposition's chronic internal disputes, Ellenborough did not believe that the Government could survive. Sir Henry Hardinge reckoned that in losing the Canningites and Brunswickers (Ultras) the Duke had forfeited at least fifty parliamentary votes. There were continual discussions about how to gain an access of strength. It was hoped that Lord Rosslyn, a Whig, would bring over some fellow Whigs when he consented to enter the Cabinet. Nobody followed him. Nor could the Duke 'coquette' – to quote Hardinge – with the Whig leader himself, Lord Grey, because of the King's personal animosity.

With his deep king-consciousness, Wellington still laid the ultimate blame for his Government's weakness on the two royal brothers, King George and Duke Ernest. 'Dearest Ernest' was generally understood to have sworn not to leave his brother's side until he had turned out the present minister. 'He *keeps the pot boiling*,' said the Duke ominously to Harriet; but she stoutly refused to believe that Cumberland would ever get the King actually to dismiss Wellington. 'I don't believe the King *dares*.'[3]

*

The cloying fondness at Stratfield Saye was hardly more attractive to the Duke than the *froideur* at Court. His suffocating post-emancipation cold had driven him down to the country for the latter part of April. Here Kitty welcomed him with what she doubtless considered a restful house-party, but which provoked bitter complaints. The house was full of company, he informed Harriet, not one of whom was known to him except his brother Gerald. 'The Duchess has certainly the most extraordinary fancy in the selection of her acquaintances.' A whiskered lieutenant, two or three officers on half-pay, a whiskered Pole relative (of his own), a lady called 'the Guinivere' and her sister. 'This is what is called Repose in the Country.' Similar criticisms were made four or five months later, when he found staying in his house Captain and Mrs Browne 'as usual', Mrs Browne's sister, Mrs Browne's child, and 'a Miss Somebody'.[4]

The fact that Kitty was First Lady had made no difference to her ideas of personal *chic*, though her niece Kate Foster, the Duke's secretary Algy Greville and her son Douro, all of whom loved her dearly, combined to reform her. Kate had written to Kitty in January:

My darling Mother, have you had your spectacles made to fit . . . if one eye was in its right place the other must necessarily be askew, till they were set a right distance from each other.[5]

Algy followed in March with a brief but urgent plea to 'brush up for the 23rd, for you will have a *deal* to go through'. Five months later Douro was having a go at Mama's head-dress:

. . . you may be sure I should never have found fault with it if I did not know *for certain* that the person whom you most wish to please is extremely hurt at your dress being inconsistent with and beneath the station you hold in the world; it was not Dr Hume who found fault with your headdress but himself.[6]

Douro added that he had hoped his mother would have allowed the lady who dressed better than anyone else in London and who was a special friend of hers, to choose a really becoming headdress for her. This would have saved him from making the present unwelcome approach.

The well-dressed lady to whom Douro referred was almost certainly Kitty's protégée of many years ago, Miss Elizabeth Hume. Douro's passion for the charming Elizabeth blossomed again when he returned home in 1829 from a long foreign tour.* During this and the following year society understood that they might marry, Lord Grey writing to Princess Lieven and Creevey to his step-daughter about Douro's engagement to 'the surgeon's daughter'. Then came what seemed the characteristically sensible intervention by the Duke.

'Ah! rather young, Douro, are you not – to be married? suppose you stay till the year is out, and if then you are in the same mind, it's all very well.'[7]

Douro had celebrated his twenty-third birthday only a fortnight before (6 February). He took his father's hint without umbrage, for according to Mrs Arbuthnot the relations between father and sons were at this time extremely good. 'I think they promise to be great comforts to the Duke,' she wrote, 'for they are both amiable & seem very fond of him.'[8] Perhaps it was a comfort to the Duke that Douro never married the doctor's daughter. He was soon falling in and out of love again with his usual volatility. Whether the result was a comfort to Douro is more doubtful. His long, blighted romance with Elizabeth Hume seems to have drained him of any constancy he may have possessed. His later marriage to Lady Elizabeth Hay was exactly what 'they' desired, just as 'they' had been enchanted by Arthur's second proposal to Kitty. Douro's marriage, being childless, was less blessed than that of his parents.

*

Meanwhile a political upheaval in France during July 1829 caused the Duke more anxiety than the prospect of a surgeon's girl as daughter-in-law. Charles x (formerly Artois) dismissed his moderate minister, M. de Martignac, and sent to England for the French ambassador, Prince Jules de Polignac, like himself a

* A letter from Douro to his mother written on 16 April 1829 in Rome shows him aching to fall in love again. Not being in love at the moment, he writes, he is in the kind of pain which an Italian vine feels when it runs along the ground unable to find a tree to rest upon. (*Wellington MSS.*)

reactionary Ultra, to take his place. Polignac's arrival provoked
an immediate outcry in France. It was a plot by Wellington and
Metternich! In England Lord Grey had to assure even the usually
well-informed Princess Lieven that 'the Duke of Wellington had
nothing to do with it'.[9] Wellington himself said the same thing to
Lady Jersey.

With enormous relief and pleasure the Duke retired towards
the middle of July to a newly discovered paradise on the Kent
coast. He was looking ill again and no wonder. His timetable had
latterly been as crammed with engagements as the Downs with
shipping. Just before the session ended he told Sir William
Knighton that he was now rising at six o'clock every morning and
a call from him at that hour would be very welcome.[10] (Whether
the invitation was welcome to Knighton is not known.)

Walmer Castle, lying between Deal and Dover and offering on
clear days a stirring panorama of sea-going traffic, was the
traditional home of the Lords Warden of the Cinque Ports. Lord
Liverpool had been the Warden until his death on 4 December
1828. On that very day Wellington, in sending George IV the news,
added that he would like the vacant office of Warden since it was
'of great influence and power but without any salary'.[11] He was
appointed on 20 January 1829. But it was the beauty of Walmer
rather than the power which entranced him for the rest of his life.
He wrote to Harriet on 13 July just before her first visit; 'This
place is delightful; very well furnished; and in a tolerable state of
repair for this summer. Everything will be ready for your reception on Friday.' The Arbuthnots were as delighted as he hoped.

Today Walmer Castle is still, in Harriet's words, 'the most
charming marine chateau',[12] though the sea has receded somewhat, leaving a wider stretch of grass between the ramparts and
the beach. But the pew close to the pulpit where Wellington used
to sit in Old St Mary's Norman church is still pointed out, as is
the yew tree where he tied up his horse. The plantations where he
walked with Mrs Arbuthnot and then with Lady Salisbury, and
after her with another Lady Salisbury, are still as leafy below
and as sliced by the wind above as they were over a century
ago.

It was at Walmer that the Duke found most time to indulge his
lifelong affection for children, one of his great charms.

That there was mutual affection cannot be doubted, nor that it was robust and on his side full of humanity. He not only delighted in rosy children with bounding energy, but also visited the victims of measles and whooping cough or sat beside the many small invalids wasting from consumption, holding their hot hands and sending meticulous reports of progress to their parents on holiday. Any child in distress could count upon the Duke. A tearful boy who had to leave his pet toad behind when sent away to school received regular notes from Field-Marshal the Duke of Wellington to say that the toad was well; a girl despised for snob reasons by her fellow pupils at a smart Kensington day-school was presented with a bouquet of flowers from F.M. the D. of W. who had driven up personally in his carriage to deliver them.

For the families staying at Walmer there were endless schemes to amuse: cushion-fights with 'Mr Duke' for Oggy and Bo Grosvenor when there was no grandmother to object – 'We had the cushion affair whenever she was not there; and when she was expected the cushions were always put in order' – football or chases round the ramparts – 'I'll catch ye! – ha, ha, I've got ye!' – games in his armchair for a younger family – 'They climb upon me and make toys of my Hair and my fingers!' – drinks of tea from his breakfast saucer, the seals off his used envelopes, diminutive letters written by him for visiting children who were disappointed at getting no post, medals made of silver shillings hung on red or blue ribbons – 'Are you army or navy?' – and promises of a place in a regiment for likely-looking boys.

'You are a very nice little fellow,' he said to a child playing in the garden at Apsley House; 'when you are old enough I will give you a commission in the Guards.'

'But I'm a dirl, Mr Dook,' replied the future Lady Spencer Walpole.[13]

*

By September the Duke had recovered his health sufficiently to enjoy the continuing battle with the King. 'He is now quite fat enough,' reported Harriet on the 12th; 'looks strong & muscular & his face, instead of being pale and wrinkled, looks quite full & florid' – like her portrait of him by Lawrence, though Peel, who had stayed with him at Stratfield Saye on the 3rd, thought his walk had lost its elasticity: 'He seems feeble and drags one leg after the other as if he was weak.'[14] Perhaps it was the contrast of

Peel's and Kitty's company at Stratfield Saye with that of the Arbuthnots at Walmer. On the 15th Mrs Arbuthnot found him roaring with laughter over a caricature of himself in *The Times*. The artist had portrayed him reading a passage from that newspaper to the King which ran: 'We have to announce on undoubted authority that a serious difference has arisen between a great personage & his prime minister.'

More than one jealous grievance against Wellington indeed afflicted the King. His wish to visit Paris was vetoed owing to the Polignac situation. ('Poor king!' said Cumberland, 'I knew it! He can never do what he likes.') Yet a week or two later Wellington had a spree in the north, receiving the freedom of Doncaster, going to the races and attending a most successful ball. 'Lady Londonderry fainted under the weight of her finery,' he told Harriet, 'before I arrived.'[15]

The Duke's September tour had not been without its political interest. 'Distress' was a sad and sinister word which had begun to feature more and more often in discussions on the state of the country. Not that the 1828 harvest had been immoderately bad. But the spring of 1829 heralded nothing remotely cheerful. Lord Sefton, a fervent Whig, wrote to Creevey in April: 'The Beau's troubles are not over yet. The distress in the country is Frightful. Millions are starving, and I defy him to do anything to relieve them.'[16]

Over sixteen million people now inhabited Britain and an appallingly large number of them could reasonably be described as starving. The postwar depression in industry which followed Waterloo had prompted the bolder spirits to organize, and to air their grievances at Spa Fields or Peterloo. But agitation simply resulted in political repression by 'gag acts'. A decade passed and acute distress was by no means confined to the great industrial towns, where beneath the bustling surface groaned an underworld of sweated labour, unemployment, squalor and disease. The countryside, also in a wretched state since the fall of agricultural prices after Waterloo, was working up for a doomsday explosion. Over the years tens of thousands of peasant proprietors had left their homes to swell the city ant-heaps, drawn by higher wages or driven by the 'enclosures' policy, often applied to common land. (The Duke, it will be remembered, had refused to enclose a common near Stratfield Saye when his agent

recommended it.) Weekly wages in the country for those who had
stayed behind could sink in places as low as three or four shillings.
But the nadir in 1829 was reached in industrial Yorkshire. A
wage reduction provoked strikes and rioting in Barnsley while
in Huddersfield, though there was no violence, an investigating
committee of employers informed the Government that thirteen
thousand workers in fancy goods were earning $2\frac{1}{2}d.$ a week.

Wellington's letters to Mrs Arbuthnot, written after his tour,
were alternately despairing and irritated. The distress of the poor
filled him with hopelessness. He could see no remedy in any of
the nostrums suggested by Opposition and friends alike –
Huskisson wanting free trade; Cobbett wishing the hard-faced
men who had done well out of the war to pay off the national
debt; Attwood, in Birmingham, advocating more paper money,
others, including some Tories, arguing for reform of the banks,
parliamentary reform, a coalition, economies. The Duke was
deeply sceptical; at the same time he resented criticism of his own
inactivity. 'There is nothing but calumny in the World my dear
Mrs Arbuthnot,' he wrote on 29 October; 'and I must make up
my mind to be exposed to it!' Two days earlier he had been
intensely irritated by the moans of great landowners at the state
of agriculture. 'I hear of nothing but complaints from all quarters.
But somehow or other we do not see any Man refuse himself any
gratification or Luxury.' He would not believe that the Dukes of
Norfolk, Rutland or Beaufort had reason to grumble until they
ceased giving huge parties in their castles or at the races.[17]

Many of his political colleagues hankered after a coalition
with the Whigs. But the Government in his eyes would only lose
character by such a move, considering they were by far the strongest of the five parties now operating in Parliament – Ultràs,
Huskissonites, Radicals, Grey's Whigs and his own moderate
Tories. Next day he brought his analysis to a rational if mistaken
climax:

Men are tired in England of novelties in Trade Agriculture — foreign
and domestic Policy. They wish to go on quietly; they will support any
Govt. that will act upon those principles.[18]

The truth was that Wellington had reached a point familiar to
many successful governments, when difficulties and a certain
lassitude have dimmed their reforming ardour. They become

convinced that the right policy is 'consolidation', not further advance. Nor are they always wrong. The Duke had special reasons for thinking he was right.

Some reforms which he might personally have welcomed were bitterly opposed by the bishops, and after the upheavals of Catholic emancipation their lordships' bench needed time to quieten down. One such reform involved a new Anatomy Bill to provide bodies legally for dissection by medical students, thus thwarting future body-snatchers and murderers like Burke and Hare, who had been profitably employed at the average rate of 16 guineas per corpse until 1829, when they were caught.[19] But the bishops were more frightened by dissection and its supposed threat to religious belief in the resurrection of the body than they were by the dreadful 'Resurrection men' themselves. Proposals that a Jews' Relief Bill should follow up Catholic relief were at this stage turned down by the Duke mainly because of episcopal opposition.

A major reform in the army was obstinately rejected by Wellington himself. Corporal punishment had come up regularly since Waterloo. Even his friend Sir Henry Hardinge wanted a switch to the reformed Prussian system in 1829, but Hardinge failed to shake him. As long as Britain had an empire Wellington believed that her battles would be fought abroad in horrible colonial climates; so long, her soldiers could not be conscripted as in Prussia; only 'the scum of the earth' would volunteer for such unpleasant service; 'the scum' must be controlled ultimately by corporal punishment. This pitifully static view of human nature had a superficial realism which influenced Wellington for many a long year to come.

Was he correct even on the main question of consolidation versus advance, 'quiet' versus 'novelty'? The answer must be no. He had mistaken the spirit of the times. Discontent in autumn 1829 was not, as he supposed, the subsiding groundswell of Catholic emancipation but the sign of oncoming storms.

He saw out his great year of 1829 in an ambivalent mood. 'I should say that matters were looking upwards,' he wrote to the Duke of Rutland on 3 December. Revenue was keeping up, arrears of taxes falling. Whether or not the reports of distress were exaggerated, the country was improving everywhere. In agriculture, manufacture and commerce, in building of houses, roads and bridges, progress in the last few years had been 'astounding'.[20]

Sometimes he would feel over-confident. 'If Lord Grey opposes us he will destroy himself in the opinion of all the Quiet People in the Country.' At other times it was he himself who was going under. 'If I do not get some relief I shall be destroyed. . . .' But he dared not delegate: 'I feel myself to be situated as I was in the Command of the Army; without resource excepting in my own Mind and knowing that where I was not myself to give directions matters would go wrong.'[21]

It was Charles Arbuthnot, whose home was temporarily out of bounds to the Duke because of press innuendo, to whom the Duke poured out on 13 December the most eloquent of his tales of woe:

I certainly admit that I am anxious to quit office. Till I became First Lord of the Treasury I never had a dispute or a difference with any body; excepting the Scum of the Earth, who defrauded the Publick or who would not do their Duty. In my Office I am necessarily put in Collision with every body. The King the Royal family every Nobleman & Gentleman in England, every foreign sovereign, every Ambassador or Foreign Minister.

Apart from Clarence, not one of the royal family spoke to him.

Then I am obliged to keep every thing and every body in order and in His Place; and I have a quarrel open with Mr Huskisson and Lord Anglesey; and another ready for Lord Combermere; and all for what?

How could the Duke paper over all these cracks? In the old days a prime minister would have used patronage. But it had been the Duke's own policy to abolish every sinecure as it fell in.

I have nothing to give to any body excepting Smiles and a Dinner; and I cannot excuse myself, or write and answer in a hurry or make any mistake without giving offence!! I should be more than Man if I did not feel the Misery of my Position.[22]

And Wellington, in his own words, was 'but a man'.

Even his faith in the great Hoby, maker of his Wellington boots, withered during this December month of trials. 'I shall be very much obliged to you,' he told Charles Arbuthnot, 'if you will write me the direction of the Man who makes your Waterloo boots.' Mr Hoby had made him a pair which left him lame.*

*

The Duke expected what he called a 'warm session' to open on 4 February 1830. He had not expected the icy winter – the worst it was said for ninety years – which still held the country in its grip, squeezing the life out of the poor. A group of 110 desperate memorialists marked the opening of Parliament with a petition to the Government to devise effective measures for an immediate thaw.

His political opponents, both Radicals and Ultras, denounced him mercilessly throughout February and March for ignoring their terrible plight. Resentment at his autumn tour had grown into furious abuse of his heartlessness in 'gadding about' (Greville's words) on shooting parties while the poor starved. Greville himself was shocked by such sniping. Did not a prime minister need outdoor recreation? He was also struck by the Duke's short temper with the not so poor. To a deputation of West Indian planters complaining of distress he had given 'a very rough answer . . . cut them very short and told them they were not distressed at all and nothing could be done for them'.[23]

In March there was an outburst from the Duke against the whole race of inventors, who constantly badgered him to buy their projects for the nation. 'There are thousands of them at present in England,' he fumed; 'as well as I believe elsewhere; the offspring of the march of intellect. Their object is money; which, please God, they shall not get from the Publick Treasury.'[24] Though the Duke was never tired of pointing out that machines did more good through increased production than harm through unemployment, he could not forgive their inventors. March of machinery, yes; 'March of Intellect', no.

How far was he genuinely moved by the distress of 1830? At Stratfield Saye he was known to be a sympathetic landlord,

* Many years later there was again trouble over the famous boots, according to a story about Sir Charles Locock, Queen Victoria's doctor.
'Locock,' said the Duke, stopping the doctor one day in the Park, 'I have a bad headache from taking your damned lozenges.'
'Well, I might as well say', returned Locock, 'that I am lamed by wearing your damned boots.' (*Medical Times & Gazette*, page 137, 31 July 1875.)

willing to knock off part of the rent for hard-pressed tenants. One was excused £200 during this year. Much rural misery was caused by the old Poor Law (though by no means all) and he laid to heart a letter from James Hogg, M.P. for Kettering, in which the evil effects of low wages subsidized by a parish poor-rate were graphically described. While keeping the poor on a bare subsistence level, the parish dole nevertheless prevented them from leaving their parish to look for work elsewhere. 'Present Poor Laws are like a wall of brass round each parish,' wrote Hogg, 'enclosing the inhabitants until they are ready to devour each other and are yet hungry.'[25] The Duke also showed awareness of other reasons for rural poverty; enclosures, the results of war, shocking harvests, no work for an exploding population.

In Parliament during spring 1830 he frequently deplored specific instances of distress, noting the ruinous cost of getting in an appalling harvest, the fall in fat-stock prices, especially in Ireland, and the wretched prices obtained for manufactures. (A Mr Thomas Wright had sent him a dramatic bag of hardware, naming the fantastically low cost of each object – $1d.$ for a 4-inch bolt and staple; $1\frac{1}{2}d.$ for a $3\frac{1}{2}$-inch box lock and key; $1s.$ $9d.$ for a 6-inch mortice lock, key and brass plate; $2\frac{3}{4}d.$ for an outsize key. You could lock up your property four times over for the trifling sum of 2s. $2\frac{1}{4}d.$) Nevertheless he would not let go of his conviction that there was over-all progress. 'In all other respects,' he would repeat endlessly in letters and speeches, 'we have reason to believe that the country is improving slowly, as all great countries must improve; certainly.'[26]

There was one matter, moreover, on which the political philosophers of both sides agreed: Parliament could do nothing to relieve many kinds of distress, 'Can this House prevent competition by foreign markets with our own?' the Duke asked on 4 February. 'Parliament cannot, by any act of theirs, raise the price of the manufactured goods,' he declared on the 25th. Parliament could of course cut taxes, and his party had reduced taxation by £3,500,000 in three years. Parliament could also increase the circulation of money; but this might cause speculation mania again. Or it could abolish the Corn Laws or reintroduce income tax; but neither of these things would be acceptable to the Duke's particular supporters, the country gentlemen.

If he continued to lead he must march, as before, straight

ahead. Of course he could drop back into second place. That would mean giving the lead to Peel, with all the 'libertizing' it would involve – certainly a coalition, for Peel was getting desperate about the lack of Tory debating power in the Commons. He had no one but himself to put up against such masters as Brougham, John Russell, Huskisson and Palmerston. Was it Wellington's duty to be first or second?

The tense uncertainties of his position were revealed in full only to the Arbuthnots. On 4 March he wrote to Harriet,

I think that at the end of this Session the Country will be clear of its financial and Political difficulties. . . . That will be the time for me to retire and I will go at that time, never to return to office again.

But by 9 April his spirits had sunk. 'I am not well. I fell asleep in my carriage on Wednesday which is always a sign of being unwell. . . .' And exactly a month later, on 9 May, he was actually telling the Arbuthnots, 'he was *determined* to write to Peel in a few days & resign the Govt into his hands'.[27]

Harriet was aghast. She made him promise not to send Peel any letter without showing it to her first. What would the country think of his self-sacrifice? It would seem the opposite: 'It will be felt by the whole country as an unfair abandonment of his post in a moment of great difficulty.'

The 'great difficulty' to which Harriet referred was the serious illness of the King.

Her arguments seemed to prevail, after she had spent an hour and a half with him on the 16th, walking and sitting on the spring grass of Buckingham House (later Buckingham Palace). 'He seems now willing only to draw up a paper for Mr Peel, pointing out to him the obstacles to a junction with any party.'

The paper for Mr Peel was duly drafted. But instead of restricting himself to discussing the disadvantages of a coalition, the Duke made a definite offer to retire in Peel's favour as soon as the King died. 'I have long been of opinion,' he wrote, 'that it is desirable that the power of the government should be concentrated in one hand, and that hand that of the leader of the House of Commons.' The letter was never sent.[28]

Why did the Duke, an exceptionally selfless statesman, decide against resignation? Such self-sacrifice could not fairly be expected and would indeed have been unique in history. But if he

had served under Peel in 1830 instead of waiting four years, he
would have saved himself and probably the Tory party from an
impending disaster. Throughout these critical days from 3 to 16
May Peel had been absent in Drayton, Staffordshire, supervising
the funeral and legal affairs of his father. (Old Sir Robert had
died on the 3rd.) Absence made the Duke's heart grow less
irritable. But when his second-in-command returned to London
as Sir Robert Peel, Bt, the graces of an inherited baronetcy were
far from investing him, at least in the Duke's eyes, with the aura
of a prime minister. Could the Duke in truth hand over to this
morose man, so lacking in courteous manners, so austere, above
all so demanding, since his return, of absurd new schemes for
reform, slanted at the Whigs? Like Queen Victoria eleven years
later, the Duke took another look at this strange person and
decided no. Harriet swiftly rubbed in her point. 'I told him it
only proved how necessary it was for him (the Duke) to remain
at his post.'*

Meanwhile the King too hoped to remain at his post, and was
struggling desperately to do so.

*

After an audience in mid-April, Wellington said that but for the
bulletins he would have diagnosed His Majesty's complaint as
unwillingness to attend the Levée and Drawing Room; except
for occasional congestion in his chest, his chief trouble was too
good an appetite and being too fat. Even those who saw most of
him thought that a quiet, healthy regime might yet save him. But
wine, ether and 'the black drop' (laudanum) with its high alco-
holic content were now apparently essential to his health. 'It
seem'd to depend on drink,' wrote Knighton in his diary.[29] In
May and June, apart from two miraculous blazes, the big bonfire
was clearly going out.

There was the moment in mid-May when the swollen legs were
successfully punctured and in mid-June the disease was again
arrested; all his old affection for Wellington returned, the
Duchess of Cumberland's offer to nurse him was declined, he was

* All the adjectives applied to Peel above were used by Mrs Arbuthnot in
her journal and were evidently a transcription of what the Duke had said to
her about Peel. (Vol. ii, p. 359.)

given until the autumn or beyond, and the betting was on Clarence's eccentricities landing him in a strait-jacket before HM was in his grave.

At 3.15 A.M. on Saturday 26 June King George IV died.

The immediate cause seems to have been a ferocious purgative or, as Mrs Arbuthnot heard, from the bursting of a blood vessel in his stomach. 'My boy,' he said, clutching his doctor's hand, 'this is death!' It was a sad end for one whom Wellington had seen bravely breakfasting only eleven weeks before on two pigeons in a pie, three steaks, three-quarters of a bottle of hock, a glass of champagne, two of port and one of brandy – with laudanum as his *apéritif*.[30]

In this same month of June 1830 the first incendiary fires were lit in the English countryside by those who had neither pies nor port and often no bread.

*

The death of the King was the first act in a drama which was soon to engulf the Duke. Before the explosion, however, there was a curious private interval when the Duke showed his devotion to a royal family whose individual members he did not always love.

With Sir William Knighton and Baron Gifford (since dead), Wellington had been appointed executor of King George IV's will six years before. The Duke now decided, in 1830, to be '*custos*' of HM's papers and to keep them, as before, at Apsley House. This was because of the inflammatory material in more than one bundle.

His greatest anxiety was not centred on HM's debts, though it took him five years to deal with all of them. Nor was he worried by the case of 'Lady Conyngham's jewels', as the public wrongly supposed. The late King had indeed bequeathed to her gems which, being family heirlooms, were not his to give, but she refused the whole legacy in a manner which the Duke described as admirable and high-minded. (The kindly William IV later gave her, with 'His Best Regards', a sapphire and diamond clasp which was his brother's property. *The Times*'s attack on her for wearing this jewel the Duke and Knighton agreed was for purely 'Revolutionary Purposes').[31]

Far less was the Duke disturbed by the business of dispersing HM's jackdaw collections of snuff-boxes, walking-sticks, wigs, boots and furs, most of which were absorbed without difficulty by the Pages of the Backstairs. His serious concern was with the secret affairs of the late King and one of his brothers,

King George IV's clandestine and illegal but canonical marriage with Mrs Maria Fitzherbert was the more easily dealt with. There could be no doubt in the Duke's mind about the King's enduring nostalgia for his long-abandoned Maria. Her miniature, hanging on a black ribbon and half-hidden under the royal nightshirt, had been detected by the Duke's famous hawk eyes when he saw the Sovereign's body two days after his death. It explained why the King had commanded that he should be buried in his night-shirt undisturbed.[32]* Wellington had little difficulty in persuading the amiable Maria to accept an annuity of £6,000 from the new King in settlement of her claims. Her secret must be consigned to perpetual oblivion. During the next few years at least, if not in perpetuity, Wellington was to find Mrs Fitzherbert's affairs satisfactorily quiescent.

*

The Cumberland papers were another matter.[33] For three or four years after the birth of a certain Thomas Garth in 1801 there had been strange rumours about his parentage. No one in the know doubted (or can now doubt) that Princess Sophia, the Duke of Cumberland's sister, was Thomas's mother. But was his father really, as well as legally, the royal equerry General Garth, whose name he bore? Or, horror of horrors, could his father be none other than the wildly unpopular Duke of Cumberland? After seeming to dissolve, this murky rumour was revived in March 1829 by young Garth himself, now an army captain on half-pay. Immediately everyone remembered the old story of incest; and though Princess Lieven thought the friends of Catholic emancipation had deliberately resuscitated this 'terrible charge' in order to drive Cumberland out of the country, the press loudly demanded to know the secret of the Garth papers.

As King George IV's executor, the secret was now in Welling-ton's hands.

He held among the other royal papers at Apsley House a very

* The lead coffin was said to have bulged because the body was not pro-perly embalmed. This may have been due to the King's command while alive.

agitated and undated letter from a lawyer named C. F. Williams, addressed to the retired judge Lord Wynford, formerly William Best, the Prince Regent's Attorney-General. In this letter the absolute necessity of obtaining and destroying the Garth papers *at once* was eloquently urged. Captain Garth's 'infirm' and 'malign' nature, wrote Williams, had led him to the criminal act of making copies of the originals he had got from his father General Garth, before surrendering them again to him. At present Captain Garth's copies were in the safe hands of a 'Mr Howard'. but Garth had the key to the box and 'some individual' was already intriguing with Garth to obtain them for publication or blackmail.

The box contained letters from Princess Sophia. But it was not the facts relating to her conduct and its 'unhappy' results which so upset Mr Williams. (The unhappy results were Captain Garth.) Mr Williams was concerned only with the Duke of Cumberland, whose case 'transcends a thousandfold' the other. Williams proceeded to describe it:

Several of the letters convey grave and alarming charges against HRH in the most unequivocal terms – Charges of a description that would awaken and direct an overwhelming burst of popular Indignation against the illustrious Duke, which Explanation, denial or natural improbability would perhaps ineffectually stem or control.

(According to the *Morning Chronicle* of March 1829, Cumberland's friends adduced 'the stubborn evidence of facts and distances' to prove that it was 'a *physical impossibility*' for the royal Duke to have fathered Thomas Garth on Princess Sophia. But the press were unconvinced.)

Now comes the crux, put here in italics for the sake of making clear the actual situation with which Wellington had to deal:

An accusation by a Sister that Her Own Brother had more than once attempted to violate her Person, rouses such horrible Emotions that Reason is generally over powered & explanation or refutation are either heard too late, or rejected!

It was therefore a matter of supreme urgency, 'in the present Crisis', to suppress these copies 'at even a considerable sacrifice!'

Lord Wynford must have sent this political dynamite to the Duke, for a letter among the same royal papers at Apsley House, dated 17 June 1830, is evidently the Duke's reply to the Williams appeal.*

Wellington's letter amounted to a plan of campaign outlined with military precision. First, his objective: to prevent publication of the Garth papers. Second, to find out if there were more than two sets of copies. Third, to observe strict priorities when contemplating the payment of Government money in a case of this kind.

If money is given with facility and in large sums it is almost certain that the Copies of these Papers will be multiplied; and as all these payments of Money are at the least of doubtful Legality we should at last have to pay Money in order to conceal the fact we had paid any for the suppression of these papers.

In fact, Wellington's *first* duty to 'the Royal Family and to the Public' was to do everything else except pay the blackmailer. He would not even *consider* money until 'every vestige of the papers are destroyed'.

Captain Garth was routed. Every vestige both of the papers and of Captain Garth himself disappeared without trace. After 1830 nothing more is heard of them. It is a tribute to Wellington's efficiency that the secret of exactly how he bought and burnt or burnt and paid for the papers – if this is what he did – has never leaked out. But judging by his future actions in analogous circumstances, one may guess that he first demanded the two sets of copies; then burnt them, perhaps in the presence of Garth; after which Garth was given money, or what the Duke would have called a *'pont d'or'* to cross the Channel. The Garth papers, burnt it is assumed in 1830, were to be paralleled by the

* Assuming that Williams's undated letter can now be assigned to May or June 1830, 'the present Crisis' must refer to the expected death of King George IV. One of the past successes in suppressing the Garth papers is mentioned in the Greville memoirs. On 22 March 1829 Greville noted that Sir Herbert Taylor, the King's secretary, had told him about the fate of the *original* letters: 'Old Garth has assured the Duke of York that they were all destroyed. Taylor also told Greville who was the father of Princess Sophia's 'unhappy' mistake. 'The papers prove that old Garth is the father, of which Taylor says there is not a doubt.' Finally, 'Mr Howard' may have belonged to the banking firm, Messrs Paul & Co., where the Garth papers were deposited; while the 'individual' who was intriguing to publish the copies may have been Captain Garth's friend C. M. Westmacott, editor of the scurrilous *Age*, who had read and made abstracts of all of them.

Fitzherbert papers, burnt in 1833; and the golden bridge across the English Channel for the Duke of Cumberland's enemy, Garth, was to be followed later by another *'pont d'or'* for Queen Victoria's enemy, Conroy.

Because Wellington chose to take on the responsible duty of *custos* the truth about the Garth scandal is known at last. Up till now it has generally been assumed either that the 'terrible charge' was monstrously untrue, having been fabricated by Princess Caroline; or that it was horribly true, Princess Caroline having been let into the secret by the Duke of Kent.

Williams's letter, quoted above on p. 264 shows that the 'terrible charge' emanated not from Queen Victoria's father but from Princess Sophia herself. Nor was it so unutterably 'terrible' as the gossips hopefully supposed. Cumberland was said to have 'attempted' rather than achieved his object. If Williams's letter tells the whole truth, General Garth is left in the undisputed but unenviable possession of Thomas.

Happy the family that has lost its annals; or even better, that has a servant as formidable and single-minded as Wellington to spirit them away in the nick of time. Did it ever occur to the great Duke that the infamous Garth had delivered Cumberland, arch-enemy of his policies and determined wrecker of his career, into his hands? Not for a moment.

Five years later it is no surprise to find the Duke paying £50 to an excellent Mr Jackson for handing over another box, this time an iron chest bought by Jackson at a sale in Buckingham House. On opening it Jackson found his box contained letters written between the Prince (George) and Princess (Caroline) of Wales which, as the Duke remarked, 'would have been most agreeable food for the Radical Revolutionaries of the present time.'[34]

The Duke was now to face the 'Radical revolutionaries' of 1830 unencumbered at least by royal scandals.

15

Reform

King William IV, formerly Duke of Clarence, wanted to make Wellington happy, as indeed he wanted to make all his subjects happy: 'he is an immense improvement on the last unforgiving animal,' wrote Emily Eden in her famous welcome to the new reign. 'This man at least *wishes* to make everybody happy. . . .'[1]

His method of bestowing happiness upon the Duke was to confirm his Government in office. He was as energetic in doing the business which the Duke submitted as George IV had been dilatory, and as willing to take the Duke's advice in appointing gentlemen to his Household as George IV had been recalcitrant. On one of his last rides with George Seymour before ascending the throne he had expressed his resolve to keep the Duke at the head of his councils, ban all 'Back Stairs influence' and promote 'the fullest confidence between a Sovereign and his Ministers'. He would do the right thing, and see that others did too. At his brother's funeral he had fussed and barked,

'Generals, generals, keep step, keep step! Admirals, keep step!'

He did not intend to fall out of step himself, especially with the Field-Marshal, his Prime Minister.

Sometimes the King's confidence was given with embarrassing plenitude. At a dinner held in his honour at Apsley House on 25 July, the twenty-first anniversary of Vimeiro, King William committed a series of *bêtises* with the best possible intentions. In proposing the Duke's health he offered some clumsy congratulations on his victories over the French; then, suddenly remembering the French ambassador was present, attempted an even clumsier cover-up. The ambassador, who understood no English, added to the confusion by constantly darting forward to thank His Majesty for his compliments. King William wound up with the startling remark that as long as he reigned he would continue to give his confidence to the Duke. Afterwards the Duke was laughingly congratulated by Princess Lieven on this ratification of his power to all eternity. He replied drily that 'he would far rather the King had not made the speech'. Princess Lieven saw his point. Nevertheless, with her passionate interest in his rival, Lord Grey, she felt that he had scored unfairly, especially on the eve of a general election.[2]

*

The general election, necessitated as usual by a new reign, began after the prorogation of Parliament on 23 July and proved to be the Opposition's chance for demonstrating that they, at least, had not been made happy. Some of them had expected Grey to enter Wellington's Cabinet, once the late King's objections had died with him. Others had hoped a new reign would mean a new ministry. George Seymour was convinced that during the first debate in the Lords after the announcement of George IV's serious illness Grey, from having been a consistently moderate opponent, had suddenly turned sour. The Duke did not miss the signs, for he wrote to Peel that he expected more 'active opposition' from Grey in the future.[3] Nor did it escape Seymour's notice that Grey's change of tactics coincided with a petition to the Lords on reform. Not merely reform of the laws governing agriculture, commerce, finance or poverty but the reform of Parliament itself.

This was Reform with a capital R. Away with rotten boroughs! Votes for the great cities! An end to the land-owning magnates' monopoly of the franchise! Parliamentary reform was ready to take over from all other battle-cries. Grey had advocated it as long ago as 1793; several Reform Bills had been introduced quite recently and killed, including John Russell's in February 1830; outside the House Thomas Attwood and Francis Place were able radical politicians. Reform became the Opposition's inspiration. But if the whole country was to take fire, reform must somehow be blown up to truly gigantic dimensions – the healer of every social sickness and panacea for all ills, for which the people hungered. Electioneering was not yet over, with the borough votes cast but 40 county seats to come, when in Paris occurred the blow-up (a favourite word of Wellington's) which was afterwards

labelled the French Revolution of the 'Three Glorious Days', or
'July Days'. It succeeded in firing hundreds of thousands of
Britons and in revolutionizing much of Europe.

*

On 25 July at Saint-Cloud Charles x and his chief minister
Polignac, whom some believed to be his natural son, promulgated
the notorious Ordinances or Royal Decrees. Liberty of the press
was suspended, the Chamber of Deputies dissolved and the
electoral law emasculated. Political opinion in France at once
realized that these drastic projects showed a resolve to wipe out
not only Louis xviii's constitutional charter but all that had been
won since the Great Revolution of 1789. An English painter living
in Paris, William Bennett, instinctively understood the people's
violent reaction. 'Man,' he wrote, 'feels in fact *he is* Man.' No
longer would Man be degraded by 'partial Laws' or allow his
country's wealth to be swallowed up by 'the luxurious living of
idle and designing knaves'.[4] Such thoughts were soon to be
faithfully reproduced across the Channel.

The Three Glorious Days, 26–8 July, began and continued
under the direction of the commercial middle classes, with a
maximum of tumult and minimum of bloodshed. Marshal
Marmont, who had faced Wellington at Salamanca, made no
serious attempt to hold the Tuileries with his Royal Household
troops against the singing crowds of exuberant artisans, led by
students and intellectuals waving tricolour flags. He evacuated
Paris on the 29th. In a matter of days the King and his family had
fled to England.

Meanwhile Adolph Thiers, the able and ruthless manager
behind the Paris street scenes, had appointed the King's cousin
Louis Philippe 'Lieutenant-General of the Realm'. Once the old
King was out of the way Thiers sent the young revolutionaries
home. Then on 7 August he strode into Louis Philippe's study
at the Palais-Royal and told him that he would be made, not
King of France and Navarre by divine right, but King of the
French, *tout court*.

So ended the Three Glorious Days and their immediate aftermath. The volcano of French politics had been in travail and
finally given birth to a Citizen King who walked about the
streets of Paris with a huge tricolour on his hat, an umbrella in

his left hand and the right outstretched to shake the hands of passing citizens. It was not unlike King William IV walking up St James's Street. Power had merely been transferred, however, from the land-owning nobility to industrialists and bankers of the bourgeoisie. They established their own supremacy beneath the convenient umbrella of a domesticated monarch. He happened at the same time to be France's richest capitalist.

Neither Wellington nor Peel could be expected to feel particularly elated by the bourgeois home life unfolding at the Tuileries, begotten as it was of a profoundly perturbing revolution and coinciding, moreover, with the middle of a year which had long echoed to cries for reform. They were more likely to sympathize with the *émigrés* reaching England, who spoke in anguished sarcasm of the 'charming family' now ruling 'thrice-happy France'.[5]

*

As after Waterloo, it was a Rothschild who brought the first news to the Cabinet. Wellington at once forwarded the account to Peel. They were both staggered. Wellington was particularly startled by Marmont's failure to hold the Tuileries against the mob. As British Prime Minister, it gave him food for thought. Marmont's spirits, however, were only temporarily dashed. Like the ex-King he escaped to England, where he was characteristically entertained by the Duke. On a visit to Woolwich the Duke arranged for him to meet the English soldier who had shot off his arm before Salamanca and then lost his own at Waterloo. 'Ah, my friend,' said the Marshal, 'every man gets his turn.'[6]

In the international tension caused by Louis Philippe's usurpation Wellington was not one to lose his head for ideological reasons. 'There is need for anxiety and there is need for watchfulness,' he told Princess Lieven, 'but there is no need to exasperate France by making her think there exists a tribunal sitting in judgement on her.' It would not do to ostracize the new regime. 'We shall recognize King Louis Philippe tomorrow,' he wrote to Mrs Arbuthnot on 24 August, adding grandly but truly: 'All the other Powers will follow our example.'[7]

The hopes roused by the Three Glorious Days lived on in Britain. 'What a glorious event this is in France!' wrote Palmerston to his fellow-Huskissonite, Charles Grant.[8] As Henry

Brougham rampaged round Yorkshire and Henry Hunt round
Lancashire on their election campaigns, the message got home.
If the French could achieve the Parliament they wanted, so could
the English. For France, the 'Limited Liability Revolution'; for
England, reform. A 'wild and indiscriminating' injection of
reform, according to the *Annual Register*, suddenly transformed
the Whig campaign. This was equally 'wild and indiscriminating'
exaggeration. All the same, there was great excitement, no
excitement like it since the first French Revolution. Meetings,
petitions, addresses multiplied; deputations of sympathy rushed
to Paris and subscriptions poured in to succour the families of
Frenchmen who had fallen in the streets. In the Midlands the
fever ran particularly high, the Birmingham Political Union
having been founded during the previous January for the express
purpose of forcing reform on Parliament. Brougham won a stunning victory in Yorkshire, considering that he 'had no earthly
connection' with the county, as the *Annual Register* wittily remarked, meaning that he did not own an acre of land there.

Throughout the campaign the Duke had refused to be stam-
peded into exerting the pressures open to the party of the landlords,
and Brougham wrote many years later that the Whigs owed much
of their success to the Duke's 'admirable conduct at the General
Election. No minister ever abstained more scrupulously from the
exercise of undue influence.' Part of the Duke's calmness, though
not his scrupulousness, stemmed from the curious Tory view that
the July Revolution would actually benefit their cause. He wrote
on 21 August:

Events now going on in France will aid in convincing the well in-
tentioned at least that we enjoy at least the benefit at present of having
no question depending about political Right, in which large Classes of
the People are interested.[9]

'No questions pending of political rights in which the masses were
interested. . . .' If the last three lines of that cautious sentence
proved anything, it was the Duke's utter failure to appreciate the
dynamism of reform.

Nevertheless the overall election results were not stark enough
to destroy his optimism. As Professor Gash has shown, the
effects of events in France were much exaggerated.* Lord Grey

* 'English Reform & French Revolution', *Essays Presented to Sir Lewis
Namier.*

might correctly calculate that his side had won the substantial increase of 50 votes on a division; the Duke still had a majority, and his party managers even worked out a gain of 17 seats by counting in neutrals and such devices. But they had to gloss over the fact that the country squires, who had come to represent an important part of public opinion, were ratting. At most 28 of the 82 county members could be absolutely relied on. Peel, Ellenborough and Lyndhurst were despondent, the last telling Princess Lieven that all but the Duke now recognized the crying need for Cabinet reinforcements.

During July an abortive attempt had been made to interest Palmerston and Melbourne in an alliance with the Duke. He had been emotionally against the project at the time and still was, as Mrs Arbuthnot found to her cost when she tried to put the case for reinforcements in August at Walmer. The Duke had gone to Walmer with one idea only – 'I want more Sea Bathing.' He did not want more catechizing about coalitions. Mrs Arbuthnot had to desist. She wrote in her diary, 'He got into a great rage & abused Peel & I saw there was no use. . . .'[10]

It was significant that Mrs Arbuthnot, with her ear habitually to the ground, had at last come round to the majority view. Less than two months before (6 July) she herself had lambasted Lord Rosslyn for proposing that the Government should take in Lord John Russell and Sir James Graham, both Whigs. Were they not pledged to currency and parliamentary reform? 'Oh God! that's nothing,' replied Rosslyn airily. 'They'd throw all that overboard. No principles of that sort would make any difficulty.' Harriet had recorded this in her journal with two exclamation marks and a disgusted, 'It makes me sick.'[11] Now only the Duke of Wellington was left to feel sick at the necessities of the party political game.

*

At the Kentish village of Lower Hardres, not many miles away from Walmer Castle where the Duke was still restoring his vital energies, a group of labourers destroyed a threshing-machine on 28 August. This was an early case of machine-breaking in what soon became a major tragedy for the poor. Desperate agricultural workers felt they could not face another winter like the last, with machines taking away their employment on the threshing-floor just when they needed it most. In September the movement spread, as labourers in adjacent areas of Kent and East Sussex rose up in protest against the same or other local grievances. At Robertsbridge in Sussex there was a disturbance because the two chief ratepayers and overseers of the poor paid their labourers in mouldy flour instead of money. They were insulting into the bargain. 'They never call a man Tom, Dick, etc., but you damned rascal at every word.'[12]

A day or two before the Kentish machine-breaking began the rocket of revolution exploded for the second time, exactly a month after takeoff. The Belgians suddenly decided to be a Dutch province no longer. They would achieve independence, either absolute or leaning towards France.

Compared with the numerous small plots uncovered by Wellington in Brussels in 1817–18, this was a colossal challenge. Was France to begin once more at Antwerp? That would indeed make all the fighting since 1793 a mockery. Yet the last thing Wellington wanted was to fight France again. Fortunately for his pacific designs the new French ambassador appointed to London by Louis Philippe was an old friend and even older political manipulator, if not sage.

Talleyrand might be received in England with shrieks of horror from right, left and centre: 'varlet' to Eldon, 'monster' to Cumberland, 'really hardly human' to Harriet Arbuthnot; reptile, death's-head, prince of darkness. To the Duke he was a diplomat of perfect probity and matchless skill when it came to warding off an international situation which they would both regard as calamitous. It was due mainly to Talleyrand that Louis Philippe refrained from exploiting the Belgian revolution after the Princes of Orange had been extruded; and to Wellington and Talleyrand together that an armistice was arranged between Belgium and Holland, with a five-power conference to follow in London. True, the immensely protracted negotiations begun in November 1830 were to be Palmerston's task and triumph. Nevertheless Europe owed Wellington a debt of gratitude. He had resisted the warmongers and showed once again that he preferred the olive to the laurel.

As far as the Duke's responsibilities at home were concerned the Belgian revolution hit him hardest in Ireland. If Catholic Belgium could break its enforced union with Protestant Holland, why could not Catholic Ireland get the union with Protestant England repealed?

'What the youth of Bruxelles has affected the boys of Dublin can perform!'

Repeal was soon to be O'Connell's heaviest gun, heavier even than reform of tithes, poor relief or the franchise. Known since Catholic emancipation as 'The Liberator', O'Connell was to see the future liberation of Ireland more and more through the political end of the telescope. That end was for Wellington a blank. Politically he had no more to give.[13] But through the economic end of the telescope the Duke saw the distant features of a promised land, though obstructed by terrible hazards nearer at hand.

'I confess that the annually recurring starvation in Ireland, for a period differing . . . from one week to three months,' he had written to the Lord-Lieutenant on 7 July, 'gives me more uneasiness than any other evil existing in the United Kingdom.' When the starvation occurred there was no relief except public money. The landlords who ought to be providing relief were away 'amusing themselves' in London, Cheltenham, Bath or abroad. Even the public money donated was misappropriated by their agents and applied to 'payment of the arrears of an exorbitant rent'.[14]

The Duke as a young man had not represented Trim in the old Irish Parliament for nothing, nor supervised his eldest brother's estate without learning about arrears. He continued to the Lord-Lieutenant with a striking forecast:

The chances of a serious evil, such as the loss of a large number of persons by famine, will be greater in proportion to the numbers existing in Ireland. . . .

In 1847 the numbers of the Irish, by then more than eight million, were indeed to heighten the disaster. But in 1830 the Duke still saw a chance for salvation through reform of the landlords – hire of a potato patch in return for labour to be forbidden by law; all work to be in return for a money wage. He had said it before and he said it again:

The only remedy that ever occurred to me is to endeavour to bring the people to the markets, by the prohibition of bargains for the payment of labour by letting land to the labourer.[15]

It would be instructive to consider whether O'Connell with his emphasis on repeal of the Union, or Wellington with his reform of the land system came nearer in 1830 to assessing Ireland's needs.

*

Early in August the Duke had asked permission of the King through Sir Herbert Taylor, his secretary, for leave of absence from 6 to 20 September. He wished to visit Lancashire for the opening of the Liverpool–Manchester railway. Dutifully he hoped it would not 'derange HM's projects'.[16]

The Duke's own projects in the north went far beyond railways. The new parliamentary session was to open on 2 November. He would feel the pulse of northern industry, perhaps strengthen it, and possibly strengthen also his Government in ways that 'Black Billy' Holmes, the party agent, was already exploring.

When he reached Manchester on 11 September his welcome was unexpectedly, even deceptively, warm. 'As far as I can judge,' he wrote to a friend in Paris, 'people are in very good humour here,' despite 'something like a turn out [strike] at Stalybridge' (the scene of a serious cotton strike in August).[17] Cheering crowds did not seem to spell industrial distress or dissatisfaction with the Government. The Duke failed to realize that his vast personal prestige could still conceal the unpopularity of the ministry.

Some criticism was caused by his visiting a factory owned by Major 'Hurly-Burly' Birley, one of the villains of Peterloo, and this only a month after 'Orator' Hunt had celebrated its eleventh anniversary on the 'battlefield'. Hunt assured his cheering audience that since the 'Glorious Days' in France no peaceful meeting could be attacked without swift and terrible retribution. Severe comments on the Duke's tour came also from Lord Grey. How dared he leave the capital on his 'progresses' at such a time of peril in Europe? Huzzas and toasts were undignified and unwise. Grey consoled himself, however, with the thought that two could play at that game. Henry Brougham, intoxicated by his sweeping electoral victory in Yorkshire, was preparing for the Duke at Liverpool the hottest reception of his life: 'A scene awaits him,' wrote Grey, 'for which I do not believe him to be prepared.'[18]

On 15 September Grey was writing to Princess Lieven that rumour had cast Wellington for the new role of a parliamentary reformer. It ought to be good fun, added Grey ironically. That same day the bizarre prospect of this good fun evaporated. The 15th happened to be the opening date of the Liverpool–Manchester railway.

*

The large ducal party clambered gaily into the first coach, a sprightly gilt affair standing at Liverpool station, and settled down under its scarlet velvet awning, edged with tassels and draped pelmets of gilded wood, for the joy-ride to Manchester. The awning would save its passengers from being burned by flying sparks, as had happened the year before when Creevey first rode in a train and a pelisse, gown and cheek had been holed. Entering into the spirit which had prompted Creevey to call his journal 'a *lark* of a very high order', the Duke was suitably impressed with the cheering crowds along the embankments, as well as with the iron horse's breakneck speed. It averaged sixteen and sometimes travelled at thirty miles an hour, so that he could not read the figures on the mileposts along the track. As for the crossing of two trains going in opposite directions, a diversion which was frequently staged for the Duke's amusement – 'It was the whizzing,' he gasped, 'of a cannon ball.'[19]

After an hour's activity the iron horse reached Parkside at 11.30 A.M. and stopped to be watered. The passengers must not descend on to the track, warned the directors of the company. 'Black Billy' Holmes, however, had been assigned the congenial task of presenting a distinguished fellow-traveller to the Duke at this moment of general euphoria: none other than Huskisson who, as M.P. for Liverpool, was riding in the directors' carriage. It was intended to be the beginning of a grand political *entente cordiale*. The Duke and Huskisson had met less than a year ago at Lord Hertford's, so there was no personal difficulty.

Eye-witnesses said that Huskisson had already grasped the Duke's hand when a loud shout went up. 'Stop the engine! Clear the track!' The *Rocket*, Stephenson's prize-winning engine, was dashing towards them, eager to show its paces. Caught between the lines, about a dozen strolling passengers made for safety. But Huskisson, heavily built and enfeebled since the Duke of York's funeral, could not make up his mind whether to run for his own carriage or scramble for the Duke's.

As once before a muddled decision had cut short his ministerial career, so now it terminated his life. The *Rocket* struck him as he stumbled, flung him down, ran over his leg at the thigh and in Croker's words 'crushed the limb to a jelly'. Lady Wilton distinctly heard the crunching of the bones. Croker, an enthusiast for the new railways, explained to his patron Lord Hertford that such an accident could have happened as easily in the Strand if a man slipped from the kerb while the stage-coach was passing. The Duke did not take this philosophical view.

Perhaps it was the tragic utterance of Huskisson – 'It's all over with me; bring me my wife and let me die' – or the piercing shrieks of poor Mrs Huskisson; or the roaring of a loud-hailer to stop their train; or the cries from carriage to carriage to know what had happened; or the screams for surgical aid; or the tourniquet applied unavailingly by Lord Wilton; or the news of Huskisson's agonized death at 9 P.M. – perhaps it was a combination of all these horrors which prejudiced the Duke for ever against railways. He was later to find added reasons for disliking them, but his friend Gleig always believed that Huskisson's death had really done it.

Deep gloom fell on the company. Shocked as after Waterloo, the Duke was persuaded with difficulty to go on to Manchester rather than disappoint the huge crowds already assembled, who might otherwise riot. But he avoided the collation afterwards and postponed the Liverpool ceremony next day where he was to have received the freedom of the city.

The sudden removal of this formidable political character would plainly affect the Duke's Government. A stronger position was predicted for him by the Whigs. 'Here again fate is on the side of the Duke of Wellington,' wrote Grey; and Greville gave the same thought an eerie twist: 'As to the Duke of Wellington, a fatality attends him, and it is perilous to cross his path.'[20] Notwithstanding these tributes to his star, the Duke's position was in fact weakened by Huskisson's death. It left the Canningites without a shepherd who could be relied upon to lead them, if anywhere, back into the Tory fold, and necessitated further attempts to whistle up Palmerston for high Cabinet office.

That the Duke was sceptical about such political manoeuvres can be taken for granted. It is more surprising to find him equally sceptical about the increasingly dangerous state of the disturbed southern counties. No one ever doubted the possibility of trouble in the north, and with a wave of industrial strikes the Duke was sending more troops to the garrison towns; indeed Lord Francis Leveson-Gower was glad to get him out of Lancashire – 'The spirit of the district was detestable.' In Manchester there was even a threat to assassinate the Duke, and though he commented on it in somewhat oracular style – 'I never neglect and never believe these things' – he did not fail to take the north seriously. It was different in the south.

'The Gentlemen in Kent, so bold in Parliament, are terrified out of their wits with the burning of a few cornstacks and the breaking of a few threshing machines,' he wrote contemptuously to Mrs Arbuthnot on 15 October. But the truth was that hardly had the Duke returned home before the outbreaks in the countryside entered a new, more violent phase. In October incendiary fires, rick-burning and machine-breaking all occurred together. At Ash in Kent, a village considerably nearer to Walmer than Lower Hardres, a local magistrate and overseer had his property completely destroyed for 'unfeeling conduct' towards the poor. (The Oxenden family of Canterbury, however, were known for their compassion and as a reward had only one shaft of their threshing-machine sawn off.)

The rioting spread. The Duke of Wellington was disgusted when Lord Camden, another Kent landowner, sent him a terrified letter implying that everything was lost unless he satisfied the people by strengthening his Government with reformers. Not for the last time the Duke privately commented, 'I am more afraid of terror than I am of anything else.'[21]

A no less terrified and far longer letter than Camden's arrived from a Mr James Hamilton in Dublin, describing the whole of Connaught and Munster as depots of anarchy and rebellion, while O'Connell's party were all designing incendiaries. Would the Duke please return forthwith to his command of the army and bring it with him to Ireland? 'Alas! My Lord, that the Necessity ever existed for your descending . . . to mix yourself with English Politicks.' The Duke replied curtly that his correspondent should descend from opinions to facts:

The Duke begs leave to observe to Mr Hamilton that he misapplies his own time as well as the Duke's by writing invectives against any Men or Parties. That which is desirable is to state facts shortly and clearly and how and where the Evidence can be procured. The Duke can assure him that it is not worth while to state his opinions.[22]

Under which heading did the need to woo Palmerston come? Was it a fact – or merely the opinion of a lot of frightened ministers?

*

A council of war had taken place at Peel's home, Drayton, shortly before the senior ministers returned to London. The authority which Peel gained under his own roof, plus Arbuthnot's urgency, brought the Duke round to an agreement. Palmerston should be approached through a common friend of his own and the Duke's, Lord Clive. It is odd to think of old 'Puzzlestick' (the nickname given to Clive by the Wellesleys in India), now seventy-six and stone deaf, being chosen to manage the abrasive Lord 'Pumicestone', as Palmerston was called until he achieved the genial image of 'Pam'.

During the interview with Clive at the beginning of October Palmerston was apparently not unfavourable to entering a reconstituted Cabinet in company with a couple of Canningite friends.

It had been agony for the Duke to contemplate pushing his Peninsular colleague, Sir George Murray, out of the Cabinet and into the Blues to make way for Palmerston. He lacked a born prime minister's toughness about giving the sack. But he had faced it. Could he now face sacking two more? 'I cannot change Ministers more frequently than I do my coats on my back,' he wrote passionately to Mrs Arbuthnot.[23] Nevertheless the painful juggling had to go on in his head throughout October, with Murray, Beresford, Calcraft and even Rosslyn as possible victims of the deal. There was a moment of exquisite irony when the busy Arbuthnot received an insulting anonymous letter asking him to make room himself: 'You cannot but be aware,' wrote this snake, 'that you are of no *oratorical* use in the House of Commons. . . .'

Arbuthnot, always selfless and gentle, insisted on offering his resignation after sending this horrible communication to the Duke, and Harriet's stouter heart stood still until the 'kindest possible' answer arrived saying that such a thing was quite out of the question.

Three days before the opening of the session (30 October) the Duke himself made a last-minute bid for Lord Palmerston. It was a dead failure. Palmerston rejected the three Canningite places now firmly offered to him unless they were accompanied by further places in the Government. Wellington assumed this to mean filling up his Government with 'Whigs & Liberals [Canning-ites]', since old Puzzlestick understood Palmerston to have been thinking of the Whigs at his interview four weeks earlier. (It is not clear that Puzzlestick had got this right.) The prospect of the Prime Minister, Home Secretary and Chancellor becoming figureheads, or rather prisoners of a Whig ministry run by the haughty Grey, ferocious Brougham and reforming Russell, brought the negotiations in Wellington's mind to an abrupt end. Peel agreed with him that they must go on alone.

True, one final interview was held between a Canningite and a Wellingtonian before the King's Speech and as late as Monday, 1 November. Edward Littleton, M.P., the Duke's Canningite nephew, suggested to Charles Arbuthnot that though Palmerston did indeed demand three or four more Canningites there was no wish for Brougham whose electioneering had made him an object or terror. As for Russell, it was not Russell the man but Russell's Reform Bill which was required. Could the Duke promise to take up Russell's bill, defeated last February, and make it his own? If so, the 'Liberals' would support him as never before. If not, they would fight him to the death – his death, not theirs. Arbuthnot duly reported these proposals to his leader.

The only effect on the Duke was to heighten his hostility to any bargain on reform. 'I saw that it was a question of noses,' he recalled to Lady Salisbury six years later, '– that as many as I gained on one side I should lose on the other: the Ultra Tories were beginning to take great alarm at the idea of reform. . . . Peel declared on the Saturday (30 October) to Arb: that he would resign before Xmas. . . .'[*24]

All in all, Littleton's approach merely put the Duke more keenly on the alert for the debate next day. He had already expressed his private views on reform in no uncertain terms. A distinguished acquaintance, Sir James Shaw, had asked him on 17 October if he could not introduce moderate reform as 'an

* On this last point there was probably a misunderstanding, since Peel later told Croker he had no such specific plan. (Parker, Vol. II, pp. 171-2.)

act of grace & justice'. The Duke replied flatly:

Not only do I think Parliamentary Reform unnecessary but that it would be so injurious as that Society, as now established in the Empire could not exist under the system which must be its Consequence.

Then came the punch-line, even more significant on 1 November than when he wrote it on 17 October:

I shall therefore at all times and under all circumstances oppose it.[25]

Next day, 2 November, he would be answering Grey's speech on the Address in the House of Lords. What he had said in private, as it were yesterday, he would tell the world tomorrow.*

* Professor Gash in his authoritative *Mr Secretary Peel*, p. 646, attributes the Duke's notorious attack on Reform on 2 November (see below pp. 282–5) to the effect of the Palmerston–Littleton proposals of the 1st. 'The effect on the Prime Minister' writes Professor Gash, 'was curious and disastrous . . . he made up his mind that the best way to check the drift towards parliamentary reform was to throw up an immovable opposition, a kind of political Torres Vedras before which the Whig *sansculottes* would come to a halt.' It is clear, however, from the Duke's letter to Shaw that he had made up his mind and had entered his Torres Vedras well before the last-minute proposals. One might say that these proposals caused him to strengthen his redoubts.

16

Release

The night of Tuesday 2 November 1830 in the House of Lords. Debate on the Address. Earl Grey had wound up for the Opposition and the Duke of Wellington rose to wind up for the Government. He wore his familiar white stock with the plain silver buckle behind and quiet, well-cut dark clothes. For once nobody said he looked worn or ill.

There seemed little to expect in the way of sudden drama, judging by what had gone before: a King's Speech preaching firmness at home and abroad, coupled with conciliation; the usual attempt by the irreconcilable Winchilsea to make capital out of the people's suffering; Grey paying a handsome tribute to the Duke's extraordinary ascendancy and introducing reform only towards the end of his speech as a remedy for distress.

Even then Grey admitted that he personally was not tied to any particular measures of reform – a hit at the radical Brougham who, in another place, was clamouring for universal suffrage, the secret ballot and annual parliaments. So far so good. There was an atmosphere of which no prime minister could complain.

Wellington began as graciously as Grey. He congratulated the noble Earl on many of his sentiments and sincerely regretted that he could not assent to them all. However, some considerable time spent in differing from Grey on Portugal, Holland and Ireland seemed at last to give an edge to the Prime Minister's oration. When he reached the outrages in Kent and Sussex he roundly denied that they were caused by distress, since greater distress in the past had produced no outrages. Were they then due to evils resulting from the recent disturbances in France? And if they were, was this country to be protected from similar revolution only by reform? The noble Earl Lord Grey had been candid enough to admit that he was 'not prepared with any measure of reform'. His Majesty's Government, declared the Duke, speaking more vibrantly than hitherto, 'is as totally unprepared as the noble Lord'. Suddenly he was launched into his great onslaught on reform. That at least was prepared.

Nay, I, on my own part, will go further, and say, that I never read or heard of any measure . . . which in any degree satisfies my mind that the state of representation can be improved. . . .

Both sides were now listening with rapt attention as the Duke, entering upon his peroration, moved from the imperfections of reform to the perfections of the present system. His voice rose, his tone became challenging. He was pushing himself further, further, further – towards what?

I am fully convinced that the country possesses at the present moment a Legislature which answers all the good purposes of legislation, and this to a greater degree than any Legislature ever has answered in any country whatever.

The Government benches began to look uneasy, the Opposition incredulous.

I will go further and say, that the Legislature and the system of representation possess the full and entire confidence of the country. . . .

What of the packed reform meetings, the Birmingham and other political unions, Brougham's election walkover in Yorkshire, the largest county in the whole of England? But the great Duke was sailing into the empyrean like an aeronaut who has slipped his moorings and no one could save him.

I will go still further, and say, that if at the present moment I had imposed upon me the duty of forming a Legislature for any country, and particularly for a country like this, in possession of great property of various descriptions, – I do not mean to assert that I could form such a Legislature as we possess now, for the nature of man is incapable of reaching such *excellence* at once, – but my great endeavour would be, to form some description of legislature which would produce the same results.

The face of Lord Aberdeen, the Foreign Secretary, who was sitting next to him, looked more like a tragic mask than usual. For the Duke even now had not finished. The special excellence of the present system, he emphasized, consisted in its being heavily weighted in favour of the landed proprietors.

Under these circumstances, I am not prepared to bring forward any measure of the description alluded to by the noble Lord. And –

further, further, further –

I am not only not prepared to bring forward any measure of this nature, but I will at once declare that . . . I shall always feel it my duty to resist such measures when proposed by others.

The Duke sat down. He had said exactly what he meant. In this age of reform, no scheme of his own and damnation to anyone else's.

There was not an immediate uproar as there would have been in the Commons. Only a brief stunned silence followed by a rising murmur of bewilderment. The Duke noticed and turned to Aberdeen.

'I have not said too much, have I?'

Aberdeen's long lugubrious face became still longer as he thrust forward his chin in a gesture reserved for extremities.

'You'll hear of it,' he warned.

George Seymour was aware of a friend convulsively grasping his arm.

'That he should have taken the Bull of Reform by the Horns at such a moment!'

As the House emptied someone outside asked Aberdeen what the Duke had said. The Foreign Secretary, having heard the bell toll for the Government, replied hollowly.

'He said that we were going out.'[1]

*

What had come over the Duke? Why did Grey's very moderate references to reform have such a catastrophic effect? No one could understand. The House got the impression that he had unaccountably lashed himself into a fury and Brougham in his memoirs recalled that it was the Duke's autocratic tone as much as his matter which had shocked the peers. Lord Granville charitably suggested that his defiant delivery and whirling words were all part of his inexperience as a speaker, leading him to exaggerate.

The Duke's uncompromising language was not only premeditated but almost a repetition of what he had written about reform to Shaw only a fortnight before – 'I shall therefore at all times and under all circumstances oppose it.' No doubt his raptures over the constitution, though extremely inopportune, would not have sounded quite so fulsome to his contemporaries as they do today. Men still vied with each other in extolling the British constitution as if it were quasi-divine. Wordsworth described its sublime principles as 'archetypes of the pure intellect'. But the Duke's paean of praise sounded defiant rather than lyrical. The further question is, then, why not the brilliantly urbane manner in which he had conducted the debates, for instance, on Catholic emancipation?

Partly because, as has been seen, he was trying to reassure the Ultras whose 'noses' he had counted, by beating a big drum; some of them had even flirted with the idea of reform. But the figure of Lord Palmerston must also be again invoked. And not only because of what Palmerston had demanded on 1 November – reform – but because of what Wellington had offered – a place in the Cabinet.

The Duke was suffering on 2 November from guilt. His vehemence was partly self-flagellation. All along he had felt untuitively it would be wrong to take in the 'Liberals' when the Government had a majority without them and had won an election only three months before. Peel, however, was adamant. When the manoeuvres failed, and failed in a fashion so humiliating, he could only kick himself. The one step he regretted having taken in autumn 1830, he told Lady Salisbury two years later, was 'making an overture to Lord Palmerston to join him with the Canningites'.[2] Often and often had he said in the past that a reputation for manly, straightforward dealing was his great asset. What was he doing, playing Palmerston's sibylline game? It had made him fall from grace. At all costs he must climb back. In doing so he was to climb out.

Less subjective but equally relevant was the Duke's attitude to reform itself. This also contributed largely to the debacle, seeming as it did to give his emotions a rational base. He saw parliamentary reform as the next stage before revolution: 'Beginning reform,' he told Mrs Arbuthnot, 'is beginning revolution.'[3] That he himself had given the country a taste for Tory reform through his Test Acts, Corn Laws and Catholic relief did not strike his political imagination. All his life the first French Revolution had been vividly present to his imagination. For him, its destructive ideas had never been modified. They had merely been kept at bay, by British arms and British institutions. In a year like 1830 who would exchange an English borough, even a 'rotten' one, for a revolutionary commune? Not he. Looking at France's '*Journées Glorieuses*' in July, his final reflection was that Britain should be 'more and more satisfied with its own institutions'.[4]

A Radical like Cobbett would no doubt discover a few more rotten boroughs on his rural rides as bad as Old Sarum, where a grassy mound, bare of all human habitation, was represented in Parliament. Votes for mounds but not for Manchester? The Duke remembered instead the number of pocket boroughs which had stuck to him, when the Ultras defected, and helped him to push through his great 'imperial measure', Catholic emancipation. He regarded them as an independent element in Parliament with a wider outlook than most. They were ready to consider the Empire as well as home interests. This element must be reassured as to its future safety in Tory hands.

The question finally resolved itself into one of fundamentals. Why did the Duke's mind work in this way? Why did he equate the 'March of Intellect' with what he now called the 'March of Insurrection'? There is no room for argument here. His most fervent admirers from Sir William Fraser onwards have agreed that he was totally lacking in political imagination. Battlefield imagination, yes; it was his forte. A favourite carriage-game often played with Croker as they bowled along the English roads together was to guess what kind of terrain lay 'on the other side of the hill'. Croker was always astounded by the Duke's accuracy. His guesses seemed to be inspired. Not so in politics. If genius is an infinite capacity for taking pains, imagination may be defined on a similarly practical level as an infinite number of past experiences projected forward in a sudden flash. The Duke's mind was already formed when he entered high British politics. After a dozen years he had not yet learned to divine the lie of the land. Was it surprising that on some of his political excursions he wrongly guessed that revolution lay on the other side of the hill?

*

The effect of the Duke's speech was prodigious. Wild rumours circulated in the City. Had he acquired secret information of

some conspiracy emanating from abroad? Funds fell four points.
Bets were laid among the Whigs on his resigning immediately
or becoming a reformer before the end of the week. Lord Wharncliffe, a moderate Tory, allowed his Whig acquaintance to see
him 'holding up his hands and eyes' in horror. Nameless fears,
cynicism and silent gestures were not the way of the radical
mobs, who raged about London in paroxysms of fury, hooting
and hissing the Duke whenever they saw him and shouting, 'No
Polignac!' 'No Police!' The rumour-mongers of a year earlier
who had hinted that the Duke installed Polignac in France now
credited him with inspiring the Polignac decrees. An English
revolution from the right was what the radical crowds professed
to fear. Nearly a week after the speech Greville found the town
still ringing with the Prime Minister's 'act of egregious folly'.[5]

The Duke remained perfectly composed. He assured his
alarmed colleagues there was no conspiracy, 'or we should have
heard of it', but every intention to do mischief. (The scare about
a conspiracy had reached his ears as early as September, when a
Dorset postmistress sent him the directions left with her by 'a
mysterious Frenchman' for forwarding letters.) His impassive,
even cheerful demeanour in the hostile streets flummoxed
Princess Lieven. 'This is to me unintelligible.'[6]

Perhaps the most striking effect of the Duke's speech was seen
in his post-bag. The usual flow of anonymous letters, both
friendly and scurrilous, suddenly became a torrent. 'Well-wisher'
on 4 November entreated him to concede reform:

I wish you could have heard all that was said on 'Change today by
the hitherto always supporters of Government – do take the advice . . .
to save us from ruin – Do Do consider the terrible precipice we stand
upon.

The whole town, 'Well-wisher' insisted, was in the most dreadful
state over reform but –

The opinion of the mob is nothing – the opinion of the educated portion of Society is at all times *strong*, but backed by the Mob it is
irresistible. . . .

In other words, 'Well-wisher' saw the March of Intellect and of
Insurrection as one. Even the 'respectable & thinking part of the
community' had expected the Duke to give the vote to the great

towns. 'I am sorry for it,' concluded 'Well-wisher' desperately, 'I see a *terrible* crisis.'

Commercial paralysis and bankruptcy were predicted by 'Humble Servant' because the 'grace of conciliation' had been lacking from his Grace's speech: 'Crown the Laurel with Olive, and Rule for Life . . . a too lofty bearing, Noble Duke, is not politic in this nation of shopkeepers.'

Among the hundreds of offensive letters came the Duke's first personal experience of 'Captain Swing'. This legendary character was really nothing but a name, though a marvellously potent name standing for the unknown leader or leaders of the rioting agricultural labourers; the true King Ludd. No one had ever seen 'Swing' for certain, though he was believed to ride about in a gig setting fire to hayricks with a strange blue spark. Within a few weeks 'Captain Swing' was to confront the authorities with a crisis in the countryside such as they had never known before and which their successors would never have to face again. Threatening letters from 'Swing' had been scarifying the land-lords since September. On the day after his fatal speech, 3 November 1830, the Duke received the first directed against himself:

Secret committee BEWARE – we are coming to London. Signed Swing.

On 4 November came a longer warning:

. . . take my advice act openly and nobly as becomes a Briton: reform that vile nest of corruption which is bred in Downing St. destroy those vultures that prey on the public liver or beware! I say beware! BEWARE BEWARE! ['Swing had now changed from black to red ink] Signed Swing.

Four days later 'Swing' struck again, in a bold, well-formed black script:

Parliamentary Reform in a full and fair representation of the people or Death!!!
Mark this thou Despot.
Swing.

An undated letter referred to the mob having jostled Wellington n the Park during the weekend:

Allegory of Wellington at the Crowning of Peace, with War lying slain at his feet. Water-colour by Thomas Stothard, 1815, designer of the Wellington Shield.

Wellington as Master-General of the Ordnance, 1819. Ladies watch him exercising his 'hobby horse'. 'Bless! what a Spanker!' says one, 'I hope he won't fire it at me'. 'It can't do any harm', replies her friend, 'for he has fired it so often in various Countries, that it is nearly worn out!'

Wellington in 1818. The Duke commissioned this portrait as a gift for his godson, Lord Arthur Russell, and kept a stock of engravings to give to friends who asked for a picture.

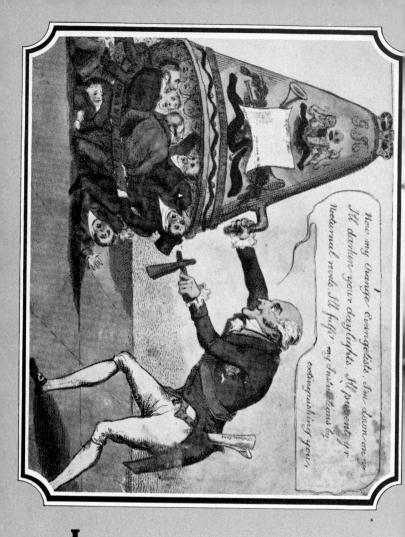

Lord Wellesley, as Lord-Lieutenant of
Ireland, extinguishing the Orange Clubs.

Lord Castlereagh.

George Canning.

Robert Peel.

Wellington 1824. Portrait painted for Peel by
Sir Thomas Lawrence. The artist began by
putting a watch in the Duke's hand, as if waiting
for his Prussian allies, but the Duke expostulated,
'That will never do. I was *not* "waiting" for the
Prussians at Waterloo. Put a telescope in my hand,
if you please'.

'Killing Time'.
Wellington eyeing a lady in the street. An
unsigned undated print, probably by 'HB' (John
Doyle) though it is not among his collected works
and may have been withdrawn. Harriette Wilson,
the 'demi-rep', published her Memoirs in 1825,
containing a number of stories about Wellington.

Wellington 1829. 'Leaving the House of Lords – Through the Assembled Commons'. The mob yells 'No popery – No Catholic ministers' – as Wellington gallops home after a debate on Catholic emancipation.

The Duel 1829. Wellington challenges
Winchilsea on 'the field of Battersea' over
Catholic emancipation. The Prime Minister wears
a priest's robes and rosary, with the head of a
lobster, symbol of a scarlet-uniformed soldier. He
says, 'I used to be a good shot but have been out
of practice for some years'.

Framed but not yet glazed.' Wellington
looks through his broken windows at
Apsley House.

'A sketch in the Park.' Wellington and Mrs Harriet Arbuthnot.

A Celebrated Commander on the Retir'd
List.' Wellington relaxed and elegant.

'Wellington musing on the Field of Waterloo.' Imaginative scene painted by B. R. Haydon in 1839, showing the Lion Mound and monument to Sir A. Gordon in the background. 'They have spoilt my battlefield,' said the Duke when he first saw the Mound in 1821. Count D'Orsay, who himself painted the Duke in 1845, touched up Copenhagen's hind quarters, but after he had left the studio Haydon obliterated his work with the words, 'This won't do – a Frenchman touch Copenhagen!'

Wellington with his grandchildren, in the
library at Stratfield Saye. From left to right:
Henry (afterwards 3rd Duke), Mary (Lady Mary
Scott), Arthur (4th Duke), Victoria (Lady Holm
Patrick). The miniature was painted by
R. Thorburn for Angela Burdett-Coutts in 1853,
though the Duke's head may have been taken from
life the year before and copied here. Miss Coutts
had wanted the Duke at breakfast but the 2nd
Duke suggested the breakfast-table would be a
'terrible stumbling block'. Would she not prefer
him opening his letters in the library before
breakfast 'and giving as he did the covers to the
children'?

Sir Pride not yourself upon your Late escape . . . Signed By Order of the Commander in Chief of the Bellingham Society in honour of that patriot named SWING.

On the back of this note was scribbled 'Remember Percival [*sic*] of old' – Perceval being the Prime Minister assassinated by Bellingham in 1812. Another anonymous writer about the Park incident advised the Duke to 'quit the Country in the quickest ship out of Port'.

But instead of quitting the Duke braced himself to face a new challenge.

*

In the flood of agitated letters to both Peel and the Duke special emphasis was laid on the dangers of a state visit to the City, due to take place on Lord Mayor's Day, Tuesday 9 November, exactly a week after the Duke's speech. The King and Queen accompanied by their ministers were to drive to the Guildhall and dine with the new Lord Mayor of London. But would they ever reach their destination? This was to be the occasion, warned scores of citizens, for a most stupendous riot, culminating in mass murder of the Cabinet. As soon as HM entered the City, Temple Bar would be lowered and he would be held prisoner until he dismissed his ministers or promised reform. If necessary the City would be set on fire. The cutting of gas-pipes was planned, destruction of London factories and a mutiny in the Life Guards. Birmingham was sending three thousand men to join the insurgents and there was another body of armed rebels known as the Five Hundred. 'Beware of men in the backstreets of Knightsbridge' – seen carrying a placard with tricolour streamers and the slogan 'Bread or Blood'.

A printed placard was brought to Peel, attacking his new police:

PEEL'S POLICE RAW LOBSTERS BLUE DEVILS or by whatever other appropriate Name they may be known:-

Notice is hereby given of a subscription to arm the people with STAVES of a superior Effect [against] a Force unknown to the British Constitution. . . .

The placard was signed in ink, 'Swing'.

Postmarked 9 November, the actual day of the proposed

procession, came a short sharp message from 'The Avenger' for the Duke. 'I and many more bold spirits mean to rid the World of [a] *Madman* and a tyrannt [*sic*].' But the 'madman' was not so demented after all. He had taken steps to cancel the whole royal proceedings.

*

On Saturday 6 November the Lord Mayor elect, Alderman Key, had written urgently to the Duke and Peel: they must bring a strong military force with them on Tuesday or he could not answer for the consequences. The Duke at once consulted Peel and then called an emergency Cabinet meeging for 4 P.M. on Sunday the 7th at 10 Downing Street. A message had already been received from St James's Palace: 'The King is inclined to think that the Visit to the City had better be postponed.'

The moment the Prime Minister and the Home Secretary entered the Cabinet chamber Lord Ellenborough knew from their faces that the visit was off. Lyndhurst attempted a remonstrance, but with a quiet 'Listen', the Duke read aloud a selection of spine-chilling letters received by the Home Secretary. All showed that an attempt was to be made on the way to or from the Guildhall.

'The feeling in the Duke's mind,' noted Ellenborough sym-pathetically, 'was that we should not be justified in giving an occasion for the shedding of blood, by means of a crowd *of our own making*.'[7] It might even spark off a riot which, combined with the disturbances on the farms, would spread all over England.

The Duke and Peel went off at 7 P.M. with a letter of advice to the King. They left behind a group of still unconvinced ministers who dreaded the effect of retreat, particularly the appearance they would give of saddling His Majesty with their own unpopularity. But with tears in his eyes at the thought of his ministers' peril, the King agreed to cancellation. The announcement was made next day, Monday the 8th. Cancellation did not mean peace and calm for the Duke.

There was an immediate crisis in public confidence. The funds fell another 3 per cent. Shopkeepers put up their shutters and barred their doors. Commerce came to a standstill. To the Whig politicians it was the last step in Wellington's road to ruin. Lord

Wellesley convulsed Greville with a crack against his brother for preventing the King from moving freely among his faithful subjects – 'the boldest act of cowardice he ever knew'.

A new flood of furious letters descended on the Prime Minister. The flavour of two must suffice, the first coming from 'Tax-payer for Thirty-five Years':

> My Lord Duke you have disappointed the Loyal citizens of London!!! look to it . . . I say again look to it – Take off TAXES – cause reduction in every department of the state, beginning with YOURSELF first. Give to the BEST of Kings the BEST of advice. . . .

The second, strangely signed '*Amicus*', added its quota of gloom and panic:

> Doctors Commons. My Lord
> The insult offered to the Citizens through your advice will be attended by the most direful consequences. Beware of *your* own safety. I caution you.

By the 9th Lady Granville was anxious for the Duke. 'Everything is dropping beneath his feet.' If only he would resign and get it over. He looked 'low, *abattu*, downfallen', but scoffed at any personal danger saying,

'It is not so easy to kill a man.'

His carriage doors had bolts on the inside and when Hardinge had hinted that he would take a pistol in each pocket on *the day*, Wellington replied,

'Oh! I shall have pistols in the carriage.'[8]

Lord Mayor's Day was still to be celebrated, though without the King and ministers. Would a disturbance take place none the less? London, particularly the Guildhall, had to be protected by cavalry, guns, five hundred marines, the New Police and City police, soldiers and eight hundred volunteers. With all these precautions to organize the Duke was at the Horse Guards on the 8th and in the evening went down to the Rotunda at Blackfriars to see for himself one of the great radical meetings which were taking place there nightly. He found two thousand people inside the building (where the speeches were 'not very seditious')[9] and an overflow of thirty-four thousand, most of whom the New Police managed to send home at about 10.30 P.M. Six hundred demonstrators, however, got away and galloped towards Downing Street at such a pace that a police officer dashing on ahead to warn Wellington and Peel, now conferring at the Home Office, beat the charge of the six hundred by only one minute. Wellington just had time to get into the Horse Guards by the back entrance when the Light Brigade swept past the front of the building and on up Whitehall.

He decided that next night – the key night – things must be different. As soon as the Rotunda was full the overflow must be dispersed by four hundred New Police, and a hundred soldiers from the Horse Guards if necessary. And instead of these forces being lined up in front of the mob, as on the 8th, they must be kept ready but out of sight. Many more nights like the 8th would destroy the police morally and physically.

Apsley House also was to be put into a state of defence: all shutters on ground floors and in Waterloo Gallery to be closed: gates into yard and stable to be locked; armed men to be stationed at various windows, especially the Duke's little ground-floor bedroom which looked on the Park; if a crowd collected they should be told that the house would be defended and they 'had better go somewhere else'; no one to fire unless the gates or railing were broken down.[10]

Tuesday the 9th came and went. There was no insurrection. Only riots and injuries to police, with hooting in Parliament Square, mobbing of ministers as they entered and left and Lord Ellenborough glad to get a lift home.

If it is probable, as many observers believed, that Wellington overestimated the crisis, at least there was none of the bloodshed he was determined to avoid – no Manchester of eleven years before, no Bristol of one year ahead. His poor Kitty, lying ill in her beleaguered bedroom and able only to pencil the news to her sister in Ireland, understood his point well:

In my heart I think that in the Duke's warlike life, he never did any-thing so valiant, and that no Government ever did a wiser than prevent-ing the Lord Mayor's dinner. . . . London might have been flowing with blood that night and all England drowned in tears now![11]

Or as the Duke asked, would it have been right to risk so much for so small a triumph? 'Would this have been well or humane for a little bravado . . .?'[12]

The greatest test of all was still to come. After the double shock to public confidence of the speech and the cancellation, what were the Duke's chances of surviving the new session?

Greville met Mrs Arbuthnot on the day of the cancelled royal visit (9 November) and walked with her to Downing Street, intending to get from her the Duke's views.

'Well, you are in a fine state; what do you mean to do?'

'Oh, are you alarmed?' returned Harriet. 'Well, I am not; everybody says we are to go out and I don't believe a word of it.'

Greville proceeded to drag from her an admission that she regretted the Duke's speech, but even so she was sure the Opposition would be beaten on reform, when a motion by Brougham was debated on the 16th.

Meanwhile the Duke had met Lady Jersey. Would he have to resign?

'Lord, I shall not go out,' he laughed; 'you will see we shall go on very well.'

At 9 o'clock that night he sat down to repeat his assurance in a letter for Harriet. The Government would get through its difficulties – 'and I dare say that I shall again be the most popular Man in the Country'.[13]

*

Nearly a week passed with things steadily getting better. The funds recovered. Sir Thomas Lethbridge, the Duke's most importunate admirer, took a sample of City opinion and reported universal relief at the cancellation of their Majesties' visit and the Duke's firmness on reform; to which the Duke replied as firmly to Lethbridge: 'You may rely upon it that I will not alter my course.' There was no more mobbing of the Prime Minister, but had there been, a Mr Henry Grosvenor was prepared to form a ducal bodyguard of friends, 650 strong. ('The Laws of the Country are strong enough to protect me against the Brutal attacks of any,' replied the Duke, after extending suitable thanks.) And the Duke 'at last convinced himself', according to Harriet Arbuthnot, writing in her journal on 15 November, that for Peel's sake there must be a Tory–Liberal alliance. Peel could not go on any longer in the House of Commons alone.

On that very morning, 15 November, a gale which was suddenly to sweep through the Commons and flatten the Government to the ground began to blow.

A meeting of ultra-Tories chaired by Sir Edward Knatchbull resolved to cast a bold vote against the Government that evening. There was to be a debate on the Civil List, a minor affair, the grand collision over Brougham's Reform Bill being scheduled for the following day. The collision came twenty-four hours earlier than expected.

Sir Edward Knatchbull seconded a motion by Sir Henry Parnell, an Irish M.P. and kinsman of the future Irish patriot, that a commission should look into the Civil List accounts. Goulburn, for the Government, refused. The vote was taken in a packed House, from which many anti-Government M.P.s were excluded through lack of space. Members, swarming together and buzzing like wasps round an overripe plum, waited for the Speaker to declare the result: 233 for Parnell and Knatchbull, 204 against. A Government defeat by 29 votes. There was an exultant roar, despite the Whig leaders' tactful order that their rank and file should not cheer. They need not have worried. Peel's purgatory was over and he longed to join in.

The Duke was entertaining the Prince of Orange to a large dinner in the Waterloo Gallery at Apsley House when a note was sent up to him giving the news and saying that Peel, Goulburn and Arbuthnot were waiting to see him downstairs. With a whispered word to Harriet alone the Duke went down.

Peel was still radiant with relief. All three insisted that the Prime Minister must hand in his resignation to the King next morning. Why wait twelve hours to fight Brougham on reform? If and when they were beaten, it would be Brougham's radical bill which occupied the field for the future, by right of conquest. To accept defeat on the Civil List was surely to place the country's fate in Grey's more tender hands? Reluctantly the Duke agreed. He and his ministers went to St James's Palace shortly before 1 P.M. on Tuesday 16 November – the third dramatic Tuesday in a row. Their resignations were accepted by His Majesty with tears, and a promise to the Duke that his two young political secretaries should each receive a pension of £250 before losing their jobs. Greville met the Duke coming out. For once he did not like to speak. The fallen minister nodded, however, from his cabriolet, 'but he looked very grave'.[14]

*

To fall from power three months after an election victory needs some doing. How did the Duke achieve it? In one sense he was his own executioner; in another, the country forced him to meet his political Waterloo. From 1830 onwards the British people were resolved that something radical should happen.

The Duke himself pointed an accusing finger at the Continental revolutions. Not the reform agitation but the barricades of July, he told Francis Leveson-Gower, brought him down. A review was held in Hyde Park the day before the barricades went up in Paris and this review, said the Duke, was the last occasion on which an English crowd exhibited loyalty and good temper. Ten years later, however, he told Stanhope that it was Cumberland who had destroyed him, quoting with approval Lord Grey's saying: 'No government can last that has him either for a friend or an enemy.'[15] The Duke saw the vote of 15 November as the Ultras' revenge for 10 April – payment for Catholic emancipation. Some even wanted reform lest RCs captured the pocket boroughs.

Most devastating of all was the blind spot in his own political imagination blotting out reform. A time had come when the country wanted reform more than they wanted Wellington – if they could not have both. The blind spot had always made this impossible, and his speech of 2 November rammed the fact home into people's faces. Though his cancellation of the royal visit on the 9th showed that, despite the blindness, he was still a masterly tactician in the prevention of avoidable bloodshed, what was wanted now was an inspired leap in the dark. He could not make it.

Could he have ridden the surf if he had been as adroit a politician as he was a great public servant? He did not altogether want to, and his temperament did not help. Peel's uncomfortable yet relentless 'liberalism' made him feel isolated in his own Cabinet, and this in turn sometimes provoked the arbitrary and incorrigible side of his nature. For weeks the Cabinet had not been a happy one.

For months, even for years, his party had not been a thriving one. After eighteen years of their rule (1812–30) it was time for a change. If not exactly Prime Minister of a 'fag-end government', Wellington was undoubtedly the inheritor of a fag-end party dynasty. In certain moods he shared the dehydration and weariness of his colleagues, especially Peel, longing only to resign as

soon as he could do so 'with honour'. In other moods he had more
kick left than they, firmly repeating his slogan, 'We shall go on
very well.' As things turned out his fall, though far from dis-
honourable, lacked the compensating grandeur of great tragedy.

'We shall go on very well. . . .' Those words were to come true,
though not in the way or at the time he expected. Of his own
choice, he never held the highest office again. But his last twenty
years of active life increased the impact of a uniquely powerful
personality. They also sharpened in retrospect the profile of an
unforgettable Prime Minister.

*

After nearly three years at the top, the general shape of his states-
manship was firmly blocked in. To begin with, it was always
obvious that he had once been Europe's most successful soldier.
He brought to his civil office both the strength and weakness of his
past: the great soldier's devotion, acumen, resolution, calm,
steadfastness, courage and readiness to take responsibility at all
times, but especially when he judged the safety of the State or of
innocent lives to be at risk. There is also no doubt that the
authoritarian nature of military command had left its indelible
stamp. Even the devoted Mrs Arbuthnot commented more than
once on his 'savage' rages when contradicted – rages for which
he made quick reparation with a stronger than usual application
of his charm. Less than five years were to pass before he was
explaining to Lady Salisbury the difference between Cabinet
ministers and his staff officers, to the formers' disadvantage:

One man wants one thing and one another; they agree to what I say
in the morning, and then in the evening up they start with some crochet
which deranges the whole plan. I have not been used to that in all the
early part of my life.

It is possible to feel sympathy for the Duke when the 'crochets' of
Huskisson and Peel are recalled. His complaint, however, was
followed by a less engaging account of how 'we did things', so to
speak, in the army:

I have been accustomed to carry on things in quite a different
manner; I assembled my officers and laid down my plan, and it was
carried into effect without any more words.[16]

That treatment had been good enough for an old general like Erskine, as blind as a beetle and not very sober; but it was not good enough for Peel.

Half in jest he would often subscribe to the image of himself as an Iron Duke determined to get his own way. He was once staying with Lord Hertford for a shoot at a time when there was trouble with the Portuguese constitutionalists. 'These gentlemen little know this iron hand,' he said, 'and it will never allow them to do what it does not wish.' (The iron hand had accidently just winged a keeper.)[17]

The habit of deluging political leaders with advice was another trait of British democracy not found in the army. 'I have come to the conclusion that the English are the most officious people that I have yet met with,' he wrote after nine months of the premiership – but he answered every letter personally, 'to a degree which is not only unprecedented,' said Greville, 'but quite unnecessary, and I think unwise, although certainly it contributes to his popularity'.

Despite his enormous correspondence, the Duke had not learned to communicate. He distrusted the press, often with good reason. Nevertheless papers like *The Times* were increasingly listened to and no statesman in 1830 could afford to speak to 'the *Gentlemen*' in Wellington's tone of voice. Disraeli was also to observe failure of communication in regard

to those unconstitutional speeches, full of naivete and secret history, which the Duke of Wellington was in the habit of addressing to the peers when his grace led the house of lords. . . .[18]

As for 'the mob', or 'mobbikins', as Maria Edgeworth called the smaller groups of demonstrators, Wellington was beginning to show a touch of the Coriolanus-type hero towards them. Charlotte Brontë, whose happy obsession with her great Duke did not diminish with the years, published her novel *Shirley* in 1847, and called one chapter 'Coriolanus'. Her fictitious hero, Robert Moore, a harsh but dynamic and lovable mill-owner, has something of Wellington in him.* Always referring to the poorest of his work-people as 'the mob', he is none the less a great man. But

* In this same novel, *Shirley*, the Duke is also compared explicitly with Mr Helstone, a rugged parson, father of the heroine and founded on Charlotte's father, the Rev. Patrick Brontë. See below, pp. 459–60.

why this fault? Charlotte turns to Shakespeare's *Coriolanus* for
some possible answers:

> *Whether was it pride,*
> *. . . whether defect of judgment,*
> *. . . or whether nature,*
> *Not to be other than one thing, not moving*
> *From the casque to the cushion but*
> *Even with the same austerity and grab*
> *As he controlled the war?*

'*From the casque to the cushion. . . .*' If Wellington in fifteen
years had not made the transition, the presumption was that he
would never fully make it. Yet his entire lack of pride, his far
from defective judgement, and above all his abhorrence of
cruelty were arguments on the other side.

The sanctity of public life, even in its most secret corners, was
always scrupulously observed by him. When Talleyrand's
nephew was imprisoned in 1829 for huge gambling debts incurred
in England, everyone except the Duke implored the French
ambassador to obtain diplomatic immunity for the delinquent
by taking him into the French embassy. Wellington was prepared
to pay the debts himself rather than have the diplomatic service
discredited.

Those who obtained pensions through the Duke were more
often the young or the old than the powerful – his two secretaries
and seventy-four-year-old Miss Sarah Ponsonby, survivor in
1829 of that inimitable, romantic partnership, the Ladies of
Llangollen.

Notwithstanding the two most remarkable innovations of
Wellington's premiership (Catholic M.P.s and the New Police)
there has always been a tendency to see him as a modernizer
malgré lui. Professor Turberville, who has many penetrating and
generous things to say, at the same time gives him a curious
label: the well-known, 'None go so far as those who do not
know whither they are going.'* Wellington, however, had contemplated a new police force and Catholic rights for years. In

* Turberville, p. 228. Wellington, he continued, 'brought the Tory ship
into some strange and alien ports of call. That the Ministry of the Duke of
Wellington would pass down to history as one of the great reforming
Ministries did not seem conceivable; but the inconceivable happened.'

each case he knew where he was going and got there. Over parliamentary reform he thought he knew where the reformers were going, namely towards the revolution, and got it wrong. His mistake was to bar that road and go nowhere.

In those years of misery a new lead was vital. Never mind if parliamentary reform could not by itself cure 'distress'; at least it could give the cause of the distressed more punch in Parliament. To argue as the Duke did that Britain's over-all wealth was increasing, even if certain unfortunate individuals on $2\frac{1}{2}d.$ a week were destitute, was to fail to see the trees for the wood. With all the criticism, some justified and some not, no one ever accused him of opposing parliamentary reform for selfish reasons. He never consented to be a borough-monger himself, pointedly rejecting the additional offer of a borough when he was extending his estate at Stratfield Saye. Proprietors who constantly added to their bag of boroughs for the sake of the money he considered detestable. The conviction that as Prime Minister he had acted only for the public good, as he saw it, gave him his incomparable strength. A 'nest of corruption' as denounced by Captain Swing might or might not exist in Downing Street or other inviting sites along Whitehall. Nobody ever thought the nests were built or feathered by Wellington. It was this incorruptibility together with his shining honesty of purpose which made him a towering political leader, and caused so many of his countrymen to feel he could never be replaced.

'If people think I like this station,' he had said to Colin Campbell soon after becoming Prime Minister, 'they are mistaken. The nation has rewarded me and over-rewarded me. My line is to command the army, but if I think I can do any good by being Minister, I am willing to . . . do what I can.'[19]

A letter has survived among the Duke's private papers written by an unknown Radical to a famous Tory, Lord Ashley (afterwards the great Lord Shaftesbury), on the victory of Catholic emancipation. 'I am constrained to tell you,' said this Radical, 'my admiration of your Duke, who is now my Duke & every man's Duke, who has a mind in him, throughout the World. . . .'[20] What comes through in this letter is not so much the Radical's natural fervour for the triumph of Catholic emancipation, as his happiness at being united at last with a national hero and very great man. It had been a personal deprivation not to be able to speak like other men of 'my Duke'.

After all the calculations have been made and the debits and credits duly balanced, such greatness suddenly reduces to rather small proportions the conventional question of whether he was a 'good' or 'bad' Prime Minister.*

* C. M. Cruttwell calls him 'the worst Prime Minister of the nineteenth century'. (*Wellington*, p. 101.)

Part III

17

Interlude II: Tower, Cinque Ports and Wicked William

Like many a wife before and since, Kitty was not sorry that her husband had become a fallen minister. From her sick-bed at Stratfield Saye she pencilled her thoughts to her sister Elizabeth Stewart in Ireland:

> My Bess, depend upon it, the Duke having found it advisable to Resign . . . was the direct Hand of that God who has ever protected him in the more evident though not more real dangers of Battle.
> Everybody saw that the Duke's health was altering, that his countenance was acquiring a drawn and fallen look, his figure to shrink, and many other appearances that precede the breaking up of a constitution from over work.

He was fallen and looked fallen. But, added Kitty, 'Thank God he has resigned in time. . . .' Here at Stratfield Saye his friends assured her his looks were already beginning to mend. Not that he was resting – 'You know dear Bess, that unlike others of the name of Wellesley, the Duke cannot be idle. . . .'[1] He had left London for his country home on a mission. Wherever his presence as Lord-Lieutenant was needed to pacify the countryside he would appear.

For 'Captain Swing' had reached Hampshire.

Samuel Rogers, the poet and financier, remembered him sitting over the Arbuthnots' fire and outlining his post-resignation plans.

'I will go down into my County,' he said, 'and do what I can to restore order and peace.' Nor were politics to be neglected. 'And in my place in Parliament, when I can, I will approve; when I cannot, I will dissent, but I will never agree to be leader of a faction.'[2] For the sake of principle he would fight reform but not for party. Meanwhile there were many other duties of a public or personal nature to occupy every hour of his day and exorcize any remaining signs of a fallen minister's particular demon, the aching void.

*

In 1830 he had become a governor of Charterhouse and an Elder Brother of Trinity House, and had been Constable of the Tower since 1827, Lord Warden of the Cinque Ports since 1829 and guardian, first official and then unofficial, of three wards in Chancery since 1825.

These positions gave him some welcome opportunities to answer the all too vehement calls for patronage. Trinity House, being a nautical corporation with almshouses and lighthouse appointments, could not be bent to serve the Duke's own beloved family, the army. But with Charterhouse he laid down a strict rule for himself; to help only the families of his veterans, and only those in need. So when General Beatson's widow, left with eleven children, wanted nominations to the school, he had to turn her down, though with soothing tact:

> General Beatson was a gentleman of large fortune. It is true that the Duke devotes to the families of the officers with whom he has had the happiness of serving all the patronage which may appertain to any office held by him. But he believes that it is his duty to look for those in preference who are most in need of assistance; and he cannot but hope that the family of General Beatson are not among them.[3]

He received at least one direct request from the boys of Charterhouse in 1830, which was conceded. Would he ask HM King William IV to grant them a holiday on his accession? Signed, John Wellington Freese, Captain of the School. John was a younger brother of Arthur Freese, the Duke's godson and himself an Old Carthusian. As children of a penurious Indian army officer and a very pretty mother, both boys were perfect candidates for the Duke's patronage.

*

There had been considerable excitement among the cocked hats when it was learnt that Lord Hastings, Constable of the Tower of London, had died suddenly in December 1826. At least one royal duke was interested, while Lord Londonderry entreated Wellington as his 'best friend' to get this plum for him. The best friend, however, was already booked by the King to take it on himself.[4]

The new Constable set to work at once to master and reform his domain. As a royal palace, the Tower was a picturesque combination of ravens and execution site on Tower Green, historic armoury, jewel house and mint to which the public had access, and the thousand or so local inhabitants who lived within the ancient 'Liberties of the Tower'. The Duke found that these favoured citizens, especially the Beefeaters in their Tudor uniforms, were taking considerable liberties with the law. Because no bailiff could enter the 'Liberties', debts were deliberately left unpaid. Money was extorted from the visiting public by warders and from the taxpaying public by sinecurists.

Licensed corruption of this kind would have scandalized the Duke anywhere. How much more when it undermined what he saw as the serious purpose of the Tower.

The Tower was a fortress in his view. Though it had not served as such since Sir Thomas Wyatt's attack in 1554, he saw it as the modern revolutionary mob's bastille, for whose possession they and he would never cease to fight. 'The fortress' fielded a lieutenant (sinecure), a tower major who lived in the medieval Queen's House and was the Constable's chief-of-staff, a medical officer, a tower chaplain, a garrison of 100 Beefeaters and Yeoman Warders, a battalion of four hundred guards at disturbed periods like the thirties, a motley crowd of 'lodgers', and an arsenal of ammunition and muskets, besides the swords, spears and halberds in the armoury which the Constable felt would be an especial temptation to the mob. Even the regular tourists whose entry fees were reduced to 1s. (Crown Jewels 2s. extra) by a Whig government in 1837 seemed to him a potential menace. 'What is to prevent some thousands each with a shilling from going there if they please, and when once there from doing what they please? Who is to keep them in order? Or to turn them out?'[5] It was obvious that the Tower as a fortress would always clash with the Tower as a show.

When William IV proposed visiting his palace in 1830 the new Constable took steps 'to prevent the *people* getting into the Tower'.[6] *No carriages to set down inside the gates unless it rained.* Joseph Hume, the Radical M.P. for Middlesex, fought his proposal to increase the Tower Hamlets militia. What would happen to London, the Constable asked himself, if a Reform bill were carried and Parliament filled with *Humeites*? 'This idea haunts me. . . .'

The remains of the Tower's original moat, known as 'the Ditch', was a matter for practical reform. One odious but inevitable liberty taken by the whole Tower population was to throw all their refuse into this dreadful sewer. When the Duke arrived there were noisome banks of ordure 8 feet deep which prevented the River Thames from entering it freely. He at once had 10,000 cubic feet of filth removed in barges at a cost of £1,000, after which the Ditch was regularly flooded, dammed, stirred about, drained and scraped by men in 'mudboots' at each spring tide. Just as the engineering department were boasting that the Ditch was 'purer' than it had been for fifty years, a new enemy struck – the cholera.

So poisonous was the stench caused by scraping the moat that residents in neighbouring St Katherine's Dock decided the smell itself had caused the disease. They therefore petitioned for 'the Scraping Process' to cease. In vain the indignant Constable wrote a minute beginning, 'All bad smells are disagreeable. But I very much doubt their being unwholesome'[7]; Charles Greville wrote on behalf of the Privy Council ordering no more scraping until the autumn.

The proper solution of filling up the Ditch with earth and laying sewerage pipes was ruled out by the allegedly enormous cost. When cholera invaded the Tower again, however, in 1849, the Duke immediately demanded main drainage, abolition of the ancient cesspools (one of which had already burst) and a dry ditch. He got them all in a matter of weeks for well under £400.

It was also through the cholera that the Constable rid the Tower of its most disgraceful absentee. The 'resident' medical officer, Dr Thomkins, was an old gentleman of eighty who resolutely refused to perform his duties. The Constable's first fierce reaction was that Dr Thomkins must either attend or resign. Dr Thomkins promptly demanded lodging money. The Constable was stymied. Lodgings and lodging money were among the greatest sources of graft in the Liberties. By paying lodging money to Dr Thomkins he would be buying inefficiency at extra expense. He therefore retreated on a Wellingtonian base of humanity and common sense, writing to the Tower major,

'There are no cases so difficult to deal with as those of Abuse in which the interests of Individuals of great Age and long standing in the Service are involved.' Dr Thomkins must be granted his sinecure officially for the sake of his 'reasonable comfort', and Dr J. Hunter appointed to do his work.[8]

The most striking declaration he ever made of devotion to the men in his old armies was apropos of the Tower warders. Lord Burghersh, married to his favourite niece, had requested a wardership for a sergeant at the Academy of Music. The Constable read him a sharp lecture on patronage:

My dear Burghersh, I conceive that what I have to dispose of in consequence of having used my bloody hands, belongs exclusively to those who assisted me ... my Choice must be in reference to their Conduct as Soldiers, and not at the Academy of Musick.

The whole world watched how he distributed his patronage, and the NCOs were 'a very important Class of Men'.

It is not unimportant that they should feel there is somebody who thinks of them, who regards them when they behave well. . . . I will not deprive myself of the Power of doing that good at least to a respectable Class of Men for the pleasure of gratifying the Ladies and Gentlemen of Society.[9]

If this letter had been published in Wellington's despatches it is unlikely that charges of his caring nothing for the army after Waterloo would have stuck.*

*

A second major preoccupation from 1830 onwards was the Duke's Wardenship of the Cinque Ports.†[10] With Walmer as his residential centre he rode forth to Dover or Deal in much the same crusading spirit as from Apsley House to the Tower. Cinque Ports business, however, was vital to the safety of human lives in a way that Tower business was not. And because the stakes

* See above, p. 31.
† The original Five Ports were Dover, Sandwich, Hastings, Hythe and New Romney, to which the 'Ancient Towns' of Rye and Winchelsea were later added, as well as other smaller member ports. In return for civil privileges they guarded the coast.
Among the Duke's successors were to be Sir Winston Churchill and Sir Robert Menzies.

were higher, the Lord Warden was that much more infuriated than the Constable by the perversity of human nature.

His duties were to supervise the various harbour works, life-boats and salvage; to appoint and regulate local magistrates and Dover Castle prison; above all to see that the system of piloting commercial vessels through the narrow seas and into the Thames estuary ran smoothly. Instead of a Tower major and his often absentee staff he had to rely on a lieutenant-general of Dover Castle and his underpaid and usually incompetent satellites. Instead of courts martial there was the ancient Court of Lode-manage. Instead of the Tower Ditch he had Dover Harbour to give him headaches. (In 1830 the Lieutenant-General kindly said the Duke could send a substitute to Harbour sessions. 'I will attend them if it should be in my Power,' replied the Lord Warden.) Instead of seeking out loyal and meritorious warders, he had to discover skilful and sober pilots. But he found himself deafened by exactly the same clamour for jobs and entangled in much the same mesh of archaic custom. At the beginning of his second decade as Lord Warden (1839) he was writing in a black rage:

I will force these Pilots to do their Duty, as long as I have any thing to say to them. But I . . . must give up the Business altogether if I cannot get a little more Assistance from the gentlemen of the Cinque Ports, and of Dover than I do. They are confoundedly mistaken if they think that I care one Pin for the Patronage of the office of Lord Warden. I will pitch it to the Goodwin Sands. . . .[11]

The pilots did in the end learn that chronic drunkenness would lose them their jobs; that they could not with impunity take out somebody else's ship in the dark before daybreak, run her on rocks and send her to the bottom of the Straits; that they must drop restrictive practices such as keeping only one pilot-cutter off Dungeness and the North Foreland respectively; and that they must be fair to their poorer competitors, the local boatmen.

The Lord Warden himself tried to be fair to the poor. In 1830 some forty salvage men from Bexhill petitioned him about a wrecked Dutch ship buried in sand since 1740 from which they had extricated valuable timber and glass, only to hear that the Customs officers and Lord Warden had a legal right to everything. 'I wish to further the views of the poor Men,' the Lord

Warden informed his officials. Let them keep the first £100 this year and share the rest with the Customs, without prejudice to future Lords Warden. Wellington refused his salary of £2,973 12s. 6½d. in accordance with a finance committee recommendation, and had the first year's payment returned to the public funds. No payments were made thereafter.

One factor which hampered reform of the Cinque Ports but scarcely featured at the Tower was party politics. The reason was that the Cinque Ports' area covered many key south-eastern constituencies. Pilot Gosley, for instance, was accused in 1832 of deserting his ship to go ashore during an election. His excuse was that he had food poisoning. But he had not been too ill to vote for the Tory, Mr Grove Price, at Sandwich, who was beaten. Grove Price, defending Gosley to the Lord Warden, complained that the whole affair was a manoeuvre to deprive the good cause of Pilot Gosley's support.[12] A terse reply from the Lord Warden advised Mr Grove Price that his protégé should look into the facts about his sickness before his case came up in the Court of Lodemanage.

At the beginning of the same year the Lord Warden had been asking for information about a change in the incumbent at Dover Castle who ran the beer canteen for the staff and for prisoners who could pay. What was at the back of this change? Rival brewers? Or a split in the Dover Tories? 'I enclose you a letter,' wrote the Lord Warden to the Lieutenant-General, 'regarding a person about to be turned out and another about to obtain the Canteen at Dover Castle.'

All this may be and I dare say is perfectly right. But I confess that I have not much Confidence in the attachment of our Gentlemen of the Cinque Ports to the good Cause, and I should like to know what the reason for this turning out and putting in is.

I must confess to prejudice against changing old servants.[13]

*

Whatever the demands of politics, the Duke generally regarded the Tower and Cinque Ports as congenial side-lines. Very different were the duties devolving upon him from a notorious family scandal.[14] As if by design, the performers in this melodrama became peculiarly frenzied at crucial moments in his career, thus adding substantially to the strains of his position. While in opposition and also while wrestling as Prime Minister with national problems, he tried to sort out a maddening private tangle which was always a prime nuisance and occasionally a threat. The villain of this piece, still known in the family as 'Wicked William', must have seemed to the Duke a natural for the Tower of London or the dungeons of Dover.

The story begins in 1809 when Sir Arthur Wellesley took his nephew William Wellesley-Pole, aged twenty-one and only son and heir of his elder brother William, later Lord Maryborough, out to the Peninsula on his staff. Deeply apathetic about everything except drink, gambling, horses and women, young William was rapidly returned to his father. One idle morning he woke up with an idea. Why not ask Catherine Tilney-Long, the heiress, to marry him? Marry him she did in 1812, having turned down the Duke of Clarence (also after her money) the year before. William changed his name to Long-Wellesley, and as such he goes down to history, or rather to the sub-area reserved for delinquent relatives of famous men.

The Long-Wellesleys' three children, William, James and Victoria, had 'a terrible upbringing' according to their aunt, the Duchess of Wellington, for their father was 'at open war with every relative on every side. . . .' Having disgraced the family name by squandering his wife's fortune and getting into debt, William fled with Catherine to Italy, where in 1823 he seduced the wife of Captain Bligh, a Guards officer, and eloped with her. The Duke had known the lovely Helena Bligh since her childhood; he had introduced her to her father's Essex neighbours, the Long-Wellesleys, and after Waterloo had entertained her and Captain Bligh at Mont-Saint-Martin. Whereas Bligh's uncle, Lord Darnley, quickly washed his hands of the whole present disagreeable affair, William's uncle entered upon a lengthy correspondence with all the families involved, in an effort to mend William's marriage. He sent Helena's father a cheque for £100 to fetch her home from Italy and again and again begged William to return separately, having first done the 'manly' thing and paid his debts. All these sheaves of letters were written while he was deep in his researches and correspondence on Ireland.

By 1824, however, Helena was pregnant and Captain Bligh had brought a case against William full of spicy details provided by Italian servants: that his wife's seduction had taken place on the slopes of Mount Vesuvius during a midnight excursion of fifty persons in carriages, and that Mr Long-Wellesley had rented a villa next door from which he could climb into her bedroom window, having hired one of the late King Murat's gigantic bodyguards to bar his own door. Hopeless as the case for a reconciliation now seemed, the Duke still worked assiduously to heal the breach between William and his father and wife. His advice to William in August 1825 was 'to act towards Mrs Wellesley in the most gentle manner; and in that least likely to irritate her feelings and to impress upon the Minds of the Children any return of the differences between father and Mother'. It was too late. On the day before Wellington wrote, 22 August, Helena Bligh had temporarily secured Wicked William by giving birth to a natural son, William Wellesley-Bligh.

Catherine Long-Wellesley, meanwhile, had found asylum with her two unmarried sisters, the Misses Long, in Hampshire, and hoped to make her children wards in Chancery after divorcing William. Death intervened. A violent letter from Wicked William on 12 September 1825 demanding the return of his children brought on fatal spasms of the heart and she died raving a few hours later. The family agreed William had killed her. Lady Maryborough warned the Duke and Duchess of Wellington not to attend the funeral as a mob were preparing to insult anyone with the name of Wellesley.

*

On 25 November 1825, in accordance with their sister's deathbed instructions, the Misses Long made the three Long-Wellesley children wards in Chancery with the Duke as a guardian. In accepting, the Duke said his object was 'to take care that those destined hereafter to become head of my family should be properly educated'.* He therefore promised to execute his guardianship of the children 'zealously . . . for their benefit and welfare, and in *opposition to all mankind*'.

Three weeks later the opposition materialized. Wicked William

---

* The Marquess Wellesley, as the eldest of the five Wellesley brothers and therefore head of the family, had succeeded to their father's title of Mornington (2nd Earl). However, since all Lord Wellesley's sons were illegitimate, the Mornington title would pass to the second Wellesley brother, Lord Maryborough, and his descendants.

descended like a wolf on England, to demand the custody of young William, James and Victoria – and if he could not obtain it by law he would get it by '*stratagem*'. 'A Man and his children ought to be allowed to go to the Devil in his own way,' he told the children's tutor. These words did not help his case when it came to be considered before Lord Chancellor Eldon. Judgement was given against him on 1 February 1827. Wicked William at once appealed and also entered upon a series of 'stratagems' to reverse it; for custody of his children would enable him to get hold of young William's money. That was the end of his devious road.

Just when Lord Liverpool's sudden stroke had started Wellington off on his collision course with Canning, he became engaged in a series of acrimonious exchanges with his nephew, trying to bring home to William that there could be no reconciliation with his father, and therefore no custody of his children, until he withdrew certain threats to attack and 'expose' his whole family in the press. At the height of the duel with Canning in May 1827, it appeared that William contemplated not only defaming his father but murdering his uncle.

In that month a Colonel James Grant was dining with Long-Wellesley when the latter burst out with an account of what he would do if the Duke defeated his appeal and was confirmed in the guardianship of his children.

'By God, I will shoot him.' Grant could not believe his ears.

'Do you know what you are saying? You must be mad.' Long-Wellesley replied calmly, 'I am fully aware of what I am saying and I will expiate the Crime on the Scaffold.'

Next morning Grant again met Long-Wellesley and saw by the 'sullen earnestness' of his manner that his words had been no 'idle menace'.

This story reached the Duke in July, shortly before the crisis of Canning's death and his own illness, having been sent to him by a confidant of Colonel Grant's. After the dinner with Long-Wellesley Grant had rushed round to his friend's house in a state of collapse, warning him shortly to expect 'a most awful Catastrophe'. But presumably owing to Grant's pressure, William dropped the assassination plot and instead circulated a pamphlet against his uncle. This 'odious' document, as Fitzroy Somerset called it, well illustrated the mad ingenuity of Wicked William's mind. If he could prove that all members of the Wellesley and

Long families, beginning with the Duke, were as vicious and immoral as he was himself, the Court of Chancery would have no choice – or so he believed – but to grant his appeal for custody of the children.

The pamphlet therefore asserted that the Duke of Wellington's association with the Misses Long sprang from his wish to obtain control of his eldest ward's money. Of his morality, the less said the better. Everyone knew Mrs Arbuthnot was now living with him in Apsley House, as they knew of his intrigues with the present Marchioness Wellesley when Mrs Patterson, with her sister Lady Hervey which had killed 'poor Sir Felton Harvey [*sic*]', with Lady Charlotte Greville and Mrs Freese, 'whose son he educated with his own'.

This is the man who wants to be guardian of Mr Wellesley's children, and who pretends to be a more MORAL man than their father.

Having subjected most of the Duke's nieces to the same kind of treatment in his pamphlet, Wicked William turned to the Long family and produced his *chef d'oeuvre* on 23 August.

He laid an affidavit against the Misses Long and their relatives together with other libellous material for the Lord Chancellor's perusal. The affidavit was a string of invented horrors: that the Misses Long had picked a playfellow for their nephews who was having intercourse with his aunt; that their niece's governess and her sister were prostitutes, both living with the Misses Long's uncle; that the younger Miss Long had committed incest with this same uncle, that all the rest of the Long family were drunken blasphemers (they were pious Evangelicals) and that finally the children's two aunts had 'a libidinous relationship' with one another.

It only needed for William's uncle to become Prime Minister for the pamphlet to be prominently displayed in the shop-window of a publisher off Drury Lane, as part of No. 18, *The Rambler's Magazine or Frolicsome Companion*, advertising more 'Amorous Scenes' and 'Voluptuous Anecdote' between its covers than any book, not excepting Harriette Wilson's Memoirs.* The magazine was a bawdy and grotesque production offered at 1s., with William's highly coloured contribution standing out

* First published in 1825 and containing many choice lies about the Duke. See *Wellington: The Years of the Sword*, pp. 208–215, 220–222; Panther, 1971.

from the well-worn amours of Lord Byron and Lady Hamilton.

Besides these repeated attacks the new Prime Minister had to deal with indignant letters from Mrs Bligh's father, accusing him of being out to wreck her parliamentary bill to obtain a divorce from Bligh. (In fact she got her divorce and William married her in August 1828, to her incalculable cost.) At last he decided to break off direct communication with his paranoiac nephew. But despite the crisis with Huskisson and all his other preoccupations he refused to abandon his wards. The solution was obvious to him. The Duchess.

*

William lost his appeal in 1828, after which the Duke set about putting the guardianship on a permanent basis. Finding a second guardian was no easy matter, since no one wished to undertake the hateful duty of dealing with the children's father. Early in 1829, however, the Duke took enough time off from Catholic emancipation to persuade Sir William Courtenay, of the distinguished Devon family, to act with Kitty 'under the Shield of my Protection'. Kitty accepted her trust almost as if her husband were the Angel of the Lord: 'I with the greatest pleasure agree to that which you propose, and will do as you wish' – and in August 1829 the Duke assured William that he would find the Duchess 'disposed to conduct the duties entrusted to her by the Lord Chancellor in the manner most likely to be approved by all those interested in the welfare of the Children'. It was a sincere uxorial compliment, richly deserved. In return, having paid off Kitty's debts, he relieved her of handling the household books.*
At the same time he cut himself off from William, though with surprising mildness. He explained to William that the threat to shoot him, followed by the libellous pamphlet, put him in an awkward position. He might have to prosecute, particularly if the libels were published in a newspaper with a wider circulation than the *Frolicsome Companion*. The Duke ended his letter, 'It is not desirable that there should be much intercourse between us. Believe me ever yours most affectionately Wellington.'

Banned – most affectionately.

Over the next two years, while the Duke was in the throes of the reform battle, an excellent working partnership developed

* See below, pp. 346–7.

between Kitty and her Arthur, she protecting him from the endlessly tedious negotiations with William, he advising her on how to handle her correspondence as guardian. Apart from Kitty's neglect of her health and restless activity, which caused two bad falls, the Duke had nothing to criticize during these years. Their frequent, friendly letters to each other about the children had no beginnings but ended in his case 'Ever yours W', and in hers 'God bless you, Most affectionately yours'. There is no reason to doubt that there was affection on his side too.

Despite crippling rheumatism and an internal complaint, Kitty did her best for two of her charges and made a brief but spectacular success of the third. Little Victoria lived mostly with her Long aunts and grew up as pious as they, to build a large church in Eastbourne out of her Long fortune. She died a spinster. The father's demon, on the other hand, completely possessed fourteen-year-old James, and he and his parent did indeed go to the devil in their own way. Wicked William enticed James away from Eton and took him on the razzle-dazzle in London. It was his plan to use James as a decoy for his elder (monied) brother.

Young William, abysmally retarded (he could not read at ten) and undisciplined, had begun his relationship with Kitty as badly as James, swearing at her, refusing to get up and happy only in the stables. He was removed from Eton by his guardians and sent with the Duke's approval to a tutor in Cheshire.* Here, with introductions from the Duke to the surviving Lady of Llangollen, the Grosvenors of Eaton Hall and the Glynnes of Hawarden,† William settled down. Except for an open addiction to alehouses and a secret one to cock-pits, he gradually lost his faroucheness and fell under Kitty's gentle spell. He had even been known to say, 'Well, I will *sap* [swot] since the Duchess wants it' – and to read history for two hours on end. Then came the enticement, almost kidnapping, of James by his father.

Neither the Duke nor Duchess could bear the thought of Wicked William triumphing. The Duke would not say that Courtenay's decision to leave James with his father was wrong but – 'I cannot but lament it'. Kitty lamented also, with spirit:

* Sir William Courtenay, his second guardian, strongly disapproved of the unruly Eton of that period and put his own two sons under Dr Arnold of Rugby.
† Parents of Catherine Glynne, the future Mrs W. E. Gladstone.

Ill as I have been, weak as I am, violent as are the wretched Boy's threats, I would rather take my Ward home this moment, than leave him to the certain ruin of the House in which I fear he now remains. Good God, I think of this with horror.

Sir William Courtenay, however, having tried in vain to winkle James out of his father's house, eventually convinced the gallant Kitty and sombre Duke that short of sending two Bow Street officers for James and imprisoning his father in the Fleet, they could do nothing – and even then Long-Wellesley might manage to receive James at the Fleet.

The real struggle was over young William, and as long as Kitty lived she triumphed. All James's advances were warded off: the promises of cigars and jewellery from their father if young William joined them, the taunts that he would be considered 'an old *school girl*' rather than an Old Etonian if he consented to be 'a Toad-Eater to the Duchess of Wellington, the Duke and his sons'. Surely he realized, asked James, that the Duke was his father's 'most inveterate Enemy'?[15] Kitty was rightly proud that notwithstanding young William's faults – his deplorable weakness, odious habits, wretched incapacity – he maintained his attachment to her. A touching account had gone to her sister Bess in Ireland of the boy secretly buying her a wheelchair so that for the first time in six months she dined downstairs.

'Don't you think she looks *better for the drive*?' murmured young William, choked with emotion at the sight of the fragile charioteer circling the dining-table. And this was the same boy who only a few months ago had loaded her with curses.[16]

Young William's tutor told her that for her ward's sake she *must* get well. Kitty replied with a short statement of her creed. 'I have read somewhere, I forget where, never to despair of any human creature while you can discover as much *Heart* as you can rest the point of a pin on.'[17]

*

The problem family on whom the Duke had spent so much time and ink came to a universally sad end.

There had been one gleam of hope for them in July 1830 when Wicked William was arrested for debt. But five people put up bail of £200 each in time for him to get himself elected to Parliament and, naturally, to vote as a reformer against his uncle. A year later he was sent to the Fleet Prison for kidnapping his daughter Victoria, and on relinquishing her used his freedom to accuse his wife Helena of a plot to trap young William into marrying her illegitimate half-sister aged twelve. In 1835 he was demanding money from the Duke to enable him, as it turned out, to provide for a girl he had seduced in Calais.[18] Meanwhile he had deserted Helena in Paris, carrying off her Italian maid as his mistress and the maid's lover as young William's valet. The Duke adhered to his resolve not to intervene in 'Mr Long-Wellesley's concerns', though he often sent Helena money. Her son William Wellesley-Bligh lived to be only twenty-six. She herself survived until 1869 as 4th Countess of Mornington, but the Duke's last recorded news of her was bleak. She was living by choice in the Wanstead workhouse – perhaps to disgrace her husband, if further disgrace were possible.

The Duke was appealed to once more on young William's behalf. In 1834 a stranger signing himself 'An Old Soldier' wrote dramatically that his Grace must rescue his ward William from his father, who had already run through over £30,000 of his fortune in eight months, and when he became twenty-one in October would rob him of the rest. The boy had nearly died from what Lord Byron modestly called 'a general subscription of the ladies'. 'Old Soldier' would send his Grace his real name if an advertisement were put in a Brussels paper merely signed 'Waterloo'.

No time was lost by the Duke and Courtenay in contacting 'Old Soldier', who turned out to be a Mr Rochefort; but the eminent legal adviser they sent over to Brussels was promptly checkmated by Wicked William publicly accusing him of having seduced his son.* This fantastic stroke seems finally to have convinced the Duke that he could do no more.

Young William lived to be fifty; James thirty-six. Their father died in squalor at Brussels in 1857. If the Duke's unfortunate wards did not actually disgrace the Wellesley name, their lives were a poignant commentary on the fate of a loveless family with a drive towards self-extinction. Like their sister, neither of the

---

* The explanation given later to the Duke was that a prostitute who had visited the eminent legal advisers, dressed as a boy, had been mistaken for young William.

Long-Wellesley brothers married, so that the Maryborough title became extinct, while the Mornington earldom devolved upon the Duke's elder son.

The cautionary tale rubbed in the Duke's repeated warnings of an idle aristocracy's doom.

18

Killed by the Bill

'He has literally been hooted down by the people,' wrote Cobbett on 20 November 1830. This harsh travesty of the Duke's defeat was none the less a true picture of the next eighteen months. Indeed, the sixteen years of active politics still before him were never to recapture a sense of 'bright confident morning'. The world was changing round him. He was the last of the national leaders who saw themselves primarily as servants of the Crown. His fall paved the way for party chiefs and the party system as we know it.

In Peel's opinion Wellington had been misled by females of the most 'mediocre' kind. 'No man has any influence with him,' he said speaking of the Duke's fatal declaration against reform; 'he is led by women; the foolish ones envelop him with incense, and he has fallen a victim to this weakness and to his own vanity.'[1]

One of the 'mediocre' females to whom Peel referred, Mrs Arbuthnot, naturally took a different view of the Duke's fall. She felt he himself was to blame for refusing to admit more talent in his team. Soon Harriet was more sorry for herself than for him. With his reading, riding and county affairs he was 'much happier out of office', but politics for her had lost their savour. 'I shall write very seldom now, I dare say, in my book.' She broke off her first entry for 1832 in the middle of a sentence. An '&' was left hanging in mid-air, as if to symbolize her disenchantment with the unfolding drama of Whig politics.[2]

*

'Everybody seems to be charmed,' wrote Lady Granville of the new regime.[3] And well they might be, for Grey had something for everyone. His Government found room for Whigs like Althorp, son and heir to Earl Spencer, and Lord John Russell, younger brother of the Duke of Bedford; Radicals like Brougham and the 1st Earl of Durham, Grey's son-in-law; Canningites like Goderich, Melbourne and Palmerston; and the Tory Duke of Richmond. The spectacle of Brougham, idol of the 'rabbleo-cracy', sitting on the Woolsack had a special charm. Radical Lord Sefton invited him and the Grey family to dinner one night and after the port preceded the Lord Chancellor out of the room carrying a fire-shovel for the mace.[4]

Once the new ministers were installed, Parliament adjourned till February. Harriet Martineau, the extraordinarily plain and deaf but enthusiastic radical historian of the period, spoke of the year beginning with November 1830 as 'Year I of the People's Cause'.[5]

*

The Duke was off to Hampshire on 22 November on the King's business. The county had been invaded by 'Captain Swing' and must be cleared. 'Swing' had made a start on the 15th with an incendiary blaze in the Duke's pew at Stratfield Saye church. This was quickly extinguished; but on the 18th and 19th the property of several neighbours, including the Baring brothers, Bingham and Frederick, sons of Alexander, was fired and machinery wrecked. Though the Prince of Waterloo himself lost nothing, £2,000 of damage was done to the Waterloo Iron Foundry not far away, because it made agricultural machinery.

What part did the Iron Duke play as Lord-Lieutenant of this exceptionally riotous county? According to Kitty, he 'made Regulations that have already [the 29th] tended to the Peace of the Neighbourhood. Indeed his appearance in the country was of the most essential use & about Stratfield Saye is perfectly quiet.' Some weeks later (8 December) 285 Hampshire prisoners were sent for trial at Winchester before a Special Commission. The setting up of this body, accompanied by offers of £500 reward for information about 'Swing', had been Melbourne's first official act as Home Secretary. The Commission operated in Hampshire with great severity, condemning six men to death (of whom two were actually hanged) and giving sixty-eight no more than a sporting chance of life by ordering them to be transported to Van Diemen's Land.

Wellington was far from shocked. There is no doubt that he

shared the outraged feelings of all landowners, whether Whigs or Tories, at the rioters' threats, extortions and fiery midnight visitations. Like his colleagues, he was kept informed about sinister figures in '*drab great coats with velvet collars* and TOP *Boots*' scouring the country in gigs. But though he thought the bankers who had dethroned Charles x were now subsidizing the British rising, he did not succumb to the fashionable theory that the agitators themselves were foreigners.[6] 'It is supposed by some noble Lords,' he told the House on 29 November, 'that they are foreigners. I do not believe, however, that there is any evidence whatever of that fact.'

The names of the indigenous folk-heroes – 'The King', 'The Counsellor' and the numerous 'Captains' – may even have reminded him of other guerilla leaders – 'The Shepherd', 'The Doctor', 'El Empecinado' – who had arisen from the heart of the Spanish people. The English 'Captains' did not shed the blood of a single landlord.

Because of that last fact the Duke has been criticized for cruel boasting by Hobsbawn and Rudé, the graphic and compassionate chroniclers of *Captain Swing*: 'The Duke of Wellington boasted of having hunted down Hampshire rioters like game or cattle.'[7] His actual account of the proceedings ran as follows:

I induced the magistrates to put themselves on horseback, each at the head of his own servants and retainers, grooms, huntsmen, game-keepers armed with horse-whips, pistols, fowling pieces and what they could get, and to attack in concert, if necessary, or singly, those mobs, disperse them, destroy them, and take and put in confinement those who could not escape. This was done in a spirited manner, in many instances, and it is astonishing how soon the country was tranquillised, and that in the best way, by the activity and spirit of the gentlemen.

There are two interrelated boasts here.

First, that Hampshire was 'tranquillised' unusually quickly. The rioting ended on 27 November, having lasted only sixteen days. Second, that this was due to the landed gentry bestirring themselves, instead of frolicking in London while the Yeomanry or Dragoons sabred down their mobs for them. 'I sent all the Hampshire gentlemen out of town last night,' Wellington wrote proudly to Peel on 21 November.[8] While far from glorious, neither of the Duke's boasts was unjustified.

Such rises in the agricultural wage as 'Captain Swing' achieved (from 8s. to perhaps 12s. a week here and there) were cancelled as soon as the landlords thought it safe to do so, permanent rises being brought about only by labour shortages in the 1850s. Much unctuous propaganda was addressed to rioters by publications like *The Labourer's Friend*. 'Englishmen! I honour your characters; I feel for your wants; and I do hope your distress may be alleviated.' But what was the good, asked the writer, of burning the corn which fed them or turning to agitators like Cobbett, who kept in the background while sending others to 'disgrace and death'?

Cobbett, as it happened, was not in the background; he was in the dock himself by the following April for inciting rioters to felony. The prosecution failed.

Not long afterwards one of the Duke's gamekeepers was shot dead in an affray with poachers. His reaction was to cease preserving game, since all the pheasants in the world were not worth one human life.

*

Despite the 'spirit of the gentlemen' in Hampshire, the Duke's first months after his fall were dispiriting. He frankly disliked his new role. 'The Duke said today he could not bear the idea of being in opposition,' noted Lord Ellenborough on 27 January 1831. 'He had supported the Govnt. for nearly 40 years & he did not know how to set about opposition.'[9] Croker, another fallen minister, attended a magnificent banquet given by the Duke to fifty Tories, presumably in order to raise their spirits; but the dinner, reported Croker, was 'too fine to be lively'. It is more likely, however, to have been the weight of foreboding rather than of plate which dispirited them. In proposing Wellington's health the Duke of Gordon hoped he would soon give them the command, 'As you were!' Wellington made a wry response. 'No, not as you were, but much better.'

According to Croker the Duke meant that in the recent past his party had been none too comfortable. There may also have been in the Duke's mind a sense of his present dilemma. Should he try to stop the hands of the clock by leading a reunited party, including ultra-Tories, against reform? Or should he pursue his life-long principle of 'no factious opposition' – assuming that opposition to reform would now seem factious? The Duke's repeated transference of his position from one horn to the other of this dilemma never left him free from malaise during the next eighteen months.

By the end of January 1831 his worst suspicions of the Government were realized, though he did not yet know it. They had persuaded a reluctant Monarch to accept an 'extensive' measure of parliamentary reform. For another month their plan was a closely guarded secret; but the Duke could feel the movement of the tide. Nevertheless he raised his voice only when high Tories implied that his leadership should be more vigorous. 'I assure you that I have discouraged nobody,' he wrote petulantly to Mrs Arbuthnot on 12 January:

> You draw false conclusions from what I write to you, either because I do not express myself clearly, or because you do not read with attention what I write, or because you don't like what I write. . . .[10]

The last point was right. None of them liked what he wrote. He told the Duke of Buckingham, intermediary for the Ultras, that his policy must be to 'remain quiet'. He did not expect them to like it. 'It will not suit the activity of many.' He did not care.[11]

*

The Duke's instinct for consensus was most pronounced over Ireland. Who was he to snipe at a government which, for the sake of law and order, had banned as many repeal meetings as ever he could wish, had arrested O'Connell for sedition and was prepared for coercion? The liberal-minded Anglesey, returning to Dublin as Lord-Lieutenant, denounced the Irish as 'a very ungrateful . . . a deluded People'. Could he himself have said more? As for the Whig Chief Secretary, Edward Stanley (later 14th Earl of Derby and a Tory prime minister), he wrote of O'Connell to Melbourne, 'I think he may be dealt with – *and transported* – and if he were, I really hope Ireland would be tranquil.' Would Wellington have suggested as much? Instead he wrote that everything must be offered which could conciliate the Irish, especially employment on their own soil. Government must 'put forth the whole force of this empire' on that project; repeal of the Union was out of the question.[12]

Meanwhile, what had happened to the Duke's generous personal project for buying his brother's Irish estates and showing, as he had clearly intended, what a good landlord could do? He had decided by August 1830 that he could not afford Lord Wellesley's high price.[13] True, the Duke had been let in for some very heavy expenses during the last two years; first, by his architect Wyatt, whose original estimate of £23,000 for renovations to Apsley House suddenly rose to £66,000 and was finally settled at £42,000; second, by his Stratfield Saye agent John Payn, who juggled the books of the various estates he managed and succeeded in losing the Duke a good deal of money. Nevertheless, money cannot have been the only factor at work in his decision against buying an Irish estate. There was disillusionment. Catholic emancipation appeared to have sown the seeds not of peace but of repeal.

*

With the approach of the Government's Reform Bill, Wellington found that on one point at least he was moving towards more forceful if not factious opposition. This was in respect to the press. Hitherto he had always maintained that the right way of dealing with a vituperative radical press was to ignore it. Now he admitted that he had made a mistake. He had let his case against reform go by default. Henceforth he drew a distinction between press abuse of individuals and of institutions. Institutions, he felt, were both more vulnerable and more important. Disraeli was to write: 'The rights and liberty of a nation can only be preserved by institutions,' adding significantly that the 'march of intellect' alone would not prove sufficient safeguard in a crisis. The Duke perceived, however, that the march of intellect enabled many more of the public to read, and to read the newspapers.

Individuals, he still held, were rarely damaged by scurrilous attacks and so should not as a rule defend themselves. A peculiarly unpleasant set of verses, sent to him just before Parliament reassembled on 3 February 1831, merited no comment but the word 'impertinent' written across the page.

> Thy life must be one loathsome pest,
> Thou jibe, & laughing-stock, & jest,
> And jack-pudding, & crack-a-joke of all.
> How could'st thou nightly thus appear,

And be the butt, & scoff, & jeer,
And universal shuttlecock, & ball?
In God's name, ne'er resume thy seat,
Or thou will be to mummy beat.

He intended not only to resume his seat and fight in the Lords to conserve the old institutions, but also to organize their defence through an opposition press. To all his other cares was now added the task – an utterly uncongenial if essential one – of discovering what papers were for sale, which were least likely to collapse as soon as bought and converted (the Duke later turned down a preposterous idea of buying the *Morning Chronicle*, of all papers),[14] and how to raise the necessary cash. No Tory fund existed until 1835. The operations of his friend the Rev. George Gleig in these muddied fields were still hardly begun when, on 1 March 1831, Lord John Russell rose in the House of Commons to introduce his great Reform Bill.

*

Suspense but not undue alarm was the mood of the House as Lord John began. How many rotten boroughs were to be purged? Some peers hoped for no more than a dozen. Wellington expected about thirty. But with at least two hundred Commons' seats – one-third of the whole – controlled by a hundred great landowning peers, Russell was determined to administer to Parliament a really strong purgative. No more should a notorious borough-monger like the Duke of Newcastle own *nine* constituencies, their members being known as his 'ninepins'. Nor should Parliament, at least, hear again such words as Newcastle had used after evicting tenants for voting the wrong way – 'Have I not the right to do what I like with mine own?'

Disfranchisement of enough pocket boroughs would enable Russell to enfranchise the large towns, thus satisfying the two main objects of popular fervour. The third object, a fairer property qualification for the vote, would be achieved by extending the franchise to all £10 householders in the boroughs and £10 leaseholders in the counties. There would then be a new total of half a million upper- and middle-class male voters. A marvellous advance? With not a working-class voter or a woman of any class among them? When it is asked how people not very different from ourselves could have allowed boroughs like Old Sarum and behaviour like Newcastle's to exist as long as they did, the reply must be that a race of totally voteless women lingered on well into our own century.

Russell read out his list of doomed boroughs and the whole House reeled with shock, some in ecstasy, others in agony. He had kept his secret on reform as successfully as the Duke had kept his on relief. There were to be 60 wholly disfranchised. It was as if a Socialist minister today read out a vast list of industries to be nationalized. Tories writhed and squirmed on their benches. Radicals felt their cup of joy was overflowing when they suddenly heard Russell adding that 46 more boroughs were to be partially disfranchised. After the number of M.P.s had been reduced from 658 to 596, the large towns were to get 42 of the disposable seats.

'I have kept my word with the nation,' wrote the well-satisfied Grey to the stupefied Princess Lieven. London buzzed with speculations. 'What is said now? How will it go? What is the last news? What do you think?' The Duke prophesied that if the bill went through, 'a shake will be given to the property of every individual in the country'.[15]

For some time before the bill he had blamed Peel for persuading him to resign in November 1830. ('I confess that I regret my consent to the resignation more than I do any Act of my Life.') Now he felt that if only Peel had refused to give the bill a first reading the moderate Whigs would have combined with the Tories to oust the Government. Instead, Peel had made an eloquent speech pointing out that Old Sarum existed even in the sacred year of the Glorious Revolution, 1688, and that a whole string of dazzling young men from Pitt to Grey himself had first entered Parliament through gates now declared rotten and unhinged. After which the bill had been read a first time. With the second reading almost upon them, the Duke desperately foretold the absolute destruction of government 'by due course of law'.[16]

But in the Commons each side expected victory, as at 3 A.M. on 23 March 1831 the vote was taken on the second reading. There was dead silence followed by a storm of Whig shouts, cheers and even weeping when the Speaker announced a Government majority of – one. Wellington could have been forgiven if he had regarded his nephew as that one, for 'Wicked William' had again voted with the Whigs against his uncle's cause. The brilliant young Whig M.P., Thomas Macaulay, observed the havoc on the Tory benches. The face of Twiss (Eldon's future biographer) was that of a damned soul, Peel's jaw dropped and Herries, taking off his tie, looked like Judas preparing for the 'last operation'.

Next day the Duke went down to the Lords and made his first speech on the bill. It lasted only two or three minutes, but his concluding words were effective.

> I possess no influence or interest of the description which will be destroyed by the measure now proposed; but I am an individual who has served His Majesty for now nearly half a century –

and he could not but feel it his duty to say that,

> from the period of the adoption of that measure will date the downfall of the Constitution.

No one could doubt his sincerity; nor that he was correct in forecasting the end of a constitutional machine powered by the aristocracy. His reference to his own freedom from 'influence or interest' in the borough-mongering system requires some explanation.

Why did he tell Gleig, for instance, that he would never dirty his fingers with so vile a job as borough-mongering, – 'I hate the whole concern' – yet still go on fighting to the death for the borough-mongers' unqualified right to operate? 'I know of no concession that could be made,' he wrote to Charles Arbuthnot on the same day as he spoke in Parliament, 'that would not be inconsistent with Principle.'[17] So his answer was 'Principle', and property was one of the principles for which he fought. The pocket boroughs were property. Worth thousands of pounds to their owners, they represented property just as much as, say, racehorses. The Duke did not covet these things for himself, but he abhorred dispossession.

His other principle was strong government. This, in the absence of a modern party system, patronage helped to provide. 'I want to know how Government is to carry any measure,' he asked in the House on 28 March, 'on the appointment of a new Parliament?' It was an argument which deeply impressed his hearers.

'They are all dead men by this bill,' wrote Creevey of the borough-owners.[18] Though not a borough-owner himself, the Duke was ready to be killed by the bill – on principle.

*

As the Duke saw things, the committee stage of the bill, reached
on 18 April, would give the country time to 'come to its senses'.
The Commons he felt were doing so when they voted in committee more than once against the Government. There were moments
now when the Duke was hopeful. He had written to Lord Falmouth on 3 April: 'The King of this country is (thank God) still
a tower of strength.'[19] Unfortunately the tower was about to be
occupied by the enemy.

What was Lord Grey to do? Defeat in committee meant subsequent destruction of the bill. In the spirit of the times, the
Prime Minister decided on a *coup d'état*. William IV should
descend like a *deus ex machina*, dissolve Parliament and enable
the Whigs to accumulate an unbeatable majority at a general
election.

The King at first jibbed and scribbled on a scrap of paper,

> *I consider Dissolution*
> *Tantamount to Revolution*

But when on 22 April he heard that a Tory peer, Lord Wharncliffe, proposed to pre-empt his royal right to dissolve by putting
down a motion against it the very next day, the Sailor King
swung round into the teeth of the gale and ordered his royal
equipage forthwith. And if his cream ponies could not be
groomed in time for him to drive to Parliament in state, he would
go in a hackney coach. Lord Albemarle, Master of the Horse, was
called from a late breakfast to prepare for His Majesty's sortie.

'Lord bless me! is there a revolution?'

'Not at this moment, but there will be if you stay to finish your
breakfast.'[20]

Lord Albemarle buckled to, the crown was rushed from the
Tower and the King's robes from Sir William Beechey's studio
in Wimpole Street, the cannon boomed and King William rolled
down in his coach to dissolve Parliament, where a revolution 'by
due course of law', as the Duke would have said, already seemed
to be in progress.

Bawling rather than debating occupied both Houses. In the
Lords the Ultras were rampant, Mansfield shouting abuse and
Londonderry brandishing a whip at Richmond while five peers
clung to his coat-tails. What was all the hubbub? asked the King
of the Lord Chancellor.

'If it please your Majesty,' replied Brougham smoothly, 'it is the Lords debating.'[21]

Next door Peel, in an ecstasy of denunciation, his auburn hair blazing like Ney's at Waterloo, refused to give way even when Black Rod was banging on the door, though his scorching periods had long been punctuated by gunfire signalling His Majesty's approach. Finally the King put an end to this bedlam by 'taking Parliament by storm' (in Buckingham's outraged words to Wellington), his crown as wobbly and crooked on his head as the Sword of State was stiff and straight in Grey's hand. Some saw it as the sword of an executioner.

*

The Duke of Wellington that day was not in his place in the House of Lords.

Kitty was dying. He had rushed up to town earlier in the month, to spend unbroken hours at her bedside. Otherwise he would have been happier at Stratfield Saye. 'I feel growing upon me a desire to live out of the World,' he had written to Mrs Arbuthnot. 'The truth is that this Reform Question breaks me down as it will everything else. . . .'[22] Now it was Kitty who was to leave the world.

'She is better certainly,' he told Harriet on 9 April; 'but she is still very unwell; and I shall not go out of town again.' Two days later he wrote sombrely: 'It is impossible to calculate upon the duration of her life.'

Maria Edgeworth believed that Kitty's last illness was cancer. It may have been cholera, though the family records throw no light on the subject. By January Kitty had seemed already very near her end when her old friend visited her at Apsley House. Maria marvelled at the contrast between the waxen figure resting on a high white sofa-bed and the glittering array of her husband's trophies which surrounded her in the spacious ground-floor room. Following her friend's gaze, Kitty raised herself up so that she too could see the magnificent china and golden shield of Achilles.

'All tributes to merit – there is the value!' she exclaimed; 'and pure! pure! – no corruption – ever *suspected* even. Even of the Duke of Marlborough that could not be said so truly.'

Despite Maria's dislike of Wellington, she could not help rejoicing that Kitty's enthusiasm still fed on her hero's glory. 'I hope she will not outlive the pleasure she now feels, I am assured, in the Duke's returning kindness,' Maria added. 'I hope she will not last too long and tire out that easily tired pity of his.' The hope, however uncharitably expressed, was realized, and three months later the Duke's last vigil began.

His wife and the old order were slipping away together. When he heard that more and more country gentlemen were becoming alarmed at the Reform Bill, he felt no surprise. 'They are right. Their order will be annihilated even sooner than any of them expect.' It was the same when they told him that people were cutting down their establishments in preparation for 'the expected Storm'.

'They are very right. If the Bill passes we shall have it.'

In the ground-floor room Kitty clung to a hand that was no longer iron. Once she ran her fingers up inside his sleeve to feel if by chance he was still wearing an armlet she had given him long ago.

'She found it,' said the Duke to a friend, 'as she would have found it any time these twenty years, had she cared to look for it.' How strange it was, he reflected sadly, that two people could live together for half a lifetime 'and only understand one another at the end'.[23]

The end came on 24 April, two days after King William dissolved Parliament. The Duke and his sons immediately went down to the country, black edgings were ordered for his writing-paper, Apsley House was shut up and nothing remained but for the small coffin to make its journey to Stratfield Saye for burial in the family vault. Before the hearse was ready 'the expected Storm' broke.

*

The Lord Mayor of London ordered illuminations on 27 April in honour of the dissolution. From Westminster to Piccadilly there were sparkling pyramids of candles in the fine sash-windows of the wealthy. But not in all. A roistering reform mob marched up Piccadilly, breaking the windows of those who showed by their dark fronts that they regarded the dissolution as a black day for Britain.

Apsley House was in darkness because of the Duchess's passing rather than Parliament's. But the Duke would certainly not have illuminated for reform even if he had been at home. Stones smashed immense quantities of his new plate-glass on the ground floor. When the crowd pulled up the railings on the Piccadilly side the Duke's servant fired two blunderbusses over their heads (though loaded with gunpowder only). At once the crowd, who were out for a lark rather than a riot, turned their attention to fresh windows and pastures new in Grosvenor Square.

I think my Servant John saved my House [wrote the Duke] or the lives of the Mob – possibly both – by firing as he did. They certainly intended to destroy the House, and did not care one Pin for the poor Duchess being dead in the House. . . .

Having consulted his lawyers about compensation from the Hundred in which Apsley House stood, he found there was 'No Redress'. (These words were blazoned on the cover of his legal file, followed by twelve exclamation marks.) Compensation could be paid only if he proved felonious intent to demolish, pull down or destroy. Two days running he trumpeted forth his indignation to·Mrs Arbuthnot. 'The people are rotten to the Core.' 'The people are gone Mad.'[24]

*

The reformers in this unreformed Parliament swept home to a tremendous election victory. With a Whig-Radical-Irish-Scottish majority of 140 against them, the Tories were utterly routed. According to the Duke, it had been achieved by sheer terrorism. 'I confess that I am much more alarmed about Terror,' he wrote to Charles Arbuthnot, 'than I am about Reform. It is not to be believed how far it goes, and what it has done.'[25]

There was indeed some violence, one Tory candidate, his nephew Lord Worcester, being saved from drowning by a reform mob only through the prompt action of John Frost, a future Chartist. But the Duke's exaggerated view of the terror merely showed how far his imagination still was from distinguishing between the deep current and the stinging surface spray of reform. In the world of slogans alone, the anti-reform press was defeated by the *Spectator*'s brilliant watchword for the election: 'The Bill, the whole Bill, and nothing but the Bill.' Mrs Arbuthnot complained that even the Duke now wrote about nothing but the bill. 'It is very true,' he replied. 'But what else is there to think or write about?'

Harsh bulletins to Harriet and more moderate jottings for his own eye enabled him to sort out his thoughts. She could not have liked the letter she received just as the elections were finishing:

There is no occasion for talking to me about the future prospects of the country. You may believe me or not as you please. I recommend you to provide Means or Subsistence for yourself in another Country. My opinion is that we are on the Eve of a great Change. . . .

All incomes from pensions, salaries, the land and finally the Funds would fall, the King would take fright and break with the Whigs – 'and then if we are in luck we may have a Civil War'.[26]

A memorandum he wrote on 'the Press and Reform' showed that the only change he approved was the increase in the people's 'indirect influence' on Parliament through the newspapers. 'Publick opinion has *found, not forced*, its way into the counsels of Parliament . . . and has exerted its influence *surely* . . . more surely . . . by reason of the soberness and calmness of its march.' Grey, however, would not have agreed that in practice the Duke approved even that much change. The Duke was 'a man who does not understand the character of the times, and who thinks public opinion may be subdued by power.'[27] In the great argument the Duke would have retorted that public opinion, when corrupted by agitators, should indeed be ignored, if not subdued.

From June onwards, without a break, the Government chained themselves to the oars, resolved that their second Reform Bill should be propelled through all its stages in the Commons by September. The Duke meanwhile stood in the Lines above the Tagus, or so it seemed, his motto 'They shall not pass' and his policy one of waiting. To Ultras like Lord Wilton who implored him to put himself at the head of 'a party of Conservatives',* he wrote doggedly:

I think that we are now in one of those situations in which it is most desirable to look about us to ascertain the opinion of public Men particularly in the House of Commons . . . and above all to give time for the Public Mind to become calm. . . .[28]

When he rode between outposts he was always well armed. In August a plot to waylay him on the Dover road between London

---

* The name was first used by Croker in the *Quarterly Journal*, January 1830. Wellington wrote to Lord Wharncliffe in 1831 of the 'conservators of the constitution'. (*Wellington MSS.*, 23 April 1831.)

and Walmer was disclosed by a spy named Underdown. The Duke was sceptical. 'Is it quite certain that these informants do not suggest the very Plan of which they give Information?'[29] He relied on the law, fortified by a brace of double-barrelled pistols in his carriage and an armed servant on the box. However, he could not prevent volunteers escorting him to the gates of his castle in a whirl of hooves and hunting-whips.

September came and with it the King's coronation. A loud spontaneous cheer went up for Wellington as he took the oath and the shout which the Whigs then tried to raise for Grey was far from triumphant. But there were to be triumphant majorities for Grey's bill in the Commons.* Suddenly the Duke found his static policy untenable. If the enemy would not withdraw he must plunge to the attack. For the next eight months he struggled in a breathless mêlée hardly less stubborn than the eight hours of Waterloo.

The Tory decision to oppose the terrible bill in the Lords had been taken at Apsley House on 21 September in an atmosphere of solemn tragedy. It was turned to farce by Lords Eldon and Kenyon, who came in 'drunk as porters', from a dinner at the Duke of Cumberland's and ranted furiously. (Lord Kenyon apologized to Wellington next day for the effects of HRH's punch.[30]) The second reading debate was more memorable, however, for Lord Brougham's advocacy of the bill than for the Opposition's resistence. His emotion carried him to heights of oratory which all agreed were 'superhuman'. So was his intake of negus. George Seymour said that he drank like a preacher regularly turning his hour-glass.[31] Though roaring drunk by the end, the final scene was wildly exaggerated in the account given by Tory Lord Campbell: how Brougham fell on his knees bfore the Duke's squares and having pleaded with them to retreat was unable to regain the Woolsack without assistance.

The Duke had begun too loudly for a speech which consisted of cannister-shot rather than 12-pounders: that the new, elected members would be mere delegates instead of independent-minded M.P.s; that the people wanted universal suffrage, so if the

---

* Young Mr W. E. Gladstone, a student at Oxford, went to hear the Reform Bill debate and could find no vacant stool or chair in the Chamber, only an iron railing which gave him occasional 'cutting repose'. (Gladstone Papers, p. 96.)

Government's self-confessed policy was to please the people, why not radical reform?

If the Duke's shots were not very damaging, his troops needed no mighty cannonade to strengthen their resolution. They voted down the bill on 8 October by a thumping majority of forty-one. Twenty-one out of the twenty-three bishops opposed the bill. Because these twenty-one by changing their votes could have given the Government another majority of one, popular opinion saddled them with defeat of the Second Reform Bill. 'The Bishops have done it,' declared the militant free-thinker Richard Carlile; 'it is the work of the Holy Ghost.'

Immediately the pent-up people broke into every kind of retaliation, legal and illegal. On the morning after the defeat Wellington's particular foe, the Morning Chronicle, came out with borders as black as his own writing-paper. His effigy and that of Cumberland were burned at Tyburn (Marble Arch), while the Bishop of Exeter's was thrown on a diocesan bonfire on 5 November along with Guy Fawkes and the Pope.* John Russell told the agitator Attwood, some thought rashly, that the voice of the nation could not be drowned by 'the whisper of a faction'.

Apsley House was stoned for the second time in one year, on 12 October. This time the Duke was at home. In broad daylight the stones came hurtling through the plate-glass windows for fifty minutes before the police arrived on the scene. One narrowly missed the Duke's head as he sat at his writing-table and broke a glass-fronted bookcase behind him; another cut through the canvas of Lady Lyndhurst's portrait by Wilkie, hanging on the wall. The garden was full of stones, though the stone-throwers themselves were kept outside the railings by the sight of armed men posted round the house. Having withdrawn to the Park, the mob circled menacingly round the Achilles statue but found it too heavy to overturn, 'It is now five o'clock, and beginning to rain a little,' the Duke wrote to Mrs Arbuthnot from his beleaguered citadel, giving her a blow-by-blow account of the affair: 'and I conclude that the Gentlemen will now go to their Dinners!'[32]

---

* Wellington's promotion of Henry Phillpotts to be Bishop of Exeter had caused a storm in 1830, since Phillpotts retained his stipend from a northern parish. The practice of holding a parish in commendam, i.e. in absence, was later abolished in 1836, the bishops' incomes being adjusted upwards where necessary.

Thank God for his new shutters even though Lord Grey, riding past a few days before, had taken them as a personal affront.

The Duke had been well prepared and he got off relatively lightly. In Derby anti-reformers' houses were wrecked; in Nottingham the castle belonging to the Duke of Newcastle was burned down; in Bristol the worst catastrophe since the Gordon Riots of 1780 took place, due to an incredible combination of evils. Provocative authorities insisted that the hated Wetherell's entry as City Recorder should not be postponed; timid magistrates delayed the action of the military; a humane but ineffectual colonel lost his nerve during the crisis and committed suicide during his court martial; and thieves out only for plunder joined the reformers' demonstration. Half the city centre was destroyed, hundreds of demonstrators were killed and wounded by the soldiers and many drunken pillagers burned to death in the cellars of houses they themselves had set on fire. Madame Tussaud's famous waxworks, which she had just brought to Bristol, narrowly escaped destruction; and Wetherell himself was said to have got away only by donning the disguise of a wash and a clean suit.

On the propaganda front, pamphlets and broadsheets with the theme, 'What ought to be done with the Things called "Lords"?' spread over the great towns. The answer was, Down with them. 'No Lords!' Better to die a republican of the *cholera morbus* than survive that plague, a slave of lords.

The Duke was in constant touch with Fitzroy Somerset and other officers over military support for the police. His aim was to create security without alarm, and a suggestion for removing the display guns from Walmer Castle received the cold reply that since there was no ammunition no one would steal them.[33] A secret report from Melbourne of an impending attack on Dover Castle was similarly discounted. But when a partly fictitious story of arms being sold by a London dealer to the Birmingham Political Union reached the Duke, he rushed headlong into the fray. On Guy Fawkes' Day he warned the King about this conspiracy, so reminiscent of the July Days in Paris, and was gratified when the Government squeezed out a proclamation against armed unions.[34] Of far more importance, however, to the Duke's subsequent actions than the Birmingham affair was the secondary purpose of his letter to the King.

This purpose was to let His Majesty know that if he wished to escape from the thraldom of the Whigs, the Duke of Wellington would 'assist him to do so'. The retained servant was ready once more to serve the King as Prime Minister. However, 'our poor King', as the Duke now called him, was not yet ready to throw over Grey.[35]

Nor did the Duke feel sure of Peel's support. 'I did pretty well with him while we were in office, but I cannot manage him at all now,' he wrote to Lady Salisbury on 21 November. 'He is a wonderful fellow – has a most correct judgment – talents almost equal to those of Pitt, but he spoils all by timidity & indecision.'[36]

*

Meanwhile the little Napoleon of reform, Johnny Russell (only 8 stone in weight, marvelled Creevey), deployed on 12 December his Third Reform Bill in the Commons. Its terms were a shade less drastic than before, mainly as a result of negotiations with a pair of moderate Tories, Lord Wharncliffe and Lord Harrowby. Known as the 'Waverers', in November they had wavered towards supporting the bill, by now had wavered away from it and next spring were to waver back again. Their manoeuvres did not appeal to the Duke. 'We are surrounded by difficulties and dangers,' he wrote on 12 December. 'God knows how we shall extricate ourselves! but I am convinced that the straight course of principle is the best.'[37]

The latest danger was Napoleon's threat to throw in his last reserves. They might be called the Young Guard. For if enough younger sons of Whig aristocrats, supplemented by Irish and Scots peers, were raised to the British peerage, Russell could close his gap of forty-one votes overnight. By January 1832 the Duke knew that His Majesty had been brought to agree. What was it, asked the Duke, but an unholy alliance of monarch and mob, as utterly unconstitutional as the Reform Bill itself and no less destructive of the Lords? Yet when the Ultras urged him to seek a personal interview with the Sovereign (the right of every peer) he refused to dishonour the political struggle by such a trick. Over Catholic emancipation the Ultras had disgusted him by privately lobbying King George iv; he would not do the same to Grey. Nor is there any evidence that two months later he took advantage of the King's revulsion against a mass creation of peers. The ultra-

Tories in his Household had been working hard for this revulsion, and by March one of them was writing to Wellington: 'Pray, my dear DUKE DEPEND UPON THE KING. Assure your party, if they will be *staunch*, he will be so.'[38] From Wellington there was no encouragement.

Opposition to the bill's third reading in the Commons was now led by two particular friends of the Duke, young Lord Mahon (future recorder, as Earl Stanhope, of the Duke's *Conversations*) and Sir John Malcolm, whom the Duke had once said was big enough to 'stand alone'. Now he was doing so. The majority against him and his party was 116. The date was 22 March 1832. It was up to 'the Things' called Lords.

Wellington never left his post from the moment the Lords' second reading began on 9 April until the vote was taken at 5 A.M. on the 14th, with the blue light of day flowing over the orange candle flames. Tightly buttoned into his dark coat, his long nose curving down towards the equally long chin supported by the white stock, he listened intently to all the old arguments, deafness adding to the rigours of duty. The bill passed by no more than nine votes, despite the support of an augmented band of Waverers and converts among the bishops. The prospect for Grey was bleak. What could happen in committee but defeat? On Monday 7 May the Lords duly defeated the third attempt at a Reform Bill and the May Days began.

*

With King William playing the part of Charles x in his subjects' imagination, by refusing to create peers as Charles had refused to withdraw the Ordinances, the July Days of France seemed in a fair way to reproduce themselves in Britain. Wellington would of course be Polignac. Radical agitators had often equated the two in the past and now the Duke was to give them some excuse for doing so again.

The May Days raced past like the mileposts he had watched from the Liverpool–Manchester train. Close at hand, the flying shapes of Throne and Parliament with King, Cabinet and Opposition merged in remorseless struggle; in the background, the people roused to a passion of petitions and monster meetings, to dark narrow conspiracies and broad radiant dreams.

7 May: 150,000 Birmingham Unionists sang their hymn, 'We will, we will, we *will be free!*'

8 May: Grey demanded the creation of at least fifty peers.

9 May: The King refused a mass creation, Grey walked out and the King, through Lyndhurst, commissioned the Duke to form a government. At the same time the Duke must bring in the extensive measure of Reform to which HM considered the country since the dissolution was entitled. 'The King appeared to think all this day,' wrote the courtier George Seymour, 'that he had done with the Whigs . . . for the next forty years.' There was heavy enrolment in the political unions.

10 May: The Duke complained privately at the King's tying him down to a reform programme.[39] And well he might. The King had set him an impossible task. Nevertheless, as HM's retained servant he wrote with quixotic loyalty in reply to Lyndhurst's approach, 'I am perfectly ready to do whatever his Majesty may command me.'[40] Not so Peel, who was in closer touch with reality. In the interests of consistency and public confidence, he declined not only the premiership but any office whatever. He could not repeat on reform his performance over Catholic emancipation. While the Duke negotiated undeterred for support elsewhere, the news of Grey's fall reached the provinces. Liverpool Stock Exchange closed. Business everywhere faltered. Placards appeared in windows, 'No taxes paid here till the Reform Bill is passed.'

11 May: Reform leaders from far and near met at Francis Place's house in London to plan resistance to a Wellington ministry.

12 May: Revolutionary arrangements for barricading Birmingham, Manchester, etc., were put in hand. Funds continued to drop despite Rothschild's efforts to hold them firm. A brainwave came to Place and he wrote out his famous poster: 'To Stop the Duke Go for Gold.' Other things, however, might stop the Duke first. Only his veterans, Hardinge and Murray, seemed eager to serve. This was Saturday. 'Well, we are in a fine scrape,' he told Croker, 'and I really do not see how we are to get out of it.'[41]

Right through until Monday he continued his anxious interviewing and succeeded in finding a Chancellor of the Exchequer in Alexander Baring. Greville wrote in his diary, 'The town is fearfully quiet.' It was what the Duke had called at Waterloo the dreadful pause.

13 May: The Scots Greys were ordered to rough-sharpen their sabres; not all were prepared to use them. A meeting was being organized for the next day on the field of Peterloo, where rough-sharpened sabres had been employed thirteen years before. These facts, together with a widely quoted and sinister remark of 'Wicked William's' about his uncle having 'a way' of keeping the people quiet, convinced reformers that there was to be a *coup d'état* by the Duke.

14 May: With a run on the Bank of England already begun, Parliament met. There were wild rumours that Wellington was to be assassinated on the way there and his niece Priscilla begged him to go incognito in her carriage. 'I could no more go to the House of Lords in your Carriage after such Reports,' he said, 'than I could crawl [on] all fours.' Hobhouse, one of the Whig ex-ministers, told Taylor, the King's secretary, that Wellington's only chance was to 'try what another dissolution would do'.[42] Perhaps Hobhouse was right. At any rate, there was no chance whatever for the Duke to head a government with the present House of Commons. The violence was extreme. One after another M.P.s flayed him for opposing reform, destroying Grey and then resurrecting the very bill which he had killed. When the Whig Lord Ebrington called it 'gross public immorality', all was over with the Duke. Three times Alexander Baring tried to speak and was drowned by uproar. The fourth time he proposed that ex-ministers should resume their seats on the Government front bench and carry the bill. He would rather face a thousand devils, he told the Duke that evening, than such a House of Commons.

15 May: The Duke informed the King that he could neither form a government nor find support in the Commons. His retreat was absolute. When a group of Ultras urged him to call a peers' meeting and think again, he answered stiffly that he had not acted for their sake but for the King's. Meanwhile Grey, recalled to Windsor, adjourned the House till the 17th, while he set about bringing the King to heel.

16 May: A burst of premature rejoicing on the assumption that all was over bar the shouting. By evening doubts had set in and there were renewed suspicions of a ducal *coup d'état*.

17 May: Grey, however, confronted the King with a ruthless dilemma. HM must either promise to create peers or face the possibility of insurrection. He crept out of the dilemma with the help of the Duke, who promised to abstain from further opposition to the bill and make his friends do likewise. But the Duke would not disclose his promise in Parliament. Such a public admission, he considered, would amount to condoning Grey's coercion of the King. Instead he eased his conscience by delivering an apologia in the House for his recent conduct, which shocked and misled by its angry tone. Nevertheless, there was one sentence which deeply moved his hearers and rang in their ears as long as he lived:

If I had been capable of refusing my assistance to His Majesty – if I had been capable of saying to His Majesty, 'I cannot assist you in this affair' – I do not think, my Lords, that I could have shown my face in the streets for shame of having done it – for shame of having abandoned my Sovereign under such distressing circumstances.

In the streets. . . . If the Duke had shown his face in the streets at that moment he would have felt the pressure building up again. For no one guessed he was making his farewell speech on reform. Every reformer thought he had double-crossed them again. One of them proposed to assassinate him, he was warned. 'The Duke knows of old,' he replied, 'that assassins and those who employ them are not the boldest of mankind.'

18 May: Britain as near as it had ever been to revolution – so much all agreed. The *Morning Chronicle* announced 'the eve of the barricades'. But Grey and Brougham were at Windsor extracting a written guarantee from the King to create peers if necessary, and the Duke, backed by a hundred other Tories, kept his promise to abstain. Both Houses met and Grey announced victory. The Duke was not without his share in it.

On 4 June the bill was read a third time in the Lords by 106 to 22. It was a dismal moment for the King. What had it gained him in the last hectic month? A noose round the marble bust of his Queen, whose supposed Germanic influence was hysterically resented, and a new slogan for the times, placarded in the streets, 'Put not your trust in Princes'.* He refused to give the Royal Assent to the bill in person. It became law none the less on 7 June by Commission, and the radical Francis Place rejoiced that all the silly people who looked forward to such 'absurd displays' as royal processions were bitterly disappointed. He prophesied that the King's 'ridiculous show of popularity as "William the Reformer" ' would come to an abrupt end. In the Lords the radical Duke of Sussex said out loud, 'This is the happiest day of my life', to which an old Tory roared back, 'O Christ!' After the Clerk of Parliament had pronounced the words of assent, *'Le Roi le veult'*, he was handed a note which read, *'La Canaille le veult'*.[43] Twelve days later at Ascot a stone hit the King hard on the head.

*

Resistance had crumbled and the Britain of big and small capitalists, professional men, journalists and all the rest of the middle classes except the lowest, were out of their shackles at last and free to march wherever intellect or interest might lead. Working men hoped that the march would lead to them. 'When the Bill is safe,' wrote the *Poor Man's Guardian* on 26 May, 'we cannot think so ill of human nature as to think that those who will have gained their own freedom, will not aid us to gain ours.'[44] Human nature nevertheless managed to withhold full manhood suffrage for another eighty-six years.

Wellington and his friends saw out the May Days 'skulking in their clubs and country houses', as Greville ungratefully put it. On Waterloo Day, 18 June, a mob lay in wait for the Duke while he was sitting to Pistrucci at the Mint. They greeted him as he emerged with such apt slogans as 'Bonaparte for ever!'[45] and,

---

* George Seymour thought Queen Adelaide's reactionary beliefs had little effect in general on the King. He remembered the King once saying to her, 'Madam, English Politics are not to be understood by any German.' Seymour implied, however, that her influence may have grown during the reform agitation. (*Confidential Memoranda*, George Seymour, 28 May 1832.)

refusing to be shaken off, gave him the longest five-mile ride of his life. There were critical moments when he sighted loose paving-stones and then a loaded coal-cart.

'Here's the Artillery coming up,' he joked; 'we must look out.'[46] But the mob were too intent on their quarry to notice the coal-cart and by now he had acquired a small bodyguard to save him from being dragged from his horse. Two Chelsea Pensioners had offered their services.

'Then keep close to me now,' he said, ordering them to stand with their backs against his stirrups whenever his horse was stopped. A magistrate and some police joined his escort, a man in a buggy protected his rear, and after failing to give the mob the slip by a diversion through Lincoln's Inn, he reached clubland to find the worst was over. The men in the bay-windows marvelled at the set face looking straight ahead. A *'visage de fer'* was one's only choice, as he told Mrs Arbuthnot two months later apropos of life in general.[47] They said that the iron mask had slipped a little when an apothecary with whom he had had dealings rushed out of Surgeon's Hall shouting 'Waterloo, Waterloo!' and he himself admitted to being touched by the many women who waved their handkerchiefs from upper windows and implored him to come indoors. But he would not stop.

'If I were to get in, in what manner was I to get out again?'

At last he reached Apsley House, and turning to Lord St Germans, who had joined him outside the United Services Club, raised his hat:

'An odd day to choose. Good morning!'[48]

Each window of Apsley House had its own iron shutter, behind which the broken glass of October 1831 had not been replaced. Both he and his house maintained their *'visage de fer'*.*

*

The summer days passed with the Duke still only too willing to prophesy wholesale doom. In November 1831 he had predicted that six weeks after the reformed Parliament met Lord Grey's own 'caste' would cease to govern, while 'the race of Englishmen will not last long afterwards'. He found no reason yet to change

---

* The glass was mended in time for the Waterloo banquet of 1833, but the Duke retained the shutters and to the end of his life was apt to raise his hat ironically and point towards them if a crowd began cheering him.

his mind. Much as Burke had seen France handed over to 'sophisters, economists and calculators', the Duke saw Britain at the mercy of 'lawyers, Physicians and shopkeepers'.[49]

There was an added reason, moreover, why he should feel low. Many people could not forgive him for his conduct during the May Days, particularly between the 9th and the 14th. Why had he not taken the honest and uncompromising line of Peel? A 'right-wing' Whig like Lady Cowper was at first in a minority when she praised his 'straight forward' apologia of 17 May.

He quite cleared himself for his conduct, that is to say, not the wisdom of it, but as to the integrity of his intentions. . . .

Emily Cowper believed there were only two parties in England, 'the Conservative' and 'the Destructive', and the great Duke had rightly demonstrated that he did not belong to the second.[50]

That Wellington's volte-face of May 1832 did not prove his end was due to his remarkable character's being recognized for what it was. After the first shock, there were few who believed that he had acted for the sake of power or party advantage rather than loyalty to that Sovereign in whose person he saw the country embodied.

On a more practical level, rigid consistency had never been the Duke's creed. He would no more hesitate to alter his course in politics than in battle he would refuse to change his tactics. For the purposes of war, he had his simile of the rough-and-ready harness made of rope, which might break but could be knotted and used again. His policies had certainly snapped during the May Days. He tied one knot on the 10th for the King's sake and on the 15th had to untie it. But life was not finished, and a fighter may have to knot, knot and knot again.

Back in March 1831 the Duke had made one of his fiery resolves against the Reform Bill. 'I certainly never will enter the House of Lords from the time that it passes.'[51] John Wilson Croker, M.P., his close comrade-in-arms during the reform struggle, may have known of this dramatic decision. At any rate, two months after the bill passed he wrote to Wellington declaring his own firm determination not to stand for the reformed Parliament. At great length he explained that it was a '*usurpation*', a new version of the Long Parliament, a means of subverting 'the Church, the Peerage & the throne'. No doubt Croker expected a pat on the back from Wellington. But the Duke meanwhile had begun to get a grip on the ravelled rope. In reply to Croker's four pages he drafted four lines.

My dear Croker,
   I have recd. your letter.
   I am very sorry that you do not intend again to serve in Parlt.
   I cannot conceive for what reason.[52]

In the Duke's eyes it was never impossible to serve.

19

The Duke on Elba

A brief but fervent reaction in the Duke's favour resulted from his mobbing on Waterloo Day 1832. From all parts of the country came huge sheets of vellum, sometimes several feet square, ornately inscribed with loyal sentiments. Even reformers signed. While not agreeing with him, they recognized that his conduct as a minister of the Crown was of that 'unbending and honorable nature which evidently characterizes your Grace as an upright and truly independent Man'.

The Duke none the less sensed a continuing personal hostility and felt himself banished to an Elba of his own. The situation produced occasional glooms, particularly as he had no intention of returning like Napoleon with the violets of spring. These moods, however, were exaggerated by his intimates. Thomas Raikes,* who had been abroad, found him philosophical about the political changes. 'His whole mind seems engrossed by the love of his country. . . . His language breathes no bitterness, neither sunk into despondency.'[1] The Arbuthnots, on the contrary, found his language breathed such deep discouragement that they asked Croker to show him the bright side. Yes, admitted the Duke, the aristocracy still had great stamina; but what would happen when new shocks gave democracy fresh powers? Croker, swamped by the grey mood, prophesied anarchy followed by dictatorship. Gleig thought the Duke was more than half in earnest when he threatened to buy foreign securities and retire from public life. But the Duke's own recollections of that kind of talk, as relayed to Lord Mahon (Stanhope) on 17 April 1840, showed that it was not to be taken too seriously.†

* Thomas Raikes (1777–1848), the diarist, wealthy dandy and clubman.
† The Duke remembered Talleyrand saying one day, at the time of the re-modelled Parliament, 'Duke of Wellington, you have seen a great deal of

When the problem of emigration arose in his own family circle the Duke came down against it. His wife's favourite niece, Kate, had married the Rev. William Foster, a Church of Ireland clergyman who quoted their famous uncle's views about reform and was therefore disliked by his parishioners. Should he emigrate for his family's sake?

'Is not your duty to remain at your post and hope for better times?' asked the Duke in reply. 'Make every exertion, every sacrifice, to enable you to do justice by everybody, including your family; but I confess that if I was in your situation I would not quit my post.'[2]

*

If the Duke's pessimism darkened the surface only, its causes were not entirely in politics, 'They say, by-the-by, that his private affairs are in disorder,' wrote Princess Lieven to Grey on 28 August 1832, 'and that it is this that is annoying him so much.' She was right. The management of both his Spanish and Netherlands estates was unsatisfactory. He wished he could have sent Douro over to deal with the latter, but his son was not that kind of person. The 'rascal' Payn was still ruining him at Stratfield Saye. (But when Payn once bought a farm for his employer for a sum far below its value, and boasted of his success, the Duke sharply ordered him to pay the full price.) Everyone thought he was made of money and no one thought of repaying a loan. Culling Smith, his brother-in-law, owed him £1,200 and Samuel Briscall, his curate, £500. He had to turn Smith's loan into a gift three years later to prevent him from being arrested for debt, and Briscall died without repaying. Nor had poor Kitty carried a good conscience to the grave, at least over money affairs.

She died with her husband and Douro at her bedside (Charles, stationed at Dover, was too late) and even Miss Edgeworth felt that her end had been happy and perhaps her life also. 'Happy, I should think, *through all*; happy in her good feelings, good conscience, and warm affection, still LOVING on!'[3] To spoil

---

the world; can you point out to me any one place in Europe where an old man could go to and be quite sure of being safe and dying in peace?' The Duke was on the point of suggesting Malta when he recollected that the Government was just about to 'remodel' Malta also. He broke into laughter.

such a moving epitaph, in which there is much truth, is an ungrateful task.

Though all Kitty's disclosed debts had been wiped out by 1828 and she had not had to pay any house bills since that time – they had been put into the scarcely more reliable hands of Mr Payn – she had still managed to die with concealed debts of £10,000. Included in that sum was a bond for £2,000 taken up by her in 1822, which now caused her brother Colonel Hercules Pakenham and her husband considerable pain. Colonel Pakenham had to explain that his sister, of whose 'line' he could not approve, had resorted to the bond because she did not wish the affair to come to her husband's notice. What was the affair?

Hercules had been told by her it was the usual tradesmen's bills; the Duke was pretty sure, however, that the money had gone to her in-laws, the Stewarts, whose Dublin bank had failed. Miserably the Duke wrote that the discovery of this bond 'revived the recollection of many transactions which I had wished and determined to bury in oblivion'. Moreover, all those who had known about the bond must have believed the legend that he kept her short of housekeeping money; yet he always paid her what she asked for, 'generally with an Overplus'. He had made one last effort in 1828 to get her to admit that the money was being given away. 'I entreated her to tell if the fact were true; and promised that I would never notice it to Her or to any other Human being. She always denied it.' So the debts 'preyed on her mind' while she was alive, as he told Mrs Arbuthnot, and on his after she was dead.

Nevertheless, the light of early morning and of sunset which had played over their first and last years together was not entirely blotted out. Croker noted that it was the death of his wife and mother in the same year which partly accounted for his low spirits; yet the world said he had no feeling for either. And why did he not marry again?

This question was actually put to him by the bold and devoted Kate Foster. His reaction, she wrote, 'puts a final answer, not only to the supposition that there were grounds, but even to the idea that there *ever could be* grounds for believing such a step could enter his contemplation'. It was not for lack of opportunities that he failed to select 'from the brightest of England's fair treasures, one who would consent to share his high position and the glories of his name'. No, said Mrs Foster, her aunt remained 'his only chosen bride beyond the grave!'[4]

Allowing for Mrs Foster's sentimental prose, there is still little doubt that the Duke maintained a special feeling for Kitty as his wife. Though not logically definable, this feeling belonged to the whole body of his ideas on life in general as it should be lived: on loyalty, on duty, on what was proper, on the right order of things. It was of the essence of his being.

Kitty's single-minded devotion also contributed to her final victory: 'With all my heart and soul I have loved him straight on from the first time I knew him (I was not then fifteen) to the present hour.'[5] Shortly after her death he told Mrs Arbuthnot with a kind of awe that the Duchess could not bear his being out of her sight. It was none the less a problem to both of them. On his side, her obsession irritated. On her side, she sometimes wondered whether she was not setting up an idol of a forbidden kind.

There is evidence that Kitty's fatal fear of him gradually melted away in the strength given to her by illness and her battle for his Long-Wellesley nephews. A striking contrast is presented between a series of hysterically nervous letters written by her to the Fosters' Irish uncle, Lord Oriel, in 1825 and one to her sister Elizabeth Stewart four years later. In 1825 she entreated Lord Oriel to prevent the Fosters at all costs from paying her a visit in England. 'There can hardly exist a case in which it is wise in any Woman to fill her husband's house . . . with her own Relations however dear they may be', but in this case it would be 'totally destructive of every hope of happiness'.[6] (To this period belongs the legend of young people using the backstairs of Apsley House rather than risk an encounter with the Duke.) Yet in 1829 Kitty was gaily telling Elizabeth that she insisted on putting up her son Tom at 10 Downing Street: 'This house is enormous . . . & you see it can possibly be no inconvenience to invite Thomas to stay and I will answer for the Duke's kindly feelings towards your child. . . .'

In her last years Kitty could answer for the Duke's kindly feelings towards herself. After her death and despite the debts, there was only one subject which reawakened in him the carping spirit of old – their son Douro.

*

The Duke was not the first noble father to be disappointed in his son and heir. There was criticism of horses being dumped in his stables and fed at his expense without a 'by your leave', so that he was no longer master in his own house.[7] Douro for his part believed the fiction of his father's harshness over money, and had secretly offered to lend his mother part of his own very handsome allowance when he came of age. Kitty while alive was probably something of a buffer between father and son, for after she died there was a spate of complaints to Mrs Arbuthnot, often about trivialities. Douro, for instance, had not paid a formal call on his father when stationed at Dover Castle.

> The truth is that he is incorrigible. His Manner when I spoke to him and his shuffling excuses provoked me, because it put me in Mind of his Mother when she was in a difficulty. . . .[8]

Or he would spend idle days at Walmer and Stratfield Saye without speaking to his father.

> First he is afraid of me and dislikes to be in the House with me. Secondly he inherits His Mother's lightness of character. I really believe that she poor Woman! would, if she could, have had me at all times in her sight. But she could not recollect from day to day what she had been repeatedly informed I disliked.[9]

The Duke disliked being ignored in his own house. His gloom over Douro and over politics coalesced towards the end of 1832, when his son stood as a Tory candidate for Hampshire in a general election which showed all the signs of going wrong.

*

It was a crucial election. By the new year, 1833, members destined to sit in the first reformed Parliament would have been chosen. The Duke heard that Douro was very active. 'I hope he is so,' he remarked dubiously. Local enquiries about his son's chances did not diminish his suspicions. The Tory 'Hunting Gentlemen' said it would be a walkover but the Whigs predicted a close run thing.[10]

The truth was that for several months past the election prospects throughout the country had given him cause for concern. There was a lack of proper organization, and his mind was relieved by the appointment in November of a new *éminence grise*, the first Conservative party manager. (An earlier, amateurish attempt by Gleig, Arbuthnot and others to set up a Tory HQ in Charles Street had run into financial trouble.) Francis

Robert Bonham, the new man, was socially a cut above 'Black Billy' Holmes the party agent, and for the next fourteen years he built up the party machine. Unduly elated perhaps by Bonham's advent Sir Henry Hardinge foretold to the Duke a muster in the Commons of 240 'staunch Conservatives, exclusive of loose fish'.[11]

Alas, by December Douro himself had become a loose fish and slipped through the net. Hearing worse and worse reports of his chances, he resigned before the poll took place without consulting his father. His action started a ripple of despondency in neighbouring constituencies and of anger against the Duke. 'But it is like everything else,' wrote his furious father, 'I am supposed to be the *Head*! I am in reality the *Tail* of the Party. *Servus Servorum!*'[12]

The 'slave of slaves' knew in fact that all the results so far were horrible, the Reform Bill having wreaked havoc in the towns. Only one seat had been carried by the Conservatives without an expensive and 'bloody contest' – Peel's at Tamworth.[13] In Winchester they had the 'advantage' of a Political Union, explained the Duke sarcastically to Harriet, which intimidated voters by physical outrage. 'In truth the Revolution is effected.'

If 'Revolution' meant the Whigs winning 320 seats with a substantial leaven of Radicals, and the Conservatives only 150, the Duke was right. They asked him what he thought about the remodelled Parliament, when for the first time he surveyed the new MPS from the Peers' Gallery.

Think of them? 'I have never seen so many bad hats in my life!'[14]

Hats could be a symbol of social status. When the Duke was Prime Minister one of his self-appointed advisers had seen salvation in a graduated hat tax. Not much tax would have been raised from the middle-class hats now submitted to his inspection. Old Cobbett was present for the first time, looking like John Bull up from the country. But Orator Hunt, the owner of the bad white hat signifying revolution, had lost his seat.

*

The Duke, in agreement with Peel, decided not to harass Grey's Government until another was fit to take its place. To do so earlier would have been contrary to all his principles: 'Our course in the House of Lords,' he had announced in the previous December, 'ought to be very firm and uncompromising, but very moderate' – an example of what has since been called the politics of the extreme centre. They must attend assiduously and argue every point, 'but avoid dividing except upon occasions of great importance'.[15] The great occasion did not arrive until June 1833. Meanwhile a '*piano*' leader again had to face ultra-Tory criticism.

Cumberland badgered the Duke to call immediate party meetings, some large to gratify the inconspicuous members, some '*smaller* meetings of the GREAT GUNS' to initiate action. But the greatest gun of all refused to fire. The last thing he wanted was to stoke up the party fires at Apsley House. Lord Londonderry's hopes that the Duke's health would stand up to the 'perilous trials' ahead were deliberately extinguished. There were to be no perilous trials. It was no good the House of Lords holding fierce debates until they were 'opportune'.[16] Similarly, all suggestions that he should create constitutional associations to counteract the political unions were snubbed. 'I feel a great disinclination to recommend to any class of the King's Subjects,' he wrote to a Devon farmer, 'to associate or combine for any purpose which is not . . . recognised by the Laws and by the Government of the Country.' Gleig was told more brusquely, 'It is very easy to turn the Society with the *best* Name and rules and regulations to the worst purposes. . . .'[17] Such an attitude could never satisfy a busy character like Gleig, far less Cumberland.

Nor was Wellington as yet friendly with Peel, though their cautious and moderate policies exactly coincided. The sulphurous fumes of the May Days were still in their garments. In public no doubt they each congratulated the other on having taken the course he had chosen, Wellington for serving the King, Peel for not serving. But the contradiction could not be agreeable to either. Wellington met Peel in February at the Carlton Club. Peel did not speak to him and after dinner sat reading by one of the fireplaces while the rest of the company conversed round the other. The Duke suspected Peel was jealous, though why? 'I have repeatedly told him I would not stand in his way.'[18]

*

The King's Speech of February 1833 at once showed the Duke

that during the coming session he must give the Government qualified support on more than one subject. The 'great occasion' for a full-scale attack would none the less arise – Ireland.

From the Speech it appeared that the Government's policy on Ireland was two-edged: repression and concession. Repression meant a Coercion Bill to restore law and order.* Where O'Connell called the Speech 'brutal and sanguinary', the Duke found nothing to criticize. Concessions, however, on the Irish Protestant Church could and must be opposed. Admittedly six million Catholics were required by law to pay tithes in support of eight hundred thousand Protestants. Grey planned in the course of this Parliament to abolish ten redundant Protestant bishoprics, to phase out Protestant clergy who had no parishioners and lastly to commute the tithes, appropriating surplus income derived from the streamlined new system to lay purposes. In all, a sweeping programme, a 'great occasion' indeed.

How could the Duke applaud concessions, and such concessions, to Catholic peasants who were taking the law into their own hands, refusing to pay any tithes whatever and murdering the police who distrained on their cattle? Besides, 'Lay Appropriation' (of tithes) was an attack on Church property. The men who seized Church property one day would seize yours and mine the next. Was it not the first step towards repeal of the Union? 'It will put an end to the Protestant Interest in Ireland; and if the Connection is to be maintained it must be by the Bayonet.'[19]

It would be July, however, before the first Irish Church Bill reached the Lords. With growing confidence in his policy of the extreme centre, Wellington suddenly felt able to divide against the Government in June. Even Greville was impressed by the return of his crowd-magnetism. As they rode through St James's Park on 19 May hats were lifted to him and people stood up. 'I like this symptom,' wrote Greville, 'and it is the more remarkable because it is not *popularity*.' It was a much higher feeling – 'great reverence'. The Duke's surprise attack on the Government, an attack upon Lord Palmerston's foreign policy during the debate of 3 June, was to try the people's reverence very hard.

*

* Coercion was the method of putting down political disturbances by replacing the ordinary law of the land with a special act which introduced an element of force.

The so-called War of the Two Brothers in Portugal, with Dom Pedro fighting for his young daughter, Maria da Gloria, and Dom Miguel for himself, had reached a critical stage. Funds and volunteers raised in Britain looked like giving victory to Dom Pedro and the constitutionalists. In Tory opinion, Grey had committed a breach of non-intervention by turning a blind eye to British aid for Pedro, and the Duke on 3 June called on the Government to enforce their official neutrality.

His Majesty's Ministers have declared that neutrality is the policy of the country. If all this be so, in the name of God, let His Majesty recall every one of his Subjects who has engaged on either side of the contest.

The Duke pressed his motion to a division and beat the Government by seventy-nine to sixty-nine votes. Dismay and indignation in the Whig ranks. What did the Duke think he was doing? Grey called it a vote of censure intended to overthrow his Ministry. The Duke denied any such intention, so the Ministry was not overthrown. But his motives seemed nevertheless questionable. Was it wise to demonstrate the independence of the Lords? In fact it again brought the very existence of 'these Things called Lords' into question, convincing many people that the Duke's true motive had been to please the wild men he could not control.

That he was serious about British neutrality seems to have made little impression. Yet it was so; and a private letter written to a certain Captain Logan proved it in a manner that probably caused the Captain surprise. Asked to lend Logan £50 so that he might enlist with Dom Miguel's forces, the Duke replied with an iron disapproval not expected from an alleged Miguelite:

Sir, I have received your letter. You are perhaps not aware that you are about to undertake a service the performance of which is contrary to the laws of the country. It is impossible for me so far to encourage you to undertake this service as to lend you money to enable you to set out. . . . I have the honor to be etc. etc. Wellington.[20]

*

Exhilarated by the derring-do of June, the Duke rough-sharpened his sabre for the Irish Church Bill in July. He and Peel were still in accord over preserving the Whigs as long as the only alternative was a Radical coup. But short of actually destroying Grey, the Duke felt no inhibitions about brinkmanship. He went down to the House on 11 July and proceeded with great vehemence to pour out the thoughts he had collected from sheaves and sheaves of historic notes on Ireland covering three centuries. 'I consider the Bill utterly inconsistent,' he summed up, 'with the policy of the country since the period of the Reformation.'

The Duke's speech had the worst possible effect. Inflamed beyond endurance, the High Tory peers called a secret meeting at Buckingham's house two days later and resolved to turn out the Ministry on the Irish Church Bill, even if Peel refused to join in forming a new Tory Government. This was mutiny. One of their number, Lord Strangford, got cold feet and warned the Duke at 8 A.M. next morning to tackle the rebels at a party meeting already scheduled for the following day in Apsley House. 'If something be not done, I fear (from the language held last night), that we shall again witness *a split*, worse than that of 1829.'[21]

The Duke acted promptly. On Monday 15 July he steadied all but the irreconcilables at the party meeting, arguing that for the Church's own sake the bill must go to committee. He did not intend to oppose the second reading. Four days later, 19 July, his bugles were publicly sounding the 'Recall' to his over-excited troops. 'It appears to me absolutely impossible,' he declared in the House, 'that the Church of England established in Ireland can continue to exist for a day if some measure of this description is not passed to relieve it from its present unfortunate situation.' He admitted that had he been asked to establish the Protestant Church in Ireland for the first time in 1833, he might not have found it necessary to have three archbishops and twenty-two bishops to two thousand clergy – 'but they are there' – and he could not vote for their withdrawal or contemplate a scene where a Catholic bishop might occupy the palace, 'and probably use the very furniture', of the Protestant bishop. At the same time he could not vote against it.

The Ultras, foaming with rage when he abstained, ignored his bugle-call and though outnumbered by 158 to 96 dug in their heels & voted 'Not Content'.

Though the Duke had saved the bill, the crisis had been partly due to his earlier tactical error in exciting the heavy cavalry beyond recall. It was a mistake which he would never have committed on the battlefield. Peel was determined that it should not happen again on the floor of Parliament. He wrote to the Duke next day making it clear that their joint strategy of pricking rather than puncturing the Government must not itself be punctured in the Lords. The Duke agreed with all Peel's points, explaining only that it was hard for the Lords to realize all of a sudden that they no longer counted. 'The true sense of the position will be inspired at last,' he added grimly, 'when they will become more manageable.'[22]

After the excitement had subsided the Duke was able to please the ruffled bishops by helping to vote down the Jews and Dissenters in their respective attempts to enter Parliament and the ancient universities. Unlike many of his followers who had left long ago for the grouse moors, he stuck out the session to its end, proposing reasoned amendments to the Bank Charter bill on 26 August. Not everyone admired his zeal. Grey spoke irritably of his 'strange conceit' in appearing to understand every question better than all the world besides and thereby often cutting 'a sorry figure'.[23] Listening to the Duke's indistinct enunciation and looking down on so many bald heads (not his) and trembling limbs – Lord Eldon on someone's arm, Lord Holland wheeled in – the radical Lady Morgan would have liked to see the House of Lords abolished, 'barrier against progress' as it was, manned principally by the aged and infirm.[24]

Notwithstanding these strictures, the Duke had achieved his difficult task of bringing their lordships safely through the session in a state verging on sanity. Neither so badly demoralized by retreats as to make no contribution, nor so dementedly euphoric over successes as to invite condign punishment, their House had avoided the head-on collision with the Commons which the King above all dreaded.

The King had a further reason for being grateful to the Duke. One of those delicate assignments from royalty, which the Duke knew so well how to handle, had helped to keep him in London when others left.

*

The secret of Mrs Fitzherbert's marriage to the late King had lain dormant with her papers for nearly two years. By the spring of 1832, however, she had begun to regret that her letters were accessible to Sir William Knighton, one of George IV's executors and a man she loathed. Supported by King William, who loved her and also detested Knighton, she requested the other executor, Wellington, either to hand over her letters or destroy them. Knighton refused point-blank to betray his 'sacred Trust'[25] to George IV by handing over any letters, and even the Duke was much alarmed at the possibility of this explosive material afterwards being wormed out of a frail old lady and published. The lie which Fox had been deceived by HM into telling the House – that the Protestant heir was *not* married to a Catholic – must never be nailed.

The Duke began, therefore, by suggesting to Mrs Fitzherbert, with King William's approval, that all the letters and documents exchanged between her and George IV (she possessed his to her) should be destroyed in the presence of a third party. This time it was she who refused. The Duke was baffled, until he discovered that she really wanted to preserve only one love-letter, her marriage certificate and a few other documents of that kind. He devised a solution satisfactory to all. Two peers, Lord Albemarle, the Master of the Horse, and Lord Stourton, her Catholic relative, were appointed by her early in August 1833 to act with the Duke and Knighton. The four agreed to destroy all the papers except those precious few, which should be sealed and locked up in Coutts's bank.

Then followed one of the great letter-burnings in history. The Duke and Albemarle met at Mrs Fitzherbert's house in Tilney Street off Park Lane on 24 August, and for several industrious hours fed Mrs Fitzherbert's drawing-room fire with the records of a long-dead passion. 'I think, my Lord, we had better hold our hand for a while,' said the practical Duke at last, 'or we shall set the old woman's chimney on fire.'[26] Next day the burning was completed, poor Mrs Fitzherbert collapsed and the Duke retired to Stratfield Saye.

With the royal event well over (he had no more trouble with the Fitzherbert papers for four years) and the session closed he should have felt liberated, especially as he professed to like being alone. Yet there is a curiously autumnal feeling in a letter he sent to Harriet Arbuthnot on 30 August.

I am quite alone. But as I have now to be in a new course of being bored by artists . . . my Life is a Burthen to me.[27]

Worse than sitting to artists was entertaining a large house-party in December.

I am ashamed to feel the Bore of it so much as I do. But I think that there is something so degrading in passing a whole Week in an useless effort to amuse people who cannot be amused by any thing.

At the end of it all, what was there but a huge accumulation of unanswered letters?

I think that I ought to be allowed to be either a Man like another with the Affairs of the World to transact; or I ought to be made a *Shew* entirely! It is impossible that I can continue to be both.[28]

The artists of course helped to make him a '*Shew*' and he had many skirmishes with them, once complaining that he had been painted in every position except standing on his head. Yet it was through a request to sit to yet another artist that the Duke got his first clue to an impending '*Shew*' which was soon to bring him the purest pleasure.

*

The Professor of Poetry at Oxford, the Rev. John Keble, had asked the Duke in March 1833 to be sculpted by the famous Francis Chantrey. Keble and some university colleagues wished in this manner to express their sense of his noble loyalty to the King during May last. Unexpectedly touched, the Duke replied that though no one had approved of his conduct then but himself, he would gladly sit to Mr Chantrey or anyone else they liked.

The next thing he heard was that Lord Grenville, Chancellor of Oxford, was gravely ill and *he* would be nominated to succeed him. The Duke was overwhelmed. That the golden plum of academic honour should be offered to him, the backward boy who had been sent by his mother and eldest brother to the barrack square instead of an Oxford quadrangle, and afterwards had removed his own two sons and sent them to Cambridge! He could not resist writing to Harriet Arbuthnot: 'What will Lord Wellesley say?'

Sir Robert Peel was deeply hurt. He still had his following in Oxford but others did not like the way he had refused to serve the King in May 1832. In any case most of Oxford wanted a peer. Though the Duke wrote pressing his own disqualifications and

Peel's claims, they wanted *him*.[29] He was elected Chancellor on 29 January 1834.

The boyish pleasure came bubbling out when he described to Harriet the first installation ceremony of 7 February at Apsley House and how well he had understood the Latin. 'This shows what attention to a Language for a few days will do.' The royal family were present and 'did no harm'. He continued in a cheerful vein to Lady Shelley, 'I think I shall get to the Woolsack at last!'[30]

His triumph at the Installation of 11–13 June in Oxford was a high Tory carnival, a Tory 'Three Glorious Days'[31] – Peel absent but Newcastle, Wetherell, Winchilsea and Eldon there in force, the latter wildly cheered because 'he never ratted!' The Duke, robed in black and gold, stood outwardly unmoved among the scarlet doctors and bewigged bishops as the surges of enthusiasm rolled round him and the stamping feet raised a huge cloud of dust. Young Lord Maidstone of Christ Church was cut short by thunderous applause as he declaimed,

> *Heroes succeeded heroes, year by year,*
> *We have one only – and that One is here!*

Britain had challenged the master of the universe, declared Joseph Arnould of Wadham College next day, winner of the Newdigate prize poem,

> *And the dark soul the world could scarce subdue,*
> *Bowed to thy Genius, Chief of Waterloo!*

Wellington himself had to raise his hand to bring the shouting to a close.

Two false quantities in his own Latin oration did not upset the Duke's poise, though they may have shown what attention to a language for only 'a few days' could do. One of his future tips on public speaking was never to use Latin.

On the last day of the carnival he called at the colleges to render thanks. Mrs Yonge, wife of a Waterloo officer, pushed forward her son Julian, aged four, and daughter Charlotte, eleven, to shake hands. To the immeasurable pride of Julian's family, the Duke kissed him. But afterwards Julian's friends, if they wanted to tease him, would say,

'Show us the place where the Duke bit you.'[32]

*

The intoxication of Tory Oxford gave Wellington's political position a lift at the right moment. Grey's Government had entered an agonizing final phase. There were painful divisions between right and left as well as between personalities. A report of three angry voices, identified as Grey's, Palmerston's and Althorp's, heard wrangling at the Foreign Office into the small hours about whether to send troops to Portugal, reached Wellington shortly before Parliament reassembled on 4 February 1834.[33]

Wellington himself was still preaching against 'fruitless Collision' with the Commons. He had been persuaded against his better judgement to invite fifty peers to an eve-of-session party meeting at Apsley House. Huffily he told Lord Roden, the die-hard Ulsterman, that some peers answered his invitation uncivilly, others not at all. If only they could have met at a club or the house of some other noble lord. Nevertheless, the Whigs' disputes over the next instalment of Irish Church reform could not but stir up their enemies, including the royal family. Wellington and Princess Lieven agreed that the King's anxiety about the Church was driving him mad, while Cumberland's modest requirement of his leader was to *'blow up'* the Government at once, *'when* or *how* I care not'.[34]

The Duke did not need to blow it up. Through its own contentiousness it detonated the first bomb on 6 May, when John Russell made a vigorous plea for the transfer of tithes to lay purposes. As soon as the orator sat down, Edward Stanley, the former Canningite, passed a note to his colleague Graham, 'Johny Russell has upset the coach.' Three weeks later (27 May) Stanley and Graham resigned, followed by Ripon and Richmond.

With the Government's 'right wing' gone, the ultra-Tories sniffed victory: 'a crisis cannot be far distant,' wrote Londonderry to Buckingham, planning to see Wellington immediately he returned from Oxford and to press on him a winning combination with the Radicals against Grey. But there was still no change to be got out of the Duke. 'I also am for a fair *Stand up fight*,' he announced. But he would not be a party to any combination of discontented Whigs, Radicals or others to bring down the Government.[35]

Again such action was not needed. The Prime Minister, already deserted by his 'right,' now suspected treachery from his 'left'. Some confidential pledge or appearance of a pledge against coercion had certainly been made by the 'left' to O'Connell. Edward Littleton, the Duke's well-meaning but unskilful nephew, had got himself embroiled and had involved Althorp also. It all came out in the wash and a wretched wash it was. Althorp resigned on 7 July. This was the end for Grey. He wound up the Ministry next day. Of the two major subjects before this Parliament, the coercion of Ireland and the Poor Law, coercion had brought down a government. It was not to be Ireland's last achievement in this line.

The King sent for Lord Melbourne, hoping however that it would be a coalition government including Peel and Wellington. To the Duke, a coalition with Melbourne would no more promote that fair stand-up fight which he desired than would the machinations of the Ultras with the Radicals. All three of them, Melbourne, the Duke and Peel, told the King that a coalition was impossible.

*

Though there was no such 'community of purpose' between the Duke and Melbourne as the King had hoped, he was right in believing the two had much in common. The new Poor Law brought it out.

In the great and growing argument over how to deal with poverty, they were on the same side: Whigs, Liberals and Conservatives versus Radicals, Tory Radicals and some ultra-Tories. The Duke has already been seen supporting the Home Secretary in 1830 against the political unions. In 1834 there was much agricultural distress and a spurt of trade union activity to keep up wages. The Duke expressed indignation in an emphatic memorandum on 26 February:

We have no Govt. in England. We are not able if we are willing to protect men . . . in their Bargains with their Labourers . . . the consequence is that the latter are paid much more than the value of their Labour. They *will* be so paid. They will burn and destroy until they are so paid and the Govt. will not possibly cannot, now protect the Gentlemen and farmers in resistance to these demands. . . .[36]

So when Lord Melbourne had the Tolpuddle Martyrs transported in April (they had been arrested in their Dorset village two days before the Duke wrote his memorandum) it seemed that England had a government at last. What could the Duke give but support?

To be sure, there was a period when Richard Oastler, the Tory steward of Fixby Hall in Yorkshire, hoped to range the Duke on the Tory Radical side. Known as 'the King of the Factory Children' for his work in limiting hours of child-labour, Oastler posed the question: Could not the aristocracy make common cause with the poor against the cotton-spinning capitalists? Many impassioned letters reached the Duke in 1834, describing how the 'poor working class' was enchained by the same plebeian capitalists who 'spindle-ized' the aristocracy by buying up the title deeds to their estates: '. . . aye, my Lord Duke, you may smile, but these men know how to spin PARCHMENT, signed by the noblest hands in Britain, into yarn, as well as my poor factory children's sinews and bones.'[37]

The Duke did not smile; he had invited Oastler to Apsley House the year before and learned that the aristocracy and the poor misunderstood one another, the former expecting to be plundered and the latter to be sabred. Oastler found the Duke agreeably devoid of grandeur and glad to assure his guest that he had renounced cold steel since Waterloo.[38] He and his party voted for the Factory Bill in 1833 (children of nine to eleven restricted to a nine-hour day) and for the bill of 1834 to prevent 'climbing boys' of under ten from sweeping chimneys. Seven years later the Duke's architect, Benjamin Wyatt, asked permission to send a little sweep up a particularly obstinate chimney in Apsley House. The Duke wrote back angrily, 'The Employment of climbing Boys is prohibited by Act of Parliament.'[39]

Nevertheless, when Disraeli published in *Sybil* a vision similar to and just as romantic as Oastler's, it was clear that the Duke had never belonged to their side. Disraeli's dream was of a Tory-Radical alliance which would unite the 'Two Nations' of the rich and the poor. In his imagination he heard 'the voice of a noble, who without being a demagogue, upheld the popular cause'.[40] (The alliance was symbolized in *Sybil* by the marriage of the noble Egremont with Sybil, the Chartist's daughter.) Yes, but where were the votes for that nobleman's new party? As Robert Blake points out, no politician could lead a party half of which – the poor half – had no votes until 1867.

The Duke may have seemed close to Oastler in the days when he used to deride 'the economists'. But things had changed. The

Tory-Radicals' failure to win him was inevitable when Oastler wrote in June 1834 attacking financiers and businessmen: '*Who keeps the aristocracy and people enemies?* Messrs. Rothschild, Louis Philippe, Morrison & Co. – cold blooded capitalists.'[41] In the world of finance which the Duke understood and valued, Rothschild was a king. In vain Oastler went on to denounce the Whigs' heartless Poor Law Commission. By their new Poor Law, Oastler's little Yorkshire village of Fixby and its small neighbours would be formed into a Union and attached to the teeming mill-town of Huddersfield. What for? Simply to bail out bankrupt mill-owners, according to Oastler, with the rate from the countryside.

The steamlining into Unions appeared to the Duke desirable; the true reason being, as he saw it, to rescue agriculture from the old system of relieving the poor in their homes or in a parish workhouse out of the parish rates, which amounted to subsidizing low wages.

His view of the new Poor Law was that of all 'reasonable persons', to quote Harriet Martineau, namely, favourable. It was indeed a public servant's *chef d'oeuvre*, remarkable for its good intentions, thoroughness and efficiency. Not that the Duke accepted its every detail. The new bastardy laws, which threw responsibility almost entirely on the mother, seemed to him harsh. Others thought that these and similarly rigorous changes applying to the family were either beneficial or very small sacrifices to make for the curtailment of 'out-door relief', as the old method was called, and the reorganization of workhouses.[42]

These Union workhouses were to be run on the principle of 'less eligibility', meaning that life inside should be less eligible than life outside. Their opponents called them 'bastilles'. Men and women were segregated, parents were separated from one another and from their children. A good thing too, said Miss Martineau; why allow children to be corrupted by parents who were possibly hardened criminals? Rations were often so mean that even when the quality of the food was disgusting a brave spirit might ask for more. Nevertheless, in many Unions the administration was humane and sensible, and the food 'the best' of the lowest kind, as the Duke noted approvingly, reading the proposed menus of porridge, soup and bread. Today, both the reasons for Poor Law reform and its results are questioned by historians. They are the subjects of intensive research. Suffice it to say here that in the Duke's time, responsible people like himself and Peel found, from the information available to them, that the case for reform was clear enough to merit their support. They can hardly be blamed. Having duly voted for it, the Duke felt free at last to lead the Lords in total war against the crumbling Whigs and the rest of their handiwork.

When their new Jew, Dissenters and Tithe Bills came up from the Commons he charged and routed them all.

With the proviso that Lord Roden throw overboard the Orange societies, he felt confident at the end of this testing session of preserving not only the Irish Church but an independent House of Lords. 'I consider the destruction of the House of Lords to be now out of the question,' he wrote to Aberdeen on 23 August; 'and we have only to follow a plain course with moderation and dignity, in order to attain very great if not preponderating influence in the affairs of the country.'[43] Plain, dignified language, if perhaps immoderately sanguine. But a sanguine opposition was just what suited the King.

*

King William had prorogued Parliament in person on 15 August in a mood of dynamic despair brought on by Russell's Tithe Bill. Was there no possibility of upsetting this dangerous coach, if indeed it could be regarded as ever having been properly righted since the upsets of June and July? The country seemed to share his intense irritability. 'There exists a general uneasiness about something, nobody knows what, and dissatisfaction with everything,' wrote the Duke on 5 October to the King's brother Cumberland, now abroad.[44] Later that month the Houses of Parliament were burned to the ground, through a load of old rubbish – used Exchequer tallies – having set fire to a chimney. 'Sweep!' shouted opponents of the Climbing Boys Bill ironically, as they watched the blaze and drew their own moral; but was it not rather a portent that the first reformed Parliament would never sit again, either in that building or any other?

Soon afterwards Providence seemed to hear the King's cry. Melbourne announced to him that the lynch-pin of the House of Commons, Lord Althorp, had suddenly been removed from his position as Leader. His father, Earl Spencer, had died on 10

November and Althorp would succeed to the Lords. This was made by Melbourne to sound like the end. If King William persisted with the Whigs, it would mean his having the terrible Lord John Russell himself for coachman in the Commons. He summoned Melbourne to Brighton and on 14 November told him that he need not trouble to reconstruct his Government. But he accepted Melbourne's most civil offer to summon his successor – handing him a letter addressed to the Duke. The King, sure of release, was very affable to his former gaoler. That the dismissed Prime Minister had a substantial majority in the Commons did not worry him. Nor that he would go down to history as the first king who had deliberately set out to be a constitutional monarch, and the last who had succeeded in dismissing a government supported by the popular vote. A curious paradox.

The Duke of Wellington was in Hampshire about to go hunting when the King's summons reached him at 8 o'clock next morning. He hurried to Brighton as soon as his carriage was ready. His sudden arrival took all but the King completely by surprise. The Court had been told nothing about the crisis. With the delivery of *The Times* newspaper, however, it became clear that HM's confidential interview with Melbourne was no longer a secret in London, and indeed had been leaked by Brougham to *The Times* with a punch-line of his own invention: 'There is every reason to believe the Duke of Wellington has been sent for. The Queen has done it all.' Holding out the obnoxious passage to his retained servant, the King exclaimed,

'There, Duke! You see how I am insulted and betrayed . . . will your Grace compel me to take back people who have treated me in this way?'[45]

The Duke was too old a hand to feel sure that His Majesty had not got himself, by premature action, into a constitutional jam. Nevertheless, what could he do but go to the King's rescue? His willingness to waive his own doubts about the constitutional issue, moreover, gave him the whip-hand over the King on another matter. Peel must be Prime Minister, not himself.

Peel happened to have left England on 14 October for a long holiday abroad; 'just like him,' muttered the Duke, feeling that he must have known about the King's state of mind and ought to have stayed at his post.[46] A lesser man than the Duke might have been tempted to exploit the situation and accept the King's offer. But it was one of the Duke's greatest hours. He had promised Peel not to stand in his way or thwart the country's need for a prime minister in the Commons. Peel must be recalled at once. The Duke declined to form another Wellington administration. Meanwhile as caretaker, he would keep the King's Government going single-handed, until Peel arrived to appoint his own Cabinet.

The Duke's nominal eminence was dazzling: First Lord of the Treasury, Secretary of State for the Home Office, Foreign Affairs and War. The date was 15 November 1834, exactly four years to the day since his fall. If Elba were followed by no more than the prescribed hundred days, they would be a hundred days to take his mind off a tragic personal loss.

Mrs Arbuthnot, for twenty years his dearest friend and confidante, had died of cholera just over three months before.

20

A Hundred Days

July 28th 1834

My dear Mrs. Arbuthnot,
    I have received your Note and am delighted to learn that you are better. . . .[1]

It was the Duke's last letter to Harriet and the end of a most unusual, subtle and successful essay in triangular friendship.
    On the evening of 2 August, while staying with the Salisburys at Hatfield, he received an express from Sir Henry Halford, Mrs Arbuthnot's doctor:

My dear Lord duke! . . . my amiable friend was taken from us at six o'clock this morning. Did not suffer but wandered when was conscious. . . .[2]

The Duke threw down the fatal paper and flung himself on to a sofa. Then he walked about the room for a few minutes almost weeping aloud before he went to his room. Next morning he left at 8 A.M. to be with Charles Arbuthnot.
    The first letter from the stricken husband to the Duke was written in a pathetically shaky hand immediately after this visit (5 August) and explained much of their previous relationship.

I am very glad you came to me instead of writing to propose it; for had you, I must have said no. There was no one I so much dreaded seeing for the first sad time – She had no friend to whom She was so much attached as She was to you. . . . I believe I may say that you never had such a friend before & you will never have such a one again. As for myself I without murmur feel the conviction that life to me is from this day a blank. . . . I am writing all my thoughts to you, for we were *three*, & you will understand – O my dear Duke you feel for me I know – you feel for yourself also –

He then went on to describe his utter dependence on her.

I got into agitations & anxieties which made me unfit for everything; but she relieved me from all troubles . . . all my income was paid in her account – I even went to her for mere Pocket Money – It was my delight & joy to feel that I had such a guardian angel –[3]

In the Duke, Arbuthnot found his new guardian angel, as he never ceased to declare: a guardian who handled his business affairs, got him through a protracted nervous breakdown, took him to live in his house and finally, as will appear, restored him to a state of authority in which he was able to advise the guardian himself.

That the Duke 'felt for himself' also, to quote Mr Arbuthnot, needs no stressing. Mrs Arbuthnot's special gift lay in devoting herself exclusively to whatever subject occupied her at the moment – her estate and garden, her stepchildren, society, politics. She was a person to be uniquely missed. Nevertheless, after the first uncontrollable burst of grief the Duke suppressed his emotion except in the presence of Harriet's husband and stepsons. Immediately after the tragedy he appeared in Parliament. Young Lady Salisbury, to whom he turned for the next four years, believed the loss of Mrs Arbuthnot to be no more than that of a sincerely loved friend, whatever liaison may have existed in the past. In her opinion he was more concerned with Mr Arbuthnot's distress than his own – 'so much is he in the habit of directing his mind to whatever are the exigencies of the present moment, rather than of regretting the past'.[4]

There was much truth in this, even allowing for the writer's natural twinges of jealousy. Apart from finding consolation in Lady Salisbury herself, the Duke continued as before to be amused by the designs of ambitious girls. There was the Hon. Maria Tollemache who married Lord Ailesbury, having put it about that she had refused the Duke. He laughed at not being invited to her wedding 'presumably because I had been rejected!'[5] Then there was Miss Mary Ann Jervis, daughter of Lord St Vincent and called by the Duke 'The Syren'. She pursued him for seven years hoping to ensnare him with her beautiful singing voice. But he never admired her except as a queen of song. 'I am going to give her a crown for singing the Cenerentola; mind – *not a coronet*!'[6] Frances Salisbury nevertheless became gravely concerned by the scandalous gossip which the Syren caused to focus upon the Duke. At one point the gossip touched even the irreproachable Frances. After a visit to Walmer in 1836 she received a disagreeable anonymous letter. It was shortly followed by another in the same hand addressed to the Duke himself and this time attacking Miss Jervis's presence at Walmer. In answer to Lady Salisbury's questions he laughed off any possibility of his being in love with the mad Miss Jervis. 'What is the good of being sixty-seven if one cannot speak to a young lady?' [7]

In the course of the next year, however, the attacks persisted and the Duke felt bound on 10 July 1837 to warn Lady Salisbury: 'I shall be delighted to see you at Walmer with all your children. But I strongly recommend you not to come without Lord Salisbury.' [8] One particularly vicious attack on Miss Jervis dated 27 September he kept 'for handwriting':

The lady is *enragée* at the sudden termination of her hopes. The castle once cleared of guests, the day was her own, her victim clenched. – 'If four-and-twenty be not an overmatch for sixty-eight, the devil's in't –' and thus she brawls like a billingsgate, and utters indecent threats with the audacity of a W[hore]. 'He is the best dangler in the world'. – she cried, '. . . never out of my bed-room, but when I am in his' – a singularly delicate boast from a lady, truly. 'Not let me stay! If I had no objection, why should he? – What's come to him? He was not wont to be so nice. – But no matter – I have a project, and will fix him yet –'

The writer then explained that Miss Jervis planned to catch the Duke by pretending to be *enceinte*.

Faugh! – And the Duke submits to have his name thus degraded, because *she can sing*.[9]

It is necessary to quote such rubbish now and then in order to explain the legend of the Duke's life-long libertinism. Though he suspected Miss Jervis of circulating the rumours about his matrimonial intentions, he jocularly assured Lady Salisbury on 7 November that they were neither true nor injurious: 'I confess that I have no feeling about them; as I have no pretensions elsewhere either to the Queen or anybody else!' – Victoria being at this date an unmarried girl of eighteen.[10]

*

A last look at Mrs Arbuthnot and the Duke shows that her loss to him was great in the sphere of his own family. Lady Salisbury took over the long political conversations which he called 'thinking aloud' and the copying of his memoranda;[11] Mr

Arbuthnot provided the companionship. With his sons it was different. Mrs Arbuthnot had nearly always championed them. Though in her last months the Duke was still describing them to her as going about 'like two Scamps . . . scarcely clean' and fonder of parties given by the local tenants than by the *ton*, yet he had to admit to her that they were free from real vices.

I certainly think my Sons the most extraordinary Young Men that I ever saw. They detest good Company. Yet they do not frequent, and have none of the vices or the follies of those who do frequent bad. What they like is what is second best.[12]

He was one of the famous fathers who failed to see that small stars cannot shine in the same sky as the sun.

After Mrs Arbuthnot's death the situation for a time deteriorated. The gentle and loving Fanny Salisbury, with children of her own (unlike Mrs Arbuthnot), was deeply shocked by what seemed to her the young men's·neglect of their father. Her prejudices were not removed by Douro one day declaring his love for her, a thing he would never have dared to try on Harriet Arbuthnot. Altogether the next five years were vexing ones – the Duke passionately longing for his sons to marry and give him daughters-in-law and grandchildren, while Charles went on his cheerful way without recorded affairs and Douro let slip Lady Mary Herbert and the Hon. Louisa Stuart through what appeared to his parent to be sheer dilatoriness. An end to these frustrations, however, was in sight.

It was perhaps the beginning of Lady Salisbury's fatal illness in the summer of 1838 which released Douro for serious courtship. In April 1839 he married Lady Elizabeth Hay, the lovely daughter of the Marquess of Tweeddale, who had served under Douro's father in the Peninsula and had supported him faithfully in all his political battles, including Catholic emancipation. This marriage may have been arranged by the two families. Bessie, as they called Douro's bride, was a mere child. But for the Duke she was a daughter at last, perfectly loving and unutterably simple.

*

It was impossible in that age of religious revival for Mrs Arbuthnot's death to leave no mark on the Duke's spiritual life. By nature his religious feelings were sincere but quiet and unaffected as Harriet's own. Mr Arbuthnot described how she would unostentatiously slip away into her closet for meditation and prayer. In the same spirit the Duke had been used to attend St James's Church, Piccadilly, for early service, where he was often almost the only person present. In view of such inconspicuous conduct, it was too much to hope that zealous clerical voices would not sooner or later demand from the great Duke of Wellington more public demonstrations of devotion to church-going.

The first determined attack had been launched by a former political adviser on religious affairs, Henry Phillpotts, Bishop of Exeter. During the winter of 1831–2 the Duke was struck down with pneumonia. The Whig press took pleasure in announcing his imminent death and the Tory bishop in recommending more frequent approaches to the 'Throne of Grace'. The Duke replied with exemplary meekness to the throne of Exeter. He was anxious to disabuse the bishop of the rumour that he was a person 'without any sense of religion'. If true, it was unpardonable, since he had read and talked about religion a good deal. The truth was that he did not boast about this knowledge or about his charity or about his regular church attendances on Sundays at Stratfield Saye and Walmer – London churches were now generally too cold for his bare head and injured ear – and in these days people who did not boast stood condemned.

Then in private life I have been accused of every vice and enormity; and when those who live with me, and know every action of my life and every thought, testify that such charges are groundless, the charge is then brought 'Oh, he is a man without religion!' [13]

The Duke concluded humbly with the remark that there was room for amendment in every man, 'in me as well as in others'; his lordship's advice would not be thrown away.

The year 1834 opened for him in loneliness. Lord Francis Leveson-Gower remembered coming into the library at Stratfield Saye one January evening to find the Duke reading alone by the light of a single candle. [14] His snow-white hair, chiselled features and worn expression caused by the effort to hear made him begin to look old at last, and he was thin now rather than slim. But his eyes were as piercing, his complexion as clear and his mind as incisive as ever.

He returned to Apsley House where a letter was waiting for him from a Miss Jenkins, dated 15 January 1834. It was about his soul. He acknowledged it immediately on the 18th, making one or two blots on his reply and dating it '1833', which Miss Jenkins thought betrayed his agitated feelings.[15] On the anniversary of Kitty's death, 24 April, she therefore delivered a bible at Apsley House with St John, Chapter III, verse 5 marked in pencil: 'Except a man be born again . . . he cannot enter into the kingdom of God.'

The Duke did not answer. Four months later, however (27 August) the death of Mrs Arbuthnot prompted him to thank the bible lady whose name he had misread as *Mrs* Jenkins. She informed him that she was single and invited him to call. He answered her summons on 12 November 1834 after carefully explaining that he was not in the habit of visiting young ladies with whom he was not acquainted. It was just three days before the royal summons arrived from the King. The extraordinary interview that followed was described by Miss Jenkins in her diary. But first, who was she?

Anna Maria Jenkins, aged twenty and blessed with charms as imperious as her piety, was the orphaned only child of middle-class parents. She lived with a companion, Mrs Lachlan, on a slender income in Charlotte Street. Hitherto her claims to fame had consisted in bringing a murderer named Henry Cooke to a condemned-cell repentance the year before. Now she asked the Lord, what next? 'Greater things than these', came the 'precious' reply. She realized in a flash that this could mean only one thing. The Duke of Wellington must be given 'a new *birth* into righteousness. . . .'*

---

* I shall not refer to Anna Maria Jenkins as 'Miss J', the name invented for purposes of anonymity by Christine Terhune Herrick, the editor of *Letters of the Duke of Wellington to Miss J, 1834 to 1851* (London 1889). Through the kindness of Mr J. Thomas Eubank Jr of Houston, Texas, and Rice University I have seen photostats of a number of the original letters from Wellington to Miss Jenkins, ranging from 1835 to 1851. Not one of them opens with the coy words 'Miss J' but all with 'Miss Jenkins'. Unfortunately the Duke's biographers have adopted the editorial 'Miss J', as though the Duke used it himself. Some readers may be sorry to know the truth. On the other hand, it is totally unlike the Duke to resort to a nickname for a lady he hardly knew. The Rice Collection also shows that Miss Jenkins's christian names were Anna Maria. When referring to Miss Jenkins's companion, the Duke called her Mrs Lachlan not, as the editor makes him write, 'Mrs L'.

The Lord prescribed that Anna Maria should wear her old, *turned* merino gown at the interview. She was not unaware of her beauty. After a fervent prayer she came downstairs to meet her distinguished sinner. 'Now if the Lord should send his arrow into his soul!'[16]

Both of them were struck dumb by the sight of the other: Anna Maria by the Duke's 'beautiful silver head', the Duke by the lustrous young beauty where he had expected an elderly, spinsterish 'Saint'. An arrow had certainly pierced him. He could not speak, so Anna Maria planted a bible between them on the table and raising her lovely hand in the manner which had been so successful with poor Cooke, began to read aloud, '*Ye MUST be born again. . . .*'

The Duke suddenly got his voice back and seizing the uplifted hand in his, repeated over and over again with mounting energy – 'Oh, *how* I *love* you! *how* I *love* you!' Astonished by the vehemence of his expression, Anna Maria asked who made him feel thus. He had the presence of mind to reply, 'God Almighty!'

The Duke was in the midst of intense political preoccupations when they met again on 23 December. He spoke rapidly. 'This must be for life! This must be for life! . . . Do you feel sufficiently for me to be with me a whole life?' The lovely young evangelist deceived herself into misunderstanding his proposal and replied demurely, '*If it be the will of God*'.[17]

After he had gone she began to feel doubts and on 10 January 1835 wrote that he had seemed to forget he was speaking to a virtuous woman. They had better part. By return came a short note repeating his proposal and agreeing that since she could not answer yes, her decision was entirely correct.

Two days later, 12 January, fire and brimstone were prepared for his 'beautiful silver head' and the volcano continued active throughout that night and the next day, pouring out pages of burning indignation. How dared he make such a profession of affection to her? If she were to bestow her hand on a Prince, *his* would be the honour. The Duke had offended 'one of these little ones'. Oh, that this letter might sink into his rebellious soul: for the Lord alone could 'make crooked things straight'.

The crooked thing again replied by return. Showing himself a better politician than on other occasions, he evaded the issue of whether he had proposed to seduce or marry her and answered a question in the affirmative which she had not asked: yes, he was strongly impressed with veneration for her virtues, attainments and sentiments.[18] So ended the first act of a play which was to continue with intervals on its half-ludicrous, half-touching course until the last year in the Duke's life. After accepting the brimstone on 13 January, he added a worldly thought for Anna Maria's consideration: 'The commands of all others which we ought to obey are those dictated to us by our social relations.' She was asking him to flout them. 'What would be said, if I, a man of seventy years of age, nearly, were to take in marriage a lady young enough to be my Granddaughter?'[19]

Again Anna Maria refused to let herself see the point. '*Alas! Alas!*' she reflected sadly in her diary, was there a single moment when he would have thought her too young for his 'most sinful adulation'? The Duke recognized and was tender towards her naivety. When she told him that his being the *Duke of Wellington* meant nothing to her, since she had never even heard of Waterloo (the second fact was true), he believed her. 'I know it, I know it, I know it and I respect you for it.'[20] What he did not know was that once she had decided it was better for him to marry her than to burn, she would never stop trying to become the Duchess. For his part, the intoxication was quickly over and he would gladly have dropped the whole thing. There was indeed a gap of five months in 1835. But when Anna Maria again raised the torch of salvation, his irresistible instinct to answer letters, his courtesy, his loneliness, his pleasure in feminine society, his humble gratitude to a young girl whose apparent interest was in his soul rather than in his dukedom, forced him to respond.

Sir Herbert Maxwell, his biographer, robustly writes it all off as 'twaddle'.[21] But the Duke had more to him than common sense. He could suffer and grope for consolation. Life without Mrs Arbuthnot had to answer for life with Miss Jenkins: the calls, the tiffs, the tracts received and the notes sent – all 390 of them. With Mrs Arbuthnot alive, he would not have needed to write more than the first.

There was, however, one advantage in Mrs Arbuthnot's dying at the precise moment when she did. Politically, she had not always been a good influence, particularly in her contempt for

Peel. This had been noticed by Wellington's other friends.* Lady Salisbury now saw in Peel the country's gift from God – a *Dieudonné*.[22] With turbulence and unrest feared for the future, it was vital that Wellington should see this also. At any rate, his conduct as caretaker through the delicate three weeks and more of waiting for Peel was strikingly magnanimous.

*

Though it was mid-November 1834, London pulsated, carriages bowling to and fro, crowds thronging the streets, clubs humming with political guesswork. What would the Duke do? What would the new Government be? Would it be the rule of 'Humbug' [old Toryism] or of 'Hum-drum' – 'an Enlightened-Spirit-of-the-Age Liberal-Moderate-Reform government'? Disraeli, who imagined these pertinent questions in his novel *Coningsby*, also imagined the Duke's answer. 'Nothing could be pumped out of him. All that he knew, which he told in his curt, husky manner, was, that he had to carry on the King's government.'[23]

In fact from 15 November until 9 December 1834 the Duke put into operation his own original method of caretaking. He took care of everything himself. He was everybody from Prime Minister downwards, holding five major and three minor offices. People laughed delightedly or groaned with anger to see the determined figure 'roving' about Whitehall, now at the Home Office, his HQ, now at No. 10, a turn in the Foreign Office, a spell in the Horse Guards or Colonial Office and back to the Home Department. The advantage was that government proceeded regularly, but nothing else. No appointments, no decisions, no policy, no legislation; all free and ready for Peel to do as he liked. Only one exception was permitted, the Chancellorship, of which the seals were *lent* to Lyndhurst. It must be admitted that this was a brief paradise for the Duke also. He was one of those who believed passionately in government and coolly in legislation. Now it was his duty to act strictly as he felt.

The Whigs' astonishment had been great – 'kicked out' by the

* 'I had a good deal of conversation with Sir H. Hardinge,' wrote Lady Salisbury in her journal (17–20 November 1833). '. . . He told me he thought Mrs Arbuthnot did mischief by setting the duke against Peel, and agreed with me that it is the duty of every friend of either to unite them as much as possible.' (Oman, p. 95.)

King, as Greville put it, 'in the plenitude of their fancied strength, and utterly unconscious of danger'.[24] As soon as they had got their breath back they used it to denounce Wellington. Not Caretaker but Dictator, was the cry. 'His Highness the Dictator,' Grey wrote indignantly to Princess Lieven, 'is concentrating in himself all the power of the State, in a manner neither constitutional nor legal.'[25]

It did not wash. The people knew their Duke well enough by now to acquit him of personal ambition. A few raised the cry, 'Reform in danger!' but most enjoyed the engaging absurdity of the situation and the current jokes. 'At last we have a united government,' said one wit. 'The Cabinet council sits in the Duke's head and the Ministers are all of one mind.' The Duke laughed with them, and enjoyed referring in later years to his brief period of 'Dictatorship'.

Seriously, he no longer doubted that the King had the constitutional power to dismiss ministers as he had dismissed the Whigs. (Whether he had been wise to use it was debatable.) 'I may be constitutionally responsible for enabling the king to carry on a Government without the aid of his popular Ministers,' admitted the Duke.[26] But that was his only personal involvement. If the King was within his rights, so was the Duke in serving him.

At the same time as the Duke defended his action, he showed exceptional enthusiasm in getting the party organization going, ready for Peel's return and a probable general election. Forgetting his usual aversion from such activities, he congratulated two East Anglian magnates on holding a Conservative dinner in Ipswich and 'entreated' them to stir up all their friends, while an indirect offer from the *Standard* to support his caretaker Government was actually described as candid and fair.

He naturally found no difficulty in turning a deaf ear to the siren or importunate voices of strangers and friends. To the gentleman from Bedford Square, for example, who advised 'a Radical reform' with Disraelian seductiveness: 'The natural allies of the nobility are the common People. Do not, therefore, fear them. They will rally around you to a man. . . .' Or to Lord Londonderry, who urgently demanded the Paris embassy for himself. 'I have not given a single office,' answered the Duke calmly. 'I don't propose to give one. . . .'[27]

There was one anonymous writer who was not snubbed. This

man congratulated the Duke on shedding no blood, causing no tears, persecuting no one for former opinions, yet saving the State from anarchy.

Anarchy was in the news. A few months later the great Whig Duke of Bedford, master of Woburn's incalculable wealth, said the nation's choice was now between anarchy and despotism, and he preferred anarchy.

'I can tell Johnny Bedford,' commented the Duke, 'if we have anarchy, I'll have Woburn.'[28]

*

Peel brought the Duke's 'despotism' to an end by landing at Dover on 9 December, after a dash home across Europe from Rome, where he had been eventually located. He saw the King that same day and with his usual ill luck was able to offer nothing but a display of 'awkward' manners in response to His Majesty's glowing welcome. Peel turned immediately to Cabinet-making. The Duke slid gracefully out of his seven redundant skins, retaining the office of Foreign Secretary; Lyndhurst stayed on as Lord Chancellor, while Peel was Prime Minister and Chancellor of the Exchequer. There were other worthy men in Peel's Cabinet, but not the two he needed to give permanency to his Government – Stanley and Graham.

These two Canningites had left the Whigs but were as yet unable to make the further transition to the Conservatives. They both refused to serve. Without them the fort which Wellington had held might turn out to be built on sand. Perhaps, indeed, Wellington had held the fort a shade too scrupulously. There had been a moment when the royal secretary passed him two letters containing personal appeals to Stanley and Graham from the King. But to ask for their services at that juncture would have meant the Duke's breaking his trusteeship and compromising Peel's liberty of action. His Majesty's letters went into the Duke's pocket. In any case, the Duke could see nothing to keep Peel and the former Canningites apart, now that reform, slavery, the China trade and Stanley's own Irish Bill were 'irrevocably settled'.[29]

The Duke's final words on the Stanley–Graham affair illustrated the contrast between his personal sensitivity and his failure to discern the nuances of parliamentary debate. He heard afterwards from the diehard Lord Wilton that Stanley had been chiefly put off by a speech of the Duke's last session in which he again denounced reform and all its works, including Stanley's.

'I don't believe that I was the real difficulty,' reflected Wellington. 'If I should have thought that I was, I should have been too happy to have gone out of the Way.'[30]

A Stanley for a Wellington? Peel's was not an easy task.

Despite their failure with the Canningites, the Duke and Peel set out bravely to educate the Tories into becoming true Conservatives. It was Peel's first ministry and the choices before his party were still the same three which had faced them since the Duke's crash in 1830. To step back out of the reform flood and try to rebuild on the old Tory rock; to go forward with the (voteless) people under the phantom aegis of a paternal aristocracy; or to become a reforming party hardly distinguishable from the Whigs. Except that Peel's and Melbourne's names were not very amenable to a semantic marriage, the last choice faced Peel with the risk of becoming 'Pelbourne'. Yet this was the choice he made. Moderate reform.

He had returned from his holiday to find everybody expecting an election. He duly called one and prepared for the occasion by a distinctly liberal programme named, from his own constituency, the Tamworth Manifesto.

*

The Duke was impressed by the Manifesto's spirit, and the proposals for which Peel asked 'a fair trial' were indeed far from unattractive: 'careful' reforms in the old areas of pensions and economy; commutation of Church tithes in Ireland without the old enemy, Lay Appropriation;* above all, conservation of the country's old institutions.

Just round the corner, however, lurked another political event which packed a much heavier punch than Tamworth, and was in fact to render Tamworth nugatory. This was the Lichfield House compact. An organic arrangement between Dan O'Connell and the Whigs grew up over several meetings at Lord Lichfield's mansion in St James's Square, by which the Irish and Radicals would vote solidly with the Opposition. Without the two Can-

* Lay Appropriation: transfer of particular Irish Church rents and other property, which had been made redundant by reorganization, to lay purposes.

ningites, and with Lichfield in the field against it, Tamworth could count its future in days rather than years.

Nevertheless the general election went reasonably well for the Conservatives. The Duke's son Charles was out by only one vote at Rochester and since that one was in dispute and the returning officer a stalwart supporter of 'the good cause', Charles half expected to get in. The Conservatives increased their total vote, though still a minority government – roughly 273 for the Government and 280 for the Opposition. The exquisite dandy, Disraeli, was proud to have fought at Wycombe under the Tamworth banner and furious at having been defeated by fourteen votes. He pledged himself to the Duke: 'If the devotion of my energies to your cause, IN or OUT, can avail you, your Grace may count upon me, who seeks no greater satisfaction than that of serving a really great man.'[31]

The great man had authorized £500 to be paid towards Disraeli's election expenses.

Deeply as the Duke disliked 'the duty of tax-gatherer', his contribution to the electoral battle had been collecting and allocating funds.[32] While lamenting the far greater resources of the Whigs, he was able in December to inform Hardinge that he had £3,000 for disbursement: £2,000 from the Duke of Northumberland and £1,000 from himself. Hardinge and Lord Granville Somerset, two of the party managers, were warned not to promise too much.

'The Party of Cottage, Throne and Altar' (as the Tories liked to call themselves) began to look solid again. Though the Game Laws still kept cottage and mansion at loggerheads, the throne exhibited vivid partiality, while the altar was loyal through self-preservation if nothing else. Many Whigs still wanted to see all bishops expelled from the House of Lords. With one such iconoclast Lord Alvanley pleaded that *two* bishops should be left. The Whig smiled.

'To keep up the breed, I suppose?'[33]

That was just about what Peel's first, short-lived ministry of 1834–5 was to do for the Conservatives. Keep up the breed.

*

Having in mind the Duke's return from his political Elba in November 1834, the Ministry in which he now sat as Foreign

Secretary might well be called his Hundred Days. Certainly it lasted little longer. From the dissolution of Parliament on 28 December 1834 to Peel's resignation on 7 April 1835 was exactly one hundred days. Its interest, however, rarely lay in the Duke's performance as Foreign Secretary, though one of the Foreign Office clerks later paid him a handsome tribute. Charles Scott, younger son of Sir Walter, in comparing foreign secretaries under whom he had served, described the Duke as 'one by himself "superior and alone" – of the fewest words but those few always straight to the point and doing the business to be done at once – in writing minutes or directions of any kind – short and full and *clear* . . . so simple that almost any one would think "I could have written that" – till he tried. . . .'[34]

The Duke found many old European problems already settled by Palmerston, though not always according to his taste.* Prince Leopold of Saxe-Coburg was now King of the Belgians; in Portugal the War of the Two Brothers had ended in June 1834 with young Maria de Gloria as a relatively constitutional queen; and the Carlist Wars were starting up in Spain between the girl queen Isabella II and Don Carlos, her uncle whom she had displaced from the succession. The Duke had a low opinion of Don Carlos – 'he is a fool'[35] – but a still lower opinion of Palmerston who had engineered a quadruple alliance between the Spanish constitutionalists, Britain, France and Portugal against the 'northern' powers, Russia, Prussia and Austria. The Duke did not like Europe being divided up in this way, or Britain abandoning non-intervention. (Palmerston repealed the Foreign Enlistment Act of 1819 in 1834, so that British volunteers might participate in the Carlist Wars.)

But if the Duke could not make much impact on foreign affairs neither could Peel on the statute book. No memorable reforms marked his first premiership. His was a minority Government, harried, thwarted.

The interest of this ministry lay primarily in its being the stage on which the new Wellington–Peel partnership opened. In the Commons, Peel's hand rocked the cradle of Conservatism and

* Palmerston, however, was full of bumptious praise for 'the most fair & honourable manner' in which Wellington had kept his, Pam's, foreign engagements, calling him a 'great practical statesman'. (Bell, vol. I, pp. 208–9.)

should therefore have ruled his world. But there was the shadow of the Lords. Even Wellington was not always willing or able to protect the young party growing up in the other place from its wicked uncles, Londonderry, Newcastle, Cumberland, Buckingham and the like. As Lady Granville put it later, the poor Beau had to 'seesaw' between Peel and the Ultras.[36]

The seesaw's first violent oscillation came early in March 1835. As Foreign Secretary, the Duke nominated to the Russian embassy in St Petersburg his strident and widely detested colleague Lord Londonderry. In answer to immediate protests the Duke, who did not mind a colleague's unpopularity as long as he could do the job, replied that he knew of no one who sent home such excellent dialogues from foreign capitals. This literary gift, however, was not enough for a House of Commons up in arms. Londonderry had to withdraw and the Government's prestige suffered a blow from which it never recovered. Greville echoed the general indignation and blamed the Duke, saying on 15 March that it was 'the old story of ignorance and disregard of public opinion'.

Nine days later, 24 March, a series of shocks was initiated by Peel which completed the havoc begun by the Londonderry blunder. After continuous opposition on his Irish Tithe Bill, a despairing conviction swept over Peel that he could carry on a minority Government no longer. He summoned the Duke to Whitehall Gardens and told him so. The Duke strongly objected, begging Peel to hold on at all costs. What he described as 'a dreadful scene' ensued.[37] The scene achieved little or nothing for next day, 25 March, Peel announced his intention of resigning in a circular letter to the Cabinet. The Duke again implored Peel to fight on or at least to wait for defeat on an issue which the country would recognize as crucial.

'But surely,' interposed Lady Salisbury, to whom the Duke was telling this story, 'does he not see that his own reputation must be sacrificed if he gives way without absolute necessity?'

'I don't know. He has very bad judgement on these points,' said the Duke, thinking of his own forced resignation in 1830; ' – and some people are so wonderfully sensitive. But I think he'll stay.' Nevertheless the Duke could not forget the way Peel's face had worked during that 'dreadful scene' of 24 March – his awful agitation and features 'twisting in a thousand ways', while he himself sat as coolly as possible telling him not to resign. Something of Peel's despair had infected the Duke by the 29th and he too began to yearn for a new solution, the one he had so flatly rejected five years earlier – coalition.

> The only thing that I can see a chance for the country is that the King should try and compose a Ministry out of the different Parties, Lord Grey, Stanley and Peel and so on. And yet that is a dream – a mere vision. . . .

It was indeed. Peel saw his chance neither in coalition nor long-drawn defiance, despite the colourful pleas of two of the wicked uncles, Kenyon and Newcastle, to nail his colours to the mast and mount the scaffold rather than give in. Peel saw his chance for release in the Opposition's attack on his Irish Tithe Bill and in the steady reappearances of that old Whig sin, Lay Appropriation, introduced by the inveterate sinner, Lord John Russell. This was an issue on which even the Duke agreed Peel might resign.

The first critical debate came on the night of 2 April. Lady Salisbury told the Duke that Lord Lyndhurst had offered to send her the result at the earliest possible moment next morning.

'I am quite satisfied to have it when the newspapers come in at 10 o'clock,' said the Duke. 'If I could do any good by having it before, I would; but as I can't, I had just as soon wait.'

'You always look at these things coolly,' said Lady Salisbury, 'Now! you never lie awake with anxiety?'

'No, I don't like lying awake – it does no good. I make it a point never to lie awake. . . .'[38]

It was the temperament which had carried him calmly through the last anxious hours before so many victories. Now it prepared him for defeat. He read in his newspapers on 8 April that Peel, after defeats three days running, had lost on 7 April by twenty-seven votes. This was Peel's fighting finish. He resigned on the 8th. The Hundred Days were over and the Duke had held office for the last time.

Peel's administration had had its uses. First, the wound caused by past reforms had healed and there was now a good chance of a united instead of a brawling Conservative Opposition. Second, Peel had made the party follow the Tamworth signpost, and if it had been possible only to travel rather than to arrive, at least the party knew it was not going to travel backwards. A gentleman from Hampshire had sent the Duke a New Year's message for 1835: 'The Tories must now glide into the stream of public opinion.' This was precisely what had happened. Though the Duke sent only 'Compts.' in return, they were the compliments of a new political season.

*

With Melbourne again shouldering the burdens of office, there were signs that Wellington's summer months in opposition might be halcyon. At least he was no longer plagued by the Ultras, of whom, according to Lady Salisbury, he had 'a nervous horror'. Applause greeted him wherever he appeared; at a Cambridge festival, in Vauxhall Gardens or at a Hyde Park review. The diarist Raikes thought the Whig ministers were received with contrasting neglect. 'After the experience of the past,' wrote Raikes on 15 July 1835, 'it would be rash to be sanguine,' – but it really seemed as if the country was at last becoming 'indignant' with the reckless destroyers of its institutions. The Duke himself had been heard to say some time ago that the country was *on its legs again*.[39]

The Duke had a little more time for friendship, both of the incredible and the admirable kind. Calls and correspondence were reopened with Anna Maria Jenkins in June 1835. But she picked a quarrel in September, returning all sixty of his letters because he had insulted her by sealing the last one with a plain seal instead of his ducal coronet. He thereupon burnt the letters she had written to him, much to her indignation – 'one and all being more or less marked with *Divine* Truth' – and in October she sent him a farewell hymn entitled 'The Shortness of Time and Frailty of Man':

> *VAIN* his *AMBITION, NOISE and SHOW!*
> *VAIN are the cares Which rack his mind!*
> *He heaps up treasures MIXED WITH WOE*
> *And dies, and leaves them all behind!*[40]

A month later Miss Jenkins found that it was her own ambition which looked like being vain, for the Duke was reported in the papers as having had a grave seizure. She hastily wrote to enquire

after his health. He replied coolly in the third person that the
newspapers exaggerated and that he had been unwell only one
day.[41] Warmer letters soon followed.

These seizures were a terrifying feature of his later years and
were generally thought to be caused by too much violent exercise
on an empty stomach. The Duke took pride in riding as hard at
seventy as he had twenty years earlier, but his luncheon was now
a jelly or biscuit and his period of sleep short. When Lady Salisbury once protested that from midnight to 6 A.M. was not enough,
he said, 'I am perfectly well, and whether a man has a little more
sleep or a little less, what does it signify!'[42]

Next year, 1836, there were more letters to Miss Jenkins and
more of what she called 'Dissension'. After suffering from an
injured knee in July – 'I am getting the better of it' – he called on
her in October, the first visit for a considerable time. She began by
chiding him for irreligion, then enquired tenderly after his knee.
At this he brightened and drew up his chair nearer to hers.
Promptly she moved hers back, *'due* to Christianity'. Unabashed
the Duke paid another visit in December, but four months later
foolish Miss Jenkins overplayed her hand. She referred to his
'brushing up his chair'. Back came the third person and an icy
reply: 'The Duke is not aware that he has been guilty of *presumption*: of *daring presumption.* . . .'[43] There was a long gap in
the visits ('little did the poor Duke think . . . that the great Lord
of lords had decreed he should not behold me again for nearly
eight years. . . .') but not in the letters. Miss Jenkins had become
one of his duties.

There was also Charles Arbuthnot. Nothing could be more irk-
some, thought Lady Salisbury in September 1835, for a man of the
Duke's active mind than to keep on visiting a 'solitary broken
hearted man like Mr Arbuthnot who had lost all energy and
interest in everything'. Here she was mistaken. The widower had
maintained an energetic interest in his saviour's career, particularly when personal strains threatened it. Soon after these
autumn months Arbuthnot was to become an important mediator
between Peel and the Duke.

*

The Whigs' debonair and leisurely leader, Lord Melbourne, was
by temperament no reformer. In his opinion good seldom came

of interference. The earnest violence of the age of reform made
no appeal to his easy-going, careless, cynical geniality. Nevertheless, he had one heavy-weight reform ready for the 1835 session –
a Municipal Corporations Bill powerful enough to clear the
ground of feudal debris and then to lay the foundations for the
city and town councils of today. For the first time councillors
were to be elected by the ratepayers. What would the House of
Lords say? Customs which some people called feudal debris
might be regarded by others, especially lawyers, as the rights of
property. Tory lawyers were well represented in the House of
Peers. Property was one principle; the 'independence of the
House of Lords' was another. Defended together, they could
provoke a spectacular collision with the Commons. Lord
Lyndhurst's rakishly brilliant oratory, moreover, was more than
a match for Melbourne. Everything depended on Wellington.

The hero of Waterloo had told Lord Lyndhurst at the very
beginning of the session that he wished to lead 'a quiet life'.[44]
The usual spate of letters from Londonderry and Cumberland
demanding a more aggressive policy left him cold. 'Life is not
long enough for this description of correspondence.' Nor did a
suggested series of shadow-cabinet dinners for Opposition peers
seem to him 'an advisable measure or a profitable way of passing
one's time'. Then came the Whigs' great Municipal Corporations
Reform Bill, introduced by them on 5 June. Because Peel and his
followers supported it, the bill received a second reading, and
after it reached the Lords towards the end of July the Duke's
'quiet life' was over. There was scarcely a moment of controversy
which did not result in an Apsley House meeting. It was the peers
against Peel, if not against the people. The Duke was active
again on his seesaw.

Determined to be loyal to Peel's leadership and aware that
some kind of municipal reform was necessary, he persuaded his
large, vociferous and very awkward squad to vote for the Government bill's second reading. Then he wrote to warn Peel of possible
mutiny at the committee stage and to ask his advice. But Peel was
in deep despondency, high dudgeon and a state of physical
exhaustion. He knew that certain gusts of demoniac laughter,
which were apt to sweep the ultra-Tories during debates, were
directed as much against himself as against Lord John Russell,

the mover of the bill. 'Peel! what is Peel to me? Damn Peel!'[45]
There were rumours that the author of these words, Lord Lynd-hurst, would be the next Prime Minister and that the Duke had lost control. Peel wrote back to Wellington with a pen like a ramrod: 'The Lords must do as they please.' Then, without telling the Duke, he vanished to his home at Drayton early in August, prepared to work off his sulks over a hundred miles from the scene of operations.

Meanwhile the bill reached the peers for the committee stage on 12 August. At once the famous 'independence of the House of Lords' showed itself in a species of auto-intoxication. Carried away with furious excitement, Newcastle demanded that Russell should go to the Tower, Winchilsea choked himself with rage and Lord Lyndhurst massacred the bill clause by clause with the thoroughness of a Herod. Unfortunately the Duke himself was not quite immune to the contagion. There was one class of muni-cipal dignitary which he considered the epitome of innocence and usefulness – the ancient life-aldermen. It seemed right to him for once to disobey Peel, seize the clause which would liquidate the aldermen and cut it down. Truth to tell the Duke disliked the whole idea of elected mayors and corporations, with their power to levy money. He foresaw 'a little Republic in every town,' and brooded darkly on the Civil War and disloyal London and Charles I's severed head. (Sir Henry Halford had told him he had seen the head for a moment in the royal vault when King George IV was buried, before it vanished into dust.)

The peers had enjoyed their Saturnalia from 12 to 25 August. The real world reappeared when the Commons debated the Lords' amendments. It was a real world in crisis. Would this be the end of the Thing called Lords? John Russell, with the wealth of Woburn behind him, though not in his pocket, had no such wish. He rejected most of the amendments but without rancour. And with the return to reality Peel, the *Dieudonné*, suddenly re-appeared in his place on the front bench. He 'threw over the Lords', as Greville was delighted to record, by voting with the Government against the peers' amendments. Some baying was heard from the Ultras at the last Apsley House conference on 3 September, called to make a final decision. Old Lord Harrowby, however, his handwriting become more wavering as his views stabilized, made the running for Wellington by arguing that

Municipal Reform was not the right ditch for their lordships to die in. Despite the Duke's personal dilemma, he allowed a compromise to be reached even over his precious aldermen. They were given a tenure of six years instead of life, roughly the same privilege which they enjoy today. No doubt he felt that in the next civil war each little republic would be curbed by its big aldermen.

Lord Melbourne had to make the most of his Municipal Bill, for nothing so satisfying was to appear again for months, even years. The Tory peers vetoed local self-government for Ireland, regarding a country dedicated to Dan O'Connell as lost. And indeed tithes were withheld by O'Connell's order from penurious Protestant parsons and those who paid them were sent pictures of coffins, though not on O'Connell's orders. 'Captain Rock', Captain Swing's Irish brother-in-arms, rode again. Many years ago Rock had sent at least one letter to England wishing his Grace's long nose to the Devil. It was not surprising that the peers preferred the old corrupt Irish corporations to be replaced by some form of direct rule from Westminster. An appreciable concession was made to Irish peace, however, when the Orange Lodges beloved of Cumberland were closed down on the suggestion of Lord Mulgrave (afterwards Normanby), now Lord-Lieutenant.

*

The recent extraordinary happenings between Wellington and Peel – seesaw, sulks and the aldermanic crisis – could not but leave their bruises. As the new session approached the Duke found he was ignored. It was now January 1836 and there had been no contact whatever between him and Peel since the previous August. The Whigs observed the situation with pleasure and calculated on a new Conservative split raising their own party from the doldrums. Arbuthnot noted it also, especially his friend's hurt feelings. He and Hardinge decided to act. Through their good offices Peel was persuaded to include the Duke there and then in his house-party at Drayton. The host made a splendid effort to be friendly. Afterwards the Duke told the overjoyed Lady Salisbury that Peel had behaved 'more rationally' than ever before in response to his own customary display of 'unaffected good temper and cordiality'. This was the occasion when young Mrs Gladstone met the great man for the first time. His impressions are worthy of notice, for both the Wellingtonian matter and Gladstonian manner:

The Duke of Wellington appears to speak little and never for speaking's sake, but only to convey an idea commonly worth conveying. He receives remarks made to him very frequently with no more than 'Ha!' a convenient suspensive expression, which acknowledges the arrival of the observation and no more.[46]

Gladstone went on to marvel at the Duke's energy and ability to make transitions from business to pleasure and back again with no 'encroachments' on either side. Peel, he added, was also a 'thrifty dealer in his time'; but such self-command was far more astounding in a man of the Duke's age.

*

The first result of Wellington's *rapprochement* with Peel was an awkward request. In Peel's exhausting struggle to keep the party together, he felt the evil influence of Cumberland was a cross he should no longer be asked to bear. Could the Duke get him ostracized? The answer was blunt: 'There is no person who feels more than I do the inconvenience of the Duke of Cumberland. I feel it every day, and all day. Others feel it only occasionally. But I can't see a remedy.'[47]

The fact was that the King's brother still had a sizeable following among the peers. Within the House of Lords Wellington was conducting the same arduous campaign to educate and unify as Peel within the party as a whole. Sudden ostracisms would help neither leader. There was a difference, however, between his and Peel's exertions. While Peel's heart was wholly in them, there was a small place in the Duke's which still yearned for the old days when Tories were Tories instead of 'liberals', as he used to call Peel, and there was no such thing as a Conservative. 'It is now said there is no longer such a thing as a Tory,' Greville had written on 16 June 1835. This was the kind of saying which knocked hollowly on the Duke's heart. Though he kept that chamber firmly closed to the world, there were a few deep-dyed Tory friends who obtained occasional insights. Mr Chad, a retired diplomat, was one.

'We have nothing left now but the House of Lords – God knows how long we shall keep that,' groaned the Duke to Chad in April 1837.

'But is there no reaction – no conversion?' asked Chad. The Duke refused to see any sign of it: only perhaps the signs of more courage on the part of those who had long been secretly anti-Whig, to speak out.[48]

Meanwhile the Duke in his normal political relations was slowly moving forward into the new age. At least he no longer opposed the formation of Conservative associations for party political purposes on his old ground that all sectional organizations, however well-intentioned at first, might be used to harm the State. When asked to sponsor a newly-founded Conservative association he still withheld his patronage but gave his approval. In these times, he said rather sadly, he could not do otherwise.

In other respects he was being turned into an ancient monument, willy-nilly. Every Waterloo Day he was wreathed with verses in the antique vein, all laudatory and many ludicrous. Shoals of people applied and were refused permission to see the Waterloo banquet being prepared the morning before. How could his servants deal with a crowd of spectators while arranging the silver plate for *boeuf à la Wellington* and the crystal glasses for champagne? A Mr Beer was told politely to come again another day.

Sometimes events in themselves strange were embellished with whimsical *graffiti*, any excuse being good enough to create a legend. On 8 October a letter apparently signed 'J. C. London' of Bayswater, informed the Duke that the writer was compiling a book on British trees and wished to see the 108-foot cedar of Lebanon and giant hemlock spruce at Stratfield Saye, apparently the highest and largest in the land. The Duke, wrongly assuming his correspondent to be the Bishop of London (possibly misled by the initials J.C.), warmly welcomed the prelate to a view of his trees. An enlightening answer arrived from the Bishop's Palace:

My Lord Duke I have been honoured with a letter from Your Grace which at first rather perplexed me, as the subject of the only communication which I have lately made to Your Grace was not that of *Trees*, but of *Churches*. But it occurs to me, that the letter, which Your Grace has received, must be from Mr Loudon, the well-known writer

on Horticulture, who is publishing a book called *Arboretum Britannicum*. . . .
> signed, C. J. London.*[49]

*

By the spring of 1837 Lord Melbourne's defeat seemed to be at hand. One half of the country found his measures insufficient and the other half extreme. William IV longed to get rid of him. Old, asthmatic and devoutly supported by his reactionary German spouse, he had been since 1832 'a true King of the Tories'. Some people had pinned their hopes to June 1836 when Mrs Norton's husband cited Melbourne in a divorce case. There had been eager speculation on the result if the suit succeeded.

'Would Melbourne resign?' Greville asked the Duke.

'O Lord, no! Resign! Not a bit of it. I tell you all these things are a nine-days wonder . . . it will all blow over and won't signify a straw.'[50] In any case the suit failed.

Now in 1837 the pressure on Melbourne was political. The battlefields were perforce the old ones, Irish Tithes and Municipal Corporations with a little new skirmishing for the Whigs over Church rates and property. But if the terrain was familiar, the tactics were not. Nothing quite like them had been seen since Wellington and Marmont twisted and coiled round one another for week upon week before the Battle of Salamanca, each trying to drive the other into a fatal position. That Melbourne's resignation was coming no one doubted. 'Is not the probable resignation of the Government the great Question of the Day?' wrote the Duke to Peel in March.[51] But to the Government and Opposition the question posed itself in contrary ways.

Melbourne's aim must be to trap Wellington into making him resign on a defeat of his Irish Corporations Bill – his one relatively popular measure on which the people would support him against the peers. Then what would Peel do? If he became Prime

---

* The Victorians, with their headstrong instinct to exaggerate, built on these modest but pleasant foundations a truly noble legend. It was said that John Claudius Loudon, famous author of the *Arboretum*, had asked to see the Duke's Waterloo *beeches*, upon which his Grace invited Dr Bloomfield, Bishop of London, to examine his Waterloo *breeches*, thereby causing the Bishop and his acolytes considerable embarrassment.

There is no mention of 'Waterloo beeches' at Stratfield Saye. The famous avenue of *Wellingtonias* (Sequoia Gigantica) was planted after the Duke's death and still stands.

Minister, the Commons would neither let him introduce a comparable bill himself nor substitute an inferior one.

Peel's policy, on the other hand, must be to manoeuvre Melbourne into accepting a humiliating bargain; in return for an Irish Corporations Bill Melbourne would have to drop Lay Appropriation from Irish Tithes. This solution of course meant that the Lords must keep the detested Irish Corporations Bill in play instead of defeating it as soon as it reached their House: 'our game is to postpone it as long as possible,' Wellington firmly informed one of his Ultras. But the game caused the Duke much tribulation on the Westminster seesaw, putting Peel's case to the Lords and the Lords' case to Peel. 'I don't believe that the House of Lords had any desire to appoint a government,' he wrote to Peel on 22 February, launching into a passionate defence of the peers' unselfish behaviour ever since November 1830, all to promote 'the general objects of the Country and to preserve Peace' between the two Houses. What was the Lords' only offence? 'It is an Independent and now an Insulated Assembly.'[52]

Peel sometimes wondered uneasily whether the Duke was not more fatally 'insulated' by his deafness than the Lords by their loss of pocket boroughs. At the end of March the Duke began to think Melbourne would resign anyway, thus freeing him from the obligation to keep the Irish Corporations Bill afloat. At a Shadow Cabinet meeting on 8 April, however, his duty to get a second reading for the bill was reaffirmed. The Duke misheard this decision. He thought the matter had been left open. Peel learned that he intended to kill the bill at last. In a great state he wrote to the Duke on the 15th going over the decisions of the week before. In an even greater state the Duke replied by return:

Your letter just affords another instance how unfit I am to go into a council or conference upon any subject. The fact is that I don't hear half that passes.[53]

Nevertheless, once the Duke had again got the correct line, there was none to equal him in putting it across. The skill of his arguments and the reverence in which he was held persuaded a crowded meeting of peers at Apsley House on the 24th to give the bill its second reading. In May the second reading passed and, pursuant to his renewed game of postponement, the committee stage was put off till 9 June. Twisting and coiling together, the two serpents continued to perform their evolutions in the dusty parliamentary plain. Suddenly Providence intervened to give one side the victory.

When 9 June arrived the 'true King of the Tories' was desperately ill. He died on 20 June, thus cutting the serpentine knots.

Awaiting the event at Kensington Palace was his successor, the young Princess Victoria, her fair hair neatly braided into a small coronet. Her blue eyes like bubbles on a clear stream searched for the happiness which had so far eluded her youth; but would she find it with the Tories? Lord Melbourne's romantic personal aura and unruffled kindness seemed on the face of it more likely to attract the King's niece.

On the King's instructions Wellington had held the Waterloo banquet as usual, feeling he dared not disobey his Sovereign's last command; but he gave the royal toast with deep melancholy. Afterwards he still had time to do two necessary things before the new reign began. He took his annual 'rent' for Stratfield Saye to Windsor, a small tricolour flag fringed with gold, symbolic of his gratitude to Crown and people for the honours they had done him. The old King buried his face in its folds, happy at having lived long enough to see the sun of Waterloo set on 18 June 1837.

Then the Duke saw Cumberland and gave him a piece of advice, at least, this was Grevilles' story. Let him leave the Castle and the country.

'Go instantly, and take care that *you don't get pelted.*'[54]

21

Our Gracious

Surely the young Queen's first act would be to send for the Duke?
On Waterloo Day 1837 Lady Salisbury bet 5s. on its happening.
But there were rumours of radical and other influences at Kensington Palace. 'I shall lose,' she added.[1]

Lose she did. The Duke was not sent for. He felt no surprise. A
week before the accession he had heard that 'Radical Jack'
Durham was hastening home from the Continent to establish
Victoria as a radical Queen. He thought it not unlikely that 'the
transfer of the Crown to the Head of a Young Lady of eighteen
years' would go to that young head, making her choose the
Radicals 'and the Race for Popularity!'

Soon he and everyone else realized that it was not the Radicals
but her Whig Prime Minister for whom the Queen had fallen
headlong, her dear, wise, witty Lord Melbourne. The Duke was
simply an old hero whom her Mama had entertained now and
then at Kensington. For his part he followed the current stories
from well outside the magic circle. 'She is surrounded by Whigs
and Whiglings male and female,' he wrote in July; 'and Nobody
knows any thing excepting Gossip'[2] – gossip about the Queen's
dislike of her mother the Duchess of Kent, her loathing for Sir
John Conroy, the Duchess's majordomo, and her devotion to a
foreign lady, formerly her governess, the Baroness Lehzen.

At the Queen's first Privy Council on 21 June the Duke told
Greville 'that if she had been his own daughter he could not have
desired to see her perform her part better'. Her part at a Hyde
Park review, however, he decided must not be to caracole between
himself and Lord Hill. He had been privately consulted by the
Court about her wish to ride on a horse instead of in a carriage
with her ladies. The Duke reported back to Windsor on the '*un-
suitableness*' of her being attended on horseback 'by men *only*'.

What a target she would present to the caricaturists by surrounding herself with 'such youths as Lord Hill and me'. She was trying to do a Queen Elizabeth at Tilbury, he suspected; but as there was no threat of an Armada in 1837, what was the point?[3]

This was the first clash between the old hero and the young girl. The girl won. In August she was prancing between the two venerable 'youths', thin bent Wellington and 'old Fatty Hill', as Creevey called the Commander-in-Chief.

There were other signs that the little Queen intended to ride a high horse. At a Buckingham House banquet on 19 July the Duke of Wellington was the only Tory present, and he had not been admitted in his own right. 'Chancellor of Oxford' was on his place-card. 'It is curious that she should not be able to venture to invite the Duke of Wellington to dinner excepting as Chancellor of Oxford,' he wrote to Arbuthnot next day. 'I keep the Card as a real curiosity.'[4]

*

The affairs of an older royal generation were still regulated by the Duke. In 1837 shortly before the new reign began, Lord Stourton, Mrs Fitzherbert's Catholic relative and trustee, heard rumours that a slanderous biography of her was projected. Would it not be right for the trustees to obtain the correct facts from the secret documents in Coutts's bank and even to consider an authorized biography? The Duke resisted, beginning what was to be a long defensive action. He saw no reason to satisfy 'the curiosity of the public' and begged Lord Albemarle, a co-trustee, to make Stourton abandon his intention. Mrs Fitzherbert's lawyer agreed with the Duke, further suggesting that all the documents in Coutts's should be destroyed, since the fact of her marriage was now 'notorious to all the World'. This her trustees flatly refused to do.[5]

In 1841 after Mrs Fitzherbert's death and again in 1842 Lord Stourton reopened his crusade and the Duke continued to resist. There had been no scandalous biography; if one appeared he promised to kill it on publication; until then he would not risk the revival of an ancient scandal. Poor Lord Stourton went on gamely until he fell ill and died in 1847, to be followed in 1851 by his brother-in-arms, Lord Albemarle. Having lived just long enough to defeat them both, the Duke died next year, leaving the treasure at Coutts's undisturbed until it was removed to the Windsor

Archives in the next century. So ended one of his less publicized defensive engagements.

*

The Duke was not the only man to find defensive action necessary in 1837. The statesman whose beloved name appeared so frequently in the Queen's journal that it soon had to be shortened to 'Lord M' made a poor impression on the electorate. At the general election there were ominous demands from the left that Melbourne should repeal the Corn Laws and push radicalism further by introducing the secret ballot, frequent parliaments and universal suffrage. But the Leader of the House, John Russell, in his new role of 'Finality Jack', refused any further extension of the franchise. The Radicals none the less went on singing defiance:

> Then rise, my boys, and fight the foe,
> Your arms are truth and reason
> We'll let the Whigs and Tories know
> That union is not treason.

On Melbourne's right, the Tories made overall election gains of thirteen, leaving the slim Whig majority further attenuated. Tories were returned *en masse* for the English counties, a result which compensated them for defeat in Ireland. Foreseeing this situation, the Duke was delighted to have persuaded the gentlemen of Northamptonshire, of whom Arbuthnot was one, to hand over their election fund to Dublin. Behaviour as handsome as it was rare, he wrote, 'There is nothing so selfish as the collection of money for the purposes of an Election.'[6] Altogether the Tories were in good heart. The Duke particularly liked the story of the Tory candidate at Canterbury (first told about Wilkes!)

'Sir,' said a man he was canvassing, 'I would as soon vote for the devil.'

'But, Sir, if your friend should not stand,' pursued the Tory Candidate, 'may I then hope for your support?'

Lord Melbourne was in no such lively mood. Indeed the autumn found him groping towards that refuge of weak ministries, a coalition. The approach was made to Wellington through a feminine intermediary, his clever niece Priscilla Burghersh. The Duke and Priscilla had been in particularly close touch since the year before, when they appeared to be the only rocks in a sea of family dissension. There was a mingle-mangle of marriages in the new generation which awakened memories of things best forgotten. Priscilla and the Duke agreed that the sins of the past ought not to be visited on the young.*

He and Priscilla understood one another. Lord Melbourne showed sense, therefore, in contacting the Duke through her. On 8 September she had been sent for by the Prime Minister and had seen him next morning. 'He has just left me,' she wrote to her uncle. She had the strong impression that Melbourne wanted a coalition with the Duke. In any case Melbourne's policy would be as moderate as possible, though he could not retract anything. 'If he did he was gone!' Melbourne also asked her what Peel would do in the coming session. 'I suppose he will be forced to take more actively hostile measures against us – or else he won't be followed – for a strong party won't stand a backward Leader. . . .' The Prime Minister then swore her to secrecy about this conversation, except for telling the Duke.[7]

Her uncle responded crossly. How could Melbourne contemplate a coalition yet retract nothing?[8] Hastily Priscilla explained the Prime Minister's position. It was weak, in that he was a party politician, a handicap from which her dearest uncle did not suffer. Priscilla believed that Melbourne saw his duty in a very different light from Wellington. Melbourne's object was to keep in office, no doubt to govern the country as well as possible, but if he were once out of office she doubted his caring much about the country.

He told me (& I have heard him say the same thing long ago) that he believed you to be entirely above Party feelings, & to be actuated solely by a 'passionate Love of his Country, & a desire to do what he thinks best for the Country' – but he added, he believed you to be the only man in the world in whom such feelings were genuine & unalloyed by any other consideration.[9]

Priscilla had told Melbourne she quite agreed with him and it was because of these feelings in her uncle that the passing of the Reform Bill had almost broken his heart.

* Viscount Chelsea, son and heir of Lord Cadogan, and Emily Wellesley, daughter of Gerald Wellesley and his separated wife Emily, née Cadogan, wished to marry. The Cadogans objected, which the Duke considered most unjust. At the same time Emily Bagot, grand-daughter of Lord Maryborough and known as 'The Tigress', married Lord Winchilsea, the Duke's opponent in the duel. (The other pair did marry.)

Melbourne had countered on the Reform Bill, that 'the *good sense* of the Country' would enable the Queen's Government to be carried on, even in a crisis of foreign war or civil disturbance, despite the Duke's fears.

Priscilla concluded her analysis of Melbourne's policy with a neat summary. It was to do as little mischief as possible while allowing mischief to be done '*if he can't help it*'. For the rest, all he hoped was to keep his place and to '*tide on*'.[10]

Tiding on, or tiding over, was not the Duke's idea of a prime minister's function. It smacked altogether too much of soothing syrup for the times in which they lived.* No whit appeased, he ended the discussion with an uncompromising note to his niece on 14 September. Melbourne's conversation with her was certainly 'to try the ground of Coalition':

Some of His Colleagues have that object in view. But in these Times it is impossible.

It is astonishing that a Man with the good sense of Lord Melbourne should not feel ashamed of talking of the *good sense* of the *Country*. There is no such thing.

The Conservatives of the day, he argued, would no doubt support Melbourne when he deserved it; but soon they would have passed from the stage. (The Duke was now sixty-eight.) Their successors, having been alienated by Whig measures, a Whig Court and the exclusion of their caste from government by the Reform Bill, would refuse to give a future Whig government the support which 'good sense' dictated.[11]

This was the Duke despairing of the future. Fortunately these moods never made him any less assiduous in helping the present to 'tide on'.

His decision to stand alone, pursue a straightforward course and wait for a fair stand-up fight (to use a few of his favourite expressions) involved him in all the old problems of leadership over again.

It meant that while Peel was mysteriously *incommunicado*, Lord Wilton would be embarrassingly vocal. What was Peel up to? demanded this aggressive Ultra. The Duke confessed he did

---

* On 12 May 1837 Lord Melbourne had told Waverer Wharncliffe that he thought things were 'soothing down'. (Clark, p. 355.)

not know. But whatever Peel's plans, he felt sure he agreed with them. Moreover, he had nothing to do with affairs in the Commons, nor really understood them. 'Old Men ought not to chatter of things that they don't understand any more than *charming Women*!' – reference to Lady Wilton.[12]

It meant that while the Ultras remained dissatisfied on one side, the Irish became increasingly disgusted on the other. Irish Tithe, Municipal and Poor Law reform still dragged their weary lengths along the corridors of the House of Lords, the first not settled until 1838, and then shorn of Lay Appropriation, and the second not enacted at all. Daniel O'Connell denounced the Duke with the violence expected from an admirer of Napoleon; indeed they each invoked the memory of the French Emperor to expose the other, O'Connell describing the Duke as 'a Man whom nature intended for a stunted corporal', and the Duke declaring Napoleon to have been 'not a personality, but a principle; that is what O'Connell is at this moment'.[13]

It meant above all that when a major new issue of policy arose on which the Duke differed profoundly from the Government, he was torn by the old conflicts. For the sake of the country he must prevent 'mischief': for the sake of the constitution he must prevent a clash between Lords and Commons; for the sake of his authority with the Ultras he must let the tail wag a little but not wag the dog.

Canada, where insurrections had broken out in both the Upper and Lower Provinces, proved to be this major new issue.

*

On the last day of 1837 another of Priscilla Burghersh's animated letters reached the Duke. She had just seen the Russian ambassador, Pozzo di Borgo. (The Lievens had been recalled to Russia three years earlier.) Pozzo predicted joy on the Continent over Britain's troubles in Canada. How would gentlemen like to find in their own house what they tried to stir up in other people's? – a reference to Palmerston's support for European liberal movements. Hardly had Priscilla got beyond this point in her letter to her uncle when the Prime Minister was announced.

In a great state about Canada, he said he wanted to know the Duke's opinion of the army's strength out there. Could he write

direct to the Duke? Why not? said Lady Burghersh.[14] He duly
sent a private letter to the Leader of the Opposition in the Lords,
asking him whether the Government were to blame for starving
Canada of troops.

Meanwhile the elated Opposition had already seen the Canadian
rebellion as their chance for a political triumph.

On 18 January the crisis was debated in the Lords. The Government were on the mat. In a happy state of suspense the Opposition peers waited for the great Duke to pulverize Melbourne for
the disgraceful inadequacy of the armed forces in Canada. But
the Duke had Melbourne's question in his file. And he had given
his answer to the Prime Minister privately that the Government
were not to blame. Now he neither evaded the issue nor prevari-
cated. He said to the House exactly what he had said to Lord
Melbourne, namely, that in this context he could not blame
them.

Collapse of Conservative hopes. Lord Mahon rushed from the
Carlton Club saying that the Duke had floored the coach. Lord
Londonderry declared that the Duke's speech had stopped Ellenborough and Aberdeen from making 'mince meat' (his favourite
dish) of the Government. Aberdeen agreed that but for the Duke's
fatal intervention the Government might have fallen. Angry Lord
Wharncliffe was reminded of Wellington's anti-reform speech and
thought he had again gone further than he meant, 'not having a
perfect use of his weapon when he speaks'. Peel climbed into his
pulpit and wagged a cold finger at Wellington. He was risking the
unity of the party.[15]

The Duke sizzled with resentment. At first he told the shocked
Lady Salisbury that he did not care sixpence about the party
turmoil. He had done the right thing. But in the following week
he revealed his sore feelings by telling her that he did not wish to
take office in any future Tory government – 'I have no influence.
There is no respect for my opinion, *none I assure you.*' Lady Salisbury wisely tackled the problem at Peel's end, begging him to
treat his colleague in future openly and frankly. 'Straightforwardness and direct communications are the only way with the
Duke.'[16] By the beginning of February the storm in the party was
subsiding but not the storm in Wellington.

He had helped to restore his popularity by preaching prepared-
ness: 'There is no such thing as a *little War*,' he said, 'for a great

Nation.'* In his own mind, however, contempt for the party zealots only deepened when there was a move to join with the Radicals in a vote of censure on the Colonial Secretary, tabled for 7 March. Here was an unrivalled opportunity, argued the Ultras, for bringing down the Whigs. Great was the Duke's scorn for such a scheme, particularly when the Ultras went on to say that the party would break up unless led immediately into battle. 'I have always been and always shall be in front of the battle. I cannot hold back,' he wrote heatedly to Arbuthnot on 15 February. 'But it is a little too much for noblemen and Honble. gentlemen to call upon Sir Robert Peel and me to put ourselves at their Head to carry into execution a course of policy of which we disapprove and see the danger' – the danger being that the Conservatives, even if successful in their coup, would not be able to form a government. 'They talk of breaking up the Party; the fact is it never existed.' He meant it never had the cohesion given by loyalty.[17]

Four days later, sitting far back in his chair at Lady Salisbury's, biting his finger and avoiding her eyes, he suddenly burst out:

'The party! What party? What is the meaning of a party if they do not follow their leaders? I don't care sixpence if they split! D – m! 'em! let 'em go!'[18]

Fortunately for the Duke's sixpences Peel found a cunning solution to the dilemma of 7 March. He avoided voting with the Radicals by devising an amendment of his own which the Radicals in turn were unable to support. The Radical motion was withdrawn, Peel's amendment was duly defeated at 3.30 A.M. on 7 March by twenty-nine votes, the Government was saved and the Duke satisfied.

There happened to be a chivalrous as well as a rational reason why the Duke had shrunk from a Tory *coup d'état*. In common justice, in common morality, could he press his party upon an unwilling young Queen? It was not fair to force 'this poor girl' into all the embarrassments of a change of government against

* This famous remark was first made to Fitzroy Somerset on 5 January by letter. The Duke repeated the words in Parliament on 16 January and again on 2 February, afterwards explaining to Sir Willoughby Gordon by letter what he meant: namely, a great nation's interests were so wide that they were bound to touch the interests of other nations at many points. (Maxwell, vol. II, p. 319; *Wellington MSS.; Speeches.*)

her will. 'That's the thing – *against* her will. With William IV it was different.'[19]

The Duke of Wellington might not be a pillar of the party. 'There is nobody who dislikes so much as I do, and who knows so little of Party Management. I hate it,' he wrote to a saddened party whip.[20] Royal management, however, was his vocation, and if a headstrong girl of nineteen ever needed a pillar of strength, there was one at hand.

*

The Queen hardly noticed the Duke's gorgeous but stooping figure at her coronation in June 1838. But Lady Salisbury did. The applause was so tremendous as he touched the crown that 'Ld. Melbourne coloured, and grew pale again'. As the procession preceded Her Majesty out of the Abbey, Wellington's were the loudest cheers and he looked anxiously back over his shoulder towards his Sovereign, as if the applause were really her due, not his. Her journal said nothing of his historic meeting with Marshal Soult at a coronation concert in her music-room, though Lady Salisbury again recorded how benevolently the two heroes had shaken hands and how much brighter was the Duke's eye than his old antagonist's. Before Soult's arrival in England Wellington had expressed the hope that his first day would not fall on the anniversary of one of his 1814 defeats.

'Soult would be puzzled to find a day at the present season,' pointed out George Seymour, 'in which he might not have a disagreeable recollection.'

'That is very true,' agreed the Duke; 'yes' – his eyes beginning to sparkle – 'we licked him in June, we licked him in July & well into August.'[21]

*

The Duke was not dwelling in the past but great changes in his life were no longer acceptable. Next year he would be seventy. He had now lived at Stratfield Saye for twenty years. The idea of building a Wellingtonian Blenheim had gradually faded, until by 1838 it was abandoned. Henceforth he put all his energies into improving Stratfield Saye. A conservatory was added where he read and wrote his morning letters, kept warm by patent 'Arnott' stoves which he also installed in his tenants' cottages. The house itself was already centrally heated by indestructible iron pipes (still there) and the nine guest-rooms were now fitted with a water-closet each. Finally a courteously worded notice was put outside the front door:

Those desirous of seeing the Interior of the HOUSE, are requested to ring at the door of entrance and to express their desire. It is wished that the practice of stopping on the paved walk to look in at the windows should be discontinued.

Rheumatism had become an inveterate enemy, though one he never ceased to bully. It was rheumatism which accounted for the bouts of irritability which were becoming noticeable. There was the respectable baronet who was lucky – or unlucky – enough to obtain a personal interview at Apsley House.

'You stated you had something to say to me.'

'Yes, my Lord, I have a question to put. I wish to ascertain whether, if your Grace were to return to office you would support principles of moderate reform.'

'That is your question, is it?'

'Yes, my Lord.'

'Then allow me to put a question in return. What right have you to ask me?'[22]

His patience with Miss Jenkins was all the more remarkable. She still covered scores of pages with moralizing. He continued to thank her for the spectacle-wipers, pen-wipers and what might be called soul-wipers with which she presented him.

No less courteous was his handling of Lady Hester Stanhope, that high-powered woman who said she would as soon live with pack horses as with other women, and who became the bane of statesmen after she fell heavily into debt. Self-exiled to the Lebanon, she received a pension as Pitt's niece which the Duke while in office had refused to have taken from her. But Lord Palmerston and a new reign had changed all that. 'Your Queen,' wrote Lady Hester to Wellington in the course of frantic appeals for justice,

. . . has no business to meddle in my affairs. . . . There is nobody more capable than your Grace of making the Queen understand that a Pitt is a unique race: – there is no trifling with them. . . . New coined Royalty I do not understand; nor do I wish to understand them, nor any of their proceedings.[23]

The Duke did not altogether understand the royal situation

either. Poor Lady Hester was beyond saving; pensionless, she walled herself up on Mount Lebanon and died in 1839. But the young, new-coined Majesty of scarcely twenty years old was also walled in, at Buckingham Palace, by tragic pressures. Her he might help to save.

*

'The Queen is as great a wonder in her way as Fair Star or any other enchanted Princess,' wrote the dazzled Emily Cowper in September 1838: the fairies had given her the Gift of Pleasure.*[24]

If the fairies had given it, they had certainly taken it away again by the end of the year. Early in 1839 Wellington was twice consulted on the same day about a serious problem. The Duchess of Kent and the Tory Marquess of Hastings came to him separately with a tale of monstrous scandal and injustice at the Palace.

Lady Flora Hastings was the Duchess's lady-in-waiting and Lord Hastings's unmarried sister. She had returned from her Christmas holiday ill and swollen, and was said to be pregnant by Sir John Conroy, the Duchess's majordomo. The indignant Lady Flora submitted herself to an examination by two royal doctors. Though the doctors admitted that the swelling was possibly a tumour and the lady indubitably a virgin, neither they nor Melbourne, nor indeed the Queen herself were convinced the Lady Flora was not with child: 'It might be possible.'[25] A drizzle of royal tittle-tattle continued to fall until Lady Flora's two champions, the Duchess and Hastings, rushed in a rage to the Duke. As Greville said, in desperate cases he was always 'the doctor they rely on'.[26] He could not have been less reliable than the doctors poor Flora had consulted. Her condition steadily deteriorated. Meanwhile, the Duke urged each of his visitors to hush the whole thing up. Judging that the scandal had begun in coarse jokes and loose talk, he saw every reason why silence should now swiftly descend to save the two women who would suffer most from further gossip – Lady Flora and the Queen.

He had not reckoned with the press. By the middle of April the newspapers were full of the scandal and the Duke had the affair in better focus. 'The greatest rascal', as he put it, was Conroy and he realized that an ancient split between the two camps – Queen Victoria, Lehzen and the royal ladies versus the Duchess, Conroy

* 'Fair Star' was a character in a popular Harlequinade.

and the Duchess's ladies – would never be healed with Conroy
still around. Lady Flora was fast becoming a persecuted Queen
Caroline in the eyes of the people and Queen Victoria's court as
unpopular as George IV's. Wellington told the Queen to her huge
relief that he would disembarrass her of Conroy. But just as he
was searching for the golden bridge over which Conroy might
pass from the story, a fresh drama overtook them.

*

In the House of Commons the dreaded conjunction between
Conservatives and Radicals happened at last. On 7 May the
Whigs, at loggerheads with the Jamaican planters, asked Parliament to dissolve their House of Assembly. At once both Conservatives and Radicals raised an outcry. Caught in this crossfire, the
Government survived with a majority of only five votes. For a
party already staggering, this was a fatal fall. Melbourne resigned
next day.

The Duke realized something of what it would mean for the
Queen to lose her Whig ministers. 'I have no small talk,' he said,
'and Peel has no manners.' But he could not foresee the depth of
the Queen's misery at the changes, or the kindly foolishness of
Melbourne's plan for alleviating it. He advised her to keep at least
the ladies of her Household unchanged. The distraught young
Queen snatched at this straw. Beleaguered as she already felt by
the Hastings set, how could she open her palace gates to them and
their like as Tory ladies-of-the-bed-chamber? Five votes in the
Commons blew up the Flora Hastings scandal into the Bedchamber Plot.

Queen Victoria has described with inimitable panache her
deplorable but highly diverting victory over Wellington and Peel
combined. Let Wellington give the story from his angle, as he told
it to Greville three months later.

The Queen saw him for twenty minutes in the Yellow Closet on
8 May. Coached beforehand by Melbourne, she began by asking
him to be Prime Minister. He explained that his years and deafness
were prohibitive. Peel was her man.

'But what am I to do if he proposes appointments that are
disagreeable to me?'

'Fight upon the details as much as you please,' advised the
shrewd tactician, 'but make no conditions as to principles, and

depend upon it, there will be every disposition to consult your wishes and feelings in every respect.' She agreed. Then she said:

'You must promise me to be Secretary of State for Foreign Affairs.'

The Duke again demurred. This was the same constitutional error which her late uncle, William IV, had tried to perpetrate in 1834. He did not think much of the Queen's political education, but gently told her that the Prime Minister must make his own appointments. Once more she agreed.

'Will you desire him to come to me?' She must write to Peel herself.

Would he then tell Peel she was writing? He would.

The first interview left the Duke 'excessively pleased' with HM's docility and frankness. Peel reported himself perfectly satisfied by his own subsequent interview. When the Queen brought up her Household he promised that no changes should be made without her agreement. But if he was satisfied, she was distraught. She wept passionately after the two interviews. Lord M. had warned her she would find Peel close and stiff. He had in fact minced and shuffled like a dancing-master. But the dancing-master should not send *one* of her ladies – not Baroness Lehzen above all, her beloved friend and Conroy's enemy – off the floor.

Next day Peel returned to the palace in 'perfect security' of a tranquil arrangement. Instead the Queen catapulted her famous stone into the middle of Goliath's forehead. She must retain *all* her ladies.

'All?'

'All.'

'The Mistress of the Robes and the Ladies of the Bedchamber?'

'All.'

Peel was suddenly unnerved. He fell back on the obvious remedy. The Duke must see her next day. She consented; but this time the Duke told Greville she was not only in high passion and excitement but extremely naive and girlish.

'Well, I am very sorry to find there is a difficulty,' he opened.

'Oh, *he* began it and not me,' she retorted. 'It is offensive to me to suppose that I talk to any of my ladies upon public affairs.'[27]

'I know you do not . . . but the public does not know this,' he answered. He went and fetched Peel from the room next door, where he was waiting, close and stiff.

Where the Duke had failed Peel was powerless, though never before had the Duke seen him 'so gentle and conciliatory'. On 10 May everyone knew that Peel had thrown up his commission. Melbourne stood by the Queen as the Duke had stood by the King five years before. He reconstituted his Whig Government. To see the two old Tories, Wellington and Peel, looking very much put out at her ball on the 10th, gave 'Little Vixen', as Creevey had once affectionately called her, immense pleasure.

Greville and his Establishment friends did not try to hide their feelings of disgust. The pillar of state had been overthrown. There was something peculiarly shocking in 'this mere baby of a queen setting herself in opposition to this great man, the decus and testamen [sic] of her kingdom'. It was all a terrible 'Scompiglio'.*[28] Someone rounded off the affair with a good, simple Tory joke: 'One has often heard of the country going to the dogs – but never before of a country going to the bitches!'[29]

*

Little Vixen had to expiate her sins in many months of unhappiness before her engagement to Prince Albert of Saxe-Coburg-Gotha that autumn broke up her old, stifling circle and let in fresh air. The Duke had returned to the Conroy problem in May and finally persuaded him at an Apsley House party to leave the country. But there was still Baroness Lehzen, the other factor in the disastrous equation.

The press, in a mood of xenophobia, were convinced that Lehzen, the Queen's 'foreign lady', had led the Palace pack against Lady Flora. The Duke, therefore, set to work on softening the Duchess of Kent towards Lehzen. The results of his intervention were set out by him in a characteristic memorandum:

In respect to Baroness Lehzen HRH asked me what she should do if the Queen said to her Mama! I wish you would shake hands with Lehzen! I said Take her into your Arms and kiss Her! I added I don't mean Lehzen but the Queen! She laughed excessively.[30]

The increasingly desperate illness of Lady Flora, however, prevented any kissing; instead there was hissing for the Queen at

* Greville found relief in bizarre language. Decus et tutamen (glory and guardian) were on the 'Crown' coins of 1689. 'Scompiglio' was an Italian word for confusion or disorder.

Ascot. Said to be the work of Tory ladies, it widened the Queen's rift with the Opposition. Lady Flora's death on 5 July (1839) completed the devastation and launched a new wave of press attacks. Then the tide turned.

With the Queen's idyllic marriage on 10 February 1840 to the good young German, the Tories gradually moved up into their correct constitutional place, ready to take a second bite at the cherry. However, Lord Melbourne still had one more unwise concession to make to the Queen, now as obsessed with Albert's position as before she had been with Lehzen's. Foolishly agreeing to grant Prince Albert an income of £50,000 rather than the £30,000 insisted on by the Tories, Melbourne was thwarted by Wellington in the House of Lords. As guardian of the old royal family, Wellington also opposed, equally foolishly, Prince Albert's precedence over the royal dukes. Queen Victoria completed the foolishness by calling the Duke of Wellington 'that Old Rebel' and refusing until the last minute to invite him to her wedding. The Duke commented drily: 'I hear that our Gracious is very much out of Temper.'*[31]

*

The Duke's first speech in the House after the return of Melbourne to office, on 14 May 1839, struck his friends with dismay. It was not only the subject-matter – he spoke of 'anomalous influences' at the Palace – but the delivery. This was a good deal more anomalous: the emphasis on unimportant words, the whispers alternating with shouts, the 'drop by drop' pace, the swaying on his feet. But nothing happened this time. By July he was telling Lady Douro he was very well and could continue the session for another twelve months if need be. He was also telling Lord Aberdeen with angry sarcasm what he thought of his leaving early for Scotland: 'With all my heart be it so! I will not desire anybody to *stay*! I have before now stood; and I can *stand alone*!'[32]

Then came 15 October. Young Lady Salisbury died, that perfect confidante of the Duke's who had rivalled Mrs Arbuthnot for good sense. Just over a month later, on 19 November, he had a stroke and was found by his valet lying on the floor of his room at Walmer. He recovered consciousness after three-quarters of an hour and then his sight and speech. He had been starving a cold the week before and also hunting. When he felt the attack coming on he had tried to 'walk it off'. After a few days he insisted that he was quite well and got to the Privy Council on the 23rd for the Queen's declaration of marriage.* She looked round for him kindly and was glad to see him there.[33] But everyone noticed that his mouth and right arm were still slightly affected.

By Christmas the after-effects had disappeared. In this year, however, he first developed his beast-of-burden theme. He declined a Pitt Club dinner in April with the words:

> Every Animal in the creation is allowed some relaxation from Exertion . . . except the Duke of Wellington. All that the Duke can say is this: that if such relaxation is not allowed him; he must take the Liberty of giving it to Himself.[34]

After Lady Salisbury's funeral he coined his half-ironic, half-serious phrase about being a costermonger's donkey. Lord Mahon had suggested his resting:

> Rest! [he echoed] Every other animal – even a donkey – a costermonger's donkey – is allowed some rest, but the Duke of Wellington never! There is no help for it. As long as I am able to go on, they will put the saddle upon my back and make me go.[35]

The real truth was that he needed neither carrot nor stick to make him go; just sense of duty.

Three months later, in February 1840, he was smitten again, first with giddiness in the House of Lords and soon afterwards with another seizure while riding over to Lady Burghersh in Harley Street. He could not read her door number and only just reached home with his groom holding the reins of both horses. This time Croker predicted the end of the Duke's public life, Lady Palmerston (formerly Emily Cowper) thought he would not last long, and M. Guizot, the French ambassador, recognized in his empty and extinct eyes a sign that 'the soul, about to depart, no longer bothers to show itself'.[36]

Miss Jenkins offered to come to Apsley House and nurse him. He replied frostily: 'The Duke is much obliged to Her. He is quite well. He has no reason to believe that he will have occasion to trouble Her upon any object whatever.' At which Anna Maria

* Melbourne forced the Queen to invite Wellington by saying, 'There were some things the people of England would bear and some things they would not' – one of the latter being a ban on the Duke at a royal ceremony. (Lord Cowley to Arbuthnot, 11 February 1840; Aspinall, *Arbuthnot*, p. 217.)

swotted him with a text. 'Let NOT Him that girdeth on his harness *boast himself* as he that putteth it off. I Kings, XX. II.' In August he told her that he would write no more. Whether he wrote again or not depended not on him but on the Lord, she retorted. No more letters, the Lord decided, for four years.[37]

Meanwhile Sir Astley Cooper, the Duke's neurologist, was amazed by the completeness of his recovery. He resisted a spell at Bath or Auschowitz but agreed to take fluid magnesia for his stomach as recommended to the army and navy after hard drinking and for 'Irritability of Pregnant Females'.

*

The forties were upon them. What would the Duke offer to the Tories in the way of leadership? Precious little. 'If the House of Lords act wisely,' he wrote curtly to Croker, 'they will not be in a hurry to attack the government. I can say no more. . . .' The peers wanted him to say a great deal more. Even Peel was beginning to think like an activist. At the end of January the Duke did indeed admit to Lady Wilton, his new confidante, that there was 'a screw loose in the machine' – the Government machine.[38] But he still preferred offering a screwdriver rather than summoning the demolition squad. By August his bipartisanship had been carried so far that he jokingly looked forward to attending Whig Cabinet dinners. This was all very difficult for a renaissant Tory party which meant to win and win soon. When he did attack it was contrary to Peel's wishes.

An important Canada bill was before the House of Lords in 1840. Though the Government had quarrelled with the new Governor-General, 'Radical Jack' Durham, they had adopted his solution as propounded in his famous Report and Declaration of 1839. Its object was to settle the crisis by uniting the two Canadian provinces and introducing self-government. The Duke's whole being rejected the report. He felt that it had let down the Canadian loyalists and instead of uniting Canada would separate the colony from Britain. His solution was to maintain the two Canadas' independence and pacify the Lower (French) Province by direct rule: 'They wanted this iron fist to command them.'[39]

But in common with the majority, Peel accepted the Government's bill, and the Duke ultimately found himself in the extraordinary position of denouncing the bill while advising his

followers to support it. It can perhaps be said for him that the
Canadian union did not in fact prove permanent. Fifteen years
after his death (1867) Canada had a federal constitution.

At the end of 1840 the Duke sent out peremptory notes to
various dilatory peers, including Earl Beauchamp, which suggested that he too had at last picked up the scent of victory.

Considering the importance of the subjects likely to be brought under
the consideration of Parlt at an early period of the Session, I venture to
submit to your Lordship that it will not be creditable to the House of
Lords if that House should not be well attended.[40]

*

There was indeed a good deal of bellicosity left in the Duke.
Other events besides Canada had combined to awaken his old
fires. When he was not lying speechless like 'monumental marble'
on his camp bed at Walmer, he was shaking his iron fist at the
Chartists, whose radical Charter had appeared in 1838 – 'Oh! If I
were twenty years younger!' – and longing to have a go at those
blackguards and scoundrels, the French.[41]

Consecutive bad harvests and rising bread prices had told the
poor, if they needed telling, that they were about to enter the
'hungry forties'. Chartism reached its plateau of power. Thousands trooped at midnight to the moors above Manchester, there
were riots in Birmingham and a march of three thousand miners
armed with sticks, pikes and cutlasses on Newport. Their leader,
John Frost, who had once saved the Duke's nephew from drowning, was captured and transported. Many great cities saw in Frost
their martyr-hero. Chief Chartist leader was tall, tub-thumping
Feargus O'Connor, whose father had been the last tenant at the
Duke's old Irish home, Dangan. The Duke was to hear more of
O'Connor. Meanwhile some of the more militant Chartists
advocated violence and produced bloodthirsty placards:

> Let England's sons then prime her guns
>   And save each good man's daughter
> In tyrant's blood baptize your sons
>   And every villain slaughter.

Birmingham, busy with its own riots, had managed to bemuse
its magistrates through the clash between the duties of their office

and their liberal convictions. The rioters methodically gutted four houses under their eyes. The Duke was rather short with one victim who wrote to him personally for compensation. He had lost a diamond brooch (£9 2s.), studs, pencil cases and his hat. It had been a good hat (£1 4s.) and was now a bad hat – 'broke to pieces'. But the Duke defended the victims in Parliament with spirit. Birmingham had been treated like a town taken by storm:

Taken by storm, did I say? I have, while with the armies of my country, seen many towns taken by storm; but I never saw, never heard of, such outrages as were committed last night under the eyes of these magistrates. . . .

Many people felt that the 'grand blow-up' was coming and plied the Duke with ammunition. Bishop Phillpotts of Exeter discovered a socialist colony in Hampshire, of all places, where large audiences were urged to support Chartism and hold all things in common except their wives. The Duke advised against a prosecution, but thought a close watch should be kept on them, and gentlemen's servants discouraged from visits. The magistrates, however, issued a warrant. When the police arrived the socialists, their furniture, wives, pamphlets and all had vanished. Hampshire was saved.[42]

Not that the Duke himself expected the Chartists to take over, provided the Government did its duty. As General Charles Napier, Northern Command, put it: 'Poor people! They will suffer . . . We have the physical force not they . . . What would their 100,000 men do with my hundred rockets wriggling their fiery tails among them, roaring, scorching, tearing, smashing all they came near?'[43] Napier's radical sympathies and soldierly firmness prevented revolution. The Duke had another, very characteristic theory as to why the Chartists were no real danger, and why a mob of thirty thousand would run from thirty troops. The English had consciences and knew when they were doing wrong, unlike the French.

Yes, it was the French who had always been the real danger and now their ambitions in the Middle East looked to him like causing a catastrophe. They were backing the Egyptian rebel, Mehemet Ali, against the Sultan and the Great Powers. Wellington lamented the increase in French insolence since his day. 'When I was in Office in the year 1830, I held up my finger and told Prince

Polignac . . . that I could not allow Charles x to make use of
Mahomed Ali . . . They did not avail themselves of his services.
But now there is no such finger!' However, where the Duke's
finger had succeeded in 1830, Palmerston's gun-boats prevailed
in 1841. A European war was averted.

The Duke himself had been torn between a nostalgic longing to
be up and at the French himself, and fear lest Pam's gun-boat
diplomacy should precipitate the crisis. Another war, said the
French minister, Thiers, would mean the end of the world. 'We
should become Nations of Wild beasts on two legs,' said the Duke
more accurately, 'destroying each other!'[44]

His nostalgia had been fanned by two unprecedented proposals
from abroad. In the event of war, the King of Prussia asked him
in 1840 to command the armies of the German Confederation.
Next year he was approached with a similar and even more remarkable request by the three Great Powers. 'Mine is a most
extraordinary Position,' reflected the Duke truthfully. Here he
was at nearly seventy-two, still the greatest warrior-name in
Europe. He must listen to his conscience and remember to be
humble, he told Lady Wilton, or he would have the Soothsayer
after him, sending him a 'Memorandum' like the one he had sent
Caesar. 'Beware!'

*

The Ides of March, 1841, brought Wellington nothing worse than
fears and forebodings. His professional expertise told him that in
these perilous times his country was not adequately armed:
'We are not and are not likely [to be] in a state to defend ourselves. . . .'[45]

For the Whigs, things were desperate. They did indeed get
through March and even as far as June, but always in a hubbub of
old and new cries which they could neither appease nor ignore.
Corn and sugar duties were assailed with peculiar ferocity. The
Duke heard of a meeting in Salford where a Tory speaker had put
Free Trade before all political parties. 'The gentleman was prepared to be Tory, Conservative, Whig, Radical or Chartist – (Hear)
– to accomplish this great object – (Loud cheering).' The minds of
both leaders, Peel and Russell, were stretched and harassed by the
new situation, but Russell was in the hotter seat.

Two years earlier, when Samuel Rogers had remarked to Wellington upon the host of Conservative talent in the Commons against one talented Whig, Russell, the prompt answer came, 'John Russell is a host in himself.' Now the host had literally dwindled to one. At 3 A.M. on 5 June 1841 the Government were defeated on a vote of confidence by 312 to 311 – one vote. All the good hats flew up into the air and the bad ones were crammed down on anxious faces. Would their leader resign? Not Melbourne. He decided to wait till Parliament was prorogued and then try his luck, as the Queen wished, at the polls. It would at least give her a few more weeks of his company.

Raikes said it was just like the Whigs not to go out like gentlemen.

'They will only go out,' said the Duke, 'when compelled by the police.'[46]

They were compelled by the people.

22

Interlude III: Schism at Oxford

'Let these boys loose,' said the new Chancellor of Oxford University, astonished by the joyous bedlam at his installation in June 1834 – 'Let these boys loose in the state in which I saw them, and give them a political object to carry, and they would revolutionize any nation under the sun.'[1]

Curiously enough it was not the boys of Oxford who were to be let loose during his first stirring decade of office. These young men of good family, a large proportion of whom would enter the Church, chose to show the indiscipline of youth in private extravagance and debts. Various attempts by the University to introduce stiffer laws against student luxury received short shrift from the Duke. His quarrel with Christ Church over his own son Charles had taught him a lesson. By 1838 he believed that better discipline in the home was the answer. Not that he disapproved of college discipline – far from it – but 'the liberal World of the day' insisted on fewer rules, not more. Therefore to a complaining parent the Duke offered his own solution: 'If a Youth is not fit to be treated immediately as a Man under the Discipline of a College in the University, he should be kept in his Father's House or at a private tutor's till he becomes sufficiently ready.'[2] He had little sympathy with those who could not keep order in their own house. When he heard that the flogging headmaster of Eton, Dr Keate, boasted of having subdued an insurrection among his boys, the Duke expressed nothing but contempt:

'You might as well talk of an insurrection in a fishpond. The fish might just as well talk of an insurrection.'[3]

Only once during the Duke's tenure at Oxford did the boys break loose. It was at a public degree-giving in the Sheldonian Theatre. A deafening uproar earned the four ringleaders a grand total of twelve years' rustication. But on this occasion, 1845, the small fry behaved no worse than the big fish. They were mainly barracking a don who had hired private detectives to pry into their rooms. The big fish, the professors, fellows and tutors, joined in, raising a hubbub that wrecked the bestowal of an honorary degree upon Mr Edward Everett, the American minister and a Unitarian.

Here was the clue to the turbulent Oxford of the thirties and forties – religion. The Christian theologians were the ones to be let loose. Within the fold there were wild bleats and battle-cries, sheep biting sheep to right and left, and coming away with great lumps of wool in their teeth.

*

The Duke's Oxford was less like its descendant of today than any other institution with which he had to deal, for the majority of its dons were in holy orders. Parliament, the army – changed as they are, he would still know them if he returned. In Oxford he would no longer find the prevailing wind of clerical draperies swishing round every corner and softly nudging one another at every high table, nor the rings of white clerical collars singing together in planetary harmony or discord.

German scholarship had already begun to revolutionize religious thought, introducing ideas of history and literature into Revelation. Revelation could be only the Church's province; history might be shared by laymen. Between these two poles lay a third rich tract of country fiercely claimed by both, the Scriptures. If one cared enough about religion, it was also possible to dispute with passion the boundaries between Scripture and Revelation. In this domestic theatre of war, violent fighting did indeed flare up at Oxford towards the end of 1835. It was here that the Duke as Chancellor got his first taste of the Church militant.

Dr Renn Hampden, reported by his friends to be a singularly inoffensive person though undoubtedly ugly, was one of the great controversial figures in Oxford.* He had begun his career in that centre of intellectual brilliance, Oriel College, where he was friendly both with liberals like Dr Arnold and High Church Tories like Keble. When he delivered his famous Bampton Lectures in 1832, however, the High Church or 'high-and-dry' party, as their enemies called them, were scandalized to hear from him that the

---

* Renn Dickson Hampden (1793–1868), Bishop of Hereford (1847).

authority of the Scriptures was of greater weight than the authority of the Church. From that moment his only friends were the Broad Church, Evangelicals, or Low Church – 'low-and-slow', as their enemies later called them. Slow they were not in 1832; for next year this College Hampden was appointed President of St Mary Hall and, two years later, Professor of Moral Philosophy. Hardly had the 'high-and-drys' digested these hateful mouthfuls than the Whig Prime Minister, Lord Melbourne, decided to foster the cause of free thought at Oxford by offering to make the Whig Dr Hampden Regius (Crown) Professor of Divinity.

Wellington was not the man to welcome as Professor of Divinity one who had questioned the authority of the teaching Church. Nor was he alone in his attitude. High Tories, led by bewigged Dr Routh, President of Magdalen, turned Dr Hampden's appointment into a *cause célèbre* by petitioning the Crown against it. On 16 January 1836 the *Globe* exposed the Chancellor's wickedness in permitting the 'persecution' of Dr Hampden and demanded a parliamentary commission to rescue Oxford from bigotry.

This was a challenge well suited to the Duke. He would rescue Oxford himself, not from bigotry – a danger which he did not yet fear – but from unorthodoxy, that evil effluent of 'these modern times'.

His first important letter to his official secretary at Oxford, Dr Cardwell, was practical if not altogether politic. He would champion the anti-Hampdenites but they must drop their petition. Those who had been foolish enough to think of appointing Hampden would not alter their intention in response to such a move. Why not instead introduce a new University statute, making unnecessary for youths studying divinity to attend the Professor's lectures? 'I am not disposed to sit quietly,' he concluded with spirit, '& see the pure doctrine & practice of the Church overturned by the basest and most foolish conspiracy.' In return Dr Cardwell sent him a useful pamphlet entitled *Elucidations*, setting forth the errors of Dr Hampden's 'peculiar opinions'.[4] It was written by the young High Church Fellow of Oriel, Dr Newman.* Who would have imagined that when the sheep next fought each other within the fold the Chancellor would be on the side of the Lows and against this all too elucidatory High?

Meanwhile gusts from the Hampden affair continued to rock

* John Henry Newman (1801–89), Cardinal of the Church (1879).

Oxford. The High Tories proposed that the episcopal bench should accept certificates from young candidates for Holy Orders signed by the Lady Margaret Professor of Divinity, a reliable High Tory, instead of by the Whig Regius Professor. Wellington nipped this particular madness in the bud. Two or three months of active Oxford politics had convinced him that to 'sit quietly' after all had its merits. 'The object,' he now wrote to Cardwell, 'is to avoid Schism in the Church.' Yet this plan would produce schism not only at Oxford but everywhere else. 'We should have had Lady Margaret's Clergymen and Dr Hampden's Clergymen throughout the country; and orthodox and unorthodox Bishops in our several Dioceses.' No doubt the alternative of having all Hampden clergymen was deplorable. 'However we must make the best of it.'[5] This was once more the Duke's true voice.

It was not listened to. Though the obnoxious proposals were dropped, Convocation, the assembly of all senior members of the University, found another way of punishing Dr Hampden. On 5 May 1836 they passed a temporary statute depriving the Regius Professor of his powers to nominate University preachers. The Duke was again alarmed. 'The most desirable thing of all,' he wrote insistently, 'is that these Discussions in the University should be brought to a close.' Alas, in November Dr Gilbert, the Vice-Chancellor, announced that he would not sign testimonials for any young men who attended Dr Hampden's lectures.[6] Many High Tories followed him.

This was too much for the Chancellor. He rapped the Vice-Chancellor hard, lecturing him on the three great evils of Heresy, Impiety and Schism, the greatest of these being Schism. Even such a mischievous appointment as Hampden's might be got the better of by moderation and prudence, whereas Dr Gilbert's plan smacked of 'party Motives'. He begged to remind the Vice-Chancellor that there was such a thing as a powerful Whig party in Parliament which supported the Prime Minister's appointment of Hampden, and bishops who belonged to that party. Just as the Vice-Chancellor gave in and the Duke hoped that Oxford had been soothed down and tided on, the High Tories found a new chink in Dr Hampden's armour which they hastened to exploit.

For reasons of prestige, he had not immediately resigned from St Mary Hall when appointed Regius Professor; but neither did he keep his statutory residence at the Hall. His professorship entitled him to a canonry at Christ Church, and the Tories discovered that he was living there with his wife but repairing four nights a week after 11 P.M. to his bed at St Mary Hall. How dreadful that the Regius Professor should degrade himself by such a quibble. The case was too 'low' for the Vice-Chancellor to enquire into himself, but he proposed to employ a solicitor. The Duke felt obliged to send Hampden an official *monitio* (warning) about keeping his residence. An acrimonious correspondence ensued in which the Duke said he was not treated by Hampden like a gentleman, far less a Chancellor.[7] It ceased only with Hampden's resignation from the Hall and the end of his nocturnal wanderings.

It remained for the Duke in 1842 to try to get Dr Hampden out of everybody's hair by expunging the offensive statute against him of 5 May 1836. Since those days, the Regius Professor's Evangelical opinions had become less repugnant to the authorities than some other High Church views fashionable in 1842. The Chancellor hoped that Convocation, following the advice of their own board – the Hebdomadal Board, which governed the University – would repeal the anti-Hampden statute. Instead Convocation, led by the bellicose Tory Bishop Phillpotts of Exeter, voted against repeal. As in Parliament, so at Oxford, the Duke found that the Tory party would not follow their leaders. The heads of Church and State agreed that good sense and the cause of peace demanded repeal of the offending statute; 'It appears otherwise to other Wiser Man,' wrote the Duke sarcastically.[8]

Meanwhile there was acute trouble on a new front.

*

The anti-Catholics of Oxford, reported Dr Cardwell sadly to the Duke in December 1838, wished to erect a provocative memorial to the three Protestant martyrs, Cranmer, Latimer and Ridley, who had been burned at the stake in the reign of Bloody Mary. In this they were strenuously but vainly opposed by a pro-Catholic group which included Mr Froude and Dr Newman. The former said he could see no good in the martyred Bishop Cranmer except that he 'burned well'.

Today the Martyrs' Memorial stands like a rock of tranquillity in the roaring currents of the twentieth century, an occasional challenge to the climbing skills of students, pot in hand. But a hundred and thirty years ago it roused the fury of those who were soon to call themselves Anglo-Catholics, Tractarians or members of the Oxford Movement. By the Duke their activities were designated, 'the new schism in the Church', or simply, 'the Schism'. Just as the Low Church schism was healing, Dr Newman, from having been the skilful and orthodox 'elucidator' of the Hampden heresy, had become in 1841 the anonymous author of an equally pernicious publication called *Tract XC*, the ninetieth in a series of pamphlets entitled *Tracts for the Times*. Newman's *Tract XC* was understood to argue that the Church of England was compatible with Rome. *Tract XC* created ecclesiastical uproar. Two years later another violent tremor from the same quarter shook the University. Dr Edward Pusey, the Anglo-Catholic Regius Professor of Hebrew, preached a sermon on the Lord's Supper which contravened the doctrines of the Church of England. A copy of the sermon was sent to the Duke with two heretical passages marked in pencil. Such things, said the Duke sombrely, were bad for the University in the eyes of the public and of foreigners.

It had become clear to him that these enthusiasts for the pristine purity of Christian belief – for such they were – thought little of the Reformed religion as set forth in the Thirty-Nine Articles. In returning to the medieval Church, they claimed to have found a middle way between the Anglicans and the Catholics. But their *via media* seemed to the Church of England its Via Dolorosa, littered with the torn-up articles of their faith and lined with crucifixes, candles and confessionals. The time came when the Duke felt himself impelled to descend into the arena wearing the full panoply of office and save the Church of England.

The Tractarians' strategy in 1844 for strengthening their movement revolved around the election of a new Vice-Chancellor. Wellington had been advised to nominate Dr Benjamin Symons, a doughty Evangelical known as Big Ben. Fearing lest Big Ben should make Oxford too hot to hold them, the Tractarians decided to challenge Wellington's nomination through a vote in Convocation. This indeed was a bold and intriguing course, worthy of their academic ingenuity, for no one knew whether the University statutes permitted such a challenge or not. The Duke learned from *The Times* of the threatened challenge to his authority. A stinging letter was forthwith composed behind the battlements of Walmer Castle and despatched like a bullet to Oxford. If a vote were taken in Convocation the Duke of Wellington would resign. Had he solicited the office of Chancellor? He had not. Would he now submit to the disgrace of a vote? He would not: 'I *will not* submit to an Indignity on the part of any authority whatever. . . .' The moment the news reached him of such an indignity, he would resign his office of Chancellor 'by return of the post'.[9]

Unhappy Dr Wynter, the retiring Vice-Chancellor, was forced to explain all. The situation was worse than the Duke imagined. At the handing-over ceremony in the Sheldonian, Dr Wynter would have to resign before the Proctors could administer the oath to his successor, Dr Symons. Even if Wynter ignored the hullabaloo which would attend this stage of the proceedings, the Proctors, being Tractarians themselves, would probably refuse to swear in Big Ben. The University would then be left with no Vice-Chancellor at all. The Holy Ghost had certainly inspired the Tractarians.

The Duke was inspired also. He had his motto: 'If you want a thing done well, do it yourself.' The agitated Wynter received a despatch from HQ Walmer announcing that on the crucial day the Commander-in-Chief would enter Oxford, occupy the Sheldonian Theatre, seat himself in the Vice-Chancellor's chair and after Wynter had resigned, personally nominate Symons. When he put the question to Convocation, '*Placetne Domini vobis?*' (Content?) and there were lusty roars of '*Non placet*' (Not Content), the C.-in-C. would simply ignore them, make over the Vice-Chancellor's chair to Big Ben and march out of the building.

This splendid general order took Dr Wynter's breath away. Rather than risk the consequences of such a military coup, he suggested that a vote on Wellington's nomination should be voluntarily granted, 'always saving the Authority and Power of the Chancellor'. The phrase struck the Duke as eminently suitable to the dignity of his office. He readily agreed to have it used. The great day arrived, 8 October 1844. The theatre was packed out. When the Tractarians raised their shout of '*Non placet!*' the vote was duly taken, excitement rose to fever pitch – and the Tractarians were beaten by the enormous majority of 699 votes.

The battle for Convocation had been won by the Establishment. On his own initiative the Duke performed a small mopping-up operation. Having discovered that Convocation's vote on Dr Symons had been unstatutory after all, he wrote to say that if ever such a vote against the Chancellor's nomination were demanded in the future, it should not be granted. It never was.

Dr Symons ventured to hope that the peace of the University might not be disturbed again for some time. 'But the disturbing party,' he added, 'whose object is to revolutionize the University and the Church, is restless and perpetually aggressive.' The Duke, however, found that with the lapsing of some Tractarians and the conversion of others (especially Dr Newman) to Rome, this particular 'revolution' gradually died out. Meanwhile there were new disturbers of the University peace. Their accents were harsh and they spoke from Parliament. The Duke was not altogether unsympathetic to their message.

*

Before introducing the Duke's political work for the University – a labour which began in 1834 and ended only with his life – it will be as well to see him for a moment in the general setting. There is no need to linger over the problem of patronage and letter-writing. The costermonger's donkey bore these burdens wherever he travelled, from the army to the Hampshire Yeomanry, from Westminster to Oxford. The dons recommended themselves for promotion with matchless eloquence, though not always with corresponding efficiency. One suppliant wrote four times, finally lamenting that the great man, so famous for replying by return of post, had sent no answer whatever to his three letters. The Duke answered the fourth by return, telling his correspondent that this was the first time he had sent his address.

That some of the requests for patronage would be extremely odd was only to be expected. But even the case-hardened Duke was surprised at being asked by an unknown man named Roger Dyson to recommend a relative, now a cook at Balliol College, to be a cook at Worcester.

If the Duke was in the Habit of partaking of the Dinners of Worcester College [he replied], there might be some excuse for his interference. But as it never happens for him to dine there, he must say that the act on his part would be as extraordinary as it appears to him that the application is on the part of Mr. Dyson, a gentleman of whom the Duke of Wellington knows nothing. The Duke suggests to Mr. Dyson that if he has a female relation unmarried; who is desirous of being married; he might as well desire the Duke to recommend her as a wife! The application would be just as reasonable as that which he has made to the Duke to recommend his son-in-law . . . of whom the Duke knows nothing to be appointed cook at Worcester College!!![10]

It seemed that the costermonger's donkey got a certain kick out of bearing his burdens.

The burden of Oxford's religious disputes, already examined, generally fell on the Duke indirectly. In this sphere his task was to discourage polemics and keep the peace. There were occasions when he went beyond mere pacification and strongly advised the University not to interfere in matters which did not concern it. On 16 April 1845, for example, he heard that the Board were preparing a petition to Parliament against a bill to remove Jewish disabilities. This bill, the Chancellor pointed out, was of a quasi-political and party character and he wondered why the Board felt 'constrained' to give it their attention.

Wise and reflecting Men such as the Hebdl. Board is composed of would do well to consider all the circumstances attending a political Question . . . before they deliver an opinion which is not required from them, and it is not their duty to give.
    Signed, Wellington.

In a lengthened postscript, Wellington warned the Board that certain subjects might be coming before the House of Lords 'in which the University really has an Interest and upon which it has undoubtedly Duties to perform! I only hope that it will be found that these Questions have really been attended to. . . .'

Great was his relief when he heard a week later that the petition against the Jews had been dropped. As Chancellor, he would have had to present it if required, but with a public expression of his own disapproval. He was anxious, he explained, not to 'stultify' himself in this way. For what could be more humiliating than to serve the University 'with zeal & fidelity for ten years' and then to be seen exposed as having insufficient influence to stop the Board from delivering opinions on public questions 'over which it can have no Control'.[11]

The last few words represented one of the great negative principles on which the Duke based his career: never to give opinions on practical issues over which one had no control.

*

The reforming spirit which Wellington always dated from 1830 was unlikely to bypass Oxford and Cambridge. He was not surprised therefore when the radical 3rd Earl of Radnor raised the question in 1835 of reforming some of the Universities' statutes with a view to admitting dissenting sects. As a pillar of Church and State the Duke was opposed to reform in this direction. He automatically decided to defend Oxford against an aggressive Parliament. At the same time, as a sensible man he could not but agree that one of the conditions for admission to the University, namely 'subscription' to the Thirty-Nine Articles, was indefensible. How could a callow youth of seventeen be expected to understand and subscribe to such intricacies? On this matter, he urged, Oxford must accept reform. Either the ancient statute must be altered 'to suit the altered Circumstances of the times', or, if kept unchanged, explained away by a new statute: 'We shall not long be able to resist some alteration, and I earnestly entreat the University to make it themselves.' Lord Radnor's bill was so moderate, and so many moderate men including himself agreed with it, that his task in speaking for the University would be infinitely easier if he had behind him an assurance that Oxford planned her own reform.

As it happened, the House of Lords defeated Radnor's bill. Undeterred, he struck again in 1837 on a wider front. He proposed an enquiry into the college statutes of Oxford and Cambridge through which, as interpreted by College Visitors, the individual colleges ultimately controlled entry into the Universities. At once all the storm-signals were flying. How describe the enquiry, demanded the Vice-Chancellor of Oxford, then Dr Gilbert, but as an unjust invasion of the rights of private foundations and an indecent interference with the jurisdiction of College Visitors? The Board in great perturbation besought the Duke to send the strongest possible petition against such an outrage.

The Duke made his own enquiries. It appeared that College Visitors were no safeguard against ancient abuses. Some colleges had statutes drawn up centuries ago which restricted candidates for scholarships to 'founder's kin' or a county of England whose supply of eligible young men had long dried up. Others in accordance with their statutes adopted a system of 'false and heedless swearing'; others again ignored their unworkable medieval laws but 'under circumstances of mystery' which aroused deep suspicion. Lord Radnor was on to all this. The Duke's answer to the trembling yet defiant Board was a trumpet call for reform:

The Colleges have but one course to follow. That is to look into their own Affairs, and to put them in order themselves. Let each of them which has a Visitor and the Power of Legislation consider its Statutes, repeal all that is anomalous and obsolete, and frame a code suitable to the University and to the times.[12]

The University was half-coaxed, half-frightened into action. A committee of the Board was set up to revise the whole body of University statutes and many letters arrived from the Vice-Chancellor for the Duke saying that it 'laboured indefatigably'. Laboured? asked the Duke. This was not what he wanted to hear. In order to stave off Lord Radnor, he must be able to assure Parliament that the committee had actually *revised*.

In June Lord Radnor dropped a new bombshell. He intended to move for a committee to examine those college statutes which were deposited in the British Museum. There was a crisis of alarm and despondency at Oxford. Not only were the 'British Museum colleges' vulnerable to research but almost all the colleges one way or another. Poor Dr Gilbert wrote to the Duke that at least six or seven had lodged their statutes in the Museum, a dozen more were available in the University's Bodleian Library and others could be picked up secondhand on bookstalls. In most instances the conditions laid down by medieval benefactors neither were nor could be obeyed.

The Duke, therefore, pounded away at the colleges, doing his best to dispel false hope, extremism or procrastination. Some colleges had leapt to the conclusion that the Conservative success in the 1837 election would save them from the need to reform at all. The Duke wrote sternly:

There is not in Oxford a Gentleman who dislikes innovation and change so much as I do. But I live in the World, I know the Times in which and the Men with whom I live. Even the best Friends of the University . . . will not support the existing order of things.[13]

It was easy enough to say 'no surrender no compromise'. Those who said it were usually the first to run away. For their opinions the Duke did not care 'one Pin'.

The moderate tone of politicks in general should be an inducement now to make the alterations which are essential, and that the universities and their Colleges should place themselves in a position in which they can stand permanently before the Publick.

Among the extremists for whom the Duke cared not one pin was the Rev. William Sewell, a Tractarian who propounded the delectable principle, 'Obsolete laws are no evil'.

The progress reports of 1837–40 which the Duke demanded and received sounded like nothing so much as the parable of the Marriage Feast, since every college had a perfectly good excuse for refusing the Chancellor's invitation to act.

Wadham alone had gone ahead. The Master of Pembroke in 1838 had seen no immediate hurry and had therefore set aside his labours during the long Vacation; Brasenose's Visitor had not yet been approached, as both Principal and Vice-Principal had been ill; Oriel was waiting to find leisure to make a digest of its statutes; Dr Jenkyns of Balliol had been engaged upon the 'unremitting occupation' of revising the University code, and so had no time for his college statutes; Merton preferred, with the greatest respect, to report progress to its Visitor, the Archbishop of Canterbury, rather than to the Duke; Dr Fox of Queen's was predictably not aware of any 'system of abuses'; Trinity found only one weakness in its statutes, namely, that certain fellows seemed to get excessive leave of absence; Worcester's statutes had a long way to go through special committees; New College, Christ Church, Exeter and Magdalen had sent in no reports whatever by the end of 1838 and the Duke summed up their situation tersely on a half-sheet of writing-paper: 'Subject under consideration.'

Magdalen College turned out to be the greatest sinner of all, and the most indebted to the Duke for its salvation. It had obtained an injunction against the Tractarian, W. G. Ward, for translating its statutes without permission. Work on revision therefore seemed to the aged and obstinate Dr Routh and his colleagues superfluous. After waiting till the end of 1839, the Duke decided to wait no longer.

I wish that the Gentlemen of Magdalen would look steadily at their situation [he wrote to the Vice-Chancellor]. The Abuses which prevail there have been notorious for above fifty years. Gibbon the Historian noticed them early in his life. These gentlemen are quite mistaken in their estimation of the Symptoms of the Times, if they think that there is a chance of their continuance, much less of their Endurance for another half Century.[14]

No man or power in the land was capable of defending them. Whatever happened in their case against Mr Ward, let them alter their statutes in accordance with the University's present view on education.

The Duke's letter was read aloud to the College's representative in the new year, 1840, and made a deep impression. The injunction against Ward was eventually dropped, and any progress Magdalen then made into the nineteenth century was entirely due, in the Vice-Chancellor's words, to 'your Grace's wisdom and influence'. His Grace replied simply: 'It frequently occurs that I cannot do more than let them know the truth.'

In the course of his first seven years as Chancellor, 1834–41, the Duke had spoken often and often about the spirit, circumstances or symptoms of the times. When he returned to political power in the summer of 1841 as a member of Peel's cabinet, the University and its colleges were not yet reformed.

The battle had none the less enabled him to see the spirit of the times in a new light. By contrast with some of the colleges' obscurities, it seemed a spirit to be tolerated, even fostered. The lesson was a valuable one for the next five years with Peel.

23

Rightabout Face!

What was to be the Duke's position in the new Government? The 1841 election had given Peel a Conservative majority of ninety-one. It also gave him the opportunity to form a superlatively strong Cabinet, including five prime ministers past, present and to come: Wellington, Ripon (Goderich), Peel himself, Stanley (Derby), Aberdeen. Another future prime minister was Vice-President of the Board of Trade, Mr Gladstone. There was one absentee premier-to-be who offered his services but was turned down, Mr Disraeli. The man who regarded Peel's refusal as 'intolerable humiliation'[1] duly became the black-ringleted fairy at the feast.

The Duke had clarified his own requirements well in advance of victory. 'The truth is that all that I desire is to be as useful as possible to the Queen's service,' he wrote to Peel on 17 May 1841, ' – to do anything, go anywhere, and hold any office, or no office, as may be thought most desirable. . . . I don't desire even to have a voice in deciding upon it.'[2] But in case Peel wished to know his opinion, he gave it: the best thing would be for him to continue in the Cabinet as Leader of the Lords but for the first time without office. He would thus be free to deal with any trouble-spots.

Thanks largely to the Duke, the Palace was no longer a trouble. His personal success with the Queen was of great use in dispelling any Whig miasma that might remain. As early as August 1840 she had shown him incipient favour. He sat next to her at dinner. 'She drank wine repeatedly with me,' he reported; 'in short, if I was not a milksop, I should become her Bottle Companion.' Six months later the milksop (he concentrated on iced water these days) was invited to stand proxy for the Queen's father-in-law, the Duke of Saxe-Coburg-Gotha, at the Princess Royal's christening: 'I must be in favour to be thought of as a Beau Père!' On the same principle, he became Her Majesty's half-brother in 1843, when at Prince Alfred's christening he represented Prince Charles of Leinigen. Meanwhile he had lent Walmer Castle to the Queen and her young family for a blast of sea air during the preceding November. There was only one untoward event, when her postilions failed to negotiate the Castle entrance. 'She Stuck in it, and was obliged to get out of the Carriage.'[3] Even in old age the Duke was accustomed to drive himself and his guests at breakneck speed along the narrow lanes of Walmer. Sometimes they trembled; they never stuck.

Two years later, in January 1845, the Queen conferred the most daunting favour of all by inviting herself to stay at Stratfield Saye. The Duke was for once staggered by a problem of logistics. How fit HM and all her train into a gentleman's residence which, though undoubtedly the most comfortable, was not the largest in the world? He put these points tactfully to HM. 'She smiled and continued to be very gracious, but did not give a Hint of postponing the Visit.'

So he had to break to Mrs Apostles, his housekeeper for a quarter of a century, the appalling honour which was awaiting them. She dried her tears after he said: 'What cannot be prevented must be borne.' By dint of many ingenious makeshifts culminating in a proposal to harbour any high sheriffs, mayors and corporations who might turn up, in the tennis court, an unexpected success was made of the visit. 'I thank God!' he wrote to Lady Wilton afterwards, 'the visitation is concluded. I have just now returned from attending Her Majesty on Horseback to the Borders of the County.'[4] From Queen Victoria's journal it appears that he not only saw her off the premises but attended almost every step she took, showing her to her room, fetching her for dinner, helping her generously to pudding, talking to her confidentially on the sofa in the hearty tones of the deaf and lighting her up to bed. Prince Albert had a go at tennis when there were not too many spectators and, according to Florence Nightingale, was also 'taught to miss at billiards'.[5] The Peels were staying in the house and the Queen noted that Albert had talks with the Prime Minister.

The whole visit, like the rest of the Duke's work with the Queen, was invaluable to Peel. Only one question arose. Was it possible that the Duke had succeeded almost too well in impregnating the shy and sensitive Peel with his own enthusiasm for the Crown? If the Duke had a hand in firing Peel with excessive chivalry, he would have something to answer for at the end of the year.

*

The Duke's intense aversion to giving interviews was not growing less. Yet there was every reason why public men should be beset during the autumn of 1841 with such requests. The harvest had been bad and a terrible winter was in prospect. Deputations were on the move. One had come to London all the way from Paisley, telling of dreadful distress among the wool-weavers and seeking an interview with the Duke. He refused, alleging that he had neither time nor influence since he held no office. 'All this is lamentable,' commented Greville; 'it is a complete delusion he is under; he has nothing to do, and he has boundless influence.'[6]

Greville's assertion that the Duke had nothing to do was untrue. He was at that moment conducting a voluminous correspondence with Graham (Home Secretary) on Paisley, among other things; with Stanley (Colonies) on the defence of Canada; with Aberdeen (Foreign Secretary) on France; with Ellenborough (Governor-General of India) on India and China. Nine months later while the Paisley affair was still raging, Greville sought and was denied an interview for a hanger-on of his own. In apologizing to Greville, the Duke described how he had risen that morning at five and would sit up till two or three next morning reading papers. Providence ought to have given him two days for every other man's one, and the power to be in two places at once. 'I hope therefore that you will excuse me.'[7] Greville did not, nor, more importantly, did Mr John Giblett of Paisley.

The first Paisley approach had been made on 8 September 1841. It was naive, but none the worse for that. During the past three or four years, explained Mr Giblett, it had been the fashion for the nobility to wear black or dark green coats and trousers. Dark colours, alas, wore longer than light. At a time of acute unemployment, therefore, fashion had contributed its quota. Would the Duke give a lead himself and also persuade the Prince to introduce more transient shades? In a prompt reply, Field-Marshal the Duke of Wellington had to inform Mr Giblett that he was not a member of the Queen's or Prince's Court and it was not part of his duty to suggest the colours which Prince Albert should choose for his spring clothes.

Mr Giblett remonstrated. No further reply. Finally some of the correspondence got into the newspapers, the Duke was castigated for his acid pen and iron heart and Lord Brougham presented a petition in favour of the Paisley weavers next summer.

Of course the Duke should have received these delegates. His only excuse was that by autumn 1841 he knew official measures were already in preparation to salvage industry. As he told Lord Salisbury on 11 September, 'We are in the act of making a great experiment.'[8]

*

The great experiment of 1842–6 depended on two things: a united party and a breakthrough in legislation. At long last Peel and Wellington were leading a combined force of Conservatives like themselves, Canningites like Stanley and Ultras like Buckingham. And whither was this united force to march? Into Peel's promised land: a land of financial stability and economic growth; a land where the revenue which had fallen under the Whigs would rise again, where manufacturers would get cheaper raw materials and so increase production and employment, where consumers would get cheaper food and so buy more manufactured goods; to be precise, a land of tariff reform and income tax.

Peel had watched the horrors of the winter with painful shudders of his own. Thousands had to be fed by charity. In Paisley alone £600 a week was needed to keep the people from starving. Yet charity was a wretchedly haphazard net in which to catch the unfortunate. There was the ghastly story from the Anti-Corn Law League of a hand-loom weaver in the midst of his family found dead at his loom. Peel exclaimed passionately, 'Who was the relieving officer? Why did he neglect his duty?'[9] The Poor Law should have prevented this tragedy.

The League and the Chartists raged. Unfortunately for them, they raged at each other as well as at the system, the one being predominantly middle-class and the other working-class. But the League could count on additional support in the Commons, now that their leader Cobden had become a member. Peel's aim was to get the economy going and let the people save themselves, first from starvation and then from Chartism. To Wellington, Chartism was a greater menace than misery. Nature had made him a keeper of order rather than a creator of laws. Peel's imaginative genius for law-making was something he respected but could not imitate.

After countless exchanges of letters and Cabinet consultations, the great experiment was announced when Parliament met in February 1842. Duties on corn and meat were to be lowered while the tariffs on a mass of other products would be reformed or removed. To make up for loss of revenue, a three-year experimental income tax was to be imposed for the first time on a peacetime Britain: 7d in the £ on all incomes over £150 per annum.

Peel's vision and competence deeply impressed even a cynic like Greville. 'One felt all the time he was speaking,' wrote Greville of his great financial exposition on 12 March, ' "Thank God, Peel is Minister".' Others felt the opposite. Fat old Buckingham, unable to forget his promises at agricultural dinners to maintain the Corn Laws, had already resigned as Lord Privy Seal. Lord Hardwicke left the Queen's Household. Wellington said roundly that Buckingham and Hardwicke had been fools. 'Both will be the ridicule of the whole nation.'[10]

While the mass of Conservative protectionists gulped and swallowed the changes, the Whig and Radical out-and-out free traders declared Peel's tariff reform to be an insult and his income tax a crime. They had denounced the latter when Castlereagh tried to maintain it after Waterloo and they denounced it again now. Harriet Martineau, who carried two hearing-aids, one long and one short to scoop up radical wisdom from far and near, wrote:

There is something transcendently disgusting in an Income Tax, which not only takes a substantial sum immediately out of a man's pocket, but compels him to expose his affairs to a party [the Tax Collector], that he would by no means choose for a confidant.[11]

Nevertheless the tax collector worked away, the revenue in time began to float and even become buoyant, and in 1845 this criminal miracle measure was re-enacted for another three years.

Though the foundations of prosperity had been laid by the budget and new Corn Law, the fate of all the Paisleys was more than ever in doubt. How would they be fed next winter? To the angry Ultras Peel put the inexorable choice; they must accept further tariff reform or expect insurrection. They might get both. Britain's relations with foreign powers were by no means pellucid, after Palmerston's stirring of the waters. France was still suspect and there was still a quarrel with the United States over the Maine –Oregon boundary.* From Afghanistan came news of a positively frightful disaster at Kabul. Old Lord Hill decided he was no longer able to do himself justice as head of the army. He resigned in August and the Duke of Wellington was once more, after fourteen years, Commander-in-Chief.

*

The Duke's first instinct had been not to hold a dual position in the Cabinet and Army. According to Arbuthnot he complained of being worked to death in the Lords. The trouble was that he would not admit to being tired except to intimates like Charles Arbuthnot or women friends. To Peel he insisted he was as strong as ever, able to do anything required in Her Majesty's service. Peel, however, knew from friendly sources of his fatigue. Why then did he not cut the knot for him by offering the army to someone else?

Peel was in a dilemma. Through Arbuthnot, the Duke had made it clear that he wanted the army. One of his rare exercises in resentment was never to forgive his being deprived of it on constitutional grounds when he became Prime Minister. He was now willing, even eager, to exchange the Cabinet for the Army. Peel, on the other hand, was desperately anxious not to lose the Duke's name from his Cabinet. Great experiments need great names to float them. As it turned out, Peel was proved right. The Duke's last years in Parliament were of infinitely more service to the country than his last years as head of the army. This was no paradox. There were things in Parliament which only the hero of Waterloo could do. The years of the sword had made him the rock he was.

A slight remission of the Duke's parliamentary burden was agreed to in 1844. Lord Stanley asked for 'accelerated promotion' to the House of Lords (his father, the 13th Earl of Derby, was still living) in order that he might be trained to succeed Wellington. In answer to a tactful enquiry from Peel on the subject, the

---

* The news of its settlement arrived on the day Peel's Government fell.

Duke sent a typical comment:

> I am well as I have been for the last twenty-two years . . . and as well able to transact any business, in the House of Lords or elsewhere. But . . a great object would be attained by having there Lord Stanley.[12]

A great object was indeed attained by Lord Stanley, but whether it benefited Wellington or Peel remained to be seen.

Printed slips, or 'lithographs', had been invented by the Duke in 1842 to save time and temper in answering his mounting flood of requests from strangers for patronage. The lithographs gave delight to the inventor and amusement to his friends. They were not always popular with recipients.

> Field Marshal the Duke of Wellington presents his compliments. The Duke is Commander in Chief of the Army but he has no Patronage not exclusively Military, nor Controul over those who have. He positively and distinctly declines to solicit favors for any Person whatever, but most particularly for a Gentleman of whom he knows nothing, not even whether or not he is trustworthy.

*

August 1842 was a hungry and riotous month for the Duke to start again as Commander-in-Chief. He felt deeply responsible, and not only as the provider of soldiery. An attempt by Prince Albert to design new caps for British officers was vetoed by the Duke because it would throw the present cap-makers out of work. That spring and summer wages were cut, prices rose and a third of the working population was unemployed. So many weavers' houses in Stockport were empty that a poster was put up, 'Street To Let'. In August an anonymous letter to the Duke from strike-bound Manchester ended with the desperate words: 'The sooner an actual state of Riot, which can be so treated by the Magistrates & Military takes place, the sooner we shall be relieved. . . .' Many mill-owners and military commanders shared this view. The Duke had already sent a detachment of Guards and artillery to the North by rail. One of the paradoxes of 1842 was the sudden love-affair of the wealthy with the hitherto unpopular railways. They liked to have their property protected, noted Raikes, 'by regiments whirled down . . . at the rate of forty miles an hour'.[13]

From Colonel Arbuthnot, HQ Blackburn, came accounts of colliery and mill mobs; of famous names like Hargreaves, Wedgwood and Copeland in trouble; of eighty-nine prisoners taken; of three hundred thousand workers on strike because forced by Anti-Corn Law Leaguers or encouraged by weak Justices of the Peace to take 'this demon-step'. 'If we had good old Tory Justices things would never have got so far.'

Wellington's summary of the August crisis was uncompromising. He saw it as a pre-revolutionary situation, but only just 'pre':

> Chartism is neither more nor less than Combination to raise Wages: to force Industrious Men to discontinue Work by Violence and Intimidation . . . the ultimate object being to obtain money whether in the shape of Wages pension or any other manner without Work.

Small mobs could live on forced requisitions but large ones had to find bigger resources.

> Then commences Plunder: of the Houses of Individuals of shops etc. etc. next will come the Roosts Farmyards Fields etc. and you will find these Mobs to be Armies in fact: living as Revolutionary Armies do by Plunder. . . .

Fortunately they had not yet achieved the discipline and subordination to leaders of Continental armies.

> But Time will teach them all this. It is for this reason that I am so anxious to strike an effectual blow.[14]

The blow was struck. Chartists to the number of one thousand five hundred were arrested and fifty-four leaders transported. The Duke had wanted a Special Commission on the lines of Melbourne's in 1830–1. But without funds or leaders the strikes collapsed, while internal disputes and economic improvements brought by Peel's policy gradually reduced the unrest.

The Duke's opinions of three bodies of men on whom he relied to keep order are significant. The magistracy of 1842 he considered to be in a 'lamentable state' because of Radical infiltration. Armed pensioners he welcomed, provided they were under strict military discipline. Otherwise they were a 'Rabble' and probably a dangerous one. The Duke until now had always hoped to avoid arming the veterans. In 1830 he wrote, 'A Man who is a Constable today is a Mr tomorrow.'[15] Until 1842 the Duke did not want any armed misters. As for the army, it was absolutely reliable – no fears now lest the fire-engine should catch fire.

Then did the mobs and petitions and strikers achieve nothing?

The clamour of the destitute strengthened the hand of those Conservatives who were fighting for remedial legislation. Peel's government introduced the first Factory Bill in 1843, to be followed after much controversy by Lord Ashley's famous 'Ten Hour Bill' four years later.* Ashley had earlier tried to enlist the Duke's support for the 1842 Mines Bill. He sent him a copy of a petition against female labour underground. The petitioner dwelt on the naked squalor of women and girls down the mines, leading to vice: 'to hear the awful swearing, obscene conversation, and filthy songs, would lead any person to believe he was in a land of savages, rather than in civilised England.'

The Duke promised Ashley to give the bill fair play, but added that he must take the same line on it as the Government took in the Commons. In fact, Lords Wharncliffe and Hatherton organised a fierce resistance and the Duke assisted them, alas, to send back the bill to the Commons with severe mutilations. 'Civilised England', to quote the petitioner, believed in liberty for the free-born Englishwoman to debauch herself or starve.

*

If this was civilized England, what of the untamed neighbour whom the Industrial Revolution had passed by? Ireland had temporarily lost the limelight. Plenty of disagreeable rumours were abroad in 1842 but Peel dismissed most of them as false – especially the report of fifty thousand Americans coming to the assistance of Irish rebels, but whose transport was unspecified. The undeniable facts, however, were not reassuring.

After the defeat of the Whigs, O'Connell and his surviving Irish M.P.s renewed their demand for repeal of the Union. They developed a powerful repeal programme, with a repeal 'Rent' target of £3 million, non-payment of landlords' rent and over forty monster meetings to destroy 'spinning-jenny Peel' and 'Wellington the old Buccaneer', the two defenders of the Union. By May 1843 O'Connell's campaign was formidable and so were the Government's counter-preparations. The Duke's informants, mainly Government spies, Protestant parsons and Orange peers, reported

* Peel was for limiting children's hours in factories to 12, Ashley to 10. The Duke heard that Ashley would be Prime Minister, 'but whether for *ten* or *twelve* Hours was not known!' (*Wellington and His Friends*, 29 March 1844.)

frequent use among Nationalists of the sinister phrase, 'When the Day comes' (an equivalent to '*Der Tag*' in 1914).

In writing to Graham, the Home Secretary, Wellington spoke definitively of 'an Awful Contest impending over us' and 'this expected Warfare in Ireland'. In his view the Protestants were worse off now than during the Great Rebellion of 1798, being more scattered. He advocated 'ships of refuge' to be anchored in western Irish harbours, the preparation of food and arms depots and recruitment of more troops.[16] He was relieved when 24 Irish magistrates were dismissed for attending repeal meetings.

Piles of newspaper cuttings on these meetings reached him and for once he listened to the gentlemen of the press. Under O'Connell the Irish were becoming damned impertinent and their power of evoking laughter was particularly irritating to the British Government. So Ireland was to be sent more troops by Wellington, jeered O'Connell in a speech. All right. They would find nobody to fight with. Repealers were not going to fight. 'They knew a trick worth two of that.' (Laughter.) An account of a disrespectful priest, Father O'Keefe, came to the Duke from Kilkenny. At an enquiry into election frauds, an anti-Nationalist claimed that his voting-paper had been defaced and his initials put opposite the wrong candidate by a Nationalist. Father O'Keefe, a Nationalist witness, suggested it had been done by a friend of the plaintiff hiding under his bed. (Laughter.)

Chairman: 'An exceedingly unhandsome expression; particularly when coming from a person in the garb of a clergyman.'

Fr O'Keefe: 'Perhaps his wife signed it.'

Plaintiff: 'My wife can't write.' (More laughter.)

Prosecutor: 'What I propose to do is to give evidence of the state the paper was in. . . .

Fr O'Keefe: 'I am sure you'd get anything sworn.' (Some cries of 'Shame!')

Prosecutor: 'Does the Reverend gentleman think that I would be guilty of subornation, of perjury?'

Fr O'Keefe: 'I don't say so – Oh no; but I know – ' (Laughter).

Chairman: 'You'll please be silent, sir.'

Fr O'Keefe: 'I'm dumb.' (*Loud laughter*).

As O'Connell's huge Cork meeting assembled in Mill Street the Rev. John Mangan, a Protestant whose house overlooked the multitude, frantically seized a pen and dashed off an entreaty to

Wellington for two hundred soldiers to fill the empty barracks. CRASH. 'I am glad to be able to add,' wrote Mangan, 'that the Platform has just given way and there is a general upset among the orators. . . .'[17]

At first Graham thanked the Duke over and over again for his energy and resourcefulness. What would the Cabinet have done in this crisis without him? But as the summer wore on and there was no organized rebellion, they began to find Wellington's letters alarmist. Even at Cork, despite shouts of 'Ireland for the Irish!' and 'Repeal or Blood!', O'Connell gave the toast of the Queen. The truth was that repeal did not yet mean separation. Britain still had many years in which to save the connection with the Crown by an offer of Home Rule and land reform.

Passionately defending his military preparations, the Duke wrote: 'This is a better course than to sit down and cry out they are Alarmist! I have some practice & experience; and I avow that upon the subject of Ireland, I am the principal Alarmist! . . . If a Misfortune shall occur such as that in . . . 1798 we should be eternally disgraced!' This outburst took place at the end of July 1843. Within two months the Cabinet were again perturbed by signs of even fiercer activity at the Horse Guards.

'From something which fell from Arbuthnot,' wrote Graham to Peel on 16 September, 'I begin to suspect that the Duke wishes to go to Ireland, and believes that the winds and the waves will obey him, and that in his presence there will be a great calm.'[18] O'Connell was in fact working up for his most formidable of all monster meetings, to take place at Clontarf, near Dublin, on 8 October. Long ago in 1821 the Duke had declined to go to Ireland as Lord-Lieutenant: it would be using a big gun, he said then, to shoot a sparrow. But was it not now high time for the big gun? Should he not act like Cornwallis, go to Dublin as military and civil governor combined and end the '43 Rebellion about to break out at Clontarf?

'The Duke for Ireland' was not a slogan which attracted Peel. That great gun must not speak unless there were a mutiny or actual rising. But if the Duke could not go to Clontarf, O'Connell and his million men should not go there either. At the last minute the Cabinet issued a proclamation banning the Clontarf meeting. Six days later, on the 14th, Daniel O'Connell was arrested and condemned by a packed jury to a year's imprisonment and a fine of £2,000. Though the House of Lords later quashed the sentence by four to one (Brougham being that vengeful one) it is said that the six months which O'Connell served in prison began his break-up.

His imprisonment also broke the spell of infallibility which he had cast over Ireland. The Liberator liberated could indeed be signalized by processions and rejoicing; but why had he ever been captured? His health deteriorated, and when the next lethal blow struck a million of his countrymen, he too was dying.

*

Once O'Connell was in gaol, the Cabinet policy of reconciliation seemed for a few months to stand a chance. The common people might still print (very badly) and sing a new ballad, but it smacked of hope deferred:

> *Cheer up brave boyes from slumbers awaken*
> *As the Prophet decreed they are at a ful Period*
> *They will be conquered without cannon or baynot,*
> *As Goliah was conquered at the hands of king david.*

The Duke warmly supported Peel's remedial measures for 1844–5 affecting land and education: the Devon Commission to examine landlord–tenant laws, and proposals among others to increase the grant to Maynooth College, where the Irish Catholic clergy were educated. 'You could not do otherwise than appoint a Commission,' wrote the Duke to Peel of the Devon Commission; in Northern Ireland the law of 'Tenant right' was held to provide some protection against eviction. Not so in the South. As regards Maynooth, Wellington spoke up strongly for the increased grant. If it had been right last century to endow Maynooth at all, it was right to endow it reasonably now. Was £112 per annum a reasonable salary for its professors? It was less than we paid to a clerk. How much did the Duke of Newcastle (as usual a violent opponent) wish to economize on these poor people, the students, five hundred young men who were to be the religious instructors of six million Roman Catholics? 'Are you to put two or three in a bed?' Not only was it reasonable to raise the grant, 'there is a great Christian principle involved in it – . . . not to persecute the weak'.[19]

Nevertheless the Duke had his work cut out to prevent the

party whip, Lord Redesdale, from resigning on Maynooth. In the Commons, Peel was unable to prevent Gladstone, his right-hand man in financial reforms, from doing so. Always scrupulous, Gladstone could not forget his recent book (1841) damning Catholic subsidies as vicious. Though he now considered Peel's proposals right, it would not be right for him to support Peel except from the back benches. It can have been no consolation to Peel that he himself had very nearly done the same thing to Wellington over Catholic emancipation.

*

The news about the potatoes arrived during the first half of October 1845. In retrospect it seems a macabre irony that only a fortnight earlier the Duke had been indulging one of his impulses for martial law, to put down the large-scale rejoicings which had followed O'Connell's release from gaol. (They were not meetings now so much as shows – an excuse for O'Connell's supporters to deck themselves out ever more lavishly in plumes, green and white velvet, golden mottoes.) The evil tidings of October turned the idea of martial law into a sad charade.

Peel sent his dire news to Wellington on the 15th. The Irish potato crop was a failure. A strange potato disease had already appeared in the south of England that summer and in North America three years earlier. The difference was that English and American potatoes were food; Irish potatoes were the only food. Loss of a potato crop anywhere meant suffering; in Ireland it meant a hurricane of hunger. Lord Wellesley had once found his Irish marquessate, given as a reward for his services in India, a pitiful thing, a mere 'gilt potato'. To the Irish peasant his potato was truly gilded with the blessing of life itself. When his potato turned black, then indeed life in Ireland would be a pitiful thing.

The tone of Peel's letter to the Duke conveyed a sense of emergency:

The accounts of the failure of the Potato Crop in Ireland are very alarming. The Disease appears to be very prevalent, – and – the loss of food – where it does prevail – to be very great. . . . We shall have to give the subject very early and very serious Consideration.

He had already told the Home Secretary and Lord-Lieutenant just what he was considering – complete repeal of the Corn Laws in order that cheap grain might enter famine-stricken Ireland:

'The removal of impediments to import is the only effectual remedy.'[20]

Perhaps because the Duke was leader of the landed aristocracy who lived and moved and had their being in the Corn Laws, Peel did not yet mention to him their repeal. But others did. A letter reached him almost at once from Belfast, written in the accents of doom which few outside Ireland as yet found appropriate:

Potatoes!

Read – for the sake of the country Read. . . . No man can stop the disease; nor can any man be certain that a single tuber will remain in the island at the end of a few months! In this lies the terrific danger – The RISK is absolutely appalling. *Two thirds* at least of the peasantry have nothing – absolutely NOTHING, to depend on for existence save the potatoes. . . . If their potatoes decay they must die by the Million.

You my lord duke are far too wise & humane to incur so unheard of a RISK – you will open the ports for provisions. . . .[21]

The Duke was aware of the appalling 'RISK' (in well-justified capital letters) to Ireland. Two years earlier he had called the Lords' attention to its two million paupers – a quarter of the population* – and he had often predicted disaster in case of total crop-failure, unless the tenants' condition of labour was changed. He put their possible quandary to Peel in three sentences on 17 October. 'The potato crop fails. What is to become of their bargain? The labourer bound to give his labour must starve.'[22]

A distinctly apocalyptic note had begun to sound in some of the Duke's information about Ireland. There was the mysterious paper picked up on an exhausted carrier pigeon by a London station-master, despatched to the Duke from the 'Isle of Ichabod'. Could it be Ireland? *Ichabod* meant 'the glory is departed'. Then there was the Protestant Association of Exeter Hall, with their pamphlet entitled 'The New Interpretation of the Apocalypse'. Daniel O'Connell was to wade through Protestant blood towards that horrific event. 'POPERY the ENEMY of GOD and MAN,' screamed the handbills at 2s a hundred, 'STARTLING FACTS.' The facts about the potato blight were more than startling. If poor old Dan himself was not to ride again, the Four Horsemen were all in the saddle. Conquest, Slaughter, Judgement and Death by famine and pestilence.

Peel's first prompt public step was to call in the aid of science to

* In a speech on 14 July 1843. The true figure was probably even higher.

combat the disease. He asked Dr Lyon Playfair, the chemist, and Professor Lindley, the botanist, to go to Dublin and examine the prospects. Their verdict on the present crop, the Duke heard from Graham, was very unfavourable and anticipation for the future hardly less gloomy. The Duke contributed to botanical research by forwarding an alleged discovery made by Thomas Ingram in the royal garden at Windsor: if potatoes were steeped in lime-water, they did not decay. Lime-water was in fact irrelevant, but it would be interesting to know whether the Duke was ever in touch with the one man in England who knew the truth about the disease but could not prove it. This was the Rev. M. J. Berkeley, the perpetual curate of Wood Newton and Apethorpe, Northamptonshire, and therefore the close neighbour of Wellington's Arbuthnot and Westmorland circle. The clever country parson was convinced that the blight was caused by a fungus but his guess was not substantiated until the following century.*

Privately the Duke was assailed by propaganda from Protestant Irish sources, to the effect that the disaster was a put-up job by Nationalists and Leaguers: 'The Potato Famine is only a means to an end,' reported Lord Glengall. Another informant suggested the Jesuits were exhorting their flocks to let their potatoes rot, eat their corn if they had any instead of selling it, and pay no rent.[23] The Duke did not fall for this. At the same time he began to doubt whether drastic remedies were yet necessary.

Peel's mind, as has been seen, was already made up. Though he and his Cabinet decided at an emergency meeting on 31 October to spend many thousands of pounds on Irish famine relief and public works, these measures to Peel were mere palliatives. He never deviated from his first instinct that the ports must be opened. He had publicly travelled far along the free trade road during his two great budgets; Cobden's arguments in Parliament had carried him privately the rest of the way. In any case, he had intended to abolish the Corn Laws within a year or two. In the present crisis he could not wait six months. Nevertheless he was tragically unable to match his powers of persuasion to his sense of urgency.

Throughout November he consulted, but far from pushed, his Cabinet colleagues. With Lord John Russell's recent public conversion to free trade ringing in his ears, he sent a definitive memorandum on 29 November. A covering note with the Duke's copy,

* Woodham-Smith, Chapter v. The fungus was *Phytophthora infestans*.

however, still applied surprisingly modest pressure. In advising the suspension of the existing Corn Law for a limited period, Peel wrote: 'I will not ask you to express any opinion on the subject in returning this Paper. I only ask you to have the kindness to read it' – and to let him have it back.[24]

The memorandum itself, like all his others, made little attempt to convert the doubters, and its pedantic tone greatly irritated opponents. 'Shall we modify the Corn Law, shall we maintain it, or shall we suspend it for a limited period?' was Peel's routine formula, followed by his own recommendation of suspension.* The Duke was always urging his friends to wait patiently and see exactly what measures Peel would adopt.

His own answer to the memorandum was the most important and forthright Peel received. The Duke was against repeal of the Corn Laws but was more against a split. While unconvinced by Peel's arguments, he promised faithfully to support Peel's action. Reluctantly a majority of the Cabinet took the same decision. Two stood out. Lord Stanley and the Duke of Buccleuch stuck to protection. Stanley, indeed, criticized the Duke's logic with some asperity: 'He talked of supporting the Queen's Government, in measures of which he disapproved, as if he were not a member of the Government which is to be supported.'[25] Such a course, muttered Stanley, could hardly be adopted by anyone else but the Duke.

Stanley's opposition finished Peel. With this leading figure in the Lords vociferously against him and his Cabinet colleagues in the Commons lukewarm, he felt his mission to repeal the Corn Laws hopeless. On 6 December his resignation was accepted by the Queen at Osborne. He had behaved with absolute honesty towards his colleagues but without the slightest magnetism. From the Duke, however, he had not concealed his acute suffering in reaching the momentous decision on corn, above all his anguish for Ireland. 'I cannot doubt,' wrote the Duke soon afterwards to an incredulous Croker, 'that which passed under my view and frequent observation day after day. I mean Peel's alarm at the

---

* In a skit on these memoranda Peel was supposed to be choosing a costume for a fancy-dress ball, his choices being: 1 To go in fancy-dress; 2 To go in plain clothes; 3 To go naked. He chooses 3 with the proviso, 'I am, I repeat it, compelled on the whole to reserve to myself that unfettered right of entirely concealing . . . the measures which I may think it my duty to tread upon this occasion.'

Consequences to Ireland of the Potato Disease. I never witnessed in any case such Agony!'[26]

*

For three dreadful years every stab of sympathetic 'agony' in England was to be matched by a fresh Irish pang. The ominous new year of 1846 was to bring a recurrence of the disease in new potatoes and signs that relief measures were already inadequate. Yet a false hope that things were mending was wafted to England, where it persuaded many people, Wellington included, that the crisis would disappear with the last rotten potato of 1845. At the same time chronic evils were at work in ever more virulent forms: politicians of all parties addicted to the drug of *laissez-faire* and fearful of State interference; absentee landlords who had sub-let to middlemen and now declined to contribute to relief; evicted peasants whose potato patches were to be converted to more profitable grazing land, shrieking over the ruins of their demolished homes. For one model estate which Thackeray had seen in 1842, full of 'great blue plots of comfortable cabbages', he saw hundreds of women with no food, pulling weeds and nettles from the hedges.[27]

A year after Peel's first 'agony', when the Whigs were once more in power, an open letter to Wellington was to appear in *The Times*. Through him – the Irishman living in England who had done most for Ireland – the British public should be told of the stricken acres now given over wholly to blackened crops and 'famished and ghastly skeletons'.

*

The Queen sent for Lord John Russell, but this was kept a close secret for five days. Meanwhile the press, excited and mystified, produced their own versions of events. On 5 December *The Times* 'electrified' London with a revelation that Parliament was to be summoned in January and the Corn Laws repealed by a unanimous Cabinet, the Duke first bringing forward the measure in the Lords. Two days later the *Sunday Times* published a forged letter from the Duke to 'a zealous Free-Trader' declaring that he had told Sir R. Peel, 'it is not his business or the duke's to repeal the Corn laws but Lord John Russell's and Mr Cobden's'. That this was a clever travesty of the Duke's view became clear within the next few weeks.

The news of the Government's resignation suddenly burst upon the public when the retiring Cabinet travelled to Osborne to surrender their seals. Next day, 12 December, the Queen sent a message to the Duke which was radically to affect his last years. She began by explaining that Lord John was not yet certain whether he could form a ministry.

Whatever the result of his enquiries may be, the Queen has a STRONG *desire* to see the Duke of Wellington remain at the head of her Army. The Queen appeals to the Duke's so often proved loyalty, and attachment to her person in asking him to give her this assurance.[28]

The Duke saw in a flash that this was the boon he had coveted and been denied by Peel for over three years – to command the army free from ties in the Lords. He replied to the Queen by return:

If he were to remain as Commander-in-Chief under the new ministry, he could not 'form a political connection with Lord John Russell as it would be discreditable to both parties'. At the same time he ought not to 'belong to, or to act in concert with, any political parties opposed to the Government'.[29] In other words, he would no longer lead the Conservative Opposition in the Lords. As he had always been partially, so now he would be completely the independent elder statesman.

Meanwhile, what became known as the 'Ten Days' of waiting for Russell, between 10 and 20 December, were spent by Wellington in writing enormous letters to his bewildered friends. In answer to Lord Redesdale, the whip, who asked at great length for guidance, the Duke replied on the 16th with five pages analysing the 'most lamentable' situation. Why this general movement in the country towards free trade? Because the Reform Act of 1832 substituted for independent M.P.s others dependent on some party or faction 'professing political, or religious, or commercial or agricultural or factory or mine working opinion', and these sectional interests fed the press and were in turn nourished by it. Result, political leadership since 1832 was very difficult. What would he do himself? Leave the Lords to Stanley. As the Duke of Wellington he had never been 'a legitimate party Man'; as Commander-in-Chief 'it is still less necessary that I should become one now'. What about the Cabinet split on the Corn Laws? He believed that the whole Cabinet agreed the Laws must be suspended in the future if there developed in Ireland 'any thing in the shape of famine'. The only disagreement was on the present 'necessity of interference'. On that, members of the Government must form 'their own conscientious judgment'.[30]

From this it is clear that the Duke envisaged no break-up in the Conservative party, but varying degrees of opposition to Russell's Free Trade measure. Such a solution was not to be.

'Another *coup de tonnère* this morning!' wrote Lord Mahon excitedly to the Duke at 2 P.M. on Saturday 20 December. 'Lord John Russell's attempt to form a government is over! . . . What is to follow? I am sure it passes my powers of divination.' If Peel really had a project of total repeal, as Mahon heard, 'he will not find a great many of his party follow him in that course, & *certainly not* your Grace's most faithful & obedient *Mahon*. Nor, as I venture to hope, your Grace yourself!'[31]

The Duke had already that morning received a hurried scrawl from Peel. After having accepted, Lord John had declined to form a government and Peel was summoned to Windsor:

I am going to the Queen – I shall tell her at once, and without hesitation that I will not abandon her – whatever happens. I shall return from Windsor as her Minister – it is necessary that we should have a Cabinet as soon as possible – will you have the goodness to attend a Cabinet in my Room in Downing Street – at nine o'clock this Evening –[32]

The Duke was delighted with Peel's breathless promises of loyalty. Even more chivalrous than he dared hope was his leader's actual confrontation with Queen Victoria.

'So far from taking leave of you, Sir Robert,' began the young Queen, 'I must require you to withdraw your resignation, and to remain in my service.' She then explained that Lord John had failed because of fierce opposition by his colleagues to having Palmerston again as Foreign Secretary. Sir Robert would of course need time for reflection and communication with his friends.

The Prime Minister replied to his Sovereign's appeal with a happy oblivion of colleagues surely unique in the annals of Downing Street.

'I want no consultations, no time for reflection. I will be your Minister, happen what may. I will do without a colleague, rather than leave you in this extremity.'[33]

It might have been the Duke speaking. Perhaps in a sense it was. Peel returned to London confident of success and with no thought for the effects of his own precipitation. At the appointed hour, 9.30 P.M., he faced his colleagues at No. 10 and broke the news. He was Her Majesty's Minister, with or without colleagues; he would take all necessary measures with or without support.

Peel was throwing down a gage. Dead silence fell. The Duke waited for Stanley to speak first. Stanley picked up the gage and announced his unaltered decision to resign. He believed in protection and saw no necessity to interfere with the Corn Law. Then it was time for the Duke to spur forward: 'It was not a question of measures,' he said, 'but of Government, of support of the Queen.' Though the Duke of Buccleuch echoed Stanley, all the rest, with whatever foreboding, followed Wellington's lead.[34] The extraordinary scene was rounded off two days later by a euphoric letter from Peel, still exalted by his sudden awakening from a fortnight's bad dream. He rejoiced to inform the Duke that he had persuaded Buccleuch to remain in office and Gladstone to enter the Cabinet as Colonial Secretary: 'a good beginning'.[35] It was a good beginning of the end.

*

'The Duke says, "rotten potatoes have done it all; they have put Peel in his d—d fright"; and both for the *cause* and the effect he seems to feel equal contempt.'[36] So wrote Greville at the time when illusory hopes were rising. Nevertheless the Duke spent the whole interval between 20 December and 27 January, when Peel was to address Parliament on repeal of the Corn Laws, in trying to quell with his indefatigable pen the Tory mutineers and doubters – Redesdale, Beaufort, Croker, Salisbury, Rutland; some of them with three, four and five letters apiece. Redesdale was told that the Queen had to choose between Peel and Cobden, Russell having failed her. 'We are very sick!' he said honestly. 'God send us a good deliverance.'

Redesdale refused to help send it. He resigned as whip and sent the Duke a scorpion of a message on Christmas Day: 'Better that we should go into opposition than cut our throats.' Of course we must examine everything, retorted the Duke. 'But I do not at once declare against a Man who says to his Queen, Happen what may, I will stand by you. . . .' It was Peel's duty 'to rescue the lady from Cobden'.[37]

Wellington's relative, the Duke of Beaufort, was given a summary of all the issues, concluding that improvements in domestic agriculture would soon in any case enable the Corn Laws to be safely repealed; 'I would likewise beg you to observe, that the Provisions of the Corn Law however interesting are not the only interest of this great Country.'[38]

Croker, a more damaging critic because a contributor to the *Quarterly*, attacked the Duke's attitude with increasing vehemence: 'Whatever broke you upon the *10th* Decr. was equally in force when you reunited on the *20th*. This is *my guess* but I don't ask *yours*.' Croker's guess was right. Corn had split them then and still did. He passionately urged his Grace to give up the key of his Cabinet boxes and let Peel face the music. 'But – ' continued Croker, 'then you ask Where is a Government to be found? I reply – Let Peel answer *that*. Let him make a Government of *those who agree in his opinions*.' The voice of the Duke's old friend had become uncommonly rasping, especially about the Cabinet key. There was only one possible answer for the Duke to make: 'I am the retained Servant of the Sovereign of this Empire.'[39]

It was a pleasanter duty to write pages and pages for Lord Salisbury's guidance on Ireland, discussing public works, a market economy and imported maize, with a copy and covering letter for the Duke of Rutland. He reminded Rutland encouragingly of their Sunday morning walks when 'you and I generally take the same view of political Questions'. His message for all of them now was to have patience until Peel spoke in the new year. As long as Peel enjoyed the Queen's and the public's confidence he must be supported. 'A good Government is more important than Corn Laws.'[40]

*

Parliament met at last. On 26 January Wellington extolled in the Lords a Prime Minister who next day shone magnificently in the Commons. Showing Peel in the light of what the Duke afterwards called 'a warm-hearted enthusiast', he based his leader's claim to support on that leader's own support for the Queen. The magic word 'enthusiasm' to explain Peel's behaviour had first come to the Duke while rebutting one of Croker's vicious attacks: 'A movement of Enthusiasm induced Sir Robert Peel when sent for, to determine, before he saw the Queen that if required he would would stand by her, even alone. . . . ' 'I participated of this,' added the Duke.[41] Pleased with his idea, he drew Lady Wilton's attention to the pleasure it had also given Sir Robert:

You will be amused by my representing Him to the House a warm-hearted Enthusiast! He is much pleased with what I said, has written to me, and Lady Peel has called upon me this morning, and in tears assured me that what I said had the same Impression upon Him as what I said upon Talleyrand in the House of Lords some years ago had upon *Him*! *[42]

For the next four months, while the slow course of politics contrasted with the gathering disaster in Ireland, Wellington followed his path of duty: in public fanatically loyal to Peel, in private deeply disturbed about the party. 'I am very apprehensive that a great Mistake has been made,' he wrote to Lady Wilton on 9 February, 'though we are not told.'[43] Not told . . . There again was the old trouble of Peel's deep-seated inability to communicate. 'At all events,' he continued, 'I am certain that a Party mistake has been made, and that if we continue to be a Government we shall be without support.' Resignations were in fact pouring in. Despite this, the Duke expected the Commons to carry Corn Law repeal. Of the Lords he was profoundly doubtful.

The least he could do, therefore, was to try to win over Lord Stanley, since he was the focus of disaffection in the Lords. Admired as 'the cleverest eldest son for a hundred years', Stanley happened also to be one of the wealthiest. In these two capacities he was a natural cynosure for anxious Conservative eyes. It was he who opened the private argument with Wellington on 18 February, tackling him on Peel's leadership. Peel had 'completely dislocated and shattered the great Conservative party in both Houses'; he would never lead a united party again and there was no other leader in the Commons. But there was still the Duke. Though even his 'great name and influence' would not carry Peel's Corn Bill through the Lords, he was the party's natural leader. Stanley's personal tribute to the Duke would consist in repelling all entreaties by the Ultras to lead a faction against him.[44]

So far so good. Stanley already neutralized by reverence was

* When the Duke, in September 1831, said no man's character, public or private, had ever been so much belied as Talleyrand's, the old sinner wept. He added, according to Lady Salisbury, '*C'est le seul homme qui a jamais dit du bien de moi*' – 'He is the only man who has ever spoken a good word of me.' (Burghclere, p. 331, 17 December 1851.)

something. The Duke, however, hoped for his conversion. He replied next day, agreeing that Peel's influence was probably diminished for ever but he demolished the idea of himself leading the party, or even continuing to lead the Lords, in a typically curt and unexplained aside:

It is not easy to account for my being in the situation which I have so long filled in the House of Lords. Its commencement was merely accidental.

Finally he invoked with an intellectual vigour which would have been commendable in a much younger man a pair of powerful new arguments calculated to sway Stanley. First, he had always used his influence to prevent a collision between the two Houses; repeal of the Corn Law would get its second reading in the Commons – it did so, eight days later, on 27 February – and must not be frustrated by the Lords. Second, his policy would prevent conflict not only between the two Houses but between two classes, the rich and the poor. The great landed proprietors had a personal interest in protection which could not be concealed.

Here the Duke was probably influenced by Arbuthnot who, as a landowner himself, saw the class issue most vividly: 'The Corn Laws are considered as a class monopoly,' he had written to Peel from Stratfield Saye on 8 January 1846, 'and are thus most detrimental to the aristocracy, and to the landed interest.'[45]

While offering these new thoughts to Stanley, the Duke allowed himself a familiar peroration:

I am the servant of the Crown and People. I have been paid and rewarded, and I consider myself retained. . . .[46]

The Duke failed to convert Stanley. Two or three weeks later, on 8 March, he was elected leader of the protectionist peers. But at least the Duke was instrumental in keeping him quiet except in debate for another four months.[47] And if the Duke did not entirely succeed with Stanley, he may have more than half converted himself – to free trade. Arbuthnot was already a convert. There were many winter evenings in 1846 when the two old friends sat together over the fire, talking . . .

*

Spring came hysterically to the Commons, bursting out in ardent Government striving, violent Ultra execrations and a rush of sap

to Young Ireland and Young England – the former a rival to
O'Connell, the latter a defunct Tory hybrid reborn in 1846,
though without its name, as the creation of Lord George Bentinck's will-power and Disraeli's oratorical genius.

Disraeli's virulence against Peel had been rising for several
years past. At the third reading of the Corn Bill, in the middle of
May 1846, the invective surpassed itself in what Disraeli called
afterwards 'my great speech', torturing Peel, transporting the
Opposition and more than once drawing wicked laughter from
all sides of the House.

It was inevitable that Peel's changes of front, first on the anti-
Catholic laws in 1829, then on protection in 1846, should prove
a sitting target. In circumstances suggestively parallel he had
twice been elected to preserve a principle which he then proceeded
to abandon. He and Wellington had trounced the 'Catholics' on
emancipation and the Leaguers on corn, only to steal their policy
when in power. 'His life has been a great Appropriation Clause,'
said Disraeli, (shouts of laughter and cheers). 'He is a burglar of
others' intellect.' A halt would be called to 'this huckstering
tyranny of the Treasury bench (loud cheers) – these political pedlars that bought their party in the cheapest market, and sold us in
the dearest. (Enthusiastic cheers)'.

The pedlars nonetheless got their majority of ninety-eight for
repeal of the Corn Laws on 15 May 1846. Within a fortnight the
bill was before the Lords for the second reading.

Stanley, living up to his romantic label, showed himself a true
'Rupert of debate'. In replying to him, it was not a counter-stroke
by cavalry which the Duke hoped to produce, but the familiar
impregnable square. He began by briefly recapitulating the obligations he had felt in December last – his double duty to Peel and
the Queen. Then he entered his square.

My Lords, it is not necessary that I should say more on that subject.
I am aware that I address your Lordships at present with all your
prejudices against me for having adopted the course I then took – a
course which however . . . if it was to be adopted tomorrow, I should
take again.

I am in Her Majesty's service – bound to Her Majesty and to the
Sovereigns of this country by considerations of gratitude of which it is
not necessary that I should say more to your Lordships.

Perhaps he ought not to be connected with any party. 'Be it so, my Lords, be it so, if you think proper.' But if he never addressed them again he would give them this advice. Let them remember that he once before made them change their vote. What was the position this time? A bill had come up from the Commons, passed by a majority there and recommended by the Crown. If it were rejected, the Lords would stand alone.

He had spoken for some eight minutes, Suddenly the pace changed. The square had formed into line and it was time for the advance:

Now that, my Lords, is a situation in which, I beg to remind your Lordships, I have frequently stated you ought not to stand; it is a position in which you cannot stand, because you are entirely powerless; without the House of Commons and the Crown the House of Lords can do nothing. You have vast influence on public opinion; you have great confidence in your own principles but without the Crown or the House of Commons you can do nothing – till the connection with the House of Commons is revived, there is an end of the functions of the House of Lords.

In fact it was rightabout face, as Lord Clarendon had once said over emancipation, rightabout face with Peel or nothing. 'Attention, my Lords! Rightabout face! quick march!'

At 4.30 A.M. on the morning of 28 May 1846 the 'Contents' to the number of 211 marched out to record their votes, while only 164 'Not Contents' remained with their feet firmly under their seats: a majority of 47.* It was not the last speech the Duke made to their lordships, but it was in many ways the finest. In a matter of fifteen minutes he had routed Stanley and shown them clearly what they most needed to see – themselves.

As the Duke left the House in the bright light of the summer morning some early workers collected to hear the result. When they saw him they cheered with relief and gratitude, crowding round the old warrior.

'God bless you, Duke!'

'For Heaven's sake, people, let me get to my horse!'[48]

*

He was right not to celebrate. Retribution came to his party in less than a month.

* The present procedure of both sides going below the Bar to vote was not adopted until 1857.

In Ireland, agrarian crime had followed in the wake of hunger and destitution. It was feared that desperate peasants would kill the landlords whose rent they could not pay. Peel introduced yet another Coercion Bill. At the beginning of the year he had had the support of almost all M.P.s but the Irish. Now it was different.

Young Ireland and old Dan, young Dizzy and Bentinck, case-hardened Whigs and inveterate Tories – but especially the old ultra-Tories – combined against the political 'pedlars' who they believed had sold their party to the highest bidder, to the anti-Corn Law mob. Only Cobden and the Conservatives could be relied on.

Peel and the Duke both saw defeat coming on coercion.* The Duke's blood was up. Why not strike the first blow, he suggested, and take a vote of confidence on some popular but minor issue? If defeated Peel could go to the country on his record. 'I would not allow this blackguard combination to break up the Government,' he wrote fiercely to Peel on 8 June. 'I would prefer to dissolve the Parliament. You would then take the bull by the horns, and if your Government is to fall it will at least fall with honour.'[49]

This bizarre device was no good to Peel. It might affront the Commons. Worse still, if it failed he would fall, not without honour perhaps, but certainly without his precious Corn Bill. For the third reading of the Corn Bill in the Lords was not due until 25 June – the same date on which the Coercion Bill would come up in the Commons for second reading. In deploying his arguments against the Duke, Peel's paragraphs had a weary, hopeless ring as if he foresaw the end of his Government.

Everything happened as the Duke feared. The Corn Bill went through the Lords and Coercion was beaten in the Commons a few hours later.

'They say we are beaten by seventy-three,' whispered Graham into the Prime Minister's ear, as he waited on the Treasury bench after the vote.[50] Peel did not speak or even look round. He merely stuck out his chin, as politicians do in anger, and as Aberdeen had done sixteen years earlier after the Duke's speech on reform.

* The element of force in coercion always made the introduction of such bills in Britain controversial. Throughout the nineteenth century governments of both the 'right' and the 'left' felt it necessary to resort at times to coercion for Ireland.

Then, as now, the Government had been brought down by ultra-Tories taking their revenge. Now, as then, the Prime Minister had made a mistake. What was Peel's?

A last-minute tactical error? Ought he to have brought forward coercion before corn, to make sure of both? But the Opposition were out to get him by then and would have got him somehow. Was he broken by Disraeli's philippics, as Canning had been by the old Tories? He certainly had little fight left in him by June. Or was it the mistake of allowing John Russell to manoeuvre him into introducing controversial legislation with a split party? – the 'poisoned chalice' of Disraeli's suitably Borgia-like phrase. Peel had been under no necessity to accept. He could have insisted on leaving the chalice in Russell's hands, confident that the trouble over Palmerston would be surmounted, as it duly was half a year later.

But what if Peel was in fact under a psychological necessity, a glorious compulsion to accept? There was the Queen. There was that 'movement of enthusiasm'. The Duke had been the first to recognize it and indeed had participated in it. If that was the mistake, the poisoned chalice had been handed back by Queen Victoria herself to her two servants, now both 'retained'. Fortunately the draught injured neither of them, at least with posterity. Each has survived with his reputation for courage and patriotism enhanced.

But the old political party of Pitt, Liverpool, Canning, Wellington and Peel was poisoned beyond recovery.

24

Strange Times

The affair of the 'Archduke' seemed to Wellington a poor reward for services rendered after his party's fall in summer 1846.

The new Prime Minister, Russell, had tentatively offered him and other Conservatives places in the Government. They all declined. At the same time Wellington pledged himself to support the Whigs wherever possible. Similarly when the Queen repeated her request of last December that he should continue as Commander-in-Chief, he accepted with the proviso that he should no longer act as a party leader in the Lords. It was therefore with intense annoyance that he heard of a proposal to remove to some other site the new equestrian statue of himself recently installed upon the Decimus Burton triumphal arch opposite Apsley House.

The moment the colossal bronze by Matthew Cotes Wyatt had been hoisted aloft – all forty tons of it – and facetiously christened the 'Archduke', an outcry was raised by the art world. Burton, who had designed his arch for a four-horse chariot, declared that this 'Archduke' would be made to look ridiculous. Others bluntly said it was ridiculous anyway. Particularly distasteful to admirers of Copenhagen, the Duke's late Waterloo charger (died 1836), was Wyatt's bronze horse modelled from an animal named Rosemary. If rosemary was for remembrance, this Rosemary did not remind them of Copenhagen, especially about the ears. The best place for it, suggested Lord Strangford, the 'Coningsby' of Disraeli's novel, was the bed of the Serpentine.

Up till November the unfortunate Duke had behaved with exemplary restraint. Having decided from the project's inception to regard himself as a defunct hero in whose memory a statue was being erected – 'Upon that subject I am *Dead*!'[1] – he had steadily refused to become embroiled in any controversies. But when the

Queen and Prince Consort left Windsor for London at 9 A.M. on 7 November expressly to veto the site, his defence mechanism went into action. The dispute, he decided, was not about art but about men; not the Archduke but the Duke of Wellington. Not only the Whigs but Her Majesty also wished to degrade and disgrace him

Perhaps in reality she was as startled to see his long nose from the windows of her house as the young man in *Punch*. Not that she could see it clearly. First it was hidden by a 'forest of black deformity', as someone called the scaffolding; then during its fortnight's trial by a black November fog.

By December the Duke felt he was the victim of universal persecution, as once he had been in youth after Cintra. Eventually his distress signals got through to all concerned in this deplorably mishandled operation. Russell wrote to the Queen that the Duke's feelings formed 'the best grounds for retaining the statue as an eye-sore in its present position'. The Queen wrote to Wellington that she had countermanded removal, though she would have hoped he knew her too well to doubt her affection. Wellington wrote to the Queen that he was ashamed at troubling her by anything so insignificant as a statue of himself! all the same, its removal would have been misinterpreted.[2]

The statue remained on the Decimus Burton arch until the Duke's death and for thirty years afterwards. Then road-works were announced at Hyde Park Corner, the arch was swivelled round into its present oblique position and later given its four-horse chariot. As for the Archduke, a permanent site was found for it at the British Army camp, Aldershot, on the Round Hill, described as a steep '*kopje*'. South Africa had become the field for British arms and a hill was a *kopje* rather than a 'col', as in the Duke's time. Today man and horse still tower above their thick green coverts, dominant and sleek.

Meanwhile in 1888 a new equestrian statue, by Sir Edgar Boehm, had been set on a pedestal opposite Apsley House where it has continued to stand ever since, the bronze Duke gazing into the windows of his old home but no longer, as did his predecessor, casting a monumental shadow at certain times of day across its austere façade.

*

Command of the army from 1842 onwards undoubtedly gave the Duke a much-needed lift. His renewed vitality took everybody by surprise. 'Nothing is more extraordinary than the complete restoration of that vigour of mind which for the last two or three years was visibly impaired,' wrote Greville on 19 March 1843. 'His speeches this session have been as good if not better than any he ever made.'

Towards the end of that year he was a guest of the Duke of Rutland at Belvoir Castle during a royal visit. An account written up for Prince Albert by his secretary included the sentence: 'The Duke of Wellington was up and walking in the grounds before seven o'clock this morning.' (As the date was 6 December the Duke's promenade must have taken place in darkness.) That same afternoon, added the Prince's secretary, the 'illustrious hero' mounted his hunter and when Lord Charles Manners, the Duke of Rutland's son, offered to show him the way over a strange countryside, the hero answered: 'I am now seventy-five years old, I never yet wanted anyone to show me my way, & I don't now.'[3]

As Peel well knew, political bias over army promotions would never be the Duke's trouble. Aristocratical bias was the nearest he got, as over the Generals Londonderry and Cardigan who the Duke said needed a Commander-in-Chief all to themselves. Lord Cardigan's disgraceful and insulting behaviour towards his subordinate officers in the 11th Hussars was notorious. Why did not the Duke sweep this tormentor away? He could not stand Cardigan. Indeed in sending a plea through the Adjutant-General that Cardigan should carry out regulations 'in a spirit of Conciliation and indulgence', he penned one paragraph which the Adjutant-General felt constrained to omit. 'I must add,' wrote the Duke, 'that it will be quite a pleasing occupation to command the Army, if I am to have many such Commanding officers as Lord Cardigan!!!'[4] When in 1837 Cardigan had badgered him for a post in the Royal Household, the Duke snubbed him with the reply that he had no claim whatever, never having seen active service. That he never would see it was probably the Duke's belief. Could he have divined the extraordinary circumstances of 1854, with Britain allied to France fighting Russia in the Crimea and 'his Lordship' holding high command, he would certainly have moved him. But in the conditions of his time, the Duke felt that to deprive a great aristocrat of his regiment would shake the old hierarchical principle before another one was fully acceptable in its place.

Towards the end of the Duke's life Cardigan was told for the last time that manners between gentlemen must be 'gentle, without asperity or appearance of violent temper'.[5] The Duke positively entreated Cardigan to drop his haughty tone, otherwise he would order him to remain permanently in his HQ. He only wrote thus, the Duke explained, so that the public might not be deprived of his Lordship's 'military qualities' – qualities which were to be disastrously demonstrated in the Crimea at the Charge of the Light Brigade.

In keeping Cardigan, the Duke's attitude was admittedly out of date; his reaction towards the discovery of widespread 'Sodomitical Practices' at a military academy was eminently civilized. He agreed that the parents should be requested individually to withdraw their sons under a pledge of 'inviolable secrecy'. This would best serve the public interest and be least severe on the youths.*[6]

Within the officer class, the Duke believed in promotion by merit. He had appointed a colonel named Sale over the heads of various generals to the colonelcy of his old regiment, the 33rd Foot. When an intermediary asked what answer he could give to the angry generals, the Duke replied:

'My answer is, "go & do likewise".'[7]

*

Not for Cardigan alone, however, but for the army's general unpreparedness to face the Crimean War, must Wellington bear a heavy responsibility, since he was Commander-in-Chief for ten out of the twelve preceding years. The failure of this former master of detail and miracle of foresight was due to a variety of causes. He was old. He suffered from a historical hangover, shared by many other people, which made him see the British Army as an anomaly:

It is an exotic in England; unknown to the old constitution of the

---

* In 1818 he had interceded for a Captain Swinburne of the 93rd, who was blackmailed by two soldiers for unnatural practices. The Duke considered the evidence dubious, adding, 'He is so good an officer . . . I could wish it were possible to save him.' (Wellington to General Towers, 30 June 1818; Maggs Bros Catalogue 927, November 1970.)

country; required only for the defence of its foreign possessions; disliked by the inhabitants, and particularly by the higher orders, some of whom never allow their families to serve in it.[8]

This 'exotic' must therefore be careful not to obtrude itself upon the notice of Parliament or the public with Prussian-type plans for its own advancement. It should be seen as little as possible and heard not at all.

There was also the national drive for economy ever since Waterloo, which prevented him from saving the Royal Waggon Train from disbandment: one of the gravest losses to Crimean soldiers.

Again, his innate conservatism affected his thought on all subjects, from the officer class to specialized and scientific training. His lifelong conviction that officers should begin with an all-round 'gentleman's education' like civilians, before attending one of the military colleges, was admirable within its assumptions; and Wellington College, the public school founded in his honour, was a most fitting memorial to him. Nevertheless Wellington, even within the assumptions of the time, tended to overvalue the 'gentlemanly' side of an officer's education compared with the technical, which he sometimes feared might attract the wrong kind of candidate. This applied especially to the artillery and engineers.

In straightforward infantry training he was not an innovator like Sir John Moore. Nor, if he had lived in the next century, would he necessarily have been the first general to insist on the revolutionary tank. Nelson was not interested in a new gun sight offered by the Admiralty for trial and report. Wellington brought his genius to preparing and fighting a battle with an unbeatable combination of action and character. But once the hero himself has departed, his legacy of 'steady troops' despite everything at the Alma or Balaclava, is easily forgotten, while the deplorable examples of top-ranking 'officers and gentlemen' are vividly remembered as an all but lethal bequest. Having remembered them, no one can doubt that the old Duke should have retired earlier, taking not a few of his generals with him. As his descendant, the 7th Duke, has written with understanding and pungency:

The incompetence shown during the Crimean War is often with some justification laid at his door. No man should ever cling to a job when he is too old, and no one will ever tell him when that moment arrives.[9]

Finally there was a paradox. The very intensity of his obsession with the country's defencelessness during his last ten years forbade him to risk inventions and new ideas where old, tried methods were available.

*

Continued anxiety over the army's numerical strength drove the Duke into his most serious political controversy during the 1840s. The worrying which was characteristic of an old man and which had nagged him on and off since the thirties now got a firm grip. There were always France and Ireland to agitate him and he had often exasperated Peel with demands for an increased army budget, or for more ships, since the country was not genuinely 'at Peace'.[10] Walking on the 'platform' between the battlements and walls of Walmer Castle, he could see the French coast only too clearly. Suddenly a nightmare vision would flicker before him. 'I see exactly what the danger is; I am as certain of it as if it was passing under my view!'[11] On some brilliant morning the French invasion fleet, powered by that treacherous newcomer steam, which the Duke for reasons unknown imagined had made all navies equal, would land on Britain's south coast. Dazzled by the eastern sun, people would not at first notice them. With half an hour's start they would do anything, get anywhere. It would be too late for retaliation. What 'irretrievable disgrace' to an old soldier!

Then would come a steadying letter from Peel and the burden would lift a little. He had done his duty in protesting. Peel's was now the responsibility: 'You must decide the rest.'[12]

By August 1845 different nightmares had begun to afflict Peel also, not of invasion but of strain, overwork and perils of all kinds. As the latest fracas with Wellington subsided, the exhausted Peel enumerated to the sympathetic Arbuthnot a long list of his public burdens in the very tone and words of the costermonger's donkey. Somehow, he ended, these difficulties must be solved. 'The failure of the mind is the usual way, as we know from sad experience.' Was there to be another Castlereagh? Meanwhile Arbuthnot reminded Peel that the Duke's uneasiness had been preying on *his* mind also: 'but I am certain it is not necessary for me to say that you will ever find him, heart and soul, most anxious to lend you all the aid in his power.'[13] Every aid, except to remain silent about the country's defences. This was not in the Duke's power.

That autumn he had most of his colleagues, especially Peel, Aberdeen and Graham, chattering with rage over defence. Aberdeen, the Foreign Secretary, had formed his *entente cordiale* with Louis Philippe and dreaded the effect of new coastal defences glowering across the Channel at France. The Duke's fears of the French seemed to Aberdeen 'chimerical' and 'stultifying our foreign policy'.[14] To the Duke, the problem existed in reverse: Britain's foreign policy was being stultified by her defencelessness.

There were the Spanish marriages, for instance, by which Louis Philippe intended to get a firm dynastic grip on Spain. Despite the provocation, the Duke could not advise the new Whig Government of 1846 to resist the pretences of Louis Philippe and his sons. 'I must first see the country in a reasonable state of defence.'[15] Nor had he approved of the conditions in which Queen Victoria was previously allowed to do her favourite globe-trotting. She visited Brussels without seeing Waterloo. The British residents would not like this, observed the Duke. As for her being the guest of Louis Philippe at Eu in France for an *entente cordiale* beside the sea, that would inevitably be seized upon by the caricaturists. Britannia in a bathing-machine.

One way, however, in which the Duke as Commander-in-Chief could aid his political leaders, as Arbuthnot had promised, was by preventing waste of public money in the army. And what was so wasteful as military inventions? 'I have therefore taken the course of leaving Inventions & Inventors to themselves,' he once said, believing most inventions were fakes designed to defraud the public. He could not help rejoicing when Samuel Alfred Warner, inventor of a long-range secret weapon, failed miserably. Warner claimed his shell would hit a specified tree eight miles away on a testing ground. It travelled under three miles. 'It is quite delightful,' wrote the Duke, 'that one of the Judges of the experiment should have posted himself under the Tree. . . .'[16] Just the place the Duke would have chosen for himself.

Perhaps another inventor would also have come to grief if he had been tested. The Rev. Patrick Brontë wrote from Haworth Parsonage on 15 November 1841 about his novel sighting device for army muskets. Complete with new *iron* bullets cased in lead, it had already enabled the rector to bring down a flying bird. Of course the Duke had no idea whose father he was addressing when he sent a crushing reply. But if Charlotte ever saw the iron bulletin returned to her papa by her great Duke, she was probably amused.

Field Marshal the Duke of Wellington presents his compliments to Mr. Brontë. . . . He considers it his duty to refrain from interfering in the details of duties over which he has no Controul. . . . Much time would be saved if others would follow the Duke's example. . . .[17]

The Duke did in the end allow the army to be supplied with twenty-eight thousand modern Minié rifles. In the interests of economy, however, he insisted that the bores of the new rifles should be of a calibre which, if necessary, could take the old musket bullets. What was wrong in putting old wine into new bottles? Nor would he let the common soldiers call them rifles: 'We must not allow them to fancy they are all riflemen,' he said, crossing out the word rifle wherever it was used in the training manual, 'or they will become conceited, and be wanting next to be dressed in green, or some other *jack-a-dandy* uniform.'[18] After all, it was what he called 'the infantry of the old stamp', armed with the still older Brown Bess, who had conquered at Waterloo.

*

The affair of the 'Burgoyne Letter' seemed to recapitulate and sum up all the Duke's phobias about defence. The scene for this extraordinary episode was laid in September 1846. Britain was confronted in that month by the spectacle of France's 'Spanish marriages' policy accomplished, despite opposition,* and a famine far worse than the year before in Ireland. Each prospect held a threat to British security. The Duke's voice, which had long been crying in the wilderness, was now echoed by Sir John Burgoyne, Inspector-General of Fortifications, who wrote to the Duke in strong support of his views. On 9 January 1847 the Duke sent Burgoyne in reply a full analysis of Britain's danger. His letter became a delayed-action bomb which suddenly exploded in *The Times* of 1 December 1847. Part of its text was published early the next year in the *Morning Chronicle* with a flattering commentary

---

* Queen Isabella of Spain was married to her allegedly impotent cousin the Duke of Cadiz, while her sister Fernanda married Louis Philippe's son, the Duke of Montpensier.

by Lord Ellesmere (Francis Egerton); the *Annual Register* called it the Great Captain's 'military testament'.

Burgoyne, deeply impressed by his chief's letter, had decided to have it copied but foolishly gave the task of copying to his wife and daughters. The Burgoyne ladies, pleasurably excited, showed their copies around Sussex, not forgetting the Duke's old friend and their neighbour, Lady Shelley. From Maresfield it was an easy leap to London. Lady Shelley gave the text to Lord Ellesmere assuring him the Duke would love to see it published. By the end of the first week in December 1847 the Duke was astounded and enraged to find himself accused of having personally circulated his letter to members of the public in order to wreck Russell's Government with a defence scare.

The facts were exactly the opposite. So scrupulous had the Duke been about not embarrassing the Government that he avoided discussing defence even in Parliament, preferring to notify people like Burgoyne, Anglesey and Palmerston privately of his views. These views were drastic. Ideally in his opinion safety required the addition of 30,000 regular soldiers to the 50,000 already available. Assuming however that this would be denied, he emphasized an increase in the militia to 150,000 men. Palmerston as War Minister was certainly meant to use the Duke's letter as ammunition, but perfectly properly within the Cabinet. Even after the débâcle the Duke still allowed Lord Anglesey, Master-General of the Ordnance, to show his letters to all interested persons – except Burgoyne and his family.[19]

As a result of Lady Shelley's leak the Duke wrote immediately to the two people whom he regarded respectively as victim and aggressor. First, to Russell on 7 January 1848. No one could be more pained than himself, he began, '& I could not think it possible that a word that I should write would ever be read by the publick!' Moreover, for the Commander-in-Chief to speak, as it were, directly to the public through the press was entirely against his principles and seemed a peculiarly sinister invention of modern times: 'These important issues should be brought to public notice by the government.'[20] When the subject of national defence was raised in the Lords at the end of the month the Duke sat silent. He felt he owed it to Russell.

Second, to Lady Shelley. She received a proper trouncing from her adored Duke which saddened her life for several weeks. In the course of five furious and sarcastic letters, in parts almost illegible, he wrote on 27 January: 'It is quite delightful to live in times with your Ladyship, with Sir John, Lady and Miss Burgoyne!' Next day he again referred to 'the meddling gossip of the ladies of modern times. . . . I will not allow myself to be accused of breach of Trust and engagement by any Party without answering firmly; and loudly proclaiming that the charge is groundless, and false. . . .'[21] However, after loudly proclaiming all he felt, as was his custom, he had forgiven her within a month.

Unfortunately Lady Shelley's memory was as inaccurate as her behaviour had been indiscreet. In her reminiscences she stated that the hard-hearted Duke had refused to speak to her for two years and relented at the end of that long period only because her husband, Sir John Shelley, met him at a party and made him laugh.

'Good evening, duke,' Sir John is supposed to have begun. 'Do you know, it has been said . . . that the cackling of geese once saved Rome. I have been thinking that perhaps the cackling of my old Goose may yet save England!'

'By God, Shelley! You are right,' replied the Duke in this story; 'give me your honest hand.'

The truth is that the Duke heard Sir John's 'goose' *mot* from mutual friends less than a month after the quarrel. Highly delighted with it, he at once wrote a merry letter to Lady Shelley dated 26 February 1848, in which he ended by gallantly differing from Sir John only in calling his wife '*old*'. 'I can't think that the Word applies to a Lady fat and fair but less than forty! However Sir John knows best. Believe me Ever Yours Affectionately W'.[22]

The years of ducal dudgeon were a fiction.

*

Whether wisely or wantonly published, the Burgoyne Letter ushered in a year for which its grave tone seemed only too appropriate. Written as has been seen in January 1847, it was being widely discussed at the beginning of 1848. This was the Year of Revolution.

Louis Philippe was driven from the throne in February. So ended what Tocqueville called his 'usurping dynasty . . . the most selfish & grasping & exclusive of Plutocracies'. A few days later a letter arrived for the Duke from Lamartine, the French romantic poet turned revolutionary leader, hoping for his Grace's approbation of this very liberal revolution. After all, the English Constitution was 'the most ultra of liberal republics, having a hereditary Sovereign Magistrate, as chief'. The Duke replied that he hoped France would be happy. No comment on Britain's advanced liberal republic. 'Very judicious,' wrote Russell.[23]

Hardly were the royal fugitives from France installed in their traditional asylum, England, before the European revolutions of March began. Prince Metternich had to run from Vienna in a disguise and was seen for three hours in London by the Duke.

'What does he do?' asked the invalid Mr Chad whom the Duke was visiting.

'Oh he perorates.'[24]

The Duke himself was too busy to perorate. '*We are living in Strange Times*!' he wrote to William Spicer, a West Country friend. 'However, I hope that we may be able yet to preserve the general Peace, although it appears probable that we alone of the Nations of the earth may . . . be saved from Wreck and Destruction!'[25] According to his information, the appointed day for 'wrecking' England was Monday 10 April. Feargus O'Connor, Nottingham's M.P. since 1847, proposed to direct yet another tidal wave of Chartism on Parliament, by means of a petition with five million signatures and a vast meeting on Kennington Common to launch its processional journey to Westminster. A National Assembly on the French model would then replace Parliament until the Charter became law.

The Commander-in Chief, saying he felt as well as twenty-five years ago, rose to the challenge with a mighty effort of mind and body which gradually instilled courage into all who worked with him. During the week before the crisis Lord Campbell, Chancellor of the Duchy, did not at all like the look of things: 'Many people believe that by Monday evening we shall be under a Provisional Government,' he wrote to his brother. The Duke tried personally to calm him.

'Lord Campbell, we shall be as quiet on Monday as we are at this moment, and it will end to the credit of the Government and the country.'[26]

In the Cabinet room on the eve of operations Campbell listened enthralled to the Duke's Council of War. As in 1830, all the soldiers were to be kept out of sight but so disposed that ten thousand could be assembled at any danger-point in a matter of minutes. Lady Palmerston afterwards understood from her husband, also present, that this arrangement was to prevent them from fraternizing with the mob.[27] The Duke however, did not fear fraternization. It was to prevent provocation. As he laid out and explained his maps and plans, Campbell marvelled at his quickness and precision. Thomas Macaulay, another Cabinet minister, told Campbell he had never seen such an interesting spectacle; he would remember it to his dying day. In this thin, silver-haired old man they could all see the boundless spring and energy which had won Waterloo.

Cannon were placed on the bridges and all government offices in the Whitehall area garrisoned and provisioned. Prince Albert wanted a mass removal of the Tower guns out of harm's way but the Duke would have none of it: 'Considering that the Guns have thus been kept in security upon former occasions of the Disturbance of the Peace of the Tower by Mobs, it appears to the Duke to be best to leave *well* as it is.' Special constables to the number of two hundred thousand were enrolled, presumably one to each of the expected Chartist demonstrators. (The Duke had written to Lady Wilton on the 5th, 'I am up to the Eyes in arrangements for the reception of the Chartists on Monday to the amount of 200,000.') Among the specials were Prince Louis Napoleon, Bonaparte's nephew, and Charles Greville, with all his Privy Council clerks and messengers, their ground-floor rooms barricaded with the Council registers. The democratic Lady Palmerston was enchanted by the 'higgeldy piggeldy' mass of volunteers – peers, commoners, servants and workmen, all united 'to stand by our constitution'. In fact the Duke found many of the workmen, though willing to defend their allotted buildings, unwilling to attack the mobs. 'We think like them.'[28]

Before leaving London on 8 April at her ministers' request, the Queen asked Wellington if there was really any danger.

'None, Madam, if I am allowed to proceed with my precautionary measures.'

Then the great day dawned, and suddenly it was clear that all these preparations had been made to deal with far fewer Chartists than expected bearing rolls of signatures of which only 1,975,496 were genuine – fewer than in 1842. Among the forged names that of the Duke of Wellington appeared no less than seventeen times. By 9 A.M. Feargus O'Connor had already lost heart. The Duke, as yet unaware of this, was at the Horse Guards at 10 A.M., where he proposed to stay until it was time to go down and meet the petitioners at Westminster. At 1 P.M. he heard the procession had been formed on Kennington Common. At 1.45 P.M. an officer announced that the petition was trundling over Vauxhall Bridge in a cab, O'Connor having been talked out of his procession by Sir Richard Mayne, Chief of Police, in the nearby Horns Tavern. The Chartist M.P., gigantic in stature but no more than human in spirit, had gladly folded up his long limbs among the scrolls, agreeing with Mayne that it would be foolish to march and get his toes trodden on or pockets picked. The petitions were delivered by cab.

'I consider the heart of the Affair broken,' wrote the Duke from his office to Lady Wilton.[29] He ordered his troops back to barracks. By 3.30 P.M. it was raining. 'In short the War is over,' continued the Duke, 'and the Rain will probably keep the Town quiet this night.' He left for the House of Lords at 4.30 P.M., well pleased that the Monarch, though evacuated to Osborne with a new-born baby, was still on her throne.

'It must have been a happy day for him,' the Queen wrote to him in the third person on the 12th. 'It is a pity he is not *59* instead of *79*. Such Men are indeed now valuable in these days.'[30]

*

The Young Irelanders had been expected by the Duke to rise on the same day as the Chartists. Blood-curdling reports of their speeches had arrived, all proving that they had abandoned the voting-booth for the pike. Whereas the old O'Connellite cry had been 'Register, register, register!' Young Ireland proclaimed, 'Arm, arm, arm!' Should the whole world be free, they asked, and Ireland remain a slave? The Duke thought he saw clearly what they wanted: 'to deprive the Queen of her crown! and to establish a republick!'[31] Forgetting who had first said it, their favourite quotation was, 'Trust in God and keep your powder dry.' For those without powder, pikes were selling on the streets at 2s. 6d. to 4s. 6d. well polished.

Two days before the 10th the Duke was dreading a far worse fate for Dublin than for London:

As there are few of the Police armed with Staves in Dublin the Mob must be dealt with there by Fire Arms! . . . There will therefore possibly be great slaughter of the Insurgents! This is heart-breaking![32]

But spasmodic violence never concentrated into the single flame of revolution. Inexorably the leaders were rounded up and transported. The potato blight meanwhile struck yet again, but no signs of permanent cure for Ireland's desolation occurred either to Whigs or Tories. The Whigs tried to punish the land-lords for past sins by forcing them to bear, through the rates, the cost of salvaging the poor. Instead the landlords evicted their paupers, thus condemning the second half of the century to orgies of mutual hatred.

Conservative policy up to 1846 had been less parsimonious and doctrinaire than Whig. Nevertheless Peel and Wellington went out of office 'without having accomplished anything to make the Irish people better able to meet the calamity that lay ahead of them'.[33] The Duke, indeed, at times saw no solution at all or only a solution that would be too slow. Somehow 'the anomalous state of social life in Ireland' – the landlord–tenant relationship – must be changed.

I entertain no doubt that no Improvement can be effectual in Ire-land till the Reform in contemplation will take place in the common social Relation between employer and Workman! But the Misfortune is that the relation is so universal that the Alteration wished for is so difficult as to be almost impossible.[34]

For lack of that 'alteration' probably at least two million Irish were lost, one million by emigration and one by famine.

Also worthy of note are the population figures for the Duke's two native islands at the beginning of the century and at the end of his life. When he died the population of Ireland was fast shrink-ing back to what it had been when he was a young man in Dublin; England's had more than doubled.

*

Much personal happiness compensated the old Duke for the political confusion abroad and at home during his last years. Two pieces of bad news in particular needed some counterbalance. In July 1850 he was paying a tribute in the Lords to his late leader, Sir Robert Peel, accidentally killed through a fall from his horse.

Tears stood in the Duke's eyes and his voice broke as he testified to Peel's scrupulous veracity. Undeviating love of truth was the thing above all which he and Peel possessed in common.

The Duke had entered rarely if ever into the party complexities of 'Peelites' and 'Stanleyites' after 1846. His interventions in national politics, though far from ineffective, were made only in response to direct appeals. Brougham had once said, 'That man's first object is to serve his country, with a sword if necessary, or with a pickaxe.'[35] He still carried the Sword of State on great parliamentary occasions but it was for a sharp jab with the pickaxe that Queen Victoria more often called on him. Who should be Prime Minister, she demanded desperately in 1851, now that Russell had resigned and no one else would serve? The pickaxe came down with a thud. Russell must go on.

'Is your Majesty dissatisfied with your Ministers?'

'No.'

'Then you had better keep them.'[36]

It was at the end of 1851 that the second blow fell. Prince Louis Napoleon, who had been elected President of the French Republic in December 1848, now assumed dictatorial powers. With a Napoleon again supreme in France, the Duke was haunted anew by phantoms of a French invasion fleet. He found solace more and more in the reflected gaiety and hopes of a younger generation, represented among others by Angela Burt-detCoutts.

*

Grand-daughter and heiress of the immensely wealthy banker, Thomas Coutts, and daughter of Sir Francis Burdett, the Duke's old radical antagonist, 'Miss Angela', as the Duke almost always addressed her in the 842 letters he wrote her, was born in 1814. This plain but strong-minded young woman lived at No. 1 Stratton Street at the corner of Piccadilly, not far from Apsley House, and there was continual visiting between No. 1 Stratton Street and 'No. 1 London', as the Duke's house was now reverentially called. Miss Angela's conscientious desire to use her enormous wealth charitably gave her a common interest with the Duke. They shared the Victorian fervour for rescuing prostitutes, the Duke in particular being almost lyrical once Miss Angela had aroused his compassion. A typical outpouring was sent to her on 30 March 1849:

My young Lady fills her letters with assurances that she does all the good things which I have enjoined; in return for all the Money I have given her and paid for her! at the same time demanding more. . . . But her letters are not to be compared to those of my Irish girl who is going to Australia! . . . She is a character such as a Heroine in a Romance or Novel personified! and I feel the same interest in her fate, as I should in the story of such a one . . . and her letters to me are models of modesty, humility. . . .[37]

They were almost certainly models of duplicity. Of the Duke's large clientele of unmarried mothers who gave birth at suspiciously frequent intervals before receiving their passage-money to the Antipodes, few ever left Lambeth or Charing Cross; indeed many of them were the same person, and that a man. But when the Mendicity Society exposed a fraud, it was the Society whom the Duke heartily disliked, not the imposter: 'An Officer from the Mendicity Society called on me and gave me such a scolding, as I have never had before in my life!'[38]

From the Duke's letters to Miss Angela – most of them non-political – many racy trifles emerge concerning his last years: that he had thought of being trained to sing as a consolation in his deafness but was too much occupied; that in order to prevent colds he wore the finest Bengal muslin next to his skin and cárried a bottle of vinegar and rose-water in his pocket, to rub himself each time he changed his clothes (usually three times but sometimes seven times a day); that he dreaded the draughts of Windsor – 'I don't know where I have been more uncomfortable';[39] that he was once caught up when waltzing under a stranger's petticoat – 'She was very well looking and must have been very much surprised to find a veteran with grey Hair under her Cloaths'; and that he believed women could and should skate – 'Don't repine! My Dear! that you are a Woman! There is nothing to prevent your skaiting [sic]; excepting the difficulty of learning. . . .'[40]

There were many signs of a touching affection for one another. The Duke's pale grey writing-paper still carries the stains here and there of pressed rose leaves, geraniums or verbena sent to his young friend. One small envelope contains a tiny bow of pure white hair tied with a few brown strands. Another, labelled on the outside in Angela's hand, 'Duke of Wellington's favourite Poplins', is filled with small patterns of material: gold shot with pink (6s), gold and purple (4s 9d), checks of lilac, grey and deep violet (ditto), shot purple (3s 6d), fawn shot with rose (5s 9d). The colours the Duke preferred were gay and warm; no greens, blues, black or white.

The warmth flowed into words when Angela was abroad in October 1847:

My Dearest! for so I must call you! your constant recollection of and kindness to me, charm me; and I must express what I feel for you! . . . we think aloud! and the thoughts of the one are imparted to the other! this is the charm of our existence.[41]

Were these the words of a lover? On 6 February of that year he had written her a temporizing letter which suggested nevertheless that an emotional crisis was impending.

I am sensible of your kindness and confidence my dear Miss Angela! and of the admirable good sense and goodness of heart which induced you to write me your letter of last night. You are right! there can be no Secrets between us on such Subjects! . . . The subject is now exactly as it ought to be between us! and as every other is; one on which either can think aloud!

By the following evening, however, Miss Angela had decided that the subject was far from being exactly as it ought to be between them. She proposed marriage to the Duke on 7 February 1847 and received a refusal, she being thirty-two and he seventy-seven. He wrote to her next day:

My Dearest Angela,
I have passed every Moment of the Evening and Night since I quitted you in reflecting upon our Conversation of yesterday, Every Word of which I have considered repeatedly.

But he could not change his mind. His first duty to her was that of friend, guardian, protector.

You are Young, My Dearest! You have before you the Prospect of at least twenty years of enjoyment of Happiness in Life. [As Baroness Burdett-Coutts, Angela lived to be ninety-two marrying at sixty-seven a man less than half her age.] I entreat you again, in this way, not to throw yourself away upon a Man old enough to be your Grandfather, who, however strong, Hearty and Healthy at present, must and will certainly in time feel the consequences and Infirmities of Age.[42]

Some of the infirmities of age soon began to appear in tiffs and tantrums. But his dearest Angela never gave up hope of becoming the Duchess. He would complain of her badgering him to call more often than he could manage – 'I wish that it could occasionally occur to your Reflection, that I am eighty-two not twenty-eight years of Age'; of her calling at Apsley House while he was still dressing; of sending round a note even earlier – 'The fact is that when my servant brought me your note I was naked! and I was ashamed of his seeing me in that state'.[43] Exasperated by the multitude of his would-be visitors he invented a new, ironic name for himself – 'Boniface', the jovial host of Farquhar's *Beaux' Stratagem*. Because of his deafness entertaining was a nightmare. 'Poor Deaf old Man! obliged to pass *my days* in Society!' Small select parties were torture. 'I do very well with one or in a crowd but best of all alone!'[44] After a burst of irritability he would humbly explain what had made him so annoying, and thus annoy her again by apologizing. On one occasion some popular verses seemed the best reply to Miss Angela's sharp complaints:

> *Speak gently to the aged one*
> *Grieve not the care-worn heart;*
> *The sands of life are nearly run;*
> *Let such in peace depart.**

Nevertheless their mutual affection was strong enough to defy critics like Greville, who spoke of the Duke's 'strange intimacy' with Miss Burdett-Coutts as one of the 'lamentable appearances of decay in his vigorous mind'.†[45]

The Duke's no less innocent friendship with another young woman and his persecution by an ageing spinster were noticed with even more spleen.

*

Margaret Jones of Pantglas, wife of an M.P. and niece of Lord Campbell, was nearly sixty years the Duke's junior. She charmed

---

* Compare *Alice:*
> *Speak gently to your little boy*
> *And beat him when he sneezes;*
> *He only does it to annoy,*
> *Because he knows it teases.*

† After Wellington's death the Duke of Broglie, Mme de Staël's son-in-law, contrasted his 'position and prestige' with 'the clumsy and pressing gallantries he permitted himself towards pretty young women' even in extreme old age, over which all parties agreed to draw a veil. (Pange, p. 74.)

him during his last year. It was a delight to have someone young and new to show his sea-girt Castle, ramparts and platform. A mellowness even about house-parties crept into his letters. He agreed with her that country-house society was the most agreeable in England, the best arranged and understood. 'I have been in the habit of visiting much and enjoyed the society until I have become so deaf as to be unfit for social life. . . . '46 Now he never went anywhere excepting to Lord Salisbury's for a night.

But he was still pressed to make an appearance, however brief, in countless London drawing-rooms, and his arrival with Mrs Jones provoked acid criticism. After his death the famous Effie Ruskin, a Scottish compatriot of Mrs Jones's, wrote to her mother:

It is much better that he is dead for this Love Affair he had with Mrs. Jones during his last season was very unbecoming. He always was in love with someone but had never made himself ridiculous till this one, which was a source of great grief to his family and made him laughed at by every empty-headed fool in London. . . . At every party Mrs Jones and the 'Dook' were ushered in together as she has never been known to blush since she came to town, I daresay she will feel no remorse at all for making the last years of so great a Hero contemptible, when perhaps she might have done him some lasting service.

The year before, Mrs Ruskin had seen the Duke 'flirting away tremendously' with the noisy Miss Hattons who talked so loudly even he could probably hear them. There was a society riddle, reported Effie:

'Why is the Duke the rudest man in London?'

'Because he always comes into a room with his Hat On!'47

Lady Georgiana Fane, unmarried daughter of Lord Westmorland, was the Duke's most heartless pursuer and like Miss Burdett-Coutts and Miss Jenkins never gave up hope of catching him. At one point it seemed likely that Lady Georgiana would sue him for breach of promise. But he kept his head and also, more surprisingly, kept his special liking for the 'Bardwell and Pickwick' passage in Dickens, which he used to read aloud. Towards the end of his life the lady trapped him after early service at St James's, Piccadilly, and made a scene. On Waterloo Day, 1849, he had to ask several ladies not to bring Georgiana with them into his house. Miss Angela was one of these. 'I have refused to receive my Lady!' he wrote to Miss Angela, 'and have re-

quested Lady Charles not to receive visitors. Allow me to ask this
favour.' His letter to Lady Charles Wellesley, his daughter-in-
law, who had rooms at Apsley House with her family, was even
more insistent:

My dear Lady Charles I have long been under the necessity of declin-
ing to allow this house to be made a shew on the 18th of June! People
however still persevere! and this morning I learned that Lady Georgiana
Fane, knowing that I will not receive her visits, intends to apply to you
to receive her! I shall be very much obliged to you if you will refuse to
receive her *on this day*. . . .[48]

On a systematic plan, Miss Jenkins also still 'persevered'.

He did not see her again after 1845 but the correspondence
continued, the Duke attempting every so often to cut it off and
Anna Maria reopening by an appeal for money, a letter of
condolence on a grandchild's death, or a parcel of religious books
to be forwarded to Peel. The Peel idea earned a sharp rebuff: 'I
am not the Post Man! nor the Secretary of Sir Robert Peel nor
your Secretary!' A report in *The Times* that at the opening of
Parliament in 1851 he had seemed to 'shrink' from public applause, brought forth the comment from Miss Jenkins which
finally proved fatal to her. Was his 'precious soul' at last turning
away from The World? she asked. No, replied the Duke. While
naturally trying to perform his official duties with 'due Humility',
he felt that worldly Marthas as well as spiritual Marys were necessary.

Perhaps, indeed, this particular Mary of his was not necessary
at all. 'With due respect for Her Higher occupations,' he added
later, 'I hope she will excuse my adhering to my own Course of
duty.'[49] His duty to Miss Jenkins had finished. He never wrote
again.

*

The occasional night spent at Lord Salisbury's, which he mentioned to Mrs Jones, represented his last great friendship with a
young married woman – one which none dared to criticise. At
fifty-six the widowed Lord Salisbury had married again. His
bride was Lady Mary Sackville-West, ten years younger than
Miss Angela and known to the Duke since she was a child. She
slipped effortlessly into her predecessor's place in the old man's
affections and gave each of her children, boy or girl, the sacred

name of Arthur. Just as Fanny Salisbury's girls had walked about his garden with him arm in arm, so now their young stepmother took 'quarter-deck exercise' every day with him in St James's Park. 'It is to *the* Duke,' she used to say in old age, 'that I owe the best of the good I have learnt, and in especial, the forgiveness of injuries.'[50]

Lastly, his own daughters-in-law. Charles had married Sophia Pierrepont, niece of Lord Manvers, in 1844 and to the Duke's joy produced many Wellesley grandchildren. Though the eldest, Arthur, died in infancy, to the Duke's great sorrow, Henry and Arthur Charles grew up to become 3rd and 4th Dukes respectively. Lady Charles's children made the platform at Walmer 'quite gay', as the Duke told Mrs Jones. To his elder daughter-in-law, Lady Douro, he was especially devoted, precisely it would seem because she was childless and unloved.

Having paid her debts in October 1841, presumably in order that Douro should not repeat the Arthur–Kitty syndrome, he was preparing to receive her at Stratfield Saye in March 1842 as a much cherished invalid, after what sounded like a miscarriage. The Duke obtained a wheelchair for Lady Douro and had rollers attached to a chaise-longue. He fussed over her like a mother, entreating her to obey her doctors for everyone's sake, 'above all for your own; and I will add mine'. In June that year he offered Walmer to her for a long stay. 'I should be more than compensated by the re-establishment of your Health and particularly the Restoration of the domestic Comfort and Happiness of yourself and Douro!'

Many touching and extraordinarily frank letters were later exchanged between them. In 1849 he was praising his dearest Lady Douro's courage in deciding to have an operation in Edinburgh.

I am anxious about one thing in this world; and that is that you should be the Mother of Children! For your sake for mine: and for others! but however desirous I am that this should come to pass; I am very unwilling that you should suffer. . . .

She must be the only judge. If she decided in favour he would conceal her reason for staying in Scotland from the Queen (whose lady-of-the-bedchamber Lady Douro was) and everyone else. All to no avail.

Another two years passed by after the Duke's last hopeful letter to Lady Douro, and it was his eighty-second birthday, 1 May 1851. Miss Coutts gave a magnificent dinner party in his honour, winding up with elaborate toasts by the gentlemen in the dining-room. As briefly as possible the Duke returned thanks and suggested joining the ladies. He had just taken part in one of the greatest peacetime spectacles of these strange but stimulating times.

25

The Other Side of the Hill

I LAST STEPS

'I should have liked that man of yours for one of my generals,' the Duke of Wellington said to the Duke of Devonshire after watching William Paxton's pyrotechnics at Chatsworth in 1843.[1] But though the great architect had built Chatsworth conservatory and handled the firework display in masterly fashion, the Duke had grave doubts about both Paxton's Glass Palace of 1851 and Prince Albert's Great Exhibition it was to house.

'The glass is very thin,' he muttered; and later, 'I don't clearly understand the Benefit which such exhibition is to produce, an exhibition of Works of Art and Manufacture.' Why collect unnecessary crowds in London during the restless summer months?[2] The Duke still saw Hyde Park as a stamping-ground for Chartists, rather than as the setting for Prince Albert's crystal jewel of world peace.

Part of the Duke's scepticism sprang from his recent appointment as Ranger of the Royal Parks. He always took new duties seriously and had already discovered a great deal of jobbery connected with Hyde Park, that anomalous stretch of countryside in the West End.

With the coming of the Great Exhibition the problems of Hyde Park redoubled. The Duke fought encroachments on public rights inch by inch.[3] Why should the beer supplier drive his dray up Rotten Row? Or an Arab encampment, which had suddenly arrived from Tunis, spread all over the grass? It must be retained within a strong fence. As for the dangerous foreigners who were expected to invade the Park in the wake of Prince Albert's international brotherhood, warnings by the score reached the Ranger, one official informer calculating that a mere hundred villains armed with a pint of turpentine each could burn down the whole metropolis.

By the middle of April the Duke had all his plans completed for guarding the three buildings most at risk, Buckingham Palace, Parliament and the Glass Palace itself. Totally unacceptable to him was the Government's panic proposal that a body of Paris police should be invited over to move among the Exhibition crowds in plain clothes, identifying 'red republicans' from over the water. 'What is to be done with them when pointed out?' asked the Duke. By all means let the Government introduce foreign policemen if they felt windy. 'I feel no want of confidence in my own powers . . . to preserve the public peace and to provide for the general safety without requiring the assistance of French Officers.'⁴ Hastily Russell abandoned the notion.

Above all the Duke had dealt with the Hyde Park squatter. Mrs Ann Hicks had squatted for years in what was variously termed by the authorities a hut, cottage, stone building, booth, cave or wigwam on the bank of the Serpentine, where she sold cakes and glasses of water from a nearby fountain. On 9 October 1850 the Deputy Ranger informed the Ranger that in view of the forth-coming exhibition, the Department of Woods and Forests insisted on having the squatter removed. Next day the Duke wrote back in anger: he could not take orders from a Government depart-ment through his own subordinate officer, especially over 'the female Squatter whose eviction is now likely to give some trouble'.⁵

Five days later he decided to get upon his horse and go and see this 'Residence' for himself. (He was always scrupulously polite about the squatter's dwelling, never using a word like wigwam.) So the Ranger galloped over the Park until he found Mrs Hicks at the elegant address she had given him: 'Cottage on the Hill, Serpentine River, Hyde Park.' One glance showed him that the very simplest siege-work would be enough to reduce this small Badajoz, but he begged Lord Seymour, Minister of Woods and Forests, to try first an offer of money to make her withdraw from her 'Premises'. The department agreed to give her a year's rent if she went quietly, and by the beginning of November she had done so. Owing to their dilatoriness, however, Mrs Hicks had appar-ently received no compensation nine months later. A protest letter on her behalf from the North London Anti-Enclosure Social and Sanitary Improvement Society pointed out that this ill-used female was the sister of all of them by nature if not by law, and how would her brother the Duke like it if Lord Seymour destroyed Apsley House just because it stood inside the Park?

He does not exactly understand [replied the Duke patiently], what connection is supposed to exist between His Mansion in Piccadilly and Mrs Hicks' Cottage. The Duke purchased from the Crown his property in Piccadilly! Mrs Hicks was neither more nor less than a Squatter on the bank of the Serpentine River. . . .[6]

Meanwhile the palace of peace, brotherhood and sisterhood was facing its very last crisis. When the treasures from many lands were already on display, hundreds of London's sparrows assembled under the glass domes. Nothing would move them. It was said that the Queen at last asked the Duke how to get rid of these squatters.

'Try sparrow-hawks, Ma'am.' In a trice the enemy had fled.*

*

Prolonged huzzas, fluttering of handkerchiefs and kisses blown by gloved hands greeted the Duke as he entered the Crystal Palace on 1 May 1851 and processed for three-quarters of an hour round the building towards the central point, accompanied by members of the Government, Opposition and other notables. One of the spectators, Lady Charlotte Guest, observed the contrast between the Duke's 'hearty cheer' and Russell's 'tolerably good one'. The Duke's cheer was indeed a double-barrelled salute, for he and Lord Anglesey supported one another, arm in arm, up and down and round the long aisles, all their family and political feuds long forgotten. That the two old heroes tottered in their walk only added to the crowd's affectionate enthusiasm.

When the sightseeing began someone remembered it was the Duke's birthday. More cheers; and a round of applause from each section he visited; wax flowers to amuse Lady Douro and heavy machinery to amuse himself. Mrs W. E. Gladstone was among the lucky ladies to find herself close to him. She wrote to her husband, 'The dear old Duke of Wellington so cheered on his birthday; I got a nice shake of his hand, which did me good.' At the end of

* Even if this story, like so many others, was a contemporary *jeu d'esprit* and therefore apocryphal, it is worth remembering for its distillation of the Wellington spirit.

the dizzy afternoon, with the sun slanting through the glass on to the elm trees growing beneath, the ladies eating ices and the gentlemen drinking beer, he was whisked off to Buckingham Palace to give a birthday present to his godson Prince Arthur, one year old on the day that he was eighty-two.

He was notoriously forgetful these days about equipping himself beforehand for such occasions. There is a story in the Jersey family of his attending Lady Jersey's birthday party and finding he had no offering. So he picked up a Meissen figure on his way in.

'My dear Duke, how charming! Exactly matches one I've got in the outer drawing-room.'

Prince Arthur's birthday present, however, had not been forgotten, and the Queen's favourite artist, Franz Winterhalter, painted a picture she greatly admired of the presentation. The Duke's only surviving comment on the picture characteristically concerned the unconscionable time he had spent on sitting. Counting the journeys to and from the Palace, Winterhalter's masterpiece represented three hours' lost time a day.[*]

The Glass Palace, on the contrary, was soon drawing the old Duke like a magnet. 'Whether the Shew will ever be of any use to anybody may be questioned,' he wrote to Lady Salisbury at the end of the first week, 'but of this I am certain nothing can be more successful.' He went again and again and became so much a part of the 'Shew' that his final visit on 7 October almost ended in disaster. Unaware of the situation, he strolled in like anyone else. Suddenly eighty thousand Wellington worshippers were rushing down upon him from all quarters determined to touch him before it was too late:

> Never did I see such a mob, or get such a rubbing, scrubbing and mashing . . . I expected at every moment to be crushed and I was saved by the Police alive![7]

*

[*] The Duke presented his godson with a cup and model of the throne. The Prince, however, substituted a casket belonging to the Queen in the painting, as being more picturesque. When nearly twenty-one Prince Arthur was ragged because of a rumour that the mysterious casket contained a birthday present from his godpapa. In enlightening him, the Queen deprecated the original substitution: 'it only shows how wrong it is not to paint things as they really are.' (R.A.Vic.Add.MSS.A/15.1727.)

With the autumn of 1851 the Duke entered upon his last full year. For the costermonger's donkey it was now a fine thing to be alive, and still on the trot, though some of his friends shook their heads dubiously over reports issuing from the Horse Guards. Reports of an old, old Commander-in-Chief riding down from Apsley House every morning, who leant strangely backwards in his saddle as he held himself on by the bridle; of the sad performance in the courtyard, dismounting and mounting, his friends forced to watch his struggles but forbidden to help; of the times out of number when he fell asleep at his desk, to wake up irritable and snappish at the posing of some tomfool question. The work was not done and his subordinates spent their time, as one remarked, trying to put damned big rats into damned small bottles.* Not surprising that quite a few felt it was time for those wondrous sands to run out.

Yet there were fields where the Duke could still operate to good effect. Oxford was one. In 1850 the long-dreaded Royal Commission on the Universities was announced. The Duke realized at once that its enquiries would focus on the professorial system. With Nonconformists still barred, was it certain that there would be enough Anglicans to handle the galloping progress of science? He felt some sympathy for the critics, besides approving highly of the 'New Studies' – modern literature, physics and chemistry. How should he proceed?

His first act was to warn off the Government extremists, after which he tackled the obscurantists on his own side. There was Dr Plumptre, the Vice-Chancellor, for instance, pointing out that Oxford had not been founded directly for the education of youth but for higher purposes.

The Education of Youth has . . . been superadded to their other duties by the Heads and Fellows of Colleges, of their own free will.[8]

It was July 1852 when the Commission's report reached the Duke. He spent a week reading it and then suggested to the University authorities that they would probably wish to adopt some of its proposals. A polite reply was received regretting that

* (Albemarle, pp. 407–8.) Wellington first used the metaphor of the rat in the bottle during the Peninsular War. It was taken from a trick he had watched in India, of drawing musk rats into scent bottles by creating a vacuum. See *Wellington: The Years of the Sword*, pp. 430–1 and below, p. 497, Panther, 1971.

since the Long Vacation had already commenced, consideration of his Grace's advice would have to wait until they returned next term.

By that time his Grace was on a longer absence, but the reforms eventually went through.

For reasons great and small, posterity must be grateful to the Duke for his eighteen years' service to Oxford. Among the small reasons is that in 1845 he selected from three possible subjects for the Newdigate Prize poem the title 'Petra'. He thus had an honourable share in the creation of J. W. Burgon's winning lines, the most famous ever written for the Newdigate:

> *Match me such marvel, save in Eastern clime –*
> *A rose-red City – half as old as Time!*

How would Wellington have taken the discoveries of science about Time: that Petra was after all only a stripling, and Britain's ancient institutions which he had held up so often for public veneration, mere youthful experiments in the March of Intellect? He would have had his answer. In that case, what was the Spirit of the Age but a transient moment, to be regarded but not glorified?*

*

A crowd of social duties still pressed upon him, though the ferocity of his complaints about them gradually faded.

In August 1850 he had given away one of the brides at a double Pakenham wedding and signed the register of St George's, Hanover Square, for the thousandth time – or so he said. 'I was in my usual bride-giving dress, and I believe that the mob took me for one of the Bride-grooms!'

---

* William Hazlitt in his biographical studies entitled *The Spirit of the Age* defined this spirit in 1825 as one of change, fashion, talk and paradox. As regards the 'New Studies' which already affected the idea of time, Frances Salisbury wrote on 16 September 1836,

> The Duke seemed to lean to the theory of a different state of the world having existed previous to the chaos mentioned in the 2nd verse of the 1st chapter of Genesis. He observed repeatedly that there was nothing in the modern discoveries at variance with the account in Genesis. The Duke considers the discovery of so many animals of unknown species in the secondary strata as the strongest argument in favour of a previous state of things. (*Hatfield MSS.*)

When he escorted another young relative, Prudence Penelope Leslie, known as 'Britannia', up the aisle, the bride heard him saying quietly.

'Left, right! Left, right!' She realized it was not to keep *her* in step but himself.*

Another few days passed after the Pakenham wedding and it was time to go to church again. Charles Arbuthnot, whom he had cherished throughout a long illness, died on 16 August 1850. The Duke wrote on the 22nd to Lady Salisbury: 'It is curious shifting as I have done this year from funerals to marriages – thence back to funerals! It is the way of the World and gives occasion for Reflection. . . . '[9] He was not yet hardened to the way of the world and tears poured down his cheeks as he stood next day by his friend's grave.

Of the five Wellesley brothers and one sister, he and Gerald were the only two left. Richard had gone in 1842, Anne in 1844, William in 1845, Henry in 1846. He had not been intimate with Anne since the second Worcester marriage, which he felt disgraced the aristocracy as well as his family,† but he and Richard, to everyone's surprise, had become reconciled four years before the latter's death. By 1841 Richard was giving his proxy to Arthur and therefore voting Conservative. His son-in-law, Lord Hatherton, believed the old trouble had been jealousy, which made Wellesley 'a most difficult man to act with'. Certainly there are signs of jealousy: for instance, Richard's criticism of some ladies for presuming to destroy one of his letters. 'They would not have treated Nosey's with such contempt.'[10]

An extraordinary conversation about Arthur took place between Hatherton and his father-in-law on 12 March 1837.[11] Having been questioned regarding the Duke's faults of character, especially 'neglect' of his family, Lord Wellesley embarked on a review of all his four brothers' qualities.

'But you know,' he suddenly said to Hatherton, 'Pole [William Maryborough] and Lady Anne and I are Wellesleys, Arthur's father was Mr Gardiner.' (The Gardiners were a Meath family and this Mr Gardiner was possibly the Wellesley boys' tutor.)

---

* Told to the author by Mr William Cavendish-Bentinck, the bride's descendant.

† His niece Emily Smith created a great scandal by marrying her deceased half-sister's husband, Lord Worcester (see above, p. 107).

Hatherton then suggested that though Richard and Anne were clearly brother and sister in full blood, Arthur and Henry were not quite so much like one another.

'Oh! I believe Henry and Arthur have also different parentage,' said Lord Wellesley.

A man who could claim that his severe mother was an enthusiastic adultress must indeed have been difficult to act with, particularly as there is not a shred of evidence to confirm his statement.* Nevertheless the Duke was visibly distressed during his brother's funeral at Eton. Next day, Count D'Orsay, the dandy of genius, reported that the Duke had called Lord Wellesley 'a very gentlemanly man. A very agreeable man – when he got his own way.' But the Duke changed his final assessment: 'He had never thought any honour he had ever received equal to that of being Lord Wellesley's brother.'[12]

The circumstances in which another close associate died at the end of 1845 grieved the Duke and were the source of unjustified attacks. A word is called for here.

Colonel John Gurwood, editor of the published *Despatches* and one of the Duke's private secretaries from 1837 to 1844, committed suicide at his home in Brighton. Throughout Gurwood's life he had felt nothing but gratitude to the Duke. In 1839 the Duke appointed him Deputy-Lieutenant of the Tower, with a salary of £786, plus his pension of £2,000. He and his family would thus be 'most happily settled'.[13] Unfortunately the beginning of a fatal illness showed itself in 1841, with insomnia, disturbed vision and melancholia. On Waterloo Day 1842 Gurwood thanked the Duke for visits which had relieved his sufferings; he was now convalescent. But on 14 December 1845 the Duke was writing from Stratfield Saye:

My dear Colonel! I am sorry to learn you are unwell. I should be very happy to see you here; you will find a Warm House and great tranquillity.

Meanwhile he would not lose an instant in signing the Colonel's request for leave of absence.

* Professor A. Aspinall, the authority on the documents of this period, denies the rumour. (See also the forthcoming life of the Marquess Wellesley by Iris Butler.) From portraits all the brothers seem to have resembled one another, but Arthur was the one who chiefly inherited his father the Earl of Mornington's musical talents.

A few days later Colonel Gurwood died. Some weeks after receiving the gloomy news the Duke was informed by common friends of the fact that poor Gurwood had been collecting material for a Wellington *Life*, based on private papers and conversations.

This was a bombshell to the Duke. No memoirs ever had been or would be authorized by him. If they were, copies and even forgeries would immediately appear in Paris, Vienna, Brussels, and no one would be able to distinguish between truth and falsehood. He wrote in agitation to Mrs Gurwood asking for his papers back at once. Equally aroused, Mrs Gurwood denied the existence of any memoir whatever and felt deeply wounded. Her husband, she said, had burnt all the Duke's letters to him before he died. Thirteen pages of apology and explanation followed from the Duke and after Mrs Gurwood had accepted his assurances in a moving reply, the correspondence closed.[14]

Mrs Gurwood did not realize that her husband had indeed begun collecting material for a memoir of Wellington when he became his secretary. Illness had caused him to give up the grandiose idea of a *Life*, though he continued amassing material for posterity.[15] This material has not survived. In all probability it was burnt by Gurwood with his letters from the Duke.

Fortunately for posterity, there was still someone working away on Wellington material – Lord Mahon (Stanhope). All unsuspecting, the Duke poured out pearls for the *Conversations with the Duke of Wellington* every evening at Walmer. Occasionally he got a little fretful at young Mahon's eternal questions.*

*

The Duke was holding a Pilot Court at Dover in October 1851 and he dropped in to see Mrs Jones's children at their lodgings in Biggin Street, but missed them: 'They and the Governess must have gone as all others in Dover to see *the Shew* in the streets,'

* Lord Mahon once asked the Duke whether Napoleon created his environment or vice versa. 'It would take a volume to answer your question,' replied the Duke. 'I must go and take off my muddy boots.' (Gleig, *Reminiscences*, p. 297.) On another occasion Lady de Ros (Georgiana Lennox) tried unsuccessfully to erect a barricade of books on the Duke's table between him and the besieging Mahon. 'I don't think much of your fortifications,' murmured the Duke ruefully, as Mahon swept the books aside and moved in. (*A Victorian Vintage*, Stories from the Diaries of Sir M. Grant Duff, 1930.)

he wrote to her, 'at the very same time at which *the Shew* went to see them!'

He could joke about that phenomenon now, but got bored with what he called 'dowagering' – visiting lonely old dowagers, especially royalties, like the dear cracky Duchess of Gloucester: 'I heard this morning that the Duchess of Gloucester lives upon the visits which the Duke of Wellington pays her.'

His Christmas wishes from Mrs Jones brought forth the reply, 'I hope that I may keep my health and strength! I should be an awkward sort of old man if weak and doubled up!'[16] In fact the rheumatism in his neck gave him a pronounced stoop, and he was weaker than his indomitable spirit would admit. He spent much time in his favourite wing arm-chair, chin sunk on chest; but if something was said to arouse him from the private reverie of the old, his eyes would be alight with interest while he was still very slowly lifting his head.

His exchanges of Christmas greetings, which had been going on for ten years, were early symptoms of the new age into which he was getting his toe.[17] In the old days he had written letters dated 25 December with no comment. Another more recent symptom was the cutting of distances and scurrying from one Christmas party to another in Surrey, Hertfordshire, Buckinghamshire. 'We shall end by making one great city of the counties surrounding London.'[18] After seeing the new electric telegraph at Dover he thought he might even live to fly.

One perennial marvel, however, seemed to have come to an end and that was Lord Palmerston. He had been dismissed from Russell's Government for going behind his own ambassador's back over Napoleon III's *coup d'état*. The Duke described Pam's exit as a nine days' wonder and awaited with interest his next move. It was worth waiting for. Next February Palmerston gave Russell his famous 'tit-for-tat' by bringing down his Government. To the Duke there was a double relish in this event: Palmerston was primed by the Duke's arguments when he defeated Russell on a Militia Bill, and the defeat enabled Derby (Stanley) to give the country a Tory administration. Only one thing was not perfect. As the new Prime Minister read out the names of his Government the old Duke, wearing his white winter cape to keep warm, craned forward but still could not hear.

'Who – who?' he asked in a loud whisper. It was Sir So-and So.

'Never heard of the gentleman!'[19]

He was to die under the 'Who – who? Government', but not before he had caused the Prime Minister a headache or two. Lord Derby once returned to the Duke a peculiarly illegible letter with the request that he would decipher it.

'It was my business to write that letter,' said the Duke with a smile, 'but it is *your* duty to read it.'[20]

On 1 May 1852 he celebrated his eighty-third birthday and the greetings and cheering in the streets awakened once more his warning interior voice, even though he acknowledged them with his familiar salute of two fingers raised to the brim of his hat. The voice spoke in Cromwell's remembered words, since there was an election on in Dover and his friends wanted him to use his influence on their behalf. 'They would readily pull me to pieces if convicted of exciting undue influence in the Election of Dover. Alas! we are but men!'

Lady Charlotte Guest found him a very unresponsive old man, hemmed in by huge crowds at a ball given at Apsley House on the 14th – 'he seemed almost asleep'.[21]

That spring the circuit judges had dined as usual at Stratfield Saye and Mr Justice Talfourd, once a famous reform M.P., was surprised and delighted to see the Duke tuck into turtle soup, salmon, a patty, roast beef and 'a child's portion of apple tart and cream'. At his last Waterloo banquet his face, pink and smooth without a wrinkle, shone with pleasure. He refused to feel old. When a man one day helped him across Hyde Park Corner he ought to have been grateful but was not.

'I thank you, Sir,' he managed to say. Then the man perorated.

'My Lord, I have passed a long and not uneventful life; but never did I hope to reach the day when I might be of some assistance to the greatest man that ever lived.'

'Don't be a damned fool!'[22]

*

At last he escaped to Walmer from the hot July days where he had been 'stewed up' in drawing-rooms (though always careful to sit next to a handsome woman when there was music) and obliged to 'sneak along' the shady side of the street. The Sword of State had been carried by him for the last time at the Prorogation, when he confessed to finding it 'as heavy as a regimental firelock'.[23]

His last visitors to Walmer – the Grand Duke and Duchess of Mecklenberg-Strelitz, gracious but a strain – departed on 28 August, leaving him to his reading, rides and walks; to his great lime-tree in the garden, of course 'the finest in the world', and his head gardener, Sergeant Townsend, a Waterloo veteran who suited the Duke admirably.

'Do you know anything about gardening?' the Duke had asked the unemployed soldier who came to his door at Stratfield Saye.

'No, Your Grace.'

'Then *learn* – *learn* and return here this day fortnight at the same hour. Take the place of gardener at Walmer Castle.'

'But I know nothing of gardening.'

'Neither do I, neither do I.'[24]

Sometimes during his solitary rides there would be a little hobnobbing with country people, like the owner of Ripple Mill, who years afterwards recalled the knocking on the steps of his mill and the voice shouting up,

'That the miller? – come down and talk.'

Then the two would sit together in the rumbling, sweet-smelling mill while the soldier confessed to the miller that war was a horrible trade.* Many years later still, an old lady remembered as a girl opening the gate on the Upper Deal road for the Duke to ride through. Often he was fast asleep in the saddle and his horse would stop, wait and then continue gently along the road for home.[25] On the day after his foreign royalties left Walmer, 29 August, he wrote jubilantly to Lady Salisbury of his good health:

I am always well, never fatigued, and I can do anything! I have none of the infirmities of old age! excepting *Vanity* perhaps!

... My deafness is accidental! If I was not deaf, I really believe that there is not a youth in London who could enjoy the world more than myself or could bear fatigue better! but being deaf, the spirit, not the body, tires! One gets bored in boring others, and one becomes too happy to get home![26]

To get home . . . He was nearly there now. On 5 September he

* Told to the author by Mr John Mannering, descendant of the miller. There is another account of the Duke's hobnobbing in the *Illustrated London News* (12 September 1846). When he was temporarily stranded near Plymouth, the guard of the stage-coach offered him a lift. 'No, I thank you . . . I'd rather walk; besides, I have company', pointing to a couple of navvies and a farmer with whom he had been deep in conversation.

received his last eccentric appeal for help. He had recently sent an officer's widow in Boulogne, a total stranger, £5 for her fare home. In her excitement at receiving the money she had broken a looking-glass and now asked him to send another £5 to pay for it; 'Was there ever anything like it in the World?'

He had made two attempts on 2 and 3 September to see old Croker, who was convalescing at Folkestone. Croker had been out the first time; quite a blow, since the Duke had tired himself by walking from the station, not realizing it was three miles up and down hill. Next day he went again, only to be teased by Croker for having failed to guess that yet more hills lay on the other side of Folkestone Hill. Mrs Croker looked puzzled and the Duke explained to her:

'All the business of war, and indeed all the business of life is to endeavour to find out what you do not know by what you do; that is what I called "guessing what was at the other side of the hill!"'

As he left the house to start home the Crokers accompanied him down the two flights of steps to the road, Mrs Croker on his arm and Croker behind. He counted the steps aloud as he went down and then, turning round, repeated the numbers to Croker:

'One, two, three, and one, two, three and four.'

It was a help to a man, even to one so free from the infirmities of old age and gay as any youth in London, to watch his step and count 'One, two' or 'Left, right' as he approached the other side of the hill.

Besides, he had always asked himself before embarking on any enterprise,

'What's the next step?'[27]

*

September was in its second week and the Duke still reading hard at his standing-desk, or dealing with letters at his cluttered table and laughing away over the answers he composed. On 12 September a particularly choice note arrived by hand. 'I had one this morning,' he wrote to Lady Salisbury, 'from a Madman who announces that he is a messenger from the Lord, and will deliver his message to-morrow morning Monday at Walmer Castle! We shall see!'[28]

Monday the 13th was his last full day.

The Charles Wellesleys arrived with his grandchildren. He had got up early at 5.30 A.M. to look at his garden and was in high spirits for the rest of the day. Games with his grandchildren, venison for dinner; then up the Castle stairs for the last time, candle in hand, to the small irregularly shaped room with yellow curtains behind the ramparts. There was just the amount of furniture he needed: the wing arm-chair, his curtainless camp-bed with faded green counterpane, horse-hair mattress and pillow covered in chamois leather, copper cans and wash-basin in the cupboard, towel-horse, standing-desk, tables and bedside reading in a bookcase, including Caesar and Jeremy Taylor's *Holy Living and Holy Dying*. He liked his camp-bed partly because it was his army one – only 2 feet 9 inches wide – and partly because the sight of it had amused Mary Salisbury. She asked him how he managed to turn over in such a narrow bed and he replied,

'When it's time to turn over it's time to turn out.'*

But on the morning of 14 September 1852 there was no need to turn out, for the messenger of the Lord had come for him. It was fifty-eight years all but one day since he fought his first action at Boxtel in Holland.[29] His valet, Kendall, had knocked on his door as usual at 6.30 A.M. An hour later a maid came running to say his Grace was 'making a great noise' and must be ill. Kendall rushed in half-dressed but his master was lying quietly.

'It is half-past Seven o'clock, your Grace.'

'*Thank you*, where does the Apothecary live?'

'At Deal, your Grace.'

'Send for him, I wish to speak to him.'

Dr Hulke the apothecary left his breakfast unfinished and reached Walmer at 9 A.M.

'I am sorry that your Grace is an invalid – what do you complain of?'

'I think some derangement' – passing his hand across his chest. The pulse was irregular but Hulke was not unduly alarmed and ordered an ammonia stimulant after some tea and toast. He told

* I have assigned the Duke's famous quip to this occasion on the strength of his letter to Mary Salisbury dated 27 August 1850. 'I slept in my little camp bed without curtains, which amused you so much! Indeed I think I liked it better for the notice taken of it.' (Burghclere, p. 83.) Douro quoted the quip to Henry Hobhouse in December of the same year, 1850, that is about four months later, if indeed the Duke's quip was first made to Lady Salisbury that August. (Broughton, vol. v, p. 266.)

Lord Charles Wellesley he would return at noon. As soon as the apothecary had gone Kendall asked the Duke if he would take a little tea.

'*Yes if you please.*'

Kendall underlined these words in the account he sent to Shackle, the Queen's footman who had originally come to Windsor from Stratfield Saye, because they were the last words his beloved master spoke. They did indeed seem to underline one side of the Duke's character: his courtesy and readiness to do his duty even if it meant drinking the hemlock. The tea was immediately followed by a fit, and then another and another.

He was no longer conscious when Dr Hulke hurried back at 9.45 A.M. accompanied by his son. The two Hulkes plied him with the remedies which had been effective in the past – a mustard emetic and a feather to 'irritate the fauces [jaws]' while another manservant, Collins, assisted Kendall in applying mustard poultices to the Duke's body and legs. Meanwhile the local doctor, McArthur, had been summoned; he took over the feather while the rest went on poulticing. There was no relief. Three grains of calomel were administered and the Duke becoming restless at about 2 P.M., he was lifted into his wing-chair on Kendall's advice. Kendall felt sure this was what he wanted.

Sitting in his favourite chair he slowly sank. At 3.25 P.M. with Charles and Sophia beside him and his devoted servants and doctors around he died. The end was so quiet that Charles could not believe he had gone. Dr Hulke's son held up a mirror to his mouth. There was not a whisper of breath on the glass.

*

While the Duke was alive it had been the custom to strike the Lord Warden's flag flying over the Castle when he returned to London. His friends, watching his carriage vanish over the other side of the hill, would make their way sadly home feeling Walmer was an empty place.[30] Now the flag flew at half-mast and the whole country seemed empty. 'The greatest man that England ever knew is no more,' wrote Prince Albert's secretary to the royal family at Balmoral, confirming the news of the 14th received by electric telegraph; 'One can hardly realise to oneself the idea of England without the Duke of Wellington.' When the news was brought to the Balmoral schoolroom the Queen's niece, Princess Feo, looked up with swimming eyes: 'and what will become of the Aunt Victoria?'[31]

The Times in its leading article struck a rich philosophical note: 'The Duke of WELLINGTON had exhausted nature and exhausted glory. His career was one unclouded longest day. . . .' More realistic, the radical *Spectator* said that on one point there could be no doubt: 'As a Counsellor of his Sovereign, the great Duke is not to be replaced.' With this conviction added to the Queen's personal grief for her '*dear* & great old Duke of Wellington,' she and the Prince decided to postpone the funeral until after Parliament met in November: 'Every Englishman shall have time and opportunity to take his humble part in it,' announced the Prince.[32] In fact time was needed not by the humble but by the proud: time to organize the most superb State funeral the nation had ever known.

The Duke's body, lying quietly at first on his camp bed at Walmer, was duly embalmed ready to take its place beside Lord Nelson in St Paul's. Meanwhile his friends had him for a few weeks longer. 'Sir,' wrote his manservant, Collins, to William Spicer of Devon:

I enclose you a little of Field Marshall the Duke of Wellingtons hair which I cut of [*sic*] myself after his death . . . I am sorry its so small a quantity but the demand from his family and friends are so great. . . .[33]

The false teeth he was wearing when he died were given to Lady Douro. (On her death they were returned to the family.)*

Where did Victorian sentimentality end and the feeling for relics of an almost godlike being begin? Carlyle had once seen his wife Jane creep up behind the old Duke at a party and without his knowing kiss him very gently on the shoulder. It was even rumoured that Lord Clanwilliam, who used to keep the Duke informed of suspicious shipping off the French coast, asked not only for a relic of hair but also the hand which wrote the Waterloo Despatch. What the Duke would have thought can be guessed from his rage when it was found that someone had cut off Copenhagen's hoof as a memento. The man, a servant, dared not

---

* False teeth were sometimes called 'Waterloo teeth' because of the trade's custom of using human teeth from battlefields. The Duke's front teeth were human, the rest of gold and walrus ivory.

confess but later handed the hoof back to the 2nd Duke, who had it made into an inkstand.

More consonant with the feelings of today was Miss Coutts's decision to remember the Duke's hands in marble. 'I have placed the Hands of the Duke on a Cushion,' wrote the artist.[34] From the tone of the condolences, not least from Douro (as the 2nd Duke insisted on still signing himself to her), Miss Coutts might have been the Duke's widow. She was the only woman to whom the 2nd Duke gave a death-mask and she attended the funeral with the ladies of his family.

For poor, distracted Miss Jenkins it was very different. When her doctor broke the news her first thought was that the Duke had died after all without a 'new birth'. Then she hoped it might have happened during his last five hours of unconsciousness. In England there was nothing to stay for. She joined a sister in America and died ten years after her elusive hero in a sad state of religious mania.

'Since the Duke's death I have had nothing to write about,' Greville confessed on 22 October, as if the world had stopped.

*

For two days in November, the 9th and 10th, the Walmer people were allowed to file past the coffin. By the end of the second day nine thousand people had gone through the Castle and drifted out in a slow black line along the beach. Then at 7 P.M. on the 10th the Castle's minute guns began to boom. The Duke had said a fortnight before he died that he intended to quit 'this part of the world' before his usual date, 14 November, and quit it he did.[35] The train carried him to London, where he arrived at 3 A.M. on the 11th. He was taken by torchlight with an escort of the 1st Life Guards to Chelsea Hospital for the lying-in-state. Under the same roof where forty-four years earlier young Arthur Wellesley had stood his bleak trial for Cintra, he now lay in unimaginable and some thought irrelevant pomp.

The ceiling of the Great Hall was draped to represent a sable tent; the walls were hung with black cloth adorned by the Duke's armorial bearings; four rows of colossal candelabra in silver sconces divided the hall into five parts, and at the western end a dais surrounded by twelve candelabra and ten columns formed of spears swathed in black velvet 'powdered with' laurel wreaths and escutcheons, supported the coffin. Covered in red velvet, the coffin was raised on a black bier 'garnished' with more escutcheons, while round the rail were the Field-Marshal's batons, with heraldic banners at the head and at the foot a 'trophy' of surcoat, sword, targe, helm, crest and spurs. A silver-lined black canopy 'enriched' with cornice, vallance, tenons, plumes, curtains and lace completed the magnificently oppressive scene. Around the coffin sat the surviving warriors whose martial names were associated with the hero's great days: Ponsonby, Pakenham, Stanhope, Baring, Maitland.

The whole thing had been quite contrary to the wishes of Wellington's sons and the havoc which at first ensued among the struggling crowds did nothing to change their feelings. On 13 November Douro was writing to Miss Coutts:

The Lying in State is a really disgusting affair, seven people they say were killed by the crowd today and I shall carefully consider whether or not it will do for us to countenance such a disgraceful way of doing honor.*

Two days later the brothers' mood had changed. Though they would still have preferred a private funeral, 'we have never regretted that we placed ourselves at the disposition of the country'.[36] If the country desired what was neither reverential nor in good taste, at least it had an opportunity of displaying unexampled attachment.

As the day of the funeral approached, many shared the 2nd Duke's reservations. Lady Palmerston had never looked forward to her dearest but gouty Harry having to process for six or seven hours. She decided personally to ignore the whole thing. 'It seems to me so unnatural and so grating to one's feelings to make a festival of a funeral! It's like an Irish Wake.'[37]

Yet in the end it was neither like a wake nor anything else anyone had ever known before.

*

> Lead out the pageant: sad and slow,
> As fits an universal woe,
> Let the long procession go,
> And let the sorrowing crowd about it grow,
> And let the martial music blow:
> The last great Englishman is low.

* The *Annual Register* said three people were crushed to death.

After a wet blustery night the sun suddenly shone upon a million and a half people lining the route. They were packed together at windows, on rooftops, in trees, to watch the incredible cortège: great dignitaries of Church and State in their splendid coaches; marching bands with trumpets and kettledrums; officers carrying the Duke's standard, guidon, banners and bannerols, and eighty-three Chelsea pensioners who joined the procession on foot at Charing Cross; a black mourning coach containing Bluemantle and Rouge Dragon, their brilliant tabards worn over mourning cloaks; then the Duke's servants in another mourning coach, followed by representatives from the Tower, East India Company, Trinity House, Cinque Ports, Board of Ordnance, Oxford University; Prince Albert in a coach and six; Lord Anglesey carrying the Duke's British army baton and distinguished foreigners with the batons of their respective countries.

Now at last appeared the ducal coronet borne by Clarenceux King of Arms on a black velvet cushion, the pall-bearers in two mourning coaches, the band of the Grenadier Guards and – 'THE BODY, placed upon a FUNERAL CAR, drawn by twelve Horses, and decorated with Trophies and Heraldic Achievements. The Hat and Sword of the Deceased being placed on the Coffin.' The huge dray horses, borrowed from a London brewery, were richly caparisoned in black up to the eyes.

There followed the 2nd Duke in an immensely long mourning cloak, with his 'assistants', 'supporters', friends and relatives: Wellesleys and Pakenhams; Salisbury, Tweeddale, Raglan, Burghersh, Cowley, Smith, Worcester, Hamilton, Foster and two Arbuthnots. As the mourning coaches rolled out of sight all eyes turned towards the Duke's horse, led by John Mears, his groom. The reversed Wellington boots hanging on either side brought tears to many eyes including the Queen's. There was a subdued murmur in contrast to the profound silence which had greeted the coffin.

Inspired by Prince Albert, the designer of the funeral car had produced an earthly mansion on wheels which would somehow carry the thoughts of millions to mansions above. The car was 21 feet long by 12 feet wide and weighed 18 tons, while the coffin, though a foot longer than the Duke at 6 feet 9 inches, looked lost on its high perch. The creaking architectural mass on which it trembled was too much for even the six great wheels. They sank into the mud opposite the Duke of York's statue in Pall Mall, and the vast edifice moved again only after sixty strong men had been roped in to heave. The canopy was successfully lowered by machinery in order to pass under Temple Bar, but the mechanism for transferring the coffin to the bier at the west door of St Paul's failed to work for over an hour.

To be both monstrous and inefficient was too much. Prince Albert had chosen the 'abominably ugliest' of all designs, declared Carlyle, and Lady de Ros – Georgiana Lennox of Waterloo days – was positively appalled: 'The car! oh, so frightful! I can't describe it. I must leave it to the *Morning Post*.' Lady Morgan hoped they would have no more heroes to bury for a thousand years.[38] In the guns, plumes and martial trophies of Britain's last heraldic funeral, the evangelical Lord Ashley saw many signs of death but none of immortality.

All along, the Prince's guiding light had been 'that nothing should be wanting in this tribute of national gratitude'.[39] Nothing was wanting; except the simplicity which had been the hallmark of the hero.

As the coffin waited helplessly outside the Cathedral's open door a biting November blast whistled up the aisles, chilling those inside and forcing some with bald heads to put on handkerchiefs or even hats. Contrariwise, shafts of cheerful sunlight pierced the gloom, killing the intended theatrical effect of a cavernous cathedral soaring into utter darkness, while every spark of radiance was concentrated on the central point beneath the dome.

But when all this was said, there remained an experience for hundreds of thousands that was beautiful and unique. They wept as the catafalque passed by, showing that they did not need great art to mediate their feelings for the Great Duke. The sight of all the hats raised looked to one eye-witness like 'the sudden rising from the ground & settling again of a huge flock of birds'.[40] As the bier at length entered the nave a draught caught the feathers on his cocked hat, so that it seemed to stir. Thousands of pages turning over together in the hands of the vast congregation sounded like a drawn-out universal sigh. Six tall candlesticks stood round the coffin, three on either side, to be lighted again 112 years later for Winston Churchill. Some of the music had been composed long years before by the Duke's father.

Of the eight pall-bearers, Seaton, Maitland and Woodford had

served the Duke at Waterloo and Hardinge at Quatre-Bras;
Charles Napier and Gouch had conquered in India, the former
still tortured by his head-wound received at Bussaco; Combermere had constantly looked to the Duke for military, political
and even domestic advice, Londonderry for military and political
counsel which, however, he seldom took. Lord Seaton (Colborne
of Waterloo) judged the sonorous reading of the Duke's titles
and the throwing of the broken staff into the grave to be relics of
heraldry 'inapplicable to the present age'. But the playing of the
Dead March as the coffin was lowered into the vault, followed by
the singing of *Man that is born of a woman*, moved him to tears. 'I
was very much affected, and thought I should have been obliged
to sit down.'[41]

Suddenly, *Sleepers awake* rang out, the Tower guns crashed
and at the west door the trumpets sounded 'a wail'. It was over.

> *Under the cross of gold*
> *That shines over city and river,*
> *There he shall rest for ever*
> *Among the wise and the bold.*

II   IMMORTALITY

' – I wonder how you could suffice,' said George Chad one day to
the Duke, marvelling at his prodigies of achievement in India.

'I never should,' said the Duke, 'if I had not been very young
in command.'[42]

Early advantages were not enough to account for all that the
Great Duke had become since. In a scheme for a statue in St
Paul's it was the Duke's 'chief virtues' which Prince Albert
wished to see commemorated allegorically, rather than 'endless
marble Bayonets, swords, cannon smoke, Shakoes & Drums'.*[43]

* The magnificent monument designed for St Paul's by Alfred Stevens
was completed by John Tweed and originally placed in the Chapel of St
Michael and St George. It had its allegorical virtues of Truth and Valour
defeating Falsehood and Cowardice. When it was removed to the present
position the equestrian statue on top was omitted, because Dean Milner
objected to a horse in a church. About 1903 the equestrian statue was added
but the whole was not completed until 1912.
After a good deal of argument over where to put the funeral car, it was
finally returned to St Paul's, where it can be seen today in the crypt, in all its
grandeur and misery.

The Great Duke's chief virtues were not in dispute: the truth-fulness, courage, honesty, fairness and simplicity; the prudence and foresight; the directness, straightforwardness, decision and realism that made him so extraordinarily sensible; the repeated proofs that personal ambition, after youth was over, had no power to move him and that all he responded to was service, duty and patriotism, on whose full tide he was carried forward.

To the Victorians, sense of duty was a major virtue not because everybody possessed it but because so many did not. Wellington set the style for the great public servant of the future, single-minded and incorruptible. The most admired couplet in Tenny-son's 'Ode on the Death of the Duke of Wellington', already quoted, was in fact a verse paraphrase of what the Duke had often said himself:

> *Not once or twice in our rough island-story*
> *The path of duty was the way to glory*[44]

There was the French reviewer of his *Despatches* who complained of finding 'duty' on every page and 'glory' never. 'That,' said the Duke, 'is the difference between the French and English soldier; with the French glory is the cause; with us, the result.'[45]

*

'Come what come may, I will cling to the heroic principle. It can alone satisfy my soul.' So said Coningsby, the hero of Disraeli's novel.

Not much was known of the Duke's soul, despite Miss Jenkins. But an unsuspected interest in theology was confided to a few of his friends. Who would have thought he sat up half the night reading Keith's *Demonstration of the Truth of Christianity*? 'It is the most interesting Work upon any Subject that I ever perused.'[46] Or that he told Miss Angela a sensational book on the French Revolution would 'amuse' her less than Dr Wiseman's *Lectures on Science and Revealed Religion*?

The Duke's Christianity was tolerant. Dr Wiseman, a Roman Catholic, had become Cardinal-Archbishop of Westminster in 1850, thus causing Protestant England to smell the sulphur of 'Papal Aggression'. The Duke remained calm. To be sure, he found himself again regretting the Concordat which he had vainly proposed in the 1820s and which he believed would have prevented the present crisis. But he regretted even more the anti-Catholic hubbub. 'I hear nothing everywhere but the dangers of Popery,' he wrote scornfully. 'It is driving people mad. I have this day two letters foretelling the end of the World!'[47]

He deprecated shallow criticism of non-Christian religions. 'The whole army, while I was in India, except about 50,000 men, consisted of idolators,' he told Parliament in 1839, ' – but they were as good soldiers as could be found anywhere.' Not all missionaries, on the other hand, were good soldiers of Christ. 'I know . . . the little progress they make; and I know at the same time that their labors create a good deal of jealousy'.[48] Nevertheless, he defended missions in principle for the sufficient reason that Christ has ordered them.

'A soldier must obey orders,' he said to a man who was attacking missionaries.

'What do you mean?'

'It is orders to preach the gospel to every creature alive.'

Above all education must never be separated from religion, otherwise you would create 'so many clever devils'.[49]

Ultimately his Christianity focused upon the Lord's Prayer, in which he found 'the sum total of religion and morals', and upon the Christian virtue of forgiveness, with which he identified peace. When an army colonel asked him how he could forgive and reinstate Sir Robert Wilson, a soldier who had intrigued so much against him, the Duke answered that he himself had done many things which required forgiveness '& he hoped God who was a God of Peace would forgive him'.[50] Forgiveness and peace were not perhaps the virtues most closely associated by the outside world with the Duke; certainly they were those most prized by him at the end of his life.

*

Peculiarities are not necessarily virtues but sometimes they give as much pleasure. 'Wyatt called, and we revelled in His Grace's peculiarities,' wrote the painter Benjamin Haydon in his diary for 30 September 1839. 'Wyatt informed me he always said when people tried to persuade him to do what he had made up his mind not to do, "The rat has got into the bottle – the rat has got into the bottle." ' Odd as the expression always sounded, it conveyed the special flavour of the Duke's obstinacy: the damned large rat at bay inside the damned small bottle, from which he could not be budged.

It was widely believed by contemporaries that the Duke 'never took anybody's opinion but his own', and that this obstinacy led him into making mistakes which he never rectified or even admitted. 'The Duke has strong sense, great resolution,' wrote Knighton in 1830, 'but being wrong he has no power of setting himself right either from the advice of friends or . . . his own reflection.' Fourteen years later, however, the Duke had so far conquered this weakness as to publish in the records of Pembroke College, Oxford, a mistake he had made as Visitor, precisely through listening to only one side of a question and then making up his own mind – wrongly. The mistake had been to veto the appointment of a Dr Jeune as Provost, on the representations of his rivals. The Duke recorded his mistake, he said, as 'a Memento of warning not only to myself but to others who may have similar Duties to perform'.[51] The rat had come out of the bottle.*

In a wider context, the Duke cannot be exonerated of neglecting public opinion. Though his contempt for the press was mitigated in later years, the old fighter would be heard protesting to the end that he did not care a pin what 'the Gentlemen' said. This peculiarity was one which his circle either 'revelled in' or condoned. As Professor Brock has pointed out, the bigger the man the greater the blunders he is allowed to make by respectful colleagues.

From self-confidence in exaggerated or freak forms were derived many of the Duke's other peculiarities. His secretiveness, which saw no advantage or pleasure in taking others into his confidence, remained with him from first to last, the wound of a deprived child which nonetheless went with the proud bow of Achilles. No phrase is more striking throughout his long life than the will to walk or stand alone. He once said that if the hairs of his

---

* Mrs Jeune's comments in her diary on the unfolding drama deserve to be quoted almost in full, for their truthful picture of Wellington's contrasting impacts on contemporary opinion: 7 February 1844: Fulminations against Wellington's 'very unjust and extraordinary conduct'. 22 April 1844: 'I rejoice to see that his (Dr Jeune's) election has been confirmed by the Great Duke in the handsomest and most flattering manner, thereby enhancing the value of his success tenfold. Such noble cndour is quite overpowering and one laments ever being betrayed into an unjust thought of this great man.'

head could talk he would tear them out and wear a wig.[52]

Much of his inventiveness sprang from a wish that he and his friends might be independent of doctors, coachmen, butlers, valets. Such was the finger-bandage which he could fix himself, the infinite variety of wet-weather equipment to prevent colds, the three pairs of bath gloves in linen and tweed, the fast self-drive curricle, the individual pots of tea on the breakfast-table, the purchase of an early safety razor and, before that, the regular journeys from the country to the one man in London who sharpened his razors so perfectly that he could always shave himself.*[53]

In old age he brushed his own clothes and wished he were 'strong enough' to clean his own boots. This, despite the protocol against such practices. A group of visiting diplomats were said to have protested to Abraham Lincoln when they caught sight of him polishing away under their windows at the White House,

'In England no gentleman ever cleans his own boots.'

'Indeed? Whose boots do they clean then?'

Over the enormous chore of letter-writing, the Duke's decision to rely on self-help rather than secretaries led him into some rich peculiarities. The man who was treated with royal deference did not hesitate to order in his own hand a meal of boiled fowl and rice from the landlord of a country inn. But his lithograph system was gradually extended to cover refusals for every conceivable request: for the dedication of a book to him, for a seat in the House of Lords' gallery, for presenting petitions and for sending information about or specimens of his hair, handwriting or prose style. 'I intend to have a Lithograph answer prepared for some of these curious askers of Questions,' he wrote to Mary Salisbury on 23 January 1851, 'recommending them to attend to their own business, with which my Height, age or Weight can have no relation.' For those who persisted in sending him, unasked, poems, stories or irreplaceable family documents to read, there was a pile of return slips lying always ready on his table:

Avoid to impose upon others the care of original papers which you wish to preserve.

* 'I am vastly amused by the Bloomer discussions!' he wrote when Mrs Bloomer invented her knickers, 'I understand them, being somewhat of a Taylor!' – but finally decided they were 'impossible'. (Burghclere, p. 208, 18 October 1851). He was also, as no one needed reminding, more than somewhat of a bootmaker.

The composition of these printed slips gave the Duke immense satisfaction and he would sometimes add to them by hand either in the text or in a space left at the bottom. A favourite addition to solicitations was that he was not 'the Solicitor-General', and to those who asked him to convey messages, that he was not 'a Postman or Booking-office'.*

The flick of his logic sometimes made him sound harsh while being kind. From the unknown inmate of a workhouse came a plea for new clothes and tea. The Duke answered that a lady in a workhouse did not require smart wearing apparel but he would send the tea. Though Algy Greville, his one indispensable secretary, did his best to soften the Duke's acerbities, he was not always successful. Occasionally a bold spirit would complain of some scalding phrase. The Duke invariably replied that he had not intended to hurt anyone's feelings and would the victim return his letter with the offending passage marked?

Despite the Duke's addiction to letter-writing he maintained a carping attitude to the penny post (shared with Lord Melbourne), which had been introduced in 1840. The subsidy was wasteful, he declared, since the working classes did not write letters: one Highland regiment in the Peninsula had sent home a total of only sixty-four letters in six months. Soon, however, he was complaining that the popularity of the penny post had damaged the postal service. 'Never again will I trust wax alone, for my letter to you was certainly well sealed,' he wrote to the beautiful Lady Caroline Maxse in 1848, whose letter from him had arrived open. 'The fact is that there is a hurry and crowding under the penny postage system that there was not in the days of franking.'[54]

*

The Duke's attitude towards the 'lower orders' was certainly not peculiar to him. He was devoted to his own personal servants but had no wish to see a blurring of class edges. Ernest Bevin said a century later that the tragedy of the working class was 'the poverty of their desires'. To Wellington and his friends this was a mercy, not a tragedy. He wrote to Charles Arbuthnot:

---

* The Duke never minded adding in bits and pieces even to intimate letters, when others would have thought it better to rewrite. He once began a letter to his daughter-in-law, 'My dear Lady Douro', and then squeezed in 'est' below the line to make it 'dear*est*'.

We have educated the lower orders. They now say why should they not associate with us ?[55]

They wanted to resort to our private houses, our entertainments; have the run of our kitchens and dance with our wives and daughters. Alternatively, they would invite us to their public houses, to live with them.

They would shortly afterwards discover that they are better qualified to be Legislators Ministers Generals Holders of Large Properties than we are.

This diatribe, probably the most reactionary in tone which the Duke ever perpetrated, must be seen in context. It was written in 1832 at the height of the reform struggle.

*

It is unnecessary to dwell again at length on the Duke and his women friends. Unlike auto-intoxicated characters such as Napoleon and Byron, he was too much of a gentleman to boast of using women for pleasure, although during his early years he occasionally did so. In the prime of life he settled for clever women, but still with the emphasis frankly on what they could give to him. A snatch of dialogue recorded by Fanny Salisbury makes the point:

I asked him if he thought Ly Peel had any influence over her husband. 'No, she is not a clever woman – Peel did not wish to marry a clever woman.' I observed how extraordinary it seemed to me that a man of abilities should not wish to have a wife capable of entering into the subjects in which he took interest – 'and of anticipating one's meaning [interposed the Duke] – that is what a clever woman does – she sees what you mean.' *[56]

As he grew older the relations subtly changed. He found more pleasure in giving. From Lady Wilton, a hard woman, he received only a modest return for his friendship. Between himself and each of the Lady Salisburys a perfect interchange was established, despite the difference in age. His love for Angela Burdett-Coutts was the final stage, showing itself in the prodigal expenditure of thought and imagination on *her* interests, her talents, her future. Such a radiation of protective and eager devotion made his friendship irresistible.

* Compare Dr Johnson on the actress Kitty Clive: 'Clive, Sir, is a very good thing to sit by; she always understands what you say.'

His 'pin-up' girl at Apsley House makes a romantic postscript. She was Mrs Sarah Dowell, tobacconist, living at the corner of Wilton Place and Knightsbridge. She sent him her portrait in 1839 out of admiration for the Great Duke; he kept it on a chair in his bedroom out of kindness, and because of her great charm. They never met.

*

'Transparent' is one of the adjectives which seems to have been made for Wellington. His contemporary and friend, G. R. Gleig, wrote at the end of his biography that if anyone was still in doubt about Wellington's character it was the biographer's fault, since no great man's character was ever 'more completely free from disguise'.

Yet there are opacities, mainly in the Duke's attitude to politics and party. He put country above party. Did he, as critics have suggested, put himself above party also?

British politics claim to be grounded in a mature patriotism so that the eternal triangle of country, party and self cannot be dismembered or despised in any of its parts, however much they may war with one another at times. When the Duke saw himself as the Sovereign's retained servant he was linking two arms of the triangle – self and country – in a noble and honourable way. The third arm of the triangle, party, was not fully developed, being as much an amalgam of 'connections' (family, patronage and so on) up to 1830, as a political entity. By transcending the 'connections', Wellington did in a sense point a way forward. Moreover, he saved the party of the 'right' from disaster when he saved its major constitutional long-stop, the House of Lords. Without his reiterated commands to face about and retreat, the Lords might have been mown down and thrown like the proverbial grass into the oven.

Would that have been such a bad thing in the 1830s and 1840s? It would have saved much subsequent trouble, including the Parliament Act of 1911 to restrict their powers.

The answer must surely be that in the crucial years sandwiched between two European revolutions, 1830–48, the risk to British democracy would have been unjustified. The great landed and financial interests would hardly have surrendered their Upper House without attempting a counter-revolution. In those stormy times British democracy and the budding party system might well have vanished into the oven, along with the old constitutional House of Lords. By preventing the Upper House from dashing itself to pieces against the Commons, Wellington may have saved more than he knew.[57]

As for his putting himself above party, there was no admixture of personal ambition to this trait, which was in any case a limited one. Twice in his career – 1834 and 1839 – he made the *gran rifiuto* of supreme office. Few other British statesmen have refused the premiership once; only one more than once.*

How far was the great Duke aware that his sublime position above party and almost beyond politics could not be taken as an example by other statesmen? He was well aware. He may not have foreseen, as the younger Disraeli did, how the British party system would develop, but he fully realized that his own stance, half within and half outside, was literally inimitable: a political once-for-all, or at any rate, once in a century. 'This anomalous position' was how he described it to Lord Londonderry in 1846.[58]

*

Wellington's relations with the army were complex and unusual. As a disciplined body of men he was devoted to them, and they to him; not because he was *séduisant* in the way that people found Napoleon seductive, but for the trust he invited and never betrayed, for the guns he never lost and the armies he never threw away. Old soldiers who accosted him in the streets were rewarded with a sovereign from a stock kept ready in a special purse; it contained three when he died. Yet in the long bitter controversies over flogging he could not be brought to abandon that most abominable of deterrents. He still insisted before the Royal Commission on Military Punishments in 1836 that Prussian reforms were not suited to Britain, clinging to his old distinction between an army of conscripts drawn from every class and a volunteer force generally supplied by the lowest.

Ten years later, on 9 August 1846, the masters of Manchester Grammar School asked him his views on the subject, hoping they might have softened. He replied that he dared not yet do without flogging entirely, and people like them who lived in

* Lord Hartington refused in 1880 and 1886; Lord Halifax took steps in 1940 which prevented his being asked.

Manchester where the army was so often called in to disperse mobs ought to be thankful it was a disciplined army. In his last speech on flogging, however, delivered in the Lords two days later, he recognized that the change would come. Flogging was on the way out. Twenty years before, one soldier in fifty had been flogged per year; by 1844 the figure had dropped to one in 194.

'I hope I may live,' he said, 'to see it abolished altogether.'

His pathetic decline during the last ten years when he held the chief command has already been taken into account, together with its serious consequences to the Crimean soldiers. Nevertheless he gave to the Crimean army, and to every British army, a tradition of victory, a pride, a doggedness, an iron nerve even in the most unnerving conditions, without which they must have succumbed as in 1793–5.

*

It is usual to compare great commanders with their peers, in many ways a profitless task. With regard to the strategy and tactics of Wellington and Napoleon, 'their only common characteristic was an overwhelming tendency to be victorious'.[59] Comparisons between himself and Marlborough were often invited by Wellington's contemporaries, and though he deprecated them he was occasionally drawn into giving a view. 'I can conceive nothing greater than Marlborough at the head of an English Army,' he once told Lord Mahon.

He had greater difficulties than I had with his Allies; the Dutch were worse to manage than the Spaniards or Portuguese. But on the other hand I think I had more difficulties at home. He was all in all with the administration, but I supported the Government much more than they supported me![60]

When Mahon wished to publish this judgement, however, the Duke replied sharply:

I can't help thinking that if you avoid to make a comparison between living and dead persons you might as well not make me settle the comparison for you. I am convinced that you will see that you cannot publish what you propose without writing a History of the War and of the State of this Nation; and of Europe at each Period.

Lord Mahon hastily agreed.

In this always unreal exercise, Napoleon must be the key figure, since it was he who in his own day disputed with Wellington the supreme title. Everything was done by their respective nations to enhance their own hero and belittle his rival: the French chess set with Napoleon as white king and Wellington a mere black bishop, the English anagram of Arthur Wellesley, Duke of Wellington – 'Let well foil'd Gaul secure thy renown.'*

At their most magnanimous the rivals freely conceded one another's genius, Napoleon admitting during the voyage to St Helena that the Duke had everything he had, with prudence added; Wellington never deviating from his original dictum that Napoleon's presence on the field was worth forty thousand men. When asked who was the greatest general of the age, General Sir John Le Couteur remembered the Duke replying, 'In this age, in the past ages, in *any* age, Napoleon.'[61]

Napoleon was more dazzlingly prodigal with men and materiel, Wellington more brilliantly economical. If the French Chasseurs could be made to perform miracles, so could the Scots Greys. Napoleon created his élitist gigantic Guard, Wellington his thin red line. Wellington's stroke was a battering-ram, according to William Napier, Napoleon's the onrush of a wave. The Prussian military writer, General Carl von Clausewitz, made a brave attempt to cut down both heroes to size over the Waterloo campaign. His strictures on Wellington added up to one argument: that the British general could have stood shoulder to shoulder with the Prussians at *any point* he cared to choose, without waiting to see where the French would strike, since Napoleon was bound to seek him out in a head-on collision wherever he stood.

This criticism was rightly rejected by the Duke when he read it in 1842. It virtually demanded of him second sight, as well as a crude view of Napoleon quite out of character, at least until after the bludgeoning and pounding of Waterloo.

Napoleon's total genius exerts a more powerful attraction on the world than Wellington's, partly because the Emperor was defeated and died in exile – a tragic situation though ably exploited by the victim – and partly because he chose the nations for his footstool and Europe for his throne. 'He was a glorious tyrant after all,' said Byron.[62] Despite wide experience of dictators

* The modern French mastery of the Waterloo battlefield shows no sign of slipping. A traveller in 1971 who asked why there were no Wellington souvenirs in the shops was told, 'He does not sell.'

mankind prefers, it seems, to lie prostrate in imagination at the feet of the world's masters, rather than turn to the honest and just men of history.

The great, idealistic impulses in the Emperor do indeed shine forth in splendour: those which made him give France the *code Napoléon*, establish national education and put a field-marshal's baton into the knapsack of every common soldier. But all the fine things he was going to do in the way of liberating the European peoples if he had won Waterloo were propaganda issued from St Helena after the time for doing them had passed. In his day it was felt that despite his constructive legacies to the French he had left them with a spoilt palate for constitutional government.

Wellington handed down to his fellow-countrymen a clear mandate to make constitutional government work. His total genius was less spectacular than Napoleon's, apart from the fact that he deliberately eschewed theatrical aids to communication. Napoleon, he once remarked, was 'a great man but also a great actor'. Speaking of General Montgomery in 1944, the Permanent Head of the British Foreign Office wrote, 'I don't believe he's a general at all, but just a film star.'[63] Wellington did not belong to this, in many ways effective, school of leadership. Did he also have to manage without the gift of intuitive genius?

In his Wellington Memorial Lecture, 1969, Lord Montgomery described the Duke as 'the best soldier our nation has produced for many a long day'. This said, he failed to find in him that 'inner conviction, which at times will transcend reason'. A moment comes for boldness. 'When that moment comes, will you soar from the known to the unknown? In the answer to this question lies the supreme test of generalship in high command.'

Wellington must be allowed to answer this challenge in his own words, as recorded by Frances Salisbury in her diary:

'There is a curious thing that one feels sometimes; when you are considering a subject, suddenly a whole train of reasoning comes before you like a flash of light; you see it all (moving his hand as if something appeared before him, his eye with its brightest expression), yet it takes you perhaps two hours to put on paper all that has occurred to your mind in an instant. Every part of the subject, the bearing of all the parts upon each other, and all the consequences are there before you.'[64]

Wellington the commander was restricted by the politicians as

Napoleon never was, and his titanic tussle with Marshal Massena in Portugal put a stamp of defensiveness on his generalship which was belied by Salamanca, Vitoria and the Pyrenees. Before Waterloo itself he said, 'Now I will show the French how I can *defend* a position' – meaning that in the years before he had constantly been on the attack.

His political imagination could not compete with Napoleon's but its limitations did far less damage than his great opponent's boundless range. His temperamental objection to reminiscences, outside his official *Despatches*, had its advantages. In our over-all knowledge of the man, it adds almost as much as it takes away. What a character, who could be persuaded to write in the margins of contemporary accounts of his battles only the words 'True' and 'False'; or even merely the letters 'L.' and 'D.L.' – Lie and Damned Lie.[65]

In the halls of virtue rather than fame, the Duke makes an incomparably better showing. Goodness, in a Christian sense, did not enter into Napoleon's motivation. For the purpose of bestriding Europe it would have been foolish to choose compassion and humility as mounting-blocks. The two men's ideas of duty were radically different. Wellington's has already been examined; Napoleon wrote to his brother Jerome: 'Never forget that . . . your first duty is to me, your second is to France.'[66]

Wellington's sense of Britain's place in the world was essentially non-aggressive. 'A sort of fabulous Englishman,' he wrote after the Chinese Opium War 'is not to be permitted to go about the world bullying, smuggling, and plundering as he pleases.'[67]

His sense of mankind's place linked him with another great soldier-statesman, George Washington, to whom he was indeed likened by the American minister, Edward Everett. 'I have always felt the Highest respect for the character of General Washington,' wrote the Duke to Everett in thanking him for the comparison.[68] Curiously relevant to the Duke's refrain, 'I am but a man,' is the story of Washington riding through a small town and overhearing a girl of seven, brought out to see the hero, exclaim,

'Why, he is only a man!' The General swept off his hat, bowed and said,

'Yes miss, that's all I am.'

*

There is one last image which must be either fitted into or discarded from the Wellingtonian gallery – the Iron Duke.

Punch may be said to have coined the expression in 1845. Commenting on the regimental brevity of Wellington's epistolary style from which all 'small courtesies and minor graces' were omitted, *Punch* said: 'We cannot but think that Iron Dukes like Iron Pokers are none the worse for just a little polish.' If the term became popular only after the Duke's death, there were plenty of precedents earlier than 1845 for its subsequent adoption, from General Pakenham's admiration for 'the iron man', to his own frank pride in his 'iron hand'. His younger contemporary, the painter Frith, heard that after Waterloo he 'shed iron tears'.

Some modern military historians, however, have protested against the nickname on the ground that it gives a false slant to the qualities of a great and humane man. That may be so. The Duke was never 'iron' in the sense of unfeeling or cold-hearted; indeed the iron in his make-up was often molten. Benjamin Haydon recalled his violent imprecations against artists and how the sculptor Bailey had refused to dine or spend the night at Stratfield Saye after one of the Duke's rages. Lifting up both hands above his white head, he had cursed the whole tribe of his 'tormentors' for sentencing him to a lifetime of '400,000' sittings! There were also a hot streak which showed up less well in the cabinet than the camp. Harriet Arbuthnot referred to the 'dictatorial & arbitrary spirit' of which his enemies accused him, not always without reason.[69]

But when the iron was cool it possessed an incomparable quality. Wellington showed the army that a man could have an iron constitution not because he had been born with one but because he had acquired it the hard way. Though some of his hardness belonged to the leader's stock-in-trade, it exhibited more than common resilience. He showed the world of politics that the stern Tory need not always be unbending or the silent Englishman always stern.

Nevertheless he had a defect which was popularly associated with the cold hard side of an Iron Duke. He was insensitive to the spirit of the times and lacked the political warmth and luminosity which imagination gives. Obsessed by the first French Revolution, he was adamant that reform threatened the constitution.

He was therefore a reactionary in his revulsion from the liberal movements of Europe and in his affinity with the High Tories at home. The French Revolution, however, simply put a permanent edge on these feelings; it did not create them. He was not anxious to put the clock back, but like the aristocracy as a whole he found himself suited by things as they were. Change he disliked in his very bones. He accepted it only when he had to. At such times he was a pragmatist and did what was necessary and seemed to him right. Yet with his pragmatism the picture shifts again. He found it necessary to break with the French Ultras over constitutional government. He found it necessary to break with the British Ultras over Catholic emancipation, and despite reconciliations to give them more than one subsequent hammering. Thus he could behave as a man of iron towards reactionaries as well as radicals. For this steely impartiality even those who were most conscious of his defects had to give him credit.

Then the succeeding generations got hold of him. His arresting character, moulded by traditions and legends, or transmuted through the Brontës' genius into the Rochesters, Helstones and Moores (with just a touch of Heathcliff) was finally handed down to a later race of 'strong silent Englishmen' doing their imperial duty in pith helmets and at all times and everywhere keeping a stiff upper lip. That was not the Duke.

His iron was closer to reality: sometimes feared as men feared the 'iron-handed despotism' of the Industrial Revolution in Dickens's *Hard Times*; always honoured like the 'pillar of iron' in the *Book of Jeremiah*; once chosen by Teilhard de Chardin as the noble metal which gave him 'the feeling of full personality'. There were repressed and repressive elements in Wellington, but these did not prevent the full personality from breaking through.

It was during the second half of his life that the process came to maturity. As a young man he had heard Pitt's unforgettable words, 'England saved herself by her exertions and will, as I trust, save Europe by her example.' He himself was soon to be honoured for his exertions and his example. But his glory lay also in the fact that he did not cease from mental fight even after he had received the ultimate acclaim and seen his physical battles become legends in his lifetime. No man ever rested less on his laurels. Sometimes mistakenly, always selflessly, he continued to serve.

After Waterloo they called him the Great Captain. If he had

fallen on the field it would have been as the Great Captain that he was remembered. He lived to become the Great Duke. In those two words his countrymen, going beyond rank and honours, have paid tribute to a hero and saluted the completeness of a man.

Select Bibliography

MANUSCRIPT SOURCES

Royal Archives, Windsor Castle.

Royal Archives, the Royal House, The Hague.

Wellington MSS., in the possession of the Duke of Wellington.

Raglan MSS., in the possession of Lord Raglan, for the correspondence of Wellington, his brother Lord Maryborough (William Wellesley-Pole) and Lord Fitzroy Somerset, afterwards Lord Raglan.

Confidential Memoranda of Admiral Sir George Seymour, in the possession of Mrs Freda Loch.

Arthur Shakespear's Journal, in the possession of the Countess of Albemarle.

Arthur Kennedy's Letters, Weldon MSS.

Lady Dalrymple-Hamilton's Diary, in the possession of Admiral Sir F. Dalrymple-Hamilton.

Archives of the House of Rothschild, London.

The Wellesley, Peel, Aberdeen, Huskisson, Place and other manuscripts in the British Museum.

National Library of Ireland, for Wellington correspondence; letters of Maria Edgeworth to Lady Romilly: the Wellington Monument.

Irish State Paper Office, for Wellington correspondence.

Public Record Office of Northern Ireland, for Oriel papers and Stewart papers.

West Sussex Record Office, for Maxse papers.

Surrey Record Office, for Goulburn papers.

Frances Lady Salisbury's Journal, in the possession of the Marquess of Salisbury.

Letters of Anna Maria Jenkins, in the possession of Rice University, Texas.

MSS., copy of Lord Hatherton's diary, in the possession of Colonel R. J. Longfield.

Stewart papers, in the possession of Mr Michael Farrar-Bell.

Department of Western MSS., Bodleian Library, Oxford, for Dr Wynter's papers and Wellington correspondence.

Spicer letters, in the possession of Mrs Noel Tweddell.

A Tour of Waterloo 1815, in the possession of the Naval and Military Club.

Letters of Lord Wellesley and others, in the possession of Mr John Showers.

Letters concerning Wellington, in the possession of Lord Kenyon, Brigadier K. Thompson, Mr R. Boulind, Mr P. Skottowe, the Society for the Promotion of Christian Knowledge.

PUBLISHED SOURCES

Airlie, Mabell, Countess of: *Lady Palmerston and her Times* (2 vols., London, 1922).

Albemarle, George Thomas, Earl of: *Fifty Years of my Life* (London, 1877).

Aldington, Richard: *Wellington* (London, 1946).

Alington, Cyril, *Twenty Years of Party Politics – being a Study of the Development of the Party System between 1815 and 1835* (Oxford U.P., 1921).

Anglesey, Marquess of: *One-Leg, The Life and Letters of Henry William Paget, 1st Marquess of Anglesey* (London, 1961).

Annual Register.

Arbuthnot, Mrs P. S.-M.: *Memories of the Arbuthnots of Kincardine-shire and Aberdeenshire* (London, 1920).

Arbuthnot: *The Journal of Mrs Arbuthnot*. Edited by Francis Bamford and the Duke of Wellington (2 vols., London, 1950).

Aspinall, A.: *The Correspondence of Charles Arbuthnot*. Edited by A. Aspinall, Camden 3rd Series, LXV (London, 1941).

Aspinall, A.: *The Diary of Henry Hobhouse 1820–1827*. Edited by A. Aspinall (London, 1947).

Aspinall, A.: *The Formation of Canning's Ministry, February to August 1827*. Edited by A. Aspinall, Camden 3rd Series, LIX (London, 1937).

Aspinall, A.: *The Correspondence of George, Prince of Wales* (4 vols., London, 1963–70).

Aspinall, A.: *The Letters of George IV* (3 vols., Cambridge U.P., 1938).

Aspinall, A.: *Three Early Nineteenth Century Diaries* (Le Marchant, Ellenborough and Littleton, afterwards Hatherton). Edited by A. Aspinall (London, 1952).

Baldick, R.: *The Duel, A History of Duelling* (London, 1965).

Bamford, Samuel: *Passages in the Life of a Radical* (2 vols., London, 1844).

Bartlett, C. J.: *Castlereagh* (London, 1967).

Bell, H. C. F.: *Lord Palmerston* (2 vols., London, 1936).

Berry: *Journal and Correspondence of Miss Berry, 1783–1852*. Edited by Lady Theresa Lewis (London, 1865).

Bessborough: *Lady Bessborough and Her Family Circle*. Edited by the Earl of Bessborough in collaboration with A. Aspinall (London, 1940).

Best, G.: 'The Protestant Constitution and its Supporters, 1800–1829', vol. 18, 5th series, Royal Historical Society.

Bird, Anthony: *The Damnable Duke of Cumberland* (London, 1966).

Blake, Robert: *Disraeli* (London, 1966).

Blake, Robert: *The Conservative Party from Peel to Churchill* (London, 1970).

Blessington: *The Literary Life and Correspondence of the Countess of Blessington*. Edited by R. R. Madden (2 vols., London, 1855).

Brett-James, A.: *The Hundred Days* (London, 1964).

Briggs, Asa: *The Age of Improvement* (London, 1965).

Brontë, Charlotte: *Shirley* (London, 1849).

Brontë, Charlotte: *The Search after Happiness* (London, 1969).

Brougham: *Works of Henry Lord Brougham* (vols. 3–5, 'Statesmen of the Times of George III and George IV', London edition 1872–3).

Broughton, Lord (J. C. Hobhouse): *Recollections of a Long Life* (4 vols., London, 1911).

Bryant, Sir Arthur: *The Great Duke* (London, 1971).

Buchan, Susan: *The Sword of State: Wellington after Waterloo* (London, 1928).

Buckingham and Chandos, Duke of: *Memoirs of the Court and Cabinets of George III* (Vol. IV, London, 1853).

Buckingham and Chandos, Duke of: *Memoirs of the Court of George IV, 1820–1830* (2 vols., London, 1859).

Buckingham and Chandos, Duke of: *Memoirs of the Court and Cabinets of William IV and Victoria* (2 vols., London, 1861).

Burghclere: *A Great Man's Friendship. Letters of the Duke of Wellington to Mary, Marchioness of Salisbury, 1850–1852*. Edited by Lady Burghclere (London, 1927).

Burghersh: *The Correspondence of Lady Burghersh with the Duke of Wellington*. Edited by Lady Rose Weigall (London, 1903).

Butler, J. R. M.: *The Passing of the Great Reform Bill* (London, 1914).

Byron's Correspondence: Edited by John Murray (2 vols., London, 1912).

Calvert: *An Irish Beauty of the Regency*. Compiled from the unpublished journals of the Hon. Mrs Calvert, 1789–1822, by Mrs Warrenne Blake (London, 1911).

Castlereagh: *Despatches* (12 vols., London, 1848–1853).

Cecil, David: *Lord M. or the Later Life of Lord Melbourne* (London, 1954).

Chad: *The Conversations of the First Duke of Wellington with George William Chad*. Edited by the Seventh Duke of Wellington (Cambridge, 1956).

Chadwick, Owen: *The Victorian Church* (Part I., London, 1966).

Charles X and Louis Philippe: The Secret History of the Revolution of July 1830. By one of King Charles's officers. (London, 1839).

Chateaubriand: *The Memoirs of Chateaubriand*. Edited by Robert Baldick (London, 1961).

Clark, George Kitson: *Peel and the Conservative Party 1832–1841* (London, 2nd edition 1964).

Cobbett, William: *The Political Register*.

Cobbett, William: *Rural Rides* (London, 1853).

Colborne: *Life of Sir John Colborne, Field-Marshal Lord Seaton* by G. C. Moore Smith (London, 1903).

Colby, Reginald: *The Wellington Despatch* (Victoria and Albert Museum, 1965).

Colchester: *The Diary and Correspondence of Charles Abbot Lord Colchester*. Edited by his son (3 vols., London, 1861).

Cooper, Leonard: *The Age of Wellington* (London, 1964).

Cox, Cynthia: *Talleyrand's Successor, Duc de Richelieu, 1766–1822* (London, 1959).

Creevey, Thomas: *The Creevey Papers*. Edited by Sir H. Maxwell (London, 1904) and by John Gore (London, 1934).

Croker, John Wilson: *The Croker Papers, 1808–1857* (3 vols., London, 1884). Edited by Bernard Pool (London, 1967).

Cruttwell, C. M.: *Wellington* (London, 1936).

Davis, H. W. C.: *The Age of Grey and Peel* (Oxford, 1929).

De Grey, Earl: *Characteristics of the Duke of Wellington* (London, 1853).

De Lancey: *A Week at Waterloo in 1815. Lady de Lancey's Narrative*. Edited by Major B. R. Ward (London, 1906).

De Ros: *A Sketch of the Life of Georgiana Lady de Ros* [née Lennox] by the Hon. Mrs J. R. Swinton (London, 1893).

Dickens, Charles: *Hard Times* (London, 1854).

Disraeli, Benjamin: *Vivian Grey* (London, 1826).

Disraeli, Benjamin: *Coningsby or The New Generation* (London, 1844).

Disraeli, Benjamin: *Sybil or The Two Nations* (London, 1845).

Disraeli, Benjamin: *Lord George Bentinck: A Political Biography* (London, 2nd edition 1852).

Doyle, James Warren: *Letters on the State of Ireland*, 1825 (using the pen-name of 'J.K.L.', i.e. Bishop James of Kildare and Leighlin).

Eaton, Charlotte A. (née Waldie): *The Days of Battle, or Quatre Bras and Waterloo* (London, 1853, first published, 1816).

Eden: *Miss Eden's Letters*. Edited by her great-niece, Violet Dickinson (London, 1919).

Edgeworth: Maria Edgeworth *Letters from England 1813–1844*. Edited by Christina Colvin (Oxford U.P., 1971).

Edgeworth: *The Life and Letters of Maria Edgeworth*. Edited by Augustus Hare (2 vols., London, 1894).

Ellenborough, Lord: *A Political Diary 1828–1830*. Edited by Lord Colchester (2 vols., London, 1881).

Ellesmere: *Personal Reminiscences of the Duke of Wellington by Francis, First Earl of Ellesmere*. Edited by Alice, Countess of Strafford (London, 1903).

Elvey: *Life and Reminiscences of Sir George Elvey* (London, 1894).

Elvin, Charles: *History of Walmer Castle* (Privately printed, 1894).

Farmar, Hugh: *A Regency Elopement* (London, 1969).

Fitzgerald, Percy: *The Life and Times of William IV* (2 vols., London, 1884).

Fortesque, Sir John: *History of the British Army* (Vol. X., London, 1920).

Fortescue, Sir John: *Wellington* (London, 1925).

Fox: *Journal of the Hon. Henry Edward Fox, 4th and last Lord Holland, 1818–1830*. Edited by Lord Ilchester (London, 1923).

Fraser, Sir William: *Words on Wellington* (London, 1889).

Frith, W. P.: *My Autobiography and Reminiscences* (2 vols., London, 5th edition, 1888).

Fulford, Roger: *The Royal Dukes* (London, 1933).

Fulford, Roger: *George IV* (London, 2nd edition, 1949).

Fulford, Roger: *The Trial of Queen Caroline* (London, 1967).

Gash, Norman: *F. R. Bonham*, English Historical Review, (October 1948).

Gash, Norman: *Mr Secretary Peel, The Life of Sir Robert Peel to 1830* (London, 1961).

Gash, Norman: *Politics in the Age of Peel, A Study in Technique of Party Representation 1830–1850* (London, 1953).

George, Eric: *The Life and Death of Benjamin Robert Haydon 1786–1846* (London, 1967).

Gladstone, W. E.: *The Gladstone Papers* (London, 1930).

Gleig, G. R.: *Life of Arthur Duke of Wellington* (London, 1889).

Gleig, G. R.: *Reminiscences of the First Duke of Wellington* (London, 1904).

Glover, Michael: *Wellington as Military Commander* (London, 1968).

Glover, Michael: *Legacy of Glory* (New York, 1971).

Gordon, Sir A.: *The Earl of Aberdeen* (London, 1893).

Gower, Lord Ronald: *My Reminiscences* (London, 1883).

Gower, Lord Ronald: *Old Diaries 1881–1901* (London, 1902).

Granville: *G. Leveson Gower, First Lord Granville, Correspondence* (2 vols., London, 1916).

Granville, Lady: *Letters of Harriet Countess Granville 1810–1845.* Edited by her son, the Hon. F. Leveson Gower (2 vols., London, 1894).

Grattan, William: *Adventures with the Connaught Rangers.* Edited by Charles Oman (2nd series, vol. 2, London, 1902).

Greville: *The Greville Memoirs 1817–1860.* Edited by H. Reeve (8 vols., London, 1875–87); by L. Strachey and R. Fulford (8 vols., London, 1938).

Griffiths, Major Arthur: *The Wellington Memorial, Wellington and His Contemporaries* (London, 1897).

Gronow: *The Reminiscences and Recollections of Captain Gronow.* Edited by John Raymond (London, 1964).

Guedalla, Philip: *The Duke* (London, 1931).

Guest: *Lady Charlotte Guest, Extracts from her Journal 1833–1852.* Edited by the Earl of Bessborough (London, 1950).

Hare, Augustus: *The Story of My Life* (Vols. 4 and 5, London, 1900).

Haydon, B. R.: *Correspondence and Table-Talk* (2 vols., London, 1876).

Haydon, B. R.: *The Autobiography and Memoirs of Benjamin Robert Haydon.* Edited from his Journals by Tom Taylor (2 vols., London, 1926).

Hazlitt, William: *The Spirit of the Age or Contemporary Portraits* (London, 1825).

Henry, C. Bowdler: *The Iron Duke's Dentures,* British Dental Journal, October 1968.

Herrick, C. T.: *Letters of the Duke of Wellington to Miss J. Edited with extracts from Miss J.'s diary by Christine Terhune Herrick* (London, 1889).

Hidy, Ralph W.: *The House of Baring in American Trade and Finance. English Merchant Bankers at Work, 1763–1861* (Harvard U.P., 1949).

Hill, Rev. Edwin Sidney: *The Life of Lord Hill* (London, 2nd edition, 1845).

Hobhouse, Christopher: *1851 and The Crystal Palace* (London, 1937).

Hobsbawn, E. J. and Rudé, George: *Captain Swing* (Harvard U.P., 1949; London, 1969).

Hodson, L. J.: *A Short History of the Parish of Salehurst* (1914).

Holland, Lord: *Further Memoirs of the Whig Party 1807–1821.* Edited by Lord Stavordale (London, 1905).

Houssaye, Henry: *1815 – La Seconde Abdication – La Terreur Blanche* (Paris, 1893).

Hudleston, F. J.: *Warriors in Undress* (London, 1925).

Hudson, Derek: *The Forgotten King and Other Essays* (for Miss Jenkins) (London, 1960).

Hunt: *Memoirs of Henry Hunt from Ilchester Jail* (2 vols., London, 1820).

Hyde, H. Montgomery: *The Strange Death of Lord Castlereagh* (London, 1959).

Inglis, Brian: *Poverty and the Industrial Revolution* (London, 1971).

Inglis, Brian: 'Sir Arthur Wellesley and the Irish Press', *Hermathena*, *LXXXIII*, 1954.

Jackson, Lt.-Col. Basil: *Notes and Reminiscences of a Staff Officer*. Edited by R. C. Seaton (London, 1903).

Jeune: *Pages from the Diary of an Oxford Lady, 1843–1862* (Mrs M. D. Jeune). Edited by Margaret Jeune Gifford (Oxford, 1932).

Jones: *Letters from the Duke of Wellington to Mrs Jones of Pantglas*. Edited by her daughter Mrs Davies-Evans, Century Magazine, December 1889.

Kee, Robert: *The Green Flag, A History of Irish Nationalism* (London, 1972).

Kelly, Christopher: *The Memorable Battle of Waterloo* (London, 1818).

Kurtz, Harold: *The Trial of Marshal Ney* (London, 1957).

Lamb, Lady Caroline: *Glenarvon* (3 vols., London, 1816).

Lennox, Lord William: *Three Years with the Duke, or Wellington in Private Life* by an ex-aide-de-camp (London, 1853).

Lieven: *Correspondence of Lord Aberdeen and Princess Lieven 1832–1854*. Edited by E. Parry Jones, Camden 3rd series, vol. LX (London, 1938).

Lieven: *Correspondence of Princess Lieven and Earl Grey*. Edited by Guy Le Strange (3 vols., London, 1890).

Lieven: *Lettres de Francois Guizot et de la Princesse de Lieven* (Paris, 1963).

Lieven: *Unpublished Diary and Political Sketches of Princess Lieven*. Edited by Harold Temperley (London, 1925).

Lieven: *Letters of Dorothea, Princess Lieven, during her Residence in London 1812–1834*. Edited by Lionel G. Robinson (London, 1902).

Lieven: *The Private Letters of Princess Lieven to Prince Metternich 1820–1826*. Edited by Peter Quennell (London, 1937).

Lincoln, L. J., and McEwen, R. L.: *Lord Eldon's Anecdote Book* (London, 1960).

Longford, Elizabeth: *Victoria R.I.* (London, 1964). *Queen Victoria: Born to Succeed* (New York, 1965).

Longford, Elizabeth: *Wellington: The Years of the Sword* (London and New York, 1969).

Lutyens, Mary: *Effie in Venice, Unpublished letters of Mrs John Ruskin written from Venice between 1849–1852*. Edited by Mary Lutyens (London, 1965).

Lynch, P. and Vaizey, J.: *Guinness's Brewery in the Irish Economy 1759–1876* (Cambridge U.P., 1960).

Macintyre, Angus: *The Liberator, Daniel O'Connell and the Irish Party, 1830–1847* (London, 1965).

Malcolm: *The Life and Correspondence of Maj.-Gen. Sir John Malcolm.* Edited by J. W. Kaye (2 vols., London, 1856).

Marchand, Leslie A.: *Byron: A Critical Introduction with an annotated Bibliography* (3 vols., London, 1957).

Markham, Felix: *Napoleon* (London, 1962).

Martineau, Harriet: *A History of the Thirty Years Peace, 1816–1846* (2 vols., London, 1850).

Maxwell, Sir Herbert: *The Life of Wellington* (2 vols., London, 1899).

Medwin, Thomas: *Conversations of Lord Byron, Noted during a Residence with his Lordship at Pisa* (vol. I, London, 1824).

Mercer, General Cavalie: *Journal of the Waterloo Campaign* (Vol. 2, London, 1870).

Monypenny, W. F. and Buckle, G. E.: *The Life of Benjamin Disraeli, Earl of Beaconsfield* (2 vols., London, 1929).

Moody, T. W. and Martin, F. X. (editors): *The Course of Irish History* (Cork, 1967).

Moore, D. C.: 'The Other Face of Reform', *Victorian Studies* 1961–2 (Indiana University).

Morgan, Lady: *Autobiography, Diaries and Correspondence* (2 vols., London, 1862).

Namier, Sir Lewis: *Personalities and Powers* (London, 1955).

Namier, Sir Lewis: Essays Presented to Sir Lewis Namier. Edited by Richard Pares and A. J. P. Taylor (London, 1956).

Napier: *Life and Letters of Sir William Napier.* Edited by H. A. Bruce (2 vols., London, 1864).

Napier: *The Life and Opinions of Gen. Sir Charles Napier* by Ltd. Gen. William Napier (4 vols., London, 1857).

Napoleon's Memoirs: Edited by S. de Chair (London, 1948).

Neumann: *The Diary of Philip von Neumann 1819–1850.* Edited by E. B. Chancellor (2 vols., London, 1928).

Newman, Aubrey: *The Stanhopes of Chevening* (London, 1969).

Nowlan, Kevin B.: *The Politics of Repeal, A Study in the Relations between Great Britain and Ireland 1841–1850* (London, 1965).

Oman, Carola: *The Gascoyne Heiress, The Life and Diaries of Frances Mary Gascoyne-Cecil 1802–1839* (London, 1968).

Old Soldier: *Life Military and Civil of the Duke of Wellington digested from the materials of W. H. Maxwell and re-written by an Old Soldier* (London, 1852).

Palmerston: *The Letters of Lady Palmerston.* Edited by Tresham Lever (London, 1957).

Pange, Victor de: *The Unpublished Correspondence of Madame de Staël and the Duke of Wellington*. Translated by Harold Kurtz (London, 1965).

Parker, C. S.: *Sir Robert Peel* (3 vols., London, 1891–1899).

Peel: *The Private Letters of Sir Robert Peel*. Edited by George Peel (London, 1920).

Percival, Victor: *The Duke of Wellington, A Pictorial Survey of his Life* (Victoria and Albert Museum, London, 1969).

Petrie, Sir C.: *Wellington, A Reassessment* (London, 1956).

Physick, John: *The Duke of Wellington in Caricature* (Victoria and Albert Museum, London, 1965).

Physick, John: *The Wellington Monument* (Victoria and Albert Museum, London, 1970).

Pirenne, Jacques-Henri: *Le Congrès d'Aix-la-Chapelle et L'apogée de l'influence russe après Napoléon* (Brussels, 1953).

Plumb, J. H.: *The First Four Georges* (London, 1956).

Poynter, J. R.: *Society and Pauperism 1795–1834* (London, 1969).

Raikes: *Journal of Thomas Raikes, 1831–1847* (4 vols., London, 1856).

Redding, Cyrus: *Personal Reminiscence of Eminent Men* (3 vols., London, 1867).

Richardson, Ethel: *Long Forgotten Days* (London, 1928).

Ridley, Jasper: *Lord Palmerston* (London, 1970).

Rogers: *Recollections of Samuel Rogers*. Edited by W. Sharpe (London, 1859).

Rogers: *Recollections of the Table-Talk of Samuel Rogers*. Edited by A. Dyce (London, 1887).

Rolo, P. J. V.: *George Canning* (London, 1965).

Russell, G. W. B.: *Collections and Recollections* (London, 1898).

Russell, Lord Russell of Liverpool: *Caroline the Unhappy Queen* (London, 1967).

Saunders, Edith: *The Hundred Days* (London, 1964).

Seymour: *Confidential Memoranda by Admiral Sir George Seymour* (Loch MSS.).

Shaw-Kennedy, Sir James: *Notes on the Battle of Waterloo with a Memoir* (London, 1865).

Shelley: *The Diary of Frances Lady Shelley*. Edited by her grandson Richard Edgecumbe (2 vols., London, 1912).

Simmons, J. S. G.: 'The Duke of Wellington and the Vice-Chancellorship in 1844'. Bodleian Library Record, V (1954–6), 37–52.

Spencer-Stanhope: *The Letter-Bag of Lady Elizabeth Spencer-Stanhope* (2 vols., London, 1912).

Stanhope, Philip Henry, 5th Earl: *Notes of Conversations with the Duke of Wellington, 1831–1851* (Oxford U.P., reprinted 1947).

Stanley: *Letters of Lady Augusta Stanley, A Young Lady at Court, 1849–*

1863. Edited by the Dean of Windsor and Hector Bolitho (London 1927).

Stapleton, A. G.: *George Canning, 1822–1827* (3 vols., London, 1831).

Stevens, Joan: *Victorian Faces, An Inroduction to the papers of Sir John Le Couteur* (Jersey, 1969).

Stuart, D. M.: *Daughters of George III* (London, 1939).

Surtees, W. E.: *A Sketch of the Lives of Lords Stowell and Eldon* (London, 1846).

Tallon, Maura: *The Patriot Bishop of Kildare and Leighlin* (Dr Doyle) (Journal of the Kildare Archaeological Society, vol. XIV.2. 1966–7).

Temperley, H. V.: *Life of Canning* (London, 1905).

Thackeray, W. M.: *The Irish Sketch Book, 1842–1844* (first vol. published London, 1843).

Turberville, A. S.: *The House of Lords in the Age of Reform, 1784–1837* (London, 1958).

Twiss, Horace: *The Public and Private Life of Lord Chancellor Eldon* (3 vols., London, 1844).

Verner: *Reminiscences of William Verner.* Edited by Ruth W. Verner, Society for Army Historical Research, 1965.

Victoria, Queen: *The Girlhood of Queen Victoria 1832–1840.* Edited by Viscount Esher (2 vols., London, 1912).

Victoria, Queen: *The Letters of Queen Victoria 1837–1861.* First Series, vol. I. 1837–1843, vol. II, 1844–1853. Edited by A. C. Benson and Viscount Esher. (London, 1907).

Walmsley, Robert: *Peterloo: The Case Reopened* (Manchester U.P., 1969).

Ward, S. G. P.: *Wellington* (London, 1963).

Weiner, Margery: *A Sovereign Remedy, Europe after Waterloo* (London, 1971).

Wellesley: *Diary and Correspondence of Henry Wellesley, First Lord Cowley, 1790–1846.* Edited by the Hon. F. A. Wellesley (London, 1930).

Wellesley, Lord Gerald and Steegman, J.: *Iconography of the First Duke of Wellington* (London, 1935).

Wellesley, Muriel: *Wellington in Civil Life* (London, 1939).

Wellington: *A Selection from the Private Correspondence of the First Duke of Wellington.* Edited by the (Seventh) Duke of Wellington (The Roxburghe Club, London, 1952).

Wellington Anecdotes: (2nd edition, London, 1852).

Wellington and His Friends: Letters of the 1st Duke of Wellington to the Rt. Hon. Charles and Mrs Arbuthnot, the Earl and Countess of Wilton, Princess Lieven, and Miss Burdett-Coutts, selected and edited by the 7th Duke of Wellington (London, 1965).

Wellington: *The Despatches of Field Marshal the Duke of Wellington during his various Campaigns 1799–1815*. Compiled by Lt.-Col. Gurwood (13 vols., London, 1834–1839).

Wellington: *Supplementary Despatches, Correspondence, and Memoranda of Field Marshal Arthur Duke of Wellington, K.G., 1794–1818*. Edited by his son the Duke of Wellington (15 vols., London, 1858–1872).

Wellington: *Despatches, Correspondence, and Memoranda of Arthur Duke of Wellington (New Series) 1819–1832*. Edited by his son (8 vols., London, 1867–1880).

Wellington: *Speeches of the Duke of Wellington in Parliament*. Collected by Col. Gurwood (London, 1854).

Wellington Studies: Essays by five Old Wellingtonians, edited by Michael Howard (1959).

Wellingtoniana: Anecdotes, Maxims and Characteristics of the Duke of Wellington by John Timbs (London, 1852).

Wilkins, W. H.: *Mrs Fitzherbert and George IV* (2 vols., London, 1905).

Williams, David: *John Frost, A Study in Chartism* (Cardiff, 1939).

Williams, Helen Maria: *The Present State of France* (London, 1815).

Willis, G. M.: *Ernest Augustus Duke of Cumberland* (London, 1954).

Willis, N. P.: *Pencillings by the Way* (2nd edition, London, 1850).

With Napoleon at Waterloo and other unpublished documents of the Waterloo and Peninsular Campaigns. Edited by Mackenzie Macbride (London, 1911).

Woodham-Smith, Cecil: *The Great Hunger, 1845–1849* (London, 1962).

Ziegler, Philip: *A Life of Henry Addington, First Viscount Sidmouth* (London, 1965).

Ziegler, Philip: *William IV* (London, 1971).

References

The following abbreviations are used:
Wellington *Despatches* WD
Wellington *Supplementary Despatches, Correspondence and Memoranda*
WSD
Wellington *Despatches, Correspondence and Memoranda* (*New Series*)
WDNS
Wellington MSS. W.MSS.
Wellington and His Friends WHF
Selection from Wellington's Private Correspondence WPC
Royal Archives RA
Journal of Mrs Arbuthnot JA
British Museum BM
Public Record Office PRO

PART I

1 PRINCE OF WATERLOO

1 Eaton, p. 72.
2 Hamilton, 18 and 19 June 1815.
3 Kelly, p. 386.
4 W.MSS., 13 April 1829.
5 Richardson, pp. 384–5; Verner.
6 De Lancey, p. 14.
7 Fraser, p. 160.
8 Eaton, p. 135; Kennedy MSS.
9 WSD., X. 553, 22 June 1815; *ibid.*, 562.
10 Houssaye, pp. 13–15.
11 *Ibid.*, p. 22.
12 Stanhope, 6 October 1839; Colby, *Waterloo Despatch.*
13 Shelley, I. 87.
14 Stanhope, 6 October 1839.
15 MSS., *Tour to Waterloo.*
16 *Croker*, 28 January 1853.
17 Moore Smith, Colborne, p. 244.
18 Maxwell, II. 48; (note by Lady Hatherton, W.MSS.).
19 WD., XII. 590, 8 August 1815.
20 Stanhope, 17 September 1839; *Gronow*, p. 277.
21 *Gronow*, p. 277.
22 Gleig, *Life*, p. 490.
23 Ellesmere, p. 82.
24 Malcolm, II. 101.
25 Fortescue, X. 224.

2 CASES OF 'CRIM. CON.'?

1 Chateaubriand, p. 282; WSD., X. 673–6, 7 July 1815.
2 Shelley, I. 108.
3 WSD., X. 677 Castlereagh to Liverpool, 7 July 1815.
4 Wheeler, p. 179.
5 Broughton, I. 311; Shelley, I. 106; Stanhope, 5 November 1831, 25 October 1838; Houssaye, pp. 238–41.
6 WD., XII. 516, Wellington to Sir C. Stuart, 28 June 1815.
7 Holland, p. 220.
8 Albemarle, p. 168; Mercer, II. 180; Grattan II. 2nd series, pp. 85–93.
9 Gronow, p. 87; Shelley, I. 113.
10 Shelley, I. 99–144; Lennox, p. 166.
11 Lennox, pp. 181–3.
12 Shelley, I. 135.
13 Irish National Library, unpublished letters of Maria Edgeworth to Lady Romilly, 13 August 1815.
14 Ibid., M. Edgeworth quoting a letters from the Duchess of Wellington, 9 February 1816.
15 Edgeworth, Letters from England, p. 61, 16 May 1813.
16 W.MSS.
17 Ibid., 7 September 1838.
18 Pange, pp. 8–12.

3 AT THE COURT OF KING ARTHUR

1 Redding, II. 81.
2 WD., XII. 641–6; Williams, p. 359; Cox, p. 154.
3 Broughton, I. 325, 22 December 1815; WD., XII. 641–6.
4 Grattan, II. 2nd series, pp. 96–8; Broughton, I. 325.

5 Broughton, V. 202, 14 June 1839.
6 W.MSS., Papal letter, 20 October 1816.
7 WSD., X. 670 – I, 7 July 1815.
8 Kurtz, p. 226.
9 W.MSS., from the Dean of Windsor 1864, being the memorandum of a conversation between the Duke and Lord Alvanley. 'Lord Alvanley told me, that the Duke of Wellington spoke to him as follows at Walmer Castle, with regard to his not having interfered to save Marshal Ney's life.'
10 Ibid.
11 Kurtz, p. 314, 1 September 1849.
12 Ibid., p. 284; W.MSS., 23 February 1816.
13 Malcolm, II. 35, 19 August 1815.
14 Raglan MSS., No. 68, 31 October 1817; W.MSS., to Mrs Arbuthnot, 18 November 1817; Ibid., No. 51, 9 December 1816.
15 Morgan, p. 63, 8 May 1817.
16 Albemarle, p. 309.
17 WSD., XI. 302.
18 Irish National Library, M. Edgeworth to Lady Romilly, 9 February 1816.
19 With Napoleon at Waterloo (The Gordons), p. 166; Moore Smith, Colborne, p. 242.
20 Redding, II. 95; Berry, pp. 78–9, 17 March 1816.
21 Guedalla, p. 299, quoting from the Hamwood Papers.
22 W.MSS., 20 July 1816.
23 Bessborough, pp. 257–8.

24 W.MSS., 26 July 1816.
25 WSD., XI. 441.
26 Cox, pp. 157–8.
27 WSD., XI. 565.
28 *Ibid.*, 571–3, 11 December 1816.
29 Pange, pp. 25–6, 29 October 1816.
30 Napier, W., I. 197, 26 December 1816.
31 Pange, p. 153, 16 November 1816.

4 END OF AN OCCUPATION

1 WSD., XI. 592–3, 619.
2 Pange, p. 64.
3 Burghersh, p. 30, Schlegel to Lady Burghersh, 14 August 1817.
4 Raglan MSS., No. 59, 9 July 1817.
5 Stanhope, 18 March 1840; JA., I. 135.
6 Spicer MSS.
7 Albemarle, pp. 179–81.
8 WSD., XI. 401.
9 Martineau, I. 21.
10 WSD., XI. 632, 17 February 1817; W.MSS.; WSD., XI. 561.
11 Mercer, II. 275, 280; WSD., XII. 622.
12 WSD., XI. 502, 2 October 1816; Shaw-Kennedy, p. 28.
13 Farmar, p. 80.
14 Raglan MSS., No. 87, 13 and 29 February 1816.
15 W.MSS., 21 March 1816.
16 Edgeworth, *Letters from England*, p. 103, M. Edgeworth to Sophy Ruxton describing a talk with Lady Bathurst, 19 September 1818.

17 W.MSS., to Mrs Arbuthnot, 7 October 1816; to Wyatt, 25 February 1817.
18 W.MSS., Wyatt to Wellington, 27 July 1817.
19 W.MSS., Wellington to Mrs Arbuthnot, 8 November and 20 December 1816.
20 W.MSS., Wellington to Lady Burghersh, 6 March 1817.
21 Calvert, p. 279, 22 May 1817.
22 Lady Granville, I. 109.
23 WSD., XII. 213, Wellington to J. C. Villiers, 11 January 1818.
24 *Ibid.*, XI. 749, 16 July 1817.
25 *Ibid.*, 745, 15 July 1817.
26 *Ibid.*, 601, Wellington to Clancarty, 17 July 1818.
27 *Ibid.*, XII. 320, Police report, 15 February 1818.
28 *Ibid.*, 273–4, Kinnaird to Sir George Murray.
29 *Ibid.*, 284.
30 *Ibid.*, 363, Bathurst to Wellington, 3 March 1818.
31 *Ibid.*, 334–5, Wellington to Bathurst, 25 February 1818.
32 Spencer–Stanhope, pp. 331–2.
33 WSD., XII. 601, Wellington to Clancarty, 17 July 1818.
34 *Ibid.*, 272, to Bathurst, 12 February 1818.
35 *Ibid.*, 494, to General Fane, 24 April 1818.
36 PRO. FO. 92/35. 4307. Metternich's summary of interview with Tsar, 29 September 1818.
37 WSD., XII. 778, Calais, 29 October 1818.
38 W.MSS., 25 October 1818.
39 Shelley, I. 378.
40 *Greevey*, 11 September 1818.

PART II

5 A LITTLE *Murder*

1 WSD., XII. 813, 1 November 1818.
2 W.MSS., 22 May 1819.
3 Redding, II. 75–6; Haydon, *Correspondence*, II. 347.
4 *Ibid.*, 263.
5 WSD., XI. 660, Castlereagh to Wellington, 31 March 1817.
6 *Creevey*, 11 September 1818.
7 Warmsley, p. 168.
8 Bamford, I. 166–8.
9 Ziegler, *Addington*, p. 374.
10 Shelley, II. 68.
11 W.MSS., Wellington to Mrs Arbuthnot, 27 August 1819.
12 WDNS., I. 80, Wellington to Byng, 21 and 23 October 1819; Byng to Wellington, 28 October 1819.
13 Gash, *Peel*, p. 248.
14 WDNS., I, 89, Wellington to Sidmouth, 11 December 1819.
15 W.MSS., 5 January 1820.
16 Gleig, *Life*, p. 292.
17 JA., I. 70, 2 March 1820.
18 W.MSS., Wellington to Mrs Arbuthnot, 5 March 1820.
19 Gleig, *Life*, p. 292; Ellesmere, p. 132.
20 WPC., pp. 185–8, to Mrs Patterson, 27 February 1820.
21 Ziegler, *Addington*, p. 388.
22 Brougham, IV. 33.
23 W.MSS., Wellington to Mrs Arbuthnot, 29 July 1820.
24 WDNS., I. 128, memorandum from Wellington to Lord Liverpool, June 1820; Maxwell, II. 153; Gash, *Peel*, pp. 312–13.
25 *Creevey*, 25 August 1820.
26 JA., I. 52, 10 November 1820, quoting a letter from Charles Arbuthnot.
27 W.MSS., Wellington to Mrs Arbuthnot, 11 November 1820.
28 Aspinall, *George* IV, II. Letters 879–80.
29 JA., I. 53, 18 November 1820.
30 Shakespear MSS.
31 JA., I. 108 and footnote, 19 July 1821; W.MSS., Wellington to Countess Lieven, 29 July 1821.
32 WHF., p. 219 (translated).
33 Russell, p. 158.
34 WDNS., I. 195.
35 *Creevey*, 26 January 1821.

6 INTERLUDE 1:

ALMOST PRIVATE LIFE

1 Edgeworth, II. 174–6; Lennox, p. 270.
2 W.MSS.
3 *Ibid.*
4 *Ibid.*
5 *Ibid.*
6 *Ibid.*
7 Stanhope, 1 November 1831; De Ros, p. 175.
8 Holland, p. 295.
9 Byron, *Detached Thoughts*, 110.
10 JA., I. 105.
11 Stanhope, 2 November 1831.
12 *Ibid.*, 20 September 1839.
13 Bessborough, p. 250, 20 July 1815.
14 JA., I. 116, 119–20.
15 Gleig, *Life*, p. 297.
16 Fraser, p. 247.
17 W.MSS.

18 WPC., p. 14, Duchess to Mrs Foster, 2 May 1822.
19 W.MSS., Mrs Foster's memoir.
20 JA., I. 168–9.
21 Napier, W., I. 251 (1824).
22 JA., I. 169.
23 W.MSS., Arthur Freese to Duchess, 13 April 1821; 23 May 1823.
24 Ibid., Arthur Lennox to Duchess, undated, and 4 April 1821; Duchess to Mrs Caroline Penelope Hamilton, 30 March 1820; Charles Wellesley to Duchess, 9 March 1818.
25 Ibid., Henry Wagner to Duchess, 11 September 1819; WPC., pp. 20–1, 16 and 9 July 1822.
26 W.MSS., Douro to Duchess, undated (May 1823).
27 WPC., pp. 23–4, copy made by Duchess between 5 and 8 July 1823.
28 W.MSS., quoted in Wagner's diary, 15 October 1823.
29 Napier, W., I. 349.
30 W.MSS., Douro to Duchess from Oxford, 18 October 1824; ibid., from Weimar, 2 April 1828.
31 Hare, 13 November 1879.
32 W.MSS., Douro to Duchess, 16 September 1823.
33 Ibid., Wellington to Charles Arbuthnot, 18 May 1820.
34 JA., I. 300–1, 11 April 1824.
35 JA., I. 362, 4 December 1824.
36 W.MSS., [Col. Charles Greville to Lady Charlotte Greville], undated.
37 Greville, 18 September 1852.
38 JA., I. 85, 27 March 1821, I.

112, 28 July 1821; I. 407, 9 July 1825.
39 W.MSS., Wellington to Mrs Arbuthnot, 20 April 1824.
40 Society for the Promotion of Christian Knowledge, MSS., 6 November 1821; WDNS., I. 162, Wellington to Mr Fleming, M.P. for Hampshire, 1 March 1821.
41 Cobbett, Rural Rides, October 1822.
42 W.MSS., Wellington to Farrar & Co., Solicitors, 25 February 1816.
43 JA., I. 63, 11 January 1821.
44 Peel, Private Papers, pp. 87–8.
45 Napier, W., I. 250, Stratfield Saye, 1824.
46 Shelley, II. 73.
47 W.MSS., Wellington to Mrs Arbuthnot, 13 January 1823.
48 Lady Granville, I. 149.
49 Told to the author by Mr Harold Macmillan.
50 Hatherton MSS., 18 September 1821.
51 W.MSS., Wellington to Mrs Arbuthnot.
52 JA., I. 150, 11 March 1820.

7 ONE GENTLEMAN OF VERONA

1 JA., I. 178, 29 August 1822.
2 WHF., pp. 23–5; JA., I. 183.
3 This account is taken from five main sources: Wellington's letter to Charles Arbuthnot, W.MSS., 9 August 1822; his memorandum, WDNS., I. 255, 13 August 1822; his talk with Greville, Greville, 19 August 1822; and his later conversations with Lady Salisbury and Lord Mahon, Salis-

bury MSS., 1838, Stanhope, 1842. There is only one real discrepancy, namely between the Salisbury and Greville accounts, where Lady Salisbury says the Duke told Castlereagh to ring the bell, 'and ask if your horses are in London, convince yourself'. (Maxwell, II. 164.) The Duke's account to Greville, however, must be preferred, being contemporary, whereas his account to Lady Salisbury was given sixteen years later.

4 WHF., p. 25, to Mrs Arbuthnot, 10 August 1822.

5 W.MSS., Wellington to Mme de Lieven, 14 June 1822.

6 WDNS., I. 251–4, Bankhead's memorandum; JA., I. 180, 29 August 1822.

7 JA., I. 185, 29 August 1822.

8 W.MSS., Wellington to Mrs Arbuthnot, 13 September 1822.

9 W.MSS., Wellington to Mrs Arbuthnot, 25 March 1823.

10 *Creevey*, 14 August 1822; JA., I. 241.

11 W.MSS., 1 August 1823.

12 *Lieven-Metternich*, p. 198, 21 August 1822.

13 JA., I. 375, 9 February 1825; W.MSS., Wellington to Charles Arbuthnot, 16 November 1823.

14 Aspinall, *George IV*, II. p. 536, 6 September 1822.

15 Wellesley, H., p. 95.

16 Lever, 16 September 1822.

17 W.MSS., Wellington to Mrs Arbuthnot, 12 September 1822.

18 *Lieven-Metternich*, p. 207, 14 September 1822.

19 *Creevey*, 14 November 1822.

20 WHF., p. 29.

21 W.MSS., Wellington to Mrs Arbuthnot, 4 October 1822.

22 *Ibid.*, 30 March and 6 April 1823.

23 *Ibid.*, 12 October 1822.

24 WDNS., I. 491.

25 Rothschild MSS., S. M. de Rothschild (Vienna) to N. M. Rothschild (London), 3 October 1822.

26 Gleig, *Life*, p. 300.

27 Byron, *Age of Bronze*, lines 534–5.

28 Extract from *Résumé Historique* of the Congress of Verona, *Archives des Affaires Etrangères, Mémoires et Documents*, vols. 716–20.

29 W.MSS., Wellington to Mrs Arbuthnot, 5 November 1822; 12 December 1822.

30 *Lieven-Metternich*, p. 218, 7 January 1823; p. 227–30, 26 January 1823; p. 243, 28 March 1823.

31 Aspinall, *Arbuthnot*, p. 36, Liverpool to Charles Arbuthnot, 29 December 1822.

32 Stanhope, 19 June 1840.

33 JA., I. 375; Shelley, II. 133.

8 REDRESSING THE BALANCE

1 *Lieven-Metternich*, p. 209, 20 April 1823; WHF., p. 41, 30 October 1823; JA., I. 211, 3 February, 1823.

2 W.MSS.

3 *Ibid.*, 13 October 1823; *Creevey*, January 1823.

4 W.MSS., Wellington to Mrs

Arbuthnot, 25 November 1823.

5 Ibid., 27 December 1823.

6 Ibid., 26 January 1824.

7 W.MSS., 4 October 1824; 15 and 25 February 1825.

8 JA., I. 300, 11 April 1824.

9 Ibid., 307, 2 May 1824.

10 Lieven-Metternich, pp. 318–319, 17 June 1824.

11 JA., I. 359, 26 September 1823.

12 WDNS., II. 325.

13 Rolo, p. 134.

14 JA., I. 367, 18 December 1824; 372, 27 January 1825.

15 WDNS., II. 401, 21 January 1825.

16 JA., I. 374.

17 WDNS., II. 403, 28 January 1825.

18 JA., I. 375.

19 Lieven-Metternich, p. 345, 10 March 1825.

20 JA., II. 64, 15 December 1826.

21 W.MSS., Charles Wellesley to Duchess, 7 February 1825; Alava to Duchess 23 [March 1825].

22 Kenyon MSS., J. Williams and A. Short (Christ Church) to Hon. Lloyd Kenyon, 17 January 1834.

23 JA., I. 421, 20 October 1825. The news arrived at Stratfield Saye between 11 and 18 October, while Mrs Arbuthnot was staying.

24 BM. Add.MSS., 37415, 13 October 1825.

25 WDNS., I. 241, to Lord Clancarty, 6 June 1822.

26 Ibid., 155–6.

27 Creevey, 14 February 1823.

28 W.MSS., M. Shaw to Wellington, 20 February 1823.

29 BM. Add.MSS. 37415, Wellington to Marquess Wellesley, 21 February 1823.

30 W.MSS., 7 March 1823.

31 Gash, Peel, 371.

32 W.MSS., Keene to Wellington, 19 August 1823; Clancarty to Wellington, 23 April 1823.

33 Ibid., Wellington to Mrs Arbuthnot, 13 April 1823.

34 Ibid., 7 June 1823; JA., I 321, Mrs Arbuthnot's summary of Wellington's letter of 7 June 1823.

35 WDNS., II. 331; 380–2, 26 and 27 December 1824; 361, 6 December 1824; II. 376, 21 December 1824.

36 W.MSS., 30 December 1824.

37 Ibid., 6 April 1825.

38 WDNS., II. 592–607.

39 W.MSS., Wellington to Charles Arbuthnot, 25 April 1825.

40 Ibid., 26 April 1825.

41 Surtees, p. 125, 1 January 1825.

42 W.MSS., Wellington to Mrs Arbuthnot, 20 April 1824; JA., I. 382, 5 March 1825; I. 427.

43 Morgan, p. 356, Mrs Patterson-Bonaparte to Lady Morgan, 28 November 1829; Aspinall, George IV, III. 126 footnote; Gash, Peel, p. 372, Peel to Goulburn, 12 November 1825.

44 W.MSS., Wellington to Louisa Hervey, 1 January 1826.

45 Surrey Record Office, Wellington to Peel, 7 January 1826.

9 CANNING? 'NO, NO, NO!'

1 W.MSS., Charles Arbuthnot to Duchess, August 1824.
2 JA., II. 5–6, 26 January 1826.
3 WDNS., III. 56.
4 Sir Walter Scott's *Journal*, 15 February 1827; Rogers, *Table-Talk*, p. 222.
5 W.MSS., Lord Clanwilliam to Wellington, 16 February 1826.
6 WHF., pp. 55–6, Berlin, 19 February 1826.
7 WDNS., III. 113.
8 *Lieven-Metternich*, p. 362, 20 March 1826; p. 364, 28 April 1826; p. 268, 2 June 1823; p. 271, 20 June 1823.
9 Lever, 9 May 1826.
10 W.MSS., Westmorland to Wellington, 3 March 1826.
11 *Ibid.*, Wellington to Croker, 29 May 1826.
12 JA., II. 35–6, 16 July 1826.
13 WPC., pp. 43–53; W.MSS.
14 W.MSS., Wellington to secretary, January 1840.
15 JA., II. 36, 16 July 1826.
16 WDNS., III. 385, Wellington to Peel; W.MSS., to Mrs Arbuthnot, 22 August 1826.
17 Peel, *Private Letters*, p. 91, 21 January 1827.
18 *Ibid.*, pp. 95–6, 22 January 1827.
19 W.MSS., Princess Lieven to Wellington, 3 January 1827.
20 WDNS., III. 532–3, Wellington to Peel, 7 January 1827; Peel to Wellington, 8 January 1827; W.MSS., 11 January 1827.
21 WDNS., III. 566.
22 WPC., pp. 84–94.
23 Bessborough, p. 287.
24 JA., II. 87–8.
25 W.MSS., Wellington to Charles Arbuthnot.
26 JA., II. 89; II. 90; II. 92.
27 Colchester, III. 500–1.
28 JA., II. 98.
29 *Ibid.*, 103, 10 April 1827.
30 *Greville*, 29 September 1834.

10 ON THE THRESHOLD

1 W.MSS., Wellington to Londonderry, 10 April 1827; WDNS., III. 628.
2 WDNS., III. 629.
3 W.MSS., Wellington to Cumberland, 23 June 1827.
4 *Ibid.*, to Malcolm, 25 April 1827.
5 W.MSS., to Gleig, 9 May 1827.
6 JA., II. 138, 21 August 1827; Shelley, II. 156, Duke of Rutland to Lady Shelley, 9 May 1827; WDNS., IV. 35.
7 WDNS., IV. 68, Wellington to Aberdeen, 31 July 1827.
8 Broughton, III. 189.
9 *Lieven-Metternich*, 24 May–5 June 1827.
10 W.MSS., Wellington to Charles Arbuthnot, 19–23 April 1827; 18 June 1827.
11 *Ibid.*, 23 April 1827.
12 WDNS., IV. 75, Wellington to Bathurst, 10 August 1827.
13 Napier, W., I. 313.
14 Chad, p. 8, 10 April 1828.
15 WDNS., IV. 26.
16 Copy of a letter in the possession of Mr Gerald Liddell, from Lady Mornington to an

unnamed friend, and transcribed in the margin (p. 27) of Guedalla's *The Duke* by Lady Trotter. Information given to the author by the Countess of Limerick.

17 Morgan, p. 240; *Greville*, 10 August 1827; W.MSS., 7 August 1827.

18 W.MSS., Wellington to Charles Arbuthnot, 6 August 1827.

19 W.MSS., Wellington to Mrs Arbuthnot, 11 August 1827; WHF., p. 75, 9 August 1827.

20 W.MSS., Wellington to Mrs Arbuthnot, 10 and 14 August 1827.

21 W.MSS., Wellington to Mrs Arbuthnot, 17 August 1827; JA, II. 136–8.

22 WHF., p. 76, 21 August 1827.

23 W.MSS., Wellington to Charles Arbuthnot, 21 August 1827.

24 W.MSS., Wellington to Mrs Arbuthnot, 11 November 1827.

25 W.MSS., H. Hardinge to Duchess, 2 October 1827; WHF., pp. 77–8.

26 Temperley, *Canning*, p. 220.

27 *Ibid.*, Stratford Canning to Codrington, 1 September 1827.

28 Temperley, *Diary of Princess Lieven*, p. 131; *Lieven-Grey*, I. 89.

29 JA., II. 148–9, 2 December 1827.

30 W.MSS., Wellington to Mrs Arbuthnot, 29 December 1827.

31 WHF., pp. 80–1.

32 Holland, p. 230.

33 W.MSS., description given by Duchess to Rundell the jeweller, 8 September 1828.

34 *Ibid.*, Charles Arbuthnot to Duchess, August 1824.

35 *Ibid.*, Wellington to Princess Lieven, 13 February 1827.

36 *Ibid.*, 1 August 1826.

37 Shelley, III. 163; II. 140.

38 Inglis, *Hermathena*, LXXXIII, 1954.

39 Stanhope, 21 November 1831; WDNS., III. 451.

40 Haydon, *Correspondence*, II. 72, 5 June 1821.

11 PRIME MINISTER

1 WDNS., IV. 184, 9 January 1828.

2 W.MSS., Wellington to Mrs Arbuthnot, 10 January 1828.

3 JA., II. 158, 15 January 1828.

4 W.MSS., Charles Arbuthnot to Wellington, 23 January 1928; JA., II. 159, 29 January 1828; WHF., p. 83, Wellington to Charles Arbuthnot, 26 January 1828.

5 BM. Add.MSS. 37415. f.89; Blessington, III. 7.

6 *Croker*, 24 January 1828.

7 W.MSS., Wellington to Mrs Arbuthnot, 12 December 1828.

8 Fox, p. 274, 8 March 1828; Bell, I. 63, 71.

9 Colchester, III. 534, 28, 19, 7 and 24 January 1828; W.MSS., Wellington to Mrs Arbuthnot, 26 January 1828.

10 WDNS., IV. 269, 18 February 1828.

11 Ellenborough, I. 3.

12 W.MSS., Wellington to Mrs Arbuthnot, 7 April 1828.
13 *Ibid.*, 5 April 1828.
14 WDNS., IV. 322–3, Wellington to F. Lamb, 24 March 1828.
15 *Creevey*, 28 February 1828.
16 Old Soldier, p. 400.
17 Thompson MSS., Wellington to Sir W. Gordon, 18 July 1816.
18 W.MSS., 29 February 1828.
19 WDNS., IV. 412.
20 *Lieven in London*, p. 125, 16–28 March 1828.
21 *Creevey*, 20 March 1828.
22 Royal Archives, The Hague, Wellington to the Prince of Orange, 5 April 1828.
23 W.MSS., Wellington to Mrs Arbuthnot, 13 February 1828; *Creevey*, 6 March 1828.
24 JA., II. 162, 15 February 1828.
25 Aspinall, *George IV*, III. Letter 1545, Cumberland to Knighton, 17 November 1828.
26 *Croker*, 14 March 1828.
27 WDNS., IV. 449; IV. 456, 21 May 1828.
28 WDNS., IV. 454.
29 JA., II. 187.
30 W.MSS., Wellington to Mrs Arbuthnot, 22 May 1828.
31 Ellenborough, I. 132, 30 May 1828.

12 EMANCIPATION BY STEALTH

1 WDNS., IV., 324, 24 March 1828.
2 Anglesey, p. 195, F. Lamb to Anglesey, 24 March 1828.
3 Raglan MSS., No. 48, 7 July 1812.
4 Gash, *Peel*, p. 525, quoting Anglesey Papers, PRO, Northern Ireland, 1068/15f.125.
5 WDNS., IV. 577; W.MSS., 11 July 1828; RA. 24522, 15 July 1828; JA., II. 197, 23 July 1828; Ellenborough I. 171, 19 July 1828.
6 *Lieven in London*, p. 146, 3–15 June 1828.
7 JA., II. 198–200.
8 Ziegler, *William IV*, p. 139.
9 JA., II. 200, 1 August 1828; WDNS. IV. 565–73, 1 August 1828.
10 WDNS., IV. 581, 9 August 1828; IV. 628, 18 August 1828.
11 JA., II. 204, 28 August 1828; Seymour MSS., 19 August 1828.
12 WHF., p. 83, 10 August 1828; JA., II. 202, 17 August 1828.
13 W.MSS., Wellington to Mrs Arbuthnot, 9 August 1828.
14 *Lieven in London*, p. 152, 14–26 August 1828; W.MSS., Wellington to Mrs Arbuthnot, 24 August 1828; 20 August 1828.
15 WDNS., IV. 650, 22 August 1828.
16 W.MSS., Wellington to Mrs Arbuthnot, 29 September 1828.
17 *Ibid.*, 17 August 1828; 26 August 1828; *Lieven in London*, p. 152, 14–26 August 1828.
18 WDNS., IV. 664, Peel to Wellington, 25 August 1828.
19 W.MSS., Wellington to Mrs Arbuthnot, 21 August 1828; 31 August 1828.
20 JA., II. 206, 10 September 1828.

21 W.MSS., Wellington to Mrs Arbuthnot, 21 September 1828; Lord Longford to Wellington, 21 October 1828.
22 WHF., p. 84, 23 September 1828.
23 WDNS., IV. 674, Wellington to Peel, 28 August 1828; V. 92–3, Wellington to Anglesey, 28 September 1828.
24 W.MSS., Wellington to Mrs Arbuthnot, 29 September 1828.
25 WDNS., V. 133–6, 14 October 1828; V. 138.
26 W.MSS., Wellington to Mrs Arbuthnot, 5 November 1828; JA., II. 220, 16 November 1828.
27 WDNS., V. 240, 11 November 1828; V. 244, 17 November 1828; V, 268, 19 November 1828; V. 280, 24 November 1828; V, 290, 26 November 1828.
28 WDNS., V. 275, 20 November 1828.
29 W.MSS., Wellington to Mrs Arbuthnot, 4 November 1828.
30 WDNS., V. 268, 17 November 1828.
31 Aspinall, George IV, III. Letter 1545, 17 November 1828.
32 W.MSS., Wellington to Mrs Arbuthnot, 4 November 1828; 23 November 1828.
33 Ibid., 7 January 1829.
34 W.MSS., Wellington to Mrs Arbuthnot, 10 and 12 January 1829.
35 Ibid., 13, 15 and 16 January 1829.
36 Ibid., 16 and 17 January 1829.
37 Ibid., 17 January 1829.

13 FOR THIS RELIEF . . .

1 W.MSS., Wellington to Mrs Arbuthnot, 22 January 1829; Lieven in London, pp. 176–7, 3–15 January 1829.
2 Colchester, III. 594, 4 February 1829.
3 Twiss, III. 95.
4 Aspinall, George IV, III. Letters 1552, 1555.
5 W.MSS., Lt. Col. Fremantle to Duchess, 20 February 1829.
6 Ellenborough, I. 357.
7 JA., II. 243, 26 February 1829.
8 Colchester, III. 612.
9 WDNS., V. 516, 2 March 1829.
10 Gash, Peel, p. 568.
11 JA., II. 248, 4 March 1829.
12 Ibid., 1829.
13 Maxwell, II. p. 228, being Wellington's account to Lady Salisbury (Salisbury MSS). According to another version, the Duke received the King's letter 'soon after he arrived home from the cabinet dinner'. Gash, Peel, 569; Peel's Memoirs, I. 349–50.
14 WDNS., V. 518.
15 Ibid., 519.
16 JA., II. 249, 4 March 1829.
17 Ibid., 252.
18 Haydon, Correspondence, II. 339.
19 Bodleian Library Record, vol. III. N. 33. Dec. 1951, Wellington to the Bishop of Salisbury, 20 March 1829.
20 WDNS., V. 538. The story

of the duel is taken mainly from WDNS., V. 527–45, Dr Hume's account to the Duchess; W.MSS.; Maxwell, II. 234; Gleig, *Life*, pp. 384–9; Shelley, II. 188; and the memoirs of Greville, Ellenborough and Broughton.

21 W.MSS., Duchess to Charles Wellesley, 26 March 1829.

22 WDNS., V. 585, Wellington to Duke of Buckingham, 21 April 1829.

23 WDNS., V. 546–7, 554.

24 Gleig, *Life*, p. 349.

25 WDNS., V. 585, 21 April 1829.

26 *Ibid.*, 548, 23 March 1829.

27 Ellenborough, II. 4–6; *Lieven in London*, p. 189, 7 April 1829.

28 JA., II. 264–6, 7 April 1829.

29 Colchester, III. 614, 18 April 1829.

30 Broughton, III. 318, Wellington to Duncannon; JA., II. 260, 28 March 1829.

31 W.MSS., Wellington to Knight of Kerry, 18 August 1828.

32 *Ibid.*, Colin Campbell to Duchess, 1 April 1829.

33 *Greville*, 22 February 1829.

14 ... LITTLE THANKS

1 W.MSS., 17 September 1829; 12 December 1829.

2 WDNS., VI. 282, 3 November 1829.

3 JA., II. 295, 21 July 1829.

4 W.MSS., to Mrs Arbuthnot, 22 April 1829.

5 *Ibid.*, Mrs Foster to Duchess, 6 January 1829.

6 *Ibid.*, Douro to Duchess, 14 August 1829.

7 *Creevey*, 19 February 1830.

8 JA., II. 316, 14 November 1829.

9 *Lieven-Grey*, I. 268, 14 August 1829; 257–8, 29 July 1829.

10 Aspinall, *George IV*, III. Letter 1564, 20 June 1829.

11 *Ibid.*, Letter 1548, 4 December 1828.

12 W.MSS.; JA., II. 294, 21 July 1829.

13 Salisbury MSS., Wellington to Lady Salisbury, 7 November 1837; Haydon, *Autobiography*, II. 517; Jones, p. 172, 6 October 1851; Mountstewart Diaries.

14 JA., II. 312; Peel, *Private Papers*, p. 114.

15 W.MSS., Wellington to Mrs Arbuthnot, 1 September 1829; 17 September 1829.

16 *Creevey*, 11 April 1829.

17 W.MSS., Wellington to Mrs Arbuthnot, 29 and 27 October 1829; Moore, p. 20.

18 *Ibid.*, 30 October 1829.

19 *Ibid.*, 9 February 1829, Wellington to Dr Hume, who was acting as go-between for the medical profession.

20 *Ibid.*, Wellington to Rutland, 3 December 1829.

21 *Ibid.*, Wellington to Mrs Arbuthnot, 26 November 1829 and 13 December 1829.

22 *Ibid.*, to Charles Arbuthnot, 13 December 1829.

23 *Greville*, 22 January 1830.

24 WDNS., VI. 529, 8 March 1830.

25 *Ibid.*, 589.

26 WDNS., VI. 417; 430, to Knight of Kerry, 19 January 1830.
27 W.MSS., Wellington to Mrs Arbuthnot, 4 March 1830.
28 Gash, *Peel*, p. 634; JA., II. 355–6; WDNS., VII. 106–8.
29 Aspinall, *George IV*, III. Letter 1578, 20 February 1830.
30 WHF., to Mrs Arbuthnot, 10 April 1830.
31 W.MSS., 7 June 1830; 1 December 1830; 16 January 1831.
32 Wilkins, II. 221–2.
33 The following account is taken largely from Wellington MSS; material is also to be found in Stuart, *Daughters of George III* (Princess Sophia) and Fulford *Royal Dukes*.
34 W.MSS., Wellington to Knighton, 15 September 1835.

15 REFORM

1 Eden, p. 198, August 1830.
2 *Greville*, 26 July 1830; *Lieven in London*, pp. 230–1, 16–28 July 1830.
3 WDNS., VII. 108, undated.
4 Bennett MSS., William M. Bennett to his brother Thomas Bennett, 8 November 1830.
5 Anonymous, *Charles X and Louis Philippe*.
6 *Greville*, 28 August 1830.
7 *Lieven in London*, pp. 334–5; W.MSS., to Mrs Arbuthnot, 24 August 1830.
8 Ridley, pp. 102–3; Airlie, p. 173.
9 W.MSS., Wellington to Lord Downshire, 21 August 1830.
10 *Ibid.*, to Mrs Arbuthnot, 25 August 1830; JA., II. 381, 26 August 1830.
11 JA., II. 370.
12 L. J. Hodson, *History of Salehurst*, 1914.
13 WDNS., VII. 312, Duke of Northumberland to Wellington, 21 October 1830; Burghersh, p. 48, 29 October 1829.
14 WDNS., VII. III – 12, 7 July 1830.
15 *Ibid.*
16 WDNS., VII. 149, 9 August 1830.
17 W.MSS., Wellington to Sir John Beckett, 12 September 1830.
18 *Lieven-Grey*, II. 83, 9 September 1830.
19 *Creevey*, 14 November 1829; Ellenborough, II. 370, 28 September 1830.
20 *Lieven-Grey*, II. 90, 19 September 1830; *Greville*, 18 September 1830.
21 W.MSS., Wellington to Mrs Arbuthnot, 15 October 1830.
22 *Ibid.*, James Hamilton to Wellington and reply, 14 and 22 October 1830.
23 *Ibid.*, Wellington to Mrs Arbuthnot, 9 October 1830.
24 Salisbury MSS., 9 December 1836.
25 W.MSS., to Sir James Shaw, 18 October 1830.

16 RELEASE

1 Gordon, p. 104; Seymour MSS.; Gordon, p. 104.
2 Maxwell, II. 252, 12 October 1832.
3 JA., II. 399, 7 November 1830.

4 WDNS., VII. 223–6, memorandum.

5 Lady Granville, II. 64; JA., II. 397; *Greville*, 8 November 1830.

6 Ellenborough, II. 409; W.MSS., September 1830; *Lieven in London*, p. 265, 25 October–6 November 1830.

7 Ellenborough, II. 418–20, 7 November 1830.

8 Lady Granville, II. 64–5; Ellenborough, II. 417.

9 Ellenborough, II. 426.

10 WDNS., VII. 353, Memorandum, 9 November 1830.

11 Stewart MSS., Duchess to Elizabeth Stewart, 12 November 1830.

12 Ellesmere, p. 164; Buckingham, *William IV and Queen Victoria*, I. 114, Wellington to Knighton, 9 November 1830.

13 *Greville*, 9 November 1830; W.MSS.

14 *Ibid.*, 16 November 1830.

15 Ellesmere, p. 73; Stanhope, 25 April 1840.

16 Maxwell, II. 194, Salisbury MSS.

17 Neumann, 16 September 1828.

18 WDNS., V. 184, to Sir Charles Forbes, 29 October 1828; *Greville*, 5 January 1830; Disraeli, *Bentinck*, p. 215.

19 Broughton, III. 254, 16 March 1828.

20 W.MSS., 10 April 1830.

PART III

17 INTERLUDE II:

TOWER, CINQUE PORTS AND WICKED WILLIAM

1 Stewart MSS., 29 November 1830.

2 Rogers, *Recollections*, p. 218, 21 November 1830.

3 W.MSS. (Charterhouse Papers), 31 July 1833.

4 What follows is taken largely from W.MSS. (Tower Papers) with valuable help from the monograph of the late Mr Frank Maggs, *The Duke, the Tower and the Beefeaters*.

5 W.MSS., Wellington to Major Elrington, 19 September 1837.

6 Maggs, Tower Secretary, E. Drummond, to Tower Major, Elrington.

7 W.MSS., Wellington to Elrington, 27 July 1832.

8 *Ibid.*, 20 September 1833.

9 *Ibid.*, to Lord Burghersh, 9 March 1833.

10 What follows is based on W.MSS. (Cinque Ports Papers).

11 W.MSS., Wellington to Lt. Gen. R. Jenkinson, 4 October 1830; 9 December 1839.

12 *Ibid.*, Grove Price to Wellington, 14 December 1832.

13 *Ibid.*, Wellington to Jenkinson, 10 January 1832.

14 What follows is taken largely from W.MSS. (Long-Wellesley and Bligh Papers).

15 *Ibid.*, Duchess to Rev. J. R. Lyon, young William's tutor.

16 Stewart MSS., Duchess to

Hon. Mrs E. Stewart, 17 September 1830.

17 W.MSS., Duchess to Rev. J. R. Lyon, 22 January 1830.

18 *Ibid.*, Sir W. Courtney to Wellington, 19 January 1835; Helena Bligh to Wellington, 14 May 1833.

18 KILLED BY THE BILL

1 *Lieven in London*, p. 278, 10 November 1830.

2 JA., II. 406, 22 December 1830; II. 404, 29 November 1830.

3 Lady Granville, II. 70, 21 November 1830.

4 *Greville*, 22 November 1830.

5 Martineau, II. 32, quoting from republican pamphlet.

6 W.MSS., Isaac Harvey, Yorkshire, to Wellington, 20 December 1830; WDNS., VII. 373, Wellington to Malmesbury, 6 December 1830.

7 Hobsbawn and Rudé, p. 255. See also Williams, p. 59, and Davis, p. 224–5. WDNS., VIII. 388.

8 WDNS., VII. 366.

9 Aspinall, *Three Diaries* (Ellenborough), 27 January 1831; *Croker*, 8 December 1830.

10 W.MSS.

11 Buckingham, *William IV and Queen Victoria*, I. 188, 1 December 1831.

12 Anglesey, p. 246; Macintyre, p. 23; WDNS., VII. 384.

13 W.MSS., Wellington to Lord Wellesley's agent, 11 August 1830.

14 *Ibid.*, Wellington to Rev. G. R. Gleig, 17 September 1831.

15 *Lieven-Grey*, II. 296, 2 March 1831; *Greville*, 7 March 1831; WDNS., VII. 410, 14 March 1831.

16 W.MSS., to Mrs Arbuthnot, 9 May 1831; Brougham, IV. 360; Buckingham, *William IV and Queen Victoria*, I. 250, 19 March 1831.

17 W.MSS., Wellington to Rev. G. R. Gleig, 11 April 1831; to Charles Arbuthnot, 24 March 1831.

18 *Creevey*, 5 March 1831.

19 WDNS., VII. 425, 3 April 1831.

20 Albemarle, p. 292.

21 Brougham, III. 118.

22 W.MSS., Wellington to Mrs Arbuthnot, 1 April 1831.

23 Edgeworth, *Letters from England*. pp. 475–7, Miss M. Edgeworth to Mrs Edgeworth, 22 January 1831; W.MSS., to Mrs Arbuthnot, 8 April 1831, 6 April 1831; Mrs P. S.-M. Arbuthnot., p. 224.

24 WHF., p. 95, 29 April 1831, 1 May 1831; W.MSS., to Mrs Arbuthnot, 2 May 1831. See also Wellington to Goulburn, W.MSS., 11 May 1831.

25 W.MSS., Wellington to Charles Arbuthnot, 9 May 1831.

26 *Ibid.*, to Mrs Arbuthnot, 19 May 1831, 5 June 1831.

27 WDNS., VII. 455; *Lieven-Grey*, II. 218.

28 W.MSS., Wellington to Wilton, 29 May 1831.

29 *Ibid.*, to the Rev. G. R. Gleig, 2 November 1831.

30 *Greville*, 22 September 1831;

W.MSS., Lord Kenyon to Wellington, 22 September 1831.

31 Seymour MSS., 4 October 1831.

32 Brownlow, p. 144; WHF., p. 99, to Mrs Arbuthnot, 12 October 1831.

33 Boulind MSS., 22 October 1831.

34 W.MSS., Londonderry, 5 December 1830.

35 WDNS., VIII. 30, 5 November 1831; Buckingham, *William IV and Queen Victoria*, I. 384, 2 January 1832.

36 Salisbury MSS.

37 WDNS., VIII. 126–7, to Lord Roden, 12 December 1831.

38 Fitzgerald, II. 102–3.

39 Aspinall, *Three Diaries* (Le Marchant), p. 252.

40 WDNS., VIII. 304, 10 May 1832.

41 *Croker*, 12 May 1832; Aspinall, *Three Diaries* (Ellenborough), p. 250, 12 May 1832.

42 W.MSS., Wellington to Lady Burghersh, 14 May 1832; Seymour MSS.

43 Place Papers, BM., Add.MSS., 27795, vol. VII, Wednesday 7 June; Aspinall, *Three Diaries* (Le Marchant), p. 273, 7 June 1832.

44 Butler, p. 425.

45 Turberville, p. 295, quoting from Reid's *Life of Durham*; W.MSS., Mr Grey to Wellington, 19 June 1832.

46 Fraser, p. 226.

47 Rogers, *Table-Talk*, 22 June 1832; W.MSS., Wellington to Mrs Arbuthnot, 19 August 1832.

48 Gleig, *Life*, p. 449; De Ros, p. 168; Fraser, pp. 23–5.

49 WDNS., VIII. 110, to Lord Wharncliffe, 29 November 1831; W.MSS., Wellington to Rev. G. R. Gleig, 6 June 1832.

50 Lever, 18 May 1832.

51 Buckingham, *William IV and Queen Victoria*, I. 261, 24 March 1831.

52 W.MSS., Wellington to Croker, 11 August 1832.

19 THE DUKE ON ELBA

1 Raikes, 24 July 1832.

2 WDNS., VIII. 472–3, 4 December 1832.

3 Edgeworth, III. 57–8.

4 W.MSS., Mrs Foster's memorandum.

5 Copy of letter from the Duchess of Wellington to General Allan, thought to be in the possession of a collector in the USA.

6 PRO, Northern Ireland, D207/67/65; Stewart MSS., 16 April 1825.

7 W.MSS., Wellington to Mrs Arbuthnot, 16 February 1831.

8 *Ibid.*, 29 November 1831.

9 *Ibid.*, 21 August 1832.

10 *Ibid.*, 30 October 1832.

11 W.MSS., Hardinge to Wellington, 15 November 1832.

12 *Ibid.*, Wellington to Mrs Arbuthnot, 18 and 16 December 1832.

13 *Ibid.*, to Knight of Kerry, 16 December 1832.

14 Fraser, p. 11.

15 Clark, p. 80; WDNS., VII. 486.

16 W.MSS., Cumberland to Wellington, 30 December 1832; Wellington to Londonderry, 7 March 1833.

17 W.MSS., 2 and 26 February 1833.

18 *Ibid.*, Wellington to Mrs Arbuthnot, 16 February 1833.

19 *Ibid.*, 13 February 1833.

20 W.MSS., 16 February 1833.

21 W.MSS., Lord Strangford to Wellington, 14 July 1833.

22 Parker, II. 218.

23 *Lieven-Grey*, II. 453, Lord Grey to Princess Lieven, 26 June 1833.

24 Morgan, p. 363, 29 July 1833.

25 W.MSS., Knighton to Wellington, 9 March 1832.

26 Albemarle, pp. 376–7.

27 W.MSS., Wellington to Mrs Arbuthnot, 30 August 1830.

28 *Ibid.*, 17 December 1833.

29 *Ibid.*, to Aberdeen, 21 January 1834.

30 *Ibid.*, to Mrs Arbuthnot, 8 February 1834; Shelley, II. 231.

31 Brownlow, p. 163.

32 Fragment of unpublished autobiography by Miss Yonge printed in Christabel Coleridge's *Charlotte M. Yonge.*

33 W.MSS., Hardinge to Wellington, reporting a conversation with Croker, 21 January 1834.

34 *Lieven in London*, p. 373, 13–25 April 1834; Buckingham, *William IV and Queen Victoria*, II. 94.

35 W.MSS., Wellington to Londonderry, 17 June 1834.

36 *Ibid.*, memorandum, 26 February 1834.

37 *Ibid.*, Wellington, R. Oastler to Wellington, 19 May 1833.

38 *Wellingtoniana*, pp. 123–4.

39 W.MSS., Wellington to Wyatt, 1 July 1840.

40 Disraeli, *Sybil*, Bk. V, Chap. 1.

41 W.MSS., R. Oastler to Wellington, 17 June 1834.

42 Martineau, II. 84–7.

43 W.MSS., Wellington to Lord Roden, 1 September 1834; to Aberdeen, 23 August 1834.

44 *Ibid.*, to Cumberland, 5 October 1834.

45 Fitzgerald, II. 307.

46 Gleig, *Reminiscences*, p. 179.

20 A HUNDRED DAYS

1 W.MSS., Wellington to Mrs Arbuthnot, 28 July 1834.

2 *Ibid.*, Halford to Wellington, 2. August 1834.

3 *Ibid.*, Charles Arbuthnot to Wellington, 5 August 1834.

4 Oman, p. 133, 12 August 1834.

5 W.MSS., Wellington to Mrs Arbuthnot, 19 August 1833.

6 Maxwell, II. 249; De Ros, Wellington to Lady de Ros, pp. 376–8.

7 Oman, p. 224, 13 December 1836.

8 Salisbury MSS., 10 July 1837.

9 W.MSS., anon. 27 September 1837.

10 Salisbury MSS., 7 November 1837.

11 Oman, p. 145.

12 WHF., 21 February 1834; 16 March 1834.

13 WDNS., VIII. 147–9, 6 January 1832.

14 Ellesmere, p. 137.

15 Herrick, p. 10.
16 *Ibid.*, pp. 13–16.
17 *Ibid.*, p. 19.
18 *Ibid.*, pp. 26–32.
19 *Ibid.*, p. 35.
20 *Ibid.*, p. 71.
21 Maxwell, II. 282.
22 Oman, p. 158.
23 Disraeli, *Coningsby*, Bk. II, Chap. 4.
24 *Greville*, 16 and 17 November 1834.
25 *Lieven-Grey*, II. 47, 1 December 1834.
26 Ellesmere, p. 143.
27 W.MSS., Wellington to Lord Londonderry, 1 December 1834.
28 Oman, p. 156.
29 W.MSS., Wellington to Egerton, 11 December 1834.
30 *Ibid.*, to Lord Wilton, 19 December 1834; Parker, II. 258.
31 *Ibid.*, Disraeli to Wellington, 1 January 1835.
32 Aspinall, *Arbuthnot*, p. 175, Lord Rosslyn to Arbuthnot, 6 August 1833.
33 *Greville*, 15 January 1835.
34 Edgeworth, *Letters from England*, p. 578, Maria Edgeworth to Harriet Butler, 10 January 1841.
35 Oman, p. 126.
36 Lady Granville, p. 195, 7 September 1835.
37 Oman, pp. 158–61, 25 and 29 March 1835.
38 *Ibid.*, pp. 163–4, 2 April 1835.
39 *Greville*, 21 February 1835.
40 Herrick, p. 65, 1 October 1835.
41 *Ibid.*, p. 68, 3 November 1835.
42 Oman, p. 146, 26 November 1834.

43 Herrick, p. 81, 3 August 1836; p. 89, 18 April 1837.
44 W.MSS., Wellington to Lord Lyndhurst, 13 May 1835.
45 Peel, *Private Letters*, p. 153.
46 *Gladstone Papers*, 20 January 1836.
47 Parker, II. 323, 11 February 1836.
48 Chad, p. 20, 22–27 April 1837.
49 W.MSS., Dr Blomfield to Wellington, 14 October, 1836.
50 *Greville*, 11 May 1836.
51 W.MSS., Wellington to Peel, 23 March 1837.
52 *Ibid.*, to Lord Roden, 19 February 1837; to Peel, 22 February 1837.
53 W.MSS., to Peel, 15 April 1837.
54 Guest, p. 48; *Greville*, 4 January 1838.

`21 OUR GRACIOUS

1 Oman, p. 241.
2 W.MSS., Wellington to Sir H. Taylor, 11 June 1837; Wellington, *Selection*, p. 204, to an unknown correspondent, 26 July 1837.
3 *Greville*, 21 June 1837; RA, Stockmar Papers, No. 28, Wellington to Lord Liverpool; Oman, pp. 247–8, 9 July 1937.
4 W.MSS., Wellington to Charles Arbuthnot, 20 July 1837.
5 *Ibid.*, to Sir H. Taylor, 19 May 1837; to Albemarle, 18 May 1837; lawyer to Wellington, 21 May 1837.
6 W.MSS., Wellington to

Charles Arbuthnot, 10 July 1837.

7 *Ibid.*, Lady Burghersh to Wellington, 9 September 1837.

8 *Ibid.*, Wellington to Lady Burghersh, 10 September 1837.

9 *Ibid.*, Lady Burghersh to Wellington, 11 September 1837.

10 *Ibid.*, Lady Burghersh to Wellington, 11 September 1837.

11 *Ibid.*, Wellington to Lady Burghersh, 14 September 1837.

12 *Ibid.*, to Lord Wilton, 31 October 1837.

13 Stanhope, 16 October 1837.

14 W.MSS., Lady Burghersh to Wellington, 30 December 1837.

15 Wharncliffe, II. 289, Lord Wharncliffe to Lady Wharncliffe, 24 January 1838; Buckingham, *William IV and Queen Victoria*, II. 310–11, 28 January 1838.

16 Oman, p. 270, 26 and 28 January 1838.

17 W.MSS., Wellington to Charles Arbuthnot, 15 February 1838.

18 Oman, p. 275, 19 February 1838.

19 *Ibid.*, p. 275, 19 February 1838.

20 W.MSS., Wellington to Lord Redesdale, 28 January 1838.

21 Seymour MSS.

22 Oman, pp. 245–6, July 1837.

23 W.MSS., Lady Hester Stanhope to Wellington, 12 February and 29 March 1838.

24 Lever, 28 September 1838.

25 Longford, *Victoria R.I.*, p. 99.

26 *Greville*, 15 August 1839.

27 *Ibid.*, 15 August 1839.

28 *Ibid.*, 12 May 1839.

29 Stanhope, 17 May 1839.

30 WPC., p. 126, memorandum, 3 June 1839.

31 WHF., p. 131, to Lady Wilton, 7 February 1840.

32 Stanhope, 14 May 1839; Gordon, p. 115.

33 Croker, 21 November 1839; Stanhope, 23 November 1839; WHF., 25 November 1839.

34 W.MSS., 24 April 1839.

35 Stanhope, 29 October and 4 November 1839.

36 Croker, 17 February 1840; Lever, 19 March 1840; Guizot, 6 March 1840.

37 Herrick, pp. 114–18, 13 and 14 March, 3 August 1840.

38 W.MSS., 29 December 1839; WHF., 31 January 1840.

39 Stanhope, 8 November 1840.

40 From autograph album of Jane, Marchioness of Ely, 31 December 1840.

41 Stanhope, 13 November 1839.

42 W.MSS., 10 October 1840.

43 Napier, C., p. 69, 6 August 1839.

44 WHF., p. 130, to Lady Wilton, 5 February 1840; WHF., p. 148, 1 October 1840.

45 *Ibid.*, p. 157, to Lady Wilton, 15 March 1841.

46 Raikes, 17 July 1841.

22 INTERLUDE III:
SCHISM AT OXFORD

1 Gleig, *Life*, p. 386.

2 W.MSS., Wellington writing on behalf of Sir James Mountain to Admiral Page, 8 December 1838.

3 Oman, p. 201. See also W.MSS., 28 December 1818,

when Wellington wrote to Dr Keate that parents could remove their sons if they disliked the headmaster's rules.

4 W.MSS., Wellington to Cardwell, 13 and 15 February 1836.

5 *Ibid.*, 2 March 1836.

6 *Ibid.*, 23 March and 16 November 1836.

7 *Ibid.*, Gilbert to Wellington, 5 March, Wellington to Gilbert, 7 March 1837.

8 *Ibid.*, Wellington to Cardwell, 8 June and 12 December 1842.

9 W.MSS., Wellington to Wynter, 29 September 1844; Simmons, p. 470.

10 W.MSS., Wellington to Balliol College cook, 2 April 1841.

11 *Ibid.*, to Hebdomadal Board, 23 April 1845.

12 *Ibid.*, 12 April 1837.

13 *Ibid.*, to Dr Gilbert, 5 November 1837.

14 *Ibid.*, 27 December 1839.

23 RIGHTABOUT FACE!

1 Parker, II. 486, Disraeli to Peel, 5 September 1841.

2 W.MSS., Wellington to Peel, 17 May 1841.

3 WHF., p. 139, to Lady Wilton, 18 August 1840; p. 185, 11 November 1842.

4 WHF., p. 198, 2 December 1844, 23 January 1845.

5 Cecil Woodham-Smith, *Florence Nightingale*, p. 41.

6 *Greville*, 7 September 1841.

7 W.MSS., Wellington to Greville, 1 June 1842.

8 W.MSS., Wellington to Salisbury, 11 September 1841.

9 Parker, II. 509, Peel to Graham, 5 September 1841.

10 Parker, II. 509, Wellington to Peel, 17 February 1842.

11 Martineau, II. 538.

12 Parker, III. 157, 28 July 1844.

13 W.MSS., 12 August 1842; Raikes, 18 August 1842.

14 W.MSS., Wellington to Graham, 22 August 1842.

15 RA., M. 51, Wellington to Prince Albert, 19 August 1842; W.MSS., to General Cameron, 6 December 1830.

16 W.MSS., Wellington to Graham, 24 and 31 May 1843.

17 *Ibid.*, Mangan to Wellington, 25 May 1843.

18 W.MSS., Wellington to Graham, 27 July 1843; Parker, III. 63, 16 September 1843.

19 Parker, III. 64, Wellington to Peel, 10 October 1843; Speech in House of Lords, 2 June, 16 June 1845.

20 W.MSS., Peel to Wellington, 15 October 1845; Parker, III. 223-4, Peel to Graham, 13 October 1845 and to Heytesbury, 15 October 1845.

21 W.MSS., James Burns, Belfast, to Wellington, 18 October 1845.

22 Parker, III. 225, Wellington to Peel.

23 W.MSS., letters to Wellington, 16 and 18 November 1845.

24 *Ibid.*, Peel to Wellington, 29 November 1845.

25 Parker, III. 236, Stanley to Peel, 29 November 1845; see also Hobhouse (Broughton, VI. 162, 26 January 1846).

26 *Croker*, 6 April 1846.

27 Thackeray, *Irish Sketch Book*.
28 W.MSS., Queen Victoria to Wellington, 12 December 1845; see also Parker, III. 243–4.
29 *Ibid.*, Wellington to Queen Victoria, 12 December 1845.
30 *Ibid.*, Wellington to Lord Redesdale, 16 December 1845.
31 *Ibid.*, Mahon (Stanhope) to Wellington, 20 December 1845.
32 Parker, III. 283.
33 *Ibid.*, Peel to Hardinge, 22 December 1845.
34 *Ibid.*, 284, Peel to Queen Victoria, 20 December 1845; Peel to Hardinge, 22 December 1845.
35 W.MSS., Peel to Wellington, 22 December 1845.
36 *Greville*, 13 January 1846.
37 W.MSS., Wellington to Redesdale, 21, 28 and 25 December 1845.
38 *Ibid.*, to Duke of Beaufort, 22 and 25 December 1845.
39 *Croker*, 28 December 1845 and 3 January 1846; W.MSS., Wellington to Croker, 6 January 1846.
40 W.MSS., Wellington to Lord Salisbury, 6 January 1846.
41 *Ibid.*, to Croker, 29 December 1845.
42 WHF., p. 203, Wellington to Lady Wilton, 27 January 1846.
43 *Ibid.*, p. 204, Wellington to Lady Wilton, 27 January 1846.
44 W.MSS., Stanley to Wellington, 18 February 1846.
45 Parker, III. 326.
46 W.MSS., Wellington to Stanley, 19 February 1846; Gleig, *Life*, pp. 567–72.
47 Blake, *Conservative Party*, pp. 66–7, quoting Derby papers.
48 Maxwell, II. 352.
49 Parker, III, 353, 366.
50 Monypenny, vol. I, bk. 2, chap. xii.

24 STRANGE TIMES

1 WHF., p. 236, Wellington to Miss Burdett-Coutts, 26 November 1846.
2 W.MSS., Wellington to Croker, 19 December 1846; RA., D. 16. 74., Lord John Russell to Queen Victoria, 9 July 1847; Queen Victoria to Wellington, 12 July 1847.
3 RA., Y. 55. 64., George Anson to Prince Albert, 6 December 1843.
4 W.MSS., Wellington to Adjutant General, 25 October 1842.
5 *Ibid.*, to Lord Cardigan, 30 September 1850.
6 *Ibid.*, to Lord Anglesey, 18 November 1850.
7 RA., Y. 55. 64, George Anson to Prince Albert, 14 December 1843.
8 WDNS., V. 593, memorandum by Wellington, 22 April 1828.
9 *Wellington Studies*, Foreword by 7th Duke of Wellington.
10 Parker, II. 575, Peel to Stanley, 19 December 1843; BM., Add. MSS., Peel Papers, 40460, ff.335, August 1844.
11 W.MSS., Wellington to Anglesey, 3 April 1847.
12 *Ibid.*, to Stanley, 1 August

1845; Parker, II. 207, Wellington to Peel, 8 August 1845.

13 *Ibid.*, 219, Peel to Arbuthnot and reply, 14 August and 28 August 1845.

14 *Ibid.*, III. 397 and 402, Aberdeen to Peel, 7 January and 18 September 1845.

15 Stanhope, 16 September and 12 October 1846.

16 W.MSS., Wellington to Anglesey, 17 July 1844; WHF., p. 204, Wellington to Lady Wilton, 6 October 1846.

17 W.MSS., Wellington to Rev. Patrick Brontë, 15 November 1841.

18 Gleig, *Life*, p. 398

19 W.MSS., Wellington to Anglesey, 17 June 1848; Anglesey, pp. 324–5.

20 RA., E. 42. 28. Wellington to Russell, 7 January 1848.

21 W.MSS., Wellington to Lady Shelley, 27 and 28 January 1848; Shelley, II. 278–86, 317 and 411. (The editor has made several slips in copying the Duke's frantic script.)

22 W.MSS., Wellington to Lady Shelley, 26 February 1848.

23 RA., I. 67. 93, Wellington to Lamartine, 3 March 1848; Russell to Palmerston, 4 March 1848.

24 Chad, p. 22, 29 April 1848.

25 Spicer MSS., Wellington to William Francis Spicer, 22 March 1848.

26 Maxwell, II. 368, 7 April 1848.

27 Lever, Lady Palmerston to Mrs Huskisson, 14 April 1848.

28 RA., C. 56. 7., Wellington to Prince Albert, 8 April 1848; W.MSS., Wellington to Lady Wilton, 5 April 1848; Lever, Lady Palmerston, 14 April 1848; Chad, p. 21.

29 Guest, p. 210, 10 April 1848; WHF., pp. 210–11

30 RA., C. 8. II., Queen Victoria to Wellington, 12 April 1848.

31 W.MSS., Wellington to Lord Glengall, 25 March 1848.

32 *Ibid.*, 8 April 1848.

33 Nowlan, p. 107.

34 W.MSS., Wellington to Edward Booth, Irish Ordnance Office, 29 June 1848.

35 *Greville*, 4 January 1838.

36 Broughton, VI. 275.

37 W.MSS., Wellington to Miss Burdett-Coutts, 30 March 1849.

38 De Ros, p. 147.

39 W.MSS., Wellington to Miss Burdett-Coutts, 19 October 1848.

40 WHF., p. 238, I January 1847.

41 W.MSS., Wellington to Miss Burdett-Coutts, 17 October 1847.

42 WHF., p. 242, 6, 7 and 8 February 1847.

43 W.MSS., Wellington to Miss Burdett-Coutts, 27 August 1851; 4 September 1848.

44 *Ibid.*, 11 October 1848; 23 August 1850.

45 *Greville*, 13 July 1847.

46 Jones, p. 174.

47 Lutyens, footnote, p. 164, 16 September 1852; 29 April 1851.

48 W.MSS., Wellington to Lady Charles Wellesley, 18 June 1849.

49 Herrick, pp. 211–17, 6 February and 10 March 1851.

50 Burghclere, p. 4.

25 THE OTHER SIDE OF THE HILL

1 Hobhouse, p. 25.

2 WHF., p. 283, Wellington to Miss Burdett-Coutts, [late December 1849].

3 W.MSS., Wellington to Lord Seymour, Dept. of Woods and Forests, 2 October 1850.

4 W.MSS., Wellington to Russell, 2 April 1851.

5 W.MSS., Wellington to Deputy Ranger, 10 October 1850.

6 W.MSS., Wellington to Henry Griffiths, 25 August 1851.

7 Guest, p. 270; Burghclere, p. 180, 7 May 1851; Jones, p. 172, 7 October 1851.

8 W.MSS., Dr Plumptre, Vice-Chancellor of Oxford, reporting to Wellington on the Hebdomadal Board's statement to Russell, 18 May 1850.

9 Burghclere, p. 63, Wellington to Lady Salisbury, 6 August 1850; p. 76.

10 Jeune, p. 68, 9 November 1856. Lord Wellesley MSS., Lord Wellesley to Lady Montgomery, 26 December 1840.

11 Etoniana, 1965, extracts from Lord Hatherton's Diary.

12 From the typescript notebooks of Geoffrey Madan.

13 W.MSS., Mahon to Wellington, 16 November 1839; Gurwood to Wellington, 20 November 1839.

14 Ibid., letters exchanged between Wellington and Mrs Gurwood, 27 January and 2 February 1846.

15 W.MSS., letters exchanged between Gurwood and Basil Hall (brother of Lady de Lancey), November 1841.

16 Jones, 23 October, 20 and 27 December 1851.

17 W.MSS., 'A merry Christmas' from Wellington to Lady Wilton and her children, 25 December 1842.

18 Jones, 4 January 1852.

19 Fraser, p. 52.

20 Maxwell, II. 288.

21 Burghclere, p. 269, 1 May 1852; Guest, p. 297.

22 Fraser, p. 108.

23 Burghclere, 3 and 6 July 1852; Old Soldier, p. 87.

24 Elvin, p. 24.

25 East Kent Mercury, 26 September 1852.

26 Burghclere, pp. 314, 321.

27 Croker, 4 September 1852; Ward, p. 138.

28 Burghclere, 12 September 1852.

29 This account of the Duke's death comes mainly from (i) a long letter from his valet Kendall written on 21 September 1852 to Kendall's friend Shackle, a footman at Windsor Castle (RA., Mixed Correspondence III. M. 53. 1848/1853, 189.) (ii) memorandum by Dr Hulke, senior (W.MSS.), (iii) a shorter memorandum by Dr John W. Hulke, his son (published in The Complete Guide to the Funeral of the Duke of Wellington, C. M. Archer, p. 78, London, 1852).

30 Stanhope, 22 November 1839.

31 RA., E. 2. 3, Col. Phipps to Prince Albert, 15 September 1852; Bolitho, p. 45.

32 RA., T. 97. Queen Victoria to King Leopold of the Belgians, 17 September 1852; RA., E. I. 21, Col. Phipps to Rev. Gerald Wellesley, 17 September 1852.

33 Spicer MSS., 4 October 1852.

34 W.MSS., Mr Campbell to Mr Willian Brown, 30 August 1854.

35 Jones, 31 August 1852.

36 W.MSS., 2nd Duke of Wellington to Miss Burdett-Coutts, 13 and 15 November 1852.

37 Airlie, 4 and 11 November 1852.

38 De Ros, p. 49; Morgan, p. 522.

39 RA., C. 61. 117, Prince Albert to 2nd Duke of Wellington, 24 November 1852.

40 Miss E.. A. Napier, letter on the funeral of the Duke of Wellington, 18 November 1852, Bodleian Library MS. Eng. Misc. H. 96. f.333.

41 Moore Smith, *Colborne*, p. 348.

42 Chad, p. 19, 3 July 1836.

43 RA., Vic. Add. MSS. 119, 20 January 1859.

44 See Lord Holland's *Further Memoirs*, pp. 230–2 and Princess Lieven's *Political Sketches*, p. 111, for critical assessments of Wellington's virtues.

45 Briggs, p. 450; *Wellington Anecdotes*, p. 60.

46 WHF., Wellington to Lady Wilton, 20 December 1840.

47 Burghclere, p. 153, Wellington to Lady Salisbury, 20 November 1850.

48 Speech in House of Lords, 13 August 1839.

49 Stanhope, 23 December 1840.

50 Gleig, *Life*, p. 428; Rogers, *Recollections*, p. 289; Seymour MSS., Col. Grisewood to Sir George Seymour, 14 March 1841.

51 Aspinall, *George IV*, III. Letter 1577, Knighton's diary, 10 February 1830; Stanhope, 21 October 1844; Jeune, pp. 3 and 5.

52 Kelly, p. 386.

53 Edgeworth, *Letters from England*, p. 592, M. Edgeworth to Harriet Butler, 20 April 1841; Ellesmere, pp. 77–8; Fraser, p. 33.

54 Maxse Papers, 411, West Sussex Record Office, Wellington to Lady Caroline Maxse, 18 November 1848.

55 W.MSS., Wellington to Charles Arbuthnot, 17 January 1832.

56 Salisbury MSS., Lady Salisbury's diary, 2 April 1835. (Sir H. Maxwell's transcription contains some small verbal changes.)

57 See a penetrating study of this issue, M. G. Brock, *Wellington Studies*, pp. 75–6.

58 W.MSS., 7 July 1846.

59 Michael Glover, 'Wellington and Napoleon,' *History of the English Speaking Peoples*, p. 2748 (London 1971).

60 Stanhope, p. 80, Lord Mahon's rendering of Wellington's views on Marlborough, sent to him for comment on 17 September 1836; W.MSS., unpublished reply from Wellington to Mahon, 18 September 1936. Wellington also sent a memorandum comparing himself and Marlborough, which appears in Stanhope, pp. 80–2.
61. Stevens, p. 99.
62 Medwin, p. 9.
63 Gleig, *Life*, p. 428; *The Diaries of Sir Alexander Cadogan* (London, 1971), 22 July 1944.
64 Wellington Memorial Lecture by Field-Marshal Montgomery, *Journal of the Royal United Service Institution*, No. 656, Vol. CXIV, December 1969; Maxwell, II. 112, quoting Salisbury MSS.
65 W.MSS., Croker to Wellington, 9 February 1850; Glover, *Wellington as Military Commander*, Preface (1968).
66 Glover, *Legacy of Glory*, p. 165 (New York, 1971).
67 Burghersh, p. 145, 27 March 1843.
68 W.MSS., 12 September 1842.
69 Haydon, *Autobiography*, 30 September 1844; JA, II. 339.

Index

In this index W = Duke of Wellington. Numbers in *italics* refer to illustrations.

Hampden Clubs, 67–8

Hampshire: W as Lord-Lieutenant of, 103–4, 320–2; agricultural unrest in, 169–70, 320–2; Chartism in, 410

Hard Times (Dickens), 195 n., 509

Hardinge, Sir Henry, 1st Viscount, 188, 209, 249, 256, 291, 338, 350, 378, 386; as second at W's duel, 237–8; considers Mrs Arbuthnot bad influence on W, 374 n.; pall-bearer at W's funeral, 494–5

Hardwicke, Charles Yorke, 4th Earl of, 430

Hare, William, 256

Harrowby, Dudley Ryder, 1st Earl of and Viscount Sandon, 27–8, 92, 336, 385–6

Harrowby, Mary, 28

Hartington, Lord, 503 n.

Hastings, Francis Rawdon-Hastings, 1st Marquis of, 304

Hastings, Lady Flora: wrongly suspected pregnancy, 402–3; death, 405–6

Hatherton, Lord (formerly Edward Littleton, q.v.), 434, 481–2

Hay, Lady Elizabeth – *see* Douro, Lady

Haydon, Benjamin Robert, 86, 194–5, 497, 508

Hazlitt, William, 480 n.

Hely-Hutchinson, John, 54

Herbert, Lady Mary, 369

Herrick, Christine Terhune, 371 n.

Herries, John Charles, 189–90, 198, 327

Hertford, Francis Seymour-Conway, 3rd Marquis of, 144, 276–7, 297

Hervey, Colonel Felton, 23, 57, 313

Hervey, Mrs Felton (Louisa Caton), 57, 73–4, 161, 313

Hicks, Mrs Ann (Hyde Park squatter), 476–7

Hill, Rowland, 1st Viscount, 392–3, 431

Hobhouse, Henry, 488 n.

Hobhouse, John Cam, 38, 181, 339

Hobsbawn, E. J., 321

Hoby, Mr (bootmaker), 257

Hogg, James (Kettering MP), 259

Holland, Henry Fox, 3rd Baron, 60–1, 98, 99, 189, 355; on W, 190, 191; Anglesey's secret communication with, 209

Holmes, William ('Black Billy'), 275, 276, 350

'Holy Alliance', 55–6, 79–80, 135

Hook, Theodore, 99 n.

Hopes (bankers), 62, 64, 65, 78

Hougoumont, 28, 29

Houses of Parliament, burnt down (1833), 363

Huddersfield, 255, 362

Hulke, Dr, 488–9

Hulton, William, 88–9, 228

'Humble Servant', and W's anti-Reform speech, 288

Hume, Dr John Robert, 115, 136–7, 144; at W's duel, 237–8

Hume, Elizabeth, 115–16, 251

Hume, Joseph, 305

Hunt, 'Orator', 67–8, 246, 271; and Peterloo, 87–9, 275; criticizes W's northern tour (1830), 275; loses seat in 1833, 350

Huskisson, William, 133, 172, 180, 187, 189–90, 255, 257, 296, 314; and Corn Law reform, 182, 203, 204–5; Colonial Secretary, 198; resigns over redistribution of disfranchised seats, 206–9; accidental death, 276–7

Hyde Park: Achilles statue in, 81, 180, 334; reviews in, 295, 392; Great Exhibition in (1851), 475–8; squatter in, 476–7

income tax, 66–7, 259; first in peacetime (1842), 429–30

industrial unrest, 87–8, 166, 169, 254–5, 277–8, 409–10, 428, 432–4

Great Life Stories in Panther Books